"One might question why we need another book on the Be[atles,] countless books, films, artistic pieces through the decade[s] ... [but this one is truly] outstanding from a unique perspective, a worthy undertaking that Meyers has chosen to tackle—the psychological, astrological and spiritual dimension of the Beatles. This book is a delight to astrologers who are also Beatle maniacs, a double bonus. Further, this book reveals charts, stories and facts about the Beatles that you will find nowhere else. Thank you, Eric, for writing this book!"

--Arielle Guttman, author of *Venus Star Rising: A New Cosmology for the 21st Century*

"A treat for Beatlemaniacs young and old, this book explores the history of the 'greatest band in the world' from a fresh perspective. Fueled by love and a commitment to in-depth research, Meyers brings unprecedented psychological and astrological insight into the Beatles, their music as well as their message. He illustrates the special alchemy that defined an era and produced music that is still dear to our hearts today."

--Mark Jones, author of *The Planetary Nodes and Collective Evolution*

"There's something special about The Beatles. At least that's the way many of us feel. While there are other great bands, there always seems to be a little 'extra' quality to The Beatles. In this book, Eric Meyers has tried to capture - or at least describe - what that extra factor is. For those who are into The Beatles, it can read like a great conversation about your favorite band, and whether or not you 'get' the astrology, you'll be amazed by Eric's insights and observations. For astrologers, the book is a treasure chest of startling connections that will astound even seasoned mundane astrologers. *The Spiritual Dimension of The Beatles* comes about as close as anyone ever has to putting their finger on that ineffable quality of The Beatles, and what they mean to us all."

–Armand Diaz, author of *Integral Astrology*

"Right when my young son obsessively delved into the musical world of the Beatles, my friend and colleague, Eric Meyers, was in the middle of writing out his love and fascination for the band in this monumental work. This writing has deep relevance for all who grew up with them, as well as for future generations. Eric demonstrates a mastery for astrological analysis and understanding with a deep and profound level of spiritual understanding and insight. This is a must read for any astrological student and even more so if you are a lover of the Beatles. Be prepared for a ride through time!"

--Sol Jonassen, evolutionary astrologer

THE SPIRITUAL DIMENSION OF
THE BEATLES

ERIC MEYERS, M.A.

The Spiritual Dimension of The Beatles

Published by Astrology Sight Publishing

Camas, WA

ISBN Number: 978-0-9747766-5-1

Printed in the United States of America

For more info about Eric's astrology services, please visit the website:

www.SoulVisionConsulting.com

email: eric@soulvisionconsulting.com

Cover art by David Holtz.

Graphic design and interior figures by Bill Streett.

Back cover photograph taken by Corrina Porterfield.

For Alan & Lois Meyers:

who provided me a loving home and family,
complete with Beatles albums.

Also by the author:

The Astrology of Awakening Volume 2:
Chart Application & Counseling
(2016)

The Astrology of Awakening Volume 1:
Eclipse of the Ego
(2012)

Elements & Evolution:
The Spiritual Landscape of Astrology
(2010)

Uranus: The Constant of Change
(2008)

Between Past & Presence:
A Spiritual View of the Moon & Sun
(2006)

The Arrow's Ascent:
Astrology & The Quest for Meaning
(2004)

"The great thing about 'Yesterday' is that it kind of wrote itself. People say to me, 'Do you believe in mysticism or magic?' With that story, I kind of have to….I just *dreamed* it, what a gift."

–Paul McCartney

Regarding "Across the Universe": "[The words] were purely inspirational and were given to me as boom! I don't own it you know; it came through like that."

"My joy is when you're like possessed, like a medium."

–John Lennon

Dedicated to Julia Lennon and Mary McCartney,
aviatrixes of dreamscapes.

Table of Contents

	Part 1	Part 2
Introduction	20	261
Chapter 1 – The Musicians	24	264
John Lennon	24	264
Paul McCartney	26	266
George Harrison	28	268
Ringo Starr	29	269
Chapter 2 – The Band	31	271
Soul Group Dynamics	31	271
Sibling Hierarchy	33	272
Band Dynamics	33	273
On the Nature of Beetles	36	---
Chapter 3 – Relationships & Influences	38	276
John—Paul: The Leaders	38	276
John—George: The Mystic Guitarists	39	278
Paul—George: The Improvisators	40	280
John—Ringo: The Tricksters	41	282
Paul—Ringo: The Performers	42	283
George—Ringo: The Followers	43	285
Major Influences	44	286
Chapter 4 – Setting the Stage	47	291
The Uranus-Pluto Interchange	47	---
The Arc of Awakening	48	---
Neptune in Scorpio	51	---
4 Phases to the Journey	52	---
5 Major Themes	53	---
Jupiter & Saturn	---	291
Venus & Mars Retrogrades	---	292
Eclipses & The Nodal Axis	---	293

Chapter 5 – Beginnings   56   295

The Lennon Family Comes Apart   56   295
Ringo's Battle   57   297
Mary McCartney's Death   57   298
John & Paul Meet   58   301
Enter George Harrison   59   303
Julia Lennon's Death   60   305
Two Routes of Grief & Redemption   62   ---
Foreshadowing   64   ---

Chapter 6 – Coming of Age   65   308

Hamburg   65   308
The Cavern Club   66   308
Stuart Sutcliffe   67   309
First Recording Session   68   312
Discovery & Brian Epstein   68   312
John's New Beginning   ---   313
The Audition & George Martin   70   314
Enter Ringo Starr   71   316
The Marginalization of Pete Best   71   317
John Gets Married   73   320

Chapter 7 – Lift Off   74   322

Love Me, Please Me   74   322
Twisting & Shouting   75   323
Album #1: *Please Please Me*   76   324
The Birth of Julian Lennon   78   325
Paul Meets Jane   78   326
John Pummels Bob Wooler   79   327

Chapter 8 – The Meteoric Rise   80   328

The Beatlemania Astrology of the Musicians   ---   328
Hysteria   80   330
Album #2: *With the Beatles*   82   331
Opening Salvo of the British Invasion   83   332
The Sun Begins to Rise   84   333
The Muse   86   ---
Reunion and Soul Contracts   88   ---

Another Unanswered Call   89   335
At the Movies   90   336
Album #3: *A Hard Day's Night*   91   337

Chapter 9 – Growing Up   93   338

A Starr Has Fallen   93   338
George Accepts His Path   94   339
Grieving Losers   94   339
Beatles & the Bard   96   341
Still No Answer   96   341
Rain and Sun   97   342
Ill Feelings   97   342
Album #4: *Beatles for Sale*   98   343
Ringo Gets Married   99   344
Ticket to Pride   100   344
The Reflection of Clowns   101   345
Words of Hidden Love   101   346
Opening the Doors   102   347

Chapter 10 – Inspiration   104   348

Major Eclipses: Consciousness Expands   105   ---
Yesterday: The Melody of Dreams   105   348
A Face in a Dream   108   ---
Album #5: *Help!*   109   351
Twinkle Twinkle Little Starr   111   352

Chapter 11 – The First Peak: Resilient Souls   112   353

Dead Little Girl and Lighting Fires   112   353
In John's Life: The Dead & Living   114   355
Working it Out   115   356
The Land of Nowhere   115   357
The Muse in Beatles Astrology   ---   359
The Mercurial Songs   117   359
Album #6: *Rubber Soul*   119   362
George Gets Married   121   363

Chapter 12 – The Second Peak: The Mountaintop   122   364

    Controversy   123   365
    The Sermon from the Mountaintop   124   365
    Sex & Drugs   127   367
    Paperback Rain   128   ---
    Taxes & Birds   129   ---
    Living the Dream   130   368
    Mind Aches   133   ---
    Sailing to the Sun   133   371
    George is Telling   134   ---
    Being Present   135   ---

Chapter 13 – The Third Peak: Gunfire   137   372

    Dead Woman Talking   137   372
    Album #7: Revolver   139   373
    Beyond Touring…   143   374
    …And into War   144   375
    John Meets Yoko and Paul Crashes   145   ---

Chapter 14 – The Dream of Lonely Hearts Part 1: Inception   147   378

    Metamorphosis   148   ---
    Fields of Dreams   150   380
    A Journey through Time   152   381
    Cleansing the Window of Perception   154   381
    The Realization of Soul Intent   156   ---
    Tea with John   158   ---
    Heart Repairs   159   ---
    The Synchronistic Landscape   160   383

Chapter 15 – The Dream of Lonely Hearts Part 2:   164   384
The Aeronautics of Consciousness

    Mystical Kite Flying   164   384
    Tea with Paul   168   ---
    As Above, So Below: The Girl Who Bridges Worlds   168   385
    Heeding the Word   172   ---
    Saving the World   174   386
    She's Having Fun   175   ---
    Singing Soul Family   176   ---

Comedy Call Song   177   ---
Tea with George   177   387
Album #8: *Sgt. Pepper's Lonely Hearts Club Band*   178   388

Chapter 16 – Descension   182   389

Paul's New Beginning   ---   389
Relaying the Message   183   390
Baby, Mother and Guru   184   390
Confronting Death   185   391
The Fall of 1967   186   ---
Hello Walrus   187   392
Clearing the Fog   188   ---
The Muse in Flight   189   392
The Sun Going Down   190   393

Chapter 17 – Amusement   192   395

Album #9: *Magical Mystery Tour*   192   395
The *Magical Mystery Tour* Movie   194   396
Depiction of the Dream   195   ---
Inner Visions #1: Mary's Transformation   197   397
Inner Visions #2: Julia's Poetry   198   398
Inner Visions #3: The Light Within   200   399
Barking in the Rain   201   ---

Chapter 18 – White Heat Part 1: Musings & Meltdown   203   402

Inner Peace & Outer Confrontation   204   ---
The Awakening of Anger   205   ---
Changing the World   206   403
The Muse in the Shadowlands   207   404
Ringo's New Beginning   ---   404
Blackbird #9   209   405
Sleep Tight   213   407
Ob-La-Disaster   214   408
Screaming Babies   215   408
Making it Better   217   410
The Mother Lode   218   ---

Chapter 19 – White Heat Part 2: Rivalry & Rawness ... 220 ... 411

Showdown at the Hoedown ... 220 ... 411
Turbulence ... 222 ... 413
Playing in the Sun ... 223 ... 413
George's Weeping Guitar ... 224 ... 415
Birthday Piggies ... 226 ... 415
Finger on your Trigger ... 227 ... 416
A Song of Love ... 228 ... 417
George's Wonderwall ... 229 ... 417
They Became Naked ... 229 ... 418
Album #10: *The Beatles* ("The White Album") ... 230 ... 419
Manson & The Collective Shadow ... 232 ... 420

Chapter 20 – The Come Down ... 234 ... 422

Album #11: *Yellow Submarine* ... 235 ... 422
Jamming in January ... 236 ... 423
Don't Let Me Get Back ... 238 ... ---
Singing on the Rooftop ... 238 ... 423
Paul's Summation: The Ultimate Answer ... 238 ... ---
Moving Forward ... 240 ... ---
Marriages & Divorce ... 241 ... 424

Chapter 21 – Coming Apart & Together ... 243 ... 427

The Ballad of John, Yoko & Paul ... 243 ... 427
Ringo's Summation: The Safe and Happy Garden ... 245 ... 427
Monetary Desires ... 245 ... ---
John's Summation: Giving Peace ... 246 ... 428
George's Summation: The Radiance of Being ... 247 ... 429
Summer of '69 ... 248 ... ---
The Beatles Summation: The Awakening of Love ... 249 ... 430
At the Crossroads ... 249 ... 431
Daughter Mary Comes to Paul ... 250 ... 432

Chapter 22 – The End ... 251 ... 433

John's Departure ... 251 ... 433
Album #12: *Abbey Road* ... 252 ... 434
Paul is "dead" and John's in "hell" ... 254 ... 435
The Return to Self ... 255 ... ---

Letting It Be   256   436
Declarations of Independence   256   437
Album #13: *Let It Be*   257   438
Final Thoughts   260   ---

Extras   439

Summaries of the Threads   439
The Muse Process   466
John as Muse?   469
Chart Data   471
Notes   476
Bibliography   486
Acknowledgements   488

Introduction

The Beatles: iconic, celebrated and likely the most influential musical phenomenon of the 20th Century. Thousands of rock bands have come and gone, but this one is lodged in the collective imagination like no other. They have become part of us, impossible to ignore and compelling as ever. So much so, they have also been the most studied.

In the last 50 years, there have been numerous books, documentaries and even courses designed to reveal their magic. People play Beatles albums backwards, attempting to glean some kind of hidden message. Others dissect every lyric, or look for clues on the album covers. Much of the pursuit has been microanalysis, as if the answers are found in the minutia. What makes this study different is the exploration of the macro. We'll be zooming out and examining them through another level or *dimension* of perception. My intention is to help answer the timeless question, *why*. Why have the Beatles made this enormous impact? What is the broader meaning?

A band noted for their eternal questing, they were continually seeking broader meaning. As Beatlemania was gaining momentum in 1964, their adventures brought them to the United States. They famously met Bob Dylan in a hotel room in New York, a meeting of musical minds shaping Western culture. Talking through billows of smoke, the conversation became philosophical. Paul shared the insight that "There are seven levels"[1] to this existence, a notion John would make reference to in "And Your Bird Can Sing" a couple years later. It's a fun anecdote for the Beatles fan and a good starting point for our journey. Let's have a look—how many levels are there?

Well, it depends on who you ask. There are numerous models of the universe put forth by philosophers, theorists, mystics, sages and perhaps other bleary-eyed young musicians. Though there is no agreement about seven, there is almost universal consensus that there are various levels. Aside from physical, emotional and intellectual levels, most conceptualizations include a spiritual level (or levels). There are a multitude of definitions and perspectives on spirituality. The view here is non-denominational and universal—including the idea that the universe itself is alive, intelligent and in meaningful connection with everyone and everything.

Imagine if it was possible to tap in to the spiritual dimension and understand the themes, issues and dynamics underlying the manifest world. Imagine there's an elegant, sophisticated system that clarifies such information...

Another Dimension

Astrology reveals the spiritual dimension in striking detail and serves as the main tool I've employed in this study. I've been a professional astrologer for 20+ years and my great passion is to communicate this sacred knowledge. Don't worry if you are not an astrologer or student, I've written this book to be accessible for you. Though astrology is an amazing tool, it's also complicated and shrouded in misperceptions. I'd like to briefly address a few of the issues.

Astrology's legacy includes fortune-telling and popular simplifications, but most present-day astrologers understand it's *co-creative* (we play a hand in our fate) and quite complex. Astrology can be seen as the celestial or cosmic weather. Like a forecast helps us plan for the day, astrology informs us of the spiritual conditions, so we can navigate consciously. Since the metaphysical dimension is archetypal and energetic in scope, it doesn't detail precisely what occurs in the manifest world. Through our co-creative response, we ground it through our behavior choices on a broad spectrum of possibilities. Astrology asks the questions of our growth, and it's our job to find the answers.

As will be detailed, the astrological weather in the 1960s emphasized the process of spiritual awakening. We tend to experience the familiar weather in the background, hardly ever knowing the exact barometric pressure or wind speed. The same holds true with the astrological weather. We may not be completely conscious of it, but the spiritual dynamics inform our experience. The Beatles served as musical conduits who expressed the energetic themes of their day.

My job is to clarify such dynamics, to interpret the overarching dimension. The information complements the familiar story by adding an additional layer. It is not intended to suggest greater validity, or as a replacement, to the well-known facts. The reader is encouraged to hold the perspective that *there are many levels operating simultaneously*…who knows, maybe Paul was right and there are seven.

The Beatles run occurred when astrology was proliferating into the mass consciousness. However, its use tended to be simple. People would ask, "What's your sign?" reducing the vast complexity of astrology to just one factor, a caricature of its potency and potential. The subject was often discussed as entertainment or as a pseudoscience, not for "serious" people. There has been a backlash from the "serious" people (academics, educators, scientists, etc.) who rightfully criticize the simplifications of astrology's popular version. It has remained controversial in the collective mind, attracting substantial interest, while largely being dismissed by science and mainstream religion. Furthermore, there are many different uses and astrological approaches, adding to the confusion of what it is and can do.

The Beatles became open to and interested in astrology, reportedly having an in-house astrologer at their Apple location.[2] Yoko Ono has been an astrology enthusiast for years and it was a part of her relationship with John.[3] Paul has mentioned astrology in relation to his song, "Hello Goodbye," which plays on the theme of duality—relating it to his Sun sign Gemini.[4] George was the most immersed in the subject matter. On his posthumous album *Brainwashed*, he sang of being a "Pisces Fish." Ringo has been open to a wide variety of metaphysical pursuits as an active voice for the counterculture.

Our Journey

The book begins with a spiritual overview of the musicians, their interrelationships, musical influences and the band itself. The unique condition of the celestial weather in the 1960s is introduced. This sets the stage for the bulk of the book, the chronology. All of the major events in their history, ranging from significant childhood experiences through the entire life of the band, are discussed. The chronology ends when their break-up became public (1970), to keep the scope of the book manageable and most relevant to The Beatles as a band.

The overarching theme is spiritual maturation, which is examined in a variety of ways: personally, the group, musically, lyrically and culturally. There is less focus on the sordid business, financial and legal entanglements they got themselves into (however, these things are noted). Since there is so much material already published about these more mundane matters, our emphasis is spirituality. Though this book enters metaphysical, philosophical and psychological areas, it never strays very far from the music, the musicians and their message.

Due to copyright law, only very small excerpts from the lyrics (usually a few words or a phrase) are found here in the text, in strict accordance with "fair use." Legal advice has informed me the minimal reprinting of lyrics qualifies because the usage involves commentary, as well as being part of original research (connecting the time the songs were developed and/or released with astrology). The use here is unquestionably "transformative" (adding new meaning, insight and understanding) and does not infringe on the commercial viability of the music. To the contrary, readers are encouraged to listen to the songs and read the full lyrics as you make your way through (and if you don't own the music, go get it!). Not only will this make the overall content clearer, it will add to your enjoyment. It's amazing to hear and experience the spiritual dimension emerge into consciousness.

It turns out that the Beatles example has relevance to us all—a remarkable coming of age story depicting universal themes of spiritual development, even including important teachings. Whether they were conscious of it or not, their story and music incredibly portray stages of growth, paralleling the astrology of their time. They exemplified spiritual discovery, while making a terrific soundtrack about it too!

The book is organized in 2 main sections, aimed to accommodate the various levels of astrological background of the readership. Part 1 is written in an accessible, story-telling style mostly free of astrological jargon. Most of the included astrology terms are in {brackets}, which can be ignored by the layperson. Major points informed by my astrological research are linked to Part 2 for further discussion through subscript notation like this$_1$. There are, however, some key astrological points and ideas which are so crucial and central, they must be brought in. I take great care in thoroughly explaining them. Part 2 contains technical astrology, including deeper chart analyses involving the astrological language. The reader can choose how much astrology to consume, or not.

For those without too much background in astrology (or none), your experience will become increasingly rewarding should you familiarize with the subject. I decided that this book cannot also serve as an introductory astrology text, so information on the basics (planets, signs, houses, elements, etc.) should be found elsewhere. Part 2 begins with a brief outline of the *Astrology of Awakening* approach, thoughts from my perspective.

My Role

     I am truly humbled and honored to present this material, thrilled to add to a spiritual understanding of this cultural phenomenon. My aim is to tell the story without any agenda, judgement or bias—to capture some of their unique spark and enchantment. I write from a place of service and deep appreciation for the fabled musicians. The Beatles return us to the simplicity of our innocence, while tantalizing us towards the dizzying heights of innovation. They have given the world a magnificent gift and it is my most sincere intention to honor it.

     Before I get out of the way, I'll share a few words about my passion for this band. I arrived on planet Earth in 1971, a year after they disbanded. I got into the music around age 5 and listened endlessly. The Beatles were a loyal friend and companion as I developed, shaping the contours of my psyche. They made an indelible mark on me, and only through this project have I come to truly understand it. During the years of research and writing, I experienced a second wave of passion, this time from the consciousness of midlife.

     At first a fun project, I followed where the story led, allowing the lens of astrology to inform my view. The deeper I looked, the more something miraculous came into focus. I was shocked and delighted to see how it unfolded, as surprised as you might be. The creative process was a uniquely special time. It brought me much joy, amazement, laughter and tears. I hope you will be similarly moved.

     I invite you to share in the magic, this truly remarkable story. Thank you for joining me in this exploration (and celebration) of the most regarded musical act the world has ever produced. With love to John, Paul, George and Ringo, let's explore the spiritual dimension of The Beatles…

Chapter 1
The Musicians

The opening chapter provides a summary of the astrology charts of the band members. I imagine people thinking, "Where is he getting this information?" As found throughout the book, the reader can follow the points being made to Part 2 for more discussion and information. For those not familiar with astrology, it does reveal a lot! However, my objective is to keep the flow moving as there is a lot of ground to cover. Most essays are actually quite condensed, focusing on the major points that have the most significance.

For the summaries in this chapter, the discussions are organized to illustrate a trajectory of spiritual growth. The assumption is that we are works in progress, enrolled in a spiritual curriculum of evolution and awakening. Therefore, all of us have lessons we are resolving, as well as opportunities for further growth. The opening section of Part 2 includes the spiritual philosophy that informs this approach. There are notes on reincarnation (which is assumed) and it is encouraged to be read here at the start.

John Lennon

John's main spiritual focus was the development of leadership skills. He had a karmic background of a visionary, a soul with big-picture perspectives and intuitive insight. He carried an unquenched desire to occupy visible positions to showcase his brilliance. He sought a career pushing innovative cultural trends, wanting recognition for his talent[1].

As a youngster, the leadership drive manifested with confidence and self-assertion. In his teenage years he founded and led the skiffle band The Quarrymen. He named an early iteration of The Beatles after himself, Johnny and The Moondogs. Interestingly, John's astrological Moon is precisely what is being referred to. He positioned himself as the alpha dog, literally playing out his emotional desires {Moon} for authority {in the 10th House}. He initially sees others as part of his pack.

On the road towards maturation and steadying his brilliance, John's emotional disposition was restless and unpredictable. The issue was disconnection from a continuity of nurturance[2]. Instability and abandonment are noted in his early childhood. John's father Alf (or Freddie) was an absentee father who left John's life when he was only 5. His mother

Julia was young and undisciplined and deferred to her sister Mimi to raise him. These experiences reflect the most painful part of his chart—John's deep wounds with family. His need for achievement was rooted in the issue, an attempt to earn love and appreciation through public roles. The spiritual work was to discover love within, a transformation into more joy and centeredness in the self[3].

In particular, the familial wound specifically concerned maternal issues; hurt from a perceived lack of love due to abandonment. Not only did Julia have Mimi serve as John's primary caretaker, she was killed in an accident when he was a teenager. The tragedy triggered the deepest wounds and horror in his soul, a feeling of desertion with intense upset. John's pattern was to play out his maternal issues in relationships, an attempt to reestablish intimacy[4]. However, the more he might find love within, the more he could relax the projection of this complex. The early developmental spiritual struggle will be discussed throughout the book as the "wounded child" area of his chart[5]. It was activated when Julia was killed and upon other occasions of emotional upset and transformation.

John was known as the "smart Beatle," an intuitive and inquisitive intelligence that understood psychological complexity. His potential was to think deeply and catalyze truthful, intimate exchanges. However, this style was entangled with his emotional defense system. His mind and speech were steeped in the psychology of pain and loss[6]. John was famous for his sharp tongue, which may have been giving voice to his inner turmoil. His song lyrics featured many examples of him calling out for reconciliation and connection. Gradually, communication transformed into a message promoting peace and love, reflecting a more established inner poise.

From a spiritual perspective (assuming reincarnation), we all create karmic patterns while less conscious and mature. John's initial emotional upset contributed to a pattern of conflict, the playing out of pain with others. His chart reveals themes of belligerence, perhaps even in the arena of war[7]. These historical patterns tend to play out when we are developing, in order for us to become aware of them and resolve. He is portrayed in his biographies as an intimidating presence in his youth, one who had his share of brawls.[5] Also, the issue of war would enter John's artistic and public life in dramatic ways.

Though astrology charts don't provide specifics, the general theme is the warrior (or soldier, leader) who is lost, defeated or confused, perhaps in an existential crisis about conflict/war itself. Karmic resolution is found by becoming a more conscious leader, to fight for the most noble of causes. Astrology often involves work with polarity—the present lifetime had a major emphasis on peace, the arts and developing the ability to harmoniously collaborate[8]. To heal prior loss and estrangement, John was energetically attuned to romance and relationship[9]. He wrote numerous love songs and Beatlemania had a flavor of romantic longing and intrigue.

Every chart has extraordinary potential gifts, which are actually necessary for our growth. With a background of instability and conflict, John carried the gifts of likability and charisma, creativity and aesthetic sensibility[10]. His end of the deal was to become more focused and diligent, to ground such potential into a body of work. Specifically, areas of entertainment and performance were the realms his soul chose to put his brilliance towards. Creative outlets were ideal for his unrealized ambition and innovative ideas, but also for emotional catharsis[11]. In his astrological area of artistry and performance was also the muse, a source of inspiration (which will become increasingly significant and further discussed as we go)[12].

John was naturally very talented (an innate gift), but grappled with the technical facets of his trade.[(6)] Finding creative partnerships to assist him was the intention[13]. The potential of his artistic development carried broader, collective themes. Using music to change the world would fit. The tightest aspect (connection between planets) in his entire chart involved the transformation of culture, to transmute deep buried psychological issues into highly charged, compelling and innovative artistic contributions[14]. More than the others, John was a trendsetter and his cultural impact became astounding.

John's transformation was miraculous. At the beginning of the Beatles he was the leader, driven to dominate and become famous. When the band ended, he was invested in social activism. He radically changed his appearance from the gruff leather jacket image of his youth (reflecting his belligerent karma), to the long-haired peacenik singing songs of love. His spiritual maturation was made possible by taking responsibility for his emotions. John grew from defensiveness to greater humility, self-preoccupation to global concern, and empowered others to similarly be more connected to love. His ability to dynamically grow was reflected in the enormity of his cultural contribution. With his innate gift in style and trendsetting, John was the "art" {Libra Sun} of The Beatles[15].

Paul McCartney

Paul appears on this planet to entertain the collective, in a very big way. He carries a pronounced need to be seen by the world, to become recognized and appreciated. He has the soul of a performer, and he has likely developed creative and artistic skill for many lifetimes[1]. Paul's disposition is agreeable, collaborative and optimistic. He has developed a charming and likable personality structure, but there are layers of complexity. Underneath the sunny disposition is significant angst and frustration[2].

The central karmic issue in Paul's chart is the surrendering of his creative vision to handle necessary responsibilities[3]. His ethic of responsibility (to the wishes of others, to help out financially) has undermined his ability to manifest his personal aims. In the band's early days, Paul faced the tension between employment and a musical career. There were financial difficulties in his home life, which he felt obligated to help remedy. The frustration in his shadow may overcompensate into being overly self-promoting, an exaggerated sense of self-importance. The spiritual lesson is to become more *healthily* self-aligned, to rightfully develop leadership in realms of entertainment and smooth out his edge from karmic sacrifice. The associated astrological signature will be referred to as the "I'm in charge" area of his chart[4].

Another dimension of his spiritual work involves grief. Sacrificing performance desires is connected with familial strife, strongly and emphatically pointing to maternal loss[5]. His mother Mary died when he was just 14. The repetition of the karmic pattern is seen in Paul's statement at the time of her death, "How are we going to get by without her money?"[7] This remark not only reflects his financial issues, but also reveals his reluctance to deal with painful emotion[6]. Paul's pattern is to handle pragmatics, rather than grief and loss. Therefore, to resolve the past, the work is to embrace his vulnerability and hurt. By so doing, he can inform his creative output with greater depth and make an emotional impact with his audience.

The dominant astrological configuration in Paul's chart is his "expression of grief" signature[7]. The first song Paul wrote was "I Lost My Little Girl," penned not too far after his mother's passing. Though the song concerns the loss of love, Paul's chart strongly suggests the projection of his maternal issues onto relationship, the major similarity he shares with John. It has been noted by biographers and critics that their songwriting may be influenced by childhood trauma of maternal loss, an attempt at the reclamation of love.[8] Paul's "expression of grief" signature makes dynamic connections to the archetype of the muse. He has this mysterious energy of divine inspiration also in his area of artistry, another key similarity he shares with John.

Paul's unresolved issue with death and loss lingers as a spiritual question: can he somehow find the spiritual understanding or experiences to heal his heart? The soul intention is to become more contemplative or intuitive, to learn how to raise his consciousness to other realms or dimensions[8]. His chart emphasizes communication, which seems to have three different purposes. First, is to learn how to communicate intuitively with what is beyond our usual comprehension. Next is to communicate his findings through performance. Finally, to learn how to communicate more effectively interpersonally from a place of authenticity, instead of desiring approval or being driven by resentment.

Due to lifetimes of service and drudgery, sacrificing himself for necessary responsibilities, Paul has earned what may be described as "karmic credit[9]." In this incarnation, he has a most public chart, one with extraordinary potential for success and recognition[10]. He is perfectly positioned to satisfy his needs to be seen and perform. However, his end of the deal is to inform his role with spiritual purpose and a philosophy of love. If not, he would be at risk for clamoring for attention and validation.

One of Paul's assets is a tireless work ethic[11]. Instead of the prior pattern of working for others, the present intention is to craft his own body of work. Due to the karmic background of drudgery, Paul now has the gift of dazzling variety and ingenuity for novel contributions. He's blessed with an improvisational style and great flexibility. Paul became proficient at many instruments and wrote songs in multiple genres.

With so much need to resolve the past, his mindset is oriented to yesteryear[12]. This enables him to release his personal grief, while his creativity might connect his audience to their roots. As he develops his own voice, Paul becomes the storyteller. The intention is to become more intuitive and tell stories which have broader spiritual, archetypal or mythological relevance[13]. Paul has the ability to tap into sources of inspiration from other dimensions.

His accessible people-pleasing demeanor, combined with his inherent dreaminess, form the persona of the "cute Beatle." His maturation involves transcending the self-gain available with such a persona, to become a creative bridge describing our connection between worlds. The potential of his chart is to invite the collective into shared emotional expression and, ultimately, catharsis. He is able to unite the world family through both love and good cheer, all made possible by his ability to heal his heart.

Paul has the soul of the frustrated performer, a compassionate humanitarian who wants everyone to be happy. The present lifetime emphasizes healthy self-alignment, to claim his light in the world. There is a message to find and share with significant mental energy to create a body of work. Paul's gift is bringing inspiration and the dream world into form. As a lead songwriter, singer and spokesman for the band for decades, Paul is the "voice" {Gemini Sun} of the Beatles[14].

George Harrison

Bringing spirituality into public arenas through creative pursuits was the central theme of George's chart. The intention was to entertain, inspire, raise consciousness and deliver a message. The development of this promise hinged on his ability to resolve a complicated emotional pattern.

George arrived into his life with an urgent need to make more loving contact with Spirit[1]. He was clearing up the discord between dogmatic teachings and a much more compassionate and fluid experience of divinity. The karmic legacy of being hurt or disempowered by teachings has been taken personally, creating a component of fear in his psyche. The internalization of limiting beliefs left George upset and brooding, creating a somber mood and need to be left alone. The corresponding part of his chart is discussed as "dark George[2]."

The defensive pattern avoids conflict, often a tendency to give power away to others[3]. George was very supportive and compassionate, a karmic pattern of being a follower. Underneath was an urgency to claim his own power and stature, a rebellious streak which wants to upset the apple cart. Upon claiming his own unique light through a more conscious spirituality, deeper and more meaningful human contact becomes possible. He no longer is so impacted by others or defers to them, rather he connects from a position of inner strength[4].

George's spiritual work also involves family and home issues, finding a more stable foundation of love and security[5]. He was the youngest child in a poor household and faced bleak prospects for the future. Often ignored or marginalized, he carried a detached pattern, a defense mechanism of protection. He had distrust of authority and was uninterested in conforming to their expectations. He was resistant to schooling, wary of repeating a karmic pattern of indoctrination. George dropped out of school[(9)]—he was learning to think for himself and find his own way.

He was learning to deepen into his emotional upset and express it artistically[6]. Being creative naturally invites him out of hiding and into sharing. In fact, George's soul intended to become commanding, maximally visible and a leader in entertainment pursuits. His gifts included charisma and originality, which helps rectify the pattern of being secondary. George was learning how to become a mystic, made possible through his emotional work as much as any spiritual practice[7]. The more he found healing and compassion internally, the greater his impact collectively.

George's chart emphasized humanitarian and global issues. He carried an intention to be part of broader movements, to raise and shift consciousness through togetherness and artistic collaboration. The corresponding part of his chart will be referred to as "spiritual George," which was catalyzed into action in the latter part of the story and beyond[8]. His spearheading of the Beatles trip to India and leadership in the world music trend serve as examples.

The karmic legacy of being misled by others is remedied by finding more resonant and meaningful spiritual teachings. More than the others, George was oriented to philosophy, which became influential to The Beatles message[9]. His philosophical intention had a cross-cultural orientation. George served as a bridge between old and new, East and West, a translator of spiritual principles into creative expression.

As he developed spiritually, a point of integration is in relationships[10]. He was healing from detachment, learning to be more engaged and intimate. As he finds deeper love within, he is able to connect with others without petitions or demands. A more transcendent perspective could inform a romantic message. The spirit of the 1960s included the questioning, and potential redefinition, of relationship. George's chart conveys progressive notions about relating, which could influence cultural and collective assumptions[11].

George's mind was unconventional, questioning and organized to see things differently[12]. He was a broad thinker and very clever, with undertones of both comedy and sarcasm.[(10)] He got people to think, just as he was learning himself. The more he learned to walk the path of the mystic, the less of an edge he carried. George was emerging into radiant visibility, learning to stand confidently in his authentic spiritual truth. He could be considered the "soul" or "conscience" {Pisces Sun} of The Beatles[13].

Ringo Starr

True to the name he adopted, Ringo arrived on the planet with the desire to be a star. He has a very deep and passionate need to perform and communicate through creative expression[1]. It will be discussed as "playful Ringo," but this part of him hasn't always been able to shine. In fact, there is great angst, lots of intense and unsettled energy about sharing himself[2]. The karmic lessons portray the reason for his frustrations.

Ringo's central issue is loneliness[3]. His chart speaks of isolation, the inability to connect with others and the resultant aggravation. He was learning to manage his feelings, to find greater self-love which would heal his isolation[4]. By deepening into himself, he was able to develop the more conscious potential of his chart. His contribution involves emotional and familial support, a continuity of love and nurturance.

Hanging in the balance of Ringo's spiritual lessons are substantial health issues, which contribute to the isolation and angst[5]. He had severe health problems in his childhood which separated him from others.[(11)] As a youngster, he developed appendicitis, which required a long period of treatment. As a teenager, he spent significant time in a sanitarium, being treated for tuberculosis. He passed his time by learning percussion in the hospital band. In contrast to "playful Ringo," who wants to perform and connect, there is also "inside Ringo," who is stuck and limited[6].

Similar to Paul, Ringo carries a surprising (albeit hidden and protected) level of anger in his shadow[7]. The defense mechanism is to convey the exact opposite, an agreeable and pleasing demeanor. The spiritual work is to deepen into emotional authenticity, to find love inside. Then he can find true happiness, rather than the appearance of it. The intention is to direct his passion and anger into vigorous performance[8]. Ringo's choice of the drums was ideal as the instrument supports emotional release through physical expression.

Similar to John, Ringo was also working along the axis of war and peace[9]. However, Ringo's war is with himself, the refusal to be with painful emotion. As he softens and deepens, the intention is to become an advocate for peace and connection in the world. Ringo's trademark is the peace gesture (two raised fingers) and he's been active with peace movements and causes. The intention is to also bring such sweetness to domestic arenas, thereby healing his issues with family[10]. Ringo created a family with 3 children. Instead of keeping feelings bottled-up, he carries the intention to learn communication skills. Ringo wrote the least amount of Beatles songs, but he had the second most prolific solo career as a songwriter. Also shy about singing in the band, he grew to be the lead singer for much of his solo output.

Another major issue in Ringo's chart is simply confidence, having personal value and inner strength[11]. Challenges with feeling safe and secure were present in his home. He grew up in pronounced poverty (like George) and his parents divorced. He was an only child and had an absentee father (like John). The poverty issues of his childhood reflect an initial paucity of self-worth. The resolution involves making something of himself, to claim his power in the world. The potential gift is to be highly successful, to use such abundance for selfless reasons. As the personal work resolves, a more worldly focus emerges. The next step involves finding broader purpose or mission, to become an advocate for something meaningful[12]. With a karmic history of aloneness and frustration, the present life has an expansive and inclusive quality. In short, Ringo gets to spread good cheer and joy wherever he goes.

Sometimes Ringo's contribution to the band is underestimated or unappreciated because he was not a main songwriter. However, the Beatles were a type of family and they referred to each other as "brothers." Ringo's main gift and contribution was to emotionally anchor the family system, just like his drums anchored the music. Also, his drumming is widely deemed to be unique, engaging, innovative and influential, perfect for the musical sensibilities of this band. The drums establish the beat (in the Beatles), and Ringo can be considered the "heart" {Cancer Sun} of the band[13].

Chapter 2
The Band

The four members share some similarities while their differences were complementary and sometimes frictional. In this chapter, the dynamics of the band as a "soul group" will be explored. Also, the individual musicians combine to form the overall gestalt to the band itself. In astrology, there is a "composite chart," which blends individual charts together. This chapter will discuss and summarize the Beatles group chart (with greater astrological detail in Part 2, p. 271).

Soul Group Dynamics

A soul group is an assemblage of people drawn together to work through spiritual lessons. The Beatles had unresolved needs to perform and use artistry for broader cultural and spiritual reasons.

John had a visionary background and his soul chose music and the arts in this incarnation as a means of creative expression. Paul arrived in this life a natural entertainer. His issue is to free himself from obligations to represent his talent. George's intention was to share spirituality artistically. Ringo is a frustrated performer who wants to be healthy enough to get out and rock and roll.

In order to rise into their full creative empowerment, all of them had significant emotional work to do. In particular, loneliness is a uniting thread. It's extraordinary to see how much the issue appears in the song catalog. Each of them had a somewhat different component of loneliness, but together, they are a lonely hearts club.

In "Strawberry Fields Forever," John writes, "No one I think is in my tree/I mean it must be high or low." These lyrics point to loneliness—he's either a genius (high) or completely mad (low), but disconnected from others just the same.[12] Paul's flavor of loneliness is tender, like a child who misses his mom and wants a hug. He asks in "Hold Me Tight" to be "the only one" so he can "never be the lonely one." George's loneliness is existential, the pain of being away from the Oneness of Spirit. He ponders in "Long Long Long" (a song about spiritual reunion with the divine[13]), "How could I ever have lost you?" For Ringo, loneliness involves feeling separate from others. He writes in "Don't Pass

Me By," "I wonder where you are tonight/And why I'm by myself." The loneliness of brilliance (John), grief (Paul), spiritual separation (George) and social isolation (Ringo) bond them together[1]. As evidence of their growth, they created brilliant, healing music which brought them, and the entire world, together.

Each of their respective charts portrays significant emotional wounds and fears[2]. The intention was to share such feelings to form personal connection and find resolution through creative catharsis. The way their charts interact, there can be incredibly tight bonding or they might profoundly trigger one another[3]. The astrology conveys the energetic channels, which become filled with the consciousness of the actors involved. For better or worse, Beatles astrology is profoundly emotionally-focused.

Each of the band members had significant issues in their home lives. John and Paul lost their mothers in their teen years. John and Ringo had absentee fathers. There were significant financial concerns in the homes of Paul, Ringo and George. Ringo spent years of his childhood in the hospital. John was primarily raised by his aunt and her husband and didn't receive a continuity of care from either of his biological parents. All of them desired to attain success as a remedy for these early struggles. As the Beatles formed when they were in their late teens (Ringo joined in his early 20s), it was easy for them to latch on to the band as a source of nurturance and family[4].

Naturally we would find a preponderance of performance-related energy in their charts. Paul and Ringo were most oriented towards performance, with the strongest needs for attention. John and George were using creative talent as means for broader cultural and spiritual reasons. All of them were using music for emotional catharsis and finding connection[5].

They were also part of a much larger astrological generation {Pluto in Leo: 1939—1956}, which loosely correlates with the Baby Boom generation. Among several evolutionary lessons, this group could deepen entertainment to make it psychologically or spiritually impactful. The blind spot is grandiosity and narcissism, using the vessel of the personality to attain adoration and self-gain. The soul work of this generation is to find love within, then to joyously share it without urgency or demand for applause[6].

Another theme of this soul group is found in intellectual and communicative areas. They were learning to progressively use speech as a catalyst for social change. In just seven years (from their first album to the last), there was incredible maturation in their writing. On the darker side, there was also a lot of sniping and bickering. Whether consciously managed or not, they had access to the power of words[7].

They were also developing more mature management of masculine energy. All had outstanding karmic challenges with leadership or effectiveness. John had a pattern with war or intense personal conflict, which led to defeat/loss or existential crisis. Paul and Ringo had their will subjugated by trying conditions. George was disempowered by limiting teachings. The remedy was to show up with a conscious and mature use of power. They could support one another, rallying together as teammates, or they might devolve into competition and rivalry. Either way, this soul group had a brotherly dynamic[8].

Sibling Hierarchy

The Beatles were a type of family and they brought their issues to work. They saw each other as "brothers"[14] and a sibling hierarchy was established. The pecking order was influenced by their biological families and reflected in their astrology[1].

John was the only child of his biological parents (he had half-siblings), and carried the independent and leadership streak which often accompanies the condition. Paul has a younger brother, so he was in a dominant role in his family of origin. Both desired leadership, which set up the rivalry. George was the youngest in his family and also in the Beatles. He was lower on the proverbial totem pole, cast in the role of follower, which is a theme of his astrology chart. Ringo was an only child. Birth order theory suggests that only children sometimes become authoritative (like John), while other times they can simply be independent (like Ringo).

John was 1.5 years older than Paul, which is quite significant for teenagers (when they met). Paul respected the age difference and he joined John's already established band. John played the role of the "older brother," the one who called the shots. Paul was the "middle brother," initially deferring to John, yet also challenging him too, especially as time went on. Paul played with John as part of The Quarrymen, while also knowing George. He was in the middle and brought the two guitarists together.

Paul asserted his dominance towards George, wanting to keep him in a less powerful position. In fact, Paul would literally refer to George as a "baby brother."[15] In birth order theory, the youngest sometimes becomes a "slider," one who catches up and/or slides ahead of the older siblings through significant accomplishment. George's rise at the end of the Beatles fits this pattern, which disrupted the hierarchy.

Ringo's route as an only child differed greatly from John. He was alone and sick for much of his childhood, and he just wanted to perform and share his talent. Over the years, Ringo has referred to the other Beatles as his "three brothers."[16] He joined years after the others established their "sibling" hierarchy. Though the eldest Beatle, he agreed to a follower position, which suited his self-sufficient nature. The position of drummer was tenuous in the band's history and he sought to fill it without rocking the boat.

Band Dynamics

The band's composite chart reveals the spiritual dynamics of this soul group, the themes, lessons and intentions. The group chart is featured in this book more than any other. Many of the events in their chronology will be related directly to it. Below is an introduction to it and a deeper dive can be found in Part 2 (p. 273).

Every chart originates with a desire, some kind of motivation which sets up an evolutionary trajectory. However, this initial desire tends to be launched from innocence and naiveté (the immaturity of the spiritual "childhood," see notes on this in Part 2). As youngsters in the early days the Beatles had a rallying cry, an aspiration to get to the "toppermost of the poppermost." Their group chart depicts this desire to climb the proverbial mountain of artistic success {10th House Moon}, to become recognized and celebrated. To get there, the strategy is to be as pleasing as possible {in Libra}. The initial motivation is discussed as their "love me" signature[1].

Directly connected to this underlying ambition is the "Beatles signature" {a Venus-Jupiter conjunction in Gemini}, the energy most central to their identity and spirit[2]. It captures their buoyant, optimistic and inviting vibe, an abundance of creativity with unlimited variety. The spirit is endlessly communicative (singing, songwriting, wit, message) with a knack for garnering popularity. It is ideal for spreading good cheer through creative and cultural pursuits. The caution is a penchant for "selling out," hedonism and initial superficiality before spiritual maturation.

Picking up on the centrality of communication, their chart directly pairs voice with romance {Mercury conjunct Juno}, as seen with their numerous love songs. The combination is smooth, pleasing and accessible—noticed in their delicate melodies and layered harmonies. This "love songs" signature is also under friction to emotionally deepen and convey a more mature understanding of love[3].

Their style and orientation to the world {Ascendant} involves travel and adventures, the pursuit of discovery fueled by purpose {in Sagittarius}. Early on they wore leather jackets, smoked cigarettes and wielded guitars as they quested the world for fame and fortune. Accompanying this style is fiery "warrior" energy {Athena in Sagittarius}, an approach like "musical gunslingers." As they matured, they grew their hair and presented a more philosophical {Sagittarius} appearance. The "warrior" energy is involved with rivalry and competition {opposite Venus}, which played out with other bands (Rolling Stones, Beach Boys, etc.) as well as within the band dynamics[4].

The core life energy of the band {Cancer Sun} gradually awakens into depth and love[5]. They had significant emotional energy to work with and resolve, matching their individual circumstances. People *love* the Beatles, and they loved each other. And also, when matters were difficult, lots of upset feelings were easily provoked. The band famously created a protective shell {Cancer} for privacy and security, which also brought confinement. Their songs and personas invite their audience to feel personally engaged, as if they are a part of us. The potential was to bring the world together as a family.

Their core soul group lesson specifically involved the ongoing development of a spiritual message {3rd House Pisces South Node}[6]. In particular, the emphasis was on universal notions of love (in contrast to the initial demand for personality adoration and self-gain), spiritual awakening and a transpersonal perspective of reality. The developmental trajectory was to become writers and messengers, serving as spiritual channels or conduits. The permeable nature of their openness allows for all sorts of input into their music. They could absorb and synthesize the currents around them, integrating threads from many influences, genres and cultures. The potential was incredibly imaginative and ethereal. However, they were also prone to flights of fancy, overindulgence and unproductive excursions leading to dead ends. They're often discussed as one group mind[(17)], which had extraordinary intuitive potential[7].

A facet of this multi-dimensional openness can be ambiguity in their lyrics and message. There are potentially many layers or dimensions, an impressionistic quality which connects subjectively to the listener. Not formally trained as musicians, they brought some

34

degree of randomness and unpredictability to the music as seen with unorthodox chord changes and use of instruments, as well as subliminal effects. The songs developed into soundscapes, while the lyrics grew to increasingly reflect spiritual ideas and teachings. Also, there is the projection of the sacred onto the group, and they have received their share of hero worship and idealization[8].

The evolutionary work was to walk a more devoted path, with an eye towards mastery and more healthy routines {9th House Virgo North Node}. There was the intention to have cross-cultural experiences, further engaging the spiritual quest. To complement their visionary and intuitive mind, growth involved technical precision[9]. The more polished and precise they became, the greater the impact of their art. They were fortunate to enlist key players for support. In particular manager Brian Epstein, producer George Martin and the technical staff at EMI provided necessary structure and discipline[10].

Also noted is a redefinition of the masculine {Mars conjunct North Node}. Born in the 1940s, they were raised as males in traditional society and initially played that role in their personal lives. Beatle wives and girlfriends were expected to be supportive, subservient and look the other way from their infidelities. As they matured, they learned greater parity and sacredness in their romantic lives, transforming the masculine role as public figures. They were learning to bring more consciousness to masculine expression through humility and service, rather than to promote self-interests[11].

Innovation with projects is strongly represented {Saturn conjunct Uranus}—a focus on grounding their visionary brilliance into concrete form. The potential was to bring inventive sparks into the work space through writing, sound, cultural leadership and collective trends[12]. Revolutionary energy is involved with business and financial areas. They founded their own record label (Apple) and sought new ways and means for financial management. As this energy can be challenging to ground, they did have some significant problems in these areas too.

There was profound spiritual work with the psychological shadow {8th House Pluto}, particularly with death[13]. In addition to resolving issues and wounds about death, this signature also involves hidden dynamics: sexual indiscretions or unwanted pregnancies, the underside of business dealings or wounding dramas we don't know about. It also relates to their sexual magnetism, the intense response from their fans. Also involved are issues regarding health {Chiron conjunct Pluto}—physical, mental or otherwise[14]. As noted, Ringo had significant health problems, John had problems with his eyesight, original bassist Stu Sutcliffe become fatally ill and biographers note that sexually-transmitted diseases were also part of their history. [18]

Within this group chart, the principle role of the 4 members can be seen. John's life energy {Libra Sun} sits right on the band's initial drive towards the "toppermost" and he was the early leader. Paul {Gemini Sun} connects with the "Beatles signature" most powerfully. Perhaps more than any member, he embodies the band's lively energy and has represented it most vocally. George's attunement {Pisces Sun} connects with spiritual direction and message, while Ringo's role {Cancer Sun} is to solidify the group as a family. He anchors the team through support, a counterbalance to the competitiveness. With his inclusion in the band in 1962, the composite chart itself became manifest, and their success occurred immediately after he joined. He fit in so well because his energy {Cancer Sun} matched the frequency of the unit itself[15].

On the Nature of Beetles

The name "Beatles" is a pun, which blends the insect with "beat," a component of music. They were briefly "The Beetles," "The Silver Beetles," "Long John and the Silver Beetles" and "The Beatals," before arriving at the familiar spelling. As fans of Buddy Holly and the Crickets, using an insect reference was also a nod to his influence.[19]

Stu Sutcliffe came up with "Beatals," and it grew from there. Stu (featured in later sections) had a Cancer Sun, which was right on the Beatles Cancer Sun. Astrology speaks in a broad archetypal language, the signs have varied and multi-dimensional meanings and underpinnings. For instance, Sagittarius involves the Centaur, and relates to the philosopher, politician, gypsy or explorer. Scorpio relates to the Scorpion but also to the eagle, phoenix or snake, as well as a host of Underworld symbolism.

The Crab is the most associated totem for Cancer, but the sign also relates to turtles and yes, to beetles, and other similar insects. Beetles carry a protective shell, the defining characteristic of the sign. Egyptians related Cancer to the scarab beetle,[20] which has connotations of immortality. Beetles deposit their eggs in the earth for 28 days, the time of a lunar cycle, and the Moon serves as the "ruling" planet of the sign. The 29th day is resurrection, when a fledgling beetle emerges from the water, the element associated with the sign.

Cancer begins at the summer solstice when the Sun is most visible in the sky (highest north declination). Similarly, the scarab beetle god Khepera pushes the Sun through the sky like a beetle pushes a ball of dung to the highest elevation on a sand ridge. For the Egyptians, beetles were thought to use the lofty position to fly into the celestial planes and bring back messages. As we'll explore, that turns out to be a theme with these musicians.

The scarab beetle was famously part of Carl Jung's fascination with synchronicity—the insect appearing on his office window when a client was mentioning its appearance in a dream. Like the Egyptians, he discussed the scarab in his *Red Book* as the "classical rebirth symbol," linking the insect with eternity and transformation.[21] Other species of beetles are saprophagous (feeding on dead organic matter), which also promotes rebirth. Saprophagous beetles convert what has been decomposed into food. *These beetles are literally nourished through death, while they facilitate the completion of the lifecycle for the dead.* The parallels to this story will become increasingly relevant and interesting as we go.

There are more beetles on our planet than any other animal. Approximately 40% of all insects are beetles, and they total about 25% of all animals. Similarly, the Beatles are likely the most popular of all rock bands and perhaps musical acts altogether. Beetles are endopterygotes, which go through a metamorphosis between childhood and adulthood. Likewise, the band experienced a metamorphosis in the middle phase of their career as they matured into adulthood. The album cover to *Sgt. Pepper's Lonely Hearts Club Band* features the mature adults in the center of the image, while their younger selves are hunched over (appearing lifeless) towards the left.

Some species of beetles are particularly competitive, fighting each other for dominance to secure mating partners. The parallel is the band's competitiveness and they had their share of sexual conquest. Beetles are also known for their bright and diverse colors and the Beatles adopted the wild, hippie wardrobe of their times. Their costumes for *Sgt. Pepper* are also noted for being bright and shiny.

Chapter 3
Band Relationships & Influences

There are 6 different dyads in the band. This chapter will summarize the unique spiritual dynamics of these pairings, both personally and musically. The analyses address how each pairing fit into the broader culture of the band—the purpose of these connections, as well as the gifts and challenges. Additionally, this chapter will detail The Beatles major musical influences.

John & Paul: The Leaders

John was a charismatic and cocksure free spirit, while Paul is more measured, agreeable and diplomatic. John could be hilarious with a wild streak, totally content staying in bed all day. Paul liked to practice and work, finding delight with method and precision. These personality characteristics are well-known. However, their astrology illustrates how these traits stem from their underlying soul work.

John was naturally intuitive, drawn to visionary processes. His soul came in to this life in a state of alarm, healing from the toll of war or conflict[1]. His famous laziness might have been a preference to explore his consciousness in favor of dealing with the pain of human connection and the drag of mundane matters. Time spent resting and in retreat allowed him to heal and develop his big-picture perspectives. As a result, he was less focused on technical matters and needed assistance with details. His soul intended to learn how to collaborate with others to share his vision.

Paul is a natural performer, a charmer with a human touch. He has developed a likable disposition with lifetimes of cultivating a focused work ethic[2]. His eagerness to work and create is driven by an unmet need to be appreciated for his talent. His soul intended to learn contemplative and intuitive skills, to inform and deepen his creativity. John was a visionary learning to be a performer, and Paul, a performer learning to be a visionary. They blended spectacularly, creating visionary entertainment.

Whereas Paul seeks affinity and positivity, John's tendency was to rebel and push the envelope[3]. The opposing styles can polarize or come together, and this central polarity can also be understood in terms of rock & roll. Paul's fiery exuberance for entertainment {Leo Moon} blends with John's desire for edginess, innovation and the transformation of culture {Aquarius Moon}[4]. Furthermore, both of these men had the energy of craftsmanship {Vesta} along this "rock & roll" axis {Leo-Aquarius}, configured in an I—thou {opposition} way[5]. When collaborating, they would sit opposite each other. With John being right-handed and Paul left-handed, they reflected each other as they played their guitars and crafted songs.

They enjoyed a supportive competitiveness and a complementary sense of artistry[6]. Of particular note was John's support for Paul's development as a visionary, what some might term a "destined" partnership[7]. Their charts reinforced the abundant potentials of the "Beatles signature." They had energetic channels which were flowing with ease, evident in areas of communication and ideas[8]. In fact, their astrology reveals rare dynamics of brilliance, made increasingly available through intuitive development[9]. Romantic energy was highly involved with writing[10]. The greatest similarities they shared were the projection of maternal issues into relationship and the muse in the astrological realm of creative performance[11].

The central challenge was divergent emotional styles and personalities. John was learning to be more deferential and collaborative, while Paul was learning how to be a leader. Each had what the other was learning; it played out with incredible synthesis as well as frictional polarization. In the final analysis, Lennon-McCartney is considered among the finest songwriting partnerships in world history.

John & George: The Mystic Guitarists

John and George were the primary guitarists and the members most involved with spiritual exploration. Though becoming a "mystic" is an ongoing (and advanced) process, they brought a focus to the metaphysical and led the walking of this path. Their contributions were the most ethereal and pushed the envelope of experimentation, often with an exotic or cross-cultural orientation[1].

As John was nearly 3 years older than George, there was a hierarchical component to their connection. John was initially reluctant to allow George into the band, so the relationship was formed with an expectation of George in a supporting role. In the early days, George deferred to John's leadership and mainly helped provide the music to his songs. Though George was younger, he was the lead guitarist, an interesting dynamic. There was a delicate negotiation of power and partnership that was tested as they individuated, particularly when George increased his creative output.

They had an extremely tight bond, but negotiating very different attachment styles was the work. John's difficulty with emotion and tendency to detach was in stark contrast to George's profound need for depth and intimacy[2]. When not feeling met in this way, George could easily feel misunderstood, seethe and carry resentment. Underneath was a stew of unspoken feelings, which reached a boiling point at the end of the band.

John and George were learning to communicate emotion. There was a rare and fascinating dynamic between them in this regard, an intuitive feeling of each other[3]. Whether or not it was managed consciously is another question, but their astrology suggests a subtle and empathic connection. It played out musically as a seamless blending of their sound, lead and rhythm guitars in synch. Making music was the way they bonded, providing a therapeutic element to the creation of Beatles music.

Collaboration and artistry were highly accentuated in their exchange[4]. The work was to ground vision through innovation, consistent with creating original soundscapes (for example, "Tomorrow Never Knows"). The transcendent (or consciousness raising) element between them was profound[5]. It might manifest as inspired music, excessive drug use, or both! John and George were the biggest consumers of LSD in the band, which was one way their highly experimental astrology might manifest. Approached consciously, their boundary-breaking attunement helped stretch the limits of popular music. Also, they could introduce elements of incoherence and unnecessary discord.

Both men had a rebellious streak, the members who most questioned fame and the myth of The Beatles[6]. They placed a premium on authenticity, which could clash with the trappings of stardom. John and George were the Beatles who most challenged their fans and the dictates of society. The transcendence of the mind became a fascination and both put forward several songs along these lines[7].

Their astrology portrays an artistic passion combined with competitiveness, a broad spiritual scope and revolutionary intention. John specifically supported George's development as a performer, while George supported the healing of John's family issues[8]. They were like brothers and will forever be bonded as the most radically experimental members of this historic musical act.

Paul & George: The Improvisators

Paul and George were arguably the most talented musicians in the band, the ones most responsible for the complexity and diversity of the actual music. Though Paul played bass (a rhythm instrument), he was a multi-instrumentalist and brought in countless other sounds, effects and musical ideas. He played piano, keyboards, both acoustic and electric guitars, and even drums on a couple tunes. George was the lead guitarist, while occasionally playing bass, keyboards and other instruments. Astrologically, both men had a mutable quality, which is improvisational, spontaneous and adds variety and ingenuity[1].

As to be expected, Paul and George had myriad artistic contacts between their astrology charts, suggesting overall flow[2]. An example was the naturalness of George's guitar flourishes which adorned many of Paul's songs. In return, Paul's musical intelligence greatly supported George's development. Paul also advocated George's inclusion in the band (despite John's initial reluctance). Both men were naturally collaborative, eager and willing to be teammates[3]. During the touring years, they would often stand next to each other on stage and sing into the same microphone. As they matured, their musical styles dramatically diverged from the cohesion of the early days[4].

The "sibling" rivalry between them became increasingly intense (and sometimes even bitter) as time went by. It's questionable whether Paul gave George the credit he deserved. George would stay in his follower role and hold a grudge. Both men carried strong soul intentions to emerge into creative leadership[5], and each forged a very successful solo career. During the last phase of the Beatles, the maturation into this promise clashed.

Paul took over creative direction on *Sgt. Pepper*, right at the time George came into his mature voice. Not only was he writing more prolifically, George's immersion in Eastern philosophy and music diversified the Beatles sound and message. His more serious, introspective and unabashedly spiritual focus was in stark contrast to Paul's upbeat, playful, sentimental and conformist tendencies. These musical styles have root in their emotional landscapes, a contrast between George's inward disposition {Scorpio Moon} and Paul's extraverted one {Leo Moon}[6].

In addition to their emotional styles, the energy of will and assertion was also a challenge between them[7]. The purpose was to prod each other to rise to their potential like sparring partners. However, should competitiveness turn into perceived antagonism, defensiveness and hurt feelings could result. The work of the Beatles was to transmute emotion into compelling creative projects.

Paul and George brought an important and critical piece to one another's growth, by activating each other's "karmic destiny." George was learning to be more visible, particularly in realms of entertainment. Paul's positivity and attunement to performance hit this area of George's chart, helping to launch his career. In return, Paul had unfinished business with spirituality and George supported his bandmate's development[8]. As seen throughout Beatles astrology, there is also healing and growth regarding family dynamics. They played out a rivalrous sibling dynamic but had a deep brotherly love and affection for one another.

John & Ringo: The Tricksters

John and Ringo added a comedic and irreverent facet to the band[1]. Paul was called the "cute" Beatle, while George was the "quiet" one. In contrast, John and Ringo brought a playful, trickster quality to the group. Ringo was the actor of the bunch, and John often served as the ringleader of revelry. They could be jokesters, but the trickster characteristic has more to do with an underlying *cleverness*. Their ingenuity was apparent musically and with language. They both served up zingers at press conferences, which added to the reputation that these lovable lads were also sharp[2].

John and Ringo were exceptional at adding craftiness to the music[3]. It's been said that if you isolate the drums, you can identify the Beatles song. Ringo adds uniqueness, just as John did with rhythm guitar and vocal innovations. Their flair for language is seen in the song titles "A Hard Day's Night" and "Tomorrow Never Knows," a couple examples of "Ringoisms" which are both John songs. Critics frequently cite "Rain," "She Said She Said," and "A Day in the Life" for their notable drumming—all primarily John songs.

This pairing also had very strong emotional energy, along with the irreverent and playful quality[4]. John was the visionary, while Ringo was happy to play along. The challenge of their astrology would be polarization or competition, but their roles were understood and followed. John was unquestionably in a more powerful position because the Beatles began as his band. Ringo was a replacement drummer who entered 5 years later. The frequent listing of "John, Paul, George & Ringo," conveys the hierarchy; and John and Ringo were at opposite ends. Therefore, instead of the astrology presenting a lot of difficulty, it manifested primarily as comradery. John invited Ringo to enter the band, and frequently stated that he made an excellent Beatle.

Both had childhoods with pronounced heartache and struggle. Whereas John and Paul lost their mothers, John and Ringo were only children with absentee fathers. They were creating new dynamics of affection as a remedy for the previous lack[5]. Once again, a family dynamic is seen in the astrology, and they were both eager to cultivate such bonds.

In particular, Ringo was learning about social inclusion and John supports that soul intention more than any other Beatle[6]. It was John who invited Ringo into the band, which almost immediately made him famous. In turn, Ringo supports John's healing of self-worth and insecurity issues[7]. Ringo was the emotional anchor who was committed to John's musical vision. When band relations became strained towards the end, Ringo was in John's corner. He even played drums for John's Plastic Ono Band after the Beatles broke up.

Born just 3 months apart (July & October 1940), Ringo and John were the Beatles closest in age. Therefore, they had more astrology in common compared to the others[7]. Out of all the interrelationships in the band, this one was the least competitive[8]. John and Ringo both had loner issues and were glad to be friends and bandmates. Ringo was not a threat to John, which made their relationship smooth. Their emotional dispositions and skillsets were completely different, which was mutually respected and therefore complimentary[9].

Paul & Ringo: The Performers

Paul and Ringo were the only Beatles with the same underlying emotional disposition and need structure {Leo Moon}, one which desires talent to be validated[1]. Both men have karmic histories of being frustrated entertainers, so were motivated to get out and be seen[2]. They are the members most interested in performance and bringing people together in positive and engaging ways. They enjoyed jamming and touring, and likely would've continued after the band stopped. They are Beatles fans themselves and love to bask in the delight the band has created.

Whereas George and John could be overtly experimental, Paul and Ringo kept the music accessible to the mainstream. In fact, they often had a sing-a-long quality as seen with "Yellow Submarine" or "With a Little Help from My Friends," songs Paul wrote for Ringo to sing. Paul also penned "All Together Now" and "Maxwell's Silver Hammer," which both have a bouncy feel, similar to Ringo's "Octopus's Garden." They brought a youthful element which appeals to the child in us all. Paul is charming and open, while Ringo brought a lovably quirky flavor to his songs and acting. Together, they added a lot of character to their music and films.

Consistent in much of Beatles astrology, the dynamic between Paul and Ringo also emphasizes romantic themes[3]. They have chart contacts connecting them in a familial way as seen with the others[4]. Paul and Ringo have a unique energetic exchange involving great potential abundance. The expansive, celebratory and uplifting vibe of the "Beatles signature" is highly reinforced in their astrology[5]. The potential is for great artistic expansion, while the unconscious version is some degree of being overly pleasing or catering to an audience. Some people criticize the band for being "campy" at times. Nevertheless, Paul and Ringo add good cheer and spirit, much of the reason why the Beatles are so lovable.

Underneath the sunny disposition there is another similarity, one which usually remains hidden. Both have anger issues in the shadow, a remnant of their karmic performance frustration[6]. The spiritual work involves the transformation of anger into leadership, which is exactly what they did. Paul and Ringo went on to become the Beatles with the most prolific solo careers, each serving as band leaders in their own right. However, during the band's decline they played out their shadow with each other.

Ringo temporarily quit the band during sessions for "The White Album," in a moment of both insecurity and angst. Among the reasons for his departure was the perception of Paul's behavior as patronizing and officious.[22] Paul took over drumming responsibilities until Ringo returned. When the band was breaking up there was an incident where Paul kicked Ringo out of his home in a dispute over the release of solo albums.[23]

Despite these conflicts, Paul and Ringo almost always functioned as teammates with great affection[7]. In fact, their relationship has endured for almost 60 years, the longest duration of any pairing. After the deaths of John and George, they have represented the band publicly, inviting new generations of fans into the magic of The Beatles. With their charm and accessibility, they have become the spokesmen for the group. In fact, the life energy of their bond {composite Cancer Sun} is closest to that of the band itself[8].

George & Ringo: The Followers

If John and Paul were the leaders, George and Ringo were the followers. Until the later years when this organization was disrupted by George's ascendancy, the two tiers created a workable musical and social structure. George's soulfulness and Ringo's emotional anchor provided a foundation. Ringo had an innate feel for the music, while George added spirituality and depth[1].

George often felt marginalized by the leaders and Ringo was there to support him. George was the main advocate for Ringo's inclusion and continually encouraged his musical development[2]. In particular, he played a key role in assisting Ringo on "Octopus's Garden." When Ringo returned from his temporary departure in 1968, he found an assortment of flowers on his drum kit, courtesy of George.[24] After the band broke up, they supported each other's solo albums and projects more than any other pairing. When the Beatles were inducted into the Rock & Roll Hall of Fame, they were the two members in attendance (Paul declined due to the legal squabbles at the time, and the induction was after John was murdered).

The connection had layers of complexity, with divergent temperaments[3]. Ringo played the actor and performer, while George was contemplative and quiet. After the touring years, Ringo was often bored and restless while George relished the opportunity to deepen into himself and his work.

Their artistic, creative and social styles were quite different. George's impressionistic, metaphysical and subtle sense of artistry {Venus in Pisces} could be at odds with Ringo's rhythmic, quick and upbeat style {Venus in Gemini}$_4$. Another facet of this dynamic played out in their personal lives. George's meandering style also manifested with porous romantic boundaries. He had an affair with Ringo's wife Maureen,[25] which brought the more conflictual dynamics of their astrology forward. However, consistent with the laissez-faire attitude of the times, it didn't seem to damage their relationship (and both men went through divorces not too far after).

Ringo's chart speaks of inclusion after loneliness, having sweet and simple fun to heal his soul. In contrast, George had far more complicated existential and philosophical questions to unravel and address$_5$. Their astrology portrays opposite tendencies with the mind, voice and teachings. The difference can be seen with Ringo's cheery and welcoming singing of "Yellow Submarine," compared to George's mysterious, complex and challenging "Within You Without You." George saw his writing as means to capture metaphysical truths, while Ringo approached songwriting as a part of creative performance$_6$.

A major facet of their relationship chart is learning creative skills$_7$. The songwriting brilliance of Lennon-McCartney needed adept musicianship to bring it to life. Lead guitar and drums are of immense importance in the rock format. George and Ringo were not just able, but ideal musicians for the artistic sensibilities of this band. They both overcame insecurities (another motif in their astrology), and came into substantial creative empowerment$_8$. As is the case throughout Beatles astrology, they too had a strong and enduring "familial" connection$_9$.

Major Influences

The Beatles had dozens of musical influences, mainly British and American. They came of age during the skiffle craze in Britain in the 1950s, led by Lonnie Donegan. Skiffle was stripped down and simple (acoustic guitar, washtub bass, washboard, kazoo, banjo, knee slapping or other basic percussion, etc.), perfect for beginners. John founded The Quarrymen as a skiffle band and they covered Donegan, as well as performing other standards. The astrology between Donegan and The Beatles illustrates a connection with roots, in a most emphatic way$_1$.

Skiffle's relatively primitive form had limitations. The more juiced-up electric guitar had a jolting impact on the boys and the emerging rock & roll genre captured their imaginations. The Quarrymen shifted to eventually become The Beatles, with the skiffle guys falling away. George's inclusion in the band emphasized the electric lead guitar, which sculpted their sound.

Their blues, rock and pop influences are numerous. Some notables include: Chet Atkins, Gene Vincent, The Everly Brothers, Cliff Richard, Eddie Cochran, Fats Domino, Jerry Lee Lewis, Bo Diddly, Bill Haley, The Cookies, The Shirelles, The Isley Brothers, The

Marvelettes, Smokey Robinson, Larry Williams, Ray Charles, The Coasters, Arthur Alexander and Joe Turner.

Additionally, there are 4 figures who stand out in importance: Elvis Presley, Chuck Berry, Buddy Holly and Little Richard. The first is the "King," Elvis Presley, who embodied the iconographic pose of the rock star like no other. His influence was not just stylistic and musical, but reached far deeper into the psychology of creative expression.

Elvis and The Beatles both had an expansive, fiery, cross-cultural and romantic flavor to their presentations {Sagittarius Ascendants}. Elvis oozed his brand of sexual magnetism through his approach {Jupiter in Scorpio}, while The Beatles projected a lighter, more bouncy and witty vibe {Jupiter in Gemini}₂.

Like the Beatles, Elvis had spiritual lessons with dark and wounding elements in family and nurturance areas₃. Elvis and John had very similar combinations of astrological factors regarding maternal death issues₄. Elvis's mother Gladys died from heart failure, less than a month after John's mother was killed in an auto accident. Also, Elvis had an identical twin brother named Jesse, who was delivered stillborn shortly before him₅. [26]

The intention in Elvis's chart was to literally "burn up" the emotions inside for release {fire element: expression through singing, dancing, etc.}, just like exercise does with what we ingest. The Beatles had similar spiritual work—channeling emotion into creativity for catharsis₆. Another similarity was the defense mechanism of escape from painful emotion. Elvis was devastated after Gladys died—the event would influence the remainder of his life. He coped through excessive substance intake; a trend similar to the Beatles₇.

Buddy Holly's contribution was more technical but no less important. He was a song craftsman, an original writer who adorned his songs with cleverness and wit. He focused on melody and story, creating a distinct singing style with "hiccups" and falsetto. Paul claims that he and John started to write because of Holly. [27] He set the standard for a rock group to feature 2 guitars, bass and drums, and the name "The Beatles" was influenced by Buddy Holly and The Crickets. His chord progressions and somewhat jangly and percussive guitar style would influence the rhythms seen in the early Beatles catalog.

For those interested in the astrology, it is striking and amazing, illustrating a profoundly important and central spiritual connection₈. To summarize: Holly nurtures the "Beatles signature" through writing, cleverness and innovation, while also stimulating issues of life direction and purpose. Additionally, he adds a technical angle, the tools of the trade. His influence assisted the grounding of inspiration into form, the invitation to realize the dream.

Holly was learning to sing from his heart, to make a body of work stemming from emotional expression₉. As he died so young, he wasn't able to fully complete that intention. However, the astrology suggests a passing of the torch to The Beatles₉. Additionally, Holly's focus on writing {Mercury} was exactly on The Beatles public persona {Midheaven}, influencing their sound and song catalog. They performed a dozen of his songs, including a cover of "Words of Love" on *With the Beatles*. Words {Gemini} of love {Moon} perfectly encapsulates their shared connection—the singing from the heart. Dead at 22, Buddy Holly was an early rock tragedy. His death was another loss which upset John and they shared the same death-related signature[10]. Paul had an energetic connection to Holly with writing[11], and he obtained the publishing rights to his songs.[(28)]

During their performing years (1957—1966), The Beatles covered Chuck Berry more than any other act or artist.[(29)] Berry was a rocker, a true innovator of the electric guitar and showmanship. He helped bridge racial divides with his contagious enthusiasm and monster hits. He also helped connect rhythm and blues, pop and rock into a thoroughly unique and explosive sound. He was one of the first to incorporate full-scale guitar solos and his stage antics thrilled audiences. Berry wrote songs about growing up (cars, girls, school, etc.) shaping the artistic contours of the emerging rock genre. With more octane (guitar riffs, heavier sound, attitude), he was particularly influential to John, who also had the ability to shape cultural trends[12]. John's singing of Berry's "Rock and Roll Music" reveals the major influence on his vocal approach. He also got in legal trouble for treading too close to Berry's "You Can't Catch Me" on "Come Together," another example of their musical reflection.

The astrology between Berry and the Beatles had a cultural scope, the seizing of sheer ambition. Berry's chart had a reflection of the "Beatles signature," and he too expanded the reach of music into the collective[13]. Like Holly, Berry also supported the Beatles construction of musical craft. Additionally, he modeled a testosterone-infused quality to showmanship. He also supported the possibilities of imagination, and like Holly, a passing of the torch[14].

Finally, there's Little Richard, flamboyant pioneering architect of the rock style, most noted for his powerful vocals, high energy and piano theatrics. He synthesized soul, blues and even gospel into the rock structure. His influence is obvious on Beatles tracks such as "I'm Down," and the head-shaking "wooooos," which punctuate their early hits. Little Richard directly influenced singing style and upbeat energy like a musical cheerleader. He was famous for his sexual magnetism and influenced the use of seductive appeal. He was also a figure of inspiration and supported issues of creative direction[15]. In particular, Richard sets off Paul's chart in an uplifting way and George too was influenced by his virtuoso[16].

The Beatles were excellent at assimilating all sorts of stimulation into their sound and message. Amazingly, each of the 4 major influences all hit the Beatles sponge-like receptivity to influences {Pisces South Node}, as well as their trajectory of further growth {Virgo North Node}[17]. The Beatles appeal to America was largely due to their ability to integrate these influences and radiate them back.

Chapter 4
Setting the Stage

This chapter clarifies the unique spiritual conditions of the Beatles' day, the big-picture setting. Also, an introduction to the 4 phases and 5 major (and 5 minor) threads is provided. The overarching spiritual context of the story is tied to astrological factors. Therefore, this chapter contains more astrology in order to sufficiently explain it. It details the relevance of the transpersonal (beyond the personality) planets in the 1960s. These planets are collective and spiritual in scope, structuring the energetic themes, dynamics and soul lessons that were alive at the time. Part 2 provides additional detail about other astrological activity.

The Uranus-Pluto Interchange

Perhaps the most used keywords for Uranus and Pluto are respectively, revolution and transformation. Orbiting beyond Saturn (organization of the material realm, linear time, consensus reality), Uranus and Pluto involve metaphysical perspectives and processes. Always pushing the evolutionary envelope forward, their scope includes innovations which are "far out," meaning outside our current understandings in consensus reality. The 1960s are often characterized as being "far out," as consciousness was being stretched into the unknown. The astrology can manifest clearly or chaotically, depending on how we partner with it. The decade saw plenty of both.

Uranus is an airy energy involving metaphysical concepts and paradigms that don't fit within conventional (Saturn) systems. An example is quantum physics, which shatters the more orderly realm of classical physics. Astrology too is Uranian, as it challenges the underpinnings of traditional paradigms, including the worldviews of science and many religions. Uranus correlates with the future and technology, the crackling and electrifying wizardry of invention. It also relates to broader themes of democracy and equality, leveling favoritism or elitism, opening the grip of centralized power for all.

Pluto is a watery energy with a psychological scope, often paired with the Jungian concept of "the shadow." As the archetype of the Underworld (Hades/Hell), Pluto resides in the realm of darkness (it orbits about 3.6 billion miles from the Sun). Though this material is sometimes characterized as "evil," a more accurate way to view it is unconsciousness—being away from the light of spiritual awareness. As we resolve darkness, both individually and collectively, we become more awake or enlightened. If not, in the grips of darkness, we may sabotage evolution. Pluto involves the deepest emotional resonances, truths and experiences; the regenerative power of love, as well as the sexual instinct which propagates the species. It relates to our collective survival. Managing it adeptly is necessary for us to continue evolution—we have to heal our darkness.

The combination of these planets is often a volatile mix which awakens (Uranus) the unconscious, taboo, repressed or hidden (Pluto). Plutonian material tends to be buried, while Uranus (called the "Great Awakener") brings it up to the light, the rising (Uranus) from the depths (Pluto). All types of instinctual desires are roused, which might create incredible art and social change, a more raw and authentic tenor of life. Pluto involves death, while Uranus can offer a broader metaphysical perspective to stimulate healing and acceptance of mortality. There can also be breakthroughs (Uranus) towards the regeneration (Pluto) of deep soul bonds.

The interchange tends to correlate with explosive times of evolutionary growth. As transpersonal planets, their energetic exchange potentially raises awareness beyond the ordinary towards the extraordinary (metaphysics, spiritual illumination, levels of consciousness beyond our usual comprehension). The promise is to reveal the spiritual dimension which envelops all of life.

The Arc of Awakening

Throughout the remainder of the book, the "arc of awakening" will play a central role. It illustrates the trajectory of evolutionary growth occurring in the 1960s. As we move year by year through the chronology, we'll be following the motion through the "arc." All the music and events occupy a position within this spiritual context and will be explained within its scope.

The "arc" is created by the degree of connection between Uranus and Pluto. These astrological titans form a conjunction about once every 125 years (with variation due to Pluto's irregular orbit), so it's notable when they meet. They formed a conjunction (occupying the same position in the zodiac) in the middle years of the 1960s.

When the 1960s began, Uranus was applying (or catching up) to Pluto. Traveling about 3 times faster than the dwarf planet, it gradually closed in. The motion of the "arc" began to elevate in October 1961, when Uranus first came into a 10° orb of influence (degree of closeness) to Pluto. The closer the planets become, the more they interact. During the first half of the decade, the orb between them tightened, which is depicted by the rising motion of the "arc." The Beatles rode this wave to stardom with a massive collective impact.

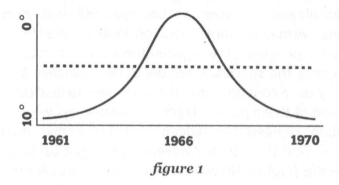

figure 1

The planets were precisely conjunct in 1965—66 (no separation between them), depicted as the peak or top of the curve. The dates of the 3 exact conjunctions were 10/9/65, 4/4/66 and 6/30/66. There are 3 conjunctions because planets move direct and retrograde, so they traverse the zodiacal degrees in a back-and-forth manner. Due to this motion, they can form aspects to other planets more than once.

After the exact conjunctions, Uranus gradually separated from Pluto in the latter half of the decade. The separating motion creates the "arc's" gradual descent. The last time they were within a $10°$ orb was July 1970. The duration of the event was just under 9 years and correlates precisely with the band's run. At the start, they met manager Brian Epstein, while the public became aware of their break-up as it was closing. In between was quite the ride.

The motion of the "arc" moves through a spectrum from denser and darker in the lower sections, to lighter and brighter in the upper. It portrays the awakening (Uranus) from darkness (Pluto), the elevation of consciousness. It's important not to assign value judgements to the trajectory. Every position within the journey is an indispensable part of a universal rhythm. It's not "better" to be at a lofty position, any more than it's "better" to be in summer versus winter, or noon instead of midnight. The purpose is to rise towards spiritual insight, then bring the awareness discovered down into reality—the illumination from "heaven" might inform our experience on Earth.

The "arc" has 2 halves, an upper and a lower. In the lower section, the orb of influence is looser (more than $5°$), while tighter in the upper section (less than $5°$). The halves are separated by the "line of inspiration" (the dotted line) as the demarcation. Above this line is increased opening to loftier levels of consciousness, the heights of intuitive receptivity. Below it pertains to life in the "everyday" world. Significant spiritual developments occur in this story when the "arc's" motion crosses this line.

The upward segment of the "arc" involves *development*. It is characterized by enthusiasm and initial immaturity like an acorn becoming a baby tree. The peak of the "arc" is *realization*, a flowering or fruition. There is maximal amplification and climax, consciousness potentially vibrant and awake. The downward segment concerns *integration.* We must return to the world of darkness on the ground, ideally bringing what was discovered into manifestation and embodiment.

Below are some ways that we can see the "arc of awakening" in the Beatles and the '60s. The rising and descending segments tend to mirror each other at the corresponding positions of elevation.

Musical & Lyrical Development: The band developed their musical proficiency in the applying stage, put forth their great works at the climax and descended in a period of individuation in the final years. They began with straightforward instrumentation which gradually became more complex, reaching greatest sophistication at the climax. The separating phase returned to simpler instrumentation and song structures, including a return to early songs and influences. The song lyrics are simpler and less mature in the applying stage and become loftier and metaphysical at the peak. They became more accessible once again at the conclusion, integrated with the wisdom of the journey.

Beatlemania: As the "arc" began to rise, the first singles were released (1962), followed by the first record (1963). Beatlemania exploded in 1964 and climaxed in 1965 with their largest crowd at Shea Stadium for the "arc's" peak. They discontinued touring in August 1966, right when the "arc" began descending. There was a cultural backlash with John's "Jesus" remarks at this time, paralleling the coming down from the heights. Although they maintained great popularity in the latter part of the decade, the previous adolescent fervor of the rising phase was over. They were less public for the descent, retreating from the limelight to be a studio band with more investment in their personal lives.

Maturation and Appearance: In the early part of the decade, they looked (and acted) like boys, reflecting the cultural adolescence of the time. They sported the "mop top" haircut, no facial hair, and wore matching suits in concert. After the peak of Beatlemania and the "arc's" rise, they traded in their conventional suits for multi-colored psychedelic outfits. They grew mustaches, John wore glasses, and they had an air of sophistication like rock & roll professors. For the descent, each member forged his own unique look and style. Some members had long hair and/or facial hair at times, and sometimes they didn't. The American released "Red Album" and "Blue Album" showed the band in the exact same place (the balcony image copied from *Please Please Me*) at the beginning and end of the "arc's" trajectory. These compilation albums illustrate how the motion returns, though the band members appear (and were) completely different.

Drug Use: In the early years Preludin (speed, a stimulant) was the drug of choice, reflecting the rising motion. In 1964, use of marijuana to "get high" became regular, upping the ante. In 1965, they started to get "incredibly high" by using LSD, which reached a peak in 1966. In 1967 they renounced the use of it and extolled the virtues of meditation. As the "arc" descended in the late '60s they were using depressants (coming down). Ringo's alcohol use increased and Paul became a heavy drinker as the band was breaking up. John was using heroin (a depressant) in 1968-1969 and had bouts with depression. Although they drank in the early days and marijuana was present in the later ones, the overall pattern remains. The drugs of choice, the ones which significantly shaped the story, reflect the "arc's" motion.[30]

Cultural Development: In the early years of the decade, culture was basic and sanitized. The Beatles appeared in black and white on the Ed Sullivan show in 1964. 73 million people watched the program because there weren't many other choices. Color television proliferated in 1965-66 at the height of the "arc," while music and entertainment diversified. For the descent, a new cultural sensibility was being grounded, one which had a bevy of options with more realism and rawness.

The Civil Rights movement built momentum in the early 1960s. The middle years had protests, riots and demonstrations with legislation to change society. The closing years dealt with the implications of integrating the changes. The countercultural movement follows the same trend. In the early 1960s, signs of an alternative lifestyle began to emerge. The word "hippie" debuted in 1965.[31] The later part of the decade brought the movement down into reality, where it clashed with opposing (more conservative) forces as it permeated deeper into culture.

Neptune in Scorpio

Neptune is the planet of inspiration, consciousness, dreams, spirituality and transcendence. It also involves glamor and cultural trends, what is considered exotic. With Neptune occupying Scorpio during the 1960s, the decade is known for having a seductive and erotic component. Neptune in Scorpio has sexual magnetism, a charisma and depth which is unforgettable and engaging. Culture and art of this time are known for their authenticity and allure. In contrast to the sterile and safe 1950s, the '60s were a time of touching in, and giving voice, to the taboo and mysterious. The Beatles evolved from a glamorized, sanitized media concoction into a conduit for a deeper spirituality and a message of substance.

This planet-sign combination involves the spirituality (Neptune) of death (Scorpio). Spiritualism is a term used to describe the connection between worlds, moving beyond our material (Saturn) reality. The '60s saw a surge of interest in the occult, including séances and mediums, people making contact with those who have departed. The idea that we have "spirit guides," essentially non-embodied helper beings, gained significant traction in the collective. Belief in reincarnation, the afterlife and interest in Eastern and non-dual spiritual paths rose substantially. Many became open to the idea that consciousness has multiple potential layers or levels.

The darker possibilities include charlatans and others who distort or confuse this territory. Another hazard is getting lost (Neptune) in drama (Scorpio), or losing one's bearing as seen with the dizzying fervor of Beatlemania. Manipulation, coercion, and duplicity are also on the list. It can be unsafe (Scorpio) to obliterate one's consciousness (Neptune) with substances. Porous sexual (Scorpio) boundaries (Neptune) can result in shattered relationships, hurt feelings and also health consequences. We also might create false gods and give away our time, energy and focus to chasing illusions of wealth, fame or power. It is easy to get ensnarled in Scorpio's web, and with Neptune, we might become hypnotized and led in. The Beatles story features some of the shadow side of Neptune in Scorpio, both within the dynamics of the band, and in what they catalyzed collectively.

Neptune entered Scorpio in 1956, when the musicians were boys learning their instruments. It moved into the following sign (Sagittarius) in January 1970, signaling an end to the phase. Neptune transits each sign for 14 years, which almost perfectly correlates with the history of the Beatles, from when John met Paul (1957) until the break-up (1970). The Beatles phenomenon is marked by the unique energetic stamp of this planet-sign combination.

4 Phases to the Journey

The chronology chapters organize the story in 4 phases, consistent with the trajectory of the "arc of awakening." It's a coming-of-age story, reflecting phases of spiritual maturation. The first 2 phases occur during the ascending motion, while the last 2 are paired with the descent. The movement is from a personality orientation, to its transcendence, then back down to the everyday wiser from the journey. The phases parallel the release of their albums and the songs give voice to each stage of this process.

Personality Expression (1963-1964) includes the first three releases: *Please Please Me*, *With the Beatles* and *A Hard Day's Night*. These early albums express the youthful desires of romantic love and the personality's trials and tribulations in finding it. The songs are a window into adolescent yearning for satisfaction, security and connection. They were able to craft an appealing product with enough undercurrents of sexuality and rebelliousness to elicit fascination. The music is generally upbeat, mirroring the "arc's" rising motion. The phase is noted for its enthusiasm and eagerness.

Personality Reconciliation (1964-1965) includes *Beatles for Sale*, *Help!* and *Rubber Soul*. These albums continue to reflect the desires of the personality, but show a more reflective mood. They address attachments, fears and insecurities, illustrating greater maturation and humility. There's an increased awareness of self, a more informed perspective on life. The issues which underlie the spiritual childhood are recognized, made conscious and potentially worked through. The music is still generally upbeat, though it was becoming more artistic and complex.

Transcendence (1966—1968) includes *Revolver*, *Sgt. Pepper*, *Magical Mystery Tour* and *Yellow Submarine*. This phase began precisely at the "arc's" peak, and is the only one including 4 albums. The songs on *Yellow Submarine* were written during the Transcendence period (though the album was released in 1969). The urgency of personality desires gives way to a broader experience of spiritual uplift and freedom, the receptivity to inspiration from beyond. The music was the most ethereal, psychedelic and experimental. This time is often called their "acid period," as LSD use was a factor and is part of the story. Now a studio band, they focused on special effects, a wide palette of instruments, noises, vocal styles and enhancements to arrive at particular sounds.

The Individuation phase (1968-1970) includes *The Beatles* (referred to as "The White Album"), *Abbey Road* and *Let It Be*. After the expansiveness of the Transcendence phase, the work was to integrate the wisdom. The music returns to worldly matters, a more "stripped-down" feel, how we might exist in the everyday. These albums address the personal implications, responsibilities and challenges of being whole within oneself, expressing one's authenticity. Often reflecting their blues and pop influences, they were weaving back to the previous phases from a more mature perspective.

Every Beatles album is discussed, including singles (with astrological charts and additional analyses in Part 2). Each of the 13 album releases are framed in a few ways. 1) information about the album, 2) discussion of musical development, 3) discussion of lyrical development, 4) an astrological summary.

Phases 1 (Personality Expression) and 2 (Personality Reconciliation) are comprised of 6 albums and feature the "early formula," songs which are fresh, lively, catchy, relatively simple and maximally accessible. Including the singles, the band put out 76 original songs during these phases.[32] Out of those 76 songs, at least one of the following words (or a slight variation) appear in *every* song they wrote (except for "Nowhere Man"): love, sad (crying or tears), lonely (or loss, gone, apart), misery, miss you, holding tight or feeling blue (or down).

The first 4 albums were composed entirely of love songs using this formula. "Help!" was the 56th original song and appeared on the 5th album of the same name. It was the first Beatles song that didn't involve romance. However, it speaks of "feeling down," a motif of the early formula. "Nowhere Man" was the 69th song, the first to completely move beyond the formula. The song appeared on the 6th album, *Rubber Soul,* which successfully concluded the Personality Reconciliation phase.

There was a dramatic development between Personality Reconciliation and Transcendence as seen on *Revolver.* Instead of the early formula, subject matter opened to any topic and the music became far more experimental. They matured into storytellers, with an emotional depth far exceeding the earlier phases. *Sgt. Pepper* and *Magical Mystery Tour* exemplify the highly artistic, experimental and lofty reach of this period.

"The White Album" was the first album in the Individuation period, a notable shift from the prior phase. Instead of ethereal music, complex production and soaring subject matter, the focus was on realism and simplicity. Instead of a group effort, the Individuation phase featured the unique voice and style of each musician. The phase was typified by creative tension, which ultimately led to the conclusion of their work. Amazingly, each member put forth a song in this phase which captured and summarized the spiritual work of his astrology chart.

5 Major Themes

The song lyrics reveal a process of spiritual maturation. Word choices are seen as meaningful, stemming from inner processes which may or may not be conscious. There are reasons why certain words were floating around their psyches and appearing in the songs. In fact, there is a broader design to it all.

There are five major themes (or threads) which are woven through the songs. Imagine that all Beatles songs collectively compose a great outdoor landscape, such as woods or a forest. Though the songs address many subjects, the five lyrical themes provide a trail system through the woods. Certain songs serve as markers on these paths.

The first thread is **solar songs**, ones with the language of solar radiance (words such as "sun," "light," "bright," "shining" or "warm," which will be in **bold**). These words were largely absent early on, indicating some initial stumbling around in darkness. The path became increasingly more illuminated as time went by. Astrologically, the Sun is the energy of soul, our energetic connection with Spirit. It involves presence, awareness, vitality, awakening into connection with all of life.

Each **solar** song contains a teaching about awakening. Surprisingly, they form a comprehensive guide for spiritual development. Teachings are discerned through astrological research, which provides the context to understand the spiritual dimension of the songs. Some are more influenced by how the solar words take expression in the song lyrics. So yes, they are my interpretations, offered as *possibilities to consider rather than declarations*. (These interpretations are designed to provide food for thought. You are invited to come up with your own if you like.) The songwriters appear to have intentionally put forward certain ideas and teachings in several cases. For the most part, it was done instinctually. The working hypothesis is they were conduits during this unique time of intuitive receptivity. The receptivity might be to other dimensions of consciousness, their soul wisdom or the muse.

The second major lyrical thread is *dream songs*, with the dream-related words appearing in *italics*. Spiritual awakening involves the recognition of the dreaming process, an awareness of the subjectivity of personal experience. Astrologically, the Moon is "the dreamer," who we essentially are inside. Its highly individualized contents (emotions, impressions, imagination, issues of the inner life) become projected onto life (through our solar radiance) for us to play out and potentially become aware of self.

Anais Nin is quoted, "We don't see things as they are; we see them as we are." An astrology chart illustrates the map or organization of a person's dream. Just like a movie screen is reflective, the world is an enormous canvas for the dream or "movie" of our consciousness. This dream perspective is the fantastic reality that we experience our own personalized version of the world. Life as we know it has a quality of make-believe, just like nighttime dreams. We cast others as characters in our spiritual theater, everyone playing roles in each other's drama.

Dream songs can have a conventional use of "dreams," as something we do in nighttime sleep or as being anticipatory about the future ("in my dreams"). The more spiritual use is the dreaming *process*, how we exist in the theater of our soul work. In addition to using dream terminology, some of these songs portray life as a "game" or a "play." Sometimes, a character is described as a "fool" or a "clown." Other dream songs employ water imagery, the element of the Moon. The projection of the dream has been called the "*stream* of consciousness," and water references are found in many notable dream songs. Additionally, this category includes lyrical references which take subjectivity further, as seen in altered states of perception and unusual perspectives on life.

At the start of the "arc's" ascent, dream usage tended to be more conventional. It progressively shifted to the more spiritual use, portraying the dreaming process in the Transcendence phase. Dream terms returned to the conventional use as the "arc" completed its descent.

Solar (Sun) and *dream* (Moon) songs involve the universal process of becoming more conscious or awake. The next two threads are more specific to this soul group. First is the issue of death, which is paramount in this story. Not only do several key people die, death also emerges in ways which are silly ("Paul is dead"), shocking (Charles Manson's interpretive distortion of Beatles lyrics to justify murder) and ultimately redemptive (the bridging of worlds with those who have passed). <u>Death</u> songs are surprisingly numerous for a band noted for their upbeat energy. The relevant lyrics ("die," "gone," "dead," etc.) will be <u>underlined</u> for emphasis.

The fourth thread is "call" (or reunion) songs, typified by a desire to bridge estrangement. Reaching out via verbal pleas, telephone, writing, or in the imagination occurs frequently during the early phases. Initially, these calls (or attempts for reunion) are unsuccessful and the lyrics describe loneliness. As the "arc" reached its peak, not only do the calls become answered, the authors write about receiving calls themselves! As the "arc" descended, the call theme became integrated in an unexpected way.

The fifth and final major thread is "dark" songs, ones which include the word "dark," "night," "black" or "shadow." In contrast to the **solar** theme, "dark" songs express the initial condition of unconsciousness. The theme is consistent throughout the catalog, though the relationship to darkness changes over time. The context and usage of "dark" terminology is another illustration of their spiritual maturation.

Some songs involve 2, 3, or 4 of these threads. Amazingly, there is one song at the conclusion which integrates all 5, a grand finale. **Solar**, *dream*, <u>death</u>, "call" and "dark" songs are the spiritually-significant songs in the catalog, the ones most central in this particular study. Most of the famous songs tend to occupy these categories.

There are also 5 minor threads. The "early formula" is not categorized as a thread since it encapsulates practically every song on the first 6 albums. The minor threads are "rain," "mother," "bird," "flute," and "violence" songs. "Rain" and "mother" songs include those words, while "bird" songs make a reference to the animal by word or sound. "Flute" songs feature the instrument in some way. "Violence" songs involve a violent scenario or references war or guns. Additionally, love is perhaps their defining message and it appears in numerous songs in a wide variety of contexts (too many to be a thread). All of these themes will be further addressed in the chapters to come, while a complete list of songs in both the major and minor categories is included at the end of the book.

The final motif which runs through the story is the muse. Unlike the threads, her presence is not solely detected through specific word choices. Rather, there are certain songs which point to her in various ways. The songwriters' process of awakening to her inspiration and subsequent collaboration is discussed as a 6-step process (1: description, 2: expression, 3: connection, 4: collaboration, 5: healing, 6: conclusion). Her role was discovered through astrological research and more about this incredible phenomenon is provided as we go. She turns out to be the spiritual star of the show.

Chapter 5
Beginnings

In this opening chapter of the chronology, significant events which shaped the story are introduced and explored. The musicians' soul work played out in dramatic fashion during childhood and adolescence. Though often painful, these seed events were the critical foundation for an eventual spiritual flowering.

The Lennon Family Comes Apart

The exact events in late June 1946 remain somewhat unclear. One of the challenges in Beatles literature and biographies is the story is told in different ways. We know that John was 5 years old. He spent a couple of weeks with his father Alf, who was planning to take him away to a new life in New Zealand. Julia tracked him down to claim her son before they would depart. Some kind of dramatic scene unfolded. One account is Alf made John choose between him and Julia. After initially choosing Alf, John had second thoughts and ran after his mom as she walked away. Another version is Alf and Julia arrived at an agreement that the boy would be raised by his mother.[33] Regardless of how it actually unfolded, the prospects of having a cohesive family upbringing came apart. John would not see his father for the next 18 years (when Alf unexpectedly showed up on the movie set of *A Hard Day's Night*).

A defining moment of his childhood, John's core nurturance issues were activated. His emotional pattern of estrangement and loss, his "axis of conflict," was being set off$_1$. Nourishment and early developmental (particularly maternal) dynamics {Ceres} were highly accentuated. At this tender age John's "wounded child" dynamic was in full relief, triggering his deep-seated anxieties and emotional vulnerabilities$_2$. Though devastating, the opportunity was to ultimately work through his emotional work in the present incarnation. As he matures, John might learn to embrace his vulnerability and share feelings personally and creatively. The astrological activation at this time specifically pointed to communications, alluding to both The Beatles group chart and Paul's$_3$. There was a deeper dimension to this heartbreaking scene—a valuable seed moment.

It would take some time for the seed to blossom. In the meantime, the profound activation of his "wounded child" signature would last for years. There is a direct link between the early emotional trauma and John's belligerent tendencies[4]. According to biographers, he increasingly became a bully and fighter at school. He taunted others, did nasty practical jokes and was especially unkind to those who were weak or disabled.[34]

Alf, Julia and John share a striking similarity of astrological factors concerning familial instability and a wild streak[5] (a deeper analysis is found in Part 2, p. 296).

Ringo's Battle

Ringo had a severe, potentially deadly condition of peritonitis which landed him in a coma as a child. For days it was uncertain if he would live, and his family was told to prepare for the worst.[35] Then, on his 7th birthday, on 7/7/1947, little Richie fluttered his eyes and opened them. The doctor said he was "lucky to survive," though he would deal with problematic health for years to come.

The health issues ripened in his astrology chart at this early age, depicting a literal battle to survive[1]. At this time, he was experiencing the hiddenness and fear of "inside Ringo," the inability to be in his playful expression[2]. The emotional dynamics were intense, particularly in Ringo's astrological area of death, which is also the realm of potential regeneration. The doctor's fear that his life was in jeopardy is starkly reflected in his astrology[3].

In his early teens, Richie spent 2 years in a sanitarium for tuberculosis,[36] a replay of his isolation karma. However, a major shift occurred at the age of 16, precisely when he became obsessed with music. At this time, there was major astrological activation of "playful Ringo," the unquenched desire to perform and engage with the world. Richie decided on drumming as his life path[4]. The experience of playing percussion in the makeshift hospital band gave him the tools and courage to emerge from isolation and loneliness.

In mid-1956 (age 16) Richie got into skiffle and began his amateur musical career. His drumming equipment was primitive, but his spirit caught fire. The activity to the performance area of his chart would be highly amplified for the next several years[5]. Richard Starkey became Ringo Starr and was recruited by Rory Storm and the Hurricanes. He got on the touring circuit and first met The Beatles in 1960.

Mary McCartney's Death

As Ringo was transforming teenage loneliness into creative performance, Paul would similarly go through a life-changing passage. On October 31, 1956, Paul's mother Mary died of breast cancer. Only 14 at the time, the event would define his childhood. Earlier in the year, Paul was gifted a trumpet on his birthday in June.[37] He would have no idea that he'd eventually compose a song about his youth called "Penny Lane" featuring a trumpet, precisely 10 years later. In 1966 he would also spearhead the *Sgt. Pepper* project, which portrays Ringo holding a trumpet on the cover. Paul would go on to introduce all sorts of brass, woodwind and other instruments and sounds into Beatles music. His musical passion was moving to the next level of focus right when his mother got sick and died.

Astrologically, eclipses signal major spiritual passages, turning points that often have breakdown and/or breakthrough meaning. Eclipses are notable evolutionary markers until the next ones come along. On June 8, 1956, there was a significant solar eclipse hitting Paul's chart, in the sign of Gemini, which involves communications. Mary's death occurred during the passage initiated by the event. As Paul is a Gemini Sun, this eclipse profoundly energized his chart in terms of communications {exact on his Mercury}, and its influence was extremely pronounced in the charts of Mary herself, Julia Lennon, The Beatles group chart and the Lennon-McCartney chart (all in terms of communication)[1]. The "call" theme {Gemini} which appears in Beatles lyrics is rooted in this major celestial event.

When Mary died, mothering energy {Ceres} in Paul's astrology was understandably emphasized—a transition from ending to a new beginning[2]. He was learning emotional self-sufficiency, a lesson he would grapple with for years. It was time to learn how to be alone and focus on his creative craft. Most interestingly, there was an uncanny echo of the "Beatles signature" animating his chart, inviting skill development for eventual creative presentation. Additionally, themes of death and loss were very active[3].

Mary McCartney loved her son dearly, a timeless form of sacred love. Though her death was undoubtedly tragic and profoundly devastating, the astrology conveys another dimension of meaning. Paul's central soul intention is the transformation of grief into performance, to not only inspire and bring people together, but to deliver a message from beyond. Paul and Mary have an incredibly profound spiritual connection, with some of the most striking astrology in this entire book[4]. The working hypothesis is her soul had the willingness and wisdom to play a catalyzing role in Paul's spiritual drama. She may have been supporting his development from both sides of the boundary of death. It is a beautiful form of selfless, soulful love.

Mary herself carried the intention and attunement of a romantically-oriented songwriter, precisely connecting with the "Beatles signature[5]." Interestingly, the solar eclipse in 1956 was triggering her writing intentions, but it's only one step in the journey. Nine years later in 1965 would be another {Gemini} solar eclipse, a BIG one that more strongly hit off the astrology between Mary and Paul with communications. It would prove to be the dramatic crescendo of both their relationship and the "call" theme—the climactic astrological event of this story.

John & Paul Meet

After Mary's death, Paul channeled his emotion into musical development. He spent his time learning the guitar and became proficient quickly. As mentioned earlier, he has likely been a musician/entertainer in prior lives, but unable to fully put it forth in the world. In the present incarnation his innate musical talent developed easily, like tying his shoes.

The next solar eclipse was on December 2, 1956 {at 10° Sagittarius, on the eventual Beatles Ascendant}. On the spiritual level, the wheels were in motion. The following

58

summer, shortly after turning 15, Paul went to see a local musical gig. It was an event that would ultimately change the trajectory of Western culture. John's childhood friend Ivan Vaughan introduced him to Paul as he knew them both.

The idea of destiny can be a tricky concept for the personality to grasp. Instead of predetermination, another way to see destiny is the realization of soul intentions. There are 360 degrees in a circle, the same as the zodiac. When John and Paul were first in the presence of each other (7/6/1957), the Moon was at the very same degree {10° Scorpio} as they have it in their relationship chart, a striking synchronicity[1]. Additionally, the Moon was conjunct the Nodal Axis, which is the signature of spiritual "destiny[2]." The astrology at this moment matched the John-Paul dynamic, which specifically involved writing about maternal death issues for emotional resolution. By so doing, they could claim visibility, even celebrity, to catalyze collective emotional processes and healing[3].

The other significant themes present when the songwriting team first met include romance, family, as well as fire power around new, innovative creative trends[4]. Paul was beginning to find life direction, with an emphasis on writing. John's signature relating to creative partnerships was being called into action[5]. The boys became friends and musical partners, spending countless hours listening to records and the radio, joking around, smoking and talking about girls. They tried to replicate with their guitars the music they were hearing and began jotting down some ideas as a writing partnership. They began their "bromance," spending many hours together in John's room located on Menlove Ave.

In many ways John and Paul would parallel one another. John's first song was titled, "Hello Little Girl," while Paul's was "I Lost My Little Girl." John's song depicts rejection with lines such as, "I send you flowers but you don't care," and "You never seem to see me standing there." Paul's central issue is located right in the title of his tune. Biographer Phillip Norman writes of Paul's first song, "it seemed to be in the usual idiom of teenage heartbreak, but actually was a way of channeling his grief over his mother's death."[38]

These early songs reflect their central issues, mainly loss, dejection and loneliness. They can be thought of as "seed songs." John and Paul would write numerous songs along these lines (much of the "early formula") during the next phase of their lives. Also, George and Ringo would compose "seed songs," giving voice to their root issues. Through maturation and healing, the seeds would blossom into magnificent gifts. At the conclusion of their work together, all 4 Beatles wrote songs that illustrated their spiritual flowering, the "summation" songs.

Enter George Harrison

John and Paul were collaborating in 1958 amidst much change. The Quarrymen was a skiffle band, and John became more interested in the emerging genre of rock & roll. He would eventually break away from the initial Quarrymen bandmates, and 1958 was the transitional year. The next addition to the band was ready for inclusion.

There is no exact day George became a Beatle. He had 2 auditions in early 1958; biographers note March as pivotal.[39] After the second audition, John was warming to him, but he wasn't officially in. Instead of being a full-fledged member, he would tag along. There was another guitarist named Eric Griffiths, and George would sometimes fill in for him. Eventually they parted ways with Eric and George was accepted as a full member.

At the time of the auditions, George's astrology was emphasizing issues of self-worth and confidence[1]. He was proving his value to himself and others, answering a challenge to be more assertive. He would eventually become the lead guitarist of the most successful rock band in world history. At this very early stage, he was replaying the seed state of his karmic issues. George was deferential to others, seeking their acceptance, not yet claiming his light and power[2]. The "probation" period he went through before his full inclusion contributed to the "younger brother" dynamic in the sibling hierarchy. It would take George almost 10 years to fully emerge from it to claim his rightful stature as the musical leader and creative visionary of his birthright.

His astrology reflected many other exciting new opportunities[3]. It was a major new beginning in his creative life, a time of seizing greater spiritual purpose and meaning. George would grow to become the spiritual conscience in the band, the most philosophical and thoughtful. The planets of spiritual discovery were at a new beginning for George when he joined the band, foreshadowing his contribution[4].

Just after the March auditions, there was a lunar eclipse on April 4th {at 14° Libra, the degree of The Beatles Moon}. As seen with the previous eclipses, the major components of the eventual band chart were being called into action, like the rousing of dormant potential. Though the chart wasn't fully realized until Ringo joined, the pieces were coming together at the soul level.

Julia Lennon's Death

As breakdown/breakthrough events, eclipses sometimes have an ominous reputation. However, there is nothing inherently positive or negative in astrology—all events play out contingent on how we work our spiritual lessons. Since we're all awakening from prior immaturity and unconsciousness, it is generally the case that substantial challenges pave the road towards a more enlightened way. Eclipses tend to bring our spiritual work to a climax.

It can be tricky to simultaneously approach life from two different perspectives. On one hand, many events are understandably devastating to the personality. On the other, there might be great value for spiritual development. The personality tends to judge events as either "good" or "bad," while the soul is invested in learning necessary lessons. At the soul level, we can look at events not as happening *to* us, rather as opportunities *for* us to grow. What John went through in the summer of 1958 was his ultimate test, a lesson that would dominate the rest of his life. It was absolutely terrible for his personality, while also supporting his spiritual awakening.

There was a lunar eclipse on May 3rd, 1958, in Scorpio, sign of death, psychological issues and ultimately the transformation into a new way of being. During the passage initiated by the event, John's mother Julia was killed in a car accident. She was crossing Menlove Ave in the evening of July 15th, hit by an allegedly drunk off-duty policeman.[40]

60

Recall that before Mary McCartney died, there was an eclipse on Paul's writing signature. As discussed in Chapter 1, John's chart has a link between communication, death and his mother. As seen in Beatles lyrics, he repeatedly calls out for romantic connection or reunion with emotional urgency. The astrology suggests it's extremely likely to be rooted in his desire to reunite with his mother. Similar to Paul's chart when his mother died, the eclipse was on the corresponding writing signature {Mercury} in John's! Part 2 provides more detail of the astrological activity to his chart when Julia died$_1$.

Julia's death (and Mary's) brings forward some important spiritual questions about soul contracts. The astrology provides the spiritual context for us to make sense of it. For those interested in the energetic details, Part 2 provides a discussion of the John-Julia bond$_2$. Below are some philosophical musings.

With many years of service as a counselor, I have seen two very different reactions to the spiritual idea that life is ultimately a benevolent teacher for our growth. Some find great comfort and meaning in it, especially when the astrology is so clear and supportive of this notion. Others find the idea that there is any love, grace or meaning in tragedy to be obscene, poisonous or ridiculous. I empathize with such a position as I used to share it too! We all teach what we are learning ourselves…I ask those who have this view to consider that there could be many dimensions or levels to our experience.

John's chart portrays a marked guardedness against feeling pain. The tendency was to stay in his mind, to develop his brilliance with an external focus on the world. The pattern was a defense mechanism, which ultimately required a breakdown into the emotion being avoided (for theoretically many lives). By so doing, he could release the energy and heal his heart. Then, he becomes more able to be a visionary connected with deeper compassion and love. John's message would ultimately become rooted in love, though the process to get there would be rocky.

Not too long after the accident was a solar eclipse on October 12th {at 19^0 Libra} on John's Sun. The Moon (related to the past) obscures the light of the Sun (related to the present) during a solar eclipse. There's a temporary creation of darkness, a thematic replay of unresolved issues from the past (in order to work them through in the present). Similarly, John entered a very dark chapter in his biography. After Julia's death, he entered a period of acting out aggressively. He apparently beat up other teenagers and was emotionally (and sometimes physically) violent towards girlfriends.[41] In full regression mode, with a sizable chip on his shoulder, he coldly took his pain out on others.

At the conclusion of the 1950s, John was mired in his karmic situation. He was still a kid, and he was playing out the challenging facets of his spiritual childhood. What we now know of The Beatles was nowhere near his reality. He was angry, insecure, afraid to feel, and terrified about his future. It was enormously helpful to find family with his bandmates as he now lacked a relationship with both his father and mother.

Similar to Paul and Mary, the astrology between John and Julia also reveals a deep spiritual bond, an intention to work through outstanding emotion. They were learning how to communicate, both with feelings and ideas. There was even the intention to collaborate and structure such communications through projects. However, there is a notable difference between these mother-son relationships.

Like her son, Julia Lennon was a carefree spirit, comedic and engaging. She was a youthful soul who felt unready or ill-equipped to raise her own child. She had her own wounds and issues {Moon square Pluto}, which were not being addressed with focus. The John-Julia bond involved the spiritual necessity to deepen into psychological realism, including emotional wounding.

Mary McCartney was a nurse, someone who gave of herself selflessly with a sense of grace, even divinity. She was a mature soul with a vision. Paul was learning how to become like his mom, to take the next steps of growth towards spiritual insight and connection. Their dynamic involved the restoration of faith after tragedy, a reunion with the divine and each other. Astrologically, John's experience relates more with the planet Pluto, while Paul's is Neptunian. The following section provides greater depth and detail about what this means.

Two Routes of Grief & Redemption

The deaths of their mothers were the defining events of John's and Paul's childhoods and would shape their psyches in different, but complementary, ways. Through astrology, we see a direct link between these experiences and their spiritual paths, including their creative contributions. These planetary energies {Neptune, Pluto} would dominate Paul's and John's respective biographies.

The maternal signature in Paul's chart {Ceres} is strongly connected to the Neptune archetype and losing his mother had elements of sadness, loss and disillusionment. His process of spiritual awakening {Sun} is to transform sadness into compassion, loss into reconnection, and to communicate the process publicly to inspire a collective healing through performance. Paul embodies a dreamy quality {Neptune on his Ascendant} and his music tends towards softer themes, poignant melodies and ballads. His mother died of cancer, and he watched her slip away {Neptune} with the corresponding Neptunian activity to his chart.

Paul developed intuitive gifts he channeled into his music. In his relationships (particularly with Jane Asher), there were elements of estrangement, experiencing the bond just slipping away. He may have also felt this with John when the band was breaking-up. A Neptunian song that illustrates his experience is "Let It Be," which is a call for grace. It also mentions his mother by name and signifies reunion or redemption.

John's maternal energy was in the sign of death and psychological transformation {Ceres in Scorpio, and also square Pluto}, and his experience was much different. After losing his mother, he was volatile and unstable, taking his pain out on others. He is quoted, "I was in a sort of blind rage for two years."[42] He experienced deep emotional angst, a need for intense purging or catharsis. His path of awakening involved the transformation of wounds into shaping culture. John's demeanor was powerful, even intimidating, seeing what he might evoke in others. His music tended towards edgier themes, jarring us towards what is real and authentic. His mother died suddenly and violently with the corresponding Plutonian astrological stimulation {John's p-Sun in Scorpio, exactly on his "wounded child" T-square}.

As a Plutonian, John would grow to make a powerful impact through his music and activism. In his relationships, he would play out elements of abuse and betrayal, a projection of the wounding drama. At the end of The Beatles, he would instigate conflict and drama. A Plutonian song that captures John's core issue is "Mother," from his solo catalog. He was literally screaming in pain, finally the catharsis he so urgently needed to express. Note that this song was after the Beatles. Throughout John's participation in the band, he carried this underlying intensity internally.

These complementary paths of spiritual development synthesized, creating a partnership that addressed both grief (Neptune) and transformation (Pluto). Beatles music was so compelling because it was transcendent and visionary (Neptune), while increasingly becoming deep and powerful (Pluto). John and Paul connected with these potent energies: in dreams, meditation, and journeys of consciousness into the heights (Neptune) and depths (Pluto).

Ideally, any tragedy can be worked through and resolved. The universe did not set it up for us to eternally suffer. Quite the contrary! We can think of Earth like a school where we learn how to grow and consciously reconnect with healing spiritual nourishment. Part of the lesson is to process hurt feelings, which requires acknowledgement of such feelings and the ability to communicate them. As young males existing in a time and place that did not promote a psycho-spiritual focus, they kept it inside. Paul has stated, "We had a bond there that we never talked about—but each of us knew what had happened to the other."[43]

Instead of discussing their common bond overtly, they channeled the emotion of their shared experience into music. Whether they were conscious of it or not, they could not escape from writing about it. In one way or another, themes and issues related to their mothers absolutely dominate the song catalog. At the beginning, it was cloaked in romantic yearning. In the middle, it was depicted in stories and veiled references. Towards the end, they wrote songs mentioning mothers. At the conclusion, they would write songs that specifically mention these courageous, beautiful women by name. Julia and Mary were the only people from their personal lives directly mentioned in Beatles lyrics. Also, when the first Beatles album was released, John named a child after his mother. Paul did the same when the final collaboration completed.

Julia Lennon and Mary McCartney are the heroines of this story. Consistent with the astrological lessons of the times, their roles raise questions about the metaphysical nature {Uranus} of death {Pluto}. Initially, the personality generally isn't aware of other realms of consciousness beyond the ordinary and mundane {Saturn}, but the gift of astrology {Uranus} is to reveal the soul level.

As we follow the rising motion of the "arc" towards the transcendent, questions with astounding implications become part of the story. Could there be "soul contracts" to stimulate particular spiritual lessons for others? Is there life after death? Is it possible to connect with those who have parted? Could we even collaborate with those beyond the veil?

Foreshadowing

At the end of the 1950s, John and Paul were beginning to become songwriters, experimenting with early attempts at the craft. They would not officially release their own works for a few years. Many of these early songs were unfinished or seen as too immature (or inappropriate) so they didn't appear on the studio albums. However, some are part of the Anthology and other collections.

As will be discussed in great detail, the 5 major threads dominate the song catalog, providing a spiritual context to their body of work. John and Paul composed songs along the lines of the 5 major threads in these early writing attempts. Though not made public for years, they foreshadowed what was to come.

Paul first song, "I Lost My Little Girl," was written soon after Mary died (1956) and can be considered a <u>death</u> song. He writes that he "<u>lost</u> my little girl." The song also has the phrase *"woke up,"* foreshadowing the *dream* thread.

John's first song, "Hello Little Girl," (1957) was inspired by a song sung to him by Julia.[44] It foreshadows "call" songs, typified by communications aimed at securing personal connection. He writes, "When you're passing on your way/I say, 'Mm mm hello little girl.'" As would be the case in the early years, his call is not answered. She passes him by and he experiences loneliness and dejection. Also at this time was another song John wrote that wasn't completed. Mark Lewisohn writes that John wrote it with "Julia in mind" and he quotes John, "I did one which had the line 'My love is like a bird with a broken wing.'"[45] "Broken wing" foreshadows major developments in the "bird" theme.

"One After 909" is an early John song (estimated 1958) in the "call" or reunion thread, the anticipation of a lover returning. It would be picked-up at the end of their career and find a home on the *Let It Be* album. The gap between conception of the song and its eventual realization parallels the subject matter—the necessity of having to wait for a conclusion.

"Like *Dreamers* Do" is one of the earliest written songs credited to the Lennon-McCartney partnership (1959). Penned primarily by Paul, it strongly foreshadows the *dream* thread to come, even including the word in the title. Most notably, Paul writes of seeing a girl in his dreams, a notion that will have primary significance in this story.

"You'll Be Mine" is an early Lennon-McCartney collaboration (1960). Though humorous (outright silly!), it nevertheless foreshadows a few threads. The brief mishmash of lyrics previews **solar,** <u>death</u> and "dark" songs. It features the words "**shine,**" "<u>die</u>" and "night."

"I'll Follow the **Sun**" was originally conceived by Paul in 1960. It was resurrected and completed in 1964, released on the *Beatles for Sale* album. The Sun is foreshadowed early on, but the song's completion fits synchronously with the development of the **solar** thread.

Also of note is the cover song, "Besame Mucho," which was part of their early rotation. Though they didn't write the lyrics, the band was drawn to this tune featuring reunion with the beloved with both *dream* and "wings" references (the latter goes with the "bird" theme).

Chapter 6
Coming of Age

The new decade brought a fresh start. The boys had excitement and anxiety about their musical career, a palpable desire for breakthrough. There was much to figure out, mainly who was going to be in the band and playing what instrument? And what about the band name? A lunar eclipse occurred March 13, 1960 on their point of spiritual development {Virgo North Node}. Once again, the sleeping giant of their potential was being roused to fulfill its destiny. In their late teens, they were striving to master their instruments and craft their sound {Virgo}.

Hamburg

In the spring and summer of 1960, the band was playing gigs at the Jacaranda (a coffee bar) and agreed to be managed by the owner, Allan Williams. Williams was able to secure them several bookings and also brought in Pete Best as the drummer. The next year they had a falling out due to a financial dispute[46], but Williams brought them to their training ground, Hamburg, Germany.

As legend would have it, the Beatles became The Beatles there, the proverbial coming of age. They arrived on August 17, 1960 and agreed to a grueling work schedule, playing several sets a day. Pete Best (reviewed later) was new, still learning the ropes. Stu Sutcliffe (also reviewed later) was on bass, though his skill was questionable. Paul was playing guitar along with John and George. The astrology for their arrival in Hamburg (p. 308) had a cross-cultural emphasis and a focus on skill development, interpersonal dynamics, hard work and growing up. They were learning how to be visible entertainers, resolve questions about sound or communication and sort through issues of romance[1].

The romantic issue hanging in the balance concerned Stu. He met German photographer Astrid Kirchherr and fell in love, eventually getting engaged and leaving the Beatles to pursue a career as a visual artist. Another romantic issue was the sex business, which was in full operation around them. Prostitutes (and their clients) were regulars at their shows. The attitude in Hamburg was "anything goes," with many delights and hazards of licentiousness.

They were gobbling Preludin ("prellies"), a stimulant that gave them energy to perform such long hours. Their excitement was also dispersed through practical jokes and delinquency. They were college age and Hamburg was their version of being in a fraternity. Biographies tell an assortment of colorful stories including lighting fires with prophylactics, carousing in the streets, clashes with their audiences, mooning, vandalism, theft, fights and other mayhem. Notable Beatles historian Mark Lewisohn cautions that many accounts may have some degree of exaggeration and mythologizing.[47] Nevertheless, it was a wild time. John played the role of ringleader, the main instigator of drunken revelry and outrageousness.

The culture of the band was becoming more established, an emphasis on wit, teasing and fun. Pete's personality was quieter, not quite fitting in. He would often choose to spend his off time away from the others.[48] John was fiercely loyal to Stu despite his subpar musicianship. Paul was frustrated with Stu's playing and was allegedly envious of John's friendship with him.[49] Matters came to head with an on-stage fight, instigated by the usually mellow Stu who charged at Paul in a moment of frustration.[50] They weren't sleeping much or eating healthily, ingesting their share of booze and pills. Simply stated, they were kids working through adolescence.

The Cavern Club

It was time for the boys to grow up. November 20, 1960 through February 6, 1961 was an astrological passage highlighting themes of masculinity, leadership and maturation {Mars retrograde in Cancer}. It involved working through inhibition, and hit Paul's astrological area of career. After returning from Hamburg, there was pressure from his family to get a job.[51] His karmic pattern of work and financial responsibility undermining his performance desires was being triggered. After a period of balancing employment with music, Paul broke free to fully dedicate himself to his musical passion, strongly urged by John. Paul assisted John with musical know-how, while John supported Paul with bravado and confidence.

A major cultural cycle in the mainstream began in February 1961 {Jupiter-Saturn conjunction in Capricorn}. The world was ready for something new. Though they played at the Cavern Club before under different names, their first show as "The Beatles" was on February 9, 1961 {just after Mars turned direct}. It began a run of hundreds of shows at this venue over the next two and a half years.

The astrology for "The Beatles" first Cavern performance (p. 308) had an emphasis on shared purpose, how workmates get along and create a well-oiled machine. It suggests a critical period, perhaps the need to make some changes for the realization of their vision. Though there is a lot of pizzazz in the chart, it also suggests they were not fully ready for prime time. It points to a need for developing more mystique and allure, learning how to embody the persona of performers. They would heed this lesson, which soon led to the explosion of Beatlemania₁.

In addition to working through maturation themes, there were also personnel issues to sort out. The planet of relating was triggering an important review of social

66

dynamics {Venus retrograde from March 20, 1961 – May 2, 1961}. There were lingering interpersonal and musical questions, particularly about Stu's role in the band.

Stuart Sutcliffe

During this time of social review, it became clear that Stu would leave the band.[52] He was a far more talented painter than bass player. Engaged to Astrid in Germany, he desired to make a life with her. Stu's chart (p. 309) had an overwhelming focus on the arts, though substantial challenges figuring out creative direction[1]. Like John, he had difficulty being with his emotions {Aquarius Moon}—therefore, was unclear about living from his heart[2]. Stu's underlying issue was unprocessed trauma, due to karmic participation in conflict (and possibly war, just like John)[3]. His astrology strongly suggests conflict intertwined with health issues. A leading possibility is karma involving injuries as a result of fighting[4]. Indeed, that is exactly what unfolded.

On January 30, 1961, Stu was horrifically beaten by a group of thugs outside a gig in Liverpool.[53] He was punched and kicked repeatedly, ending up drenched in blood, severely bruised. The attack likely contributed to the brain hemorrhaging, headaches, blackouts and overall decline which ultimately ended with his death the next spring. John also sustained injuries rushing out to defend him, including a broken finger and sprained wrist.[54] The astrology for the attack (p. 310) clearly shows the return of violent karma to be worked through[5].

Stu and John had the exact same violent signature in their chart, one consistent with fighting and defeat[6]. One possibility is they shared karmic roots as fellow soldiers, being part of an infantry or fighting together in some way. John's bond with Stu had a different dynamic compared to the others. Their link is often described as "intimate," each boy desiring to protect the other.[55]

The two men also had conflict between them. John was allegedly cruel to Stu at times, playing out his antagonistic and hostile tendencies. Stu's sister Pauline wrote a book called, *The Beatles Shadow: Stuart Sutcliffe & His Lonely Hearts Club*. In it, she claims Stu directly told her that John had attacked him in a rage in May 1961, including kicking his head while he was on the ground.[56] The veracity of this claim is an open question. Astrology can't prove or disprove it, for it reveals big-picture themes and lessons. It suggests John and Stu had a karmic connection that involved turbulence and violence[7] (p. 310), which might play out in numerous ways.

Stu's role in the story was relatively brief, sometimes marginalized or forgotten. However, he's part of two significant developments. First, his health seriously deteriorated, resulting in his death in the spring of 1962. The death theme turns out to be a major part of the psychology, and spiritual work, of the band. Still healing from the deaths of Mary and Julia, Stu's passing was another emotionally ravaging event (particularly for John). Even more, the band was gelling into a family, so the loss was most personal. Issues of family relate to the second issue...

Stu's Sun was in the sign Cancer (family), an intention to awaken into his heart and deepen loving bonds. He is described as someone sensitive and sweet. He had a loving disposition in the present incarnation to help heal the prior emotional trauma of his conflictual karmic past. His Sun was conjunct the Beatles Sun, and Stu will forever be associated with the band. Aside from helping develop the band name, he also had an influence on their style. He played a significant role in their Hamburg days, and the movie *Backbeat* is a portrayal worth seeing.

First Recording Session

Just weeks after Stu left the band, the others entered a recording studio for the first time. On June 22nd (in Hamburg) they backed-up Tony Sheridan on a few songs. They did renditions of "My Bonnie" and "Ain't She Sweet" with Sheridan, and their own instrumental, "Cry for a Shadow," without him.

The astrology for the session (p. 312) reflects and foreshadows The Beatles group chart[1]. However, it also suggests that their sound is not yet ready[2]. These early songs were not particularly romantic or emblematic of the early formula[3]. Nevertheless, the astrology portrays their eventual leadership as the premier entertainment outfit in the world[4].

The celestial wheels were turning, pointing to new developments in the field of entertainment. Just days prior to the session, the point of spiritual focus and development entered the sign of entertainment {North Node shifted to Leo on June 10, 1961}. A few months later, another shift occurred. In October, Uranus moved forward to enter a 10^0 conjunction with Pluto, signaling the beginning ascent of the "arc of awakening." Matters would accelerate rapidly.

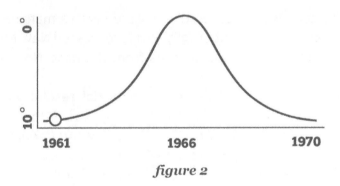

figure 2

Discovery & Brian Epstein

John, Paul, George and Pete were now a foursome with Paul on bass. At this point, they did not have a manager. They were in a time of flux and itching for breakthrough. Playing frequently at The Cavern, word of their talent was spreading. A passionate fan base was cementing, foretelling the first hints of what became Beatlemania. On November 9th, a savvy young businessman came to The Cavern to see what all the fuss was about. The Beatles met Brian Epstein (p. 312), who immediately saw their potential and had many ideas to market them. He agreed to fill the manager vacancy in December, and they officially signed a contract in January 1962.[57]

The Beatles were excellent with inspiration and improvisation, but lacked focus and organization. Brian's central contribution was providing the necessary structure for their talent[1]. His astrology chart illustrates an intention to work with creative projects and innovative trends[2]. He carried a flowing energetic circuit for expansion into culture, with an ear for what could be popular and pleasing[3]. Brian's chart also displayed a tendency to keep his personal passions hidden[4] and he was a closeted gay man.

Similar to each of the Beatles, Brian also had deep, unprocessed wounds and fears {Moon opposite Pluto}—his accompanied by criticality and self-judgment. His defensive pattern was to rise above such pain through being competent and responsible, even with an air of sophistication[5]. Fittingly, he became the ambitious manager of a soul group who similarly avoided dealing with emotion. The pattern would ultimately crash down into emotional realism and a confrontation with the shadow.

Epstein's chart precisely activated the "Beatles signature." However, the stimulation was both exuberant and potentially problematical[6]. Epstein is responsible for launching the band to stardom. Also, the relationship between band and manager would have some financial and personal issues to sort through. Epstein ended up being reckless in his private life, reflecting Beatles themes of indulgence, instability and ultimately death. Nevertheless, on a spiritual level, he played his part perfectly for the lessons and opportunities they would face.

Right when the band was discovered and signed with a manager, John entered a major new astrological cycle on December 19th, 1961 {progressed New Moon}. Prior to this new beginning, he was mired in his soul lessons from the past. Now, he was ready for renewal, an upswing of new possibility.

The new start (p. 313) involved further potential resolution of death issues, psychological dynamics and power {P-New Moon in Scorpio}[1]. These themes could now be addressed in the present, instead of a karmic replay. Additionally, the new focus involved communications {Mercury} with the mysterious and occult {Scorpio}, and John would frequently call out {Mercury} for the dead {Scorpio} in his songwriting. The new cycle also involved forming sacred partnerships and business alliances[2]. In the early 1960s John truly became a songwriter, one with a deep and involved relationship with his partner, Paul McCartney.

Astrologically, he was now finished with the painful visit to his "wounded child" complex, which correlated with Julia's death and his emotional reactivity. His troubles were receding and his overall astrology pointed to newfound opportunity and empowerment[3]. In the next phase, John would do everything he could to get to the "toppermost." He was at the wheel, eager to drive them up the hill of the "arc" with his creative passion and charisma, steady musical development, writing productivity and "yes we can" spirit. John had an unwavering determination to realize his visionary desires.

The Audition & George Martin

1962 began with a setback. On New Year's Day, The Beatles auditioned for Decca records and were rejected. They stayed determined and Brian Epstein kept busy pulling strings. The astrology in the first few months of the year featured a major emphasis on change, innovation and new trends {Aquarius}, a pileup of electrical energy desiring breakthrough. There was excitement, but also more sadness due to learning of Stu's death (on 4/10/1962).

In May, Brian met with EMI record producer George Martin, who was stationed at Parlophone, a subsidiary of the larger company. John, Paul, George and Pete arrived at the studio for an audition with George Martin on June 6th, a most historic day in their chronology. The astrology (p. 314) was suggesting a new entertainment direction being born, pointing directly to the "Beatles signature.[1]" It also involved the pairing of romance {Juno} with the maternal {Ceres}, a central Beatles theme. The transference of mother issues to romance was a dominant characteristic for both John and Paul, synchronously reflected in the sky when they officially began their recording career. Furthermore, the combination was in the sign of writing {Gemini}, situated on Paul's "expression of grief" signature and quite close to the Beatles Sun[2].

There were also recording issues to address {Mercury retrograde}[3]. George Martin had concerns about Pete's drumming (and his departure was soon to come).[58] Among the songs they recorded was "Love Me Do," which would be re-recorded before being released as their first single in the autumn. The band passed the audition, but Martin also saw the need to tighten things up.

Along with some others (notably Stu Sutcliffe, Billy Preston), George Martin has been dubbed the "fifth Beatle," for his irreplaceable role in producing their music. Especially as the music developed greater complexity, Martin's depth of musical knowledge and professionalism played a crucial role in creating the legendary sound. The partnership between band and producer became a phenomenal success, one that changed culture and history.

Not only does George Martin's chart (p. 315) feature ingenuity with sound, it connects to the Beatles chart most dramatically, precisely spotlighting their soul intention to develop visionary communications[4]. He highlights issues of craftsmanship, supporting the promise of the "Beatles signature" to develop and diversify, catalyzing their potential for artistic success[5]. Martin was the "adult" {a Capricorn Sun}, who brought pragmatic counsel and a steady hand on the helm. He connected strongly with the band's familial energy, making it easy for him to play a paternal role[6]. Considering their family issues, Martin's paternal role may have been as valuable and necessary as his musical one.

Martin's emphasis on the earth element was a necessary ingredient for the manifestation of goals. His chart illustrated a knack for finding success through business and the dominant or mainstream cultural milieu[7]. He provided stabilization, coaxing their dormant potential for stardom to ripen. He was adept with the details of production {Virgo Moon}, so the performers could concentrate on broader musical vision. He also had a flair for the theatrical, and added flashes of inspiration and creativity to their work[8].

Some have suggested that Martin is the "real" genius of the band, which he denied. His main contribution was structure and organization, a mature and experienced perspective. He brought imaginative elements and atmospherics to the soundscapes, but claims he was always responding to the band members as the creative visionaries.[59]

Enter Ringo Starr

The band was signed and ready to record. Martin suggested a session musician might be necessary to get the drumming right. He said that Pete's "drumming isn't good enough for what I want."[60] Martin found him to lack innovation and consistency. John, Paul and George weren't as chummy with Pete as they felt with each other. There was talk of replacing him and George Harrison was a main advocate for his friend Ringo Starr, who they'd known in Liverpool and Hamburg. John agreed and asked Ringo to join on August 14th. Brian Epstein told Pete 2 days later on August 16th that he was out.

In between these 2 days was a lunar eclipse {in Aquarius} on August 15th. It was right on Pete Best's Moon, who was literally getting eclipsed, and Stu's Moon, who had recently died. Two weeks prior was a solar eclipse {Leo} on July 31st, which profoundly hit the chart of Ringo Starr (p. 316). The theme of breakdown (Stu, Pete) as well as breakthrough (Ringo) is quite striking with these eclipses.

"Playful Ringo" was dramatically being called to action by the celestial event$_1$. Similar to John's, his astrology reveals that his karmic struggle was finally releasing. During the last 5 years he became a drummer and attained some success playing with Rory Storm. He was now ready for the next step, free of the prior preparatory phase. He had a major emphasis on performance and social connection for years to come, and he earned it!

Ringo was now poised to seize his karmic destiny. He was developing his creativity and confidence, forging new partnerships in order to appear on the world stage$_2$. Additionally, themes of travel, adventure and new beginnings were now available. Similar to when George became part of the band, Ringo's astrology portrays a major turning point. He had no idea the level of fame, hysteria and global impact he would soon experience.

The band is John, Paul, George and now Ringo. People not only list the Beatles in this order, it was the hierarchy within the band. Interestingly, those atop the hierarchy were responsible for bringing in the member just below their ranking. John formed The Quarrymen and invited Paul to join, which ultimately became The Beatles. Paul knew George and brought him in. George was the main advocate for Ringo. The organization of the Fab Four was in place.

The Marginalization of Pete Best

Pete Best was born in Madras, India. He arrived in Liverpool at the age of 4, where he spent his upbringing. He was a member of the Beatles for 2 years, from August 12, 1960 until August 16, 1962.

71

Regarding his removal from the band, George Martin had concerns about his playing. However, if the others were really in his corner, he would have stayed on. He was considered good looking, an able drummer, and his personality was agreeable. He was quite popular with the fans, including a sizable and passionate fan club. The other Beatles deny that he was a threat to their popularity. They claim he didn't quite fit in on a personality level, simply not as witty and engaging. When they adopted the mop top haircut, Pete kept his rocker look. He became "the odd man out,"[61] which has spiritual relevance in this story.

A unifying theme of the band is loneliness. Like the others', Pete's chart (p. 317) illustrates emotional wounds with love and connection, suggestive of loneliness$_1$. Abandonment and outsider issues are strongly emphasized. Similar to John, his pattern is to emotionally disconnect and act out in pain$_2$. (After he was dismissed, Pete had an unsuccessful suicide attempt in 1965.[62] He also took legal action against The Beatles at one point, which is discussed in a later section.) Pete's spiritual work was to venture deep within himself to find inner connection and love—to befriend, rather than abandon, himself. From a healed inner foundation, he might emerge into meaningful experiences and newfound purpose$_3$.

When he was dismissed, Pete's abandonment/disconnection karmic pattern was active$_4$. He may have represented and mirrored the loneliness issue for the others, playing the role of scapegoat. Brian Epstein was asked to inform Pete of his dismissal. After 2 years of being bandmates, the others suddenly cut off all contact. They were cold and distant, precisely what they were so upset about with their own estrangement issues.

Pete's dismissal can be understood astrologically. His chart suggests a relational and creative style that is reserved and measured$_5$. A challenge for Pete was adding more pizzazz, something George Martin addressed in his biography, *All You Need is Ears*. He claims that Pete's drumming lacked innovation. Simply stated, he was learning how to loosen up (both musically and personally), to break out of a "mechanical" style to be more engaging$_6$.

His quieter demeanor had undertones of sexual magnetism, which was compelling for many fans$_7$.[63] There is merit to the idea that he was a threat to others. In fact, the group chart with Pete is highly competitive (p. 319), including sexual and passionate themes, configured in an intense and frictional way$_8$. It is an edgy chart, one that reflects the adolescence when Pete was aboard. Their experiences together in Hamburg had edgy themes (prostitution, experimentation, wildness, etc.). The competitiveness spurred them to achieve, though the dynamic may not have been comfortable for the long term. In contrast, the group chart with Ringo features the abundant "Beatles signature," which is incredibly buoyant, optimistic and agreeable. There are no "better" or "worse" charts, rather each portrays certain spiritual lessons and energetic possibilities.

Pete's involvement triggered the lessons in his natal chart, which was helpful for him to grow. He also mirrored the core loneliness issue for the others. The group chart with him reflected the friction and challenges of the early years; he played his role perfectly. The chart with Ringo ends up being highly sensitive to the explosive astrology of the 1960s. It also connects profoundly to Mary McCartney and Julia Lennon, their important spiritual roles in this story. Ringo's addition in the summer of 1962 brought the group chart into manifestation. The sleeping giant of their potential could now rise up. With the potentially fortuitous "Beatles signature," unheard of fame would soon follow.

John Gets Married

When John found out his girlfriend Cynthia was pregnant, he felt the responsible way to proceed was to get married. On August 23rd, John and Cynthia Powell tied the knot in Liverpool. At this point, The Beatles had a growing female following and Brian Epstein wanted the marriage kept secret.

Cynthia's relationship astrology with John (p. 320) portrays undercurrents of emotional intensity centered in the home[1]. Her chart dramatically reflects John's "wounded child" signature, pairing the shadow with nurturance {Pluto-Ceres}[2]. The relationship became an outlet for John's unresolved feelings (upset, anger, abandonment, etc.). Available sources suggest episodes of physical abuse in the relationship.[64] Cynthia's tendency was to seek affinity and maintain positivity[3], to weather storms until everything is ok. Underneath this avoidant strategy was unresolved anger, fears and hurt buried in her shadow[4]. They were drawn together to work through, or simply play out, darker emotional issues, contingent on the level of maturity brought in.

The astrology on their wedding day (p. 321) activated John's vulnerable "wounded child" signature. The intention was to bring such issues to light and transform abandonment into joy and loving connection[5]. However, the chart also suggests ambivalence (and the marriage resulted from pregnancy). It strongly points to an emotional allegiance with The Beatles, and the "family" of men who were his priority[6].

Chapter 7
Lift Off

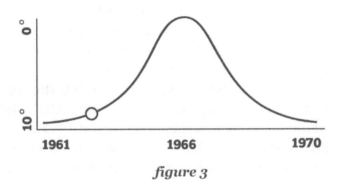

figure 3

Shortly after John got married, matters continued to accelerate in the autumn of 1962. Ringo bonded with the others both personally and musically. Brian Epstein was busy and effective at expanding their public reach through touring and appearances, while also grooming them to be most accessible to the mainstream. They wanted to make some hits, so into the studio they went.

Love Me, Please Me

In September, they recorded "Love Me Do," "Please Please Me," and "P.S. I Love You." All 3 songs have personal pronouns referring to the self in the titles, indicative of the Personality Expression phase. The lyrics to "Love Me Do" are basic and repetitive, setting up a dramatic contrast to what's ahead. They repeat the phrase "love me" 14 times, suggesting a degree of urgency.

"Please Please Me" petitions others (please) to satisfy (please) the self (me)—a most egoic demand. Some contend it has the innuendo of asking for oral sex.[65] John was the primary author of the song and he enjoyed adding subversive elements in his writing {natal Mercury in Scorpio}. Though upbeat and infectious, it's the first "dark song," mentioning "night" in the opening line. It's also the first "rain" song, which is "in my heart." In this epic journey of spiritual awakening, the lyrics begin with unconsciousness (the dark of the night) with emotional upset (rain) to work through. "P.S. I Love You" features communication (a letter) expressing the desire to bridge distance for a reunion, the first "call" song.

George Martin was not completely satisfied with Ringo's drumming on "Love Me Do" and hired session musician Andy White to have more options. Ringo carries a wound regarding performance, and this was a soul lesson[1]. He was an intuitive timekeeper who inserted himself through feeling {Cancer Sun}. At first, Martin wanted precision and consistency, which Ringo had to grow into. He was learning to become steadier and confident in himself[2].

Both a Starr and a White version of "Love Me Do" were released in different re-pressings. The planet of artistry was in a phase of review {Venus retrograde from October 23, 1962 – December 3, 1962 in Scorpio}, signaling a need to work through musical and contractual dynamics. It was traveling through the Beatles "world stage" area {11th House}, preparing to launch them into the cultural milieu.

"Love Me Do" peaked at #17, but they wanted a #1 hit. They re-recorded "Please Please Me" {during the Venus retrograde} with a faster tempo. Martin is famously quoted, "Gentlemen, you've just made your first number one record."[66] He was right. There was a lunar eclipse on January 9, 1963 in the Beatles Sun sign. The single was released 2 days later on January 11th. Consistent with the nature of eclipses, it was a moment of breakthrough.

At this time, the "Beatles signature" was receiving the most explosive stimulation yet[3]. Their "love me" desire was receiving flowing energetic support, while the astrology was pointing to mainstream inclusion with a romantic emphasis[4]. The celestial weather was also relaying a caution.

The boys may have thought that worldwide adoration could heal their loneliness. The planet of will and assertion {Mars} was in the sign of entertainment and celebrity {Leo}, but was retrograde {December 26, 1962 through March 16, 1963}. There is a "careful what you wish for" caution to the retrograde, like a cosmic warning of pitfalls and challenges. Fame would have some heavy costs including the loss of privacy, untamed hysteria, public backlash and security issues. They would eventually retreat {Mars retrograde} from the limelight {Leo}.

Twisting & Shouting

After the success of the singles, it was time to make a record. The recording of their first full-length album, *Please Please Me*, was accomplished in an all-day session on February 11th, 1963. George Martin wanted to capture them live as he found their chemistry remarkable. He instructed them to play as if they were performing for an audience. The boys entered a groove, banging out song after song, relishing the opportunity to make their first album. Martin said that despite recording throughout the day, the band got better as they went.[67]

John was battling a cold and the marathon performing was damaging his vocal cords. By late evening his voice was raspy and frayed, but he was determined to press on for a final song. At 10pm they began recording "Twist and Shout," which would become a classic, featured in movies and played at countless parties. The quality of John's singing held a unique flavor of abandon, giving voice to the wild spirit of youth. The heightened intensity and passion reflected the rising fervor of the "arc" and the times.

"Twist and Shout" is an iconic song—the astrology reveals a unique and brilliant sense of artistry (p. 323)$_1$. Though a cover, The Beatles not only made it their own, it helped define their early sound. The astrology involved the claiming of destiny, while the mood energetically shifted *just for this particular song*$_2$. The astrology for the moment pointed directly to John, the leader in the early phases$_3$. His artistic persona was solidified and the song represents his sheer passion for music, an uncanny ability to shape cultural trends. It was a turning point in John's life, marking his transformation from gruff upstart to becoming a musical legend.

Album #1: *Please Please Me*

Please Please Me was released on March 22, 1963, just weeks after its recording. A remarkable album filled with classic songs, it was an enormously successful debut, reaching #1 in the UK. (Capitol would release the slightly different American version, *Introducing... The Beatles*, almost 10 months later on 1/10/64.)

The album showcases the "early formula." Each song was around 2 minutes, typical for pop songs at the time. The music was designed to garner popularity; they were playing the part of the lovable "mop tops." The band sounds tight, though with nothing overtly experimental. It's straight-ahead early '60s rock & roll, clearly reflecting their influences. In short, this album was a ringing declaration they had arrived.

There were 8 original Lennon-McCartney compositions and 6 cover songs. Individual styles were not yet as distinct as they would become. Instead, the songs were "Beatles music," delivered in the winning formula. The album featured each Beatle singing lead on at least one track. However, the emphasis was on the band as a unit. At concerts they wore matching suits, indicative of the strong group focus at this stage.

Please Please Me was the first of 3 albums in the Personality Expression phase. Subject matter was focused exclusively on romantic yearning and desires for personality satisfaction. Many of the early songs used pronouns and simple words in the title (me, you, she, I), that express the personality. The music and message were simple and straightforward.

The album's cover image intimated the upward trajectory of the "arc of awakening." It showed the band in a stairwell at EMI's London headquarters, appearing to be positioned on the first balcony. Above them are the stairs for the upper levels, which seems to depict 6 levels. It's as if we see them starting to ascend towards the heights they would attain. Interestingly, *Please Please Me* was the first album of 6 in the rising side of the "arc."

Musical Development: The band was on their first floor musically. They would only develop from this point forward, in both surprising and historic ways. As the intention was to capture their live act, the standard line-up of lead guitar-rhythm guitar-bass-drums runs through the album. Additionally, there were harmonica, tambourine and hand claps. George Martin played on a couple tracks (piano, celesta),[68] a trend that would continue.

The raw enthusiasm of the session led to a few imperfections that can be heard—though nothing too outstanding. The album had very little overdubbing.

Lyrical Development: The writing was also figuratively on the first floor. They were still adolescent and the songs reflect it. Some of the writing even sounds younger, an expression of the unresolved and unsatisfied emotional yearnings of children. The 10 original songs (including 2 singles, "From Me to You" and "Thank You Girl") register with 8 placements in lyrical threads: 4 "call," 2 "dark," 1 *dream* and 1 "rain" song. There were no **solar** songs on the debut album. Rather, the tunes portray upset and isolation in separation (spiritual darkness), a disconnection from Source (Sun), and an urgent calling out for support. Below are notes on the songs not previously addressed.

The opening track, "I Saw Her Standing There," is the second "dark" song ("night"). External support (holding each other) is necessary in the dark of the night—love is not found within, but urgently required from others. The next song gives voice to suffering should affection not be received. "Misery" stems from the undesired decisions of others, which is taken most personally. John laments "I've lost her now," a likely projection of his mother issues. "Misery" is the second "call" song--"Send her back to me" is a plea for reunion.

The word "misery" also appears in "Ask Me Why," as something that can be avoided through receiving affection. At this egoic stage, love is experienced as positive affirmations for the personality. "Do You Want to Know a Secret" was written by John and given to George to sing. Inspired by the song "I'm Wishing" from Disney's *Snow White and the Seven Dwarfs* (which Julia sang to John as young child[69]), it's another example of maternal influence on the songwriting. The Disney song foreshadows development of the *dream* thread. "I'm Wishing" contains the line, "I'm wishing for the one I love to find me," then immediately mentions *"dreaming."*

"There's a Place" is the first *dream* and third "call" song, reunion is sought *inside the mind*. Through introspection, loneliness and sorrow recede and memories of the beloved ("I think of you") provide a nourishing experience. This relatively obscure song foreshadows the defining spiritual theme (reunion) of this story. It also intimates the Transcendence phase, "And *there's no time* when I'm alone," an alteration of ordinary experience, which is ultimately how reunion will be discovered.

The single, "From Me to You," also features pronouns in the title. It's the fourth "call" song, expressing a desire to bridge distance. The request, "Just call on me," is stated 5 times during the song. The dynamic was set up at the start. The authors were calling out for reunion, while also requesting to be called in return. The B-side, "Thank You Girl," expresses gratitude for emotional support, a continuation of the external focus to feel secure.

Astrological Summary: The astrology for the album release (p.324) reveals a bold declaration of ambition, an exuberant new beginning. It featured a blend of assertion with imagination, edginess with inspiration$_1$. The group's core spiritual work, their karmic destiny, was being set off by the planets of communication {Mercury} and craftsmanship {Vesta}. It's the realization of the Lennon-McCartney songwriting partnership and activation of the band's collective contribution$_2$. There was immensely supportive flow into the cultural mainstream with maximal activation of the "Beatles signature." The potential was an explosion into widespread acclaim. Youthful expression of fiery masculine passion was the driving force₃. As is the case in much of Beatles astrology, the maternal death issue lurks underneath {Ceres conjunct Pluto and Uranus}₄.

The Birth of Julian Lennon

Family and childhood issues were central for this group. The band itself became a type of family and has entered the home and hearts of millions. Each member would have his own children and address familial spiritual lessons in that context. John's first child arrived at the start of their run, while Paul's would come at the conclusion, bookending their musical contribution. As mentioned, both children would carry the namesake of their deceased grandmothers, illustrating the encompassing presence of these women in Beatles psychology.

Julian Lennon was born on April 8, 1963, just a couple weeks after *Please Please Me* was released. John began the relationship by passing down the same absentee pattern he experienced in his youth. He did not see his son until a couple days after he was born, then chose to go on holiday with Brian Epstein to Spain soon after.[70] A pattern of estrangement began right at the start. John and Julian would have a trying relationship for the remainder of John's life. Julian would lose his father at the same age John lost Julia, also in a sudden, violent way.

Like Julia and John, Julian too has the same combination of astrological factors regarding familial abandonment themes and wounding (p. 325)₁. The spiritual opportunity was to work through such patterns, though it could just become perpetuated. Julian brought maximal illumination to John's central karmic issues, challenging his father's tendency to check out, inviting him to grow into connection and love₂. Due to the proximity of Julian's birth to the release of *Please Please Me*, the record itself gives voice to such dynamics. John writes of sadness and loneliness, his desire to find security, love and happiness. The spiritual work was to show up for his son in such a way, thereby helping to heal his own heart.

Similar to his father, Julian also carries the intention to put emotion towards creative expression₃. Julian is a talented musician, though the comparisons to his father have understandably been a challenge. His resemblance to John can also be seen astrologically₄. Another similarity is with activism₅. In contrast to John's peace activism {Athena in Libra} Julian's activism is geared towards home issues {Athena in Cancer}, which took expression with our home planet Earth. He founded the White Feather Foundation, which involves environmental and humanitarian causes. Healing his own familial issues transforms into a broader gift₆.

Paul Meets Jane

Paul met his girlfriend Jane Asher in April, which began a 5-year relationship. He would eventually move into the Ashers' home, using it as his London location. The relationship brought up emotional dynamics for Paul, which he frequently put into song. The issue of closeness vs. distance would define the connection.

Paul initially fell deeply in love, only to experience the bond gradually slip away. They often spent significant time apart. She had a busy acting career, while he was consumed by the demands of fame. Another issue that drove a wedge between them was fidelity. It's well documented that Paul had many lovers.[71] His philandering likely created tension and may have compromised the experience of undying love and devotion his heart clearly desired (as seen in his songs).

The astrology between Paul and Jane (p. 326) clearly illustrates an attraction$_1$. It's evidently romantic, but the focus was on the idea or concept of romance. Bridging distances was the dominant and pervasive theme, one that reflects Paul's core issue$_2$. The spaciousness allowed them to focus on vocational and cultural realms, to be the socialites they were. Both of them were maturing to manage a wider range of emotion, which would have anchored the relationship$_3$. The spiritual work was to deepen into a more embodied realization of love.

John Pummels Bob Wooler

In later interviews, John himself would comment how strange it was. One of the first major news stories during the rise of Beatlemania concerned John's belligerence. However, since the Beatles did not truly explode until conquering America, this event quickly receded and was forgotten. In fact, many fans have no idea it occurred. However, it did receive media attention in England at the time.

At Paul McCartney's 21st birthday party on 6/18/63, John severely beat up Bob Wooler, DJ and personality from The Cavern Club. As part of The Beatles social circle, Wooler introduced them to Brian Epstein. Apparently, Wooler made a snide comment about John's trip to Spain with Brian, insinuating homosexual relations. In a drunken rage, John not only beat him with fists, he also used a garden shovel.[72] Wooler suffered a broken nose, collarbone and ribs. There was a financial settlement and John released a public apology. He later said about the incident, "I was beating the shit of out him, hitting him with a big stick, and for the first time I thought, 'I can kill this guy.'" He went on to say, "That's when I gave up violence, because all my life I'd been like that."[73]

The astrology between the men (p. 327) portrays the potential for violence. The tendency stems from emotional reactivity and woundedness, with both of them having violent karmic patterns. Wooler sets off John's "axis of conflict" in a most powerful fashion, while John triggers Wooler's underlying hostility$_1$. Highlighted at the time of the beating was the planet of belief systems {Jupiter}, how we defend our behaviors$_2$. At the time, John justified the attack because of Wooler's name calling. He would grow out of the opinion that some people deserve violence and become a tireless advocate for peace. He would also learn to temper his own tendency to call people names and promote love instead.

Chapter 8
The Meteoric Rise

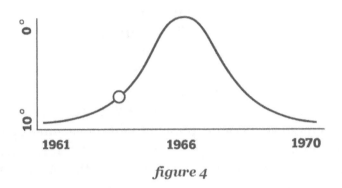

figure 4

The remainder of 1963 brought increased visibility in the UK, and they began to penetrate the American market at the end of the year. 1964 was the year that The Beatles conquered the world, largely by leading the British Invasion of America. This chapter will address the major events that transpired as they rose to international celebrity. They were touring, doing media appearances, making albums and learning to be famous. The once-in-a-lifetime ride was equally thrilling and exhausting. A summary of their individual astrological activity during Beatlemania is on p. 328.

Hysteria

During the summer of 1963, *Please Please Me* became a huge success, immediately followed by smash singles. With the "arc" stimulating the "Beatles signature," celebratory energy was being infectiously released into the collective consciousness through this 4-man musical force. Accompanying the success was a crazed adulation wherever they went, a surreal mania that was bigger than them.

The 1950s is noted for its conservatism, a respect for decorum and traditional values. As the "arc" ascended, the proverbial lid was getting blown off all restraint, unleashing pent-up desires and frustrations. In particular, the tides of change and revolution were sweeping young women into their empowerment, which played out with amorous intensity. The Beatles were a projection screen for it, and they initially couldn't get enough. On stage they would shake their heads and deliver "ooooohs," enjoying the instant response of unbridled adoration. Many girls were so enthralled, they appeared to be in pain, complete with tears.

Some early songs captured this dynamic between band and audience, evoking themes of love and desire. "She Loves You" literally describes the reception of feminine affection with upbeat energy and trademark "yeah, yeah, yeahs." The lyrics describe the facilitation of a relationship reunion after some kind of hurt and separation. It's the fifth "call" song as it involves communications designed to heal estrangement.

The song was recorded on July 1st—delayed by hijinks and mayhem at the studio. At this point they were unprepared for Beatlemania. Dozens of screaming girls crashed the studio, running down the halls and evading security.[74] It was a comical scene which pumped up the boys, contributing to their hormonal energy on the classic hit single. "She Loves You" was literally co-created by the passion between the band and their female fans, youthful libidinous fervor captured on vinyl.

The astrology for the recording of "She Loves You" (p. 330) involves transforming estrangement into redemptive intimacy$_1$. It follows what is becoming a pattern: maternal {Ceres} and romantic {Juno} energies paired, illustrating a transference. For this song, mother energy {Ceres} is literally pointing up to heaven {the Midheaven}$_2$. Additionally, blatant sexual desire is represented, which is both intense and playful$_3$.

The song was officially released 7 weeks later on August 23rd, with "I'll Get You" as the B-side. It would go on to be a #1 hit, their most successful single released in the UK. The astrology of the release day (p. 331) reveals more. There was a major emphasis on the sign of relationship {Libra}, how we play out spiritual work with others. The maternal-romantic blending was still in effect, now more prominent in the Beatles chart, accentuating their "love me" signature.

The singers give advice to an unnamed man to patch up a relationship. Perhaps they're expressing their own desires to heal emotional distance. One of the spiritual lessons of relationship {Libra} is to retract projections, to own in the self what we see in others. Upon turning "she loves you" inside out, the song could be saying, "I want her to love me." The reception of such love would make them feel "glad," and the song's upbeat energy expresses such elation. The gift of the fans to the performers was to show them they were lovable.

And they couldn't get enough.

On September 15, The Beatles played the prestigious Royal Albert Hall to a swarm of adulation. About the event, Paul said, "We felt like gods! We felt like fucking gods!"[75] He would say about these early experiences, "It was *like a dream*. The greatest fantasy ever."[76] Due to the surreal nature of such incredible overnight fame and attention, perhaps they were able to see the *dream* perspective. It likely became apparent to them that the intense reaction to Beatlemania was not really about them. It was far bigger. They were playing characters in a larger drama or process, occupying a position in an archetypal or mythological theater. A facet of the "arc of awakening" was to stimulate the awareness of such a transpersonal perspective. It was just starting to unfold—soon, they would be more in on the game.

As for feeling like gods, the band would endure mythical and divine projections, an almost religious devotion. They had many requests to heal sick children or serve as a good luck charm. They used the code word "cripples" as an alert when disadvantaged people were coming. George Martin wrote, "Every little thing they said became translated into Beatle instructions as to how we should behave."[77]

"I'll Get You" has substantial spiritual meaning as the third "dark" song ("night"), the sixth "call" song and the second *dream* song. Similar to "There's A Place," thoughts and the imagination are used creatively for emotional connection. John sings of securing a reunion with the beloved ("call" theme) through the use of consciousness (*dream* theme), foreshadowing events to come.

On October 17th they recorded "I Want to Hold Your Hand," which became their most successful single worldwide. The lyrics speak of the desire to satisfy basic security needs. Necessary for small children is touch, which is mentioned in the song's title and in the line, "And when I touch you I feel happy inside." For the song's release on November 29th, the Moon (needs) was in the sign most related to sensuality, physical security and finding calm {Taurus}. The B-Side, "This Boy," is the seventh "call" song; "This boy wants you back again" is a plea for reunion.

The planet Venus has 2 sides: the establishment of personal connection {Libra} and reaching physical calm {Taurus}. The attainment of these human functions is necessary for happiness and survival, something everyone can relate to. "She Loves You" {Libra Moon}, and "I Want to Hold Your Hand" {Taurus Moon}, gave voice to these universal needs. The Beatles used Venusian motifs brilliantly for attaining their success, charming their way to the "toppermost."

Album #2: *With the Beatles*

The second album was similar to the first in a number of ways. It contained 8 original songs, 6 covers and each Beatle sang lead vocals on at least one song. All songs were between 2-3 minutes in length and followed the "early formula." It was released on November 22, 1963 in the UK, the same day President Kennedy was assassinated in the U.S. Like *Please Please Me*, it sold a million copies and reached #1. Unlike the marathon recording session of the first album, it was created over the summer and autumn of 1963.

The cover image resembles the style of Astrid Kirchherr's photography in Hamburg, a time representative of their adolescence. It shows the musicians with their faces in half shadow, similar to the appearance of a first quarter Moon. The rest of the album cover is completely black. The illumination of faces highlights the area most symbolic of personality. As the second offering of the Personality Expression phase, they were slowly coming out of the dark. The image resembles the degree of illumination of the Moon at the release time, which was approaching the first quarter (p. 331)[1].

"I Want to Hold Your Hand" is the iconic song. Released as a single just days after *With the Beatles*, it was part of a strategy to bombard the airwaves with fresh music. Initially successful, it also placed a heavy demand on them to continually churn out high-quality material. At this stage, they were up to the challenge and *With the Beatles* (considered a weaker album compared to the debut) benefitted from the mega success of the internationally popular single.

Musical Development: Their musical palette was broadening. The album features tambourine, harmonica, handclaps, claves, maracas, a bongo and nylon-string acoustic guitars.[78] *With the Beatles* featured the first George Harrison original, and he sang lead on 2 other cover songs. Although John was the lead singer on the majority of tracks, the cohesive and collaborative nature of the Lennon-McCartney partnership was apparent.

Lyrical Development: The Personality Expression phase continues with songs similar to the debut. Romantic dynamics are rooted in the underlying psychology of maternal loss, with loneliness or crying on almost every song. The 8 original songs (and 4 singles) register with 11 placements in the lyrical threads: 6 "call," 3 "dark" and 2 *dream* songs.

In "It Won't Be Long" (the fourth "dark" song), the nights are filled with sadness. The eighth "call" song, there is anticipation for reunion ("You're coming home"). "All I've Got to Do" is the ninth "call" song, featuring the word "call" a total of 9 times. "All My Loving" is the tenth "call" song, another using the medium of the letter to bridge distance. It's also the second *dream* song: "And hope that my *dreams* will come true" is a conventional, anticipatory use.

George's first composition, "Don't Bother Me," is the fifth "dark" song ("night"), one introducing his inward disposition. A "seed song," it describes the tendencies of his spiritual childhood, mainly to withdraw for protection. "Little Child" literally reflects early developmental stages, a simple song concerning the management of "sad and lonely" feelings. "Hold Me Tight" is also childlike, a plea for security and reassurance, the unwillingness to let another go.

"I Wanna Be Your Man," repeats the words "man" and "baby" throughout. Adolescence is the time when early stages (baby) mature into adulthood (man). To get there, one must retract the need for external validation ("Tell me that you love me baby"), to become more emotionally self-sufficient. "Not a Second Time" is another song suggesting others are responsible for one's emotions ("you made me cry").

Astrological Summary: The astrology had an emphasis on emotional disconnection or alienation, the lesson of processing prior hurt and pain$_2$. The transference of maternal issues onto romance was still emphasized$_3$. *With the Beatles* had the first hints of broader contemplative or spiritual themes$_4$. The album is laced with redemptive longing, more focus on dreams and a desire for the eventual transcendence to come.

Not too long after the album's release was a lunar eclipse on December 30th near the band's Sun. As the calendar turned from 1963 to 1964, The Beatles would breakthrough into the collective consciousness with an intensity never seen before or after in the field of entertainment.

Opening Salvo of the British Invasion

Recovering from President Kennedy's assassination, the mood in America was uncertain and edgy. The Beatles offered something new and fresh and the United States was more than eager to receive them. Though heard elsewhere in the U.S. in late 1963, Beatles music first received airplay in New York in January 1964, which gave them massive publicity. The American version of their first album was also released to accompany the chart-topping singles. The British Invasion was underway, an explosion of notable bands making a cultural impact in the mid-1960s. It included The Rolling Stones, The Who, The Yardbirds, The Hollies, The Kinks, Herman's Hermits, The Animals and many others. The Beatles were the leaders of the movement and their appearance on The Ed Sullivan Show was the seminal event.

The Beatles touched down in New York City on February 7th to a swarm of people and reporters. They were the hot new thing and handled the publicity with poise, confidence, humor and accessibility. On February 9th they performed on The Ed Sullivan Show, the first of 3 appearances in 1964. An estimated audience of 73 million people watched their debut.[79]

It was an historic moment in time, one often seen in terms of destiny. On an astrology chart, the Ascendant is literally what's rising. When the show began at 8pm, Sullivan immediately introduced The Beatles (p. 332). At that time, the Ascendant was at the same degree as The Beatles point of destiny {22° Virgo North Node}!,

It was a moment when millions fell in love with them. The cosmic conditions were extremely ripe for romantic idealization,. Instead of the romantic/maternal pairing that defined much of 1963, the focus shifted to romantic glamorization or idolization. Furthermore, the astrology strongly suggested feminine empowerment, from traditional behavior standards to greater liberation,. Many were swept away by the music and the musicians, pulled into the building hysteria,.

The Sun Begins to Rise

Perhaps it had to do with being recognized by the world, coming into greater stature and power. Maybe it was from some healing of the past through creative expression. The Beatles were swiftly coming of age. The quickening pace of the "arc of awakening" was carrying them forward. At this time, the "line of inspiration" was being crossed (recall discussion on p. 49). The first inklings of spiritual awakening appeared in Beatles lyrics in the creation of the first **solar** songs.

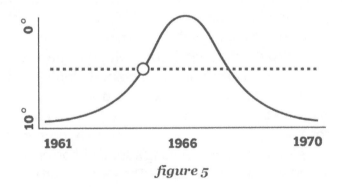

figure 5

84

At the precise time the "arc" crossed the inspiration threshold on February 25, 1964, sessions began for Paul's ballad, "And I Love Her," the first **solar** song and sixth "dark" song. It has the lines, "**Bright** are the stars that **shine**/Dark is the sky." A few months later on June 2, sessions began for the second **solar** song. John's "Anytime at All" includes the lyrics, "If the **sun** has faded away/I'll try to make it **shine**." As these 2 songs portray, the early use of solar imagery is closely paired with an initial emergence from darkness. "And I Love Her" juxtaposes "**shine**" with "dark," and "Anytime at All" mentions "faded," with a personal attempt to light up the Sun. The seed was initially struggling in the earliest stages of blossoming.

The early uses of solar imagery suggest a brightening of prospects, a renewal of hope and optimism. There will still be plenty of references to night, rain and clouds to come. However, the more awareness and trust of life (Sun) that is cultivated, the dark will be viewed much more benevolently. Ultimately, we might find that there is nothing inherently wrong with the dark, rather the issue is our fears within it. At this early juncture, the first flickers of light have been found in the abyss of unconsciousness and separation.

Each **solar** song offers a teaching about spiritual awakening.

"And I Love Her": Illumination comes from the celestial.
"Any Time at All": We are able to partner (or co-create) with the Sun.

These early teachings are foundational—necessary concepts to have established for the journey ahead. First is the idea that we are part of a larger cosmic order. Brightness, illumination itself, originates from this vast expanse of sky, heaven and beyond. We are enveloped within its reach, given vitality and awareness by something much broader than us.

The next teaching concerns our relationship with this vital expanse. It is our responsibility to consciously partner with it ("I'll try to make it **shine**"). If we do not show up and participate, we are prone to experience the darkness of separation ("If the **sun** has faded away"). Paul's song mentions stars, bringing us to the countless points of light pervading the universe. John reduces that scope to our little neighborhood, a personal connection with our Sun. Understanding the relationship between the macro and the micro, the universal and the personal, begins the journey of awakening.

"And I Love Her" is also the first <u>death</u> song with the line, "A love like ours could never <u>die</u>." They stayed away from death until this point (helpful in being lovable), but it was starting to seep in. The sentiment being expressed is poetic and sweet, but it also points to an area of the band's psyche about to become pried open.

The astrology for "And I Love Her" (p. 333) strongly triggers the core issues of Paul's natal chart. The song's {Pisces} Sun is shining a spotlight on his karmic issues of grief, stimulating his desire to find spiritual redemption[1]. The {Leo} Moon reflects his own Moon, Paul's unsatisfied need for happiness, and it's looking upwards towards heaven for connection[2]. Rising at the time of the song's creation was the sign of the Sun {Leo}, illustrative of the first **solar** song coming forth[3]. Maternal energy {Ceres} powerfully connects to Paul's "expression of grief" signature, suggesting that the transcendent longing involves his mother[4]. The muse (addressed in detail below) plays a central role in this astrology, connected to artistry, inspiration, Paul's longing, the "arc of awakening" as well as the muse attunement of the band[5].

"Anytime at All" is the eleventh "call" song, repeating the word "call" 7 times. John wants to allay sadness and loneliness through connection. The solar reference "I'll try to make it **shine**," is offered as comfort out of painful emotion. Still in the Personality Expression phase, this is the most egoic use of solar imagery, to avoid pain. Nevertheless, there is recognition that the Sun provides nourishment.

Similar to "And I Love Her," "Anytime at All" also had the sign of the Sun {Leo} rising. The Sun was in the sign of communication {Gemini} precisely on the "Beatles signature," highlighting the "call[6]." Whereas the Moon for "And I Love Her" reflected Paul {Leo}, "Anytime at All" had a lunar match with John {Aquarius}, reflecting his work to heal emotional disconnection[7]. The evolutionary motion involved the opening of his heart. By so doing, reunion with the beloved becomes more possible.

The astrological points described in terms of "destiny" are the Nodes of the Moon, which play a central role in many types of spiritual astrology. When a planet appears in proximity to this axis (North and South Node are always opposite), spiritual lessons pertinent to the planet are activated. The astrology of 1964 uniquely featured the pairing of maternal energy {Ceres} with the signature of unfinished karmic business {South Node} for an extended duration (roughly March—October). "Anytime at All" was one of several songs (and events) specifically concerning potential resolution of maternal/child and caretaking issues {Ceres}[8]. Whereas 1963 involved the transference of mother issues onto romance, the middle months of 1964 specifically involved the potential resolution of maternal karma.

The planet of communication {Mercury} was pointing to the heavens above. It was in connection {opposition} to transcendence and spirituality {Neptune}, suggesting a mystical type of communication would be necessary to complete the call[9]. John would need to further access his intuitive and visionary gifts, which requires addressing his troubled inner landscape. Similar to "And I Love Her," the muse is uncannily represented in the "Anytime at All" chart. She is in connection to the multidimensional scope of the "arc of awakening," the maternal {Ceres} as well as the awakening/presence {Sun} of the call {in Gemini}[10].

The Muse

The creation of the first **solar** songs correlated with the motion of the "arc" crossing the "line of inspiration." The astrology for these songs also featured increased involvement with the muse. At this critical junction, she is hypothesized to make her entrance. Though her presence would initially be subtle and unconscious to the musicians, her influence begins to shape the music. It's time to discuss the nature of this most mysterious spiritual phenomenon.

The muse is not a new idea with the Beatles. As seen in the literature, Julia and Mary are often discussed in this manner.[80] The question is not whether the dead mothers had an influence on the songwriting, it is the nature of such influence.

One's viewpoint is informed by philosophical or spiritual opinion. A dominant strain of modern Western thought is rationality and reason, a preference for what has clear and tangible evidence. The materialist viewpoint leaves little room for phenomena operating in other ways. For the spiritual skeptic, the muse is likely understood in pedestrian or conventional ways. Julia and Mary would be influential via John and Paul's memories and emotional longings.

As discussed in Chapter 4, conventional understandings are held within the jurisdiction of the astrological Saturn, the organization of the material world with its logic and reason. One of the dividing lines between a Saturnian and trans-Saturnian (inclusive of outer planets, transpersonal) worldview is the understanding of consciousness itself. The conventional view holds consciousness as separate and individual, while the transpersonal view posits a collective (or shared) consciousness. A transpersonal conception of consciousness (and the muse) is the view here.

The muse phenomenon is mysterious and fascinating, tantalizing us to consider some form of relationship with another realm. What exactly is a muse? An angel or spirit guide, some type of ghost or disembodied being? Could it be the consciousness, soul or spirit of a dead person? The muse is thought to inspire, but what is inspiration? The word breaks down to "in," "spirit" and the suffix "tion" involves action. To put it together, the word means "embodying spirit in action." Inspiration can involve receptivity to a muse, a way to channel the divine. These "beings," or however we wish to construe them, play this mediating role, the bridging of worlds. The muse is the deliverer of "heaven" into the realm of earth.

How the muse delivers her inspiration is the mysterious part, though here's an example that could shed some light. The novelist Stephen King is often asked how he comes up with his fantastically creative ideas. He says, "Good story ideas seem to come quite literally from *nowhere*, sailing at you right out from the empty sky… Your job isn't to find these ideas, but to recognize them when they show up."[81] King points to a creative void (nowhere, empty) in connection to our consciousness. With a transpersonal understanding of consciousness, we may connect to others in this place.

Ideas showing up involves discovery (as opposed to personal creation) through receptivity. John and Paul have uttered statements about their songwriting process (see opening quotes to this book) consistent with this notion. The work is to attune consciousness to the creative void of this nowhere land. It could occur in meditation and some report enhanced receptivity in altered states. The main way these songwriters receive their inspiration, how they connect with their muse, appears to be through dreaming.

Dreams are often nebulous, beyond the ordinary experience of time, order and reason. Their contents often become foggy or vanish upon waking. Therefore, the process may be subtle and elusive. Should greater degrees of awareness become cultivated in dreamtime (or in meditation, altered states), then the songwriters might experience the reunion of their longing. They seemed to have a gradual dawning that something extraordinary was occurring. At the conclusion of this story is the grand finale "Let It Be," a song explicitly detailing inspiration in this way (mentioning waking from dreaming with the receptivity of communications and music). On the way, the presence of the muse was more imperceptible, playing out like a game of hide and seek.

The muse process was mainly unconscious, especially early on. However, the astrology for the inspired songs provides a map through the fogginess. Her role is detected, understood and given a broader context. Other facets of the songs, including ways to decipher messages or teachings, are revealed. Existing in another dimension or plane of consciousness, the muse could have access to broader archetypal, symbolic or mythological realms. Her role is to bring such heavenly perspectives to illuminate our experience on Earth.

In Greek mythology, there are several muses including Calliope and Erato (poetry), Terpsichore (dance), Thalia (comedy) or Polyhymnia (hymns). There is also Euterpe, the muse most associated with music. Euterpe is the "giver of delight," and she's depicted holding a flute.[82] There's also relevance to bird symbolism as she descends from a lofty heavenly perch, singing her songs of love.

Astrologically, the muses can be located in the vast pantheon of asteroids. There are hundreds of large asteroids and thousands of smaller ones orbiting between Mars and Jupiter. Astrologers use asteroids for a wide variety of reasons, generally for secondary or supportive information. During the process of creating this book, I researched the role of the asteroid Euterpe in Beatles songs. What I found dramatically supports the centrality of the muse in this story. It turns out to be the most surprising and heartwarming part of it.

Reunion and Soul Contracts

The potential resolution of maternal karma in 1964 involved the muse. In early June, her travels {transiting Euterpe} came to Paul's personal point of unresolved karma {South Node} in the sign of intuitive receptivity and dreams {Pisces}, while also energizing John's muse attunement {opposite his Euterpe}. Sessions commenced on June 1st for John's "I'll Be Back," a song about estrangement and a promise of reunion. The next day Paul composed "Things We Said Today," a poignant song of utmost spiritual significance. Similar to their "seed songs" about loss, they parallel each other again about reunion. Both of these beautiful ballads are romantic, though the astrology points to another dimension, that of soul contracts.

A soul contract is an intention to partner with another for important spiritual work. At the soul level are deep and enduring bonds, connections developing for potentially many lives. These agreements are formed through love and touch us at a core level. We don't forget them—rather, our job is to consciously remember. At this point, the songwriters were getting the first flickers of awareness.

John's "I'll Be Back" is the twelfth "call" song, stating the desire for reunion in the title. It conveys heartbreak due to the necessity of going away, "you know, I hate to leave you." An eventual regeneration of love is pledged, "but I'll be back again." John may have been intuiting a message from Julia, feeling in to her process and the nature of their bond. Towards the end of the song is the phrase, "I've got a big surprise," which will be picked up on later.

Paul's "Things We Said Today," the thirteenth "call" song, is more descriptive and revealing. He is quoted about the song, "We'll remember the things we said today, sometime in the future, so the song projects itself into the future."[83] There was a prior agreement to be followed up, a soul contract.

Paralleling John's song, Paul opens with "if I have to go," also stating a necessity to depart. However, the bond remains, "You'll be thinking of me/Somehow I will know." The eternality of love is captured in "You say you'll be mine, girl/'Til the end of time." Paul reveals how the contract is completed and what's to come in the story. In this fourth *dream* song he writes, "Someday when we're *dreaming*," they "will remember" the pledge to reconvene. The more he develops intuitively, the more the reunion becomes possible.

The astrology (p. 334) features communications of a mystical variety {Mercury opposite Neptune}, consistent with a spiritual {Neptune} contract {Mercury}. The evolutionary motion is towards reunion with the beloved, specifically with familial relations {Venus in Cancer on the North Node.} The song's Sun was on the "Beatles signature," in the sign of communications {Gemini}, the "call."

"I'll Be Back" and "Things We Said Today" are prescient and haunting, offering a description of departure and return. They are Step 1 (description) of the muse process, a statement of the soul contracts. At this point, Paul's receptivity was sharper and his song more revealing. His core issue of transforming grief through dreams and inspiration was particularly highlighted. As he stated, "Things We Said Today" projects into the future. Therefore, he must go back to "Yesterday" to get to the bottom of those things that were said. John was still working through substantial emotion to reconcile.

Another Unanswered Call

The next song was an outpouring of John's heart. Through such expression and release, he might become clearer and more receptive, able to be in the emptiness of the creative void. Along with 3 cover tunes, "I Call Your Name" was released on the *Long Tall Sally* EP on June 19th (initially recorded in March). It's the seventh "dark" song ("night") and the fourteenth "call" song, a plea to rise up from darkness. "Call" now appears in the song title, emphasizing more urgency and importance. John sings of lying in bed, unable to sleep and unable to emote, simply frozen ("I can't go on") with unprocessed grief. The song is like a prayer, calling his beloved, "but you're not there."

At this point, there are already fourteen "call" songs. The repetition and intensity of the theme reflects emotional urgency. John kept his feelings after the tragedy bottled up. He did not go to therapy or discuss the issue with family or friends.[84] Emotional development requires the *acknowledgement* of feelings so one could be in charge of them (instead of the other way around). At this point, John's emotions are in charge of him, locking him in the soul cage of his past. He must free the emotional energy to liberate himself. The intensity can be transmuted into the creativity of musical expression.

"I Call Your Name" depicts a heartbreaking scene, and it's for real. Many see the lyrics of pop songs as art or fiction, not something to take seriously. Though the songs in the early catalog are often seen as light and simple, there are deep emotional and spiritual processes in these "call" songs.

The "I Call Your Name" astrology bombed John's area of communication (p. 335). The spiritual work continued with maternal issues from the past {Ceres conjunct South Node}, and an invitation for emotional expression$_1$. The unanswered nature of this call is found in a couple ways. First, maternal energy was buried at this time, literally out-of-bounds$_2$. The way to complete the call was to dive deeper into the psyche, to venture into the Underworld. Also, the planet about connection {Venus} was retrograde, signifying blockage. An internal process was necessary to complete the call$_3$.

At the Movies

1964 featured a major planetary shift. The planet Saturn is the dominant energy of the cultural milieu. It was completing its passage through the sign of new trends and fascination, modernizing culture {Aquarius}. The proliferation of rock music led by electric guitars and authentic self-expression was fitting. On March 24th, it began a passage of deeper subtlety, imagery and inspiration {Pisces}. For the next 2.5 to 3 years, the emphasis was on spirituality, which the Beatles would progressively develop throughout the passage. The *dream* thread would become more outstanding and central. At the start, they worked with the magic of the moving image (and movies are like visual representations of *dreams*).

The film, *A Hard Day's Night*, showcased the consciousness of Beatlemania, its otherworldliness and devouring mania. It featured the obligatory screaming girls and hype, depicted as comedic chases between adoring fans and the musicians. The film featured their musical abilities and personalities, further endearing them to the public. Critically acclaimed, it was hailed as joyous, timeless and culturally significant, a classic. It influenced the emerging genre of musical movies as well as television shows, music videos and even spy films.[85]

This Saturn passage presented a challenge to Paul {on his South Node}, a sluggish time in his creative output. He was still in the beginning stages of his relationship with Jane, spending his time and focus falling in love. He was deepening into the realities of his karmic grief, which he was writing about.

Though still emotionally troubled, John was in a time of expansion and abundance {Jupiter return in Taurus}. He was writing prolifically, motivated to solidify his standing as the leader. Ringo {Jupiter return as well} was also riding high, and he was the standout in the film. The plot specifically focused on him, which helped compensate for his junior status in the band. George had the expansive planet {Jupiter} enter his relationship area {7th House} during the filming, and he met his future wife Pattie on the set.

There was highly-charged activation {Mars} of the "Beatles signature" for the film's release, triggering its frenzy and expansiveness (p. 336)₁. The planet of popularity was emphasized for an extended period₂ {Venus retrograde from May 29ᵗʰ through July 11ᵗʰ, moving from Cancer back to Gemini, crossing their Sun 3 times}. The cosmic questions: How might they adjust to their good fortune and popularity? What changes might occur musically or personally₃?

A *Hard Day's Night* arrived at the 2-year mark of George Martin becoming the producer and Ringo joining. The initial dream was clearly being lived. In 1964, they held numerous positions on the Billboard Hot 100, including the top 5 spots at one point.[86] The point of karmic destiny {North Node} reached their Sun (realization) during that summer. There was a lunar eclipse on June 25ᵗʰ {at 4° Capricorn, opposite the Beatles Sun}, further signaling their explosion into the mass consciousness. The album of the same name came out just days after the movie.

Album #3: *A Hard Day's Night*

The final album of the Personality Expression phase was released on July 10, 1964. *A Hard Day's Night* featured 13 tracks, with songs from the movie filling out one side of the record. Nine of the songs were primarily authored and sung by John—this was the album most dominated by a single member. Though Paul is the primary author and singer on only 3 tracks, his offerings were all quite notable in the band's development. George does not write any songs, but is the lead singer on one (credited to Lennon-McCartney). Unlike the first 2 albums, Ringo doesn't sing a song.

The cover image features head shots of the band. There are 4 rows, each with 5 pictures for a total of 20 head shots. Every image is unique, showing a wide range of personality expression. Instead of the usual John-Paul-George-Ringo hierarchy, the top row of images is John, followed by George underneath, then Paul and Ringo. Paul contributed more songs to the album (3) compared to George (none), and his "middle brother" status was not in jeopardy. However, he was feeling the weight of his karmic issue which was bringing him down. The images of Paul do not portray his usual sunniness. In addition to his star turn in the movie, Ringo also coined the album's title. "A Hard Day's Night" would be one of several "Ringoisms" that would define his character.

Musical Development: George's opening chord of the title track became iconic, one of the most recognizable Beatles sounds. His use of the 12-string guitar added a fuller sound, while the band also employed novelties like cowbells and claves. The songs were still around 2 minutes in length but there is more subtlety, including nuanced melodies and ballads. *A Hard Day's Night* proved that The Beatles were becoming sound artists instead of just performers.

Lyrical Development: The last album of the Personality Expression phase, it gives voice to an adolescent yearning for love, happiness and connection. However, there's more depth compared to the first two albums. It features the first **solar** songs as well as intuiting deeper soul contracts (whether conscious or not). John revealed some of his emotional edge with undercurrents of angst. The lyrics were more crafted, illustrating the focus and importance they placed on songwriting.

The 14 original songs (13 on the album and "I Call Your Name" from the EP) have 12 placements in the lyrical themes. The first 2 **solar** songs suggest the awakening process was underway. However, the 5 "call" and 4 "dark" songs indicate heightened yearning and unconsciousness. The appearance of the first <u>death</u> song suggests their underlying issue was seeping through.

The title of "A Hard Day's Night" makes it the eighth "dark" song. It portrays the traditional bargain of satisfying another's needs, an exchange of financial support from the male for emotional and intimate affection from the female. Relationship negotiations continue on "I Should Have Known Better," which sets up a mutual pledge for devoted love. "If I Fell" has more relationship negotiations, wanting to move beyond "just holding hands" and avoid facing sadness. So far, this album was John's attempt to lay out his terms for a suitable relationship. He wants emotional support, an absence of problems and plenty of affection.

"I'm Happy Just to Dance with You" is the ninth "dark" song ("night"), another expressing the desire for intimacy beyond holding hands. "Tell Me Why" gives voice to emotional challenges of the personality: crying, lying, apologizing, begging for forgiveness, evading difficult emotion and doing anything to secure love from another. Paul's "Can't Buy Me Love" became a #1 hit, a bouncy song typifying Beatlemania. Regarding the dynamic between materialism and intimacy, it reflects a core issue in his chart[1]. John reveals his "chip on my shoulder" in "I'll Cry Instead." The lyric, "I just lost the only girl I had," may stem from maternal loss.

John's "When I Get Home" reprises the theme of the title song, the desire to "hold her tight" upon returning to his lover. While away, there may be something underhanded. "I've got no business being here with you" could be revealing his inability to maintain fidelity. Immediately following on "You Can't Do That," he lays down the law, demanding his lover doesn't speak to a particular boy. If not, he will "leave you flat," which may have an abusive component.

Astrological Summary: There's a difference between *A Hard Day's Night* and the previous 2 albums. The planet of artistry was moving backwards {Venus retrograde}, suggesting the discovery of more substance internally and/or repetition of ideas {Gemini}. On this third album of the early romantic formula, many songs rehash the same message. The album took some modest steps towards adding lyrical depth and musical variety, so both the challenge (repetition) and gift (additional substance) was evident. As seen with the movie, the "Beatles signature" was similarly being set off. *A Hard Day's Night* was a defining work of the early phase and the album was a huge success[2].

More so than the movie, there was an emotional edge on the album. Themes of manipulation, duplicity and hostility emerge for the first time[3]. The astrological focus remains on healing mother issues, with a particular emphasis on introspective deepening to get to the bottom of it[4].

92

Chapter 9
Growing Up

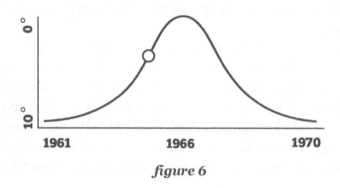

figure 6

At this point in the story, the big celestial news was the swift ascent of the "arc of awakening." In the summer of 1964, Uranus was 5° from Pluto (halfway up, crossing the "line of inspiration"). At the end of the year, the planets were only 1.5° apart. In order to keep up with the quick trajectory of evolution, issues and challenges of emotional and spiritual maturation needed to be addressed. This chapter details the shift from the Personality Expression phase to Personality Reconciliation. The first of 3 albums in the new phase was *Beatles for Sale*. Though the album is not usually part of the conversation as their best, it's one of the most important in their growth.

They were becoming exhausted by the demands of fame, including corporate pressure for more chart-topping hits. Ringo got sick and was absent for part of their summer tour, facing his performance frustration and social isolation issues. George was challenged to accept the realities and responsibilities of fame. Paul continued to reach back to the past for resolution and healing. John shifted his songwriting to become more introspective, entering his "Dylan phase."

A Starr Has Fallen

On June 3rd, Ringo was hospitalized for tonsillitis right before their Australasian Tour. Instead of cancelling the tour, session drummer Jimmie Nicol filled in. Ringo missed 8 shows and was eager to return. The setback brought up his core issue. He said, "It was very strange, them going off without me. They'd taken Jimmie Nicol and I thought they didn't love me any more – all that stuff went through my head."[87]

Ringo's astrology (p. 338) reveals a return of his social isolation issue₁. "Inside Ringo" was being triggered, precipitating a confrontation with the emotions of his karmic situation₂. Health matters were in the area of karmic cleansing and potential release.

Through maturity and poise (rather than renewing a feeling of rejection), he could resolve it. From his statement above, it sounds like he was initially triggered. However, he exercised patience and was able to work through it and rejoin the band.

It was also a lesson for the Beatles "family" as a whole. George was upset by the episode and initially didn't want to carry on without his bandmate and friend. He reportedly said, "You can find two replacements,"[88] should they go without the drummer. They felt what it might be like to have their "family" come apart.

George Accepts His Path

George was maturing his emotional defense strategy for privacy, his karmic pattern of anonymity and invisibility. At this time, he was learning to become more commanding and visible, to creatively display himself$_1$. It was now clear that the level of fame and superstardom the band had achieved would forever change his life.

He was growing up and accepting responsibility {t-Saturn on his Sun}. He met Pattie Boyd on the set of *A Hard Day's Night*, initiating what became a serious relationship. The songwriting tandem of Lennon-McCartney was clearly driving the musical direction of the band. On the first 3 albums, George only put forth 1 original song and "Don't Bother Me" was not the most inviting of messages. At this point in his development, he was wrestling with the challenge of speaking up$_2$. Dubbed the "quiet Beatle," he would ultimately end up having a lot to say.

Being famous challenged George in many ways, something he would have mixed feelings about until his death. Though fame would introduce uncared-for hassles and headaches, he also saw an opportunity to do something extraordinary. During this passage of spiritual maturation {Saturn moving through Pisces until 1967}, George immersed himself in spiritual study and experiences to ultimately claim his creative leadership and message. Some additional notes are found in Part 2 (p. 339).

Grieving Losers

Beatlemania was in full swing. The band was touring extensively and doing public appearances. Their brand was now solid gold, so naturally the powers that be wanted to cash in on it. Just as they had put out 2 albums in 1963, another LP was expected in late 1964 (to coincide with the holidays). Balancing public life with creative musical development and their personal lives was quite the balancing act. Fans had a ravenous appetite for them to please, reflecting the "please please me" of their own desires. They were beginning to get exhausted by the 4-headed monster they'd created, but the pressures were insurmountable, so back to the studio they went.

In mid-August they recorded the first 2 songs that would appear on *Beatles for Sale*, "Baby's in Black" and "I'm a Loser." The former concerns grief, while the latter literally describes the self as a loser. The year the Beatles attained unimaginable worldwide fame and fortune they were not writing celebratory songs. Instead, they were addressing grief and loss, reconciling their core issues.

"Baby's in Black" is a unique song, one that held a special place for John and Paul. It was co-written by the pair, and both sang into the same microphone for the recording (as they did in concert).[89] Despite not being a hit or fan favorite, this song became a mainstay in their live repertoire for the remainder of the touring years. It had strong sentimental value in the John-Paul relationship mainly because it gave voice to the central spiritual lesson they shared—the coming to terms with death.

"Baby's in Black" is the tenth "dark" and second <u>death</u> song, a theme which was about to explode. It doesn't specifically have a death word, but it's strongly implied by a grieving woman wearing black for a man who'll "never come back." The lyrics concern coping with upsetting emotion, a core issue and a defining lesson of the Personality Reconciliation phase. They repeatedly ask, "What can I do?" to help manage sadness.

When sessions for "Baby's in Black" began, the planet of communications was paired with death {Mercury conjunct Pluto}, in major connection to the maternal energy in the John-Paul chart₁. Similar to the other events during the summer of 1964, there was a continuation of unresolved mother and nurturing issues on the point of karmic resolution₂. The astrology suggests they were singing about maternal grief and Part 2 provides more discussion (p. 340)₃.

John prized authenticity, which he increasingly put forward in his musical and lyrical approach. In order to become marketable, he initially agreed to the conformist persona of the lovable mop tops. After the attainment of worldly success, he felt the need to present his truth. "I'm a Loser" is a major song in the Personality Reconciliation phase, indicative of a growth spurt occurring.

The song was another example of John working through his emotions. The word "loser" has connotations of loss, his core issue. He's lost "someone who's near to me," which likely points to Julia. John sings of tears "like rain from the sky," pointing to the heavens above. In this second "rain" song, rain continues to be paired with upset.

"I'm A Loser" is also the fifth *dream* song. John reveals his public persona is akin to wearing a "mask." This song marks the point when the *dream* theme shifts to the broader context of life as theater. John suggests he's been playing a character, one wearing a disguise. He behaves "like a clown," but underneath is sadness, "a frown." The idea of acting a part (in a game or play) would be built upon for years to come, even informing the concept of an album.

The astrology (p. 340) portrayed friction between a jovial (clown-like) presentation and deeper emotional realism, including wounds₁. The "arc" was getting loftier, specifically connected with message for this song. The shift and breakthrough with communications was towards psychological authenticity₂.

Bob Dylan was a major influence at this time. The American musician was becoming a folk icon, noted for his raw honesty. Dylan influenced more introspective lyrics and played an acoustic guitar with a downbeat style. Not too long after recording "I'm a Loser," they would meet the fabled poet.

Beatles & The Bard

The band met Bob Dylan right at a significant turning point. The direction of spiritual focus {Nodal axis} shifted to a new phase involving broader meaning and philosophy {Sagittarius South Node} and experimentation {Gemini North Node} on August 25th. A few days later (on August 28th) was the legendary meeting. The American poet and provocateur is a Gemini Sun with a Sagittarius Ascendant, so he embodied the spirit of this new astrological emphasis. He was becoming the iconic American equivalent to The Beatles, and they would influence each other. The Beatles were adding lyricism and depth as songwriters and Dylan would soon go "electric" and compose songs with broader appeal.

The other influence was the introduction of cannabis (though they may have had a brief taste of it in Liverpool and/or Hamburg).[90] At their meeting, they famously got stoned and laughed hilariously.[91] Paul had his aforementioned intuition of 7 levels to this existence. Marijuana would be the drug of choice for the next couple of years, and "getting high" parallels the ascent of the "arc." It would influence both the lyrics and music in the next phase.

The astrology (p. 341) features the planet of communications moving atypically {Mercury retrograde} at the time of the smoke-filled meeting, connected to all the transpersonal planets, signaling the exploration of consciousness₁. Additionally, there was expansive energy {Jupiter} converging on the band's "artistic genius" potentials₂.

Still No Answer

At this point, the major lyrical threads began to converge. "No Reply" is the fifteenth "call," third <u>death</u>, and the third **solar** song. More awareness (Sun, awakening) was being cultivated about their core issues. "No Reply" was recorded and completed on September 30th, a song portraying a fictional scene in John's psychological landscape. He "tried to telephone," but was informed his beloved was not there, a suspected lie. He was at her house, saw her at the window, but she won't take the call. The astrology (p. 341) reflects the working through of communication issues₁.

John was desperate for the reunion, but there was blockage. He sings, "I nearly <u>died</u>, I nearly <u>died</u>," an unusually intense emotional reaction to this rebuff. It points to his underlying death issue, and getting triggered allows the energy to be worked through. In "I Call Your Name," John was frozen with unprocessed grief, alone in his darkness. Now there's greater acknowledgement and awareness of his feelings. He proclaims, "I saw the **light**, I saw the **light**," potentially leading to a resolution and another **solar** teaching.

"No Reply": Emotional awareness leads to healing.

Instead of avoiding pain, we can bring in the light of awareness. We might understand the self, have deeper empathy for our situation and see life more clearly. By working with emotions, we process through the past and can more readily be in the now.

Rain and Sun

Paul was still revisiting the heaviness of his grief-stricken karmic situation {Saturn on his Pisces South Node}. It manifested as some degree of exhaustion, compounded by their grueling schedule. With his creative output sluggish, he opened his bag of tricks. As noted earlier, "I'll Follow the **Sun**" was begun in 1960, a promising song placed on the proverbial back burner.[92] Paul was literally reaching back to something unfinished, a metaphor for the spiritual work of resolving earlier times. The time was right for its completion and assuming its place in the chronology. The first session was on October 18th. The astrology (p. 342) involved the reconciliation of melancholy, the discovery of life direction and a more engaged presence,. The lyrics reflect the melancholy of the music, one of Paul's finest ballads.

"I'll Follow the **Sun**" is the fourth **solar** song. As the first **solar**-titled song, the Sun was becoming more central, indicating the next step of blossoming. It's a somber song about moving on from unrequited love. The third "rain" song, it's another with rain signifying sadness. The lyric, "Tomorrow may rain, so I'll follow the **sun**" puts forth an important teaching.

"I'll Follow the **Sun**": Challenges are inevitable; it is the individual who must choose life.

Somber (rain) is juxtaposed with hope (Sun), the work is to heal sadness (rain) to be in the present (Sun). Paul repeats the title phrase throughout the song, reassuring himself that sunny days are possible.

No one ever said being human was easy. All of us have enrolled in a challenging spiritual curriculum. There are many hazards to incarnating in a world of initial darkness, with widespread pain and wounds. The lack of following the Sun collapses one into despair and loneliness. In their karmic histories, each Beatle had a collapse of some kind. The current work is to resolve blockage and rise again. When we follow the Sun, we may connect to the uplifting expansiveness of the soul.

Ill Feelings

On October 28th, the Beatles were interviewed by *Playboy* magazine. The topic turned to Ringo's joining the band. John said, "Ringo used to fill in sometimes if our drummer was ill." And Ringo followed with, "He took little pills to make him ill."[93] Pete Best felt this was an attack on his character and filed a libel suit against Ringo (and The Beatles), which wasn't settled until 1968. Pete was victorious and received an undisclosed amount of money.[94] Clearly Pete was still upset from his experience with the band. In 1965 he had an unsuccessful suicide attempt, allegedly trying to gas himself, but was saved by family members.[95]

Interesting that Ringo was discussing illness. His childhood illnesses made him the odd man out, a painful part of his spiritual work. The astrology between Ringo and Pete

(p. 342) portrays a link regarding health issues. Illness connects to a deeper spiritual issue, the loneliness of the outsider. Ringo and Pete both have tendencies to be removed and neither wants to be the lone wolf. Their charts clash and trigger one another in this regard, generating a heightened competitiveness between them₁. The role of the drummer is to anchor the music through measured and reliable consistency. Both Ringo and Pete sought to heal removal (due to illness, abandonment, dismissal or otherwise) to be the steady heartbeat of musical presence.

Album #4: *Beatles for Sale*

Beatles for Sale was recorded between August and October 1964. All the songs on *A Hard Day's Night* were originals, but they returned to the same format as the first 2 albums (8 originals, 6 cover tunes). With pressure to get the album out by the holidays, they needed to record material quickly. The title of the album underscores their feelings about "selling out" to the corporate machine. For the first time, the darker side of fame and business was leaking through—an issue that would only amplify. The cover image showed them fatigued, the toll of great fortune. Nevertheless, the band was on the rise and they continued to churn out their brand of music.

Like the previous offering, John authored the most songs, though this album had greater balance. George does not contribute an original song, but sang a cover. Reflecting Dylan's influence, the songs are more introspective, confessional and complicated. The first album in the Personality Reconciliation phase, it's a musical depiction of maturation struggles. *Beatles for Sale* is generally not critically acclaimed, or a fan favorite, though it features a few classic songs and reached #1. The sessions produced the single "I Feel Fine" with "She's A Woman," which are included in this discussion.

Musical Development: All the songs remain around 2 minutes in duration, with obvious country-rock and folk flavors. These genres lend themselves to more subdued subject matter. "Eight Days a Week" begins with a fade-in which gets progressively louder, an innovation not used previously. It became a #1 hit, a harbinger of folk-rock. "I Feel Fine" was the first pop song to feature guitar feedback.[96] The album had a broader range of instrumentation. In particular, Ringo used more percussion, George played more guitars, and Paul played the organ (and George Martin played some piano). It was the last album that significantly featured cover songs.

Lyrical Development: The 8 original songs (and 2 singles) combined for 11 placements in the lyrical threads: 3 death, 2 **solar**, 2 *dream*, 2 "rain," 1 "call" and 1 "dark" song. The underlying death issue was much more overt. The 2 **solar** songs suggest a continuation of spiritual blossoming, while the *dream* theme shifted towards the more spiritual use.

"Eight Days a Week" is lyrically simple, notable for the phrase, "hold me, love me," still petitioning others for security. "Every Little Thing" is the fourth death song, "love will never die." "I Don't Want to Spoil the Party" speaks of "disappointment," being "sad" and a retreat to "disappear." Though not categorized as a "call" song, John leaves a party to look for his beloved, still desperately searching for reunion.

Paul expresses frustration in "What You're Doing," a shift from his usual happy face. Similar to John, he wants to be more authentic about his feelings. The lyrics in "I Feel Fine" are simple and repetitive, secondary to the catchiness of the song. On "She's A Woman," Paul continues to reconcile the connection between materialism and affection.

Astrological Summary: The astrology for the album (p. 343) can be placed in the context of the lunar cycle. A New Moon is a fresh new start. However, the closing segment of the cycle becomes increasingly listless and lethargic until such renewal. The position of the Moon for the release of *Beatles for Sale* was just before a New Moon, called the Balsamic Moon. This listless Moon fell exactly on the band's Ascendant, the point of presentation. The band appeared tired in the cover image, a visual representation of emotional fatigue. Furthermore, this almost New Moon (a half a degree from exact) was moving into a solar eclipse, initiating the process of breakdown and potential breakthrough of historical issues[1].

The overarching lesson was to discover meaning {Sagittarius} from prior experiences, to find a broader context of understanding[2]. They were clarifying purpose. Is being heavily influenced (perhaps even manipulated or controlled) to satisfy corporate interests meaningful? Was there a need to course correct? There's a marked friction between financial and artistic issues[3]. The familiar "Beatles signature" was present for the album release, though wracked with tension[4].

The romantic formula was wearing thin. The astrology suggests a new direction is now necessary, one of greater experimentation and trying novel ideas[5]. There's unresolved emotion to process, specifically agitation and restlessness[6]. Maternal issues continue to underlie matters, residing deep in the shadow, awaiting transformation and healing[7].

Ringo Gets Married

Ringo followed John in wedding a pregnant bride. He and Maureen learned that they were expecting in December and got hitched on February 11, 1965. Brian Epstein arranged the wedding, they honeymooned for a few days, then Ringo needed to show up for the filming of *Help!*. George said, "Two down, two to go,"[(97)] and he was right; the other two would eventually tie the knot during the active years of the band.

Like Ringo, Maureen ("Mo") had a preponderance of planets in the archetype of play and performance {4 in Leo}. And like her husband, she was also working through issues in this regard. Maureen would birth 3 children in the next few years, hold down the home and assist Ringo with fan mail and other tasks as a Beatle wife. Her relationship to creativity and fun was hampered by responsibilities—her spiritual work was to develop her own outlets for joy[1]. Maureen was noted for her sexual magnetism. She was a powerhouse with a lot of intensity in her biography (including infidelities, leukemia and eventually another early death for a member of the Beatle family).

The astrology between Ringo and Maureen (p. 344) was both compelling and fractious, with questions about openness vs. exclusivity[2]. Like the rest of the Beatles, Ringo had many infidelities so Mo felt free to do as she wished (including an affair with

George[(25)]). The Ringo-Maureen marriage went through a rocky time in the 1970s and ended in divorce.

1965 brought them to a crossroads. After the humungous success in 1964, what now? The previous album had been rushed and they were feeling stressed by the burden of their success. How much would they continue to comply with business demands? The astrology brought the question of will forward, challenging them to take control of their projects and destiny {Mars retrograde in Virgo from 1/28/65—4/19/65, on their North Node}. They agreed to act in their second film, what ultimately became *Help!*. Consistent with the astrological challenge, they didn't have much control over the production.

The astrology was pointing towards the exploration of consciousness {Mars crossed their Neptune three times as it went retrograde and direct, with t-Neptune heading to their 12th House}. After so much effort and busyness in 1964, they wanted some degree of escape and were smoking marijuana liberally. Before heading out to film the movie, they entered the studio to record a few songs. Some appeared in the movie, and some were just for the *Help!* album (or singles). These songs had important spiritual significance in this crucial period of Personality Reconciliation.

Ticket to Pride

In mid-February, the Beatles recorded two John songs which were released as singles in April. "Ticket to Ride" was the A-side and would go on to be a #1 hit. It was controversial at the time due to lyrics describing a (supposedly unwed) couple living together (gasp!). John said another dimension was prostitutes (in Hamburg?) getting cleared for their business.[(98)] He has called the song, "one of the earliest heavy metal records."[(99)] It sounds light and tame compared to the hard rock and heavy metal to come in the late 1960s and beyond. In the context of early 1965 it introduced new elements, deepening the language of popular music. The drone quality, distinctive drum rhythm and heaviness was more layered and nuanced than previous works. It was the first Beatles song to exceed the 3-minute mark. These innovations would be built upon soon.

The song opens with, "I think I'm gonna be sad," reflecting the heaviness of the music and John's emotional work. It goes on to tell the now familiar story of disconnection, here a lover who needs to depart. The beloved who could not "be free, when I was around" could be alluding to Julia. She was a free spirit who didn't want to be burdened with raising a child in her young adulthood. The song ends repeating, "My baby don't care," the cries of abandonment.

The more obscure, "Yes It Is," might be another dive into John's maternal angst. He informs a girl his love is not available due to longing for another who is gone. He asks her not to "wear red tonight," as that would be too difficult a reminder. The most striking feature of his mother Julia was her red hair. He says he can't forget her due to "pride," which might exemplify Julia's central position in his mind.

The singles were released on April 9th. The astrology for the release (p. 344) is consistent with a maternal focus. It shows romantic energy {Juno} traveling over John's maternally-focused "wounded child" configuration$_1$. At this time, maternal Ceres was in

Pisces, the archetype of his mother's Sun sign (as well as longing/grief). Ceres was in major connection to John's artistic expression {opposite his Venus}₂. Some additional notes are found in Part 2.

The Reflection of Clowns

On February 18ᵗʰ, the Beatles recorded John's Dylan-inspired, "You've Got to Hide Your Love Away." There's grief, "If she's <u>gone</u> I can't go on" (the fifth <u>death</u> song), making John feel "two foot small," a surreal image. However, it's the sixth *dream* song with the line, "Gather round all you *clowns*," which picks up on "I act like a *clown*" from "I'm A Loser." Others were playing roles in John's psychic theater. Who they actually are doesn't matter, because it's not about them. John's interacting with his perception or version of what they mean to him. Furthermore, he called himself a clown in the earlier song and sees others as clowns here, supporting the *dream* idea that we are interacting with reflections of self.

"You've Got to Hide Your Love Away" is the first flute song,[100] the instrument of the muse. At this time, the transiting muse {Euterpe} was on John's karmic portal to the past {South Node}, which he had in the area of divine receptivity {12ᵗʰ House} (see p. 345). For "Things We Said Today," the muse was on Paul's karmic point, correlating with Step 1 of the muse process, the description of the soul contract. Now that she's made her way to John, we get to hear more. *The song's title speaks of love being hidden, echoing the loving and hidden influence of the muse in Beatles music.* This song begins Step 2 (expression) of the muse process. In this game of spiritual hide and seek, the appearance of the flute can be seen as a synchronicity, perhaps revealing a clue. However, this expression is only a forerunner to what Paul received later that very same day...

Words of Hidden Love

Unless a big fan of the *Help!* album, one wouldn't know Paul's "Tell Me What You See." In this study, there are a few obscure songs which have major spiritual significance. A relatively unknown song, it's one of the most mysterious and important in the entire catalog. Recorded on February 18ᵗʰ, a few hours after "You've Got to Hide Your Love Away" (the first "flute" song), it's hypothesized to reveal the answering of the "call."

Step 2 of the muse process (expression) is how the muse reveals herself. At this early point of presumed contact, she was operating beneath the threshold of awareness. In fact, Paul's later statements on the song are unremarkable. As it's not a hit or well-known, it's seen as filler on an album containing "Yesterday." Paul's astrological activity shows a time of incredible receptivity, albeit likely unconscious {t-Neptune square his Moon}. The muse was in contact with Paul's maternal attunement {t-Euterpe conjunct his Ceres}. With the "arc of awakening" nearly peaking (2° from exactitude), he was poised to learn visionary or intuitive skill, the promise of his chart. The song can be examined as if it's a message to him, words of hidden love expressed from his muse.

Paul sings, "We will never be apart if I'm part of you," echoing the timeless bond described in "Things We Said Today." "Open up your eyes now" is the instruction. If Paul's eyes were shut, he was dreaming or in an intuitive process, a place of receptivity. John's "I'll Be Back" featured the line, "I've got a big surprise," as part of Step 1 of the muse process. Here in "Tell Me What You See" for Step 2 is the line, "Is it no surprise now, what you see is me." It may be pointing to the reunion, the fulfillment of the contract to rediscover one another through dreaming. From this angle, there's even some degree of insistence from the muse to make more conscious contact: "Listen to me one more time, how can I get through?" She is trying to break through from her hiding place, "Can't you try to see that I'm trying to get to you?"

Hypothesized to be assisted by the muse, "Tell Me What You See" is the most spiritually significant song yet, registering in 4 major threads. It's the sixteenth "call" song, seventh *dream* song, fifth **solar** song and the eleventh "dark" song. Through the completion of the "call" in a *dream* state, a **solar** perspective arrives to illuminate darkness. "Big and black the clouds may be, time will pass away/If you put your trust in me, I'll make **bright** your day." The spiritual teaching regards faith.

"Tell Me What You See": We awaken through trusting life.

The emotion underlying these big dark clouds is hurt and upset. Though such pain can be consuming in the moment, all things do pass. We can trust that time heals all wounds. We become bright (awake) by surrendering to what life is teaching us, what our souls orchestrate for our growth. From another angle, the lyrics could also be interpreted as the muse inviting trust in her.

The lyrics not only involve awakening from the dark to trust life, they also reflect a religious message. Apparently, they are very similar to a sign which hung in John's childhood house: "However black the clouds may be, in time they'll pass away. Have faith and trust and you will see, God's light make bright your day."[101] Was the message in John's house consciously put by Paul into the song, or did it seep in intuitively? Could it possibly be inspired (perhaps a clue?) from the bird's-eye (muse) perspective?

The astrology (p. 346) supports the hypothesis that Paul was in communication with his mother[1]. There was an emphasis on familial roots, Paul's "expression of grief" signature, as well as his central karmic lesson to develop his intuitive gifts[2]. The following discussion is John's next step in opening to the numinous.

Opening the Doors

John becomes more open when he lets down his defensive guard, embraces his emotions and trusts. "Help!" conveys humility, a continuation of the realism begun on *Beatles for Sale*. The song is an admission of insecurity; a more vulnerable John was emerging. He sang of his past, "I never needed anybody's help in any way," his prior detached strategy for survival. As he awakens {Libra Sun}, he learns to open to connection: to others, to the world and most importantly to a partnership with himself.

Upon greater self-connection, he might grow into true empowerment and do something meaningful (perhaps transformative) with the opportunity of his celebrity.

John was changing his mind, "I've opened up the doors." Opening up (a vertical reference) the doors reflects the ascending motion of the "arc." John was shifting his mind from the consciousness of self-gain to become more open to spiritual receptivity and inspiration. He was also figuring out what he'd gotten himself into. Celebrity would challenge John in many ways, even leading to a premature death. During this next phase, pressures from fans and corporate interests would become increasingly demanding. He initially wrote "Help!" in a slower tempo, though was persuaded to speed it up to be more commercially viable.[102] This compliance is indicative of underlying pressure he was singing about. "Help!" is an emblematic song of the Personality Reconciliation phase, *the first Beatles song which had nothing to do with romance.*

The astrology (p. 347) featured themes of humility and a willingness to develop$_1$. It emphasized communication, leadership, more mature self-expression and learning to be comfortable on the world stage$_2$. The romantic focus of the early formula was shifting to more universal or metaphysical themes$_3$.

The movie *Help!* came out in July. It featured an East-West cultural divide/synthesis, precisely where Beatles music was headed. In fact, George was turned on to Indian music through the scene filmed at an Indian restaurant (which included a sitar).[103] Spiritual iconography is portrayed throughout the movie. The film is comedic, if not hammy and playing to stereotypes, often completely ridiculous. Spirituality would become far more mature in the later years.

The reconciliation of their soul lessons is depicted: notably themes of communication and conflict. There are numerous scenes featuring telephones (and the sending of a letter). In one scene, Paul grabs hold of a hose which protrudes through the wall, pretends it's a phone and hands it to John. There are many scenes of mock fighting and violence where John is the most involved. Most importantly, there is a war motif, including soldiers and battlefields. In one scene, John falls to the ground and is in danger of being run over by a tank, a portrayal of his karmic theme of defeat (which would be even more dramatically depicted in a war film the following year). The film also portrayed many separations and anxious efforts to reestablish reunions.

The band was notoriously stoned for much of the movie.[104] During the filming of "The Night Before," they hilariously couldn't keep it together. Ringo got the most screen time as his ring (and finger) played the starring role. The musicians were not very involved in the details of the production or completely satisfied with the final product. Nevertheless, the movie featured their wit, engaging style and music, and was successful. Instead of celebrating the good fortune of making a movie, it was like another scene in their own movie being directed by others for profit.

In addition to regular marijuana smoking, LSD entered their lives. John and George first took the psychedelic substance unknowingly at a dinner party in late March.[105] With the "arc of awakening" at this lofty position (and soon to peak), they were now meeting that level of elevation with the more potent drug. They would experiment with LSD at certain times from this point forward, peaking in 1966 with the culmination of the "arc."

Chapter 10
Inspiration

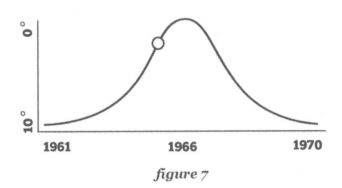

figure 7

These next few chapters chronicle the lead up and peak of the "arc of awakening." The truly once-in-a-lifetime nature of this climactic peak features incredible synchronicity and astrological revelation, a lofty reach with mind-bending connections. We will eventually return to the ground, but allow your imagination to be unleashed like an untethered kite, flying through the ethers. Have you ever become so engrossed in a movie that it's a bit surreal to leave the theater and be in the world? That heightened feeling pervades the next several scenes of this movie. All of the world was on the same ride, but the Beatles had the unique opportunity to ground it in cultural and artistic ways. We are fortunate they were so prolific, capturing the transcendent for us to eternally fathom.

The music created at this time is undeniably brilliant, though the question is whether (or how much) it was divinely inspired. The hypothesis is they were in *co-creation* with the numinous, serving as conduits and messengers. They were in touch with their soul wisdom and the muse (at some degree of awareness). Only through this remarkable tool of astrology do we get a map and guide. The following chapters have more thorough analyses and detail of the metaphysical revealing itself with utmost vibrancy and impeccable precision.

In 1965, the Beatles were still touring and the frenzy and uproar of Beatlemania continued on. Many new bands were debuting and music was becoming more experimental. Society was itching for reinvention and renewal. Young people were increasingly making their presence known through cultural participation, political demonstrations and protests. The air was thick with change and the disruptiveness that tends to accompany it.

Jupiter, the planet that broadens and exaggerates, animated the "Beatles signature" during the summer {the band's Jupiter return and it also touched their Venus}, expanding the variety of their music by adding new instruments and spreading into other genres {Gemini}. 1965 was a supersized year for them. Being undisputedly the most popular band on the planet, they were rewarded the prestigious MBEs (Member of the British Empire) from the British government. They toured the United States, including entertaining 55,000 people at Shea Stadium in New York in August, and met Elvis later that month. John would say, "Big house, big Elvis,"[106] the spirit of Jupiter, the big planet. September brought the release of the Beatles cartoon program, which further expanded them into the cultural milieu. It was the first program to feature animated versions of actual people, another milestone.[107]

Also in 1965, the planet of maturation {Saturn} was moving forward in the sign of spirituality, dreams and transcendence {Pisces}. Areas of intuition, contemplation and imagination—things we tend to call "spiritual"—were developing. Perhaps the premier Beatles theme is inspiration, which would be of major significance.

Major Eclipses: Consciousness Expands

The eclipses in mid-1965 were climactic events, the most notable in all of the chronology. As the "arc" approached the peak of potential spiritual insight, the eclipses were like turbo buttons. They were going through a profound passage of spiritual maturation, typified by further resolution of the past and a quantum leap into future possibilities.

On May 30th was a solar eclipse {9⁰ Gemini}, which was conjunct the asteroid Euterpe, the muse. This solar eclipse was also conjunct the "Beatles signature," and would play an enormous role in some key charts (including Mary McCartney's and Julia Lennon's). Two weeks later on June 14th was a lunar eclipse {spanning 23⁰ Gemini—Sagittarius, creating a cross with the Beatles composite Nodal axis}. The lunar eclipse was supercharging spiritual discovery through developing openness with *new forms of communication*.

The May 30th solar eclipse will be referred to as the Big Gemini Eclipse, the most significant turning point in the story. During this time, they would open their minds in a variety of ways. As mentioned, LSD use was becoming prevalent, especially for George and John. George was also getting into Hinduism and Eastern philosophy, spiritual practices and playing the sitar. As we'll explore next, Paul was quite busy in his dream life, heading back to face his past.

Yesterday: The Melody of Dreams

The next discussion involves the creation of the fabled song, "Yesterday." Whereas the intuitive process for "Tell Me What You See" seemed to be operating through Paul, he was now becoming more aware that something miraculous was occurring. Step 3 (connection) of the muse process is a more conscious participation. "Yesterday" has been termed "timeless," something that transcends our familiar boundary of order {Saturn}.

The melody touches us in an indescribable way. The song sounds otherworldly or divinely inspired, because it most likely is.

The story is legendary, one that Paul seems to enjoy retelling over the years. He delightfully recounts how the melody arrived while asleep, then he captured it by piano shortly after waking. He is quoted, "I couldn't have written it because I *dreamt* it."[108] The haunting melody would not let go. Paul was so concerned *the song belonged to someone else*, he asked people he knew if the melody sounded familiar. "It didn't have any words at first so I blocked it out with 'Scrambled eggs, oh my baby how I love your legs…'"[109] Regarding the spiritual dimension he says, "I think music is all very mystical. You hear people saying, 'I'm a vehicle, it just passes through me.' Well, you're *dead lucky* if something like that passes through you."[110] The preternatural quality to the song has been widely embraced by fans and commentators alike. Beatles musicologist Ian MacDonald writes, "In effect, 'Yesterday' fell, fully formed, out of the sky."[111]

On May 27th Paul and Jane went on vacation to the coast of Portugal, which turns out to be quite the synchronicity. At any place on the globe, a person's astrological attunement shifts. The natal chart is always relevant and foundational, but its expression changes relative to one's location. Out of any place on the entire planet, Paul chose to go where his planet of writing and communication {Mercury} connects with above {Midheaven}.

The image shows the path of his Mercury-Midheaven (MC) line. The Midheaven is the apex of the chart, the highest point which reaches towards the heavens. It's like he was intuitively guided to place himself where his "antennae" would receive the "call." Paul was on the coast of Portugal for 2 weeks and completed the song during that time. He was there for the Big Gemini Eclipse of May 30th, right on his Mercury line, when the words to "Yesterday" came in. In fact, he began to become inspired as soon as he arrived. Beatles biographer Bob Spitz writes, "The minute they touched down in Lisbon the words began to flow."[112] Apparently, Paul got busy jotting down lyrics as his vehicle departed from the airport!

"Yesterday" is the twelfth "dark" song. Paul writes, "There's a shadow hanging over me." Upon reconciling or healing the shadow, there is a natural opening to light (spiritual awareness, presence). It is also the eighth *dream* song (as he said, "*I dreamt it*"). The song also describes love as a "game," a common reference in the thread. Paul continues, "Why she had to go, I don't know she wouldn't say." His relationship with Jane was not yet problematic (it would officially end

106

in 1968). The words don't seem to be about her; perhaps something deeper was being stirred. "Now I long for yesterday," speaks of unfinished grief.

The Big Gemini Eclipse profoundly hit Paul's karmic signature of unresolved grief {square his Pisces South Node}, which carries the intention to craft something visionary to find completion. The next synchronicity brings us back to the time of Mary's death. As mentioned before, the eclipse that preceded Mary's death in 1956 set off Paul's chart regarding writing {at 18° Gemini, Paul's Mercury degree}. The words for "Yesterday" came to him while he was on his Mercury line {18° Gemini}. Like traveling through a portal, he was literally standing on an energetic line that linked him to the earlier event.

With a 4.5 year orbital cycle, the return of Ceres in dreamy Pisces (to Paul's natal placement) correlates with major events in Paul's life regarding his mother. At the Ceres return in 1956 at age 14, Mary died. Paul wrote, "I Lost My Little Girl" and got a trumpet, thus beginning his musical career. At the next return in 1961, he was 19 and began developing the early formula. He was having another Ceres return in 1965 for the creation of "Yesterday."

One definition of reconcile is to reach a state of acceptance, to settle previously unresolved issues. Another definition is the restoration of relations between people. In Gemini fashion, both of these definitions are apt. Paul was reconciling his outstanding emotional issues, possibly through a spiritual reconciliation with his mother. At his Ceres return in Pisces, perhaps his mother returned in his dreams.

Mary's chart (see p. 299) reveals her central spiritual intention to develop into a romantically-oriented writer {North Node in Gemini conjunct Juno}. The Big Gemini Eclipse {conjunct the muse (Euterpe)} was at *the very same degree* as Mary's point of "karmic destiny" {her North Node at 9° Gemini}, dramatically catalyzing her spiritual work in the biggest possible way.

Before now, the most striking activity to the karmic axis in Paul's chart was the astrology for "Things We Said Today." It's hypothesized the song revealed a soul contract, an agreement to remember a prior intention to reconnect during dreamtime. The muse was exactly on Paul's karmic axis for that song {t-Euterpe conjunct Paul's South Node}. She was part of the contract, inviting him back to yesterday {South Node} to complete the work. And now, for the song "Yesterday," the muse appears again on this mysterious karmic axis {conjunct Gemini North Node}. The opportunity was a writing collaboration {Gemini} to not only heal the past, but to move forward together {North Node}.

Paul wrote songs about dreaming, gazing to the stars above for connection, reuniting with a lost love. Many listen to these songs and see them as sweet and romantic, perhaps even somewhat naïve. They are generally not taken literally or seriously, rather as something to flutter the hearts of young girls. The great surprise in this study is the discovery of how literal and serious they are. The Beatles are famous for writing love songs. It turns out they have given voice to a far deeper and more sacred love than we ever imagined. Even more so, this loving reunion was not only personally healing for Paul, but would create some of the most adored and influential music the world has ever known.

Part 2 (p. 348) features additional analyses for those who want to dive deeper. Included is the astrology for the recording and release of the single "Yesterday," Mary's astrology for the Big Gemini eclipse and Paul and Mary's relationship chart. It also provides the visual to see the overlap between "Yesterday" and "Things We Said Today," how the songs are linked together through the muse process. Some highlights are below.

Paul intuited the words to "Yesterday" at the Big Gemini solar eclipse, then recorded it on June 14th, the day of the lunar eclipse! For the recording, the muse {Euterpe} was *exactly* on the "Beatles signature[1]." The Sun was precisely on Paul's Midheaven (bringing awareness to above), while his "expression of grief" signature was maximally highlighted[2]. Mercury was way up high {out of bounds north}, the furthest possible reach into the heavens[3]. The "Yesterday" astrology makes an assortment of connections to the muse {Euterpe} in Paul's chart, which is located in the area of creative performance[4]. When "Yesterday" was recorded, the degree of the Beatles "karmic destiny" {22⁰ Virgo, their North Node} was culminating in the sky, literally pointing to heaven {the Midheaven}[5]. Recall that when they first appeared on Ed Sullivan (another "destined" event), that very degree was rising. The band was having jubilant expansion to the "Beatles signature[6]" {Jupiter return}, which correlates with the massive popularity of the song.

Mary's central spiritual work was being emphasized and renewed—her chart was being highly catalyzed by the big eclipse[7]. In general, the Paul-Mary relationship chart strongly and uncannily reflects the "Beatles signature," illustrating how important their connection is for the band[8]. The Paul-Mary relationship chart reveals a writing collaboration through the boundary of death. It also echoes the "love songs" signature of The Beatles chart.

For the release of "Yesterday" as a single, Paul's "expression of grief" signature continued to be dramatically set off. Also, the brilliance of his songwriting promise was being triggered, a true moment of realization for his talent[9]. He would have the opportunity to work with transcendent and spiritual themes for the next few years, a cosmic invitation to put such inspiration into further writing projects[10].

The Big Gemini Eclipse was not only conjunct the "Beatles signature," it literally split their group chart in two {falling exactly on the horizon line: Ascendant/Descendant}. This event is so monumental, it separates the story into two volumes, a before and after. *It was the turning point in their songwriting {Gemini}, a shift towards their mature works and increased spiritual receptivity.*

A Face in a Dream

Another song was recorded on June 14th, the day of the lunar eclipse. Out of all the possibilities for song lyrics, what are the chances Paul would bring one mentioning receiving calls and dreams? "I've Just Seen a Face" provides more information about Paul's intuitive breakthrough, emphasizing *perception* {another side of the Gemini archetype}. The planet of perception {Mercury in Gemini} was exactly square motherly Ceres in the sign of intuitive receptivity and dreams {Pisces}—could it be possible that Paul was able to see {Mercury} his mother {Ceres}? The title literally suggests as much, and the song also contains the words "look" and "sight." It could be foreshadowing "Let It Be," which is overtly about seeing his mother in his dreams.

"I've Just Seen a Face" is the ninth *dream* song, "I'll *dream* of her tonight." It was speculated that in "Tell Me What You See," the "call" was answered. Now, the lyrics mention calls coming in. "I've Just Seen a Face" is the seventeenth "call" song, the phrase "she keeps calling" is repeated throughout the song! The muse was presumably coming in through both audio ("calling") and visual ("seen a face") channels. As seen with "Yesterday," the astrological muse was *exactly* on the "Beatles signature," in the sign of communication! Again, this position was precisely on Mary McCartney's point of destiny, her intention to become a romantic songwriter. "I've Just Seen a Face" is also part of Step 3 of the muse process (connection), when the reunion in dreamtime became clearer.

Album #5: *Help!*

The 5th album, *Help!*, was released on August 6, 1965 and accompanied the film of the same name. The album's title reflects the uncertainty and difficulty of the Personality Reconciliation phase. They were growing out of adolescence but unsure or unaware of what spiritual adulthood could mean. The loosening of attachments to spiritually awaken can be threatening to personality identification—"help" might be the ego's grasping for security and the familiar.

The movement on this album is towards a loftier perspective. At this elevated position of the "arc," their marijuana consumption gave this album a lighter feeling (compared to the darker and heavier prior album). *Help!* features many fresh and notable songs, an enjoyable album all around. It's a stepping-stone to the more artistic phase to come. The songs generally remain in the early formula, but it's clearly changing. Both John and Paul put forth 5 songs and George returns to songwriting and contributes 2. There are 2 covers, 1 sung by Ringo ("Act Naturally"). The album has parity and cohesion, the band is bonded and intent on developing together.

The cover image shows them waving flags in semaphore code. Their arm positions suggest the bridging of above (heaven) to below (earth). John, Paul and Ringo are all pointing towards the sky. George's arms are pointing laterally, suggestive of bringing energy to this plane. It is speculated that the muse has made her entrance, so this bridging of above to below would be a reflection.

The sequencing of the tracks reveals Paul's intuitive development towards his muse: "Tell Me What You See" is like an invitation from the muse to connect. "I've Just Seen a Face" depicts the connection, followed by "Yesterday," their premier co-creation. Listening to these songs in this order provides an excellent way to feel into this important moment of the story.

Musical Development: "Ticket to Ride" and "Yesterday" are the major works. The addition of drone, new rhythms and heavier sounds ("Ticket to Ride) and string instruments ("Yesterday") would be developed further on subsequent records. The album particularly featured keyboards, a wider range of electric guitars as well as more acoustic guitar.[113] "I've Just Seen a Face" has a country tinge, continuing the expansion into other genres. They were learning more studio techniques to also add texture and innovation.

Lyrical Development: The 14 original songs (12 on the album and 2 singles, "I'm Down" and "Yes it Is") have 15 placements in the threads: 4 *dream*, 4 "dark," 2 **solar**, 2 "call," 2 death and 1 "flute" song. The 4 *dream* songs were a marked increase, the most notable development. The 4 "dark" songs continued the process of personality reconciliation, while the 2 **solar** songs are a motion towards awakening. The 2 "call" songs signal a turning point, when the call was answered. The first "flute" song is a symbolic representation of the muse, while the death songs are just heating up.

"The Night Before" is a linguistic parallel to "Yesterday" and the thirteenth "dark" song. The title points to the previous evening, while the content likely involves Paul's maternal issue. He writes of being held near, appreciating emotional sincerity, crying due to loss and the need to say goodbye. There's a pledge to remember the connection. In contrast to "Don't Bother Me," George writes "I Need You." He's coming out from hiding, risking connection and revealing his loneliness. On "Another Girl," Paul shows a bit of the anger in his shadow, perhaps a tendency to be bossy. John's "You're Going to Lose That Girl" is another with themes of loss and loneliness. "You're going to find her gone" makes it the sixth death song.

The theme of George's "You Like Me Too Much" is commitment vs. leaving, addressing connection or loneliness. "Act Naturally" is a notable cover song (Russell, Morrison) sung by Ringo that echoes the *dream* theme. It's about starring in the movies (as a sad and lonely character no less...), which is easy for the singer as he just needs to be himself. The spiritual parallel is that we are all starring in a "movie" as ourselves. John considered "It's Only Love" to be one of his worst lyrics,[114] though notable for a couple reasons. He sang, "It's only love, and that is all," which places less emphasis on the issue compared to the prior obsession. It's is the fourteenth "dark" song ("night") and sixth **solar** song. John wrote, "Just the sight of you makes night time **bright**."

"It's Only Love": People are a reflection of soul/Spirit.

Solar energy is brought to a social context. We can learn to see the divinity in others as they radiate their soulful life force.

Astrological Summary: Similar to the previous album, there was an emphasis on resolving outstanding emotional issues from the past (p. 351)₁. These emotions remain linked to the maternal and their resolution might foster enhanced intuitive receptivity₂. Themes of the past ("Yesterday," "The Night Before") are front and center₃. Upon resolution, the promise is to awaken into greater presence, even fun₄. The theme is balancing bright with dark, joy with redemption, bringing light into the shadow₅.

The use of the mind, the nature of our thoughts, is the next suggested frontier to address for spiritual development (and the next album will pick up on it)₆. Also similar to the prior album, there is a clashing of interests, a squeeze between opposing forces. Issues of artistic direction vs. corporate interests is noted₇. The muse for this album ties directly into the Beatles attunement to their mothers {Ceres}₈.

Twinkle Twinkle Little Starr

Ringo and Maureen welcomed their son Zak into the world on September 13th. Considering Ringo's issues with family, this is a major step in his growth. His awakening involves the deepening with loved ones and a return to playful innocence. Zak grew to become a drummer like his dad and he became so good, he got to play with The Who.

The Ringo-Zak astrological connection (p. 352) depicts a similarity with loneliness issues, an intention to be more socially engaged[1]. Interestingly, there's a reflection of the "Beatles signature" between them, echoing their broader communal family[2]. Zak and Ringo have a similar focus on creative craftsmanship, cultivated in the home[3]. Their shared interest in drumming would provide them a nice way to bond and also grow.

Chapter 11
The First Peak: Resilient Souls

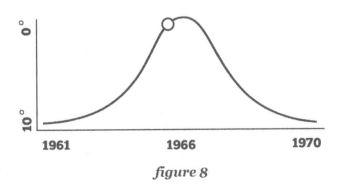

figure 8

The first peak of the "arc of awakening" occurred on October 9, 1965, John's 25th birthday. The band arrived back at the studio on October 12th, refreshed and interested in making a cohesive album of songs. For the next couple of months, they would compose tracks to fill out one of the most influential albums in music history, *Rubber Soul*. Many music historians credit it for being the first *progressive* rock album, a term which epitomizes the Uranus-Pluto interchange.

The Personality Reconciliation phase was concluding. To arrive in Transcendence, resiliency to address necessary soul lessons was required—*Rubber Soul* is an apt title. The point of unfinished karmic issues {South Node} was particularly active. In 1964, Ceres was on this point, correlating with "Baby's in Black," "I Call Your Name" and other songs pertinent to the mother. For "Things We Said Today," the muse appeared on Paul's portal to the past. For the *Rubber Soul* sessions, 3 different planets would accompany this karmic point: Mars, Venus and Mercury. First was Mars, bringing forward spiritual lessons regarding selfishness, aggression, competitiveness and independence. Venus involves issues of connection and partnership. Mercury would eventually arrive to stimulate lessons with the mind: thinking, communication, perception and understanding.

Dead Little Girl and Lighting Fires

As was often the case, sessions began with John songs. With the astrology primed to awaken contents from the shadow {Uranus-Pluto}, he brought in an infamous song. He would later disparage "Run for Your Life" and express regret about writing it.[115] Though his personality understandably had some issue with it, putting it out was a quantum leap {Uranus-Pluto} in his spiritual development.

112

"Run for Your Life" is the seventh <u>death</u> and first violence song. In the opening line John says he'd "rather see you <u>dead</u>, little girl," than have other involvements. He goes on to reveal how "jealous" and "wicked" he is, threatening "the end" should she stray. Of course, it's so outrageous, we brush it off as a fictional piece of art. However, John added, "I mean everything I've said," a line which might cause some unease. He used the phrase "little girl," which calls forth his first song, "Hello Little Girl." There, he spoke of feeling rejected by the "little girl," and now he's threatening her life.

The song can only be comfortably dismissed if John lacked violent tendencies. According to biographers, he had a well-documented and clear pattern of aggression including intimidation, brawls and domestic abuse.[5] So, why write about violence and draw attention to his shadow? As part of the reconciliation period, resolution of the past is the gateway to the transcendence to come. Bringing light to the dark allows the dark to transform.

The astrology (p. 353) illustrates aggressive karmic lessons involving a sense of entitlement and anger {Mars conjunct South Node}, echoing the exact same pattern when Julia was killed$_1$. Reconciliation involves communication and performance; precisely what John was doing. By revealing himself to the world, he was taking responsibility for his behaviors$_2$.

Later that day, John would lead an historic recording session for another of his songs. "Norwegian Wood (This Bird Has Flown)" (p. 354) would enter history as a major early influence on progressive rock, expanding the scope of Western music.[116] In 1965 George became interested in the sitar and brought its distinctive sound into John's Dylanesque tale of an affair. However, romance doesn't seem to be occurring. They "talked until two," then the singer sleeps "in the bath." He awakes alone (suggestive of the karmic issue of loneliness) and lights a fire, making it the second violence song. The underlying joke is the fire was made from her Norwegian wood wall paneling. Paul contributed to the lyrics, particularly the fire part at the end.[117] Like John, he too has anger in his shadow$_3$.

The song was designed to introduce a dark comedic element and a different musical ambience. It was successful on both counts, and nobody believes the Beatles are angry arsonists. However, the astrology suggests the healing of a selfish pattern$_4$. In "Run for Your Life," John threatens murder if there's infidelity, then a few hours later he strikes a bohemian pose and sings of having an affair. The same hypocrisy is found on *A Hard Day's Night* with "When I Get Home" followed by "You Can't Do That." The spiritual work was to release the selfish pattern and discover true togetherness and mutuality$_5$.

"Norwegian Wood (This Bird Has Flown)" is the first "bird" song as the word appears in the title. Birds are communicators who bring songs from above, a bridge between realms. They have great freedom to fly unbounded through the air, symbolic of the muse and her travels through consciousness. At this lofty position of the "arc," birds enter the songwriting, around the same time it is speculated John and Paul make conscious contact with the muse.

"I lit a **fire**" makes "Norwegian Wood" the seventh **solar** song. There is enormous power in fire. It can burn a house down or cook your dinner. Our intentions and skill, our co-creation with it, can change the world for better or worse.

Norwegian Wood: Energy (fire) can be used constructively or destructively.

Astrology works thematically, at a broad archetypal level. Though "Run for Your Life" and "Norwegian Wood" are very different songs, aggression issues are evident in both. The astrology reveals that the destructive behavior pattern {Mars conjunct South Node} stems from a very hurt place. The evolutionary motion is towards lightness and comedy, exactly what the songwriters intended to develop on this album$_6$. The same hurtful energy transmutes into being entertaining and creating good cheer. The world receives the gift of inspired music, bringing happiness to millions. This is the spiritual work of The Beatles, and they were exceptionally talented at it.

In John's Life: The Dead & Living

John's "In My Life" aims to reconcile his past. Of the people in his life, John states, "Some are <u>dead</u> and some are living," the eighth <u>death</u> song. He was approaching his underlying core issue more directly, coming to terms with the losses of Julia and Stu. Building from the humility displayed in "Help!," John touched notes of gratitude. Instead of arguing with reality or demanding that others take care of his emotions, there was mature reflection and acceptance of life.

John called the song his "first real major piece of work."[118] It evokes a poignant and sentimental atmosphere unlike any of his songs thus far. Like "Yesterday," it involved unresolved grief. Similar to Paul's masterwork, George Martin assisted the musical ambiance. He orchestrated the strings in "Yesterday" and played the piano solo in "In My Life."[119] Unlike "Yesterday," John does not claim he directly received it through intuitive channels. To the contrary, he intentionally sat down to write a song about places in his past. He wasn't satisfied with the list he generated, so he reworked it to be more feeling-based.[120] His next song would be the major intuitive breakthrough. "In My Life" is notable as the first mature <u>death</u> song.

The astrology (p. 355) set off John's "wounded child" signature$_1$. He was addressing a core spiritual lesson—the transformation of pain into joy—to arrive at a more non-attached (rather than egoic) conception of love$_2$. With such strong activation to his "wounded child" signature for this gracious and openhearted song, John had clearly grown during this important phase$_3$. He was reflecting on partnerships {t-Venus conjunct South Node} and softening his edge {Mars-South Node}.

He was working through anger issues, which circles back to Julia's death {she was killed under the same Mars-South Node signature}. Maternal death issues continue to be configured prominently$_4$. The motion was towards release and completion, allowing the energy to gently recede into the past. There was also a shift with romance. With less urgency for others to comfort his unresolved pain, John's songwriting was departing from the early formula. He was at a new beginning in his writing {Mercury return}, a fresh start with more psychological realism to address issues of death more directly₅.

Working It Out

The Lennon-McCartney songwriting partnership was the foundation for the band's success. Their complementary skills and sensibilities combined to magnificently create Beatles music. For the ascent of the "arc," they worked together to climb the mountain of success. The descent would involve the process of individuation. At this time, they were at the turning point. "We Can Work It Out" captures a delicate moment—when their skills matured and blended spectacularly, yet before they diverged.

A catchy song and fan favorite, the astrology suggests it's about their musical "bromance," this beautiful creative partnership. As is so often the case, the lyrics are framed in the context of boy-girl romanticism, but examining the song in terms of the John-Paul connection reveals another level. The song's title gives voice to the purpose of their partnership, to resolve emotional dynamics through working together. There are differences to negotiate, which can lead to polarization ("we may fall apart") or synthesis ("we can work it out"). Communication plays a prominent role as seen with "talking," "saying," and "fussing and fighting." A back and forth is noted with Paul's lead in the verses, and John's with the bridge, ("Life is very short…").

The song has a wistful undertone, the bittersweet reality that everything must ultimately end. What goes up must also come down. The impending descent of the "arc" would become marked by fussing and fighting. The question of whether they can "work it out" or when to "say goodnight" would increasingly become the issue. The reference to "night" makes it the fifteenth "dark" song, perhaps foretelling the eventual unraveling.

The astrology (p. 356) features both individuality {Mars} and togetherness {Venus} still on the point of spiritual work₁. Rivalry {Mars} vs. collaboration {Venus} defined their songwriting partnership. At this particular moment, both of these planets were exactly on the Beatles Ascendant, their presentation and identity. "We Can Work It Out" became a defining song of the Lennon-McCartney partnership, an excellent example of their individual {Mars} talents blending together {Venus}. Mother {Ceres} sits on the John-Paul point of unfinished soul work {their composite South Node}, while death sits on their point of resolution {Pluto on North Node}₂. The emotion being worked out involves their shared maternal death issue. Also represented was growth towards mystical communications, their ability to receive inspiration₃.

The Land of Nowhere

John brought the tenth *dream* song, "Nowhere Man" to the studio on October 21st. He claims he *discovered it intuitively in a dream* state, it "came, words and music, the whole damn thing as I lay down."[121] The song parallels the process Paul went through with "Yesterday." Ian MacDonald claims both songs arrived in a "quasi-mediumistic way."[122] He says "Nowhere Man" is "equally untypical of Lennon" as "Yesterday" was for

McCartney,[123] supporting the idea of discovery rather than creation. "Nowhere Man," a song that outlines the *dream* perspective, marks a turning point in this thread. It foreshadows, and has great influence on, what's to come.

Consistent with the multi-dimensional scope of this study, the lyrics can be interpreted in several ways. At the conventional level, it might be John's confession about feeling lost (incomprehensible fame and attention, alienation with family, increased drug use). The motion from "Knows not where he's going to," to "the world is at your command" might be a pep talk to himself to handle his situation with increased focus and responsibility. At this time, John's personal cosmic weather involved learning to more deeply understand spiritual perspectives and contemplative experiences. A transpersonal interpretation of the song would be consistent and is offered for consideration.

The *dream* perspective involves the idea that we exist in our own version and interpretation of the world. Like the Sun radiates its energy, an individual projects consciousness into the world (as seen in astrology charts). Each person is the writer, director and starring character in their movie. Enveloped in the theater of our soul work, we are inherently alone. Initially, the personality tends to be unaware of this perspective. Life is generally defined within the parameters of the "real" world and we are encouraged to be "down-to-earth" {Saturn}. Should the transpersonal perspective become recognized, there can be an existential crisis. At the conclusion of the Personality Reconciliation phase, the lyrics might be suggesting just that.

The "Nowhere Man" is alone in his own world ("his nowhere land") initially clueless ("knows not where he's going to") in the condition of existential aloneness ("making all his nowhere plans for nobody"). He projects his movie ("just sees what he wants to see"), but is initially oblivious to the transpersonal perspective ("as blind as he can be"). John empathizes with the situation ("don't worry"), universalizes the condition ("isn't he a bit like you and me") and gives the empowering solution ("the world is at your command"). Once we see and accept the spiritual view, we're in on the game, and the world becomes the canvas for our imagination.

Step 3 of the muse process (connection) continues with "Nowhere Man." John was aware he was receiving a vision, the message and music arrived as he "lay down." Connection with the muse informs the songwriting, but also assists the healing of John's underlying issue of death and loss. By integrating the message, he might come to see death not as a morbid ending, but a scene in the eternal dream theater. The <u>death</u>, *dream* and **solar** themes will dramatically converge during the Transcendence period, furthering such a notion. "Nowhere Man" was a stepping stone towards the synthesis, appropriately the first Beatles song which completely transcends the early formula.

The astrology (p. 357) illustrates the issue of aloneness (or independence) as a spiritual lesson {Mars-South Node}[1]. A transpersonal vision was highly accentuated for this particular song, bridging the intellect with the mystical[2]. A more mature spirituality was directly flowing into John's writing. Maternal Ceres was residing in John's mystical arena, informing him from beyond[3]. The muse continued her travels through John's area of artistic expression {5th House}, approaching his natal attunement {Euterpe return), a time of renewal and amplification of her creativity[4].

As for Julia's astrology (see her chart on p. 305), the Big Gemini eclipse in May profoundly summoned her muse {Euterpe} into action and triggered the development of writing and communications. Her nurturing style was unconventional with a metaphysical reach {Ceres in Aquarius conjunct Jupiter-Uranus}—the mature expression has broad philosophical and spiritual insight. Julia could put such insight into poetry or song {Mercury in Pisces}, which becomes communicated through death {Pluto in Gemini}. At this pivotal time, her spiritual work with John was ripening. Part 2 further examines the John-Julia connection as seen in their relationship chart, illustrating their intention for a metaphysical writing collaboration. There is also a section discussing how the muse is configured throughout Beatles astrology.

The Mercurial Songs

The band was particularly busy in early November, composing 6 songs in rapid succession, aware of the demand to get the album out by the holidays. Mars and Venus were now away from the karmic spotlight, and Mercury took its place.

The Mercury/Gemini archetype plays a major role in Beatles astrology. Not only is the "Beatles signature" in this sign, the unfinished spiritual work of the group falls in the related area of the mind {3rd House South Node}. That signature resides in the sign of mysticism {Pisces}, presenting a challenge for them to further develop their intuition to become visionary messengers. During this last stretch of the Personality Reconciliation phase, they were working through the traps and attachments of the rational mind that might impede such development.

Here's a list of the songs and the Mercury function they address: "Michelle" and "You Won't See Me" (communication), "What Goes On" (communication/thinking), "Think for Yourself" (thinking), "The Word" (understanding), "I'm Looking Through You" (perception). Since the 6 songs were recorded so close together (11/3—11/11) they have similar astrology {Mercury conjunct South Node}. The following discussion will summarize their spiritual dimension, while Part 2 (p. 359) highlights the major work for the 3 principle writers: "Michelle" (Paul), "Think for Yourself" (George) and "The Word" (John).

The astrology for "Michelle" fittingly points to cross-cultural or faraway communications and the obstacles to negotiate to truly connect[1]. The issue is framed as a foreign romantic interest who speaks another language. The theme of bridging great distances through communication makes it the eighteenth "call" song. The emotional underpinnings {Pisces Moon} of the song fall precisely on Paul's signature of karmic grief, pointing to another example of creativity stemming from his soul work[2].

The astrology also suggests an additional, more global layer. As seen in Paul's chart (and also for the Beatles group chart), a uniting message of love for world togetherness is the high spiritual promise[3]. The bridging of personal distance can be symbolic of bringing countries and cultures together. *Rubber Soul* is a bridge from personality issues to more collective themes. The simple personal message, "I love you, I love you, I love you" will become more universal, "All you need is love."

The next day they recorded "What Goes On." Ringo asks, "What goes on in your mind?" He wants to know why a lover isn't telling the truth. The resolution of heartache through open communication is both a theme for Ringo and the band itself; dialogue can heal loneliness and disconnection. It's also the ninth death song ("die").

Soul lessons playing out with personality wrangling is found in Paul's "You Won't See Me," the nineteenth "call" song. He's upset because a lover (likely Jane) is aloof towards his outreach. He can't complete a call because her line is busy. His days are "filled with tears," a need to further process his emotions. Regardless of potential reconnection with his mother in his dreams, his emotional work still needed to be addressed in the context of everyday life. Paul has trouble because his lover is "gone," pointing to the underlying issue in this tenth death song.

George addresses thinking in "Think for Yourself." Recall his issue of deferring to the thoughts of others[4]. Not only was George learning to think for himself, he was forming his own spiritual message. He had a soul history of being told what to believe and he wasn't happy about it[5]. In fact, he "has a word or two" to say in response. In the Personality Reconciliation phase, he was taking back his mind. Instead of listening to the theology from others, he says that "good things" can be found "if we close our eyes," pointing to the introspective and intuitive direction his work was heading[6].

"Think for Yourself" gives voice to the questioning of authority emblematic of the 1960s. At this time, the world was overthrowing limiting beliefs and paradigms and opening to a more humanistic and holistic global togetherness. George was on the verge of developing the philosophy that would inform the Beatles mature message and lead their spiritual quest to India and embrace of meditation.

"The Word" was a John-Paul collaboration, though John was the lead writer. It's the eighth **solar** song, one that elevates from the level of thought. The mind's stories can limit our awareness, keeping us confined in separation. Or it can be the means to understand beyond the self.

The song raises love from adolescent or romantic yearnings towards a more philosophical spiritual ideal. At this point, the proverbial flower is opening, bringing greater expansiveness and freedom. John sings, "Say the word and you'll be free." He admits he previously "misunderstood," suggestive of initial unconsciousness. Indicative of awakening, he offers, "It's so fine, it's **sunshine**/It's the word, love." The song teaches that **sunshine** is the pervasive warmth, light and energy that uplifts and connects our consciousness to all of life.

"The Word": The Sun's nurturance is spiritual love.

This song focalizes the **solar** thread, similar to what "Nowhere Man" does with the *dream* motif. The Sun is of central importance for love and connection, allowing us to engage openly in the present. An additional **solar** reference is found in, "I'm here to show everybody the **light**." Maybe the lyric is satirical, poking fun at self-proclaimed prophets. However, The Beatles were actually here to give voice to the universal process of spiritual awakening, which was now being stated directly. In "No Reply," John claimed that he "saw the **light**," further opening him up. In "The Word," he was teaching from his experience, inviting others to learn to see it.

Appropriately, the astrology for "The Word" has a major focus on message[7]. It sets off the Beatles group chart in highly dramatic ways, suggesting a significant contribution. Not only was this song representative of their message, the evolutionary motion was to bring it to the world. The "Word" is inexorably tied in to the "Beatles signature," the pivotal area of so much Beatles astrology. Also, the "arc" {Uranus-Pluto} was in the area of message or teachings for this song. The Big Gemini Eclipse in May featured the muse {Euterpe conjunct the eclipse}, suggesting that she had a breakthrough message. More than any of the recent songs, "The Word" circles back to that climactic event and is speculated to involve the muse[8].

"The Word" closes out Step 3 (connection) of the muse process and is a bridge to the next. At this time, John was renewing and highlighting his attunement to his muse {Euterpe return}. He was about to begin a new cycle with her, the doors were now open, his mind more receptive. In the spring, Paul experienced his intuitive breakthrough that informed key songs on the *Help!* album. In the autumn it was John's turn, which contributed to the spiritual reach of *Rubber Soul*. Together, they would produce a plethora of mind-bending songs in the Transcendence period, with profound teachings and insight.

The day after recording "The Word," they returned to the studio to compose Paul's, "I'm Looking Through You." This song picks up on the vision of "Nowhere Man," applying it to interpersonal relations. As we interact with our own version of the world—shifts in consciousness create shifts in perception. Paul has the experience that his beloved is not who he thought she was. He sings, "You don't look different, but you have changed." He marvels, "You're not the same" and "what did I know?"

The song is a study of projection, the perceptual side of Mercury. Paul arrives at, "I'm looking through you/And you're *nowhere*." In this eleventh *dream* song, the other has completely vanished. What remains is just personal subjective experience. Paul claims he's "*learned the game*," a notion which appears in several *dream* songs. Though the context has a mundane correlation ("playing games"), the deeper meaning is the recognition of the theatrical component, the playing of characters for each other. Whether or not the songwriters were conscious of the spiritual dimension coming through their work, the astrological conditions were perfect for it to be there.

Album #6: *Rubber Soul*

Rubber Soul was released on December 3, 1965 in time for the holidays, just 4 months after *Help!* Instead of focusing on individual tracks, the focus here was on the development of an album. Unlike the previous 2 albums, it featured all originals. *Rubber Soul* arrived when rock was shifting and exploding. It pushed the vanguard of innovation, leading what became "progressive-rock." Beatles literature often describe their music as pre- and post-*Rubber Soul* as it launched their "artsy" period. [124]

In this final album of the Personality Reconciliation period, romance is discussed from a more mature (even philosophical) standpoint. They continued to deepen with personal reflection and a wider subject range, including more wit and storytelling. Creative differences were becoming more evident. John authored 6 songs, but Paul is right behind him with 5. George contributed 2 and Ringo sings a song credited to him, John and Paul, his first writing credit. John called *Rubber Soul*, "the pot album,"[125] reflecting the drug of choice during this time. The title suggests a stretching of musical boundaries and the cover image (of the 4 of them in an outdoor setting) was stretched to give a surreal effect.

In addition to the single "We Can Work It Out" (reviewed earlier), "Day Tripper" was also created. It makes use of innuendo, "She's a big teaser," along with other ambiguous, sexually suggestive, lyrics. Also, John was dabbling with LSD and is referencing the "weekend hippie."[126] The song is notable for its guitar riff, which became one of the most iconic in the catalog. It's also the sixteenth "dark" song ("one night stands"), consistent with the shady subject matter in the song.

Musical Development: Rubber Soul was a major step forward musically, featuring elements of pop, soul, country, Indian, baroque and folk with both acoustic and electric guitars in the lead. There was sitar, fuzz bass, harmonium, French influenced guitar, new rhythms and percussion (maracas, cowbell, tambourine and Ringo even used a box of matches).[127] "You Won't See Me," was the longest song (3:22) to be recorded by the band thus far. "In My Life" had a unique piano section created by George Martin with a harpsichord effect. John, Paul and George developed more layered 3-part harmonies, creating vocal soundscapes. It is often classified as "folk-rock," but it has so many flavors, it eludes that description. Some credit the sound of "Norwegian Wood" as the harbinger of the psychedelic movement.

Lyrical Development: The 14 original songs (and 2 singles) combine for 18 placements in the themes: 5 <u>death</u>, 4 "call," 2 **solar**, 2 *dream*, 2 "dark," 2 "violence" and the first "bird" song. At the first peak of the "arc," the <u>death</u> issue was being raised and transformed. The **solar** song "The Word" revealed a major step of spiritual understanding, while "Nowhere Man" was the most sophisticated *dream* song yet. At this critical time, the "call" had been answered and the songs exhibit increased collaboration with the muse. The first "bird" song is consistent with that notion. For the first time, there are 2 "violence" songs—shadow material was emerging for catharsis and transmutation.

"Drive My Car" is lighthearted with an underlying innuendo (a euphemism for sex). In a 1970 interview, John explained that "Girl" was part of his process of reconciling Christianity, particularly the notion that one must go through suffering.[128] The girl is an idealized concept rather than an actual person. Similar to "The Word," love is more conceptual. "Girl" is also the eleventh <u>death</u> song ("<u>dead</u>").

"Wait" involves reunion, the twentieth "call" song. There's anticipation to return home, to move beyond sadness and reunite—another example of the maternal issue projected into relationship. There is now some degree of non-attachment. The beloved is given permission to "turn me away" if that's her truth. In "If I Needed Someone," George tells a suitor to retract her desires because he's taken. The twenty-first "call" song, it's another featuring greater non-attachment about connecting.

Astrological Summary: There's an interesting contrast between the cover images on *Rubber Soul* and *Beatles for Sale* (p. 362) albums released almost exactly a year apart.

Both covers featured them in an outdoor setting. For *Beatles for Sale*, they look haggard and the image conveys realism--the songs promote authenticity. On *Rubber Soul*, they look more quizzical, perhaps up to something we can't quite put a finger on. Instead of realism, the subtle stretch effect reflects the increased ambiguity of the songs.

The 2 albums feature their look and style, and display their astrological presentation {Sun on the group chart Ascendant for both albums}. *Beatles for Sale* had the very late balsamic Moon, characterized by listlessness and fatigue. For *Rubber Soul*, there was an upsurge of inspired creativity {waxing Pisces Moon}. The slightly warped, psychedelic appearance reflected the motion towards the transcendent₁.

Like the other 2 albums in the Personality Reconciliation phase, *Rubber Soul* also involved emotional resolution of the past₂. The dissolution of attachments and grief was being transformed into message₃. The album was not too "out there"—a harmonious balance of mainstream accessibility with experimental tendencies. As a defining album of this period, the "Beatles signature" was highlighted₄. The muse plays a paramount role in the astrology and the peak of the "arc of awakening" was steadily marching towards the band's point of spiritual destiny₅.

A few days after *Rubber Soul* was released, there was a yet another eclipse on the "Beatles Signature," {on December 8ᵗʰ at 15° Gemini}. The band would never be the same. From this point on, they became *artists*, not just performers. In 1966 they would cease public performing to venture deeper into artistic exploration.

George Gets Married

George and Pattie got engaged on Christmas 1965, then were married on January 21, 1966. At the time, Pattie was a model, and would go on to become a photographer and author. With blonde hair and blue eyes, she had a striking appearance, embodying the classic ideal of beauty of the day. The astrology between them (p. 363) was full of transcendent notions of love.

The glamour and idealization of the rock star and the supermodel can be astrologically located in the Pisces archetype. Not only did they both have their Suns in this sign, they also had Pisces contacts with the relational {Venus} and romantic {Juno} planets₁. Pisces is a known as a double sign, featuring fish swimming in two directions. It can be full of deception and appearances or deep compassion, love and vision. Pattie's interest in mysticism (Pisces) influenced the band to meet the Maharishi in 1967.[129] George became much more focused on his spiritual development as the bond was deepening. George and Pattie played on the Pisces archetype through both celebrity glamour and meaningful spirituality. Like a screen for our projections, we might think of them as superficial or profound, all depending on our consciousness.

A challenge in their astrology was the negotiation of boundaries. Both had the inclination to meander and seek a broad range of experience₂. True to the freewheeling nature of the times, there were infidelities.[130] George and Pattie would famously enter a triangular love drama with George's friend Eric Clapton. The marriage ended in the early 1970s.

Chapter 12
The Second Peak: The Mountaintop

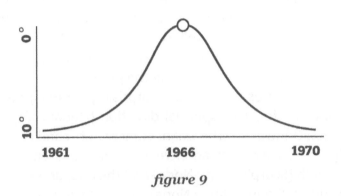

figure 9

Shortly after 1966 arrived, the celestial clock indicated a time to review artistic direction. The spiritual lesson concerned authentic creative expression vs. selling out for profit or status {Venus retrograde 1/5—2/15, from Aquarius back to Capricorn}. The reassessment of style and artistry encouraged bold experimentation into the mainstream[1]. Corresponding with the absolute peak of the "arc," 1966 would be a most revolutionary year. The Beatles brazenly pushed the throttle of inventiveness, while also instigating significant public controversy. 1966 was the year they shocked the world.

In particular, this experimental artistic invitation hit the vocational area of John's chart[2]. He was going through a personal revolution in his creative life and public status. He desired to get to the "toppermost," so what now? How mature and confident (or controversial and reactionary) would be his handling of celebrity and influence?

Underneath his commanding public persona, John was still working through his maternal wounds. Previously, he would act out his pain, blaming others for his feelings. In 1966, a new phase would commence, one where a partner would be almost like a surrogate mother[3]. John met Yoko Ono, the woman who would change his life. She was 7 years his senior and John would nickname her "mother."

After a closer look at the controversies in 1966, this chapter will explore the creation of some of their most notable songs. At this time, everything was saturated with spiritual meaning, the veil between worlds thinnest, the transpersonal maximally available. As musical conduits, the Beatles grounded it into sublime art. We have now entered the Transcendence phase, the most climactic, perplexing, astounding, soulful, multidimensional and psychedelic part of the story.

Controversy

With the "arc" at its absolute peak, the volume of 1966 was turned up. *Beatles '66: The Revolutionary Year* is an entire book on how climactic it was. The Uranus-Pluto exchange can be shocking, a combination which awakens the taboo, repressed and shadow. Authenticity is prized, the false self is eradicated through upheaval {Uranus} and elimination {Pluto}. Culture and society were becoming increasingly more progressive, violent and edgy. Many bands were now following in the Beatles footsteps, finding ways to similarly push the envelope of innovation. All facets of life were changing radically and unexpectedly. Social movements were sweeping the globe.

At this time, controversies awakened a surprising {Uranus} dark edge {Pluto} in their story. Additionally, the focus of spiritual direction {Nodal Axis} was shifting from exploration {Gemini-Sagittarius} to the management of conflict and psychological processes {Taurus-Scorpio}. There was an increasing emphasis on drama, interpersonal issues, darkness and death {Scorpio South Node} and the encouragement to ground such processes into form and art {Taurus North Node}. A new season of psychological realism began.

The biggest controversy stemmed from John's statement that, "We're more popular than Jesus,"[131] uttered in an interview on March 4th. Taken out of context, it was received poorly amongst millions of people who found it to be arrogant or disrespectful. Despite his attempts at explanation, there were demonstrations to round up and destroy Beatles records and memorabilia. John was pressured to apologize and the band's sanitized, lovable image took a hit.

John's "wounded child" signature was activated at this time (p. 365), his fears of rejection playing out₄. He was facing public humiliation, which could send him careening into his historical tendency to retreat and check out. The upcoming decision to cease touring and John's marked increase in using psychoactive chemicals are gestures along such lines.

Adding fuel to the fire was a solar eclipse on May 20th {at 28° Taurus, hitting the band's Uranus and "artistic genius" signature}, stimulating the band's revolutionary impulses in the area of work projects. Shortly afterwards, another controversy unfolded with *Yesterday and Today*, an American compilation album released in June featuring the "butcher cover." The image showed the lads adorned with slabs of meat and mutilated plastic baby dolls as they smiled for the camera, precisely fitting Uranus (shock) Pluto (deconstruction, mutilation). John said, "I especially pushed for it to be an album cover, just to break the image."[132]

Due to the uproar which ensued, a decision was made to paste a new cover over the original. The world wanted to keep The Beatles deified and sanitized, though they wanted to present deeper rawness (meat) and disassemble their youthful innocence (mutilated plastic baby dolls). They no longer wanted to be phony (plastic) little toys as they were metamorphosizing into true adulthood. Not only was the "arc" peaking, it was approaching their point of karmic destiny. They were nearing the pivotal moment of delivering their mature message. In order to rise to such promise, inauthentic facets of their past needed to be shed.

Another controversy occurred in July in the Philippines, when they unwittingly snubbed First Lady Imelda Marcos by missing a state breakfast.[133] Riots ensued, creating difficulty for them to leave the country. The experience was another indication that touring, being pulled in numerous directions, was taking a toll. Both in America and internationally, being a Beatle was now dangerous.

The Sermon from the Mountaintop

Returning back to the musical chronology, recording sessions commenced in early April for what would become *Revolver*. The absolute peak of the "arc" {the 2nd of 3 exact Uranus-Pluto conjunctions} occurred on 4/4/66. At this time, John was creating "Tomorrow Never Knows," the song boldly announcing the transcendence of ego/personality. The first session was on April 6th.

John famously gave the instructions for the sound to be like the Dalai Lama and Tibetan monks chanting on a mountaintop.[134] "Tomorrow Never Knows" was influenced by *The Tibetan Book of The Dead* as well as *The Psychedelic Experience* by Richard Alpert (Ram Dass) and Timothy Leary (which was adapted from *The Tibetan Book of The Dead*).[135] Associated with LSD, the song seeks to bring the listener into another dimension or quality of consciousness. John was experimenting with the substance and wanted to artistically represent the experience.

Critics of LSD point out the difference between true transcendence and a chemically achieved temporary state of expanded consciousness. John was not claiming LSD should be used at the exclusion of contemplative development, rather a taste of transcendence is available. Once the taste is experienced, it can motivate a person to develop spiritually; the opened mind sees a new landscape and becomes forever changed. It is also true that substances can be mismanaged, abused and lead to debilitating conditions. The term "acid casualty" is used for those who lose touch with reality, some becoming mentally ill. Beatle authors raise the question of whether John's LSD use (as well as other drugs) had detrimental consequences for his well-being or stability.[136]

For the *Revolver* sessions, Geoff Emerick was promoted to the crucial position of sound engineer and had quite the task. "Tomorrow Never Knows" was their most complicated song yet. Emerick's approach has been described in the tradition of Rube Goldberg, the art of clever inventiveness with unique solutions. The studio became a laboratory and they broke one rule after another, revolutionizing how music can be recorded. His book, *Here, There and Everywhere: My Life Recording the Music of The Beatles*, is a fascinating window into it. Fittingly, Emerick's inventiveness in sound {Uranus in Gemini} was on the "Beatles signature₁."

Sound innovations include the invention of artificial double tracking (ADT) to achieve a fuller vocal sound.[137] John's voice was filtered through a Leslie speaker to achieve the "mountain top" effect.[138] Instruments were recorded then played in reverse, including a section of the guitar solo from "Taxman."[139] Ringo's drumming was more pronounced, providing an entrancing repeating rhythmic sequence. George played sitar and tambura to create the Eastern flavor, while John played Hammond organ and Mellotron to add to the ambience.

Within the psychedelic soundscape are several tape loops creating the swirling and disjointed atmosphere.[140] One loop was made from Paul's laughing, which is sped up to achieve the "seagull" effect. Other tape loops derive from a sitar or an orchestral chord. For this study, one particular tape loop is most notable. A loop was made from a Mellotron on its flute setting,[141] so "Tomorrow Never Knows" is the 2nd "flute" song. The flute sound is hidden in the music, mirroring the muse phenomenon (and perhaps another clue in this game of metaphysical hide and seek). At this time, the muse was highly active in John's chart, pointing directly to artistic collaboration$_2$. The song features a far-reaching vision, the defining characteristic of the John-Julia partnership. It's the first of many in Step 4 (collaboration) of the muse process.

"Tomorrow Never Knows" unites the central lyrical themes. It's the ninth **solar**, twelfth *dream* and twelfth death song. Not technically a "call" song, it also has some relevance with this theme too. Instead of calling to above, John was like a prophet on a mountaintop announcing a spiritual vision. Songs on *Rubber Soul* addressed the workings of the mind, and "Tomorrow Never Knows" shifts toward what's beyond. The song title suggests presence, being in the eternal now because the future is unknown.

John instructs the listener to quiet the mind and *"float downstream,"* assuring us it's not "dying." The motion is from the level of thought (mind) to pure being (soul), bringing us to the Transcendence phase. *Floating downstream* relates to the stream of consciousness, the *dreaming* process. With a relaxed mind, consciousness can "surrender to the void," which is described as **"shining."** Dreaming is brought to the context of soul awareness, our connection with the eternal spiritual life force. The three threads become intertwined: we align the flow of consciousness with soul/Spirit, thereby transcending death. The solar teaching involves liberation.

"Tomorrow Never Knows": Beyond the mind is presence and being; there is freedom through transcendence.

Next, we are instructed to find "the meaning of within" which is pure "being." We might discover that "love is all and love is everyone," which picks up on the message of "The Word." In that song love is equated to sunshine, and here the relaxation into the shining void provides its experience. Love is found within, shifting the prior focus on attaining it externally.

John writes that "ignorance and hate mourn the dead." This cryptic line can be turned inside-out to reveal that awareness and love celebrate life. The initial ignorance about death leads to negativity and pain, which is transformed by the next instruction. John encourages us to "listen to the color of your *dreams*." The creativity of the imagination can consciously direct our dreaming, informed by the alignment with the shining (soul) void.

With greater connection to soul, we can *"play the game 'existence' to the end."* We integrate the dream perspective, willingly play our roles in the game of life. The song ends by connecting "the end" directly to "the beginning," illustrating the eternality of life, the ongoing recycling of energy. The implication is the dreaming process continues from life to life, from ending to another beginning.

To summarize: "Tomorrow Never Knows" teaches us to relax into a shining presence, which lights the direction of our dreaming. When we loosen the attachment to the mind "it is not <u>dying</u>." With the ego transcended through trusting life, we no longer need to worry about death. We surrender and flow with our soul wisdom, now connected to all of life instead of feeling separate and lonely. We are in on the game, able to embrace the grand spiritual theater of life. The dreaming process continues from life to life, allowing us to create with the colors of the imagination.

At the summit of the mountain, the major threads have been united. "Tomorrow Never Knows" holds a special place in this study, a phenomenal climax to the awakening process. The "arc" began on the ground, steadily rising to this vision at the summit. The descension involves bringing it down to earth, which has its challenging lessons and issues. At the conclusion would be another song uniting the threads on the ground.

It is staggering (almost inconceivable) that the vision put forth in "Tomorrow Never Knows" was less than 2 years after the personality entrenchment seen on *A Hard Day's Night*. Some might credit LSD for it, but the substance only interacts with one's level of spiritual maturity. Give it to a miserable and angry teenager and you will not get "Tomorrow Never Knows." John was able to mature from his youthful misery and angst. He sought help in the Personality Reconciliation phase and it arrived. The help was in the form of a special, divine love and partnership. The astrology (p. 366) strongly suggests that this striking, far-reaching vision, had assistance from his muse[2].

John had a pileup of planets in his astrological area of mysticism, consciousness and transcendence[3]. The inspirational and metaphysical dimensions were abundant, but there were also psychological facets as well[4]. Spiritual awakening is not a flight into ungrounded experience. As John sings, we have to connect to existence until the end. As the "arc" descends, the motion will ground the teachings to make them more accessible[5].

Much of the astrology for the song points to death, particularly the need to let go[6]. John was reading *The Tibetan Book of the Dead*, and he was in a process of working through the release of his dead mother. Some of the mayhem or cacophony heard in the song could be reflective of the psychic disturbance associated with the pain he was processing and releasing. (A couple years later, John composed "Revolution 9," which similarly has death-related astrology and disturbing noises.) The astrology features a tremendous amount of energetic friction, which builds for a potential release[7].

Let's assume that John was in connection with Julia, serving as his muse. He was working with her at a subtle level to not only get insight from another realm, but the experience in itself would be therapeutic. Biographers note that John became more mellow and easy-going in 1966-67, and it's often attributed to his uptake of LSD (spending time in a euphoric haze).[(142)] However, it's also possible that he was comforted through spiritual experiences with Julia (at whatever degree of clarity and awareness he brought to it).

"Tomorrow Never Knows" was the most technically ambitious of John's songs, challenging him to learn new skills and to work with others (his growth edge). The revolutionary and innovative spirit of the times {Uranus-Pluto} was entering John's astrological area of projects and work {6th House}$_8$. The message and music from the mountaintop would greatly influence the band's work in the Transcendence phase, as well as the growing progressive rock and psychedelic movements of the time. John was making tremendous strides with his healing, maybe even experiencing the reunion he so coveted. Standing on the mountain's summit, his head was in the clouds and his heart was in heaven.

Sex & Drugs

The next 3 songs address the familiar rock and roll territory of sex and drugs... but with a twist. First was Paul's "Got to Get You into My Life," a love song which is actually an "ode to pot."[143] George followed with "Love You To," a raga romp extolling the virtues of singing and lovemaking. John's "Dr. Robert" is a tale of a drug-pushing doctor. These songs feature atypical instrumentation and recording techniques, and a new lyrical bent.

Paul loved bringing new sounds and instruments to his songs and his latest featured bold sounding trumpets and saxophones. "Got to Get You into My Life" tips its hat to Motown, an influence of Paul and all of the band. It sounded unlike any Beatles song so far, and it's also unusual for the subject matter. The Transcendence phase moves far beyond the early formula and this song even pokes fun at it. The *Revolver* album would be defined by subversion, in both lyrical and musical ways.

It appears that Paul is writing his usual love song with lines like, "You knew I wanted just to hold you." However, he would reveal the song was about his appreciation of marijuana in disguise. He's no longer taking himself, or his prior romantic focus, so seriously. He lets the audience in by stating he's taking a ride to find *"another kind of mind."* This reference to an altered state of consciousness makes it the thirteenth *dream* song. The song also qualifies because it specifically toys with the consciousness of the listener. We hear what we think we should be hearing (more romance), the projection of our expectation or bias onto Paul's lyrics.

A few days later, sessions began for George's "Love You To." The previous year he played sitar on "Norwegian Wood," one of the first overt and significant innovations in Beatles music. George deepened and intensified his passion for Indian music and took it to the next level. "Love You To" achieved major historical significance as the first Western pop song to fully incorporate a mature and developed Eastern style.[144] The song featured sitar, tabla and tambura in addition to guitars.[145]

The revolutionary astrology of this time correlates with the emergence of the counterculture. The song is one of the first examples of a message consistent with the movement. George writes about the fleeting nature of time and sings, "Make love all day long," as a way to spend the moments we have. Both George and this song share a unique astrological signature (p. 367), one of elevating romance towards a broader sacred ideal₁. It's also the thirteenth <u>death</u> song ("a <u>dead</u> old man").

Later in the year, George traveled to India to study sitar with Ravi Shankar. The astrology between the men (p. 368) illustrates a mentor/apprentice dynamic in spiritual pursuits₂. Ravi played an important role in George's philosophical development, the healing of his prior wounding with dogma₃. He challenged George to live authentically and forge new directions₄. It's astounding that the lead guitarist of the world's most successful rock band would devote himself to an obscure Indian instrument at the band's peak. George's relationship with the sitar was an example of his developing courage and leadership.

Like Paul's "ode to pot" in disguise as a love song, "Dr. Robert" is also indirectly about drugs.[146] The doctor helps his patients, though the type of assistance is actually to get high. "If you're down, he'll pick you up," may have been ambiguous at the time, but the meaning is clear now. The singing of "Well, well, well, you're feeling fine," is devilishly delivered by John. Musically, the song is notable for the layering sound effects, which give a surreal quality. "Dr. Robert" is also the twenty-second "call" song. Instead of calling out for connection or reunion, the theme begins to shift now that contact with the muse has (theoretically) been established. It's the first example of this thread lightening up after so much earlier angst. It is also the seventeenth "dark" song ("night"), indicative of its shadowy undercurrents.

Paperback Rain

In April the band also completed a pair of singles, "Paperback Writer" and "Rain," which were released on May 30th, the anniversary of the Big Gemini Eclipse on the "Beatles signature." These beloved songs directly picked up on the new creative directions symbolic of that turning point.

For "Paperback Writer," Paul intentionally set out to write a song that wasn't about romance and chose the topic of writing itself. He writes, "Its a thousand pages" reflecting his own desire to amass a large body of work. He was renewing a focus on writing {Mercury return in Gemini at the song release}.

The music was becoming more complex too. The sound of the bass was boosted and Paul brought an aggressive and busy style. The bass was often marginalized in the early pop and rock format (and was previously a trouble spot in this band). Paul, as well as some others (notably John Entwhistle of The Who, Chris Squire of Yes), would revolutionize the instrument during the mid to late 1960s, making it more pronounced and creative. He also came up with the catchy guitar riff[147] and played electric guitar along with George. The song became a #1 hit.

John's "Rain" is often touted as the "finest B-side" in their catalog. It also has significance both lyrically and musically. It's the fourth "rain" song, a substantial advancement in this thread. The early association with rain was sadness or bleak prospects, a connotation of negativity. The fourteenth <u>death</u> song, ("They might as well be <u>dead</u>"), it comments on such a notion, how peoples' negativity about rain leads to despair. The song offered a resolution. Spiritual awakening involves a wider embrace—the discovery of potential beauty in all experience and openness to life's lessons. The challenge is to rise above egoic preferences to appreciate what is. In this tenth **solar** song John writes, "Rain, I don't mind/**Shine**, the weather's fine."

Ultimately, it's up to the individual to create inner peace, regardless of what's occurring outside. The weather might be a metaphor for our thoughts. John repeats "Can you hear me?" a couple of times at the conclusion of the song. He clearly has a message; one he wants his audience to understand. He sings, "when it rains and **shines**/It's just a state of mind."

"Rain": Each person creates their own experience of reality.

Through integration of this lesson, we no longer have to scurry around for (what is considered to be) "positive" experiences. The grip of the personality (its preferences and attachments) may loosen. There is some kind of value in all experience when we trust life and see it as a teacher of our lessons. The shift from expecting external circumstances to provide happiness to finding it within is perhaps their defining message.

Musically, "Rain" brings an explosion of invention. Similar to "Paperback Writer," Paul's bass playing was at an extremely high level of mastery and melodicism. George played a nimble lead guitar, while Ringo says it's his best performance on any Beatles song.[148] His energy, dexterous drum fills and overall feel is highly engaging and universally acclaimed. Like "Tomorrow Never Knows," it's considered a "psychedelic" song, one with a variety of sounds and effects. "Rain" is the first song in rock history to feature backwards vocals and pioneered their use of the fade out, fade in coda (which was later used on "Strawberry Fields Forever" and "Helter Skelter").[149]

The singles were released shortly after a major energetic shift. On May 5th, the planet of expansion, cultural enlargement and purpose {Jupiter} moved to the sign of The Beatles Sun {Cancer}, signaling a supersized new chapter for growth and potential success. Interestingly, "Paperback Writer" concerns writing {Gemini}, while "Rain" evokes water {Cancer}. The songs were composed when the Beatles "ruling planet" {Jupiter} was highlighting writing {in Gemini} and released upon the shift to water {moving to Cancer}, bridging the two archetypes.

Taxes and Birds

"Taxman" moves beyond the early romantic formula to deliver a message. The Transcendence phase not only addressed spiritual subject matter, but also collective and societal themes too. On "Think for Yourself," George challenged his listeners to question what they're told from the powers that be. "Taxman" took it to the next level with scathing criticism for those who abuse their power, calling out unfair taxation. George was naming names, the leaders of the two major British political parties (Wilson, Heath).

"Taxman" is the fifteenth <u>death</u> song ("<u>die</u>"). The death reference stems from George's dark humor, an undercurrent of his personality that was expressing itself more overtly. Though it's not related to maternal death issues (like John's and Paul's), it's an example of how death-related themes and words were a part of Beatles psychology.

The song is notable for the coughing at the beginning and the disjointed counting lead-in. Note the enthusiastic and eager counting leading off "I Saw Her Standing There" on the first album, emblematic of the early rising of the "arc." In contrast, the counting on "Taxman" sounds off and sardonic, reflective of the perplexing middle period. "Taxman" became the opening track on *Revolver*, an album featuring 3 George songs. In the sibling hierarchy he was now competing with stronger stuff, perhaps a "threat" in the rivalrous (yet still friendly at this point) Beatles culture.

On April 26th, John's "And Your Bird Can Sing" was recorded. It is the only song on *Revolver* not a part of a major thread. However, it's the second song in the minor "bird" theme, which fittingly emerged at this elevated position of the "arc." John asks if it would "bring you down" should the bird be "broken." As birds pertain to the muse, the brokenness might symbolically relate to Julia's wounded condition (fatal car crash) and foreshadows important developments along these lines...

Living the Dream

At the end of April, two *dream* songs were composed on back-to-back days. On the 27th, sessions began for "I'm Only Sleeping," the fourteenth *dream* song, one that brings the thread front and center. At the mundane level, the song is about John's preference to be left alone to sleep. And also, there is spiritual significance. While "in the middle of a *dream*," John is able to "*float upstream*," picking up on "*float downstream*" mentioned in "Tomorrow Never Knows." John was personalizing the vision from the mountaintop, modeling it for his listeners. He also provided additional perspective on the dreaming process.

John watches "the world going by my window," which has the feel of a movie. He's "staring at the ceiling," presumably lying in bed. In these lyrics, it's somewhat unclear whether he is asleep or awake. The *dream* thread blends such realities—we dream in waking consciousness. The "window" is symbolic of the subjective filter through which we view the world. These lyrics involve observation, the practice of noticing one's subjective bias.

Observation is a component of many types of meditation. Spending time away from the world in witness mode, being receptive to what emerges, allowed John an openness to divine inspiration or intuitive guidance. In this song, he might be revealing his innate visionary predilections {natal 12th House South Node}. Others might view him as lazy and detached, but in these precious moments of retreat, John may have engaged a more conscious form of dreaming.

The next day (4/28), work commenced for Paul's "Eleanor Rigby," the sixteenth death, eighteenth "dark" and fifteenth *dream* song. This haunting song blends the three threads, venturing into the psychology of darkness. Absent the awakened perspective of the solar theme, it depicts the existential crisis of being lost in the dream. In the throes of unconsciousness, life can feel lonely and disconnected, waiting inevitably for death. The song is evocative because many can relate. Ultimately, it may be pointing to the resolution of death by resolving darkness to see life as a dream.

At the outset, Paul sings that Eleanor "*lives in a dream.*" "At the window," she puts on a face from "a jar by the door," a graphic illustration of an individual playing a character in the grand theater of life. "Who is it for?" captures the existential question: if the world is a canvas for our projections, who are we getting dressed up for? The "window" (also mentioned the prior day in "I'm Only Sleeping") is the membrane between self and the world. It can reinforce aloneness should we feel isolated behind it. The repeating phrase "look at all the lonely people" gives voice to such a state.

The other character is Father McKenzie, who might be modeling the resolution to existential loneliness, the awake alternative. He is a spiritual authority, someone operating from broader awareness. He invests his heart in his work, regardless if people attend his church. As discussed in "Rain," whatever occurs in the external world is "fine." The soul work is to take care of the self, to be whole and strong inside.

Father McKenzie takes active measures to maintain his wholeness. He literally mends the holes in his socks at "night," symbolic of working through darkness. He works "when there's nobody there," (recalling the existential aloneness of "Nowhere Man"), which Father McKenzie seems to embrace. Instead of being "blind" and not having a "point of view" (like the "Nowhere Man" character), he composes sermons (a point of view) to relay a spiritual message. Whereas "Nowhere Man" and Eleanor seem lost and lonely, Father McKenzie finds satisfaction in living a life of integrity, a man at home in himself and the world.

The two characters come together by virtue of Eleanor's death. The song depicts a funeral with nobody in attendance, which may evoke a sense of tragedy. Most are accustomed to measuring a life based on personality affiliation. The song concludes by asking a question about lonely people, "Where do they all belong?" Perhaps we're finding belonging by embracing *all* of this life (including death), stemming from an acceptance of existential aloneness and the dream perspective.

On the surface, it's not surprising Paul wrote this song. Given his experience with his mother's death, a song about a woman dying and her funeral seems natural. However, there are some preternatural facets to the story. Paul didn't know that Eleanor Rigby was the name of a real woman. He chose the name "Eleanor" for the actress Eleanor Bron (who starred in the movie *Help!*), while "Rigby" stems from the company Rigby and Evens.[150] He wasn't aware that the real Eleanor Rigby had some unmistakable similarities to his mother Mary. Both women died in their mid-40s due to health complications, and both worked at hospitals in Liverpool.[151]

Many years after he wrote the song, Paul was informed the actual Eleanor Rigby was buried in a cemetery quite close to where he met John at the garden fete in Liverpool. Paul attributes the "coincidence" to his subconscious.[152] Exactly! Paul has an uncanny ability to intuit from other dimensions. Recall the "coincidence" of the lyric in "Tell Me What You See," which echoed a message in John's early childhood home. Coincidences are better understood as synchronicities, how the psyche is meaningfully connected to a vast matrix of consciousness—the very same intelligent organizational matrix of astrology. And it is through astrology we see the deeper meaning of the actual Eleanor Rigby.

Recall the discussion of Neptune in Scorpio and spiritualism on p. 51. At the time "Eleanor Rigby" was created, Neptune (in Scorpio) had its turn joining the point of unfinished karmic lessons {Moon's South Node}. This combination involves the healing of death {Scorpio} through a broader spirituality {Neptune}, to pierce through the veil and discover another dimension. Part 2 (p. 368) has some notes on the astrology of "Eleanor Rigby" with Paul's' chart, as well as Eleanor's connection to both Mary and Paul, and below are a few highlights.

The real-life Eleanor brings out the maternal issues in Paul's chart, precisely his core "expression of grief" signature[1]. There is a mysterious and compelling link between Eleanor and Mary, involving both mothering {Ceres} and the muse {Euterpe}[2]. The astrology strongly circles back to Mary's death in 1956, as well as the Big Gemini eclipse (which was conjunct the muse) in 1965[3]. Eleanor's chart connects to the "Beatles signature" along the lines of communication via death[4]. What could the message be?

Here's a hypothesis: Mary might be trying to reveal herself and deliver a message. Paul-Mary collaborations tend to involve multi-layered stories, literary examples of metaphysical themes. Mary, who has uncanny biographical and astrological similarities to Eleanor, might have influenced the character selection for the song. The synchronicities might be a clue in this metaphysical game of hide and seek. As for the message: "Eleanor Rigby" synthesizes the *dream* and death themes, which could heal Paul's heart. He was learning that he too "*lives in a dream*." The dream perspective informs us that death is only a scene in the movie. The song provides the resolution of existential aloneness in the Father McKenzie character, who shows reverence for death. He buries Eleanor with respect, just like Paul was learning to let go of his mother and respect her passing.

Paul also supports Mary, analogous to saprophagous beetles facilitating the completion of the lifecycle for the dead. Beatle Paul was helping his mother complete her soul work. Mary died in her 40s, unable to fulfill her core intention to develop as a writer. Through their partnership, Paul helped her realize that desire. It is as beautiful as the song itself. "Eleanor Rigby" is a prime example of Step 4 of the muse process, a moving example of their collaboration. It's the first of a few songs featuring Mary in some way, providing teachings through storytelling. With the multiple layers and spiritual significance, the song is a true work of inspired art; some might say it's a masterpiece.

This enchanting song also holds significance in the development of popular music. With its captivating melody, clever songwriting and hook, it is quintessentially Bealtesque. Instead of guitar, bass and drums, the only instruments are violins, violas and cellos. Similar to "Yesterday," the string arrangement was composed by George Martin.[153] "Eleanor Rigby" stretched the possibilities of popular music, bringing a rarefied artistry. It broadened the audience and appeal of the Beatles, while deeper study brings us to the numinous.

Mind Aches

Recorded on May 9th, "For No One" is a personally revealing song illustrating Paul's advancing songwriting maturity. The peak of the "arc" doesn't necessarily correlate with positive events, rather it's a general amplification of issues and potential opening towards intuitive insight. Originally titled, "Why Did it Die?," it's the seventeenth <u>death</u> song. Paul writes, "she said her love is <u>dead</u>." Paul's underlying death issue was playing out within the context of relationship. He has acknowledged the song is about Jane.

"For No One" mentions an aching mind, a general sense of ennui or despair. Paul's karmic issue is feeling impotent as love slips away. He ends the song with, "A love that should have lasted years." It was composed in the spring of 1966, 2 full years before his relationship with Jane officially ended. The love that "should have lasted" might have underpinnings in his maternal issue. At the time "For No One" was being recorded, the astrological focus was on healing the past, particularly regarding death {Neptune in Scorpio conjunct South Node}. The connection (and potential transference) between maternal and romantic energy was active again at this time {Ceres conjunct Juno}.

Sailing to the Sun

The foundation of the children's song "Yellow Submarine" was created on May 26th and was completed a few days later. A bunch of guests were in attendance and a party atmosphere was created. They made use of various musical novelties and were clever in producing an array of nautical sound effects.[154] Paul was the main writer of the song (specifically for Ringo to sing), but it was a group effort. The astrology (p. 371) illustrates that the spiritual work was to unite as a family and express the joy of togetherness₁.

"Yellow Submarine" would go on to become a #1 hit. It was the most successful song featuring Ringo's lead vocals, providing a peak moment for him as a performer. However, the song could be more notable for his spiritual healing. Ringo's soul work involves connection and togetherness. At this time, the Beatles were working smoothly as a close-knit unit and the song paints a picture of idyllic peaceful human connection. It would be made into a movie and become a prominent and colorful part of Beatles lore. "Yellow Submarine" became a sing-a-long at summer camps, recreational activities, sporting events, bars and other venues. It's an excellent example of personal growth and healing facilitating a similar process for the collective.

The lyrics would be subject to a wide range of interpretation and speculation, from drug references to nuclear submarines. Paul has said, "There's nothing more to be read into it"[155] other than being a children's song. Paul's comment suggests he was not (or they weren't?) conscious of broader metaphysical layers. It turns out that "Yellow Submarine" has remarkable and surprising significance in this study—the eleventh **solar** song and sixteenth *dream* song. Once again, a synthesis of major themes occurs at the "arc's" peak.

Paralleling "Tomorrow Never Knows," it also illustrates the spiritual journey, the voyage in the dream towards Oneness. John's song is more abstract, featuring a *"stream"* and the instruction to surrender and flow into a **"shining"** void. "Yellow Submarine" brings the same idea to cartoonlike animation.

People are aboard an aquatic vessel which is "sailed up to the **sun**." The submarine is yellow, the color most associated with the Sun, typifying the journey (in consciousness, water) back to our energetic Source.

"Yellow Submarine": Successful navigation of the dream leads back to Oneness.

The more complicated and psychedelic "Tomorrow Never Knows" was primarily driven by John and George (the "mystic guitarists"). In contrast, the simpler and more accessible "Yellow Submarine" was led by Paul and Ringo (the "performers"). The band's range was so wide, both songs are Beatlesque and fit just fine on the same album.

The dream connotations in the song are plentiful. First, the scene takes place submerged in the water, analogous to being deep in the dreaming process. Biographer Phillip Norman writes of the song, "like 'Yesterday', Paul had thought of it in the zone between sleeping and waking."[156] The song speaks of vibrant colors (blue, green, yellow), which give an impressionistic quality (and recalls the "colors of your *dreams*" in "Tomorrow Never Knows"). The *Yellow Submarine* movie (reviewed later) would take it to the next level with its sophisticated psychedelic and fantastical depiction of a dream world.

When the first session began for "Yellow Submarine," the planet of the ocean and dream world {Neptune} was rising. They live underneath the waves, and Neptune is right below the surface {Ascendant} in a transformative water sign {Scorpio}, suggesting that the aquatic journey is healing$_2$. Communication is emphasized as the means to deepen in joy with others$_3$. Not only did they write the song together, it's one of the few that features dialogue. The song celebrates a return to youthful innocence after the storms from the past are cleared. Interestingly, the jubilant feeling in the song {Leo Moon} echoes the emotional attunement of both Paul and Ringo, who primarily wrote and sung the song. Ultimately, "Yellow Submarine" expresses how we're all together in the spiritual journey, riding the waves of our dreams as we awaken.

George is Telling

On June 2nd, George composed "I Want to Tell You," which gives voice to his consciousness at the rarefied heights of this peak time. The song concerns the difficulties of communication from an expanded consciousness, the inability to articulate his mind. The seventeenth *dream* song, George sings, "The *games* begin to drag me down." He was able to see through the masquerade at the personality level, not wanting to get pulled into its traps.

George was willing to wait to be understood. He writes, "I could wait forever, I've got time," and "maybe next time around," which likely implies reincarnation. Steeped in Indian philosophy and meditation, he was finding liberation through such teachings. As seen with his other offerings for *Revolver*, his songs were now much deeper and contained message. The mention of reincarnation may have been lost on some, precisely the point of the song. The music has intentional discord and uneasiness, a musical expression of his words.

George worked through his dogmatic karma ("Think for Yourself") and found meaning through deeper spiritual experience ("Love You To"). "I Want to Tell You" informs us that his consciousness was now attuned to something transcendent. And for his next song, George will in fact tell us his mature philosophical message.

The overarching astrology at this time reflected the tension between the transpersonal {Uranus-Pluto} with the everyday {opposite Saturn}. The lesson was to synthesize these different frequencies or feel disconnection or alienation. "I Want to Tell You" brilliantly gives sound to the dynamic.

Being Present

The next 2 Paul songs involved **solar** themes. Whereas "Yellow Submarine" depicts a journey to the Sun, "Good Day **Sunshine**" and "Here, There and Everywhere" give voice to the arrival. Both songs describe life in the present moment, free of the burdens and blockages of the past.

"Good Day **Sunshine**" was recorded on June 8th, the twelfth **solar** (and second **solar** titled) song. Paul's bouncy feel-good tune is notable for its sheer innocence and openness. He sings of being in love on a "**sunny** day," complete with laughter. Gone is the loneliness, sadness, rain, shadows and clouds. There is simplicity and love in the present.

"Good Day **Sunshine**": Solar nourishment brings joy.

One astrological note: When the song was being recorded, the planet of communications {Mercury} was on the band's Sun—they were giving voice to their solar message.

The thirteenth **solar** song, "Here, There and Everywhere," was recorded on June 14th. It doesn't technically include a solar word, but builds on the theme. The title conveys unlimited expansiveness, the defining characteristic of solar energy. The Sun shines everywhere, onto everyone and everything.

The lyrics portray being in the present. Paul sings of the immediate impact of a wave of a hand or a touch of the hair. A woman is not distracted by what is happening elsewhere, she's absorbed by the intimacy in the moment. Paul sings that "love is to share," a contrast to the egoic demands and clinging of the Personality phases. Sharing connotes openness and non-attachment, wanting the other to be content as much as the self.

The eternality of the present moment is brought to love itself, "Each one believing that love never dies." "Here, There and Everywhere" is also the eighteenth death song, one that synthesizes the death and **solar** threads. Recall the first death song, "And I Love Her," which has the line, "A love like ours could never die." Characteristic of the Personality Expression phase, that song featured uncertainty and darkness ("Dark is the sky"). Notice the lyrical shift that love "could never <u>die</u>" (in the earlier, "And I Love Her") to "love never <u>dies</u>" (in the later, "Here, There and Everywhere")—what was once a hope is now the reality. Death was being resolved or transcended. If Paul was in contact with Mary at some level of awareness, then he would have the direct experience to inform the teaching.

"Here, There and Everywhere": Love is eternal.

It's a pivotal moment in the story. There was so much previous heartache and angst when death was misunderstood. Now, love is understood as something beyond the confines of the personality. We actually do stay in connection (Sun) with those who have parted (death), a sentiment which will inform more songs to come.

"Here, There and Everywhere" is a culmination of the love song—one featuring expansiveness of heart, engaged presence and a spiritual perspective of love. The seed songs of the early formula had ripened, the "arc" was peaking.

Chapter 13
The Third Peak: Gunfire

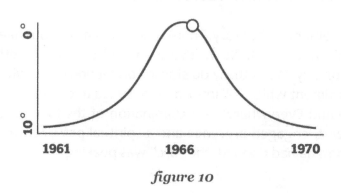

figure 10

The third peak of the "arc" occurred on 6/30/66 and correlated with a climax of the "call" and <u>death</u> themes on "She Said She Said." The song also has a connection with guns, which echoes the album's name, *Revolver*. Shortly after *Revolver* was released, John acted in a movie, *How I Won the War*, which has relevance to his war karma. In the autumn, he would meet his lover and partner, Yoko Ono, and begin peace and love activism. The violence thread would proliferate in the second half of the story, revealing an angry edge in the band's shadow. The word "Gunfire" used for the title of this chapter captures these occurrences, while also foreshadowing the intensity and conflict later in the second half.

As the "arc" began to descend, a turning point was away from the limelight. They quit touring and eventually went through a metamorphosis. For a while longer, the musical gunslingers would hit their mark with some of their most compelling works in the lofty Transcendence period. This chapter addresses the lead up to the moment of their musical realization, when the "arc" triggered their point of "karmic destiny."

Dead Woman Talking

"She Said She Said" opens with, "She said, I know what it's like to be <u>dead</u>," a suggestion of communication with a dead woman. It was recorded in one session on June 21st, the nineteenth <u>death</u>, twenty-third "call," and eighteenth *dream* song. Most cryptic, it synthesizes the threads through a surreal conversation in a psychedelic swirl. It originated from an LSD experience John had the previous summer.[157] Actor Peter Fonda was an attendee at a party where some were experimenting with the substance. Fonda allegedly stated, "I know what it's like to be <u>dead</u>," showed off a bullet wound and relayed a near-death experience.[158] Influenced by this event and intrigued by the statement, John wrote a song directly addressing death, his core wound.

At this time, John was using LSD regularly, the "arc" was peaking and he had already made incredible visionary discoveries. There is no question that other dimensions are part of this song, the issue is how to interpret them. It's hypothesized that the "call" had been answered, so "She Said She Said" will be examined as a conversation bridging the boundary of death. The question is whether John really wants to have the conversation...

John was understandably still upset by the loss of his mother. The dialogue has an undertone of incredulity, disorientation and even argumentativeness. The alternating stanzas beginning with "I said" and "she said" display a charged back and forth, as if something needs to be worked through. John seems to be resisting a message, "No, no, no, you're wrong" because when he was young, "everything was right." Julia died when John was 17, so he was a boy when she was alive.

He repeats the line, "making me feel like I've never been born," 4 times in the song. If he was communicating with Julia, it might be in the bardo, the liminal state between death and rebirth. The bardo is a core concept discussed at length in *The Tibetan Book of the Dead*, which was a major fascination to him at this time (and influenced "Tomorrow Never Knows").[159] Perhaps the experience of reunion with his mother would tempt him to spend more time with her. He repeats that he's "ready to leave" two times, perhaps to exit the game of life.

One speculation for the argumentativeness is Julia knew his work was on the ground. At this time, John was being pulled into retreat {t-Saturn entering his 12th House}, he was disillusioned by the "Jesus" controversy, had bouts with depression and was unsatisfied in his marriage. Maybe part of him did want to leave (and thereby replay his karmic pattern of checking out). He would later write in "Yer Blues," that he "wanna die," mentions being suicidal, and tells us "My mother was of the sky." A hypothesis for "She Said She Said" is his mother in the sky was telling him to stick around on planet Earth.

"She Said She Said" is musically notable. It features a backwards ("backmasked") guitar part played by George, changes from 3/4 to 4/4 time (and back again), and tails off with a flurry of psychedelic sounds. It also features one of Ringo's most acclaimed drum parts, a more aggressive "circular" type of playing which drives the song. Paul does not appear on the track (George plays bass guitar). Arguably, Paul is the Beatle with the greatest musical intelligence and skill, the most disciplined and melodic. However, "She Said She Said" is a powerful tour de force, which showcased how talented the others were too. In particular, the cohesion between John and George was remarkable, perhaps at its finest. They were taking LSD together and were on the same wavelength musically.

In contrast, Paul was yet to try the psychedelic substance. He declined to take LSD at the party with John, Peter Fonda and the others.[160] He left the "She Said She Said" session due to an argument with John, including saying "Oh, fuck you."[161] Did the argument concern his reluctance to take LSD? Did the John-George closeness and musical genius of "She Said She Said" impact Paul? He would choose to experiment with LSD soon and lead the next project in a psychedelic direction. From this point forward, the sibling rivalry would gradually shift from being friendly to territorial and antagonistic. The descent of the "arc" increasingly became marked by competitiveness and conflict as it ventured down towards realism. "She Said She Said" was at the turning point.

For this enigmatically creative song, the most brilliant astrological aspect {quintile} is featured (p. 372). It creates an ingenious link between communications and the metaphysical$_1$. The song strongly features the astrological signature of spiritualism, a permeable boundary between realms$_2$. Communication specifically involving the mother was involved with karmic resolution$_3$. Additionally, the muse was in connection with the death signature {Euterpe conjunct Pluto}$_4$. The astrology is consistent with the hypothesis that Julia was on the other end of the "call." Additionally, the muse was on the karmic signature of destiny {North Node} of the Beatles chart, representing an importance for this cryptic tune$_5$.

"She Said She Said" never became a radio staple or topped many lists of favorite Beatles songs. However, it's a work of brilliance, stunningly original with deep emotional and spiritual significance. Its splashes of psychedelic creativity and otherworldliness were indicative of the time and pushed the progressive movement forward.

Album #7: *Revolver*

Introduction: Released on August 5, 1966, just after the "arc's" final peak, *Revolver* is a striking illustration of its revolutionary and revelatory nature. Every song on the album is part of at least one thread and it has the highest percentage of songs in the threads. In short, everything on this album has spiritual significance. Now past the early formula, many songs do not address romance. The ones that do are written with greater maturity and reflection, away from the clinging of the personality.

Whereas *Rubber Soul* is the "pot album," *Revolver* was influenced by LSD. They were getting even more "high" (though Paul was still holding out). Just as LSD is more intense and vibrant compared to the milder marijuana, this forms an analogy between the songs on the two albums. "Norwegian Wood" has some exotic-sounding sitar notes, while "Love You To" and "Tomorrow Never Knows" feature ingenuity on steroids. "Michelle" is a gentle and beautiful ballad, while "Here, There and Everywhere" takes the love song into sublime territory. George's anti-establishment inclination in "Think for Yourself" blossoms much fuller with "Taxman." "The Word" delivers an important teaching about a spiritual idea, while "Rain" challenges the listener to move beyond the mind's ideas. "Nowhere Man" describes the existential situation of aloneness and "Eleanor Rigby" adds more emotional volume, literary depth and impact. "In My Life" reflects on death, while "She Said She Said" is a confrontation with it. "Drive My Car" is a jovial song, but "Yellow Submarine" has become a legendary sing-a-long. "You Won't See Me" expresses Paul's frustration, while his mind aches on the more poignant "For No One."

Rubber Soul has tasteful use of the organ, harmonium and various acoustic and percussion instruments for increased variety. *Revolver* has loud saxophones and trumpets, a French Horn, Mellotron, clavichord, tambura, tabla, a string octet, tape loops and sound effects.[162] The cover of *Rubber Soul* shows a subtle stretch effect to make the musicians look a bit different. *Revolver* features a smorgasbord of Beatles faces depicted in all types of ways. *Rubber Soul* closes out the Personality Reconciliation phase and the upward swing of the "arc." *Revolver* is at the peak and opens the much bolder Transcendence period.

Newly installed sound engineer Geoff Emerick brought an inventive streak. The studio itself became an instrument and they were breaking many "rules" of conventional music production. Stylistic differences were becoming more apparent, yet the sessions were mainly cohesive. Some are noted for being a high point of playful collaboration ("Yellow Submarine") or the assimilation of many peoples' musical ("Tomorrow Never Knows") or lyrical ("Eleanor Rigby") contributions. The cultural controversies brought them together in joint purpose as artists, and the impending decision to stop touring created focus in the studio. The album has the most equality compared to any other. John and Paul both contribute five songs, George has an unprecedented three, and Ringo sings a song.

During the creation of the album was a solar eclipse {on May 20th at 28° Taurus on their composite Uranus}, which further stirred ingenuity and non-conformity. Pretention and social expectations were no longer of concern. The first five letters of the album's title parallels the word "revolution," while also having a double meaning. The "musical gunslingers" were brandishing their weapon, and a record revolves around a turntable. Instead of the Beatles asking for adulation, they were now challenging their listeners to open their minds and ears to a new caliber of music. Unlike the inviting "mop tops" singing about holding hands, the dominant motif on *Revolver* is death.

Musical Development: The band set out to intentionally distort and innovate—to have the instruments sound unlike themselves and be used in unconventional ways.[163] Practically every track breaks new ground or does something different. "Paperback Writer" amped up the bass guitar to enhance its presence and embolden their sound. "Rain" features the first words sung backwards in the rock format.

The first few seconds of "Taxman" has coughing and off-kilter counting, opening the album in a quizzical way. "Eleanor Rigby" has no conventional rock instruments. George plays a backwards ("backmasked") guitar part on "I'm Only Sleeping," the first time such a technique had been employed. "Love You To" was the first song to fully integrate an authentic and sophisticated Eastern form of music into a mainstream rock format. Many consider the Beach Boys inspired "Here, There and Everywhere" a triumph of the pop song, adding to Paul's legendary status as a master of melody. "Yellow Submarine" features a dizzying array of effects made on a variety of instruments using a plethora of studio techniques.

"She Said She Said" shifts tempos and adds psychedelic flourishes, while "Good Day Sunshine" is piano-driven. "And Your Bird Can Sing" features an intricate dual lead-guitar part. "For No One" has a French horn, while "Dr. Robert" has a "surreal" flavor to match the song's lyrics. "Got to Get You into My Life" has a full-blown brass section reflecting the Motown sound. On "I Want to Tell You," George intentionally creates a dissonant flavor to match the song's lyrics. "Tomorrow Never Knows" sounded like nothing ever released before. The dramatic shift in sound signified the titanic shift of consciousness as seen in the lyrics. With the release of attachment to the mind, we become open to what's beyond. The cacophony portrays how anything and everything becomes possible in a world cracked open. The question is whether we are ready to embrace the apparent discord of the unknown.

Lyrical Development: Revolver and the 2 singles (16 total songs) combine for a whopping 27 placements in the threads: 8 death, 7 *dream*, 5 **solar**, 2 "call," 2 "dark," 1 "rain," 1 "flute," and 1 "bird" song (all addressed in the prior essays). The death theme reaches a climax at the summit of the "arc," while the *dream* theme is bridging this world with another. With 5 **solar** songs, the proverbial flower of awakening has blossomed into vibrant colors. Bringing such awareness into both the *dream* and death threads is testament to both greater insight and healing on their paths. The song "Rain" turns the "rain" thread completely around, empowering the individual to create one's own reality. The "call" thread reaches a climax with "She Said She Said," and a shift with "Dr. Robert." There will be fewer "call" songs as the "arc" descends, as well as the continuation of different usages. They are no longer calling out for reunion or connection, which supports the hypothesis that contact with the muse has been healing. The prevalence of "bird" and "flute" songs symbolically supports this notion and these minor threads develop further in the Transcendence period.

Astrological Summary: Revolver has the first example of a Kite configuration (p. 373), a rare signature which presents itself during the Transcendence period. In fact, several interesting and unique geometrical configurations appear during this phase. In a departure from the book's format so far, a few astrology charts with these patterns will be featured in the main text. The visual depiction of the shapes adds to the discussion, while also serving as an introduction to some astrology for the beginner.

A Kite is composed of flowing aspects {trines, sextiles}, which assist the evolutionary tension along the spine {opposition}. As the name implies, the configuration involves "flying," which could take the form of travels, journeys of consciousness or other adventures. The overall energetic flow potentially invites unlimited expansiveness, peak experiences or incredible discovery.

For *Revolver*, there are actually 2 Kites! They overlap, so it's a little difficult to distinguish them individually. The one pointing downward has double lines to make it clearer. The other is pointing towards the left.

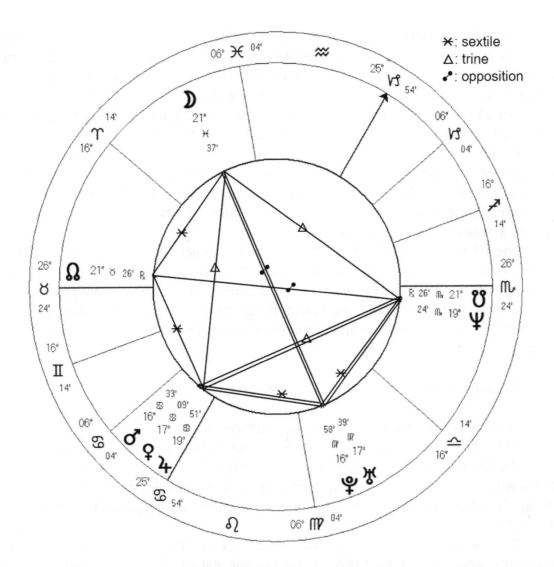

The tip of the downward pointing Kite is the "arc of awakening" {Uranus-Pluto conjunction}, the signature of metaphysical reach and spiritual transformation. At the base is an emotional desire for redemption, healing and sacred union {Pisces Moon}. For this <u>death</u> album, the death signature {Moon opposite Pluto} forms the Kite's spine. At one wing is the signature of spiritualism {Neptune in Scorpio conjunct the South Node}, while the other reflects the "Beatles signature" {Jupiter conjunct Venus, with Mars also present}. Taken together, this first Kite involves deep emotional healing through bridging worlds, expressed artistically in a Beatlesque fashion.

The base of the second Kite is the signature of spiritualism {Neptune-South Node in Scorpio}, while the tip involves the grounding of inspiration into manifest form {Taurus North Node}. At one wing is the Beatlesque artistry {Jupiter-Venus, Mars}, while the other is the longing for spiritual union {Pisces Moon}. The two Kites share many of the same points, so they are similar. The first has more to do with emotional healing, while the second emphasizes the manifestation of inspired creativity.

Part 2 features the *Revolver* chart (with all of the planets) with the Beatles group chart. The spine of the first Kite {Moon opposite Uranus-Pluto} falls along the central spiritual axis of the band₁. The "arc of awakening" {Uranus-Pluto conjunction} is close and approaching the band's point of "destiny" {North Node}₂.

The planet of communication {Mercury} was traveling backwards {retrograde}. The album contains backwards singing and instrumentation. There are various special effects and tape loops—the musicians were intentionally distorting sound. The lyrics challenged their audience to think again about several topics, to see life anew. Mercury retrograde also correlates with difficulty communicating ("I Want to Tell You," "For No One"). The *Revolver* message {Mercury} is on the Beatles planet of death {Pluto} and the album contains a peak number of <u>death</u> songs₃.

The solar theme is highlighted {Sun in Leo}, connected to the energy of dreaming {square Neptune}, illustrating the synthesis of these threads₄. The *Revolver* muse {Euterpe} is fittingly on The Beatles' planet of communication and message {Mercury}. This correlates with the "flute" and "bird" songs, as well as possible dialogue with her ("She Said She Said"). The muse appears in the sign of partnership {Libra}, consistent with collaboration₅.

Beyond Touring…

The Beatles played hundreds of live performances over the last 6-7 years. From Liverpool to Hamburg to America to all over the world, they came of age as a performing ensemble. At this time, the crazed hysteria of Beatlemania had become too much. It was adolescent, a nuisance in several ways and they could not develop their art in the concert setting. So, they decided to stop touring. In particular, George had absolutely had enough.[164]

On August 24th the band was in Los Angeles, completing their summer tour. During a press interview that day Paul said, "We know our real image, which is nothing like our image."[165] This statement reveals an awareness of the dream phenomenon, how their audience was interacting with characters in their imagination. At this point, they were growing out of being these characters. For the next album, they would intentionally take measures to shift it all altogether.

They knew they could use their celebrated and respected position in the collective consciousness to do something substantial. Building from the artistry on *Revolver*, the focus was now on expanding the limits of progressive music. They turned away from the world and into themselves, soon to deepen in a spiritual and introspective direction. Their final concert was at Candlestick Park on August 29, correlating with the shift of the "arc's" direction downwards.

Recall the discussion from early 1963. When they became famous, there was a cosmic caution about fame {Mars retrograde in Leo}. When they discontinued touring, there was a return of that initial caution, however now suggesting resolution₁ (p. 374). The planet of spiritual exploration was entering their area of retreat {Neptune entering 12th

House}, away from the world stage₂. Also, new artistic craftsmanship was strongly emphasized, as well as the lesson of maturing their message₃.

After the tour ended, the band took needed time off to reconnect with themselves. The astrological Sun is our inherent life energy, the source of our vitality. We need to "feed" it in order to grow. Each of the musicians would take measures consistent with his solar attunement. George {Pisces Sun} immersed himself in Eastern spirituality, traveled to India and studied the sitar with Ravi Shankar. Paul {Gemini Sun} learned more about the details of studio techniques and worked on a movie soundtrack with George Martin. Ringo {Cancer Sun} enjoyed time with his family. John {Libra Sun} expanded into acting and would meet a new relationship possibility.

... And Into War

John's acting debut was a supporting role in the movie *How I Won the War*.[166] He played Musketeer Gripweed in this black comedy with an anti-war message. Recall John's karma suggestive of defeat or loss in war {12th House Aries South Node}. In the movie he ends up getting shot, looks at the camera and says, "I knew this would happen." The *dream* thread is analogous to a movie, and here John is playing out his karma. The astrology suggests this karmic replay, and the intention to work through the pattern.

John's central soul intention was to become a peace advocate {Libra North Node conjunct Sun-Athena}: specifically, to use performance, arts and creativity to fulfill that aim. By so doing, he could finally "win" his war and turn his karma inside-out. The underlying message of the movie is the absurdity of war, how unnecessary the loss of life is. Ultimately John wins by no longer fighting—and a more peaceable disposition was developing in his personality and behaviors. Most interestingly, a movie poster for *How I Won the War* portrays John in a soldier's outfit {Aries, war} with a dove {Libra, peace} sitting on his helmet, perfectly illustrating the dichotomy of his spiritual lessons.

The movie was released a year after filming, on October 18, 1967. The astrology at that time (p. 375) reveals more of the story. The planet of concrete manifestation and reality {Saturn} was on John's karmic signature of war {Aries South Node}₁. He was in a time of sober examination of his pattern, taking measures to mature and rectify the past. The almost Full Moon for the movie release spanned the polarity of war {Aries Moon, suggestive of the past} and peace {Libra Sun, awakening in the present}. The Moon was approaching an eclipse, a time when spiritual lessons might breakdown or breakthrough₂.

Interestingly, maternal issues {Ceres} emerge in importance, connected with the signatures of conflict₃. Many soldiers and warriors could just be boys who feel a paucity of love and take it out on others. The resolution points to romance, peace and love₄. At this pivotal moment, John was learning the lesson. Synchronously, he was about to meet a woman who would help heal his maternal issues. They would become peace advocates using music and art, heeding the message of this astrology.

John Meets Yoko and Paul Crashes

John entered the Indica Gallery in London on 11/9/66 and flirted over avant-garde art with Yoko Ono, the woman who would profoundly influence his life.[167] She would also play a significant role in the second act of the Beatles story. Below are a few notes on her astrology chart (p. 376), as well as her connection with John.

Yoko connects emotionally with John {her Aquarius Sun in John's Moon sign}, in a way which desires innovation and activism[1]. Though inventive, the shadow of Aquarius is instability or erraticism. Yoko has a preponderance of energy geared toward creative talent and performance[2]. Combined with her unique and experimental energy {Aquarius Sun}, a point of convergence is avant-garde art.

Yoko is awakening into new mothering experiences {Sun conjunct Ceres}, a personal embodiment of the maternal energy so central in this story. Her chart details prior karmic issues of loss or disconnection with mothering. It played out in her biography with the estrangement from her daughter Kyoko and painful miscarriages[3].[168] The overlap with John's core family issues is striking and clear, and they would ultimately have a child together (Sean in 1975) as a way to heal.

She has a deep concern about the world and humanity[4]. The focus on arts is a way her personal growth can be a gift for the collective. Hanging in the balance of Yoko's soul work is the discovery of clear purpose and direction[5]. The struggle would be misguided aims or uncertainty.

Yoko is learning to become more visible, to heal soul wounding regarding a public profile. She has a somewhat rare signature of an outsider {out of bounds Moon}, in her case a foreigner {in Sagittarius}. As a result, there are intense wounds with public roles {10th House Pluto}, which can play out with reputation and/or scandal[6]. Yoko faced intense racism and sexism in her part of the Beatles story (which fortunately, has shifted and softened over the years, a reflection of her healing). The ability to create inspired art would be one way to offer the world something imaginative and therefore find greater inclusion.

John met Yoko shortly before a notable solar eclipse {on November 12, 1966 in Scorpio conjunct Venus}. The event foretells powerful new intimate dynamics with partners (romantic, business, etc.). When the lovers met, there was also a major emphasis on activism. John was starting a new cycle of peace advocacy in partnerships[7].

The John-Yoko relationship chart (p. 377) emphasizes spiritual purpose through cultural advocacy and a focus on message[8]. It is visionary, geared to broaden attitudes and perspectives in the mainstream. The intention was to ground inspiration into specific projects to make an impact[9]. The healing of nurturance wounds was their core spiritual work. They could discover new roots (and both did leave their home countries to settle in the United States)[10]. Challenges to navigate include the painful replay of grief and loss themes (which manifested with miscarriage), ungrounded focus (their substance use was problematic) and finding stability with both home and location.

Right around the same time John met Yoko, Paul was in a moped accident.[169] He was riding with his friend Tara Browne, (who would emerge again for another crash discussed in "A Day in the Life." Allegedly, Paul first tried LSD with Browne, though not on this day). Paul cut his upper lip, which was successfully hidden by the *Sgt. Pepper* mustache he would grow.[170] Changes in appearance can be suggestive of some type of inner change. The eclipse {in transformative Scorpio} hit off Paul's issues of emotional bonding {square his Moon}. The synchronicity of John meeting Yoko at the same time may have relevance to Paul at a deeper and unconscious level—John's emotional allegiance would ultimately transfer to her. Paul was about to go through a time of major reinvention and acceptance of new realities {Uranus approaching his Ascendant, applying to square his Sun}.

John was starting to become more interested in life outside the Beatles. Paul and George were growing into the leadership potentials of their charts. The group focus was gradually diminishing and the "sibling" rivalry would soon intensify. Paul had a creative vision he was excited about and asserted it confidently. The next project continues the climax of the music, message and story in the Transcendence phase. There was a unique blend of energetic factors geared towards seeing the world of dreams we inhabit. Aboard a mystical kite, we'll venture in-depth into the spiritual dynamics of their historic *Sgt. Pepper*.

Chapter 14
The Dream of Lonely Hearts Part 1: Inception

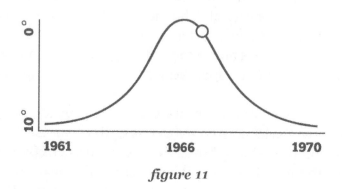

figure 11

The position of the "arc of awakening" does not necessarily correlate with the *quality* of their music. Rather, it concerns the elevation of consciousness vs. the management of matters on the ground. The Beatles' talent plays out within the context of the "arc's" position. *Revolver* is the album at the utmost peak and it's notable for the vision from the mountaintop, the climax of the death issue and overall amplification of the threads. *Sgt. Pepper's Lonely Hearts Club Band* arrives when the motion begins to descend.

Whereas *Revolver* is the <u>death</u> album, *Sgt. Pepper* can be considered the *dream* album. It has the most fantastical elements, ambiance and effects. Songs are like soundscapes evoking different qualities and feelings, taking us on journeys through time and consciousness. The musicians are intentionally taking another persona, fully aware they're playing the role of performers in the theater of our minds. They not only adorn costumes (customary in plays), they also adopted a different name. It's as if they are saying, "let us take you through the world of imagination."

Consistent with the still lofty position of the "arc," the songs are designed to look at life from on high. Snapshots of everyday life are given texture and story. Some songs are based on actual events and people, but they are dressed up in an imaginative, often surreal, way. Sometimes considered a concept album, the songs are linked by a certain mystique, as if they are different colors of a rainbow. Emblematic of the Transcendence period, *Sgt. Pepper* takes the listener beyond the self and into other dimensions. The astrology reveals fascinating information about such dimensions, perhaps the most mind-blowing part of this study.

Many believe it's their best work. In fact, some people (and rankings) say it's the best rock album of all time. The question of quality is a reflection of their development as musicians and songwriters. At this point, John and Paul had been collaborating for 9 years, the Beatles were maturing rapidly, band relations were not yet problematic and they had the engineering and technical support to progress their art. These factors, combined with the elevated position of the "arc," made for an especially inspired album.

The astrology for the creation of the songs features many notable geometric figures (triangles, squares, stars, Kites, etc.), which will be displayed in the following couple chapters. The Transcendence period can lift consciousness to other perspectives and dimensions, so the inclusion of some astrology in the main text is offered in that spirit. When the first session began, there was an isosceles triangle called a "Yod" (sometimes termed the "Finger of God"), prominent in the sky. Below is a depiction and brief description.

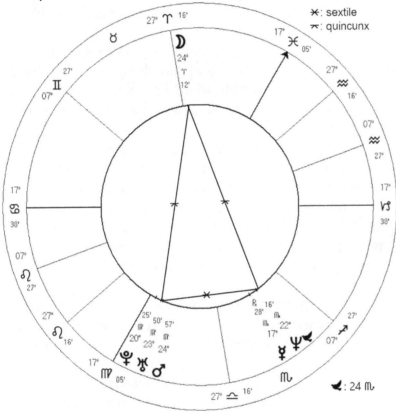

The Yod is pointing to the root issue: a need to heal emotional woundedness, particularly anger related to childhood experiences {Aries Moon quincunx Pluto and the 4th House planets}. Through healing, worldly leadership {Aries in the 10th House} is possible. Such leadership connects to performance {Moon quincunx the 5th House planets}, and the album went on to become ranked #1 on many lists. In the realm of talent and artistic expression {5th House} is the signature of spiritualism {Neptune in Scorpio} connected with the muse (and Mercury nearby). The formation reveals a creative partnership with the muse, who might be bringing communication or ideas {Mercury} from another dimension {Neptune}. Her support assists in healing childhood trauma {sextile Uranus-Pluto in the 4th House} and its resultant anger {Mars}.

Metamorphosis

The band convened in the studio on November 24th, just days after John's encounter with Yoko, Paul's moped crash and the powerful eclipse. The eclipse was in the sign Scorpio, which has deep relevance and symbolism. It's the sign of darkness and death, often characterized as the archetype of "transformation." They just completed the death album and quit touring, so it was a time of change. They were shedding the remnants of spiritual adolescence and coming more fully into their adulthood.

The eventual cover image for *Sgt. Pepper* would feature the men (with their grown-up mustaches) in the center, and cutouts of the adolescent mop tops to their side appearing smaller. In contrast to the vibrant outfits worn by the men, the appearance of the boys in these cutouts is somewhat deflated and hunched over as if they are lifeless.

Paul believed the adoption of alter-egos would give them total permission to do whatever they'd like.[171] In Scorpionic fashion, the album contains many hidden references (including to drugs), noises (such as a dog whistle) and subliminal effects.[172] There's a wide psychological (Scorpio) range to the subject matter. It also became an obsession for the "Paul is dead" hoax (discussed in detail later), another reference to death and hidden meaning.

Another facet of Scorpio is the realm of psychological dynamics between and among people. Underneath the surface (Scorpio), the band was changing. The "sibling" hierarchy was going through a process of restratification, one that had significant reverberations, perhaps even leading to the band's demise (which would occur in just 2 years after the album was released).

Paul, the "middle brother," was making a play for the top spot. His spearheading of the project was the first time a Beatles album had such a detailed vision from a single member. He wrote the most songs, played more lead guitar and had increased involvement with production decisions. George would only contribute one song to *Pepper* (compared to 3 on *Revolver*) though he had others to offer. The fantastical orientation to the album suited John's growing experimentation and his songs fit in perfectly. He was in on the project, willing to see what would develop, but there was uneasiness under the surface (Scorpio).

In his individual astrology, Paul was getting major stimulation to his "I'm in charge" signature, activating his creative drive. He was beginning a passage of reinvention and self-alignment, how he might present himself as the leader he sought to become. As seen with his recent movie role, John was grappling with his karma of surrender or defeat. His spiritual lesson involved letting things go willingly, to trust life and collaborate. It was a major step to allow Paul to take charge. However, any remnants of ego resistance would ultimately need to be addressed. The more the "arc" descends, the more a return to reality on the ground, including base personality preferences and attachments. More discussion of the activity to both Paul's and John's charts for these sessions is found in Part 2 (p. 378).

Another significant player was George Martin, the producer of such a complex and rich sound tapestry. He contributed many ideas and able orchestration of the studio to help fulfill the vision. Out of all the Beatles albums, this one had the most elegance and refinement, the hallmark of the utterly professional producer. *Sgt. Pepper* was a high point in Martin's life, and his astrology at the time reflected a climax of his spiritual work too (p. 379). There was a major focus on developing imaginative sound projects and rising to another level of innovation. Martin was interested in contributing something of lasting historical value; he had a desire to enhance culture, and did just that.

Fields of Dreams

The first song worked on was John's "Strawberry Fields Forever," which never appeared on the album. 1966 was the first year they didn't put out an album for the holidays, so the song was released as a single in February 1967 to satisfy the demand for new Beatles music. Despite its legendary status and popularity over the years, it failed to reach #1 at the time, breaking the string of singles which attained that mark. It's the nineteenth *dream* song, fitting to kick off the *dream* album.

The song opens with, "Let me take you down," paralleling the beginning descent of the "arc." (Though this may sound like a coincidence, the descent will feature many songs having a "down" suggestion, lyrically or musically.) Descending from the mountaintop, John was looking down at his childhood. He tells us that *"Nothing is real,"* so we don't have to get so upset ("hung about") how life unfolds. He was weaving the dream perspective back into the past. What transpired was not "real," meaning he was caught in his own version and interpretation of events, "misunderstanding all you see." When the dream perspective is integrated, we can trust that "it all works out" and thereby become more non-attached, "It doesn't matter much to me." It was John's prior attachment to a story which created so much suffering.

John doubts that many people really understand him, unable to join him "in my tree." He must be either a genius or an idiot "high or low," either way he experiences the loneliness of exclusion. Others aren't able to "tune in" to it, but now there's non-attachment ("all right" and "not too bad"). Then he says, "sometimes think it's me," as if he is to blame for the disconnection. However, he now knows "when it's a *dream*," which gives voice to the resolution.

"Strawberry Fields Forever" teaches that events don't need to be taken so personally, signaling the resolution of John's emotional work {a conscious and healed Aquarius Moon}. His emotional trauma might recede and the gift of his visionary potentials could awaken further. The integration of the dream perspective allows him to arrive more in the present. The past can be viewed with more clarity, assisting the release of his unresolved emotions. With the muse so prominent for this song (addressed below), the speculation is Julia was assisting her son with such a view.

"Strawberry Fields Forever" is the third "flute" song. Paul creates the flute-like atmospherics using the Mellotron,[173] producing the dreamy and impressionistic mood. George plays the swarmandal (Indian harp) and the song also features trumpets, cellos, various sounds and studio effects. Ringo's drum playing continues to sound fuller and more artistic. The song is notable for synthesizing two versions which were at different tempos, a feat that Martin first claimed would be impossible.[174] It also features a false ending and the spoken words at the end have been subject to wild speculation and interpretation. For all of these reasons, the song is rightfully considered a psychedelic masterpiece, though one that is melodic and utterly human. John has claimed it's his finest work with The Beatles.[175]

The most striking and relevant astrology for the song (p. 380) features the muse. She is inexorably tied to both the mind {Mercury} and inspiration {Neptune}, residing in the sign bridging the boundary of death {Scorpio}₁. Intuitive or dreamy songwriting fits perfectly—the intellect connecting with a metaphysical message designed for healing the past {Neptune conjunct South Node}. Communications {Mercury} are in the sign of death {Scorpio, with John having a Mercury return}₂. The planet of journeys {Jupiter} was in John's area of home, visiting his "wounded child" configuration₃. He was in a process of internal discovery, bringing perspective to his past, one that could transform wounds into warmth through creative expression {Leo}₄. Maternal Ceres was way up in the sky {out of bounds north} witnessing from above, residing in the sign of familial roots {Cancer}₅.

"Strawberry Fields Forever" is one of the most beautiful and poignant songs in the catalog. Similar to the feeling invoked by "Yesterday," there is something so moving here, the listener is taken beyond language and logic. We become transported to another plane or dimension, which could be the hallmark of true inspired genius. The underpinning of such genius is profound love, a remarkably creative soul partnership. With the muse so prominent, it's astonishing to consider that this song might be (at least partly…) not of this world. It's one of many songs to come in Step 4 (collaboration) of the muse process.

"Strawberry Fields Forever" has a rare geometric configuration that correlates with its brilliance. The aspect most associated with genius is the quintile, which is 1/5th (72°) of a circle. The song features a Grand Quintile, creating a pentagram or 5-pointed star in the sky. The song has 4 of the points and is completed by involving the muse attunement of the band. It's another example of uniquely metaphysical and inspired astrology during this peak time.

The incredible circuit of energy involves spiritual healing. This analysis begins with the Moon at the top of the chart and circles around counter-clockwise. The root issue is unresolved anger {Aries Moon}, being softened by maternal love {quintile Ceres in Cancer}. The next piece of the 5-pointed star is the "arc of awakening," and its transcendent dimensions.

Uranus-Pluto adds the multi-dimensional scope, the bridging of worlds. These planets connect to

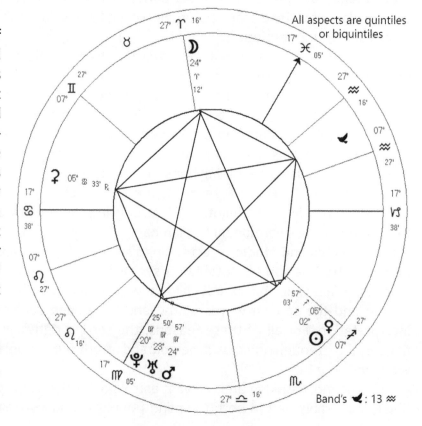

All aspects are quintiles or biquintiles

Band's ◣ : 13 ≈

151

a creative entertainment journey and long-distance partnership {quintile Sun-Venus in Sagittarius in the 5th House}.

The Beatles muse {Euterpe at 13° Aquarius}, which brings it all together, falls in the song's 8th House, the area of death. From beyond the boundary of death, the muse assists the emotional and spiritual work through creative partnership. All of the star's points are interrelated. Underlying anger {Aries Moon} and mother issues {Ceres in Cancer} are transformed metaphysically {Uranus-Pluto}, and offered as an artistic gift and partnership {Sun-Venus} with the muse {Euterpe}.

Since the song begins recording sessions for the album, this formation was in place to launch *Sgt. Pepper* itself. The entire album can be seen in such a way.

A Journey through Time

The next song worked on was "When I'm Sixty-Four." It was one of the first songs Paul wrote as a teenager and had a unique role in the early days. Its stripped-down simplicity was useful as it could be played acoustically in the event of a power outage.[176] Since this rarely occurred, the song was on the proverbial back burner until this time. Paul returned to the song, developed it further and brought it to the transcendent theme of this pivotal album. It ends up being the twentieth *dream* song, one that illustrates how the imagination journeys through time.

Synchronously, Paul's father reached the age of 64 around the time of the recording, another connection to familial roots. The jazzy music hall style evokes another era, further extending their musical palette, this time into the past. Paul is the Beatle most responsible for the "retro" flavor of their work {his natal Mercury retrograde}. His voice was slightly altered to make it sound higher, creating the impression of youth.[177] The shifting to the "younger" Paul epitomizes the time travel theme of the song: it was conceived in the 1950s, completed in the '60s and harkens back to another era, while it anticipates aging. We are taken both backwards and forwards through time!

The song has prominent clarinets, further extending the range of instruments on Beatles songs. It's also notable for the backup singing, which becomes ethereal and atmospheric on this album. Like many songs on *Sgt. Pepper*, it vividly depicts scenes in life. It's as if we are looking down at life's little vignettes (digging the weeds, Sunday morning ride, etc.), tastes of the everyday. However, with the time travel theme, these scenes are *purely in the imagination*, made-up possibilities for the future.

Interestingly, the song's initial function of being handy in a power outage has another layer of meaning. "When I'm Sixty-Four" is the fourteenth **solar** song, one that describes the utility of creative energy. The singer can be "handy" should "your **lights** have gone." He suggests his beloved, "can knit a sweater by the **fireside.**"

"When I'm Sixty-Four": Solar energy provides sustenance for our survival.

The endearing image of being cozy in old age is made possible by the warmth of our Sun, which sustains all living beings. The motion of the "arc" is down towards the pragmatics of the everyday. We can learn to use the Sun's utility to survive the trials and tribulations of life.

The astrology (p. 381) conveys an emphasis on journeys, situated in a theatrical way[1]. The planet of creativity was atypical {Venus out of bounds}, correlating with the unique artistry in the song (altered singing voice, clarinets, time-travel theme)[2]. Idealization of the past is found in the karmic signature {Neptune-South Node}[3]. The traditional values extolled in the song (staying together, Sunday morning rides, etc.) is in tension with revolution and modernization[4].

The song is a reflection on nostalgia and simplicity in a world that was rapidly changing. This tension is reflected in an astrological configuration. Called a "T-Square," there's a negotiation of different interests to find some kind of synthesis or resolution. The planet in the middle of the right triangle fittingly plays the mediating role.

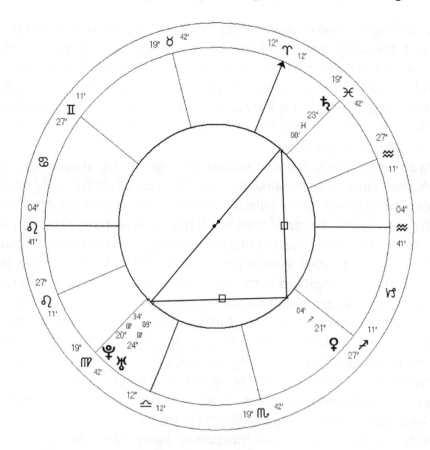

The point at the upper right holds traditional values {Saturn in the 9th House}, and is in opposition with the revolutionary ideas of the times {Uranus-Pluto in the 3rd House}. A song about knitting sweaters and feeding a loved one may seem out of place in the revolutionary 1960s. The tension of this opposition is expressed through creative performance {5[th] House Venus}. "When I'm Sixty-Four" is a brilliant work of art {Venus square Uranus} reflecting on the shifting values occurring in the collective {Saturn opposite Uranus-Pluto}.

Sessions began for "Penny Lane" on December 29th and would last into January. Forever paired with John's "Strawberry Fields Forever," it was also Paul's jaunt down memory lane. His sunniness {Leo Moon} contrasts and complements John's metaphysical panorama {Aquarius Moon}—both songs explore roots from a heightened perspective to heal the past. The presence and influence of the muse is also clear in Paul's celebrated work.

Back in 1956 Paul received a trumpet for his 14th birthday, a few months before Mary died.[178] "Penny Lane" not only features a trumpet, but a barrage of flute-related instruments including a piccolo trumpet and both flutes and piccolos. The instrument of the muse is front and center, which is precisely echoed in the astrology. At the beginning of the first session, the muse {Euterpe} was at the very degree of the Beatles Ascendant {9° Sagittarius}, the position most upfront and expressive. It's as if she's announcing her presence. Trumpets are known for their role in alerting, signifying arrivals or calls for attention.

"Penny Lane" is not only the fourth "flute" song, it's the twenty-first *dream* song, fifteenth **solar** song and fifth "rain" song, a major integrative song of these threads. Through the healing and inspiring presence of the muse, she assists in reconciling the sadness (rain) from the past by bringing radiant clarity (**solar**) to the *dream*. This could be the message from Mary, who might also have a presence in the song.

Paul sings, "A pretty nurse is selling poppies from a tray" mentioning the profession of his mother. Poppies are known for their hallucinogenic properties, so the nurse is offering a shift of perception to see life differently. The nurse "feels as if *she's in a play*," a familiar part of the *dream* motif, how we reside in the theater of our consciousness. Might Paul be recognizing (on some level) that his mother was *playing* a role in his soul work? Or perhaps it was a message from Mary to Paul that he intuited. Either way, the remainder of the song involves the integration of the perspective to the past.

The lyrics revisit an assortment of images and characters in Paul's childhood *play*: a barber showing photographs, a banker in a motorcar, children laughing, a fireman with an hourglass, etc. The "rain" thread continues to advance, seen with 2 references to the "pouring rain." First, the banker doesn't wear a raincoat ("mac") in the rain, then the fireman strangely runs from the rain under "blue suburban skies." In both situations, it may not actually be raining. One interpretation is the rain is Paul's projection. *His unresolved sadness was the rain.* His childhood grief colored his experiences, just like a smudge on the lens of a projector shows up on a movie screen.

"Penny Lane" involves the removing of the "smudge." From the more awakened view in the present, he can see his past more clearly. Though it certainly rained during Paul's childhood, the activity mentioned in the song occurred beneath the clear conditions of blue skies. Though the song doesn't technically have a **solar** word, the Sun is unquestionably implied.

"Penny Lane": The Sun provides clarity of perception.

Like John was realizing in "Strawberry Fields Forever," Paul too was understanding that what occurred in the past was his own interpretation. When we become more awake (Sun) we see life differently, the window of perception {Mercury} is cleansed to reveal another perspective. For 14 year-old Paul, the death of his mother may have been interpreted as a tragedy with nothing meaningful or redeeming whatsoever. Devoid a spiritual perspective, the event could continually reinforce sadness (rain) and pain, a belief that life is unfair and hurtful. By cleansing the window of perception, we might see potential meaning and purpose throughout life, including tragedy (though we must work through all emotion, not bypass by way of a mental perspective). If Paul was having a reunion with Mary in his dreams, then like John, he misunderstood what he was seeing in his childhood (the finality of loss).

The astrology for "Penny Lane" strongly focuses on perception {Mercury}, as well as formulating a sunnier philosophy {Jupiter in Leo} available by seeing life anew. It features another precise geometrical shape {square, a Grand Cross}, highlighted below.

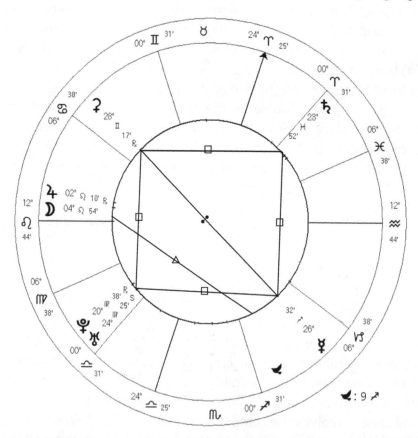

The planet of perception {Mercury, lower right} was challenged to formulate a new view-point or philosophy {in Sagittarius}. It was under heavy pressure {Grand Cross} to integrate the metaphysical scope of the "arc" {square to Uranus-Pluto, lower left}, and to spiritually mature {also square Saturn in Pisces, upper right}. The mind {Mercury} was

155

being informed by the mother {opposite Ceres in Gemini, upper left}. The Grand Cross involves the expansion of the mind—connecting with a transpersonal viewpoint as well as the perception from the mother.

A sunny new philosophy is rising {Jupiter in Leo on the Ascendant}, connected to seeing the past {conjunct the Moon in Leo, reflecting Paul}. The muse resides in the area of artistry {Euterpe in the 5th House} in relationship to such philosophy {in Sagittarius and trine Jupiter-Moon}. "Penny Lane" is the song that most prominently features the flute, consistent with the muse in the realm of creative expression. Some additional notes are found in Part 2.

In "Strawberry Fields Forever," John was seeing the *dream* of his childhood, while in "Penny Lane," Paul does the same thing with the metaphor of the *play*. John's song captures the *dream* with a sprawling impressionistic soundscape, transporting us to another dimension. In contrast, Paul assists us in seeing the *play* through a crisp and clear musical ambience, punctuated by the precision of staccato notes to rouse our attention.

The 2 singles were released on February 13, 1967, which carries the stamp of the finished product (p. 382). At this time, there was a major connection between mother and muse. The role of the muse doesn't always connect with the maternal archetype, but for these songs (and this story), they are inseparable. Part 2 also illustrates how the singles relate to the John-Paul chart. The muse is strongly featured, pointing yet again to the resolution of death.

The Realization of Soul Intent

Sessions for the introductory title song, "Sgt. Pepper's Lonely Hearts Club Band," began on February 1st. As the eventual opening track, it sets the tone for the album. The opening line, "It was twenty years ago today," references the past, a theme not only on the album, but in their spiritual work. As the musicians were in their mid-20s, 20 years ago they were small children. This album can reconnect us to our childhood innocence.

Paul invites the audience "home with us" and to "sing along." We get to be part of the Beatles "family," the lonely hearts club! Since the issue of loneliness is universal, let's all heal it together. A spiritual theme of the album is the realization of unity and each Beatle plays a unique role in this regard.

Ringo finds a sense of togetherness and good cheer. He sings an iconic song about being unified ("With a Little Help from My Friends") with his band of brothers. George realizes his spiritual musical vision ("Within You Without You"), one which specifically points to the unity (Oneness) that envelops us all. John realizes his intention for exhibiting his brilliance, inviting our minds into an unfathomably interconnected and multi-layered intelligence ("Lucy in the Sky with Diamonds," "Being for the Benefit of Mr. Kite!"). As the creative visionary, Paul realizes his intention to bring the entire world together to delight in pure musical joy, fantastic creativity and play.

For the remainder of the *Sgt. Pepper* sessions, a series of different Kites were prominent in the sky. Below is the one for the introductory title song.

156

When sessions began for the song, "Sgt. Pepper's Lonely Hearts Club Band," the Kite featured professional organization {Saturn} of the transcendent {Pisces} at the base. It was forming the spine with the metaphysical and transformative reach of the "arc of awakening" {Uranus-Pluto} at the tip. The lower wing holds the spiritualism signature {Neptune in Scorpio}, while the upper wing involves a journey {Jupiter} into heart, home and roots {in Cancer}.

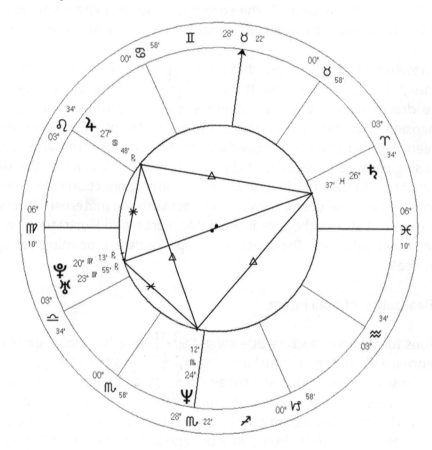

The difference between this Kite and the ones seen with *Revolver* is at the base. Here, there's stronger manifestation {Saturn} of the dream realm {Pisces} as the foundation (for the *dream* album). The similarity is a focus on deep emotional and spiritual healing {water Grand Trine}. {Also of note is the Ascendant at 6º Virgo, the same as Paul's North Node, his point of karmic destiny. Additionally, the "arc" was now exactly on the Beatles North Node at 22º Virgo (not shown here), the realization of the band's destiny.}

There was another geometric shape in the sky. A square formation {Grand Cross} featuring both mother {Ceres} and muse {Euterpe} was in effect. They were both in aspect {square} to the spine of the Kite.

Perpendicular lines form the Grand Cross. The horizontal axis involves the lesson of awakening {Uranus-Pluto} into the realization {Saturn} of spiritual unity {Pisces}, healing estrangements to come together. As heard on the album, there is an invitation for us all to be part of the lonely hearts club. The vertical axis bridges above to below. Mother, calling from above {Ceres in Gemini in the 10th House}, connects down to earth through the travels of the muse {Euterpe in Sagittarius} in the area of family {4th}.

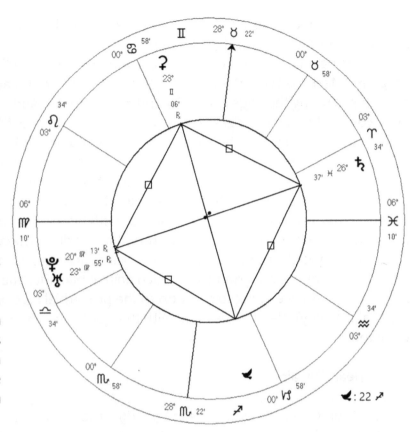

Tea with John

Sessions for John's "Good Morning, Good Morning" began on 2/8. The twenty-first <u>death</u> song opens by alluding to a man who just died ("nothing to do to save his life… "), setting a dark tone. It goes on to paint a scene of modern life through many vignettes (in town, by a school, at a show). Like the dead man, lifelessness abounds. John writes about not wanting to work, "feeling low down." The bleak picture continues with "nothing doing," the scene is "like a ruin" where people are "half *asleep*." The existential loneliness of "Nowhere Man" is in full relief.

The reference to being "half *asleep*" makes it the twenty-second *dream* song. The world is seen from the aerial perspective, as if we're aboard the Kite. We look down to see a wasteland, completely desolate and unanimated, filled with unconscious people going through the motions. The remedy is to become present and engaged, to fully embody oneself and participate. Though lacking a **solar** word, the title suggests waking up, making it the sixteenth **solar** song.

"Good Morning, Good Morning": Spiritual awakening involves being present.

In addition to John belting out "Good Morning" to rouse us awake, the song is notable for its loud, booming brass instruments (saxophones, trombones, French horn), a musical call to attention. Are we going to wake up, or not? The "town is getting dark" (the nineteenth "dark" song), but the people are "full of life." Can we awake to our vibrant selves and light up the world of darkness?

The next line mentions having "tea and meet the wife," a reference to a television program (*Meet the Wife*).[179] Consistent with the *dream* thread, it's another blending of mediums, blurring the edges of reality and make-believe. Additionally, the song is inspired by a corn flake commercial,[180] another reference to the theater of life, as seen on television. Many songs on this album make use of commonplace material in artistic ways.

Having tea becomes somewhat of a minor theme during the *Pepper* sessions. It can be thought of as a standard mundane activity, something that grounds us to the everyday. The question is whether we will bring presence to it or not (a question and lesson of the "arc's" descent). For John, tea with his wife wasn't all that exciting (and he would soon divorce). The song may be revealing his dissatisfaction with domestic life.

The song closes out with animal noise sound effects, a frenzy of activity on the ground. The sounds are arranged so each animal becomes more dominant, able to hunt the previous. Are we going to show up to the proverbial race on the ground or check out like the dead guy? We are presented with this question, which was part of John's spiritual work too.

Heart Repairs

"Fixing a Hole" sessions began on 2/9—the sixth "rain" song, another linking rain and sadness. Paul says that fixing a hole is a metaphor for healing "the hole in your makeup."[181] His "expression of grief" signature was being strongly stimulated. At this stage with the "rain" thread, there's effort to effectively manage emotion.

The holes where the rain gets in prevent his mind from wandering. Also, the cracks in the door keep his mind from wandering too. Upon patching up the holes and cracks, his mind is able to wander more freely. The metaphor points to the awakening process. When the emotional body (Moon, seed) is healthy, centered and loving, the system is more able to be present to mature (Sun, flowering). If we are preoccupied (and hurt) by what happened yesterday, it's more difficult to grow with clarity in the now.

Having alone time to be with one's heart, to grieve and process through the past opens us up. The song points to contemplative time for it. In this twenty-fourth *dream* song, Paul sings that he paints his room "in a colorful way," to host his wandering mind. Painting the room with colors is a depiction of the imagination. It recalls the colors mentioned in "Yellow Submarine" or "Tomorrow Never Knows," the fluidity of consciousness. Here, the Kite can be seen in the context of traveling through the vastness of mind. Along those lines, Paul has conceded that the song (like "Got to Get You into My Life") references marijuana smoking.[182]

Paul's heart repairs seem to be effective. He learns to take care of things "that weren't important yesterday," showing successful advancement to the present. "Yesterday" could also be a reference to the song about his unresolved grief. *Sgt. Pepper* was the turning point to adulthood and this song is Paul's testament of his healing progress.

Recording sessions for "A Day in the Life" took place over several weeks. The song that became the epic finale to *Sgt. Pepper* began coming to life on January 19, 1967. However, our discussion focuses on February 10th, the time of a legendary *event*. The astrology of the Kite was aloft for months, for all of the sessions of this song. The *event* isolates a unique situation with the "arc of awakening," while it's also one of their more famous and notable occasions.

At 8pm, they gathered a 40-piece orchestra to record the magnificent glissandos that punctuate the song. The players were given 3 instructions: to start quietly and end loudly, to start with low notes and finish with high, and to move through the range at one's own speed.[183] To have fun, the orchestra players were adorned with red clown noses, comedic hats and other novelties. Balloons were attached to instruments, a violinist wore a gorilla paw, and a bunch of celebrities and creative types were in attendance.[184] (A video with some of the footage is easily found on YouTube.)

Typical of *Sgt. Pepper*, the lyrics view everyday life from a lofty vantage point. John sings about a news story and depicts it as a surreal scene of tragedy. It is unclear what "He blew his mind out in a car" means—a crash, suicide or possibly both? John is referencing Guinness heir Tara Browne, the fatality of a recent car accident on 12/18/66.[185] Paul was friends with Browne and they allegedly did LSD together[186] (which might blow one's mind). Paul claims the verse is about a politician who commits suicide.[187] Along the lines of the *dream* motif, everyone has their own personal version and meaning.

"A Day in the Life" is not the only song in the second half that would reference a car crash (more on that later). As we know, the life of Julia Lennon ended in an unfortunate accident. It turns out that Browne (born March 4, 1945) has an astrological resemblance to Julia {his Pisces Sun was conjunct hers}. The day of the Browne accident (12/18/66), the sky displayed the Beatles "death" signature {Moon opposite Pluto}. The signature is in John's chart {opposition} and Julia's {square}, and the interchange frequently appears in Beatles astrology.

The reference to the fatal crash makes "A Day in the Life" the twentieth <u>death</u> song. It's also the fifth "flute," third "violence" and eighteenth **solar** song. The teaching relates to synchronicity, understood in the broader context of the song. However, the **solar** word "**light**" also appears, allowing for some philosophizing. John sings about the car crash, "He didn't notice that the **lights** had changed." At a mundane level, Browne simply didn't obey traffic rules. At a metaphysical level, light correlates with the eternal pervasiveness of spiritual awareness. Browne "didn't notice" the **light**, a cautionary tale of unconsciousness. He was young and driving recklessly, responsible for his own demise.

As we develop, we may become more en**light**ened, conscious of life's interconnectedness. Most of us are not aware of this, so the teaching is to notice the **light** (Oneness).

"A Day in the Life": Everything is interconnected.

Everything is intelligently interconnected. Synchronistic occurrences illustrate such intelligence and astrology is a way to study it. As reviewed below, this song features synchronicity and this teaching becomes clearer as the analysis proceeds.

Next, John mentions seeing a film about an army that "just won the war," adding to the violence theme. At this time, *How I Won the War* was being produced and would be released later in the year. John wants to have a "look" because he's *read the book*," which speaks to his own involvement with conflict or war. Reading a book suggests seeing life as story (like a play or movie). "A Day in the Life" is also the twenty-third *dream* song, a motif that has additional layers as the song carries on.

John was encouraging a more transcendent view of life, as captured in, "I'd love to turn you on." He'd love us to shift our perspective to also see it. Like many Beatles lyrics, there is ambiguity—many ways we might become "turned on." The line was controversial enough to warrant a ban by the BBC due to associations with drug use.

The shift in perspective is captured artistically in sound. The first glissando begins— the sound becomes increasingly louder (a crescendo) and higher, a musical depiction of the rising motion of the "arc of awakening." Ian MacDonald writes, "The message is that life is a dream and we have the power, as dreamers, to make it beautiful. In this perspective, the two rising orchestral glissandi may be seen as symbolizing simultaneously the moment of awakening from sleep and a spiritual ascent from fragmentation to wholeness."[188]

The glissando ends at the highest notes, reflecting the "arc's" peak that was recently experienced. The energy is elevated and intense, but inevitably must descend. An alarm clock rings. The listener is brought down to matters on the ground.

Paul enters with the "Woke up, fell out of bed" middle section, a lyrical suggestion of downward motion. There are mundane activities (combing hair) to attend to in the earth realm. Paul heads "downstairs" for coffee, further suggesting descension. After more mundane activities (grabbing coat and hat, making the bus), there is another shift up. He proceeds "upstairs" on a bus (double-decker buses are common in England) and has "a smoke." He hears someone speak and "went *into a dream*."

One interpretation is that "somebody spoke" could be an ordinary person on the bus, but why would that trigger a *dream* state? A more mystical possibility is the communication was from beyond, perhaps a call from the muse. "A Day in the Life" is the twenty-fourth "call" song. After the climax at the peak, the calls begin to come in. Consistent with dreamy dialogue, the music becomes quite transcendent. Next, we hear soaring vocals, signaling Paul's entrance into his *dream*. The triumphant "ahhh-a-a-ahhhh" refrain creates the sensation of flying, a musical reflection of the Kite.

The flying dream sequence comes to an abrupt end with (what has been described as) a sharp "brass retort," which is similar to the alarm clock in shaking us back to reality. John reenters for the final verse, mentioning 4,000 holes in the roads in Blackburn, a northern England town. He relates it to the Albert Hall, which is about 230 miles away in London. At first it sounds ridiculous, how in the world do the road conditions in a northern England town relate to a concert venue in another city? John sings once again, "I'd love to turn you on." From the view on high, we might see how seemingly unrelated events are *synchronistically interconnected.*

We are taken up to the sky once again. The second glissando becomes increasingly louder and more intense, both stimulating and cacophonous. Then, it crashes down with a powerful sustained piano chord, played at a much lower frequency. We must return to the reality on the earth plane, ideally bringing the spiritual perspective down into the everyday. The final haunting piano chord foreshadows the realities the Beatles would very soon confront.

Consistent with the *dream* thread, the song is often discussed as being visually evocative, stimulating images in our minds. Each person's images are completely unique, reflecting how we create an experience of life. The theme of interconnectedness and synchronicity is not only a major teaching, the song itself is an example of it. The band was most likely unaware that "A Day in the Life" would register so strongly in the threads (4 major, 2 minor), allude to the muse and include her instrument, as well as Julia's car crash, John's war karma and Paul's intuitive development. The song also features a musical depiction of the "arc of awakening" with the glissandos and a "flying" sequence that reflects the astrological Kite in the sky.

Astrology is a view of the synchronistic landscape from a bird's-eye perspective, providing a comprehensive way to understand it. Below is how the sky looked at the start of the orchestral event. It was not too long after the session for the title song, so the Kite and square (Grand Cross) were both still in place. Here, they are seen together.

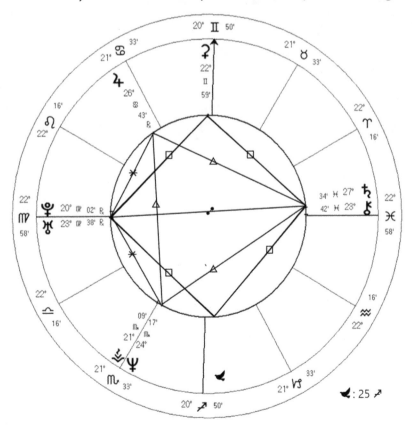

To the left in the chart on the Ascendant (9 o'clock) is the "arc of awakening" {Uranus-Pluto}. Called the "rising," it's the point that separates day (upper half) and night (lower half). Like sunrise, it is a point of expression and visibility. Through the glissandi, the orchestra was giving sound to the intensity and revelatory nature of the "arc." The top of the chart (12 o'clock, Midheaven), finds mom {Ceres} up in heaven placing her call {in Gemini}. She is opposite the muse below—the astrology is like a visual depiction of the mother flying down to earth as the muse {Euterpe at the bottom of the chart}.

The Kite is similar to that in the discussion of the title song. The "arc" {Uranus-Pluto} is grounded through professional organization {opposite Saturn} of the transcendent {in Pisces}. The upper wing includes the song's English flavor {Jupiter in Cancer}, while the lower one involves spiritualism {Neptune in Scorpio} taking form in a project {Vesta}.

The astrology depicts the premise of this book, mainly that Beatles music has many dimensions {Uranus-Pluto}, specifically including a writing collaboration with dead mothers up in heaven {Ceres in Gemini} coming to Earth in the form of the muse. Also note the Ascendant for the orchestral event was at 22° Virgo, the degree of the Beatles North Node. Part 2 (p. 383) has additional discussion about interconnectedness, how the theme is particularly highlighted in the astrology for this song.

Chapter 15
The Dream of Lonely Hearts Part 2:
The Aeronautics of Consciousness

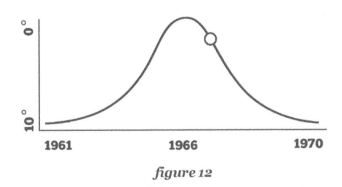

figure 12

The Kite remains the star of the show. The flying theme continues to take different expressions, all of them stretching the mind. In particular, the John-Julia partnership was at its most expansive and otherworldly, while Paul continued to strengthen leadership qualities with inspired creativity. George put forward his most musically and lyrically substantial song and Ringo brought the band of friends together as this soul group realized their destiny. Once in a while lightning is captured in a bottle, the crackling metaphysical intelligence is revealed.

Mystical Kite Flying

The themes of flying and kites reach amusingly preposterous synchronistic proportions on the next song! Sessions for "Being for the Benefit of Mr. Kite!" began on February 17th. The matching of the song title with the astrological configuration is just the beginning. We end up in another century, able to see the concordance of seemingly unrelated events.

As the legend goes, John wrote the song lyrics almost entirely from a poster advertising a circus in 1843. His vision was to portray a carnival atmosphere, to "smell the sawdust"[189] in the song's ambience. George Martin has referred to John as an "aural Salvador Dali."[190] Overtly psychedelic, the song involves some of the most sophisticated and technically rigorous sound effects on any Beatles track. The creation of the swirling soundscape was quite the task for George Martin and sound engineer Geoff Emerick. They cut up sections of the tape, threw them into the air, and reassembled them to contribute to the dizzying effect.[191] The music (especially the second half of the song), is like an auditory depiction of the Kite flying---consciousness taken away by soaring atmospherics.

Like "When I'm Sixty-Four," this twenty-fifth *dream* song also takes us on an adventure through time. Flying on a mystical Kite, we are taken back 124 years to the circus. The song depicts theater within the theater of *Sgt. Pepper*, a *dream* within a *dream*. In vivid detail it describes events, characters and plot lines that spark our imagination. The 1843 circus is animated for each listener to mentally recreate, precisely how our dreams reflect our individualized perceptions. Additionally, the song's fantastic musical swirl has a surreal (psychedelic or hallucinogenic) quality, which is often described as "dreamlike."

"Mr. Kite!" is also the seventeenth **solar** song, this time involving heat. "Over men and horses hoops and garters/Lastly through a hogshead of real **fire!**"

"Being for the Benefit of Mr. Kite!": The Sun (fire) provides animation to the grand theater of life.

The Sun is the great ball of fire that warms all of life, providing the energetic conditions for us to be vital and present. The playful spirit of the song depicts how life itself is the greatest show on earth. What character do we wish to play?

The astrology is as magical as the song. Below is the Kite when sessions began.

Similar to "A Day in the Life," the tip of the Kite was rising. The only difference between the astrology for the 2 songs was the planet of artistry {Venus} at the base of the Kite. It involves reflection and connection (like the song reflects the circus), here in a mystical {Pisces} way.

Having a song title with the name "Kite" with a Kite configuration rising in the sky is one thing, but for the circus on 2/14/1843, there was also one of these extremely rare Kite's ascending for the

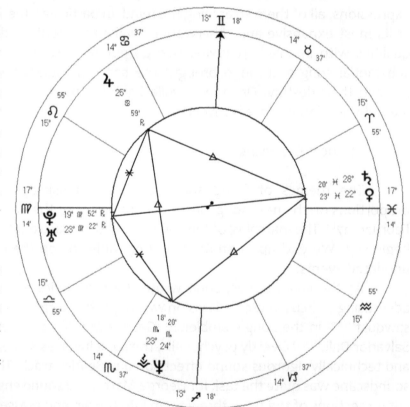

performance! Even more astounding, the Kite for the circus and the song occupy almost precisely the same zodiacal positions {base in the later degrees of Pisces, wings in late

Cancer and Scorpio, and tip in Virgo on the Ascendant}. Song and circus are fantastically connected in a mystical fashion that could only be revealed through astrology.

There is one technical issue to address. The Kite for the circus finds outlet through the Ascendant, there were no planets in Virgo at that time. The poster advertised an evening show, which John makes reference to in the song. He sings "the band begins at ten to six," perhaps having been written to rhyme with "tricks" in the next line. There is no start time on the poster that inspired the lyrics.

Since the precise time for the circus is unknown, the Ascendant degree is uncertain. However, on the evening of the circus (2/14/1843 in Rochdale, England), Virgo was rising for over 3 hours. The only way Virgo is not the Ascendant sign is if the performance started before 5:30 or after 8:30. The Kite is most perfect at 8pm, as depicted below. If the show began earlier (say 7pm), there would still be this Kite configuration and it would make sense too. 8pm is prime time, often in the heart of evening performances. After some opening acts to get warmed up, the marquee performances would be at that time. The drama in the song might have been climaxing right when the Kite was perfect.

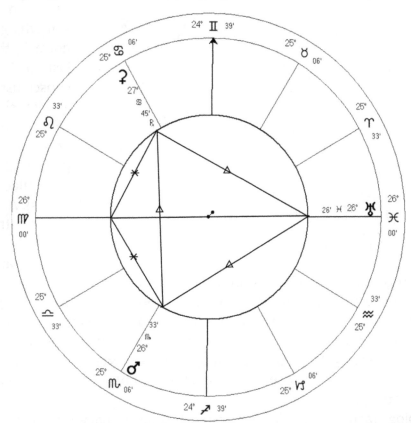

The circus Kite features Uranus in Pisces at the base, Ceres in Cancer at one wing, Mars in Scorpio at the other, and the Virgo Ascendant at the tip. The foundation (Kite's base) is the realm of imagination, the otherworldly nature of the festivities {Uranus in Pisces}. At one wing are the dangerous {Scorpio} athletic feats {Mars} in the performance. The other wing {Ceres in Cancer} adds the uniquely homegrown (in this case English) flavor to the event. The Virgo Ascendant grounds it into reality. It requires the steadiness to not

166

fall off a high-wire, drop juggling pins or miss a trapeze handoff. Taken together, the Kite depicts the "ooohs" and "aahhhs" of inspired, boundary-breaking athletic performance for a hometown crowd.

Below is a biwheel featuring the astrology for the circus (outer wheel), situated around the song (inner wheel). The overlay illustrates how these events 124 years apart are connected in this intelligent spiritual matrix we inhabit.

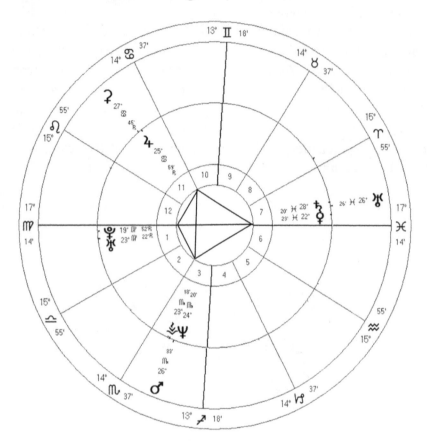

The base of the song's Kite involves grounding the mystical {Saturn in Pisces} through inspired creativity {Venus in Pisces}. The circus Kite is ethereal, breezing about in the sky. The English circus in 1843 is not something we would normally think about, it's just flying about in consciousness {Uranus in Pisces}. The Beatles song tethers it down, bringing it to tangibility {Saturn} through artistry and reflection {Venus in Pisces}. Additionally, the planets that compose the "arc of awakening" are in an earth sign {Virgo}, which grounds consciousness into specific projects.

The transpersonal dimension of the song {Neptune in Scorpio} is highlighting the athletic feats of the circus {Mars in Scorpio} in a most fantastic way. There is also additional grounding noted at this wing too {Vesta in Scorpio}, a combination pertaining to craft. The planets at the other wing {Jupiter for the song conjunct Ceres for the circus} reinforce the English flavor of the event (as Cancer involves home, roots), involving a journey {Jupiter} in discovery of the past {Cancer}.

Astrology {and the Aquarius archetype} informs us that everything exists as part of the neural activity of a colossal mind. Though events may appear random or coincidental, a more mystical perspective is synchronicity. The astrological parallels between circus and song reveal an overarching intelligence (and meaning) to comprehend our experience, perhaps to bring us to another dimension. The John-Julia partnership would produce a few more extraordinary examples of the aeronautics of consciousness. More on the muse in this song and a few additional astrological points are in Part 2 (p. 384).

167

Tea with Paul

Sessions for Paul's "Lovely Rita," the twenty-sixth *dream* song, began on February 23rd. The song begins with the vocalization "ahhh-ah-ah-ahhhh," strongly echoing the dream sequence in "A Day in the Life." The sound is an aural depiction of imagination itself, which might "fly" down to create the dramas in our lives.

The song was inspired by Paul receiving a parking ticket outside Abbey Road studios,[192] a common, unremarkable occurrence. For Paul, an entire new world becomes possible. He created an imaginary plot line with undertones of romantic intrigue. He invites the meter maid to tea, they laugh over dinner, she pays the bill and he's got it going on. None of it is reality and all of it is possible. The song itself is now part of our consensus reality. Though the drama in the song didn't actually happen, it may as well have. We have an experience of it forever etched in our imagination, just like a *dream*.

"Lovely Rita" is the twentieth "dark" song. "When it gets dark I tow your heart away" suggests playfulness in the dark, a sign of growth and shift in this thread. The song is also notable for its variety of sound effects: kazoo, comb and tissue paper and John's percussive vocal improvisations.[193] These mysterious and intriguing sounds reflect and evoke the unlimited possibilities of the imagination, something that will be helpful for the next discussion, the John-Julia masterwork.

As Above, So Below: The Girl Who Bridges Worlds

The first session for "Lucy in the Sky with Diamonds," perhaps the ultimate *dream* song, began on February 28th. It is said to have originated from a very young Julian Lennon's painting in nursery school, inspired by his classmate Lucy O'Donnell.[194] John said Julian came up with the title for the artwork and he wrote a song in honor of his son's creativity. Consistent with a theme on *Sgt. Pepper*, there is a connection to family, roots and youth. Additionally, *Alice in Wonderland* is a major influence.[195]

The public quickly made the linguistic association with LSD—Lucy (L) Sky (S) Diamonds (D)—which John says was accidental. However, the subject matter, lyrics ("incredibly high," "head in the clouds") and overtly psychedelic music has raised many skeptical eyebrows. It's well within John's character to add hidden (or not so hidden) references, double entendres and idiosyncratic meanings through his clever use of language. In fact, from this point forward, his songwriting would become increasingly daring, irreverent and individualistic. Also, John was ingesting the substance during this period.[196] Perhaps after the "Jesus" controversy the prior year, he didn't want to create any more public relations headaches and said what was necessary to put any potential controversy to rest.

"Being for the Benefit of Mr. Kite!" illustrated the preternatural reach of the Kite, its ability to "fly" through realms of consciousness to reveal a meaningful and intelligent spiritual organization. "Lucy in the Sky with Diamonds" addresses another facet of the Kite, its inherent symmetry. It can be folded along the spine, connecting the two wings. As seen in the previous discussions, the Kite's spine is along the chart's horizon line for this song too, effectively splitting it into two halves (see below). There is a famous adage spoken in astrology "as above, so below," about the concordance between the stars above and life below. Similarly, "Lucy in the Sky with Diamonds" brings the wings of the Kite together, addressing the spiritual relationship between sky and earth.

The Kite is technically a quadrilateral pattern, a geometric shape. The name "Kite" was natural because it resembles the flying objects. However, there are other things that have this shape too. A common portrayal of a diamond has a very close resemblance to a kite. So yes, there was a diamond in the sky when "Lucy in the Sky with Diamonds" was being recorded.

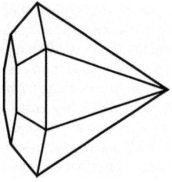

Below is the diamond (kite) shape when the first recording session began.

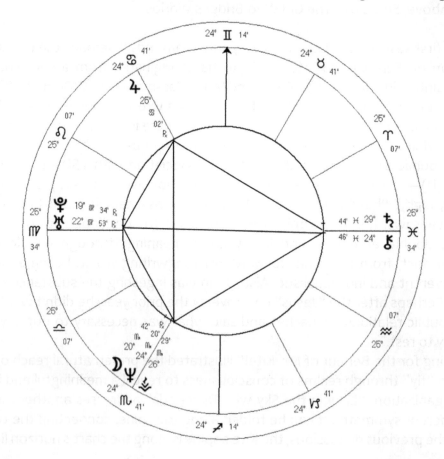

Recorded soon after "Mr. Kite!," "Lucy" has a Kite configuration that is quite similar. The only difference is that "Mr. Kite!" has creative reflection {Venus in Pisces} at the base (song reflecting circus), while "Lucy" places a greater emphasis on spiritual healing. Included in the above chart are 2 additional points {Chiron in Pisces at the base, Scorpio Moon joining Neptune at the lower wing}, which involve emotional and spiritual healing processes.

"Lucy" derives from the Latin word "lux" meaning "light." It shares the same root as lucid, to make visible. In some cultures, the name was given to girls *born at dawn*.[197] The astrological Ascendant is the point of dawn, where light is made visible. We can imagine Lucy sitting on the tip of the diamond/kite shape (on the Ascendant), where the "arc of awakening" is located. The "arc" involves the breakthrough into other dimensions or paradigms. "Lucy in the Sky with Diamonds," the song that most points to astrology itself, involves geometry (diamond) illuminated (Lucy) in the sky.

Aside from its shape, there is another facet to diamonds, that of immense value. They are considered one of the most precious gemstones, typically used for special reasons including engagements. The song might be revealing something of metaphysical (sky) value (diamond) to be seen (Lucy). We'll join Lucy on a journey and perhaps she'll reveal her riches.

"Lucy in the Sky with Diamonds" is the twenty-seventh *dream* song, an excursion through a most detailed dreamscape. At the peak of the "arc" John wrote "Tomorrow Never Knows," instructing the listener to "relax and *float downstream*" and "listen to the color of your *dreams*." Now, with the "arc" still incredibly high, he writes "Picture yourself in a boat on a river," to engage the imagination of sailing through an assemblage of colorful and dreamlike imagery ("tangerine trees and marmalade skies").

John sings "somebody calls you" (the twenty-fifth "call" song), another example of calls now coming in. It is from a girl (Lucy) "with kaleidoscope eyes." Kaleidoscopes are noted for their *shifting geometric patterns*. Lucy is also described as "the girl with the **sun** in her eyes," the nineteenth **solar** song. The teaching is to see the designs in the sky.

"Lucy in the Sky with Diamonds": The Sun illuminates a scintillating panorama of patterned meaning.

With her solar vision, Lucy invites us to see and understand the kaleidoscopic patterns in the sky (astrology) being reflected in her eyes. As portrayed in these *Sgt. Pepper* chapters, the astrology for the album showcases an unusual amount of precise geometric configurations. I included the geometric patterns in the prior songs to set up this teaching, perhaps the one most central to the spirit of this particular book. As seen in other songs from *Revolver* and *Sgt. Pepper*, "Lucy in the Sky with Diamonds" also unifies the **solar** and *dream* threads at the top of the "arc." Here, the awareness (**solar**) of astrology serves as a navigational tool for the boat on the river (*dream*). Astrology serves as guide to assist people in *dreaming* consciously by clarifying the energetic currents.

The motion continues "down" (following the "arc's" descent) to a "bridge," suggesting motion towards the earth plane. There's a visit with "rocking horse people," which also has astrological relevance. Included at the base of the Kite/diamond configuration is Chiron, a Centaur (horse-person). The Centaur bridges the conceptual (human) with the instinctual (animal), another example of bridging realms (above to below). Interestingly, Chiron is on the song chart's Descendant, part of the horizon line connecting the realm above to below.

The movement proceeds to the shore, completing the transition to the earth realm (analogous to the lower hemisphere of the chart), where "newspaper taxis" are available. Newspapers are composed of words, the contents of mind. Our thoughts are like vehicles (taxis), able to take us anywhere. John invites us to "climb in the back" of the taxi with the "head in the clouds," to stay connected to the *dream* realm as thoughts begin to shape reality on the earth plane.

The scene shifts to a train station, another location in the manifest world. At the station are "plasticine porters with looking glass ties." Plasticine is modeling clay, designed for children's play, while porters carry bags. We get to shape (plasticine) what we bring (porter) into the realm of manifestation, delivered by our mental intentions (newspaper taxis).

"Looking glass ties" references Lewis Carroll's *Through the Looking-Glass*, the sequel to *Alice in Wonderland*. Carroll intentionally designed the two books to be mirror images of each other, playing on the theme of the reflection of worlds![198] It mimics the "as above, so below" adage in astrology, effectively connecting the wings of the Kite. Lucy appears at a turnstyle (a type of gate) in the train station. Lucy is the girl at the gate between worlds (like the Ascendant), bridging the imaginal dream realm (above) with the earth plane (below).

With her travels through the sky and bridging of realms, Lucy is a depiction of the muse. John hears her call and has a fantastic experience with her presence in his mind. Through poetic symbolic language ("kaleidoscope eyes," "newspaper taxis," etc.) they create a message of epic metaphysical proportions. The strongest connection between John and Julia is the archetype of Aquarius, the one most connected to metaphysical systems including astrology. It is how Julia {Ceres in Aquarius} nurtures her son {conjunct John's Moon}. She does this through a journey that reveals the broad metaphysical paradigm of astrology {her Ceres conjunct Jupiter-Uranus in Aquarius}.

John had a need to occupy public positions which showcase his brilliance. It turns out his mother didn't abandon him after all. Quite the opposite—she may have nurtured and assisted his aims. In return, John (like a saprophagous Beatle) supported his mother to realize the potential of her chart and complete her soul work. The song is a leading example of Step 4 of the muse process (collaboration), an incredible illustration of bridging worlds: the theme of this song.

Ultimately, "Lucy in the Sky with Diamonds" involves powerful spiritual healing. John was desperately yearning for reunion and here he is, whisked away by mom for an amazing journey. What they shared could not have been experienced while she was alive. We might see that even in the most tragic events, there could be buried treasures of value and meaning, maybe even diamonds. The underlying death issue is transformed into vibrant, life-affirming joy and wondrous fascination for many of the song's listeners, the ultimate transformation.

The astrological diamond (Kite) involves a staggering level of multi-dimensional complexity and the lyrics reflect it in astounding synchronistic fashion. The music is the perfect soundtrack, and is as surrealistic as the lyrics. It features the now familiar "aaaahhh-aaahhhh" flying vocals that accompany many of these Kite songs. Like Paul's voice in "When I'm Sixty-Four," John's is distorted to give its otherworldly cadence. George plays the tambura to add the mystical tinge, while Paul's bass is so prominent and melodic, it functions almost like a lead instrument. He also assisted John with some of the lyrics. Ringo's drums are also noteworthy and distinctive, particularly his *thump-thump-thump* fill before the chorus. The band collaborated beautifully on this song and created a timeless classic, one with substantial spiritual importance. It's a phenomenally unique masterpiece that will forever baffle the mind and uplift the heart. Some additional astrological notes are found in Part 2 (p. 385).

Heeding the Word

The early days of March brought some changes in the cosmic scene. Since *A Hard Day's Night*, the planet of maturation {Saturn} resided in the sign of imagery, spirituality and the bridging of worlds {Pisces}. The passage concluded on a glorious note with the recording of the ultimate *dream* song, "Lucy in the Sky with Diamonds." Beginning on March 3rd, the next couple of years saw a focus on independence and leadership {Saturn in Aries}.

A few days later on March 8th, the planet directly associated with that change {Mars, ruler of Aries} would turn retrograde, initiating a review of leadership dynamics. It would stay retrograde for the remainder of the *Sgt. Pepper* sessions, turning direct on May 26th right before the album release. It was during this time (the spring of 1967) that leadership of The Beatles began to change.

Paul stepped forward and exercised leadership for a beautiful process. Prolific with his songwriting at this time, he was the main writer and visionary of not only a catchy song, but one of great value for his friend John. Their bond involved artistic creativity for catharsis, using the format of song for healing. "Getting Better" is one of the most important examples of such work. Usually diplomatic and seeking approval, Paul matured from those tendencies and took a risk, the mark of leadership.

On March 9th, sessions began for "Getting Better," the fourth "violence" song. Recall in the first "violence" song, "Run for Your Life," John revealed his intimidating and aggressive tendencies. For "Getting Better" there was a return of the exact same signature relating to violent patterns {Mars on the South Node}, that was also present when Julia was killed. The roots of aggressive karma, linked with the emotion of anger, are featured in the song ("I used to get mad at my school," "Me used to be angry young man"). The spiritual work was to cease taking it out on others and to do something creative with it instead.

172

The song reveals John's prior pattern of domestic abuse. Due to the sensitive nature of the subject, he may not have been ready to fully own his dark past. Paul (the "voice") would sing John's confession, assisting him with the revelation. 13 years after the song was created, John was more ready to comment on it. In a *Playboy* interview in 1980 he is quoted: "It is a diary form of writing. All that 'I used to be cruel to my woman, I beat her and kept her apart from the things that she loved' was me. I used to be cruel to my woman, and physically -- any woman. I was a hitter. *I couldn't express myself and I hit.* I fought men and I hit women. That is why I am always on about peace, you see. It is the most violent people who go for love and peace. Everything's the opposite. But I sincerely believe in love and peace. I am a violent man who has learned not to be violent and regrets his violence. I will have to be a lot older before I can face in public how I treated women as a youngster."[199]

In this statement, John speaks of the relationship between his unexpressed emotion and violent pattern, as well as his process of awakening and developing his peaceful intentions. The karmic activation of violent tendencies {Mars-South Node in Scorpio} was exactly on his "wounded child" signature for the "Getting Better" sessions. Fittingly, it was moving through John's area of partnership, and his partner Paul was of great assistance.

John's historical pattern was getting better. In addition to writing "Run for Your Life" in 1965, he also penned "The Word," which resolves the prior song. The former illustrates his darkness and the latter is an invitation to be in the sunshine of love. Though he got it conceptually, the message was becoming more embodied and integrated. "Getting Better" has the line, "You gave me *the word*, I finally heard." John heard his own message the best he could, which would soon influence his peace activism. The next step was to offer the world the ripened fruits of his personal awakening.

George, the "soul" of the group, also plays a role here. During the confessional part of the song, he created the mystical tinge from the tambura, adding an otherworldly dimension to the revelation. The atmospherics might suggest the words were being brought forward to be publicly witnessed, and such accountability might allow release. The band was working like a supportive family for John's healing, a shining example of their soul work together.

"Getting Better" is also noteworthy for an incident that occurred during its recording, one which has symbolic relevance to the Kite. Allegedly, John mistakenly took LSD (intending to ingest something else), which didn't sit well. George Martin brought him up to the roof to get some fresh air, unaware that he was tripping. When Martin returned without John, the others rushed up to prevent a possible accident.[200] The Kite's potential is the soaring heights of inspiration, while its hazard is being ungrounded. Though no accident occurred, the worry about falling from the heights would become realized as the "arc" descends.

Saving the World

George was also coming into his leadership potential. During his time in India studying Hinduism and sitar, he became further disenchanted by materialism and the attachments of the personality. Upon his return, he thought of leaving the Beatles, but knew the global stature of the band was ideal to bring soulfulness into Western music and thereby shift consciousness.

In this new passage {Saturn in Aries} George would increase his influence through more prolific songwriting and help lead an East-West musical synthesis in the emerging world music trend. He singlehandedly oversaw the orchestration of one of the most unique, haunting and penetrating Beatles tracks. "Within You Without You" creates a spiritual soundscape for reflection and contemplation. Though the lyrics were complex, it boiled down to a message of Oneness and love.

Sung lovingly yet pointedly through the drone, hums, buzz and beats of sitars, tablas, tamburas, dilrubas, swarmandal, cellos and violins,[201] George gave the world something to think about. He challenged his audience to question their very existence, to see beyond the illusion of separateness. He sings of the pitfalls of attachments, which can limit an experience of connectedness and divine love. With a deep core of inner love, we can bridge the apparent divide with others. One's value system might shift from a material to a metaphysical orientation through such introspective connection.

George teaches that inner peace can be discovered when one is able to "see beyond the self." He visions a time when humanity could experience greater unity and flow with life, made possible by such selflessness. In fact, a selfless, universal love could save the world. He delivered the message in a somewhat challenging way. He asked, "Are you one of them?" those "who gain the world and lose their soul."

"Within You Without You" is the twenty-eighth *dream* song. He states that *"life flows on* within you and without you." Upon greater spiritual realization, we are able to see the *dreamlike* nature of existence flowing through all life {a most Piscean sentiment}. We might release resistance to this flow of consciousness and partner with the currents. The music forms the perfect counterpart to the message with its meandering, impressionistic waves of sound.

Though an impressive achievement, many people were simply not on the same wavelength. It has been called "sanctimonious" with an "air of superiority" and "finger pointing."[202] The music has been characterized as "boring," and even George Martin wrote that it was "dreary."[203] Others found it to be a work of brilliance, subtlety and depth. It inspired and uplifted the consciousness for many who were open and eager for spiritual nourishment. Like a Rorschach test, it is seen in countless ways, each person interacting with their own consciousness through it. The song has a unique place in Beatles astrology. It lines up as the one which encapsulates their spiritual message. Below is the astrology for the Kite as seen in "Within You Without You," configured around the Beatles chart.

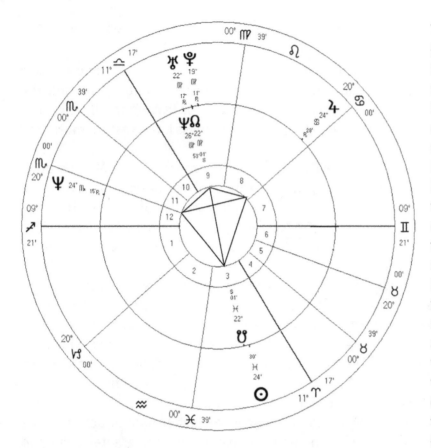

The horseshoe symbol {South Node} on the lower half of the chart relates to the band's soul intention to refine and deliver a spiritual {Pisces} message {3rd House}. The horseshoe on the upper half {North Node} assists the work through broader discovery {9th House} and focus {Virgo} on the spiritual quest {conjunct Neptune}. At this time, the spine of the Kite was situated along this central axis of the band's spiritual work. At the Kite's base was now the Sun itself (presence, awareness), in the sign of spirituality {Pisces}, in the house of message {3rd}. The "arc" {Uranus-Pluto} was at the Kite's tip, peaking on the Beatles point of "karmic destiny" {North Node}, bringing manifestation {Virgo} to their vision. The planets of spiritual questing {Jupiter, Neptune}, were at the wings of the Kite, reinforcing loftiness and reach. The discussion in Part 2 (p. 386) provides additional detail and discussion.

"Within You Without You" is a serious song, containing the most sophisticated and deepest delivery of their message. It's in complete contrast with the early formula and Beatlemania. And yet, the song ends with a burst of laughter, an invitation to paradoxically not take it so seriously. The Beatles never lost sight of playfulness and fun, which leads to the next discussion.

She's Having Fun

Paul's "She's Leaving Home" involves independence. The story is a fictionalized account of a young woman leaving the nest to find herself. Based on actual events, it captures the mood of individuation occurring in the collective. The song is notable because no Beatles play instruments on it.[204] Similar to "Eleanor Rigby," the music is composed on strings and tells a story of a female character. However, instead of an arrangement from George Martin, Paul enlisted Mike Leander as Martin was previously engaged.[205] It's an example of Paul asserting himself with production decisions, further claiming band leadership.

175

Like other songs on *Sgt. Pepper*, "She's Leaving Home" transports the listener through its soundscape. The somber and haunting atmosphere is completely unique, creating one of the more moving Beatles songs. It revisits the theme of a loss in the context of home, something dear to Paul's heart. Though not officially a "call" song, it has relevance for this theme. Instead of a call for reunion or connection, the song features the reverse—a letter to say goodbye. Paul's underlying issue might be releasing, as reflected in the poignant, perhaps melancholic, atmospherics. For this song, the celestial Kite could relate to the desire to fly the coop, to expand one's horizons towards new experiences.

Singing Soul Family

Another planetary shift occurred when nourishing Ceres entered familial Cancer on March 28th. The very next day Ceres would visit the band's Cancer Sun while they gathered to record "With a Little Help from My Friends," featuring Ringo on lead vocals. As a Cancer Sun himself, Ringo was the emotional glue or anchor in the group dynamic. This song is an example of their familial bond.

It was written collaboratively as a group, led by Paul and John. George plays lead guitar and Ringo gives voice to the shared issue of this lonely hearts club. The song begins with fears of abandonment, wondering if singing out of tune would force someone to leave. From this position of vulnerability he offers, "I want somebody to love," an honest and earnest expression of emotional needs. Then, the core Beatles issue is presented, loneliness and sadness, the need to work through feelings when love is away. It is the communal support of the group, this band of musical brothers, which helps them move forward.

"With a Little Help from My Friends" is the twentieth **solar** song. Connected to the **solar** word in this song is something outrageous, but so were the Beatles at times. The line, "What do you see when you turn out the **light**?" may stem from a somewhat comical communal experience amongst the band members. Paul told the story to GQ magazine in 2018.[206] In the early days, they would play a sexual game. They would turn out the lights and imagine certain women to fantasize about based on names being called out.

On a more spiritual level, what do we experience in the absence of **light**? The metaphysical dimension might involve the dynamic between darkness and light, from creative potentials (dark) to manifestation (light). Though the dark may be lonely or scary, it's also the void of unlimited possibility.

"With a Little Help from My Friends": In darkness is a spark of creative imagination.

Another example of group cohesion was the support they gave Ringo to sing his lead vocals. He was uncertain about singing the high part at the end, so the others gathered around him at the microphone. Also, George Martin, paternal figure of this musical family, plays organ on the track.[207]

The song celebrates their family unity while also inviting others to bond together with its welcoming vibe and sing-a-long ease. "With a Little Help from My Friends" became an anthem of the 1960s, with widespread popularity and many cover versions. Most famously, Joe Cocker's cover achieved legendary status. His rendition at the 1969 Woodstock Festival was an iconic moment in rock history. The song would gain more popularity in the 1980s through the *Wonder Years* television program, which chronicles the events of a family in the late 1960s.

Comedy Call Song

On May 17th, the band gathered for the first session of "You Know My Name (Look up the Number)." Led by John (with Paul), the song makes use of various comedic voices and includes a lounge section. It's as loose as *Sgt. Pepper* is polished, one of the most unique and unexpected tracks they recorded. As it wasn't serious, the song was placed on the backburner. It was completed and released as the B-side to "Let It Be" in March 1970, almost 3 years after this initial session.

The song is noteworthy as the twenty-sixth "call" song. It was speculated that John and Paul had made contact with their muse, having the emotional reunion they so desired. Since then, "call" songs no longer contained the same intensity and urgency. They dynamically changed in the second half of the story with this song being the most extreme.

The Beatles had a keen sense of humor and it's completely in their character to do a comedy song. It is curious and interesting that they would choose to do one about telephoning. It's evidence that the issue was front and center in their consciousness. When something intense and filled with emotion diminishes its charge, there is often a tendency to laugh at it. "You Know My Name (Look up the Number)" might illustrate a release as the "arc" descends. The contrast with the howls of pain in the "call" songs "I Call Your Name" or "No Reply" could not be more striking. "You Know My Name (Look up the Number)" is not only hilarious, given this broader context, it also might be a celebration of (some degree of) emotional freedom.

Tea with George

George's "Only a Northern Song" was put forward during the *Sgt. Pepper* sessions, but didn't make the album. It's notable as the twenty-first "dark" song ("night," "dark"), intentionally designed to be subversive. His next piece, "It's All Too Much," began on May 26th after work on the album concluded. After contributing 3 songs on *Revolver* (and having a significant role on others), George's contributions were not the priority at this time. Along with other castoffs, both of these songs would find a home on the *Yellow Submarine* album in 1969.

A psychedelic LSD-influenced "freak out," "It's All Too Much" was designed to be a countercultural sing-a-long. Instead of sitar or guitar, George's lead instrument was the organ, creating drone-like atmospherics. Adding to the psychedelia was guitar feedback and improvisation, and a cacophonous use of trumpets and bass clarinet. It exemplifies this period of drug experimentation with music, here without the *Pepper* professional craftsmanship.

The lyrics were confusing to some, especially those not on the same metaphysical wavelength. George sings, "And the more I go inside, the more there is to see," an example of the introspective direction of their message. It's the twenty-first **solar** song, "It's all too much for me to take/The love that's **shining** all around you." Here comes George's celebration of the Sun, a theme to be developed in later works. It's also reflective of "The Word" and "Tomorrow Never Knows," which pair love with a **shining** presence. He states that the world is like a "birthday cake," but cautions against overindulgence. The teaching is to show reverence for it all.

It's All Too Much: Practice moderation, humility, appreciation.

At this point, George was soon to renounce LSD in favor of the clarity of meditation. Though this song is a spirited sing-a-long in the freewheeling Summer of Love, it also reflects the gradual descent of the "arc" towards a more measured way of being. George would soon travel to San Francisco and see the excess and indulgence of the counterculture and decide on moderation and authentic devotion.

Another **solar** reference is found in, "*Sail me on a silver **sun**,*" similar to the "sailed up to the **sun**" on "Yellow Submarine." George follows with, "*Show me that I'm everywhere and get me home for tea.*" "It's All Too Much" is also the twenty-ninth *dream* song, another uniting with the **solar** thread. The idea of being "everywhere" is the projection of the *dream* onto the entire canvas of life. The need to stay connected with the personality is found with having tea, movement towards a grounded spirituality.

Like many *dream* songs, water references illustrate the stream of consciousness. In addition to the reference to sailing, George writes about "*Floating down the stream of time from life to life,*" extending consciousness (*dreaming*) to include reincarnation. Additional astrological notes are found in Part 2 (p. 387).

Album #8: Sgt. Pepper's Lonely Hearts Club Band

Introduction: As listed on the Beatles official website, the traditional and observed release day for the album was 6/1/1967.[208] *Sgt. Pepper* is considered one of the first concept albums, a major development in progressive rock. Critics argue that the songs do not have a discernable narrative, though the album has a *feel* as well as some uniting themes. Songs address aging and life changes, family and roots, the loss of innocence as well as illusion/fantasy. In the heart of the Transcendence phase, the music and lyrics are impressionistic, ethereal and have multiple layers. Drug use plays a role,[209] including some lyrical references.

The colorful and complex cover image invited the public into the realm of imagination and the theatrics of artistic rock. Along with the variety of famous people depicted, assorted artifacts and the like, stand the 4 musicians as their alter egos in colorful Edwardian military costumes. They are holding instruments (John: French horn,

Ringo: trumpet, Paul: cor anglais, and George: flute). George points the flute towards the sky, the home of the muse whose instrument he holds. The back cover featured all of the song lyrics, both a first for them and (supposedly) in the rock genre.

Whereas *Revolver* had parity, *Sgt. Pepper* is driven by Paul, who was the primary author of 7 out of 14 songs. This song total includes "You Know My Name (Look Up the Number)," but not "Penny Lane" and "Strawberry Fields Forever," which appear on *Magical Mystery Tour* ("It's All Too Much" and "It's Only a Northern Song" are discussed with the album *Yellow Submarine*). John adds 4 songs, while "A Day in the Life" is a John-Paul collaboration. George authored one song and Ringo sang lead vocals on the group collaboration.

Musical Development: George Martin gets credit for the polish and professionalism of the album, as well as some key creative contributions. Geoff Emerick was again a central figure as the sound engineer. The studio itself can be seen as an "instrument" for this album. Paul worked closely with George Martin, expanding his role from performer to incorporate facets of production.[210] There are elements of rock, psychedelia, ragtime, music hall, Indian and classical music.

A wide variety of instruments and sounds are featured. "When I'm Sixty-Four" has clarinets, "Lovely Rita" has kazoos, "Good Morning Good Morning" has saxophones and other brass, while the title song features French horns. "She's Leaving Home" has a string arrangement, while "Within You Without You" has Indian instrumentation, along with cello and violin. There are harmonicas, pianos, organs, harpsicords and harmoniums. There is comb and tissue paper in addition to a wide range of sound and studio effects (such as an alarm clock, laughing and gibberish) and an orchestra for "A Day in the Life." Compared to the amplification seen on *Revolver*, the mood on the album is turned down a notch. Like being on a cloud, the listener is able to comfortably surf.

Lyrical Development: The 13 album songs (and yet unreleased single) combine for 14 songs that claim 25 positions in the lyrical themes. It has 8 *dream* songs, the most on any album. It also has 6 **solar**, 3 "call," 2 death, 2 "violence," 2 "dark," 1 "rain" and 1 "flute" song. There's a significant drop in death songs from *Revolver* (from 8 to 2). The "call" songs now suggest receiving communication or transforming the prior upset into comedy. The prominence of "flute" songs (note the uncounted "Strawberry Fields Forever" and "Penny Lane") symbolize the role of the muse. The 6 **solar** songs reflect the continued blossoming of the awakening process. The "violence" songs suggest further resolution of the shadow, which becomes more pronounced in the liberated Individuation phase to come.

More than previous albums, the lyrical focus is on storytelling, often personal or emotional. There are a variety of characters mentioned, people involved in important turning points. Additionally, there is lighter, more observational storytelling—the transformation of the commonplace into art. The early formula has been completely transcended. In its place are more mature reflections on life, with far greater emotional and spiritual complexity.

Astrological Summary: The Kite remains the central focus, and has now been populated by even more planets. Below is its appearance for the album release with the

Beatles group chart. Also included are the muse {Euterpe} and the Sun, which both play extraordinary roles. (Additional discussion is found in Part 2, p. 388).

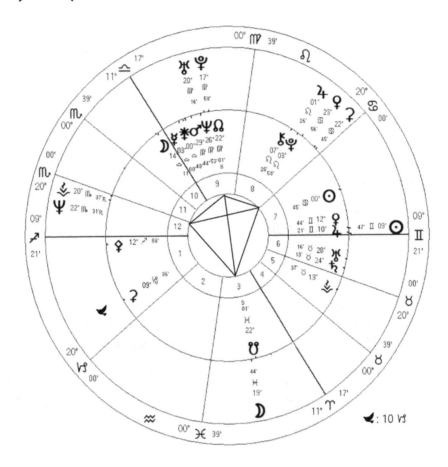

A core Beatles theme is the resolution of death. For the album's release, the signature of death {Moon opposite Pluto} formed the spine of the Kite, situated along the central axis of The Beatles spiritual work {Nodes}. At the Kite's base was unresolved emotional grief {Pisces Moon}, a need for spiritual redemption and healing. At the tip was the "arc of awakening" {Uranus-Pluto}, inviting broader metaphysical experiences and understandings. The resolution would be the emotional and spiritual reunion which defines this story.

The Kite's wing towards the right features the planets composing the Beatles signature {Jupiter-Venus}, along with maternal Ceres. There is a meaningful creative partnership {Jupiter-Venus} with mothers {Ceres} involving the home/roots {Cancer} themes heard on the album. The wing towards the left involves a project {Vesta} of spiritualism {Neptune in Scorpio}. The album's muse {Euterpe} is right on the band's attunement to mothers {Ceres}.

The *Sgt. Pepper* Sun (presence, life force) is on the "Beatles signature" and it's become a signature album. Precisely 2 years prior was the Big Gemini Eclipse {conjunct Euterpe}, the event hypothesized to bring contact with the muse. That eclipse not only lit up the "Beatles signature," but also Julia Lennon's intention to develop as a writer {her

Saturn at 11° Gemini} as well as Mary McCartney's {North Node at 9° Gemini}. The *Sgt. Pepper* Sun {9° Gemini} is at the eclipse degree! Perhaps the seed planted in 1965 had flowered, producing the album Julia and Mary had in mind. So much of the content is *a look at everyday life from above.*

Is this album a collaboration between mothers and sons connecting between worlds? It's impossible to say for sure, but one couldn't design any astrology that would point to that conclusion more emphatically and dramatically. It was upon first seeing this album's astrology that I realized the meaning of this book. Any resistance I previously had to the muse hypothesis slid away. Right then, I decided to dedicate this book to Julia and Mary, the unsung heroines of the story. These women seem to not just inspire Beatles music, they may have been co-creating it from across the boundary of death.

The Beatles wrote many love songs, but it turns out the real love story could be this bridging of worlds—the discovery of love {Moon} through death {Pluto}, and the regeneration of bonds in a new way. The "arc of awakening" involves the raising of consciousness towards other dimensions, just like the magnificent glissando that concludes the album. *Sgt. Pepper* might point us to the heavens to reconnect with our spiritual home. And yet, we need to live on the ground and play the existence game till the end.

The story reaches a climax with this phenomenal album... but what goes up must come down. The "arc's" descent will be rough, like the queasy feeling of being on a jet heading down. Growth is not always about happily ever after, but engaging with necessary spiritual lessons. There will be notes of redemption and grace, and the muse remains active. There is love too, even if it comes down from the spiritual expansion on the mountaintop to some sleepiness on the ground.

Chapter 16
Descension

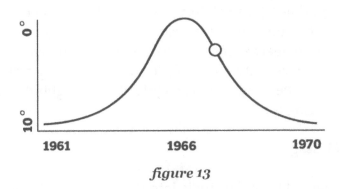

figure 13

    Sgt. Pepper signaled a shift in the band dynamic. Up until the autumn of 1966, John was the undisputed leader of the band he founded. He wrote and sang more songs than Paul, though the tally was close, making for the great rivalry. From this point on, Paul would outwrite John, including several #1 hits. Also, the *Magical Mystery Tour* movie, idea to *Get Back* to the roots, the medley on *Abbey Road* and the grand finale of "Let It Be" were all Paul's influence. *Sgt. Pepper* was the beginning of the Paul-led era. As we'll review soon, "The White Album" was in the middle of it all, where the "gunslingers" fought it out.

    John was glad the album was successful, but likely carried resentment towards Paul for the remainder of the band's active history and beyond. Shortly after the Beatles broke up, he wrote a song attacking Paul titled, "How Do You Sleep?," which appeared on *Imagine* (1971). In the very first line John mentions the album, "So *Sgt. Pepper* took you by surprise/You better see right through that mother's eyes." Interesting that he references "mother," as his maternal issues {Mars station on his Ceres in Scorpio} were activated during the recording. Perhaps he was playing out his core issue in this rivalrous context. In later 1967 John would further deepen with Yoko as his eventual partner, effectively "dumping" Paul. He was beginning to detach from the legend he created, a process that would take a couple of years.

    Paul's ascendency also impacted George and Ringo. George slid back to his historical tendency to defer {Mars retrograde during *Sgt. Pepper*} after his major contributions to *Revolver*. He didn't challenge the situation overtly, rather tensions smoldered under the surface. George played on *Pepper* and participated, but his passion was his own projects. He would say later that his "heart was in India"[211] during the creation of the album. Ringo was largely bored during the sessions as there was so much idle time with the complex studio production. He says he learned how to play chess.[212]

He felt stuck {Saturn crossed his Ascendant during the sessions}. Soon, he would take measures to free himself and come into his own.

Sgt. Pepper came at a critical moment for Paul, right when he was completing a major developmental cycle {progressed lunar cycle}. He was finishing a youthful cycle, picking up on the unmet intentions in his soul to attain visibility as a performer. When the cycle closed, Paul McCartney was one of the most famous performers on the planet. His new cycle began on 6/14/1967 (p. 389), just 2 weeks after Sgt. Pepper was released. It brought lessons about greater leadership, using public visibility to bring a message of love₁. There was major potential expansion, a convergence of his writing with the Beatles chart₂. He would be recognized internationally for his songwriting brilliance and become the most prolific writer in the band. The new cycle also highlighted frustration or anger issues, a lesson of managing conflict₃.

Relaying the Message

The Beatles emerged from the studio into the "Summer of Love," right when the quixotic mood of the fabled time was in the air. The "arc of awakening" was still aloft and the cosmic weather featured added celebratory vibrations {Jupiter in Leo}.

In touch with the spirit of the times, John wrote "All You Need Is Love," an anthem associated with this summer. On the upswing of the "arc," the message of universal love was being developed ("The Word"), delivered at the peak ("Tomorrow Never Knows") and further conceptualized in a philosophical and contemplative fashion ("Within You Without You"). As the "arc" was now descending, it was time to bring it down for broad public consumption. "All You Need Is Love" was widely accessible, in the mode of the emerging progressive-rock genre.

Indicative of the Transcendence period, the song has a broad musical palette. It features a George Martin orchestral arrangement played by string and brass instruments and an accordion. John gets credit for playing the harpsichord and banjo, and George, the violin. A cadre of celebrities and musicians receive credit for backing vocals by virtue of being at the recording.[213] There was also an *event* for this song—a rather big one.

The song was written for a performance on Our World, the first worldwide live television satellite link. The broadcast was on June 25th, and The Beatles performed in their studio. It was seen in 5 continents by an estimated 350—400 million people, the largest television audience to watch a program at the time.[214] There was a 13-piece orchestra, celebrities and other attendees, balloons, flowers, graffiti and streamers. It was a demonstration of the counterculture, a "flower power" showcase of love and optimism.

The song opens repeating the word "love," then John invites the listener to relax into life and learn to live in flow. It mentions ways to put aside the striving of the ego and trust life ("Nowhere you can be that isn't where you're meant to be"). We are encouraged to learn "how to be you in time," to understand spiritual growth (or awakening) as a process of becoming. "All You Need is Love" is the thirtieth *dream* song. "You can learn how to *play the game*" directs and grounds the *dream* perspective into everyday life. The phrase, "*play the game,*" repeats the instruction given in "Tomorrow Never Knows." At the conclusion of the song, both "yesterday" and "she loves you" are mentioned. These references to earlier works are another example of weaving back to the past for completion.

Some found the message in "All You Need Is Love" to be overly simplistic in an increasingly complex world. More edgy factions on the radical left took exception to the pacifism, an issue John would face again soon. The music was criticized for being overconfident {Jupiter in Leo}.[215] Nevertheless, the song became a #1 hit and attained massive widespread appeal. The message resonated with millions, and it's considered both a classic and an anthem, one of the most recognizable and signature of all Beatles songs. It is another example of John's influence in shaping culture. The passion he was soon to put into peace activism is forecast here in his compassion for humanity.

The astrology (p. 390) emphasized a message {Mercury} of love {Cancer}, which connects to collective spiritual unity {Mercury trine Neptune}. The underlying motivation was for global togetherness {Aquarius Moon}, radiated through heart {Cancer Sun, which was quite close to the Beatles Sun, a musical representation of their essence}. A few more notes are found in Part 2.

"Baby, You're a Rich Man" (the B-side of "All You Need is Love"), is the thirty-first *dream* song. On the A-side, John encouraged his audience to "learn how to *play the game*." Flip the single over and he asked, "*what are you going to play?*" The question is for the "beautiful people" (of the hippie movement), seen as posing in their carefully crafted roles. As the "arc" descends, issues of appearances and money, how we exist on the ground, become increasingly relevant. The band would similarly deal with both social and financial issues in the final segment of the story.

Baby, Mother and Guru

Over the summer, the band members went to Greece in search of a remote island to build their own recording studio (which never materialized). Ringo departed first as Maureen was soon to have a baby. George and Pattie left to prepare for their upcoming trip to California. George would spend time in Los Angeles at Ravi Shankar's school, then hop up to San Francisco to witness the Summer of Love in the hippie capital.

Jason Starkey was born on August 19th, adding to Ringo's growing family. Having experienced loneliness as a child, Ringo carries the intention to find abundance in his personal relations, particularly in the area of the home. The astrology between Ringo and Jason (p. 390) depicts the broadening of familial and nurturing signatures in the drummer's chart with an emphasis on creativity and play$_1$.

Meanwhile, Paul brought "Your Mother Should Know" forward for recording on August 22nd. It's the first song in the "mother" thread, a theme that proliferates in the second half. Similar to "When I'm Sixty-Four," it harkens back to previous times with its retro and music hall sound. The words are simple and repetitive, connecting knowledge with mother. The astrology (p. 391) is a literal reflection of "Your Mother Should Know." It features a tight grouping of 3 factors: the Sun (awareness, presence), Ceres (mother) and Mercury (knowledge), all in the sign of theatrical performance {Leo}. The grouping is in major flowing aspect to the muse {trine Euterpe}. Similar to "Penny Lane," the astrology suggests information from (and communication with) the mother/muse is being channeled into creative expression.

George was back in London in later August and brought John and Paul (and wives/girlfriends) to attend a talk given by the Maharishi Mahesh Yogi. After a personal meeting with the guru, they were invited to attend a weekend seminar in Bangor, Wales. When they got to the train station to make the trek, there was commotion and confusion. Cynthia was separated from John and missed the train, which was symbolic of the relationship drifting apart. While at the weekend seminar, they received news which would forever change the band.

Confronting Death

Death is a major issue of this soul group. It was raised in the ascending motion of the "arc," and death songs climaxed at the peak. Now in the descending segment, it was time to deal with its reality. Synchronously, they were beginning more intensive spiritual study with a mentor, who could be of assistance. They learned that Brian Epstein died on August 27th, putting them face-to-face with their core issue. Instantaneously, matters became serious. The fabled Summer of Love was closing and it was time to get real.

Brian had a difficult time the last couple years, especially after the band ceased touring. He was mired in drug and alcohol use and developed a penchant for gambling.[216] He made some poor business decisions that ended up costing the band. In his personal life, he engaged in risky and shadowy behaviors. He apparently enjoyed aggressive sex that was often melodramatic, including having his place trashed and belongings stolen.[217] Biographers state that he derived some kind of pleasure from it. He had mood instability, including bouts of depression where he locked himself in his room and berated himself for hours.[218] He had an unsuccessful suicide attempt in 1966, which included a note.[219]

The astrology in August involved making necessary adjustments to manage reality {on August 8, Venus went retrograde in Virgo, the sign of Brian's Ascendant, Venus, Neptune and Sun}. The passage involved turning within {retrograde} to find connection {Venus}, precisely what the musicians were doing with meditation and introspection. Without a solid inner connection, self-abandonment tendencies or erraticism may play out.

The cause of death was an overdose of sleeping pills and alcohol. It was ruled accidental, though some contend that it was suicide—either intentional or not. It was a complete shock to the band and everyone associated with them. More than any other event, this is perhaps the biggest turning point in The Beatles biography (according to John's assessment in a *Rolling Stone* interview in 1970).[220] It was the start of the unraveling and triggered the next lessons of their spiritual maturation.

Brian had deep wounds regarding self-love {Moon opposite Pluto, the Beatles death signature}. Connecting with universal love was the core work of the Beatles and precisely the message of the recent single. However, these issues run deep and were

185

something Brian struggled with for a long time. His is a cautionary tale of how emotional wounds might play out should we not mature and awaken into the healing balm of love.

At the time of his death, there was great intensity at the core of his heart {Mars in Scorpio in his 4th House}, while the proverbial "Reaper" was in his area of death {Saturn in his 8th}₁. Nurturance issues were highlighted {Ceres exactly on his Ascendant}₂. The astrology (p. 391) suggests that romantic loneliness was an underlying issue₃. Whether or not his demise was accidental, Epstein was confronting his deepest pain.

The Fall of 1967

While George was in San Francisco, he played an impromptu rendition of "Baby, You're a Rich Man." Someone handed him a guitar and he led a crowd along as if he was the star of a movie. He saw the celebratory vibe, but also strung-out hippies and drop outs, and didn't get a sense that authentic spiritual questing was the priority. There was a lot of drug use and it wasn't always beautiful.

The band was still using a lot of drugs. Paul publicly admitted experimenting with LSD in June,[221] creating a public relations mess for the band. Drugs were shifting from being enhancing to an impediment. Substance use may have been partly for medicating deeper emotional issues. At this time, it was prudent to become more focused and grounded. Brian's death was a sobering wake up call. Instead of taking time off to grieve, communicate and reflect, they decided to create something "magical."

The fall of 1967 takes on a double meaning—the autumn devolved into a downward spiral. To provide context: When *Sgt. Pepper* was released on June 1st, the "arc" was 2°18' and separating. At the end of the year, when the *Magical Mystery Tour* movie was released on December 26th, it was at 6°19'. Like a ski slope, it was a precipitous energetic drop.

The bottom was falling out and they were struggling to manage it. In particular, there was a need to become more organized with creative projects {Venus retrograde in Virgo}. Being the most diligent and focused, Paul {Virgo Ascendant} continued to step forward to help fill the management void. John was more of a conceptual visionary rather than an organized manager. Paul was more interested in technical matters and details.

They began filming *Magical Mystery Tour* on September 11th {during the Venus retrograde} and the film would ultimately become a study of its traps. Planets move retrograde all of the time, and on any given day there is likely to be a planet traveling "backwards." Nothing is necessarily doomed if it begins under a particular retrograde passage *if the spirit of the retrograde is integrated*. This particular passage {Venus in Virgo retrograde} demands a concrete and well thought out plan, and the ability to execute that plan with focused teamwork. Filming was mainly improvised, lacking foresight to deal with many logistics.[222] The sloppiness of the project made it their biggest embarrassment, contributing to their downward spiral.

They were part of the ethereal nature of the times, mixing with all sorts of groovy people and their fantastic ideas, being famous and partying. Though unable to executively manage movie production and business issues, they were still highly creative and inspired. The autumn of 1967 would produce several notable songs in the Transcendence period.

Hello Walrus

John's "I Am the Walrus" was the first song recorded after news of Brian's death. The first session occurred on September 5th, just 9 days after the tragedy. John was the closest with Brian and he processed some of his emotion on this song. Psychedelic and rambunctious, it's darker than anything on *Sgt. Pepper*. It introduces incoherence (both lyrically and musically), delivered with an edge. John's snarling singing style added to its unique rebellious ambience, driven by his emotional state.

The lyrics were intentionally confusing and nonsensical. John liked to put hidden meanings into his lyrics {natal Mercury in Scorpio}, revealing parts of himself, but also using the song platform to be provocative. Analyzing and interpreting Beatles lyrics increasingly became a fascination. Many are convinced there are deeper dimensions (and this study would of course agree!), but it's a speculative enterprise that may contain bias. (Here, the interpretations are informed by the broader organization of astrology. My translations may also have bias, a hazard in any endeavor.)

John was intentionally being mischievous. There was an assemblage of nonsense phrases, made-up words and general linguistic chaos impossible to decipher, mainly because parts may or may not have any intentional meaning. He belts out that he is the walrus, an emblematic moment in the Transcendence phase. John was playing a character, inviting us to create our own meaning. After the Beatles broke up, he wrote in the song "God" that he is no longer playing the part of the walrus, he's back to being John. For "I Am the Walrus," he was prodding us to allow the imagination to soar into levels of unreality, inside the dream where "nothing is real." Like the message in "Nowhere Man," he was in command, using the creativity of dreaming however he wants.

The song derives from a section in *Through the Looking-Glass* called "The Walrus and the Carpenter," and John said much of the other content was influenced by LSD.[223] There are 3 unfinished song fragments woven together: hearing a police siren, an experience sitting in a garden, and the fantastic idea of sitting on a corn flake. John also mentions "Lucy in the sky," a strong reference to the *Sgt. Pepper* song. Though he has taken exception to the practice of analyzing his lyrics, he was offering the bait to make linkages to other works, a practice that would continue.

"I Am the Walrus" is the twenty-second **solar** and seventh "rain" song. John writes of sitting in a "garden waiting for the **sun**." Should it not arrive, "you get a tan from standing in the English rain." Though likely unintentional, there is spiritual relevance when examined symbolically, or even psychedelically. Now that rain is no longer negative ("Rain"), the next step is to see Spirit in it as *everything* is part of the eternal flame of Oneness.

"I Am the Walrus": The entire world is ensouled.

Though one wouldn't literally get a tan from the rain, spiritual energy {fire element} is pervasive throughout life. Still in the Transcendence period, the song's opening line is also noteworthy. "I am he as you are he as you are me and we are all together," speaks of the transcendence of individual identity, the idea that we are all reflections of one another. "I Am the Walrus" is the thirty-second *dream* song as it features flying pigs, singing penguins and all sorts of disjointed mayhem and symbolic layers as we might experience in a *dream*. The music portrayed such atmospherics, which was greatly assisted by George Martin's production and orchestration.

Whereas John was pushing the psychedelic envelope further post *Sgt. Pepper*, Paul's "Hello Goodbye" is a movement towards simplicity. Recorded a few weeks later on October 2nd, the song features the interplay of duality, the tension of opposites. Paul has specifically said "Hello Goodbye" is influenced by being a Gemini {Sun}. He uses rudimentary parings (yes/no, stop/go, high/low, hello/goodbye) to illustrate dualistic interplay, and the music is similarly basic and engaging (more pop than rock). It features bongos and conga in addition to piano, which was becoming a more central instrument.

Gemini also involves communication, perhaps pointing to the deeper story. A repeating line is, "I don't know why you say goodbye, I say hello." At this point, John was starting to detach from Paul, while Paul wanted to maintain cohesion—not only with John, but also in the band. This particular song would create divisiveness between the musicians. "Hello Goodbye" was chosen by George Martin to be the A-side of a single, while "I Am the Walrus" became the B-side. John was miffed and upset, proclaiming "Can you believe that?"[224] in bewilderment. By virtue of being the A-side, "Hello Goodbye" became a #1 hit. It's another example of Paul's emerging leadership at this time, stoking underlying resentment from John. A lesson of the "arc's" descent was less ego attachment, but their rivalry would only become more pronounced.

Both songs are notable for a false ending. "Hello Goodbye" returns from a fadeout to feature Paul's vocal improvisations over a shuffling beat, while the return in "I Am the Walrus" has lines from *King Lear*. These lines mention "bury my body" and "untimely death," providing fodder for the "Paul is Dead" hoax (reviewed later).

The astrology for the release of the singles (11/24/67, see p. 392) features a tense square off between sunny (Paul, "Hello Goodbye") and dark (John, "I Am the Walrus)$_1$. There's an emotionally charged dynamic regarding communications$_2$. The rivalrous writing dynamic in the John-Paul relationship chart was being set off$_3$.

Clearing the Fog

Sessions began for "Blue Jay Way" on September 6th. The title makes it the third "bird" song and it's also the thirty-third *dream* song. George sang about his experience in Los Angeles the prior month, waiting for friends who were very late to join him. George wrote, "they've lost themselves" in the "fog" in the streets. The need to rediscover oneself by lifting the fog is analogous to clearing any cloudiness in the dream.

On the California trip, George was dismayed by the drug excess he witnessed. After telling John about it, they publicly denounced LSD and promoted the clarity of meditation.[225] Ian MacDonald calls "Blue Jay Way" a "farewell to psychedelia."[226] The atmospherics are ethereal, but the somber mood and lyrics give the sensation of coming down into realism. The necessity of George having to wait is consistent with developing the patience required to live a grounded life in the everyday world. It would follow the evolutionary trajectory (the "arc's" descent) to be drug-free. How can the vision from the mountaintop become most embodied? "Blue Jay Way" represents the pivotal lesson of fogginess vs. clarity on the spiritual path.

The music is notable for the studio effects, George's use of keyboards and also features a cello. It is influenced by Indian musical sensibilities (including a drone effect), but George creates the song using Western instrumentation.

The Muse in Flight

Instrumentals are rare for this band, as well as all four members receiving writing credit for a song. For the *Magical Mystery Tour* movie, the instrumental was originally titled, "Aerial Tour Instrumental," later changed to "Flying." The song would be used in a flyover scene, the Earth surveyed from the air. The view from above to below reflects the downward motion of the "arc."

Though all the members perform and get credit, the song was led by John who plays the lead part on the Mellotron.[227] It's the sixth "flute" song as (similar to "Strawberry Fields Forever") the Mellotron produces a flute-like sound (which is most evident in second half of the song). As the astrology dramatically reveals, it's a musical testament to the muse.

There was another Kite in the sky at this time, made possible by the inclusion of the muse {Euterpe}. It is featured below, cast for when sessions for "Flying" began on September 8th.

The Kite's spine is created by the axis of spiritual work {Lunar Nodes}, with an echo of the "Beatles signature" {Jupiter-Venus conjunction, with Ceres too} at one wing and the muse {Euterpe} at the other. Taken all together, the configuration speaks of the muse partnerships making Beatles music with a lofty, adventurous reach$_1$. The evolutionary motion is towards an earth house {North Node in the 2nd}—to ground inspiration into an embodied spirituality, following the descent of the "arc's" trajectory$_2$.

In "Lucy in the Sky with Diamonds," Lucy was positioned on the Ascendant, at the gate between worlds. Here the rising degree of the "Flying" chart {0° Pisces} is right on Julia's natal muse {1° Pisces}, pointing to her presence in this role$_3$.

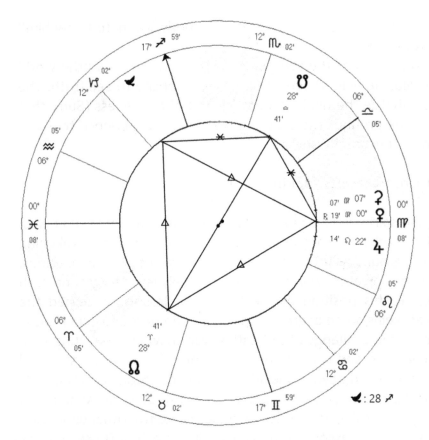

Additionally, the muse attunement of John, Paul and Mary can also be seen in the chart₄. The song may be a musical celebration of the muse as it's called "Flying" and features a Kite, contains flute-like sounds and the astrology points to the muse attunements for the songwriters and their mothers.

The Sun Going Down

Sessions for Paul's "The Fool on the Hill" began on September 25th, the major work in the autumn. It's the twenty-third **solar** and sixth "flute" song, showcasing a brilliant teaching from the Paul-Mary partnership. Indicative of Step 4 (collaboration) of the muse process, it's also a defining song for this position of the "arc."

As the "arc" descended, the work was to make spirituality accessible. Messages may come in the form of intuitions, received in dreams or noticed in synchronicities that awaken the mind. Most of the time, teachings are brought to us by teachers. In whatever form they take, they must be clear and comprehensible to make an impact in everyday life. Intuition can be ignored; dreams can be foggy and synchronicities can be missed. We might initially misconstrue a wise teacher for a fool (and sometimes there are false prophets, charlatans and misguided teachings making it tricky).

Paul claims the song was influenced by the archetype of the guru (and he recently met the Maharishi Mahesh Yogi).(228) The song depicts the wise figure who's misunderstood, not taken seriously. The Fool is alone on a hill, the proverbial mountaintop mirrored by the "arc." As discussed, the motion through the "arc" is on a spectrum from denser and darker below, to lighter and brighter above. The Fool is above, with his "head in the cloud" (ascended), "keeping perfectly still," signifying meditative receptivity. He's the "man of a thousand voices" (many teachings) who's "talking perfectly loud"

190

(delivering the message), but it's unable to be received. "Nobody wants to know him" suggests his isolation and ostracism.

From his lofty position, he "sees the **sun** going down," able to view "the world spinning round." He has a valuable heightened perspective, an ability to see truth. The "**sun** going down" might symbolize the diminishment (down) of awareness (Sun), that typifies conventional life on the ground. The teaching is everyday experience tends to have some degree of darkness (unconsciousness).

"Fool on the Hill": There are levels of spiritual realization.

Most models of psycho-spiritual development feature phases or stages of growth (like Paul's suggestion of 7 levels), an increase in awareness as spiritual awakening develops. We all begin on the ground as proverbial saplings, immature and unconscious, that's the way of it. We rise into greater awareness and ultimately learn to ground such illumination. For this song, at this position of the "arc," the lesson concerned the reintegration into life after attaining some degree of spiritual awareness and experience.

The lesson also mimics the challenges the Beatles were having connecting with part of their audience. The growth and change the last couple of years was rapid and profound, they had completely moved beyond the adolescent consciousness of the early formula and its massive popularity. Songs like "Tomorrow Never Knows" or "Within You Without You" flew over many peoples' heads. Messages which contain another dimension or perspective can bring confusion or discomfort and are easily distorted. Those who are not on the same wavelength often dismiss or sometimes ridicule what is not understood. It is the test of the "Fool" to keep perfectly still in his truth regardless. He "knows that they're the fools," willing to tolerate their projection (of being foolish) and "never listens to them."

"The Fool on the Hill" features 3 flutes and Paul is credited with playing a recorder and penny whistle,[229] part of the flute family. It rivals "Penny Lane" as the Beatles song that features the instrument most. And like that song, "The Fool on the Hill" is one of the purest and clearest examples of the muse.

Consistent with Paul-Mary collaborations, Mary might be revealing herself through the story. She could be the wise figure up in the clouds who has spiritual teachings not easily grasped. The song's astrology (p. 393) positions the muse at the pinnacle of the sky {Euterpe at the Midheaven}$_1$. She makes her message accessible by connecting down to earth through collaborative partnership in projects {Euterpe trine Libra Sun in the 6th House}$_2$. The overwhelming focus of the chart is on teachings$_3$. There is an echo of the "Beatles signature," which is being informed by deeper spirituality and complexity$_4$.

Further maturation involves the willingness to stand alone {Saturn in Aries on the Ascendant}$_5$, foreshadowing the Individuation phase to come. The evolutionary motion of the chart is towards broader spiritual discovery, which may include travels or cross-cultural experiences$_6$. Synchronously, now that the band has met the Maharishi, they will soon follow him to India.

Chapter 17
Amusement

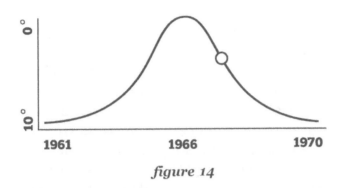

figure 14

The title for this chapter has a double meaning. The first few essays concern the amusement of entertainment products: The *Magical Mystery Tour* album and film, and the *Yellow Submarine* film. Next, the focus shifts to songs that are hypothesized to be collaborations with the muse. At this point, she remains quite active and these songs are particularly revealing of her influence. This chapter closes out the Transcendence phase with some final songs illustrating its spiritual reach.

Album #9: *Magical Mystery Tour*

Introduction: Magical Mystery Tour is another example of corporate interests pushing a product to maximize profit. A full-length album was released in the U.S. on November 27, 1967, while a shorter EP was released in the UK on December 8th. The music was available right in time for the holidays, building from the momentum of *Sgt. Pepper's* recent success. The full-length album is addressed here.

The first side contained songs from the movie, while the second was a collection of recent singles. The band was historically resistant to including already released singles on albums, so this was a business-driven decision. Nevertheless, the album features the singles "Strawberry Fields Forever," "Penny Lane," "All You Need is Love," "Baby, You're a Rich Man," "Hello Goodbye" and "I Am the Walrus" (released both as a single and also in the movie). Together with "Fool on the Hill" (not a single, but a standout song from the movie), this album is among their finest releases, with several legendary and popular songs.

Though the film was criticized, the songs remain classic Beatles. Typical of the Transcendence period, the tunes are marked by exploration, psychedelia and (critics argue) some lack focus. Most of the songs are now at least 3 minutes long and none are in the early formula. Paul contributes the most material to this album, including the title track. John only contributes one song to the movie ("I Am the Walrus"), while receiving credit for co-writing the instrumental "Flying." The single "Lady Madonna" and B-side "The Inner **Light**" were created and released shortly after this album. They will be included in this discussion (instead of with "The White Album," which has 32 songs to address).

Musical Development: There is more use of piano and keyboards, especially by Paul, who was composing this way and developing greater proficiency. Sound experimentation and a diversity of instruments set the tone. Included are trumpets, recorder, penny whistle, flutes, harp, cellos, harmonium, handbell, maracas, orchestral arrangements, a clavioline and a güiro.[230] In 1967, the counterculture had emerged amid its optimism and confusion. Similarly, the songs show brilliance and innovation and critics allege the movie songs contain some degree of incoherence. The singles tend to be more crafted and professional, leading the emerging progressive-rock movement.

The movie songs are quite unique. "Flying" is a rare instrumental with wordless vocalizations. "Baby You're a Rich Man" is applauded for its unique mood and use of the exotic clavioline. Its Indian-flavored sound is somewhat flute-like, but not counted in the thread. "Blue Jay Way" continues George's Indian-influenced experimentation with an assemblage of studio effects. "Magical Mystery Tour" draws comparisons to the opening title track for *Sgt. Pepper*, though some contend it's less inspired. "Your Mother Should Know" is a retro piece evoking the music hall style.

Lyrical Development: The collection includes 13 songs (11 on the *MMT* album and 2 singles) registering with 23 placements in the lyrical themes: 7 *dream*, 5 "flute," 4 **solar**, 2 "mother" and 1 "bird" song, creating lofty and inspired soundscapes possibly featuring a partnership with the muse. There are also 2 "rain," 1 death and 1 "dark" song, portraying further emotional work, though less urgent than before. "Flute" songs peak at this time, dropping off almost completely after the Transcendence phase. "Your Mother Should Know" is the first "mother" song, then "Lady Madonna" takes it further, adding additional *dream* and muse elements (and will be discussed shortly). George's "Inner **Light**" is a **solar** song about contemplation (also discussed shortly). "Magical Mystery Tour" is technically the twenty-second death song with the line, "Dying to take you away." Though this lyrical use may seem unremarkable, it's an example of how death-related words were easily available in their consciousness.

Astrological Summary: The astrology of *Magical Mystery Tour* (p. 395) involved issues of status and reputation, what they might do with their elevated stature as cultural leaders. Their prior conciliatory stance towards corporate pressures was being worked through. The intersection of business interests with spiritual meaning was a lesson to address[1]. Challenges of communication are also a notable theme[2].

The suggested evolutionary direction was towards self-governance[3]. Soon after this album, the Beatles created Apple records as a declaration of their independence. At this time, earthy issues (business, management, finances) were becoming more pressing. Finding spiritual direction in everyday pragmatics was the work, consistent with this position of the "arc's" descent[4].

As a whole, *Magical Mystery Tour* was a major addition to their music catalog, with strong resonance in the mainstream_s. However, the astrology is not nearly as "magical" as it was earlier; it reveals tension with business and raises questions of spiritual purpose.

The *Magical Mystery Tour* Movie

Whereas the *Magical Mystery Tour* album became a "must have" Beatles collectible, the film would not be as widely appreciated. Though it garnered poor reviews, there actually is something "magical." The movie fits perfectly with the lessons of the "arc's" descent, a visual portrayal of the spiritual work written about in recent songs. It is increasingly clear that the Beatles were conduits for spiritual lessons (and teachings) operating *through* them.

Though improvised, it was understood that Ringo would get the most screen time. He was the actor of the band and this was another chance to promote him from his junior status. Early scenes show him frustrated, arguing with his aunt. There is a back-and-forth banter, a "he said, she said" dynamic. Communication breakdown and polarization was also the theme of "Hello Goodbye."

Members of the tour competitively race around a circular track in different modes of transportation. Ringo is able to win by commandeering the bus itself. The "going in circles" theme is indicative of the aimlessness of the project and illustrative of the band functioning without a manager. John would later say that Paul led the band in circles after Brian died.[231] The theme is also relevant for the unconscious components of the broader countercultural movement. The spiritual lesson put forth in "Blue Jay Way" was being lost, the fogginess of wandering without clarity of direction.

The Beatles wear costumes of the magician or seer. They are magically able to watch over the developments of the tour from a removed location, looking down at the action from above. Removed observation from on high (while wearing the garb of the seer), depicts the situation in "Fool on the Hill."

In another scene, an army officer is shouting incoherently. An army officer is representative of order, but there is confusion about his message. On his desk a sign reads, "I you WAS," which has some resemblance to "I Am the Walrus." In that song, there are incomprehensible lyrics as well as a policeman. The issue in both the movie scene and song is the gap between communication intention and reception by a listener.

Later on, members of the tour enter a small tent. They "magically" find themselves transported to a movie theater, a visual depiction of the *dream* theme. On the screen is a video for George's "Blue Jay Way," a *dream* song. The video ("Blue Jay Way") is a movie within this movie (*Magical Mystery Tour*) within the movie of our projections.

There are two scenes featuring indulgence. In one, John shovels spaghetti onto a fat woman's dinner plate. In the other, tour members are attending a strip show. Both are illustrative of the personality feeding itself, through gluttony and glamour. "Baby You're a Rich Man" mentions the hoarding of resources ("You keep all your money in a big brown bag"), as well as the seduction of the beautiful people.

At the end of the movie, the quartet descends down a staircase for the "Your Mother Should Know" scene in the order of: Paul, John, George then Ringo. The motion downstairs is a visual representation of the "arc's" descent, while their order depicts the leadership change. Some like to note that Paul is wearing a black carnation, while the other 3 Beatles have red ones.

The movie teaches that without a plan, we are prone to going in circles. It's important to learn how to communicate comprehensibly and effectively. It serves us to come down from the proverbial mountaintop and engage the human drama. We can be aware of the projection phenomenon, realizing the subjectivity to life. By so doing, we are less prone to getting seduced by the personality's hungers and desires.

Whereas the expansive Kite configuration defined *Sgt. Pepper*, the *Magical Mystery Tour* movie had astrological stress. There was another geometrical figure in the sky, this time the more conflictual "Grand Cross" (p. 396). The cross is a circuit of friction that challenges the learning of necessary lessons, often through difficulty. This one involved issues of erratic organization, leadership and friction with business pressures.

There was also a focus on adventure, the planet of journeys {Jupiter} was moving through the band's area of travel and adventure {9th House}. However, this particular expression of the energy {Jupiter retrograde in Virgo} would require planning and attention to detail to bring out its potential. More notes are found in Part 2 (p. 396).

Depiction of the Dream

The animated *Yellow Submarine* movie was being made in 1967 during the Transcendence phase. Surprisingly delightful, it's an excellent visual representation of the *dream* theme. With unlimited visual possibilities, animation is a perfect medium. The film seized full creative advantage, synchronously depicting the spirit of several notable *dream* songs.

At its core, the film is about the imagination. It portrays the utter subjectivity of experience, how consciousness is able to shape reality. Consistent with the "Beatles signature" in Gemini, there's an emphasis on language: puns, word play and jokes, many words displayed in animation. The submarine's yellow color is reflective of the Sun. Immersed in the water, it gives a visual depiction of navigating consciousness (*dream* theme) on the path of awakening (**solar** theme), the unification of these major threads.

Regressive, immature or wounding elements residing in consciousness must be addressed on the journey towards wholeness. Such phenomena are depicted by the Blue Meanies, the *dream* material that is not conscious. They tend to be violent and cruel, both part of the shadow of the musicians. During the Personality phases, the band often wrote of "feeling blue," and this was associated with personal struggle and compromised mood. The movie can be viewed as a battle to resolve such feelings. The Blue Meanies shrink at the sound of uplifting, joyful Beatles music, their more awake gift and purpose. Ultimately, community and togetherness are established by such music, exemplifying the preeminent Beatles theme.

The beginning features their spiritual childhoods. Ringo is first depicted as a loner and says, "Nothing happens to me." He ends up finding his bandmates and experiences musical togetherness, precisely the work of his chart. John emerges from the head of Frankenstein, an illustration of his electrical brilliance. He first mentions a strange dream he had, pointing to his visionary background. George is initially depicted way up high and removed, consistent with his need for retreat. Paul is first seen receiving flowers and adoration, reflecting his early needs for validation.

George drives a car that miraculously changes colors. He utters a recurring line, "It's all in the mind," capturing the subjectivity of the *dream* thread. Throughout the movie are phenomena that morph and change, indicative of the perceptual shifts in the fluidity of dreams. The submarine first visits Liverpool (Beatles roots) for the "Eleanor Rigby" segment. For this dream song, people are portrayed as characters displaying repetitive movements, going through the motions of life. Not only does this represent a theme of the song, the lyric, "lives in a *dream*," is visually displayed.

Next, the submarine visits the Sea of Time. Here, there's a distortion of both time and space, indicative of dreams. The Beatles become smaller and younger, then older and bigger. Time travel is portrayed—the submarine sees a version of itself floating by. The time-travelling dream song, "When I'm Sixty-Four," is part of this scene.

The Sea of Science features "Only a Northern Song." Its discordant flavor is accompanied by lights flashing—the mind is like an electrical storm of connection. The Sea of Monsters features artifacts in the psyche, literally floating around in consciousness. It contains contents from the collective consciousness, our shared historical experiences that include cowboys and Indians and archetypal fears (portrayed as monsters). The old sailor delivers the line, "By Neptune's Knickerbockers, she's puttered out," referencing the dream planet.

In the Sea of Nothing they meet a character named Jeremy, with "Nowhere Man" the featured *dream* song. Consistent with its spiritual meaning, Jeremy's message is we're the authors of our own experience. Anything is possible from the creative void of nothingness. He is busy with numerous projects, a designer of creation. He uses word play and rhyme, showing how the mind is capable of endless possibilities.

Next is a tour through The Foothills of the Headlands, with the *dream* song, "Lucy in the Sky with Diamonds." Dreams form in the various heads with swirling colors and shapes, a malleability of experience. The Sea of Holes contains several references to the *dream* song, "A Day in the Life." The holes can be thought of like worm holes, showing how everything is interconnected through mysterious pathways. Also consistent with the theme of synchronicity in the song, the phrase, "causal causation," is used here.

The *dream* song, "All You Need Is Love," is a celebration of love triumphing. At the conclusion, the band meets themselves, just as we confront ourselves in our dreams. The John character says, "You're an extension of my personality," while his counterpart replies, "Yes, I'm the alter-ego man." There are many flowers blooming, in a variety of shapes and colors—a symbolic visualization of how everyone awakens in their own way. Finally, the *dream* song, "It's All Too Much," plays. It's noted for love that's shining all around, the realization of dreams. The actual band members do a live action cameo at the end, further suggestive of blending realities or dimensions.

Inner Visions

In February 1968, the 3 main songwriters composed songs with important spiritual relevance. The muse was particularly active in early 1968, seen by the travels of her associated asteroid, Euterpe. Paul renewed his muse attunement {Euterpe return in Capricorn} over the winter, while she arrived at John's intuitively metaphysical disposition {conjunct his Aquarius Moon}. She would also be active in the Beatles group chart {Euterpe return in Aquarius}, highlighting her importance for the band itself.

Paul wrote a song about mothers (with a metaphysical twist), while John received a striking poetic vision of the cosmos. George deepened his philosophical studies and created innovative music with important contemplative teaching. Below are 3 subsections for the songs created during this time of inner visionary work that concludes the Transcendence phase.

Inner Visions #1: Mary's Transformation

Paul began to discuss motherhood more directly on "Your Mother Should Know." The second "mother" song, "Lady Madonna," makes it more personal. On February 3rd, sessions started for the piano-driven boogie, an ode of appreciation to motherhood on many levels. The word "Madonna" calls forth a virtuous, idealized and heavenly version of the archetype, one with obvious religious overtones. Paul says the song celebrates motherhood in general,[232] and there's reason to believe it's also about Mary. The maternal figure in the song evokes Mary McCartney, who cared for others in a selfless way.

The song begins with the trials and tribulations of the traditional maternal role, a job rife with responsibilities and problem-solving. Among the many things to attend to, financial questions, "wonder how you manage to make ends meet," are raised. Paul was born to a family of modest means, one with palpable financial anxiety. When Mary died, Paul was worried how the family would survive without her monetary contribution.

The karmic pattern in Paul's chart suggests themes of drudgery and service related to financial hardship. Due to such responsibilities, his creative dream is sacrificed. The present lifetime involves the emergence from prior toil into the heights of imaginative creativity. Mary is a soul mate to Paul, reflecting and sharing the issue for them to work through. As she was getting increasingly more ill in 1956, Mary worked tirelessly, right up to her death to help provide for her family.[233]

"Lady Madonna" is the thirty-fourth *dream* song. The lyrics describe intuitive receptivity with music, a core Beatles theme. Lady Madonna spends time "lying on the bed," where she hears "the music playing in your head." She enters a creative meditative state, exactly what Paul and John are doing a lot of lately. Mary *dreams a life where she can do something more imaginative*, instead of just tiresome work. "Lady Madonna" is also the twenty-second "dark" song ("night"), consistent with venturing into the unconscious.

Lady Madonna's interest in intuition and music may be alluding to Mary's transformation into the muse. In this evolutionary approach to astrology, every chart is explored as a developmental journey of awakening or becoming. The astrology for "Lady Madonna" (p. 397) illustrates the trajectory from domestic/caretaking responsibility towards a reinvented metaphysical presence, specifically the muse. In fact, it *perfectly* connects with the muse attunement of The Beatles! The analysis in Part 2 provides a step-by-step discussion to see it explained astrologically.

The spiritual dimension to "Lady Madonna" is an illustration of Mary's journey. Typical of Paul-Mary collaborations (as seen in "Eleanor Rigby," "Penny Lane" and "The Fool on the Hill"), Mary inserts herself into the story, hidden in the characters and plot lines. She and Paul are the storytellers, who are also telling us their story through allegory and intimations. It is deciphered through the metaphysical lens of astrology, further revealing the amazing role of the muse.

Inner Visions #2: Julia's Poetry

In early 1968 John was developing "Across the Universe," a song he says was delivered through intuitive channels. While lying on his bed, he claims the words were "purely inspirational and were given to me as *boom!* I don't own it you know; it came through like that."[234] A few years earlier, Paul was concerned about plagiarism with "Yesterday" as he didn't feel that song was his. Of course, these remarkable statements support the hypothesis of this book. John's first attempt at capturing the song was on February 4th, the day after Paul's "Lady Madonna" session.

If John "don't own it," then who does? He says the song "came through," but from whom and how? Other songs are speculated to be inspired, meaning what John and Paul were writing may be their own personalized version of such inspiration. For reasons explained below, "Across the Universe" may be the clearest example of actual words coming directly from the muse.

The evolutionary motion in Julia's chart was towards metaphysically-oriented writing. Her potential was to bring poetry and feeling to complicated spiritual ideas. As her life was cut short, she didn't get to develop such potential. However, the astrology in early 1968 was lighting up her chart, bringing her spiritual work to a climax (p. 398).

"Across the Universe" is the thirty-fifth *dream* song as it arrived in a *dream* state. Also, it extends the usual notion of consciousness as being only personal, to having the unlimited expansiveness suggested by the title (and also reflecting George's, "show me that I'm everywhere"). John sings that "words" can flow like "rain into a paper cup." Words {Mercury} flowing like rain {Pisces} suggests the contents within consciousness (words) may travel through the air. At the time of the song's recording, the astrological weather was consistent with such an idea {Mercury at 1⁰ Pisces}. The amazing part is Julia's muse {her Euterpe at 1⁰ Pisces} was at the very same place. Yes, Julia's muse attunement was in precise alignment with the spiritual ideas being sung. John said, "I kept hearing these words {Mercury} over and over, like an endless *stream* {Pisces}."[235] More than any other combination in astrology, this particular one {Mercury in Pisces} correlates with sharing personal ideas {Mercury} through the collective consciousness {Pisces}.

"Across the Universe" is the eighth "rain" song, one bringing the thread to a spiritual climax. During the Transcendence phase, rain is no longer perceived as negative ("Rain"), it's understood more clearly ("Penny Lane") as part of healing ("Fixing A Hole"), and reconceived as part of Oneness ("I Am the Walrus"). Now it's understood as mystical nourishment, collected in a paper cup to revitalize the system. A paper cup is tangible, signifying the grounding of spiritual nourishment to the earth realm, consistent with the "arc's" descent. Rain is a metaphor for Julia speaking {Mercury} mystically {Pisces} to her son for healing, a showering from the heavens to bathe his heart.

John speaks of such nourishment with water imagery ("pools of sorrow" and "waves of joy"). More travel through consciousness is noted ("drifting through my opened mind"), which is nurturing and maternal ("possessing and caressing me"). A pool is a collection of water previously gathered, analogous to the astrological Moon, the basin of absorbed experience. John carries sorrow from the past. Waves are created by activity, the stirring of motion in the present. There are now "waves of joy" created by this downpour of divine love, made possible by his receptivity ("my opened mind").

The result of such mystical transmission is healing. The song continues with the Sanskrit line, "Jai Guru Deva Om." One interpretation is "glory to the **shining** remover of darkness,"[236] a sentiment consistent with spiritual awakening. "Nothing's gonna change my world" shows peace and solitude in the present, unperturbed by external events. Previously, John became highly reactive to the words or deeds of others (as seen in the pummeling of Bob Wooler).

"Across the Universe" is the twenty-fourth **solar** song, delivering a profound teaching. The song continues, "Images of broken **light**, which/Dance before me like a million eyes." A spiritual interpretation concerns the dance between Oneness and duality, a cosmic reunion. The Oneness of unified awareness (**light**) sees itself through a "million eyes" of separation.

Across the Universe: Spirit (Oneness) meets itself through the sacred reflection in separation.

"Across the Universe" is the twenty-seventh "call song," another where a call is coming in ("They call me on and on…"). The experience of such connection brings an increased sense of well-being. There are "sounds of laughter" and "shades of life" ringing through John's "opened ears." It's a complete turnaround from the crying about death in his prior spiritual deafness, when he couldn't hear the call. Now there's joy and presence, leading to another teaching: "Limitless undying love, which/**Shines** around me like a million **suns**." Similar to the eternality of light splitting apart in separation consciousness to meet itself, enduring spiritual love also separates in the dualistic world.

Across the Universe: Love is reflected throughout the realm of separation.

"Across the Universe" is also the fourth "bird" song, another association with the muse. The first version was released on the environmental charity album, *No One's Gonna Change Our World*. It featured 20 seconds of bird noises and fluttering to open the song. (It can be found on the Beatles *Past Masters* CD in the boxed set.) Another version later appeared on *Let It Be* (1970). On the 40th anniversary of the song's initial recording (2/4/2008), NASA transmitted the interstellar radio message "Across the Universe" towards the star Polaris, thematically repeating the essence of the song.[237]

As for Julia's possible writing contribution, the lyrics seem to have a different voice compared to John's other works. Astrologically, the song has Mercury in Pisces, like Julia. It is flowing, meandering, impressionistic and uplifting. John's style {Mercury in Scorpio} tends to be probing, subversive, clever and mischievous—especially during the later years (as seen with the recent "I Am the Walrus" and his upcoming work on "The White Album"). It's a speculation supported by the astrology, but it's offered as a possibility to ponder rather than a declaration. Part 2 has additional analysis of Julia with this song, and the song itself.

"Lady Madonna" is a prime example Paul-Mary storytelling, while "Across the Universe" is characteristic of the metaphysical reach of John-Julia collaborations. Both songs arrive when the muse is particularly highlighted, right when the Transcendence phase is concluding. Though the muse will appear for some important shadow work on "The White Album," then to say goodbye, the soaring heights of discovery is closing. These songs are the last ones of Step 4 (collaboration) of the muse process.

"Lady Madonna" went on to become a #1 hit single and bolstered Paul's reputation as a master songsmith. It was released shortly after it was recorded and gave momentum to his leadership. In contrast, "Across the Universe" couldn't be completed to John's satisfaction and was shelved for months. Nevertheless, history has been very kind to the preternatural song. Many consider it a gem in the song catalog, a fan favorite. There was a movie named for it in 2007 featuring Beatles themes, and it has numerous cover versions.

Inner Visions #3: The Light Within

George was in India in January working on his solo album *Wonderwall Music*. During recording sessions, he also developed "The Inner **Light**," performed solely by Indian musicians. It's the only Beatles recording to be made outside of Europe. George's vocals were added on February 6th back in London, while John and Paul contributed backing vocals on the 8th. Since "Across the Universe" was not yet completed, "The Inner **Light**" became the B-side to "Lady Madonna," becoming the first George song to appear as a single.

The lyrics were directly influenced by the *Tao Te Ching*,[238] repackaged to fit into a song format. They discuss meditation, while the music is designed to evoke the meditative experience. Whereas "Love You To" and "Within You Without You" were aligned with the North Indian tradition (sitar, tabla), this song was in the South Indian tradition and featured different Indian instrumentation (sarod, shehnai, pakhavaj and bansuri).[239] The bansuri is a bamboo flute, so the Transcendence period concludes with the seventh "flute" song.

The overarching spiritual lesson of the Beatles is the shift from seeking external reward for the personality to finding soul within. George sings, "The farther ones travels, the less one knows." We can get lost in the dream, perhaps what the band initially experienced in the far-reaching travels of Beatlemania. "The Inner **Light**" directs the listener inside for truth, connection and a richness of experience. It's the twenty-fifth **solar** song, one that teaches us of our inherent nature.

"The Inner **Light**": Soul is what we are.

On a spiritual level, light (awareness) and heat (vitality) correlate with the fire element and the soul. Spirit is the eternal flame, the Oneness of all energy. There is often spiritual amnesia (unconsciousness) in the state of separation, an over-identification with personality. George directs his listeners to reconnect with the light within, to rediscover the soul self.

By so doing, there is much to experience. The lyrics describe the benefits available upon such inner connection, "To know all things on Earth" and to "know the ways of Heaven"—an example of bridging above to below. The soul has access to what is beyond the confines of the personality. We connect with the soul intuitively, whereas the personality tends to be more linguistically oriented (Mercury). Making soul contact involves increasing awareness, presence and being, the awakening of the Sun. Instead of the medium of language, there is a direct knowing or feeling that doesn't require ongoing analysis (in fact, mental activity can remove us).

The intuitive knowing has no limits. We might "arrive without traveling" to "see all without looking" and to "do all without doing." The spiritual quest is turned outside-in, precisely the Beatles spiritual work and George's personal philosophical contribution.

"The Inner **Light**" is the first of a few **solar**-titled songs to come, illustrative of how spiritual awakening was becoming more pronounced, the imagery more central and direct. Meditation can greatly assist the bringing of "heaven" to "earth," the manifestation of soul, thus following the "arc's" descent towards a grounded spirituality. Soon after the song was recorded, the band would travel to India to work on that very task. More on the astrology of this song, and George's personal astrology during this pivotal time, is found in Part 2 (p. 399).

Barking in the Rain

On February 11th, the band gathered to do a promotional video for "Lady Madonna." While at the studio, they also recorded a largely improvised "Hey Bulldog." Driven by John, it turned into another playful and comedic song. Like, "You Know My Name (Look up the Number)," it also involved communications. The working title was "You Can Talk to Me."

"Hey Bulldog" is the twenty-eighth "call" song. Communication is being invited as a way to come together ("If you're lonely you can talk to me"), to heal the core underlying issue of loneliness. The song's irreverent and playful vibe invites togetherness. It's notable for the pounding piano riff and George's searing guitar solo. Sound engineer Geoff Emerick said this song was "the final time that all four Beatles were really happy being together in the studio."[240]

It is also the ninth "rain" song ("standing in the rain"), thematically representing the sadness that was healing through open communication. Once again, the work of the Beatles was to channel emotional processes into music for catharsis and resolution. Writing and performing songs was their way to communicate feeling and "Hey Bulldog" is a wonderful example of it. It's a bridge from the Transcendence to the Individuation phase, foreshadowing the liberated and highly original music to come.

Chapter 18
White Heat Part 1: Musings & Meltdown

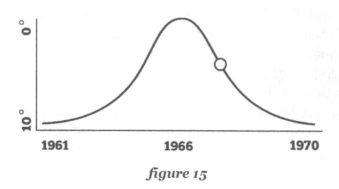

figure 15

This chapter opens the Individuation phase. The musicians were going through a universal astrological passage of maturation. For those uninterested in the astrology, this section can be skipped, though it's likely to be accessible for you.

The astrological "Saturn return" at age 29 is now part of the public lexicon. About 2 years before is another, lesser known, passage we all go through. At age 27, the progressed Moon (emotional development) returns to its natal position {p-lunar return}, highlighting family matters, emotional tendencies and issues of love. Ideally, it's the time to shed a youthful identity and incorporate a more mature disposition. The Beatles symbolically portrayed that process with their reinvented alter egos on *Sgt. Pepper*. At this point, the band members were married and raising children, or dealing with relationship turmoil and change. The family dynamic of the band was also going through a reevaluation with Brian's death and the leadership wrangling.

The p-lunar return can renew and emphasize the natal Moon's strategies, identifications and attachments. John's p-Moon returned to its home sign Aquarius in late October 1967 and was exact {at 3° Aquarius} in early February 1968. He became more detached from his wife, the band and his bandmates, replaying his core theme of estrangement {Aquarius}. He was deepening with Yoko {an Aquarius Sun}, attempting to find a new attachment pattern to match the new cycle. He became more individualistic and carried a rebellious and revolutionary edge.

Paul's p-Moon entered its natal sign Leo in March 1968 and returned to his precise Moon placement the following year. Upon entrance into Leo, it traversed the "I'm in charge" area of his chart, hitting that signature {Mars-Pluto conjunction in Leo} right when the band would have their most conflict. The others criticized Paul for being patronizing and arrogant (dark Leo), while he was trying to maintain positivity and encourage others

203

to bring out their best (heathy Leo). Ringo's p-lunar return involved his assertion of more creative expression (Leo). A bit younger, George's return {in Scorpio} would occur at the time of the band's break-up.

Inner Peace & Outer Confrontation

In this book about The Beatles and spirituality, one would think that the trip to India to sit with a spiritual master (the Maharishi Mahesh Yogi) would be the highlight. This moment is best understood through the context of the "arc's" descent, the movement towards realism. A misconception of spirituality and meditation is the objective is bliss and peace. Certainly, those elements can be a part of it. However, spirituality concerns embodiment and authenticity, the ability to be present with what is. In that regard, the trip was a success.

At this time, George was coming into his own, both as a musician/songwriter and a global advocate of spirituality. As the "soul" of the group, he led the excursion, an example of his increasing influence. The media attention the event received added to the growing interest in meditation and Eastern spirituality in Western culture.

George and John were the first to arrive in mid-February, followed by Paul and Ringo a few days later. They were accompanied by their female partners, and some other Beatles personnel came along. A few other notable celebrities and friends were also invited. The intention was to get away from the glaring lights of stardom and take spiritual practice seriously. They spent time meditating, attending the Maharishi's lectures and taking part in the community. In a most productive songwriting time, many songs that appeared on "The White Album" were conceived.[241] It was a much needed getaway.

As is often the case with spiritual processes, there was both growth and conflict. The retreat brought forward issues of their fame, lifestyle, sexual boundaries and financial fairness. How much were their egos invested in the Beatles mythology? How would they behave at the feet of someone in the position of guru? They agreed to be substance free while there, which was allegedly not honored.[242] How much were their lives organized around drugs? It was an excellent check-in and helpful for reconnection as a "family."

Ringo had difficulty adjusting to the food and culture and experienced some health issues. He missed his family and was the first to depart. Paul was next to leave citing business obligations. Then, an energetic shift—on March 28th was a solar eclipse {8° Aries}, triggering issues of personal behavior decisions and potential conflict. The next couple of weeks brought tension. It was rumored the Maharishi made unwanted sexual advances. George was not convinced of the merits of the accusations, but John was suspicious.[243] John also questioned the Maharishi's embrace of celebrities and financial motivations. Following his lead, the two remaining Beatles left abruptly on April 12th as a {Libra} lunar eclipse was approaching: one triggering relationship issues.

In his state of disillusionment, John wrote "Sexy Sadie" as a jab at the Maharishi.[244] He sings, "you broke the rules," alluding to sexual impropriety. The recent solar eclipse {Aries—passions} was on John's karmic point {South Node}, so he was likely projecting his issues. The lunar eclipse was near his Sun, highlighting his relationship patterns. On the departing flight, John admitted his sexual indiscretions to Cynthia.[245] The accusations of the Maharishi were never based on solid evidence and the Beatles eventually apologized. George would take measures to patch up the misunderstanding, while John was heading towards divorce.

It was helpful for them to explore their spirituality more deeply, to review their lifestyle choices and assess what they had become. Most of all, sitting quietly and just being tends to bring up emotion. Finally, there was deeper engagement with self and each other. Part of the work at this position of the "arc's" descent is the releasing of attachments. They were saying goodbye to Beatlemania and their youthful identity. The experience in India challenged them to release the impact of fame, to connect deeper with the core self for the Individuation phase. The music that emerged through this process was quite different, a reflection of deeper authenticity. They also had to address increasingly complicated questions about the culture in the band as well as in their personal lives. A new season of emotional realism had commenced.

The Awakening of Anger

The March solar eclipse triggered the issue of anger {Aries}, which would play out during the spring. Similar to the aftermath of the *Magical Mystery Tour* movie, there was finger pointing about the India trip.

It is completely appropriate and understandable to experience anger when we lose someone dear. If this is not sufficiently dealt with, the emotional material becomes banished to the shadow. Eclipses tend to bring up what requires attendance. The work of this soul group was to channel emotion into musical creativity. The hazard is playing out what comes up in conflictual ways. Both routes are a part of this next phase.

John and Paul announced the formation of Apple Corps in New York City on May 15, 1968. Though the band was still contracted with Parlophone in the United Kingdom and Capitol in the United States, these corporations would now distribute the music made through Apple. The death of Brian Epstein left the band scrambling for management, and this was their way to seize control of their destiny. They wanted greater creative control and a more tax-effective model, but it also loaded them with greater business responsibilities and the resulting interpersonal strain. In particular, Paul was highly invested in overseeing matters at Apple, leading to the perception of him taking over the band.[246]

In contrast, John became fascinated by Yoko. The pair made the music to what became *Two Virgins* in May. As the story goes, they "made love at dawn" after collaborating through the night. Allegedly, when Cynthia got home from a vacation (earlier than expected), she discovered them sitting in bath robes gazing at each other.[247] Divorce proceedings were initiated over the summer and were finalized in the fall. Another development in the spring was the introduction of heroin. John and Yoko became dependent on the addictive substance,[248] creating a wedge with the others. Its depressant qualities parallel the descent of the "arc."

Sessions began for a new Beatles album on May 30th {on the 3rd anniversary of the Big Gemini Eclipse}, and lasted through mid-October. When sessions began, the celestial weather was heating up {the Sun (awakening) was approaching Mars (anger)}, adding to the passions stirred by the spring eclipse. The intensity {Sun conjunct Mars} was most pronounced in June and July. In this astrologically sweltering summer, the sessions became heated and divisive, marked by frayed emotion and creative differences. In the Individuation phase, group cohesiveness was collapsing.

John brought Yoko into the sessions. It was tradition not to have wives or girlfriends in the studio, but John did not ask for permission. Geoff Emerick writes that he was "making it eminently clear that, like it or not, there was nothing they could do about it."[249] From an energetic perspective, the addition of Yoko changes the dynamics. Though Yoko was never considered a member of the Beatles, her presence can be understood astrologically. A group chart composed of the Beatles with Yoko is found in Part 2 (p. 402), and below are the main points.

As seen with the astrology for the *Magical Mystery Tour* movie, there is similarly a Grand Cross (noted for its conflict resolution) formed by Yoko's connection with the other four. The central issue was creative vision, the management of artistic direction$_1$. The chart portrays competitive and authority issues, the working with conflict$_2$. The communication of emotion was a major issue$_3$. Questions about family and bonding were pressing—how does this group deepen, or does it not?

Some argue that Yoko disrupted the group dynamic, contributing to the collapse. Certainly, the energetics with Yoko are different. However, there is spiritual purpose in all charts, and the group chart with Yoko shows major artistic potential, especially in progressive or innovative ways. It's not any "better" or "worse" than the Beatles chart, but something requiring adaptation. There was resistance to accommodating her presence, so the Grand Cross became problematic. Feelings became activated and heated, perfect for potential catharsis. Yoko might have been the ideal catalyst for the necessary spiritual work.

Changing the World

John was managing a lot of emotion, especially concerning prior trauma {p-lunar return in Aquarius}. His marriage was collapsing, a time of turbulence for anyone. He was upset his recent singles were B-sides and his masterful "Across the Universe" was left unfinished. He may have been jealous or resentful of Paul's recent successes. He certainly didn't think the *Magical Mystery Tour* movie was managed well and he left India in a huff. As the creator and leader of the Beatles, John clearly wanted to do things his way again. He took charge, fueled by "the rage that was bubbling inside."[250]

John insisted one of his songs would come first and chose "Revolution" {fitting for his Aquarian activation}. The sessions involved the initial ideas for the more laid-back version, which would ultimately appear on the album. In the weeks that followed, the edgier version with the aggressive guitar {reflecting the edgy and angry astrology} would be created for release as a single.

The song was the most overt political statement offered by the band. "Revolution" speaks of changing the world and freeing the mind {Aquarius}. John was not only getting political; he was resolving his war karma with peace advocacy. The pacifist message earned him the label of "traitor" from militant factions on the left.[251] On the album version he sang about destruction, "Don't you know you can count me out," then inserts "in." Momentum was clearly in the direction of peace, but he was covering his bases.

Soon John would commit fully to peace and become one of the most visible leaders of the anti-war movement. The planet of revolution {Uranus} entered the sign of peace {Libra} in September, correlating with the making of this song and its release. "Revolution" was emblematic of the shift, a song that inspired millions to dream of a world free of oppression. It became representative of the 1960s, a testament to the rising desire for social change. John's passionate assurance that everything is going to be "all right" (along with the memorable "shoo-be-doo-wops") stands as an iconic Beatles moment, another example of his ability to shape culture.

The astrology for the song (p. 403) featured revolutionary energy rising with an orientation to peace {Uranus on a Libra Ascendant}, a focus on message and a strong reflection of John's central work with war/peace issues. A few additional notes are found in Part 2.

On this opening day of sessions, John also began working on the avant-garde "Revolution 9," a song that would ignite tension. John sought to radically shift Beatles music, to transform the early formula as drastically as possible, even suggesting that "Revolution 9" should be a single.[252] Paul did not see it as fitting for a Beatles album and didn't participate (though it suited George's experimental inclinations and he appears on it).

The Muse in the Shadowlands

The mystical Kite ride for *Sgt. Pepper* was a wondrous exploration of the heights of spiritual discovery. "The White Album" would be equally evocative, albeit psychological and cathartic. As the "arc" was now headed in a downward motion (towards the depths), the muse entered the shadowlands. She revisited underlying trauma, going back to the proverbial (and perhaps literal) scene of the crime. The next few songs detail Step 5 (healing) of the muse process.

What unfolded in June 1968 could only be described as spooky. The synchronicities between John's and Paul's processes would be remarkable, forever emblazoned in the music for us to ponder. It was now Ringo's turn to support his friends. As the emotional anchor, he assisted the integration of the soul work. Ringo was at a major new beginning (p-New Moon, see p. 404). To kick off his new start, he brought forth his first completely solo offering.

Ringo first introduced "Don't Pass Me By" shortly after he joined the band, though it was never given much attention.[253] Complete with loneliness, feeling blue, questions about being lovable and a "poor me" attitude, it's his "seed" song and fits the early formula. However, there is a much deeper dimension, a reason why it emerged for inclusion at this time. Sessions began on June 6th, the very day Mercury {in Cancer} went retrograde. The planet of communications was exactly on the Beatles Sun, signifying an important communication. Retrograde is an inward motion towards the recesses of the psyche, to address love and family {Cancer} issues.

To understand the spiritual context of this moment, a return to 1964 is helpful. That year featured a huge spike of "call" songs, correlating with the maternal at the point of karmic activation {Ceres conjunct the South Node}. Now (4 years later), was the next time for such an astrological condition, a return of the issue in another context. This time, the muse was present to lead the way forward. She appeared on the point of karmic resolution {Euterpe conjunct North Node}, specifically to bring healing through projects {also conjunct Vesta and Saturn}. For this brief time in June 1968, both mother and muse were at the mysterious portal between worlds {Nodal Axis}, activating unresolved soul lessons. Below are these factors when recording of "Don't Pass Me By" started.

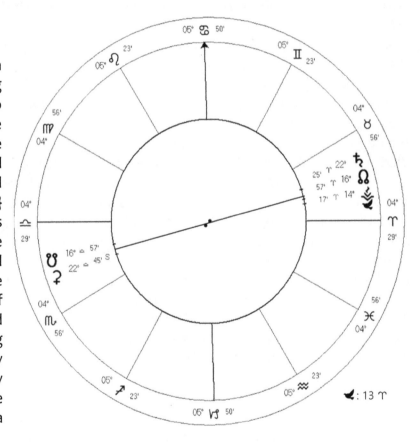

To the left is the South Node with Ceres, pointing to karma relating to mother issues. To the right is the North Node with Saturn, Vesta and Euterpe, the potential resolution {North Node} through crafting projects {Saturn, Vesta} with the muse {Euterpe}. Recall that, for a crucial time during the recording of *Sgt. Pepper*, mother and muse were bridging above to below. Now they were more personally involved with the resolution of karma {Nodes}.

"Don't Pass Me By" holds substantial spiritual significance. Mentioning a car crash, it's the fifth "violence" song, the first of 8 to appear on "The White Album." The singer is miffed by not seeing his beloved as expected, initially unaware of the crash. The karmic signature from the past {South Node} was at the very degree of John's Sun {16° Libra}. In Ringo's chart (p. 404), it falls in the area of others/partners {7th House}. As the signature is paired with the mother {Ceres conjunct South Node}, it specifically points to John's mother Julia, who was in a car crash.

Ringo was giving voice to John's spiritual drama, both by communicating hurt feelings as well as depicting the tragedy. There is anxiety about being alone, waiting to see the beloved but she doesn't arrive. The singer is concerned love is being withdrawn ("I hate to see you go," "Does it mean you don't love me anymore?").

The tone of the lyrics shifts in the second part. Ringo apologizes for his insecure reaction and acknowledges, "You were in a car crash/And you lost your hair," to account for her absence. Presumably the singer received news about what happened ("You said you would be late"), soothing the prior anxiety. "Don't Pass Me By" is the twenty-ninth "call" song, another where the singer is being contacted.

The beloved was not actually withdrawing her affection. She was in an accident and was disoriented for a bit. In England, "And you lost your hair" means being upset and anxious, understandable for a car crash. The parallel to Julia is she wasn't withdrawing her affection from John either, although he initially took it that way. It's interesting that the woman in the song is calling to say she is all right, which may have the spiritual correlation that Julia too has the same message.

The line "And you lost your hair" would become fodder for the "Paul is dead" hoax. Some speculated it referred to burns Paul received from a supposed fatal crash, not realizing the emotional context of the phrase in England. The collective may have been tuning in to the underlying Beatles issue of death. However, it's not Paul, but Julia who died in a car crash, and is the person the astrology overwhelmingly points to.

"Don't Pass Me By" vividly brings a car crash and upset forward to be worked through, but it's just the entrance into the rabbit hole of the Beatles psyche. At the same time, Paul was working on "Blackbird," while John was making "Revolution 9," a trio of songs linked in an enigmatic way. The line, "And you lost your hair" eerily connects to these other songs. "Revolution 9" has the spoken line, "My wings are broken and so is my hair," and "Blackbird" has the message, "Take these broken wings and learn to fly." The unmistakable synchronicity of these lyrics suggests a mysterious process in the Beatles "group mind." "Don't Pass Me By" introduces the spiritual work, "Revolution 9" involves further confrontation and catharsis, while "Blackbird" points to resolution and redemption. The story continues by examining the other 2 songs.

Blackbird #9

June 11th would be a very important day in this story. While John and Yoko were working on "Revolution 9," Paul was recording "Blackbird" by himself. On this day, the muse was *exactly* conjunct the point of potential karmic resolution {Euterpe conjunct North Node}, the time when she could most directly assist the healing of maternal issues {Ceres conjunct South Node}. Consistent with the Individuation phase, John and Paul do not appear on each other's songs. However, they were spiritually connected, intimately involved in a parallel process of sacred healing. First, we'll address the more straightforward "Blackbird," before venturing into the mysterious "Revolution 9."

209

"Blackbird" is the fifth "bird" song, the first of four on this album. The association between birds and the muse is most obvious here. Paul even chooses the color black for the bird that ventures into the shadow. It picks up on the earlier "bird" song, "And Your Bird Can Sing," which has the lines, "When your *bird is broken*, will it bring you down/You may be awoken, I'll be 'round," foreshadowing "Blackbird" as well as "Revolution 9."

"The White Album" sessions began on the third anniversary of the Big Gemini Eclipse, an event that brought the creation of "Yesterday." That fabled song connects with "Blackbird" in a powerful way {Suns and Moons conjunct}, which is discussed in Part 2 (p. 405). Aside from both songs featuring Paul playing solo acoustic guitar, they venture into the dark and give voice to what is there. "Yesterday" addresses the "shadow," while "Blackbird" ventures into the "night," the twenty-fourth "dark" song. In "Yesterday," Paul sings, "I'm not half the man I used to be," stating a condition of impotency. "Blackbird" has the line, "Take these sunken eyes and learn to see," a transformation of grief into the clarity of awakening.

Paul has a remarkable gift of intuition, evidenced by his having received "Yesterday" in dreams. For "Blackbird," let's imagine the song came to Paul from his muse as instructions. The blackbird is "singing in the <u>dead</u> of night," so she speaks from the wounds in his shadow {Pluto}. "Take these broken wings and learn to fly," might relate to his broken will {Paul's natal Pluto-Mars}, which was being healed. The astrological archetype related to the shadow {Pluto-Scorpio} uses the symbolism of the phoenix (a bird) rising from the ashes to take flight.

The blackbird is able to "fly into the **light** of the dark black night." The twenty-sixth **solar** song involves the resolution of shadow.

"Blackbird": Spiritual awakening is furthered by illuminating darkness.

The muse bridges above to below, bringing light to the denser and darker earthbound realm. "Blackbird" is also the twenty-third <u>death</u> song ("<u>dead</u> of night"). The descending motion ventures to the death issue residing in Paul's core. "Blackbird," a major song in this study, synthesizes the **solar**, <u>death</u>, "dark" and "bird" themes. The muse (bird) brings an awakened perspective (**solar**) straight into the darkness of the <u>death</u> issue for transformation and release. The song might have such widespread appeal because it communicates redemption and hope, the sentiment that we all might return to the light. "Blackbird" is another example of Paul's emotional work having value for a shared collective process.

Paul also says that "Blackbird" pertains to the Civil Rights movement, particularly the efforts of black women (as "bird" is slang for "girl") to rise up from oppression.[254] It's another example of liberation, the reclamation of power by emerging more visibly into life. Some additional astrological notes are found in Part 2 (p. 405).

John's avant-garde opus "Revolution 9" may also be a window into another realm. It's the thirty-sixth *dream* song, an aural illustration of the seemingly incomprehensible and utterly subjective nature of consciousness. At first listen, the disorganization and cacophony is unpleasant, so much so the song is despised by many. Some thought John lost his mind. However, it might be the opposite—a reflection of him truly understanding his mind.

John had a most complicated emotional/psychic mindscape, one marked by some degree of disorganization due to trauma {Aquarius Moon opposite Pluto}. He was reconnecting with it {p-lunar return}, in order to resolve its outstanding issues. Furthermore, his spiritual work also involved bringing his psychology to sound {his p-Moon was tightly square Mercury (sound) in Scorpio}, with a continued focus on maternal death issues {p-Sun conjunct Ceres in Scorpio}. The soundscape of "Revolution 9" eerily conveys several facets of the Julia story. First, we'll explore the lyrics, then the music.

The lyrics are mostly indecipherable and masked by the onslaught of noise. However, they can easily be found through an Internet search. They read like the blathering of someone impaired, perhaps a window into trauma. There are a few lines that pop out and point to Julia. The first is, "So I said I'd marry, join the fucking navy and went to sea." Julia Lennon agreed to marry a man who joined the navy and went to sea. The issue that drove Alf and Julia apart was his absence. The lyric circles back to the root of John's abandonment issues, the destabilization in the early home. As seen with "Blackbird," the hypothesis is John might be intuiting or "channeling" his muse.

"My wings are broken and so is my hair" makes "Revolution 9" the sixth "bird" song. The lyric could be the most haunting in this entire study. Like clicking in a puzzle piece, it seamlessly connects to the upset involved in the car crash scenario in "Don't Pass Me By," as well as the process of transformation in "Blackbird." Julia might be relaying her emotional upset from the tragedy as well as her physical injuries. *It could be suggestive of her transformation into the muse* (the forming of wings, to fly up to heaven after the accident). The song also has the spoken words, "birds for birding and fish for fishing," possibly a portrayal of Julia's two main roles in the story. She had a Pisces (fish) Sun and symbolically became the muse (bird).

"Revolution 9" is the twenty-fourth <u>death</u> song ("Afraid she'll <u>die</u>"), the sixth "violence" song (sounds of destruction), and the twenty-fifth "dark" song ("night"). The song synthesizes the *dream*, <u>death</u>, "dark," "bird" and "violence" threads—a surreal journey of the muse through John's psychological mindscape to heal the roots of his violent tendencies. "Blackbird" has hope and the promise of redemption (**solar** theme), but "Revolution 9" ventures deep into darkness. Its atmosphere is unease, confusion and a depiction of trauma in the unconscious (*dream* with "dark" theme).

The most famous part of the song is the repetition of the phrase "Number 9." It has become satirized, while also entering the "Paul is dead" hoax. Some believe it says, "turn me on dead man" when played backwards. Again, Beatles fans have good reason to be curious about deeper meanings, and death is certainly a part of the Beatles story. However, it's not Paul, but Mary and Julia who were the dead figures influencing the music. As for the number 9, there is significance to that number in Beatles astrology {The Beatles Ascendant is 9⁰ Sagittarius, and the Big Gemini Eclipse was at 9⁰ Gemini}.

Shortly after the song was released, John was asked if "Revolution 9" was about death. His response was, "Well then it is, then, when you heard it… listen to it another day.

In the Sun. Outside. And see if it's about death then."[(255)] This remarkable statement parallels how the song has both personal and collective levels. At a personal level, it could be about death. "In the Sun" (from a more awakened position), it's not so psychoanalytical, rather it's about the world around us. Like many Beatles songs, it has varied meanings (and levels) available for interpretation.

At the collective level, the song was designed to portray what a revolution might sound like. John was making it with his so-called "mother" Yoko, a reflection of his own personal revolution with his maternal issues. Together they were making revolutionary music, specifically about the idea of revolution. The personal revolution of spiritual healing is a metaphor for broader collective revolution. After moving through extreme disturbance and trauma, a new day becomes possible.

The music conveys mayhem and discord, a dramatic overturning of a status-quo. There are elements of destruction, confusion and fear. Also, it could be representative of Julia's trauma and disorganization. The soundscape from 5:00 until 5:40 is most notable, a crescendo of blaring sounds resembling a siren. Possibly, it is reflective of a car accident, with emergency vehicles arriving at the scene. The spoken line, "my wings are broken and so is my hair" is delivered when the intensity of the blaring sounds diminishes.

Listening to "Revolution 9" requires a complete shift (revolution) from what we might expect or desire in music. Using the format of the world-famous Beatles, John saw an opportunity to shock and awaken his audience into another dimension of experience. It might be revealing a sacred process of confrontation and catharsis, a collaboration with Julia for whom he mourns. If this is really the case, then "Revolution 9" is a staggering work of artistic genius, yet another boundary-stretching example of the John-Julia partnership.

Meanwhile, Paul sits alone and strums his guitar, tapping his foot on the floor to create the metronome heard in "Blackbird." Music effortlessly moves through him, just like the inspiration he's receiving. His face appears dreamy, his consciousness somewhere else. Mary takes the form of a bird, the totem of the muse, and flies into the night of Paul's darkness. At some level he feels her presence, the reunion has been made.

The great legacy of Julia and Mary is not only inspiration for the creation of music, but also to shift our consciousness. The healing work with the muse, as seen in the "Don't Pass Me By"—"Blackbird"—"Revolution 9" trio of songs, becomes more remarkable by virtue of Ringo's participation. Ringo is symbolic of the everyman like you and me. Spiritual insight and discovery is not reserved for those with heightened intuitive abilities. As the "arc" descends back to the ground, all have access to it. Everyone can live an embodied spirituality on this Earth connected to the heavens.

There is one major point to be made of the astrology for "Revolution 9" (p. 403). John's Sun {16° Libra} was *exactly* in the crosshairs of the spiritual work with mother and muse {Ceres opposite Euterpe on the Nodal Axis at 16° Libra-Aries}. It occurs in the sign of artistry and collaboration {Libra}, in service of a new beginning {Aries}. A few additional notes are found in Part 2.

212

Sleep Tight

At this point, the descending motion of the "arc" was crossing the "line of inspiration." When the motion crossed the threshold for the ascent in 1964, the first **solar** song, "And I Love Her," was composed. The muse entered the scene and the soul contracts were made overt ("Things We Said Today," "I'll Be Back"). "And I Love Her" invites us to look to the starry skies above, to fathom a broader mystery. The songwriters gradually raised their consciousness to eventually answer the call. John's song "Good Night" is the integration back down, and invitation to rest in the sanctuary of earthy comfort as the muse process concludes.

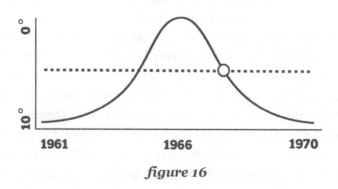

figure 16

From this point forward, the muse's influence diminishes. After "Good Night," her role will become peripheral. There will be no more far-reaching John-Julia collaborations or Paul-Mary stories to tell. Her presence remains, but her influence will be subtle and soft, releasing and loving. Towards the end, both Julia and Mary will reenter for the songs mentioning them by name, perhaps their curtain calls.

Sessions for "Good Night" began on June 28th, precisely when the inspiration threshold was crossed. It's a sweet ballad John wrote for Ringo to sing. The drama in the shadowlands was psychologically intense and cathartic, a spiritual process requiring rest for integration. Ringo, the everyman, the emotional anchor on the earth plane, continues to play his role. In his earnest and loving {Cancer Sun} way, it is he who guides us down for sleep, a return to safety and peace.

"Good Night" is the thirty-seventh *dream*, twenty-seventh **solar**, twenty-sixth "dark" and ninth "flute" song, a unification of these threads. The muse (symbolized by the flute) is literally putting the issue to rest. "Good Night" is a blessing given to experience joy (**solar** theme) in the darkness of consciousness ("dark," *dream* theme), to flow downstream safely in sleep.

As discussed, the **solar** and *dream* threads respectively relate to the astrological Sun and Moon—and both are featured in the song. John writes, "Now the **sun** turns out

213

his **light**" and "Now the moon begins to **shine**." The Sun's light is not really extinguished, but to the personality stationed on the Earth, it appears that way in our childhood innocence. The Moon's shine is a reflection of the Sun, bringing the spiritual teaching.

The Sun involves the presence, awareness and vitality of soul, our energetic connection with Spirit. The Moon is the embodied, biological vehicle of the egoic/personality self in the realm of separation. The Moon reflects the light of the Sun, symbolic of how individuals are made in the image of soul/Spirit.

"Good Night": The personal consciousness (Moon) reflects our soul connection to Spirit (Sun).

The unification of Sun and Moon connects Oneness with separation, soul with body—the bridging of worlds (paralleling the work of the muse). We may proceed through life with embodied (Moon) spiritual awareness (Sun), able to consciously "play the game" on the ground.

As the "arc" descends back to the ground, the *dream* motif returns to the simpler usage. "Good Night" refers to dreams in the conventional way. John writes, "*Dream sweet dreams* for me." He was writing for his son Julian, a return to the innocence of youth. It may have also been a message to himself and Paul, a prayer for peaceful rest after the intensity of recent processes.

The astrology (p. 407) has a nurturing message from the mother/muse, consistent with putting a child to sleep. Muse and mother are still tightly connected, with the focus in the home. There is also a cluster of planets echoing the familial theme {Sun, Venus, Mars in Cancer, all on the Beatles Sun}. These planets involve the revitalization of love and nurturance, exactly what the boys were calling out for in the early days.

"I Call Your Name" (ascending) and "Good Night" (descending) were written at similar positions in the arc's trajectory. The issue was raised in "I Call Your Name" and found resolution with "Good Night." John was unable to sleep in the earlier song and here he penned one about comforting rest, a complete transformation of the issue.

Ob-La-Disaster

Now that the "arc" descended below the inspiration threshold, the focus returned to the personality and its outstanding issues to resolve. Egoic attachments, unprocessed emotion and personal issues would need to be addressed. Having it play out provides a chance to work with it, and they would have that opportunity over the summer.

As June gave way to July, the celestial weather became extremely hot {Sun-Mars conjunction peaking}. John put forth his raucous "Everybody's Got Something to Hide Except For Me and My Monkey." Begun in India, John says it's about him and Yoko, while Paul was later quoted: "He was getting into harder drugs than we'd be into and so his songs were taking on more references to heroin. Until that point we had made rather mild, oblique references to pot or LSD. But now John started talking about fixes and monkeys and it was harder terminology which the rest of us weren't into."[256]

214

During the Individuation phase, John conducted himself as the free spirit he was. Paul saw the ship starting to sink and wanted to do something about it. He put forward what he thought was a safe and easy song to get polished off, one that could bring them together as The Beatles making charming music. It backfired and created the most divisiveness the band had experienced to this point.

Sessions for "Ob-la-di, Ob-la-da" began on July 3rd. The music is inviting and bouncy, while the lyrics mention endearing compliments, the presentation of a ring, singing, "home sweet home," kids playing and "happy ever after." John called it "granny music shit,"[257] and openly detested it. He shut down in a cold and silent protest {dark Aquarius Moon}, refusing to work on it. Paul had trouble getting it just right and dominated several days of studio time tinkering with it. The more it dragged on, the more irritated the mood became. The astrology (p. 408) illustrates the emotionality and potential conflict.

Later in the sessions, George composed "Savoy Truffle," containing the line, "We all know obla-dibla-da/But can you show me where you are?" He was not fond of the song either, desiring more substance. George might've been expressing his perception of Paul's shallowness. As part of their "sibling" rivalry, Paul was still (consciously or not) marginalizing George and his contributions, and George was almost at his breaking point (he would get there in a few months…). At this point, 6 weeks into the sessions, the band was still not working on any of his songs.

The reception of "Ob-La-Di, Ob-La-Da" has been mixed and divisive, engendering a wide spectrum of opinion. It has numerous covers, from all over the globe, and remains one of the Beatles most internationally adored songs.[258] Paul was successful in crafting his brand of infectious music, though some don't care for it. In the spirit of the song, that is life, ob-la-dibla-da.

John put his frustration into music. July 9th began sessions for the harder-edged version of "Revolution," released as a single later in the summer. The aggressive guitars and screaming reflects the emotionally intense times… and it would only continue…

Screaming Babies

On July 15th, Paul was still tinkering with "Ob-La-Di, Ob-La-Da," while John was completing (what may have been) his emotional reaction in the harder version of "Revolution." They were being competitive, playing the role of musical gunslingers. Emotions were running high and would spill over to John's appropriately titled "Cry Baby Cry" on July 16th. On this day, loyal sound engineer Geoff Emerick quit.[259] He saw enough bickering and unpleasantness and simply got up and left. His departure reflected the *fragmentation* occurring in the band; this is also a word some use to describe the music on "The White Album."

"Cry Baby Cry" thematically parallels their need to express unresolved childhood emotions. It's the twenty-seventh "dark" song, pointing down to the well of the unconscious. At the more mundane level it's akin to a nursery rhyme, influenced by "Sing a Song of Sixpence," which interestingly features blackbirds. Similarly, "Cry Baby Cry" is the seventh "bird" song and third "mother" song, both themes pointing to maternal issues. The astrology was peaking emotionally (p. 408), with a major emphasis on family dynamics.

A couple of days later on 7/18, the band reconvened and expressed emotion in a huge way. The first session for Paul's hard-rocking "Helter Skelter" was that evening, turning into an enormous catharsis—the perfect song to channel emotional energy into creative expression. Imagine the scene: in the middle of the night, in the middle of the summer, in the middle of these incredibly tense days. It was perhaps the best (and only?) way that they could bond together in their shared passion and support each other emotionally.

The session lasted from 10:30pm through 3:30am.[260] The Beatles jammed with ferocious intensity for hours, creating the loudest and messiest of songs in their entire catalog. It was pure mayhem, complete with screaming and aggressive guitars. One take lasted over 27 minutes, quite different than the early days when they didn't exceed the 3 minute mark. These sessions remain unreleased, but they would be a fascinating listen, a true window into the group psychology. The song was not completed but shelved for 6 weeks. It was redone and finished in September, yielding the version heard on the record.

The song title refers to an amusement park spiral slide, while mimicking the descent of the "arc." Paul says a dimension to the song is the rise and fall of the Roman Empire, and the song depicts the fall.[261] At the time of the session, the "arc" was separating at $5° 15'$, and it would get close to $9°$ by year's end. The song comes right when the downward slope was accelerating ("I'm coming down fast"). It's the seventh "violence" song ("Don't let me break you"). It would also inspire Charles Manson, who is addressed later.

Like the band, the world itself seemed to be spiraling down during this summer of upheaval and crisis. Martin Luther King Jr. and Robert Kennedy were recently assassinated and there were soon to be riots at the 1968 Democratic National Convention. The Vietnam War was a major, and controversial, issue and the countercultural revolution was peaking. Whereas 1967 was the "Summer of Love," 1968 was quite the opposite.

Paul's relationship with Jane unraveled when he was caught sleeping with another lover.[262] She made a public announcement on July 20th on television that their engagement was off. Paul was among the many to be surprised to learn of this through the broadcast![263] His astrology at this time (p. 409) reveals a moment of major change, adapting to new realities {Uranus crossing his Ascendant, squaring his Sun}. His emotional energy was being highly set off, including his "expression of grief" signature. In particular, his buried anger was being stimulated for release. In contrast to his usual professional, easy-going and friendly demeanor, a rawer and more intense Paul emerges on "Helter Skelter," delivering a perfect catharsis.

Recording was sparse for the rest of July. Towards the end of the month (sessions on 7/19 & 7/24) John completed his angry jab at the Maharishi in "Sexy Sadie," the twenty-eighth **solar** song. He writes, "One **sunny** day the world was waiting for a lover," and "Just a smile would **lighten** everything." John was accusing the guru of abusing his power, of not using the light of his soul admirably.

216

"Sexy Sadie": It's our task to use our light responsibly.

The Maharishi was most likely not irresponsible, but there have been plenty in positions of power and influence who have not heeded this lesson (including John himself).

George finally got to work on one of his songs at the end of July and rehearsed the basics to "While My Guitar Gently Weeps." The early version was stripped-down and acoustic, much more melancholic and reflective than how it evolved (reviewed later). In early August, he began work on "Not Guilty." After a lengthy process of more than 100 takes, the song was shelved, contributing to his disillusionment. It became part of his solo catalog, though a version with the Beatles can be heard on the Anthology collection.

Making it Better

As July was shifting to August, sessions for Paul's "Hey Jude" were the priority. He intended it to be a single to be released ahead of the album. It became a #1 hit and smashed all types of records; it's one of the most recognizable and famous of all Beatles songs. "Hey Jude" would receive massive airplay and catch on as a sing-a-long at parties, sporting events, bars and other venues. It does not register in the major threads, its importance being more personal.

"Hey Jude" is over 7 minutes long, famous for its extended, "nah nah nah nah," fadeout featuring Paul's vocal improvisations. The name "Jude" references Julian Lennon, only 5 years old and his parents were divorcing.[264] Consistent with the spirit of the "arc's" descent, the subject matter addresses a real-life situation, a return to everyday matters. It's the tenth and final "flute" song (in the orchestra). Now that the motion has crossed the "line of inspiration," we can see "Hey Jude" in this context. Instead of being inspired from above, it might signal the point when Paul was becoming the inspirer himself, the spirit of the muse embodied in his character. His loving and thoughtful words provide comfort and healing. Paul would go on to become even more of an inspirational figure for years and decades to come.

Paul's reigning need is to be a performer who brings the world together in shared emotional experience. The poignancy of emotion "Hey Jude" expresses (condolence, empathy, support) registers at a universal level. Millions of people have locked arms, swayed and sang this song in unison. It has also stirred the emotions for lonely people listening during tough times. The melody is entrancing, while tugging the heart strings. The lyric, "take a sad song and make it better" defines the Beatles soul work and contribution.

Along with lending sympathy to young Julian's situation, the song has been subject to many other interpretations. Some believe the line, "You have found her, now go and get her," is a blessing from Paul to John to shift his allegiance to Yoko. Others contend he is speaking to himself, giving permission to pursue Linda Eastman. Of note is the phrase "don't let me down." The mention of "down" follows the descent the "arc," and perhaps some resistance to the motion. The phrase became the title of a John song the following year.

Paul was criticized for his fixation on the song. He enjoyed performing it, perhaps as a way to get approval. He admits to being "bossy" about its production, overriding George's musical ideas.[265] Some feel it's self-indulgent, repetitious or overrated. Nevertheless, it is a classic and iconic, a fan favorite and one of his most adored songs of all. "Hey Jude" is a defining song of the later Beatles and a prime example of Paul's leadership. The astrology (p. 410) triggers Paul's blind spot of self-preoccupation$_1$. It also reveals how his own emotional process is the influence for the song$_2$.

The Mother Lode

The next songs developed were Paul's "Mother Nature's Son" (8/9) and John's "Yer Blues" (8/13), the fourth and fifth "mother" songs. "Mother Nature's Son" is also the twenty-ninth **solar** song, while "Yer Blues" is the twenty-fifth <u>death</u> song, so two very different syntheses.

Paul's maturation with his maternal death issue can be seen in "mother" songs over time. In 1956 at the age of 14 he wrote, "I Lost My Little Girl," after Mary died. It began the early formula of channeling his grief into song under the guise of romantic loss—a format that included numerous songs. Eleven years later he would finally use the word "mother" in a song ("Your Mother Should Know"), suggesting that he was ready to discuss the topic more overtly. Next came "Lady Madonna," a song that celebrates motherhood and one he may have been collaborating on with Mary as his muse. The song's astrology suggests movement from the conventional maternal role to the spiritual.

The evolution continues with "Mother Nature's Son," which universalizes and depersonalizes the archetype of mother. Paul is a son of the planet itself—he can be nurtured and loved, held by nature. The song contains the line "Listen to the pretty sound of music as she flies," the eighth "bird" song, the likely possibility for something that flies and makes music. It might be symbolic that his mother's presence (now as a "bird," the muse) fills his world. The line evokes "Lady Madonna" where he sings, "Listen to the music playing in your head." Now the music fills the air.

The **solar** teaching arrives with the line, "Swaying daisies sing a lazy song beneath the **sun**." The lesson is to abide in the vitality of nature, to experience the world as ensouled.

"Mother Nature's Son": Nature reveals Spirit.

In contrast, John's "Yer Blues" is the twenty-eighth "dark" song. At this point he was struggling with divorce as well as his relationship with the band. Suicide is mentioned, the eighth "violence" song. The word "<u>die</u>" (or "<u>dead</u>") appears 10 times in the song. "My mother was of the sky" parallels Paul's song, but John speaks of feeling lonely while Paul sounds fulfilled. Like Paul, John too mentions nature and animals. "The eagle picks my eye/The worm he licks my bone," is an example of John's highly individualistic word usage in the Individuation phase.

John's intention was to belt out the blues, a genre that speaks freely about feeling down and out. He intended both parody and sincerity, to have some fun with the rapidly growing blues-rock of the day.[(266)] As the "arc" was descending, he was coming down. Perhaps influenced by heroin use, his moods were more extreme. Once again, he was able to channel his emotions into music to be enjoyed by many.

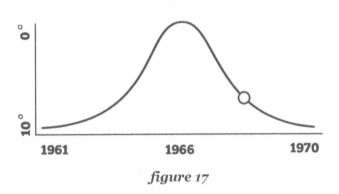

figure 17

With 30 original songs (32 including the singles), the Beatles were more prolific during the "The White Album" sessions compared to any other time. In the Individuation period, the focus was not on collaboration. Only 16 of the 30 songs featured all 4 of them.

John and Paul both put forward an entire album of songs in their own right. They relished taking all sorts of creative risks, seeing how they might venture into unexplored territory. Like musical gunslingers, they were trying to outdo each other, perhaps a musical duel for the mantle of band leader. Ringo got fed up and temporarily quit, only to return when the celestial intensity diminished and everyone agreed to get along. The remaining stretch of the sessions would be less conflictual, but the mood was raw and the music reflected it.

Showdown at the Hoedown

Despite the success of *Sgt. Pepper*, John wasn't going to easily accede band leadership to Paul. He formed the band and his character was not one to ride shotgun. Paul was more organized, managerial, and was becoming the more prolific and successful songwriter. He was too respectful of John to outright say he should be the leader. Instead of having a reasonable discussion about what was really going on, they put their feelings into the music.

Many Beatles songs involve personal processes. Sometimes this is done intentionally and other times more instinctually. Paul has the unique ability to capture spiritual or archetypal themes {a Neptunian} in words and stories {a Gemini Sun}. He may not know where he is getting his inspiration, but he's able to serve as a channel to express personal and collective processes. In stunning synchronous fashion, his song "Rocky

Raccoon" can be interpreted as the rivalry playing out between him and John concerning leadership of the Beatles.

The song was recorded on 8/15. John and Paul appear on it; perhaps they both needed to show up for this particular one. Interestingly, Paul sings and plays guitar and John plays bass—a role reversal, which was literally occurring with the leadership issue. John rarely plays bass on any Beatles songs, so it's notable. He also plays harmonica, the last Beatles song he played it on. Paul wrote the song in a folk style, somewhat tongue in cheek, but also as an homage to the genre. The song features honky-tonk piano (played by George Martin[267]), adding to the flavor.

Mentioning saloons, bibles, guns, grins and gin, Paul created a "cowboy" atmosphere for this showdown in the "hills of Dakota." {The mood and subject matter is quintessentially Sagittarian, reflective of the Beatles Ascendant like a caricature.} There's a duel to resolve a love triangle, paralleling the rivalrous tension in the group chart {Athena in Sagittarius (fighting for justice) on the Sagittarius Ascendant, opposite Venus in Gemini in the 7th House (relational dynamics involving multiple parties)}.

For this discussion, let's entertain the idea that John is Rocky, and Paul, his rival Dan. Lil is the woman caught in the middle of the showdown, just like the Beatles were in the middle of the John-Paul rivalry. The Beatles were initially John's band, his love, just like Rocky and Lil were together first. Dan is opportunistic, seeking to take Lil away, similar to Paul asserting himself as the principle visionary.

As for John being Rocky: definitions of rocky include "unstable," and "full of obstacles or problems," consistent with John's emotional instability {Aquarius Moon} and conflictual karma {Aries South Node}. A symbolic meaning of the raccoon, "to be fearless and go after what you want," precisely fits his character. Raccoons have been characterized as "masked bandits" who come out at night and seek their loot in a stealthy way. John famously preferred the nighttime, staying up late and sleeping in. He was also the only Beatle to wear glasses (masked bandit). He enjoyed exploring the dark and had secretive behaviors (infidelities, drug use, etc.).

The meaning of the name Dan is "God is my judge," suggesting a balancing of the scales of justice. The drama of the middle brother involves the leveling of hierarchies, asserting oneself in the spirit of fairness. The mindset might be, "You had your turn, now I get mine," a common dynamic between siblings. Paul's historical pattern suggests deference, staying beneath others {6th House Pisces South Node}, and wants to rise into creative leadership {Pluto-Mars in Leo}. John modeled leadership for Paul, while Paul modeled diplomacy and cooperation for John. They were learning how to reverse their roles, exactly what was occurring in the band and seen with the musicianship on this song.

The woman's name was "Magil, and she called herself Lil/But everyone knew her as Nancy." A meaning for Magil is "a flowering tree," while Lil goes with Lily, a flower. The overarching story of the Beatles is coming of age, the universal process of spiritual maturation, like a seed that grows into a flower. A meaning for the name Nancy is "grace" or "God has favored me." Might we say that everyone has a favorable impression of the Beatles, that they have the proverbial grace of God? So, in this interpretation, the lyrics

221

would be saying, "The Beatles tell the story of spiritual awakening, but everyone just thinks they're wonderful."

The Dan figure is described as "hot—he drew first and shot." Paul's disposition is fiery {Leo Moon}, with underlying suppressed aggression {Mars-Pluto}. Paul was taking a shot with greater assertiveness as the band leader (as seen with *Sgt. Pepper*, *Magical Mystery Tour*). Conflict and violence were part of John's karmic history, reflecting Rocky's injuries in the shootout. John was healing his war wounds, as seen in Rocky's need for medical assistance ("Doc it's only a scratch").

The final stanza begins with "Rocky Raccoon he fell back in his room/Only to find Gideon's bible." The phrase "fell back" is vague, either insinuating Rocky was dying or hobbling and injured. Either way, he must learn to surrender, a theme of John's chart. The song ends mentioning "Rocky's revival," connected again to Gideon, a story of unlikely military victory in the Book of Judges. Dan emerges victorious and balances the scales, just like Paul would be the more dominant influence in the second half of the Beatles story. The song ends with Paul singing, "Sorry Rocky." Though John loses the duel, he would go through a revival by becoming a peace activist and thereby balance his own scales of justice {Libra}.

"Rocky Raccoon" is the thirty-eighth *dream* song. Now that the "arc's" motion had crossed the "line of inspiration," there's an accompanying shift to the conventional dream use: "His rival it seems had broken his *dreams*." The gunfight makes it the ninth "violence" song.

The astrology (p. 411) for "Rocky Raccoon" emphasizes issues of fairness, equality and justice[1]. The rivalrous tension is pronounced, specifically pointing to productivity, the development of a body of work[2]. There are parallels to being at a crossroads or showdown, directly involving the "Beatles signature[3]." The evolutionary lesson is to work through conflict, basically to have it out. Interestingly, the signature of wounds through battle is a spiritual lesson {Chiron in Aries on the Nodes}[4]. There is a striking and uncanny parallel between "Rocky Raccoon" and the John-Paul relationship chart {Sun conjunct Sun}, an unmistakable sign that points to their connection. The John-Paul composite chart is incredibly lit up by "Rocky Raccoon," also emphasizing competition, explicitly with writing and productivity[5].

Turbulence

Sessions for Paul's "Back in the U.S.S.R." began on 8/22, giving him the opportunity to lead a unique and complicated song. As discussed in their dynamic, Paul and Ringo easily join as performers {Mars conjunct Mars in Leo}, but there can also be a competitive edginess. Allegedly, Ringo found Paul to be bossy at this time, critical about his drumming.[268] Fed up with the deteriorating relations overall, he quit the band. Ringo's astrology (p. 413) was suggesting issues with insecurity and needing validation, a return of karmic frustrations about performance. His tendency to be the loner was being triggered. Paul's "I'm in charge" signature was still highly activated. The band carried on without Ringo and Paul played drums.

222

"Back in the U.S.S.R." brings the Soviet Union to surf music, a most unusual pairing. The song's upbeat and playful vibe feels celebratory, but there is an undercurrent of unease. The first stanza describes restlessness ("didn't get to bed last night") and illness ("the paper bag was on my knee"), the twenty-ninth "dark" song ("night").

Paul was the Beatle most interested in touring. He loved the admiration his talent brought from all over the world. Much of the song is about adoring women, suggestive of his attachment to external validation. He sings about receiving love from the Ukraine and Moscow girls, making him "sing and shout," a nod to the "Twist and Shout" spirit of Beatlemania. Also featured is "yeah yeah" and "ooooh ooooh oooohh," satirizing the early days. Paul requests to be shown around "snow-peaked mountains way down south" and to be kept "warm" were likely indicating sexual connotations. How much did he enjoy the spoils of fame?

Perhaps Paul was being nostalgic about Beatlemania with a Russian twist. Shortly after "The White Album," he proposed the idea to resume public appearances.[269] This song may reveal Paul's resistance to the "arc's" descending motion. Ideally, the descent is the time to release attachments, but Paul seemed to covet adoration {Leo}. The need to purge into the paper bag might be symbolic of his inner turbulence, the reluctance to release his attachments. The band was collapsing, jeopardizing his reigning performance need. The conclusion of the song features a plane touching down, giving sound to the "arc's" descent and foreshadowing where matters are heading.

Paul's relationship just ended, his songwriting partnership with John was strained, the band had no manager and the sound engineer quit. During the recording of this song, the previously inseparable Fab Four came apart. Paul just wanted to have fun and play music, but George was not open to touring again.[270] Maybe there was a part of him that really wanted to be in Russia!

Playing in the Sun

Sessions for "Dear Prudence" began on 8/28 when Ringo was still absent. Paul continued with drumming duties on this John song written in India. The song was inspired by Prudence Farrow,[271] who was highly invested in meditation practice. It's an invitation for her to "come out to play," to connect more openly with life. John repeats, "look around," to embrace spirituality in the everyday.

Similar to Paul in "Mother Nature's Son," John wrote of the natural world. And like that song's themes, "Dear Prudence" is the thirtieth **solar** song and the ninth (and final) "bird" song. John invites Prudence to "see the **sunny** skies." He sings, "The **sun** is up," which is "beautiful and so are you."

"Dear Prudence": We reflect the beauty of Spirit.

We can enjoy and bask in the vitality of nature, thereby showing up fully on Earth and bringing presence (Sun) to the everyday. John tells us "the birds will sing/that you are part of everything." This lyric might symbolize a message of Oneness from the muse. Being part of everything is the ultimate cure for loneliness. The muse {Euterpe} just entered the sign of the natural world and physical embodiment {Taurus}, and would remain there for the rest of "The White Album" sessions.

The astrology (p. 413) invites a return to innocence, playfulness and spontaneity, an embrace of life[1]. There are cross-cultural dimensions highlighted (and the song was created and takes place in India)[2]. The Beatles message of embodied spirituality {Virgo North Node in the 9th} is strongly triggered by "Dear Prudence[3]."

"Hey Jude," backed by the harder version of "Revolution," was released as a single at the end of August. Once again there was dispute about which should be the A-side,[272] and once again, Paul's song won out. The astrology for the release of the singles (p. 413) illustrates why both are signature songs and provides a few notes.

The enormous popularity of "Hey Jude" overshadowed the release of another Apple single released in late August. "Sour Milk Sea" was written and produced by George Harrison, given to promising upstart Jackie Lomax. The song promotes the benefits of meditation as a way to lift oneself out of troubling feelings. It's not included in the official Beatles catalog, so not part of the lyrical threads. Nevertheless, it could be considered both a *dream* ("your *dreams* come true") and **solar** ("**illumination**") song. George continued to assume the role of messenger or teacher of spiritual ideas. Paul, Ringo, George and Eric Clapton performed on it. The song was not the breakout hit desired for Lomax, but became a favorite of Beatles aficionados, lauded for its hard-rock edge, musicianship and spirit.

George's Weeping Guitar

At this point the celestial intensity was becoming cooler with a focus on productivity, completion of tasks and professionalism {Virgo emphasis}. On September 5, Ringo rejoined the band. He arrived to find flowers adorning his drum kit (courtesy of George) and the band pledged to behave better.[273]

The Beatles motif of emotional expression through music takes on literal connotations next. For "While My Guitar Gently Weeps," a musical instrument is crying. George began developing the song in the spring after returning from India. He first brought it forward in late July—in its early stages it was acoustic, slow and reflective. In August it was developed further, with added substance from the full band. However, George did not feel the others gave the song the focus and support it warranted.[274] He was feeling jaded, similar to what he expresses in the song.

George was delighted Ringo returned, but also felt something else was necessary. The next day, he brought in his friend Eric Clapton to play lead guitar. Though Clapton played on "Sour Milk Sea," he was initially reluctant to appear on a Beatles track, but George was persuasive.[275] The session on September 6th was when magic happened. Not only did Clapton produce one of the most memorable and classic guitar parts and solos in rock history, George got his vocals just right. Additionally, important parts were included by Paul (fuzz bass) and John (guitar with tremolo). "While My Guitar Gently Weeps" remains one of the most beloved of all Beatles songs, a testament to George's incredible musical advancement in the band's later years. As the "soul" of the Beatles, his message is equally as poignant, capturing the bittersweet descent of the "arc."

Let's first recall the peak of the "arc" and *Revolver*. On that album, "Good Day **Sunshine**" and "Here, There and Everywhere" proclaim how the sunshine of love is immediate and abundant. "Tomorrow Never Knows" provides a spiritual context to our "**shining**" journey and "Love You To" is a celebration of presence. Everything is amplified and vibrant, almost blinding. Ideally, the "arc's" descent brings such spiritual insight, clarity and awareness down to Earth. However, on the denser earth plane, we might go back to sleep, instead of maintaining such awakening.

In "While My Guitar Gently Weeps," George sings not only of the love that is sleeping within humankind, but maybe also what he saw in the declining relations of the band. Part of George's attunement {Pisces Sun} is holding such wistfulness with compassion. Many go back to sleep and get lost in the theater of their dream. George gives it musical context in a weeping guitar, producing such longing and mourning in sound. The initial acoustic version had the line, *"play you are staging,"* giving voice to our existential situation (and would've made it a *dream* song). The line didn't make the final version, but can be heard on the Beatles *Love* album and *Anthology* versions.

The lyrics point to matters on the ground. George sings that the floor needs sweeping, there is much to take care of in the manifest world. He says, "They bought and sold you," suggesting the influence of material considerations. Like "The Fool on the Hill," he notices that the world is turning, an observance of mundane reality. Then, in a clever rhyme scheme, he poetically voices the predicament of humans who lack awareness on the ground. He points out that some become "diverted" (running off course), leading to being "perverted too" (being corrupted or distorted). They have become "inverted" (turned upside-down), which may be the tendency to maximize material gain instead of spirituality, a common motif in his writing (as seen in "Taxman" and "Within You Without You"). He finishes with, "no one alerted you," adding compassion for our naiveté. The song returns to the idea that love is sleeping in us all, waiting to be awakened.

The astrology (p. 415) portrays a robust feeling of compassion and emotion$_1$. There is a philosophical scope and continuation of an embodied spirituality$_2$. The change of personnel (inclusion of Clapton) is also noted$_3$. The overall suggestion is to find ways to bridge divides and work lovingly together$_4$.

A few days later on September 9th, the band revisited "Helter Skelter," in another barn-burner of a session. At this time, producer George Martin was absent—he needed a break and was on vacation for most of September (his assistant handled the role). The session had an emphasis on fire {Moon in Aries trine Mars in Leo}, and it was another scene of mayhem, complete with George running around with a flaming ashtray above his head.[276] Tensions were likely released in this informal session of music therapy.

The next song was "Glass Onion," a song John intentionally wrote to play with those who want to read into lyrics.[277] He makes references to prior songs and the listener is left to figure it out. At the time, the planets of creativity {Venus at 11° Libra} and words {Mercury at 13° Libra} were residing on the signature of the past {South Node at 9° Libra}, situated on the Beatles point of career contribution {Midheaven at 10° Libra} in their group chart. Therefore, "Glass Onion" specifically showcases a creative {Venus} use of linguistics {Mercury} referencing earlier {South Node} works. Next was Paul's tender ballad "I Will." This simple song has the line, "Your song will fill the air" echoing "Mother Nature's Son."

Birthday Piggies

During the Individuation phase, Paul and George continued to diverge creatively. The sibling hierarchy was in flux as Paul was claiming the top slot and George was sliding forward. In defense of their positions, John and Paul continued to marginalize George, who didn't believe his songs were being respected or prioritized. Whereas John and Paul were polarizing in revolutionary {Aquarius} vs. conformist {Leo} ways, George and Paul were squaring off between depth {Scorpio} vs. levity {Leo}. The songs in mid-September highlighted this friction.

On September 18th, Paul led the effort to make up a song right in the studio. "Birthday" is an upbeat rocker about partying and celebrating the self {quintessential Leo}. Paul sings, "It's my birthday too," voicing the personality desiring attention and recognition. His delivery of, "We're gonna have a good time" is most enthusiastic as he anticipates the "party party." The song has an infectious riff and gets the blood pumping. It has been used countless times to enhance birthday celebrations, another unique contribution.

The next day George brought "Piggies" to the studio. The song was initially created in 1966 when he was writing "Taxman,"[278] a song with obvious similarities. Both are cynical sneers about the abuse of power, but "Piggies" is more unsettling. In the tradition of Orwell's *Animal Farm*, the song reveals George's darker side. The tenth "violence" song, he writes, "What they need's a damn good whacking," and mentions that the pigs are "clutching forks and knives to eat their bacon."

George was known to have a strong and biting sense of humor, and his chart depicts issues with authority figures who abuse power. Though this song has political and social undertones, George was also having fun. The choice to adorn the acerbic lyrics with bouncy harpsichord, a string octet and baroque flavors adds satire. The song is further enhanced by pig grunting sounds, courtesy of John, who also assisted George with the lyrics.[279] Unsurprisingly, there has been a wide reaction to the song, ranging from contempt to hilarity. It is yet another original offering on an album full of surprises.

These songs are so different, one might wonder how they could have similar astrology (as they were recorded on back-to-back days). The astrology at the time (p. 415) strongly featured the signs connected to the innate dispositions of Paul {Leo Moon} and George {Scorpio Moon}, situated in a frictional way. "Birthday" is equally as intense as "Piggies," but in an upbeat Paul-like manner. He sounds forcefully {Scorpio} enthusiastic {Leo}, even pressured as he insists "I would like you to dance!" George's song is subversive and dark {Scorpio}, but he's having a ton of fun and adds lighthearted {Leo} elements. Both songs integrate intensity {Scorpio} with play {Leo} and the songwriters do it in their own styles.

Finger on Your Trigger

The Individuation phase is characterized by authenticity. They no longer played the role of the lovable mop tops, who would've never sung about taboo subjects. Sessions for John's "Happiness is a Warm Gun" began on September 24th. It's the sixth "mother" and eleventh "violence" song, continuing the current spike of these threads. It's the song with the most sexual focus and innuendo. It weaves a few unfinished musical strands together and showcases John's liberated rawness and individualistic word use.

The song was inspired by a gun magazine featuring the phrase that became the song's title.[280] As seen with "Revolution," John was working through his own aggression, here illustrating the senselessness of violence. He found the idea of feeling happiness after shooting things to be "insane."[281] The song involves the sublimation of violent desire into sexual expression. A notable line is, "I need a fix cause I'm going down." Some speculate it's a drug (heroin) reference, and it also parallels the "arc's" descent.

"The White Album" sessions were a shootout at times, but something miraculous occurred. They were able to work together as allies instead of coming apart as adversaries. Due to the song's musical complexity, they needed to work together in a focused way. The band worked for 3 solid days, got it right and brought yet another original sounding classic to their catalog. The song is revered by John's bandmates and legions of fans who place it in high regard. On an album noted for fragmentation, this song shows how their bond of brotherly love was still available to access.

The astrology (p. 416) conveys a sea change prior to this session. The Sun had entered peaceable Libra, inviting togetherness, while the planet of competitiveness {Mars} entered the sign of discipline and productivity {Virgo}, away from the ego aggrandizement available in the prior sign {Leo}. Additionally, there was a recent solar eclipse (9/22) catalyzing breakthrough with work projects {in Virgo, conjunct Uranus}. Part 2 has a few additional notes.

"Happiness is a Warm Gun" was a peak moment in a turbulent recording process, right when summer was giving way to autumn. Compared to the intensity of the sweltering summer, the autumn had a more reflective, poignant, sometimes even somber vibe. The leaves falling off the trees are symbolic of coming down to reality. The songs in autumn were of another variety.

Paul's "Honey Pie" is the thirtieth "call" song, another example of how the thread dramatically shifted from the prior heartache. It's classy and refined, a music hall number about the bridging of distance. Next, George had fun singing about Eric Clapton's love of chocolate on "Savoy Truffle,"[282] a song featuring booming brass instruments. Paul continues with his music hall influence on "Martha My Dear," an elegant piece featuring a string ensemble. The song is about inspiration, which Paul says his dog Martha provides.[283] Interestingly, Martha has a linguistic similarity to Mary. The song invites us to "take a good look around you" (similar to "Dear Prudence"), to be in the immediate present reality.

George's "Long Long Long" is an expression of longing for the embrace of Spirit, a heartfelt crying out of the seeker who feels the pain of separation. He sang, "So many tears I was searching," using the past tense. "Now I can see you, be you" shows movement into the present, an embodied integration. George is "so happy I found you," suggesting the realization of his quest.

John's "I'm So Tired" is the thirty-first "call" song. The theme returns when he feels "tired" and "upset" and needs "a little peace of mind." It's raw, another example of the psychological emphasis on this album, here addressing shadowy feelings that are normally not part of popular music.

In contrast, "The Continuing Story of Bungalow Bill" was a rollicking good time. Recorded on John's birthday (10/9), everyone banded together in good cheer (applause, hoots, whistling) for this loose sing-a-long. The song featured the only female lead singing on any Beatles track[284] when Yoko delivered the line, "not when he looked so fierce," and John followed with, "his mummy butted in," referring to the nickname for his girlfriend. The song has gun references and is about hunting, the twelfth "violence" song. John wrote it to scorn a fellow attendee in Rishikesh who had hunted tigers.[285] Given his violent history, it may be another instance where he was working out his own prior tendencies.

Paul's "Why Don't We Do it in the Road" is another where he is loud and liberated, singing a simple blues tune influenced by monkeys having sex in India.[286]

A Song of Love

There was a lunar eclipse on October 6th activating John's core spiritual work {at 13° Aries on his South Node}. Shortly after on October 13th, he recorded "Julia," the final song in the sessions, and the only Beatles song where he plays solo.[287] "Julia" was created just after the 10-year anniversary of her death. It's part of Step 6 of the muse process (conclusion), when the muse relationship is made explicit.

"Julia" is the thirty-second "call," eighth "mother," twenty-sixth <u>death</u> and the thirty-first **solar** song, unifying these threads to reveal one of the most important teachings of all. Julia, (John's dead mother) "calls me," revealing a relationship beyond the boundary of death involving communications. In contrast to the urgency of the "call" songs in the early days, this one is gentle and reflective. John sings, "Her hair of floating sky is shimmering, glimmering/In the **sun**." The teaching is that our energy (Sun, life force) does not extinguish with death.

"Julia": One's essence (soul) remains vital and present, connected to Source (Sun).

"Julia" brings a spiritual context to death, perhaps the most important lesson for John to have learned. Interestingly, he references Julia's hair, circling back to "my wings are broken and so is my hair" from "Revolution 9." Now her hair is part of the sky, echoing "Mother Nature's Son," the mergence with nature.

True to the descending motion of the "arc," the spiritual bond is felt at the tactile level. John writes, "Julia, sleeping sand, silent cloud, touch me." The muse was in the sign of sensuality {Euterpe in Taurus}, quite close to where the needs {Moon} were for "I Want to Hold Your Hand." The initial yearning for touch spoken in that song was now more

228

satisfied. Upon feeling this touch, the next line is "So I sing a song of love for Julia." "Julia" may be a much truer form of the love song compared to the early formula.

The song features images related to the astrological sign Pisces ("ocean child", "sea shell eyes"), Julia's Sun sign. John has said it also references Yoko, whose name means "child of the sea" in Japanese.[288] Though Yoko has an Aquarius Sun, it's conjunct Ceres in Pisces, reflecting the maternal energy of Julia. Perhaps this song was signaling the transference of John's heart from the past to the present, from Julia to Yoko as he lets his mother go. At the time of the recording, John was having a renewal with the maternal {a Ceres return}. A few additional notes are found in Part 2 (p. 417).

Shortly after the session on October 18th, the police raided John's house in a drug bust and he was arrested.[289] His divorce from Cynthia was finalized a few weeks later on November 8, and his album with Yoko, *Two Virgins*, was released on November 11th (discussed below).

George's Wonderwall

Solo albums debuted in the Individuation phase. George's *Wonderwall Music* was released on November 1st on the newly formed Apple label. He led the way with the first of many solo efforts by the four of them. Less engaged with both *Sgt. Pepper* and the *Magical Mystery Tour* film project, his "heart was in India." His immersion in Indian music, spirituality and culture is evident on this remarkably interesting album.

George was given creative control to make a soundtrack for the movie *Wonderwall*. The music is a bridge between Eastern culture and Western music. It contributed to the emerging world music trend, in which George was increasingly becoming a pioneer. The cover art depicts a wall separating two very different worlds, that are nevertheless connected. The songs are instrumental pieces that draw a contrast and synthesis between Indian instrumentation and Western sensibilities (including elements of rock, psychedelia, country and ragtime).[290] Eric Clapton and Ringo Starr make guest appearances. A theme of the movie is the superficiality of fame, an issue of increasing interest to George.

The astrology for the album release (p. 418) featured a leadership emphasis in George's area of work projects. There's a focus on the foreign and exotic, the bridging of cultures, but the artistry wasn't for everyone {Venus out of bounds}. Additional notes on George's astrology at this time and the album is found in Part 2 (p. 417).

They Became Naked

John & Yoko's *Two Virgins* was released in the U.S. on November 11th and was instantly controversial due to the naked album cover.[291] A potential issue with the core archetype they share {Aquarius} is going too far, which was the criticism. Another pitfall is losing accessibility, and the album was ignored by many and characterized by some as a "crazy" tangent.

To maintain his heroic, super-Beatle status, some saw John as being manipulated by Yoko. Many blamed her for his career turn, but John was fully in charge of his choices.

He was eager to overthrow heroic projections in favor of naked authenticity. He desired to use his fame and influence to further culture in a progressive direction. He supported the "butcher" cover on the American release of *Yesterday and Today* (in 1966) to obliterate the sanitized Beatles image. To take it further, he would go on to sing, "I don't believe in Beatles," in his solo career ("God"). Following the steep descent of the "arc" in 1968, he was breaking down what he saw as the phony elevation of celebrity culture. At the height of Beatlemania, millions wanted to tear off his clothes. Here, he stood naked in a stance that was utterly human and ordinary, devoid of any glamour. He was getting people to see they were in love with a story, to pierce through the trance of their *dreams*.

George's solo album was a statement of his individuation, while John was declaring his allegiance to Yoko, away from Lennon-McCartney.[292] The album's music was recorded in May during their clandestine rendezvous. Called, "Unfinished Music," it was designed to be entirely subjective to allow the listener to form their own impression, and thereby complete it (fitting with the *dream* theme). Created around the same time as "Revolution 9," it has many of the same elements: tape loops, cacophony of sound, dialogue, vocalizations and instruments being played experimentally.[293]

The astrology (p. 418) features the planet of revolution {Uranus} in the sign of artistic sensibilities {Libra}, featured prominently in the John-Yoko relationship chart$_1$. It correlates with avant-garde art and standing strong in one's authenticity (nakedness). However, like George's album, the style wasn't for everyone {out of bounds Venus as well as the Moon}, creating a feeling that John and Yoko were out of reach$_2$. However, the Sun was shining in the sign of intimacy {Scorpio}, and their togetherness was powerful. Also noted is crusader energy, and the pair would soon begin their campaign for peace$_3$.

Before they could launch their activist agenda, there was crisis. Shortly after the album came out Yoko miscarried their baby,[294] a devastating event for the couple. The very next day "The White Album" was released and the intense whirlwind of 1968 continued.

Album #10: *The Beatles* ("The White Album")

Introduction: "The White Album" was released on 11/22/1968. After the laborious studio process with *Sgt. Pepper*, it has a stripped-down feel. The cover is pure white, in stark contrast to the splendor and color on *Pepper*. Now in the Individuation period, this album takes that notion the furthest. In fact, some of the tracks might be considered solo works under the Beatles banner. Instead of collaboration, they often worked on their songs individually, sometimes playing the instruments usually played by the others.[295] George Martin had a relatively light influence compared to his enormous contribution on *Pepper*.[296]

A common adjective to describe the record is "fragmented," a state that often occurs with the individuation process. The diversity of songs, genres, musical sensibilities and directions is striking. Unlike the musical blending seen on prior albums, each song is true to its own genre, just like each Beatle was learning to be true to himself. The only double album in their catalog, it has 32 songs (including the singles "Hey Jude" and

"Revolution"). John (14) and Paul (13) dominate the writing, while George contributes 4 songs and Ringo authors 1. The John-Paul competitiveness elbowed out George, who had much more material to contribute. Many of his songs went towards later solo projects, particularly the triple album *All Things Must Pass* (1970).

It could be thought of as the "Hippie Album," with its stripped-down authenticity and acoustic guitars, focus on nature (both internal and external), rawness and realism. Whereas *Sgt. Pepper* was transcendent and driven by Paul {a Neptunian}, "The White Album" was psychological and driven by John {a Plutonian}. His strong, even intimidating, presence shaped the contours of the album into more liberated and emotionally-evocative territory, paralleling the "arc's" descent into the psychological depths. The album opens with "Back in the U.S.S.R.," featuring a plane touching down, mimicking the descent of the "arc." There are several songs that have downward references in the lyrics.

Musical Development: The music intentionally pushes the extreme, with song variety, emotional expression, subject matter and creative risks. It's also notable for soloing. Ringo is the only Beatle on "Good Night," Paul on "Blackbird," "Mother Nature's Son" and "Martha My Dear," and John on "Julia." The genres include folk ("Rocky Raccoon"), music hall ("Honey Pie," "Martha My Dear"), surf music ("Back in the U.S.S.R."), blues ("Yer Blues") and avant-garde ("Revolution 9"). Other songs have elements of country, pop or straight-ahead rock. Songs range in length from 52 seconds ("Wild Honey Pie") to 8:22 ("Revolution 9").[297]

George returns to the guitar after 2 years of focusing mainly on the sitar. Paul plays many instruments, including the drums when Ringo left. The album features acoustic guitar, piano, brass instruments and strings. Sound effects and studio techniques are kept to a minimum, used sparingly for certain punctuation instead of creating soundscapes. The exception is the experimental "Revolution 9," which relies heavily on tape loops. There are several back-up singers and guests on the album, including Eric Clapton who plays lead guitar on "While My Guitar Gently Weeps," but was uncredited.[298]

Lyrical Development: Including 2 singles, there are 32 songs that occupy 44 positions in the lyrical threads: 8 "violence," 6 **solar**, 6 "dark," 6 "mother," 5 "bird," 4 <u>death</u>, 4 "call," 3 *dream* and 2 "flute" songs. Though this number seems titanic, "The White Album" is a double album. All of the albums in the Transcendence period have a higher percentage of songs in the threads. The 8 "violence" and 6 "dark" songs portray the shadow work being addressed, while the 6 **solar** songs illustrate a continuation of spiritual blossoming. The 6 "mother," 5 "bird" and 2 "flute" songs point to the maternal and muse influence. *Dream* songs greatly diminish after the Transcendence period. Two of the three return to the conventional use (nighttime sleep or anticipation), while the other ("Revolution 9") is more shadowy than transcendent.

Practically any lyrical topic was fair game: chocolates, tiger hunting, capitalist pigs, attacking a guru, the number 9 or Ukraine girls, etc. Many songs were specifically about nature, an earthy focus. A zoo of animals is referenced: pigs, birds, walrus, raccoon, elephants, tigers, lizard, monkey, eagle and worm. There are also many references to the natural world: water, Sun, Moon, rain, mountain stream, hills, field of grass, swaying daisies, sunny skies, garden, flowers, seashell, wind, sand, cloud, snow peaked mountains, the world turning, tulips, ocean, kids running in the yard and air. There are emotional dramas depicted on the album and several tracks feature charged emotional expression (yelling, but also softness and gentleness).

Astrological Summary: The album is built on a foundation of spiritual questing and cross-cultural experience (p. 419)$_1$. Many of the songs were developed in India and reflect themes of spirituality, with an emphasis on nature. There is also a deep dark intensity, an extreme psychological quality in need of catharsis$_2$.

There is a pronounced tension between teamwork vs. leadership$_3$. The lesson is to honor individual expression within shared vision. John was having a return of leadership {his Mars return}, evidenced by his bold assertion on this album$_4$. His personal astrology was highly experimental {Uranus entering his Sun sign Libra, hitting his Mars}.

The familiar "Beatles signature" is noted, though harkening back to earlier times$_5$. Much of the music pays tribute to other genres in music history, including several references to previous Beatles songs. The album achieved mass popularity and acclaim, though some people find parts to be a challenging listen. Communications are provocative, extending an invitation for the listener to think or question$_6$. The muse was involved with themes of the natural world and arriving at greater calm$_7$.

Manson & the Collective Shadow

As the Beatles attained the toppermost degree of visibility and fame, they influenced society and culture in a wide variety of ways. They directly impacted the trajectory of music, inspired people to develop spiritually, and part of the story is also connecting with the collective shadow {Pluto}. The descent of the "arc" correlated with a confrontation with such dimensions in 1968: riots at the Democratic Conventions, assassinations (Robert Kennedy, Martin Luther King Jr.), intense Vietnam War protests, cultural movements and the backlash with the election of Richard Nixon. "The White Album" was released towards the end of this turbulent year. It would influence a particularly insidious character who was part of the cultural shadow.

Apparently, along with being mentally ill and unstable, Charles Manson was a huge Beatles fan. In his deranged mind, he interpreted messages in the music: the anti-establishment aggression in "Piggies," the call to rise from the dark in "Blackbird," the raging intensity of "Helter Skelter," and the mayhem, madness and revolutionary intent of "Revolution 9."[299] These songs and others got mixed in the psychic blender of his illness and he used them to justify his cultist crusade. The so-called "Manson Family" committed several murders, including that of actress Sharon Tate, accelerating the media fascination with high-profile crimes.

Of course, the Beatles were outraged that their music would become linked to something so abhorrent—but that's the way it went. For better or worse, the term "Helter Skelter" now has multiple meanings: an amusement park slide, a Beatles song and a phrase associated with the apocalyptic racial war of Manson's imagination, used to justify murder.[300] Unfortunately, Manson is a part of the story, so a brief look at his chart is found in Part 2 (p. 420).

Manson was particularly sensitive to the shadow components of the Beatles group chart, making it easy for him to distort their message darkly[1]. Everybody has an astrological connection to anyone else. Manson's contacts to the individual musicians illustrate their impact on his psyche. Manson's chart has a maternal wounding complex {Aquarius Moon opposite Pluto-Ceres} similar to John's, which also contains the Beatles "death" signature. Like John, he was estranged from family as a youngster and shares a strong rebellious and revolutionary desire[2]. The interaction with Paul's chart conveys possible envy of his artistry, perhaps triggering Manson's insecurity (he failed as a musician)[3]. He could easily misinterpret George's intentions or motivations in a darker direction[4]. The Beatles connection with Manson via "The White Album" is most unfortunate, though illustrative of the shadow dimensions on this record and in this story.

Chapter 20
The Come Down

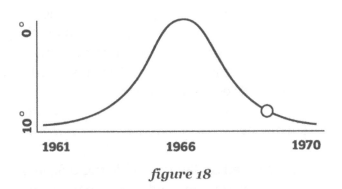

figure 18

Given the incredibly tumultuous 1968, a new year was most welcome. At the start of 1969, the "arc" was separating at 8° 53', almost fully back to earth. The band reconvened on January 2nd to commence the *Get Back* sessions. The "arc's" descent returns to where it all began—many of the songs harkened back to their musical roots and earlier times. The idea was to become a stripped-down band and jam again, to feel the joy for music that brought them together.[301] However, they were not communicating emotions effectively, so the musical direction was another context to play out their drama.

Beatles literature describes conflict in early January, shortly after the sessions began. Allegedly, George and Paul had a heated dispute on January 6th, then a few days later on the 10th, George and John had an even more serious fight.[302] Speculation was that it became physical, but this was denied. George reached his breaking point and quit the band. He told the others, "see ya 'round the clubs,"[303] and left the sessions. The planet of conflict/violence {Mars} was highly active in his chart {on his Moon, square his Pluto, and crossed his Ascendant}. Normally kept under wraps, his emotional defense mechanisms were expressed. Matters would settle down and they ended up playing numerous songs together, including playful improvisation and covers.

Paul was itchy to perform live again in some way, still pushing the idea forward (and George was still vehemently against it).[304] Paul also thought a movie could be an inside look at the band coming together, preparing to reengage as a performing act.[305] Instead, what became the movie *Let It Be* revealed some of the underlying tenseness. In contrast, a Peter Jackson movie about these sessions is close to being released at the time of this writing. In it, more of the playful and harmonious moments are seen. In their brotherly way, rivalry and love defined their bond.

John's emotional allegiance was now with Yoko, while Paul was deepening with Linda. Both couples would get married in March. John was collaborating with Yoko while Paul was now the most prolific and successful songwriter in the band. The development of George's musical talent, songwriting and spiritual leadership was profound and powerful, clashing with the prior "sibling" dynamics. Ringo agreed to a movie role (*The Magic Christian*),[306] so he too was individuating in his own direction.

Part of the issue in the Individuation phase was creating room for everyone to come into their power. Though they struggled with it in early 1969, they would rise to that occasion with *Abbey Road* later in the year. They continued on as the world-famous Beatles, trying to negotiate the limelight in their way. The public had an insatiable appetite for more music, and they were next fed some leftovers.

Album #11: *Yellow Submarine*

Yellow Submarine was released on January 13th in the U.S., less than 2 months after "The White Album." It was not an album the band sat down to make, in fact they had little to do with it.[307] It was the accompaniment to the animated movie of the same name (released in 1968), and featured 6 Beatles songs. These songs were not made to be companions to each other or with any intention to be part of a movie plot. The *Yellow Submarine* album is an example of corporate strategizing to profit from the Beatles name.

The title song first appeared on *Revolver* back in 1966. "All You Need is Love" was previously released as a single and also on the *Magical Mystery Tour* album, so it now makes a third appearance on Beatles products. George's "Only a Northern Song" didn't make it on *Sgt. Pepper*. His "It's All Too Much" and Paul's "All Together Now" were created in May 1967, after *Sgt. Pepper* sessions officially concluded. John's "Hey Bulldog" was made in February 1968 and lacked a place until now. Though *Yellow Submarine* was released during the Individuation phase, the material was produced in the Transcendence period (and is best understood as part of it).

The second side of the album featured George Martin orchestral arrangements. They're generally well-received and appreciated, though some take exception to them appearing on a Beatles album instead of another format. The band had nothing to do with the writing or performing of this music. The appearance of Martin's work on a Beatles album is a testament to his importance and influence.

Lyrical Development: "Yellow Submarine" and "All You Need is Love" are included in the thread tally for prior releases. The 4 previously unreleased songs register in 5 threads: 1 **solar**, 1 *dream*, 2 "dark" and 1 "rain" song.

On "Only a Northern Song," George speaks out against the contractual obligations the band was under, railing against the business practices he found to be unfair. Interesting that it appears on an album geared to maximize corporate profit. Paul's "All Together Now" has simple, childlike lyrics that mention colors, numbers and letters—the building blocks of the imagination. Though not technically a *dream* song, it mentions "sail the ship," connecting to the aquatic theme of the movie. "It's All Too Much" and "Hey Bulldog" were addressed earlier.

Musical Development: "Only a Northern Song" is intentionally dissonant to reflect the lyrics. George composed on the organ, instead of his customary guitar. It features trumpet and glockenspiel,[308] indicative of the variety of sounds in the Transcendence period. "All Together Now" harkens back to skiffle (with banjo, harmonica, ukulele, hand claps), the music of their roots.[309]

Astrological Summary: The astrology for *Yellow Submarine* (p. 422) shows a direct link to the song of the same name₁. Art is connected to oceanic themes {Pisces}, in an otherworldly or fantastic way. Martin's orchestral offerings are also evident in a more complex and airy sound signature₂. The astrology also describes business pressures and a need to conform to such demands₃.

Jamming in January

George's departure lasted a few days. He returned with some conditions: no touring and a return to Abbey Road studios (from Twickenham), and he also invited keyboardist Billy Preston to sit in for the sessions.[310] Not only would keyboards help fill in the more stripped-down sound, George figured the group dynamics would improve with his addition.

As seen in his astrology (p. 423), Preston's inclusion was a move towards peace. He brought togetherness and accord, activating the peaceable potentials of the Beatles chart₁. He also had the "Beatles signature" prominent in his natal chart, so he fit right in₂. His strength was supporting pleasant ambiance, precisely what the keyboards provide. With a focus on professionalism, his inclusion brought greater discipline and focus₃. George's intuition about Preston was spot on.

The band experimented with many old and new songs. They were jamming and fiddling around, sometimes telling jokes or simply waiting for each other to show up. In the musically loose atmosphere (with complex emotional undercurrents), they got back to their roots and played covers of their influences. They also toyed with older Beatles songs (even "Love Me Do," which was made at this position of the "arc's" rise). Some preliminary ideas for songs on *Abbey Road* and solo albums were also created. The *Get Back* sessions were ultimately abandoned, but several songs later appear on the *Let It Be* album (discussed at its release in 1970).

Below is how the songs developed at this time occupy the threads. Now that the "line of inspiration" had been crossed, these songs are not hypothesized to be connected to "higher" levels of consciousness, other dimensions or the muse. Instead, they reflect a return to the everyday, rooted in the personality. The lyrics may suggest how the songwriters had integrated the lessons of the journey. The focus of our analysis shifts. Part of the message from "The White Album" is that the transcendent is reflected throughout life; our job is to "look around." Similarly, we can take a renewed look at language to see if and how spiritual principles may be there for deeper reflection. Almost like solving a riddle, the question is how can we learn to see the divine in the commonplace?

Paul says "Two of Us" concerns his relationship with Linda. However, MacDonald writes, "the lyric seems to be more to do with John and Paul."[311] He sings about memories "longer than the road that stretches out ahead," and his relationship with Linda was relatively new. It's the thirty-second **solar** song and tenth "rain" song: "Two of us wearing raincoats/Standing solo in the **sun**" could have a couple interpretations. Concerning the John-Paul relationship, they supported each other in weathering the previous storms of grief. They would both stand solo in their careers to come, walking their individual paths towards realization (Sun).

A possible spiritual interpretation: "two" and "raincoats" appear in the first line, while "solo" and "**sun**" are in the second. The realm of dualism ("two") has its storms of emotion (needing "raincoats"). The Oneness of Spirit ("solo") is typified by the "**sun**." Here's a juxtaposition of the relative (dualistic) with the transpersonal (Oneness). These realms are eternally connected and simultaneously operable.

"Two of Us": Duality and Oneness coexist.

"I've Got a Feeling" is the thirty-ninth *dream* and thirty-third **solar** song. It's a synthesis of song fragments from John and Paul and features the line, "Everybody had a wet *dream*/Everybody saw the **sunshine**." John was simply being John, making a sexual reference as he was wont to do. And yet, deeper meaning can be found should we look through another lens. "Wet" and "*dream*" signify emotionality (wet) and subjectivity (dream), and can be paired with the astrological Moon. The reference to the Sun describes the spiritual flowering from the dream state.

"I've Got a Feeling": Our dreams form the seeds from which we blossom and awaken.

References to the Moon and Sun are also found in the next song. John's "Dig a Pony" is the thirty-fourth **solar** song. Of note is the line, "I pick a moon dog" calling forth the prior band name, "Johnny and the Moon Dogs." The following line is "Well you can **radiate** everything you are." The teaching could be about projection, how the psyche radiates into the external world to catalyze self-awareness.

"Dig a Pony": We radiate the dream to meet self.

Paul's "The Long and Winding Road" is the thirtieth "dark" and eleventh "rain" song, one that reflects his upset at this time. He sings of braving the night and rain in a return home. It may have parallels with working through outstanding emotion on the way towards spiritual realization. It recalls the early works by mentioning tears, crying and aloneness, but the subject matter is approached with greater maturity, reflection and acceptance. Eventually released as a single, it was their last #1 hit.

John's "One After 909" was resurrected from the late 1950s and finally brought to recording. The thirty-third "call" song, it weaves back to this important motif from the early years. The singer anticipates reunion with a lover who previously departed. John cries, "I begged her not to go" and is worried about reconnecting. "I got the number wrong" involves missed communications. It turns out she's on the train after the 909, and the song is not clear whether or not the reunion was made.

Don't Let Me Get Back

On January 27-28, sessions became more formal and structured, designed to produce a single (released on 4/11/1969). Indicative of the leadership change, Paul's "Get Back" was the A-side and became a #1 hit. John's "Don't Let Me Down" was the B-side. Though he got the secondary slot again, the song is widely viewed as one of his best offerings in the later years.[312]

"Get Back" is the title song of these *Get Back* sessions, the return to roots. It's raw and bluesy, notable for mentioning a man who "thought he was a woman." Later in 1969 were the Stonewall riots and other demonstrations for social justice and equality {Jupiter-Uranus in Libra}. The collective was beginning to address LGBTQ issues and gender identity synchronously appears in the lyrics.

Both songs have relatively simple lyrics and rely on musical grooves and feel. John sang "Don't Let Me Down" with great passion and sincerity. Recently divorced and in love with Yoko, he desperately wanted a more fulfilling romance. "I'm in love for the first time" was probably true. Much of the early catalog was a longing for love as a remedy for grief. Now there was deeper romantic authenticity, as heard in the song.

Both songs have connotations with the "arc's" descent. They were getting back to their roots (in the ground), and John's has "down" in the title.

Singing on the Rooftop

Instead of live performances, a compromise was made. The Beatles performed an impromptu concert on the roof of the Apple building. On January 30th, they played (along with Billy Preston) a 42-minute set on a cold winter day around lunchtime.[313] It was a surprise for people in earshot, as well as for the police who didn't know what to do about it. On the streets below, traffic was held up by people looking upwards. The footage can be seen in the *Let It Be* film. It was the last time the band played together in front of any audience.

The astrology for this event (p. 423) features the Moon at its uppermost peak {out of bounds in extreme north declination}, describing their heightened emotionality at this time₁. It also fits with their position on the rooftop, embodying this symbolism literally. They may have wanted to maintain their position on top of the world, perhaps a resistance to the descent. The astrology also hints at endings, consistent with their last performance₂.

Paul's Summation: The Ultimate Answer

Paul had the vision that led to writing "Let It Be" in the summer of 1968.[314] At the time, his relationship with Jane ended and relations in the band were upsetting. The "arc" was crossing the "line of inspiration," and preliminary ideas for the song were brought forward during "The White Album" sessions in September.[315] It became more developed in early 1969 and Paul filmed its "Apple Studio Performance" on 1/31, the day after the rooftop concert.[316] The release of the single "Let it Be" in March 1970 captures its essence—the astrology at that time reflects its spirit and will be reviewed later. Below is the discussion of this most spiritually significant song.

At the peak of the "arc" John composed "Tomorrow Never Knows." He was the leader for the upward motion and the song was a crowning achievement, synthesizing the major lyrical threads on the mountaintop. Paul was the leader during the descent and this song is the proverbial landing of the plane. "Let it Be" is the grand finale that also synthesizes the major threads and releases the drama. It completes Step 6 of the muse process (conclusion).

The song is important for another reason. The "seed" songs were discussed earlier, the ones that give voice to the challenges of their spiritual work from less mature consciousness. In this coming-of-age story, each of the Beatles would grow to compose a song that reflects the resolution of his astrology chart, a "summation song." Though their spiritual work was not completed, it was now fully conscious and understood. The lesson for the remainder of life is to integrate the work and walk the highest path. Being such a prolific writer, Paul has many "seed" songs. His first song "I Lost My Little Girl," as well as a good chunk of his early offerings, gave voice to his existential longing for reunion. "Let It Be" reveals the attainment of that dream, Paul's "summation" song.

Paul opens with reflection on his troubles and his "Mother Mary comes" to him. The troubling issue for Paul is loneliness and loss. Some interpret "Mother Mary" as the Christian historical figure, but Paul says it's about his biological mother, who was bringing support and perspective. Regarding the maternal visit, Paul is quoted, "I'm not sure if she used the words 'let it be,' but that was the gist."[317] He is consistently clear that the experience felt like a visitation, a non-ordinary experience, rather than a thought or memory. The song mentions her "speaking" as well as "whisper," both transmissions through language. "Let It Be" is the thirty-fourth "call" song, another involving reception of communication. It's also the ninth (and final) "mother" song and thirty-first "dark" song ("darkness").

The next part features Mary "standing right in front of me." Whereas previous contact with the muse had various degrees of awareness, now there's no doubt. As a result of the reunion, Paul's message becomes more informed. He sings that the "broken-hearted people" in the world have an answer, one that allows them to let go of those who have parted.

Paul's historical grief and turmoil resulted from not understanding death. Now he sees that life moves on, evidenced by Mary's visit. He brings the message to the entire world, to invite a collective healing. He claims that despite someone's passing, "There is still a chance that they will see." In this twenty-seventh death song, Paul's teaching from his direct experience. The dead maintain their consciousness, the ability to see.

Next is a return to the shadow in "Yesterday," here, a cloudy night. Paul asserts that within such darkness, "There is still a **light** that **shines** on me." From such illumination,

239

he will **"shine** until tomorrow," thereby moving forward from the unresolved grief of "Yesterday." The thirty-fifth **solar** song teaches that Spirit is always with us.

"Let It Be": Spiritual light is eternal.

Spiritual presence (the inner light) always accompanies us, no matter the feelings in the initial grips of unconsciousness and upset. What follows is perhaps the most revealing lyric in this study, "I *wake up* to the sound of music/Mother Mary comes to me." "Let It Be" is the fortieth *dream* song. *Mary is directly linked with the sound of music in Paul's dreams.* She is not just there to provide emotional comfort; Paul has revealed his muse.

At a similar elevation in the upward trajectory of the "arc," the line "whisper in your ear" was in "Do You Want to Know a Secret." In that song, John was paying tribute to Julia. For "Let It Be," Paul writes "whisper words of wisdom" referring to Mary. Her "words of wisdom" might be the spiritual teachings she delivers. The repetition of "whisper," and connection to Julia, could be another clue about the muse in this game of metaphysical hide and seek.

Fourteen year-old Paul might have wondered if his mother could somehow still be with him after she died. It's the ultimate question, and the elusiveness of the answer has led to much confusion and suffering on the planet. A spiritual issue shared by the members of this soul group involves deep-seated fear or wounding about death {Moon-Pluto complex}, and there is plenty of it in the story. Through the divine communication and reunion with Mary, Paul is more able to let go of the past, his fears and upset.

Paul crafted a timeless song that is healing, transformative and inspired. "Let It Be" invites us all to emotionally connect, to heal our initial spiritual amnesia, to reunite with eternal light. It moves us to feel sadness for a 14-yr old Liverpool boy who lost his mother, or for whatever losses we have experienced. If we allow it, the tears this song evokes may cleanse the past and refresh our spirit. Whether saying goodbye to The Beatles or to something else, it's haunting and poignant, utterly human in its universality. It's an iconic Beatles song and a masterpiece, a miraculous achievement that has comforted millions.

"Let It Be" is the sound of heaven coming to earth, the preeminent song of the "arc's" descent. It resolves the story, brings us grace, and provides an answer to the ultimate question—yes, life is eternal.

Moving Forward

The *Get Back* sessions were abandoned in early February. Similar to the "The White Album," the sessions were unstructured, often without clear direction. At the end of the month, they reassembled with a new plan. George Martin agreed to produce a new album, though with his customary role.[318] They began recording *Abbey Road*, what would ultimately be their last collaboration. Martin may have saved the band's legacy at this moment. He created a tighter work environment, restored direction and added his unique creativity and musical knowledge. *Abbey Road* was a return to professionalism and it became a huge success. Sessions were on and off for the next 6 months, interrupted by Ringo's acting responsibilities, business and legal squabbling, solo projects and personal issues.[319]

Though introduced during the *Get Back/Let It Be* sessions, John's "I Want You (She's So Heavy)" got a more formal session on February 22nd. The song would be developed for months to come, including the final time all 4 Beatles were at work together in August.[320] It is noteworthy for its heavy guitar, white noise sound effect, abrupt ending, simple lyrics and John's passionate singing. It is yet another highly original song in this period of Individuation.

February 25th was George's 26th birthday. For it, he chose to create demos for 3 of his songs all alone, another example of individuation. "Old Brown Shoe" was initially introduced in the *Get Back/Let It Be* sessions, but wasn't fully developed and completed. George made it his own, ultimately playing most of the instruments on the finished version.[321] The lyrics address duality, consistent with the "arc's" descent towards the everyday realm (and it has the phrase "drag me down"). In contrast, he sang about Oneness ("Within You Without You") at a loftier elevation. It became the next B-side, an example of his songwriting ascendancy at this time. "All Things Must Pass" ended up on George's solo album of the same name in 1970. Once again, his deserving work was not a priority in the band's culture.

The other song was "Something," which was not immediately embraced. George brought an early version in 1968 to rehearse during "The White Album" sessions, as well as to the *Get Back/Let It Be* sessions.[322] He completed it for these sessions and it went on to become a classic, a #1 hit and an A-side released in the autumn. It's one of George's most successful and signature songs, the most covered of all Beatles songs except "Yesterday." It doesn't register in the threads, but is personally meaningful.

George didn't write many songs in the early days. "Something" is a return to the love song, an opportunity for him to go back and really honor the genre. It has a confidence, maturity, subtlety, even a wisdom, properties the early formula songs generally lack. As the "arc" descends, this revisit completes the romantic focus of their work. George wrote, "You're asking me will my love grow/I don't know, I don't know," a contrast to the promises of everlasting idealized romantic union seen in the early formula. George makes a greater impact with emotional openness, his spirituality made him more present. Instead of being complex, philosophical or clever, he was completely engaged and accessible, totally in his heart. "Something" is a study of authenticity and the power of simplicity, a masterpiece of the love song.

Marriages and Divorce

In March, Ringo was filming his movie. Paul got married to Linda, becoming the final Beatle to tie the knot. John and Yoko went on a European adventure and also got married. In contrast, the John-Paul "bromance" was going through a "divorce." Neither man would attend the other's wedding, nor were they prioritizing the songwriting partnership. The celestial weather continued to bring forth a tension between individuality vs. relating.

On March 18th was a solar eclipse, triggering competitive and independence issues in the Beatles chart {at 27° Pisces, opposite their Mars at 29° Virgo}. On the same day as the eclipse, the planet of relating {Venus} turned retrograde in the sign of independence {Aries}, further highlighting issues of autonomy. Paul married Linda on March 12th, just before these 2 celestial events. In contrast, John and Yoko got married on March 20th, just after them. Married when Venus (partnerships) was direct, Paul and Linda had a solid and continuous marriage until her death in 1998. John and Yoko had a discontinuous marriage, one defined by a long absence when John had another lover (May Pang) and lived far away.[323] John went through a process of *recommitting* {married under Venus retrograde} to Yoko and eventually settled in to have their son Sean.

Part 2 has notes on Linda's chart, as well as the Paul-Linda connection (p. 424). The main point of convergence in the Paul-Linda bond is with Ceres, in a most uncanny and striking way. Linda also lost her mother when she was young and has remarkably similar astrology to Paul. She too had the maternal planet in major aspect to grief and spiritual redemption {Neptune}, which is inexorably tied to Paul {exact Ceres square Ceres}. Their union concerned the healing of prior loss and familial upset. A lesson was to deepen and progressively open, to establish a continuity of nurturance. Like Mary McCartney, Linda became ill with cancer. Paul was committed and loving until the end. Linda's illness may have provided a chance to resolve their karma with grief and loss. Both were confronting their core issue in a new way, courageously facing their gravest fears and deepest upset together. Linda's impending death may have fostered an even deeper experience of love.

John and Yoko got married in Gibraltar and then spent their honeymoon conducting their first bed-in for peace. It was held in Amsterdam from March 25-31, designed to protest the Vietnam War.[324] The newlyweds wanted to use the publicity of their wedding to raise peace awareness through non-violent protest. A famous image associated with the event shows John and Yoko in bed with signs reading, "hair peace," and "bed peace" above their heads, a guitar and flowers on the bed.[325] The scene is prototypical Libra (married couple, music, peace theme, flowers). John's astrology at the time (p. 425) illustrates his emergence into peace activism.

John and Paul were a partnership, operable for a dozen years. Their astrology prominently featured romantic energy {Juno} manifesting as a musical "bromance" with romantic subject matter. The March solar eclipse directly set off this particular energy {Juno} in their relationship chart (p. 426), correlating with the "divorce" of their songwriting partnership.

John played the role of the "leaver," while Paul attempted to salvage the bond. John became increasingly detached, often uninterested (and critical) of Paul's late Beatles offerings. Paul attempted to find ways to bridge divides. They later used the language of divorce in describing the band's dissolution. Paul was quoted in the Evening Standard, "John's in love with Yoko, and he's no longer in love with the other three of us."[326] John flatly said, "It feels like a divorce."[327]

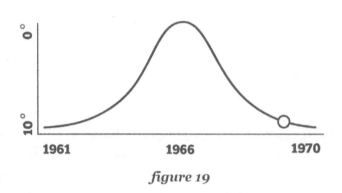

figure 19

There were headaches and disputes with business and financial issues. Apple was difficult to manage. John was now in full partnership with Yoko, campaigning for peace and composing solo material. The others all had side interests and projects too. The authors write in *All the Songs* about *Abbey Road*, "All knew, consciously or not, that the journey was at an end."[328] It wasn't always smooth, but they pulled it together to complete recording the album in the spring and summer, uniting for the sake of the band.

Ringo, John and George all composed their "summation" songs. There was one for the group as a whole too, appropriately named "The End." This chapter details the final months of active collaboration of the Fab Four, who now looked like the fathers of the boys who had that moniker. Tried and tested, they zebra crossed the final threshold as the "arc" completed its descent.

The Ballad of John, Yoko & Paul

It's often hard to say goodbye to a meaningful relationship. John and Paul grew from teenagers with big musical dreams to the realization of such dreams beyond their wildest expectations. They will forever be bonded in history with immeasurable cultural influence. Also, their shared maternal death issue bonded them at a soul level. During this "divorce" passage, there was some degree of psychodrama in letting it go. Each man was now married and had shifted his allegiance to his bride, yet the Lennon-McCartney partnership was so ingrained.

The emotional dynamic that underlies Beatles astrology {Moon-Pluto} can be obsessive, intensely passionate and dramatic. It's the same intensity seen in lovers who throw vases at each other one day and have incredible sex the next. In the latter stages of the Beatles, the John-Paul relationship was conflictual. John refused to appear on some of Paul's songs on "The White Album" and *Abbey Road*. During the "divorce," they had moments of cold disconnection and bitterness.

They also had moments of playful comradery, exhibiting the extreme nature of their dynamic. The recording of "The Ballad of John & Yoko" was an example of their shared creative passion, like a secret tryst between musical lovers. Paul joined John on his song detailing an international excursion to get married. Maybe Paul was giving his blessing for John to have Yoko as his main collaborator. Geoff Emerick was present at the session and describes it like the early days, when the two of them were alight with sheer musical joy, having a ton of fun.[329] In the midst of the band splintering apart and soon to crash, John and Paul united brilliantly, just like they used to.

The song is completely unique and only features the two of them. John sings, plays the guitar parts and percussion, while Paul plays bass, drums, piano, maracas and sings backup.[330] It was released as a single (with George's "Old Brown Shoe" the B-side) and became their final #1 hit in the UK.

"The Ballad of John & Yoko" is the twelfth (and final) "rain" ("rainy"), thirty-second "dark" ("night"), and twenty-eighth <u>death</u> song. The lesson at the "arc's" lower positions is to embody the wisdom of the journey. John grappled with the issue of death, particularly loss with outstanding grief. Here he sang, "when you're <u>dead</u>, you don't take nothing with you but your soul." In his very different way, he was paralleling the message in "Let It Be." The lyrics suggest life is eternal, providing perspective on death and perhaps also helping to remedy the prior upset ("rain" thread) and unconsciousness ("dark" thread) when that perspective was lacking.

The astrology for the session (p. 427) recalls the John-Paul partnership; their signature of collaborative writing was literally rising. However, much of the remaining factors involve self-interests, strongly pointing to John. Though the song was a collaboration (and Paul's contribution invaluable), it's about John. The heightened emotional nature that underlies Beatles astrology {Moon-Pluto} is most prominent. The combination is also the death signature, configured along the axis of karmic resolution.

In "Baby's in Black," John and Paul sang together about grief, being unsure of what to do about it. That song contains the phrase, "never come back," suggesting finality. For "The Ballad of John & Yoko," they sing together again. They were doing something about their grief, putting their process into song. In 1964 when "Baby's in Black" was recorded, they didn't seem to have a spiritual perspective on death and the hypothesized reunions with their mothers were yet to occur. Now, John claims that our souls move on when we die. If so, then Julia and Mary may actually "come back."

About a week later on April 20th, Paul began sessions for "Oh! Darling," which powerfully expressed his emotions. The song has a New Orleans rhythm and blues influence, a perfect format for Paul to unleash his increasingly liberated self. It's the twenty-ninth <u>death</u> song ("<u>died</u>"), a topic that might be part of what he was releasing.

Ringo's Summation: The Safe and Happy Garden

On April 26, sessions began for "Octopus's Garden," Ringo's summation song. The aquatic tale portrays the resolution of his karmic issue—miles away from the heartache, sickness, loneliness and relational estrangement he experienced as a youngster. It depicts an underwater sanctuary of togetherness, safety, fun and warmth. Being deep underwater, immersed in the nurturing energy of love quintessentially reflects Ringo's astrology {Cancer Sun, Pisces Ascendant}. A few years earlier, he sang lead on "Yellow Submarine," which also had an aquatic theme and flavor of childlike joy under the sea.

"Octopus's Garden" is the thirty-sixth **solar** song. "We would be **warm** below the storm" relates to the nourishing heat of the Sun, providing a vital coziness.

"Octopus's Garden": The Sun provides warmth for security, nurturance.

The astrology (p. 427) synchronously displays oceanic themes₁. At this time, Ringo's family was steadily growing (a third child coming soon) and there was powerful stimulation to his familial Ceres₂. The most represented signs in Ringo's chart relate to safety {Taurus} and happiness {Leo}, both strongly reflected in this song₃. His growth involves the attainment of comfort and joy and "Octopus's Garden" is a most buoyant expression of the promise of his chart.

Monetary Desires

As the "arc" continued to descend, issues of earthy management became more urgent. On April 29th, the planet of realism and maturation {Saturn} moved into the sign of finances and security {the earth sign, Taurus}. The spiritual work involved the cultivation of personal value and self-worth. On the mundane level, issues may play out in terms of money. The band itself was now beginning the Saturn return, a time of working with reality.

Since Brian Epstein's death, management was compromised and matters needed to be addressed. After the creation of Apple, business dealings became more complicated and they were in jeopardy of losing control of Northern Songs, their publishing company. The band fractured into different parties. Paul wanted his father-in-law John Eastman to assume management, while the other 3 preferred Allen Klein.[331] This particular planetary combination {Saturn in Taurus} can be stubborn, and the result was a stand-off. The Beatles became locked in financial and legal wrangling for years to come.

Paul had the most emotional charge around money and became the central figure in the drama. At the start of this passage, he wrote of financial tensions. Recording for "You Never Give Me Your Money" began on May 6th. It mentions negotiations breaking down and emotional upset. In 1968, they were tasked with managing anger, and now it was sadness, "wipe that tear away." Paul's "expression of grief" signature was being set off {by t-Uranus}, and this song served as an outlet. It's also the forty-first *dream* song. Paul sings, "One sweet *dream*," another return to the conventional use of dreams.

At the beginning of the "arc's" rise, they wanted to become rich. At that time, there were contractual negotiations to sort through, lots of business dealings. They covered "Money (That's What I Want)" on *With the Beatles*. As the "arc" descended to a similar elevation, financial matters were again pressing. It was also a time of major business negotiations and they composed, "You Never Give Me Your Money." The earlier song is upbeat and eager, an ode to financial conquest. The latter is somber and reflective, seasoned by the realities of financial desire.

John and Yoko released their second avant-garde album, *Unfinished Music No. 2: Life with the Lions*, on May 9th. Compared to the splash of their first album with the naked cover image, it didn't garner much interest. It would join George's 2nd solo release, *Electronic Sound*, released on the same day and also mostly ignored. They were both pet projects, indicative of the Individuation phase.

John's Summation: Giving Peace

Personal maturation and healing can become a gift for the world. The resolution of John's conflictual karma was to craft creativity and perform service to help make the world a more artistic and peaceful place. John's summation, "Give Peace a Chance," inspired and stirred the hearts of millions. The song is yet another example of his tremendous ability to shape culture.

John and Yoko did their second week-long bed-in in Montreal beginning on May 26th. John wanted it to be in New York, but legal issues from the drug bust in 1968 created an obstacle.[332] Towards the end of the demonstration, they organized a group sing-a-long to record the signature song. "Give Peace a Chance" became an iconic song of the times. It was performed at numerous protests and demonstrations and defined John's peace activism.

The lyrics reflect the individuated John who was completely unleashed. He sang about "bagism, shagism" "Bishops and Fishops," "masturbation," "flagellation," "United Nations," "Timothy Leary," "Hare Krishna," and other original word play. The words are like place holders for the chorus, which lends itself to communal singing.

At the time of the event (p. 428), a planetary combination representing an activist romantic partnership {Athena-Juno} was prominent[1]. Culminating in the sky was the sign of peace {Libra}, though with a fighting spirit[2]. The "Beatles signature" was strongly emphasized and some incorrectly think of it as a Beatles song[3]. Actually, it might be John's declaration of independence from the band[4]. It's a plea for global togetherness, and also healing from war[5]. The signature for healing battle scars {Chiron in Aries} was on John's karmic axis, suggesting his own spiritual resolution was motivating his efforts[6].

At the bed-ins in 1969, John fielded questions about presenting himself as a joke or clown (reflecting his songwriting in "I'm A Loser" and "You've Got to Hide Your Love Away"). He was willing to play "the Fool," and seemed to have great fun in the role. His answers suggested he was in on the game, completely in touch with the *dream* motif. Some saw him as "Jesus with a guitar" or a "hippie freak," and he welcomed it all because the attention supported his peace activist aims.

As the "arc" was approaching the ground, the Beatles were becoming embodiments of the spiritual wisdom they achieved. As discussed with "Hey Jude," Paul was becoming an inspirational figure himself and "Let It Be" would take it even further. John was consciously playing a character in a spiritual theater, non-attached from the projections of others. George continued to develop as a teacher of spiritual ideas in the form of artistic expression.

George's Summation: The Radiance of Being

The central challenge of George's chart is a removed disposition {Aquarius South Node}, hiding away in darkness {12th House Scorpio Moon}. He arrived in this life with fears and inhibition, adapting a reserved style (the "quiet Beatle") as a protective measure. His seed song was, "Don't Bother Me," expressing his initial tendency for retreat. Gradually, he learned to come out and engage more with life. A step forward was found in "I Need You," when he peered out from his hiding place.

In "Long, Long, Long," George gave voice to his tireless yearning for spiritual connection. He was now taking the next step towards that promise. Sessions began for "Here Comes the **Sun**" on July 7th, George's summation song. He wrote the "long cold lonely winter" {natal Aquarius South Node, a winter sign} was thawing, opening to the radiant life energy of the Sun {the dispositor of his Leo North Node}.

"Here Comes the **Sun**," is the thirty-seventh **solar** song, a titled one. The song celebrates the Sun, an invitation to be radiant and expressive, precisely what George himself was learning. He joyfully sings, "**Sun, sun, sun,** here it comes." As we engage wholeheartedly with the world, we shine our soul essence.

"Here Comes the **Sun**": We blossom into an expression of the soul.

The song is enthusiastic and optimistic, a welcome return to light. Since we all begin in the darkness of initial unconsciousness, it touches something universal. As seen in many of his later offerings, George's message was simple and accessible. The music lends itself to humming and sing-a-longs, much different than his prior complexity. George was fully open and engaged, a flowering into his more awakened potential.

The astrology (p. 429) features spiritual growth in the very area related to the Sun[1]. Darkness is connected to the past, which is resolving—the mind is learning to see life anew[2]. "Here Comes the **Sun**" is a signature song, most representative of the **solar** thread. George captured the essence of spiritual blossoming—he organized and delivered the teaching about the Sun directly. The song's Sun {reflecting the Beatles Sun, the awakening through love (Cancer)} sits right on George's astrological signature of philosophy and message[3].

247

John didn't perform on "Here Comes the Sun," as he and Yoko were in a car accident a few days before the session (on July 1, 1969).[333] Accidents can correlate with the planet Mars, which was potent in the sky {Mars stationing direct on July 8th}. Martial intensity was apparent in the sessions for "Maxwell's Silver Hammer," beginning on July 9th. Similar to "Ob-La-Di, Ob-La-Da," the song created conflict and divisiveness. With the accident as his reason, John refused to participate. He irritated his bandmates by having a bed brought into the studio for Yoko to relax on as she recuperated from injuries.[334] Ringo called it, "the worst session ever... the worst track we ever had to record."[335] George was incredulous that the song was receiving so much time compared to many of his that were being ignored or dismissed.[336]

Paul says it's symbolic of the "downfalls"[337] of life, another parallel to the descent of the "arc." The song has a bouncy, happy flavor but the subject matter is a graduate student on a murder spree, the thirty-third "dark" ("nights") and thirteenth (and final) "violence" song. It's another example of Paul's sunny disposition {Leo Moon} with repressed aggression {Pluto-Mars conjunction} in his shadow. "Maxwell's Silver Hammer" is the thirtieth (and final) <u>death</u> song ("<u>dead</u>"). The descent involves integration—and what better way to illustrate acceptance of death than having some fun with it? It's also the thirty-fifth (and final) "call" song, another with humor as seen in "You Know My Name (Look up the Number)."

The remainder of July was remarkably prolific, with far improved band relations. As astronauts were landing on the Moon and thousands were getting ready for Woodstock, the Beatles got to work. Instead of devolving as they did the previous summer, they were able to revisit unfinished songs and create new ones. They worked together beautifully, a sentiment paralleling a signature song. Sessions for John's "Come Together" began on July 21st. It's a highly individualistic tune with lyrical freedom: "joo joo eyeball," "toe jam football," "walrus gumboot" (another cross-reference to earlier works). The song has a captivating chorus and distinct shuffling rhythm. Of note is the iconic bass riff, illustrating another innovation from Paul with this instrument.

The band also began rehearsing song fragments for the medley on side 2. "Golden Slumbers" is the forty-second *dream* song, another with conventional usage. Based on a lullaby called "Cradle Song" by Thomas Dekker,[338] the song is about comforting sleep. Interestingly, "golden" calls forth the Sun, and the theme is getting "back home." Though not technically a **solar** song, it might be pointing to the integration of the 2 lyrical threads—dreaming consciously may bring us to our "golden" home of spiritual connection.

"Mean Mr. Mustard" is the thirty-fourth "dark" song ("shaves in the dark"). The song fragment concerns a "dirty" character with unseemly practices.

"**Sun** King" is the thirty-eighth (and final) **solar** song—the thread concludes with the second **solar** titled song created this month. Throughout the chronology the theme developed, and "**Sun** King" (like "Here Comes the **Sun**") showcases the pristine glory of awakening.

248

"**Sun** King": The Sun's nourishing power is magnificent.

Like many songs in the later years, the lyrics return to simplicity. Among the few words, the Beatles sing with gorgeous harmony, "Everybody's laughing/Everybody's happy." The song declares the joy of connecting with our unifying source.

The Beatles Summation: The Awakening of Love

In addition to all four members writing a summation song, the band itself also created one. "The End" is most fitting as matters were concluding. Consistent with the return to simplicity, the message is succinct: "the love you take is equal to the love you make." Their awakening {Sun} involved a connection to the personal heart {Cancer}—to fully love oneself. Upon so doing, there is less urgency, pain or drama about receiving it from external sources. Without complicated verbiage, the lyric synthesizes the **solar** and *dream* threads. The love felt within the personal consciousness (*dream* theme) is projected out (**solar** theme). In the end, *our experience of love is a reflection of this inner process---* what we "take" from the world is equal to what we "make" in ourselves.

"The End" is the forty-third (and final) *dream* song. Paul asks if you're "going to be in my *dreams*, tonight?" another conventional use of dreams. He further reveals the underlying theme of the Beatles story, the appearance of others in dreamtime. It provides a complement to "Like *Dreamers* Do" ("I saw a girl in my *dreams*"), written at the beginning.

Consistent with the Individuation period, each musician showed off his soloing skills. Ringo took the first turn and delivered his first drum solo on a Beatles record (on the last song of their last album).[339] And Paul, George then John took turns soloing a few bars, in a cycle that repeats 3 times. Paul's has a "rah rah" flavor, illustrating his igniting leadership. George's guitar licks have the furthest reach, showcasing his splashes of creativity. John's provides an anchor with down-home bluesy rawness. They mimic each other, while also deviating. The entire segment can be viewed both as one long guitar solo or 3— separation existing within Oneness.

Sessions began on 7/23 for Ringo's solo, then the guitar parts were finalized in early August. The astrology for the first session (p. 430) emphasizes the celebration of individuality linked to musical togetherness and joint purpose$_1$. In addition to forging individual expression, there is also completion in the area of message$_2$. They were collaborating beautifully and the "Beatles signature" was highlighted. The song became a standout representation of their later work$_3$.

At the Crossroads

The iconic image of the Beatles crossing the zebra walk outside of Abbey Road studios was taken in the late morning on August 8th. Many have made a pilgrimage to the site. Some saw the picture as evidence for the "Paul is Dead" conspiracy theory (more on that later). It has been replicated and parodied, but why has it resonated so profoundly in the collective psyche?

The astrology at the time (p. 431) reveals that the band was indeed at a crossroads. It depicts critical decision-making hanging in the balance—either a completion, a new beginning or some other turning point. Interestingly, the decision is connected to themes of death, and the "Paul is dead" speculation picks up on it. However, it is not Paul who is dead, but the band itself was soon to die. At the time of the photograph, John may have been mulling over his eventual decision. On the day the photograph was taken, there was a session to complete his epic "I Want You," a track that shows how potent a musical vehicle the Beatles still were. The band had defined John's life, so it's not something he was going to leave easily. And also, the passion in that song was for Yoko...

At this pivotal moment, the fate of the world's most beloved band hung the balance. In the famous photograph, John is at the front of the procession. He formed the band and it would be his decision when it would dissolve. Perhaps the image resonates so strongly because we have all made momentous decisions at a crossroads, certain moments that shaped the trajectory of our destiny.

Abbey Road was the last album they made together, and the cover image is what they looked like just a couple of weeks before the band ended. It captures a moment in history, forever immortalized. It challenges us to accept their end, just like they were learning to accept death. The familiar "Beatles signature" was in the sky when the photo was taken. True to its spirit, the cover image became immeasurably popular.

Daughter Mary Comes to Paul

Paul and Linda welcomed their daughter Mary into the world on August 28th. Some basic math reveals Linda must have been pregnant when she married Paul in March (he joined John and Ringo in marrying pregnant brides). Mary was born just before the upcoming *Abbey Road* release. Interestingly, John's son Julian was born when the first album was released (*Please Please Me*), while Mary was born at the last. Both children were named after their paternal grandmothers who lost their lives early and became central figures in this story.

Mary's astrology (p. 432) shows a link to her grandmother Mary through the energy of Ceres, the central planet of Paul's karmic resolution[1]. Paul and (daughter) Mary connect with flowing, healing aspects regarding family and nurturance. She strongly supports her father's resolution of grief and loss issues. There is also a connection to activism and she would join Paul with humanitarian causes[2].

Chapter 22
The End

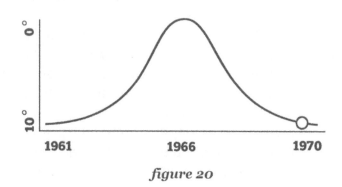

figure 20

The final chapter begins with John's announcement that he is leaving the band. In the aftermath, *Abbey Road* was released and the "Paul is Dead" hoax rippled through the collective consciousness. When the new decade arrived, the band gathered for one final recording. A few months later, Paul and Ringo released their first solo albums. In April, Paul issued a press release stating he was no longer working with John. Finally, *Let It Be* was released in May, right when the "arc" completed its descent.

John's Departure

September 20th, 1969 was the fateful day. John's decision to leave the Beatles, and thereby end the band, came in between 2 potent eclipses. On September 11th was a solar eclipse {18⁰ Virgo}, and on September 25th was a lunar eclipse {1⁰ Aries}. The former confronted the spiritual direction of the group {on their Nodal Axis}, while the latter raised questions about new beginnings and individuality₁. Also, in between these eclipses on September 13th, John and Yoko's Plastic Ono Band played at the Toronto Rock & Roll Revival. John was becoming more comfortable performing apart from the Beatles. Some believe this appearance gave him the confidence to solidify his decision to forge his own way. Additionally, the Beatles lost Northern Songs,[340] having been bought out. They would continue to get royalties, but they no longer owned the rights to their own songs.

John's announcement was made in a confidential group meeting. There was no public statement of the band's termination until the following year. *Abbey Road* was about to be released and a decision was made to keep it quiet.[341] Part 2 (p. 433) features the chart for the break-up, and below are some of the highlights.

One of the phrases used to describe their break-up is "the dream is over." The planet of death and rebirth {Pluto} was precisely on the group's dreams {Neptune}. The planet of change {Uranus} was on the band's songwriting {Mercury}, suggesting a shift in collaboration, as well as the loss of Northern Songs. John had expansive energy {Jupiter} on his Sun—he was seizing a new personal mission in his relational and artistic life {Libra}. He was also at his Saturn return, a time of accepting reality and moving into another professional cycle.

Album #12: *Abbey Road*

Named for their recording studio, *Abbey Road* was released on September 26, 1969. With George Martin running the show, the album is professional and became iconic—from the famous cover image to the classic songs filling it out. It is one of their best-selling albums, consistently ranked high by fans and critics alike.[342] Some even consider it their best, though this is far from a consensus. During the sessions, they also composed the single, "The Ballad of John & Yoko," backed by George's "Old Brown Shoe," also part of this discussion.

They put forth a marvelous work worthy of their legacy and love of music. Paul had the greatest influence on the album—the author of the most songs and director of the 16-minute medley. However, John's "Come Together" and the 2 George songs ("Something" and "Here Comes the **Sun**") have arguably become the most famous and celebrated. Many believe George solidified his stature as a songwriter and "proved himself" as an equal to John and Paul. Ringo's "Octopus's Garden" has become a trademark song, foreshadowing his prolific career to come.

The album's success could be due to its simplicity. As the "arc" returned to earth, they too came down from the heights and became more accessible. The album even touches on childlike themes, a return to the sweetness of the early days. Whereas the Transcendence phase was wildly experimental (a complete reinvention of their sound), *Abbey Road* sounds like a natural progression of the younger Beatles. However, within the simplicity is also the wisdom they had achieved.

"Come Together" and "Something" were released on October 6th in the U.S. as a double A-side single. This went against the prior practice of not releasing album songs as singles. Some made the criticism it was a money grab designed to make up for poor business management. Nevertheless, "Something" was the first George song to be an A-side, perhaps completing his slide forward to parity. Both songs reached #1.

Musical Development: The album featured greater use of synthesizer and keyboards, joining the trend in rock & roll. The 16-minute medley also paralleled the progressive-rock movement of extended pieces flourishing at this time. Critics argue the medley lacks a cohesive narrative, but the music returns to certain motifs. The harmonies on "Because" and "Sun King" receive high praise, some considering them the finest and most beautiful in rock history. The bandmates also show brilliant collaboration with the rotating guitar solos, and Ringo's debut drum solo makes news. There is also a "hidden" track, "Her Majesty," a simple song fragment from Paul. Such "hidden" songs would proliferate in rock music in the years to come. As the last track on the last album they made together, it reflects their history of being clever, playing with the audience and pointing to hidden meanings.

Abbey Road sounds cohesive and mainly stays within the mainstream rock genre, even sounding pop in a few places. "Oh! Darling" has a New Orleans rhythm and blues influence, while parts of the medley and "Octopus's Garden" have a tinge of country twang. There are only 2 non-Beatle musicians on the album, Billy Preston and George Martin, who also directed orchestral parts on a few songs.[343] Notably, Yoko does not appear on it. Sound effects or novel instruments were kept minimal, except for a white noise generator on "I Want You (She's So Heavy)."

Lyrical Development: Including the 2 singles, there are 18 total songs that occupy 15 positions in the lyrical themes: 3 **solar**, 3 *dream*, 3 death, 3 "dark," 1 "rain," 1 "call" and 1 "violence" song. The drop off parallels the return to the everyday (the "arc" completing its descent), and the lyrics are not philosophically or spiritually complex.

The 3 **solar** songs (including 2 **solar**-titled ones) illustrate a continuation of spiritual blossoming. At the conclusion of their career, the Sun is central and sung about with reverence. The 3 *dream* songs all return to the conventional use, creating a bookend with the anticipatory *dream* songs early on. The context of the 3 death and 3 "dark" songs is playfulness, suggesting some degree of resolution. The same is true for the only "call" and "violence" song, ("Maxwell's Silver Hammer"), another example of humor and lightness with these threads. The lone "rain" song ("The Ballad of John & Yoko") is also light and playful. The lack of "mother," "bird" or "flute" songs suggest inactivity with the muse.

The return to simplicity is found with minimalistic or basic lyrics on several songs, including references to the early sound. On "Polythene Pam" John sings "yeah yeah yeah," parodying the early Beatles at the corresponding place of the "arc's" rise. Paul too parodies the early Beatles on "She Came in Through the Bathroom Window." "Knew" is sung in falsetto, echoing the "ooooooohh" of the early days. The song describes a fan who came through his bathroom window, referencing their uncontrollable fame (reminiscent of the touring years). He does a similar falsetto in several places on "Oh! Darling."

Astrological Summary: The album was released under a lunar eclipse (see p. 434), a signifier of major change$_1$. The Moon is not only bursting at a Full Moon, it goes through a transformative process. It turns orangey-red, revealing the churning of emotion. The lunar eclipse spanned the polarity between individuality and collaboration {Aries-Libra}, the defining issue of the Individuation period. The eclipse confronted the Beatles chart in a highly frictional way, suggesting the band was at a most crucial turning point$_2$.

A return to previous recording production {Mercury retrograde in Libra} is indicated$_3$. Compared to the rawness on "The White Album" and *Get Back/Let It Be* sessions, *Abbey Road* is very smooth and pleasant sounding {Libra}. One criticism is sounding "artificial" {shadow Libra}$_4$. There is a workmanlike flavor, a spirit of getting the job done$_5$. The band coalesced in joint purpose, leading with a mindset of collaboration$_6$. Further evolutionary steps point to independence, interestingly, connected to women$_7$. John was partnering with Yoko in the Plastic Ono Band, while Paul would form Wings with Linda. The situation with the muse suggests her departure$_8$.

Paul is "dead" and John's in "hell"

Shortly after *Abbey Road* was released, a famous (and completely erroneous) conspiracy theory, the "Paul is dead" hoax, caused international intrigue. The rumor was he died in a car accident a couple of years prior, and was replaced by a look-alike. In September, an article published in a student newspaper at Drake University raised the issue and cited clues to the theory in Beatles music. On October 12th, the issue was discussed at length on a Detroit radio station, which sent the rumor into the mainstream.[344] The speculation was that, on the newly released *Abbey Road* cover, the Beatles were in the formation of a funeral procession. The Beatles office was flooded with calls and press officer Derek Taylor responded to debunk the claim. Nevertheless, the hoax proliferated and finding clues to Paul's "death" became a fascination for some fans.

Paul's astrology at this time (p. 435) had enormous connotations of death, certainly the strongest in his life {t-Pluto crossing his Ascendant and squaring his Sun}. Paul began his partnership with John when he was only 15 and the band defined his life. In the last couple years, he was rallying the others to make it work. He put his heart into it and was received at times as being too much. Despite his best intentions and efforts, the band was dying and he was faced with the lesson of rebirth.

Though the break-up was not announced until the following year, it's synchronous that the rumor surfaced just after John's announcement. The planet of death/rebirth {Pluto} correlates with literal but also figurative deaths. It connects to the collective unconscious, what is lurking beneath the threshold of awareness. It's amazing to think that the world was able to "tune in" to what Paul was going through, namely the biggest death/rebirth {Pluto} transit of his life.

The duration of the passage is a couple years. During this time, Paul's artistic and interpersonal life was being reborn. He got married to Linda, became a father and began collaborating with his new wife. He released a solo album (*McCartney*}, then formed the band Wings. The myth of Scorpio, Pluto's sign, involves the phoenix rising from the ashes. His new band name reflected the symbolism. Wings also recalls the song "Blackbird," the healing of broken wings and rising up.

To this day, some people believe Paul died and was replaced by an imposter. Nevertheless, the astrological activity to Paul's chart seamlessly matches the ongoing biography of Paul McCartney. It is unlikely that a replacement could have been found who not only resembled Paul, but had his incredible songwriting and musical talent. It is even less likely a replacement figure's astrology would unfold in lockstep with Paul's for decades. It is the viewpoint of this writer that the conspiracy theory has no legitimacy whatsoever. However, it places additional focus on death and a mysterious connection to one who is gone (paralleling this study).

On October 20th, John and Yoko's third experimental effort, *The Wedding Album*, was released. The record celebrates their union, focusing on their wedding and peace activism earlier in the year. On the same day, the single "Cold Turkey" was released in the U.S. (and in the UK on 10/24). Concerning the withdrawal from heroin, John continued to promote honesty and transparency. For the first time, Paul does not receive writing credit.[345]

John's detoxification from heroin was a major come down and the lyrics are a vivid illustration of the "arc's" descent. He sings, "Can't see no sky," "My feet are heavy," "I wish I was dead," "Get me out of this hell." Just 2 years ago he was singing of being "incredibly high," and now he's in "hell." "Cold Turkey" could be considered an anti-solar song as it features the line, "I'm in at the deep freeze," reflecting the coldness of the title.

John comically spoke out against the falling popularity of "Cold Turkey." He sent his MBE back to the British government with the note, "I am returning this MBE in protest against Britain's involvement in the Nigeria-Biafra thing, against our support of America in Vietnam, and against 'Cold Turkey' slipping down the charts. With love, John Lennon of Bag."[346]

Like the Beatles as a group, John also had the planet of death {t-Pluto} bringing him down from the heights {on his natal Neptune}. Like Paul, he needed to rediscover a vision for his life {Neptune} and rise again from the Underworld {Pluto}. The "Cold Turkey" cover art featuring a skeleton {Pluto} wearing glasses {vision/Neptune} is a visual depiction of such a task—as always, with John's trademark humor.

The Return to Self

When 1970 arrived, The Beatles were in limbo, caught between John's declaration to leave the band, and the public news of their split. Finishing touches were added to songs for the upcoming release of the *Let It Be* album. There was one last Beatles collaboration after the new decade began.

George, Paul and Ringo gathered to complete George's "I Me Mine" on January 3rd. Consistent with the Individuation phase, this final song concerns the individual. The use of pronouns harkens back to the early formula. "I Me Mine" captures the fixation most have on their egoic identity,[347] another George song influenced by Eastern teachings. It's a superb example of the "arc" returning to the same themes (pronouns, concerns with self) though wiser from the journey. On the upward swing, the personal self was being promoted. On the way downward, it was becoming undone.

George writes, "All I can hear, I me mine, I me mine, I me mine, even those tears..." Some contend George composed the song partly as a criticism of the self-preoccupation he saw in the band.[348] Firmly rooted in spiritual practice at this point, George was becoming less attached to his own ego. Perhaps he desired his bandmates to join him, which paradoxically may have been his own egoic agenda. "I Me Mine" is the thirty-fifth (and final) "dark" song ("through the night..."). At this final position back on the ground, the "arc" returns to darkness.

John's solo effort "Instant Karma!" was recorded at the end of January and released in early February. It became the first solo song by a Beatle to sell a million copies[349] and remains popular to this day. Though not part of The Beatles thread tally, it could be considered both a **solar** and a <u>death</u> song ("dead"). John sings the words "**Sun**" and "**shine**" throughout the song, while also mentioning the Moon and stars.

Instead of spiritual development and awakening ("arc" rising"), "Instant Karma!" brings the metaphysical law of cause and effect down to our everyday reality ("arc's" descent). Like George's "I Me Mine," it's an excellent example of how the spiritual wisdom and insight they achieved was returning to accessibility. George played lead guitar, Billy Preston played organ, Yoko and Allen Klein got credit for backing vocals and Phil Spector produced it.

Letting It Be

The single "Let It Be" was released on 3/6/1969 with "You Know My Name (Look up the Number)" the B-side. It was slightly different than the version on the soon-to-be album of the same name. They chose to have the parody "call" song as the flip side, linking 2 songs that resolve the "call" thread for their final single. "Let It Be" is sincere, beautiful and inspiring, while "You Know My Name (Look up the Number)" is disjointed, outrageous and comedic. Both songs represent facets of the band's character.

The astrology for the release of "Let It Be" (p. 436) is as miraculous as the song itself. It's conveys the resolution (perhaps a triumphant breakthrough) of Paul's karmic issues with maternal loss and redemption$_1$. There's a focus on spirituality, dreams and letting go. Not only is a partnership with the mother indicated, there is a strong echo of Mary's writing intentions and attunement$_2$. Additionally, Paul was renewing connection with his mother {Ceres return}. The issue had literally come full circle and was completing.

The astrology also points to John, the healing of emotional estrangement as well as Julia$_3$. The situation with the muse is most uncanny. It was speculated her presence was not active for *Abbey Road* and other recent songs, allowing the musicians to find their own way. However, "Let It Be" is the conclusion of the story, a song that mentions the receptivity of musical inspiration in dreams. At this time, the muse {Euterpe} was in the sign of death and deep soul partnerships {Scorpio}. It is incredible that she was at the *very same degree* as she appears in the John-Paul relationship chart, emphatically highlighting her role for them in a stunning climax and conclusion$_4$.

Declarations of Independence

Since John's announcement to leave the band, the process of individuation accelerated. Each of the Beatles quickly got busy, making solo music and forging a new path forward. Ringo's first solo album, *Sentimental Journey*, was released in March. Consistent with his familial nature, the album is composed of standards, mainly influenced by his mother's favorites.[350] Paul was distraught and drinking heavily,[351] grappling with his process of death and rebirth. He went inward and made his first solo album, *McCartney*. "Maybe I'm Amazed" was the standout song, a touching appreciation for Linda's love and support during this trying time. The album came out in April and included both songs and pictures featuring his new family life. Illustrating his musical agility, Paul played all the instruments on the album.[352]

Paul was isolated from the others, upset about the deterioration of the band and the business disputes. In particular, there was bitterness about Allen Klein's management takeover. The others thought the release of *McCartney* was too close to the upcoming release of *Let It Be* and wanted him to wait. Paul did not acquiesce, allegedly kicking Ringo out of his house when he came to negotiate.[353] *Sentimental Journey* and *McCartney* both received criticism upon their release, but are now more appreciated. Ringo has had a very fruitful solo career, including many singles, albums and his popular All-Starr band. Paul's solo career turned out to be the most prolific and commercially successful, though some Beatles fans think he was too eager to please the mainstream.

John was busy traveling, being a peace activist with Yoko and writing songs. He later participated in intensive primal therapy for several months in 1970. The song "Mother" was a testament to his process, dramatically putting his catharses into song.[354] His first album with the Plastic Ono Band, which was popular and well-received, came in late 1970. "Mother" opens the record and "My Mummy's Dead" closes it. George's triple album *All Things Must Pass* also came out later in 1970 to broad critical acclaim.[355] Many believe it's among the finest of all post-Beatles solo efforts and further cemented George's status as a songwriter. "My Sweet Lord" became a smash single and also created legal trouble for George with copyright issues.[356] Each of the Beatles would ultimately become inducted into the Rock & Roll Hall of Fame for their solo careers.

Before the band dissolved, all 4 Beatles got married and put out solo albums. Furthermore, in the Individuation phase, each declared his independence from the band. During sessions for "The White Album," Ringo temporarily quit, while George did the same during the *Get Back* sessions. John announced his departure when *Abbey Road* completed and Paul issued a press release stating he had no future plans to work with John shortly before *McCartney* and *Let It Be* were released. Some saw the timing of the press release as a way for Paul to get publicity for his solo effort.

Though Paul didn't explicitly say the band had broken up, it was widely interpreted the Beatles had disbanded through his announcement on April 10th. Part 2 (p. 437) features the chart for the press release. At this time, the astrology echoes the decision-making crossroads seen with the *Abbey Road* zebra walk$_1$. The "Beatles signature" is strongly highlighted, albeit in frictional ways$_2$. Financial and interpersonal hardship is noted$_3$, as well as a change in songwriting collaboration$_4$.

Album #13: *Let It Be*

Introduction: May is the final month in the chronology, one with a flurry of releases. The unfinished *Get Back* album was completed by producer Phil Spector, renamed *Let It Be* and released on May 8th. The album features songs directly from the rooftop performance, the *Get Back* sessions, and from prior work. The movie, *Let It Be*, was released on May 13th to coincide with the album. In between, "The Long and Winding Road" with "For You Blue" was released as a single on May 11th. Since the album, singles and movie were released less than a week apart (and have overlapping material), they are consolidated in this discussion.

Let It Be concludes the Individuation phase and the album is a return to roots. The band was not completely pleased with the final production, but matters were unresolvable at this point and out of their control. In particular, Phil Spector's work on "The Long and Winding Road" infuriated Paul as Spector added a lot of extra sound, effectively altering the song.[357] Other versions of it were released later, including on the album *Let It Be... Naked* in 2003, which captures the spirit of the album without excess production.

The cover image is the 4 of them as they looked at the time. Consistent with the Individuation phase, each musician is pictured in his own frame. The album has parity. Paul is the primary author of 4 songs, John on 3 and George, 2. John and Paul collaborate on "I've Got a Feeling," which combines 2 separate song fragments. "Dig It" is credited to all four members.

"Get Back" is credited to The Beatles with Billy Preston, a rarity to have another songwriting partner outside the band. He plays on 7 of the tracks,[358] earning the moniker "the 5th Beatle" from some. The album received criticism and it's not generally considered among their best work. Nevertheless, it's indicative of the Individuation phase, and the song "Let It Be" has utmost importance in this story.

Musical Development: The stripped-down jam orientation of the *Get Back* sessions featured blues-rock elements, reflecting their emotional rawness and return to roots. Blues influences are notable on "I've Got a Feeling," "Dig a Pony," "Dig It," "Get Back," "For You Blue" and "One After 909." "Maggie Mae" connects back to The Quarrymen skiffle days and is originally an 18th Century Liverpool folk song.[359] The sentimental "Two of Us" invokes the spirit of the early John-Paul collaboration when they were getting into their musical roots.

"The Long and Winding Road" has lush orchestral and choral arrangements from Spector. "Across the Universe" and "I Me Mine" also have musical enhancements (choral on the former, string and brass on the latter). John plays slide guitar, some lead guitar and six-string bass. Paul continues to compose on piano and keyboards. Notably absent on this album is the harmonica, which would've fit with the return to roots. On "For You Blue," John plays a bluesy guitar solo, George is at his loosest and this love song lacks the prior emotional urgency for affection. "Dig It" is only 50 seconds in duration, condensed from a far longer jam. "Let It Be" has a gospel feel, while "Across the Universe" has folk and Eastern flavors.

Lyrical Development: The album has 11 original songs that occupy 19 placements in the threads: 5 **solar**, 3 "call," 3 "dark," 3 "rain," 2 *dream*, 1 death, 1 "mother," and 1 "bird" song. (Note that "Across the Universe" was officially produced during the Transcendence phase and registers in 5 threads. Excluding it from the tally (leaving 14) would more clearly illustrate the diminishment of spiritually-significant songs at the conclusion of their work.)

The **solar** theme steadily and consistently blossomed for their entire career. The *dream* and death threads continue to diminish, while the "call" theme conveys intuitive receptivity ("Across the Universe," "Let It Be"), or a nostalgic return to the early days

("One After 909"). "Dark" and "rain" songs are evident (3 of each), but the usage suggests resolution. The exception is "The Long and Winding Road," which gives voice to Paul's crisis in the disbandment, much different than the early days.

The song "Let It Be" is the most spiritually-significant song, registering in 6 themes: **solar**, *dream*, <u>death</u>, "call," "dark" and "mother." It is the only song in the catalog that synthesizes all 5 major themes. "I've Got a Feeling" mentions *"dream,"* but lacks a transcendent context. George's "For You Blue" was written for his wife Pattie—another return to the love song. Like "I Me Mine," it includes a pronoun in the song title. Compared to prior works, the lyrics on *Let It Be* are generally simple and straightforward. The exception is "Across the Universe" (Transcendence phase). There are examples of John's liberated and unique word use ("Dig a Pony," "Dig It"), and Paul continues with storytelling ("Get Back," "Two of Us"). George was less overtly spiritual and had a lighter touch.

Astrological Summary: The astrology (p. 438) for the album's release reflects an ending in their artistry$_1$. The "Beatles signature" was strongly emphasized, highlighting the emotional competitiveness that contributed to their fracture$_2$. Communication challenges are noted, as well as a return to the past$_3$. The breakup of the "family" is evident; an emphasis on completion$_4$. The muse (Euterpe) doesn't appear to be significant for the album's release after being so prominent for the "Let it Be" single in March. It appears as if her work has completed and she's returning to the realm of death$_5$.

The "arc" was at 10° 18' separating and their work had completed. Not only were the 1960s over, but the dominant astrological configuration which defined the times (Uranus-Pluto conjunction) was history. We can look back at the 1960s and understand it's significance as a seed moment for 130 years of our collective evolution. Perhaps more than anything or anyone, The Beatles exemplified the shifting currents of culture and consciousness that defined the times, the clearest representation of this planetary interchange. Their own process of maturation and voluminous body of work captured the process of spiritual awakening and integration. The next Uranus-Pluto meeting will be in the early years of the 2100s.

Let It Be plays an important role, in ways more than just musical. The journey from Liverpool to Hamburg to Beatlemania to *Sgt. Pepper* to India to the rooftop was a whirlwind! The enormous cultural impact was unprecedented. The human toll of the journey to wealth and fame was a lot to process. The album can be seen as a plea for grace. The phrase "let it be" has a softness, even divinity. It looks above and beyond while also having gratitude for what has been. Despite the tension of poorly managed emotion at the time of its recording, these men had a deep love for each other. They were family. As is the case with most families, individual members set out to find themselves. The boys had become men and they were addressing the next stage of maturation {the Saturn return}.

Each of them would face major life challenges (including divorce, substance abuse issues, legal, financial and upsetting interpersonal dynamics) in the aftermath of the breakup and for years to come. These individuals were normal humans, with universal problems, just like the rest of us. In the end, The Beatles were not Gods, but pointed to God within us. Though this book suggests a divinely inspired dimension to the story, their example informs us that spiritual receptivity is available for all of us normal people too.

They eventually learned to accept death—of the band, and the loved ones and friends who parted. Their legacy challenges us to do the same. The "death" of The Beatles was another beginning, just as always. And for the remainder of human life on this beautiful planet, the music of The Beatles will likely be appreciated. And then someday life on Earth will end, allowing us yet again to let it be.

Final Thoughts

And here at the end of this journey, what do we make of The Beatles? My view is they have such great universal resonance because they reflect (and wrote about) our existential situation. We are all initially alone in nowhere land, misunderstanding our experience. Feeling separate from our spiritual home, it's natural to call out for love and connection. We might discover the spiritual home is in the heart. We bridge heaven to earth through becoming our most soulful self. The Beatles represent us all, the universal process of awakening (ascent) and embodiment (descent).

Each of the Beatles exemplified the reunion with self. John learned to acknowledge and embrace his wounded inner child. By giving peace to himself, his message of love shaped the trajectory of music and culture. Paul's efforts to fix the hole in his heart strengthened his resolve. The expression of his grief continues to invite collective healing and togetherness, leading us to let life be. George healed his removal to darkness, found his inner light, and blossomed into his radiant self. His example influenced the deepening of music in a contemplative direction, leading an East-West cultural synthesis. Ringo moved from isolation to finding his sanctuary of love under the sea, which is inside his heart. As a result, he was the emotional anchor of this historic musical act. And the Beatles will forever remind us that the love we experience in the world originates in what we make for ourselves.

The mystical poet Rumi is quoted, "Love is the bridge between you and everything." I began this project without any idea where it would lead. The research and writing led to the following hypothesis: from a more solid inner foundation, these songwriters bridged worlds and reunified with a lost love. The soulful love between mothers and sons motivated, inspired and ultimately led to co-creative partnerships that changed the world. Soul love poured into this incredible and beautiful music for all to enjoy, a gift of divine proportions.

The Beatles came of age at an historic moment, one that connected humanity to a broader spiritual vision and experience of the divine. They were inspired by it and delivered a message: To see beyond pleasing the self and recognize our Oneness, that life flows through us and is at our command. We sail towards spiritual realization (**Sun**) on an imaginal river where nothing is quite real, riding the colorful waves of our *dreams* with a little help from our friends.

Part 2

Detailed astrological analyses are here in Part 2. The discussions are linked to the corresponding sections in Part 1, designed to be read together. There is some work in flipping back and forth (a bookmark comes in handy). I wanted to make the reading of Part 1 most accessible to the layperson, so thanks for understanding this format. First are some notes about this astrological perspective.

The underlying philosophy of this approach assumes reincarnation. I realize that not everyone believes in, or has a framework that includes, this concept. It's important to mention this at the start, to let you know where I'm coming from. For the skeptics out there, I used to be an ardent one myself, so I get it. The Beatles themselves share a belief in reincarnation if it's any consolation (as do a majority of people on the planet). I have no interest in trying to convince anyone the phenomenon is real—it's just the assumption of this kind of astrology.

The main idea is that every person who appears on this beautiful planet has an intention to spiritually mature. We grow from a "spiritual childhood," which began in prior lives. Astrology doesn't provide information on how many lives we have had, just their impact. We tend to create familiar karmic patterns—particular themes, issues and interests that are developing. Oftentimes we behave unconsciously and have to clean something up. Usually, there are substantial wounds needing to be addressed. Universally, we are all works in progress and that's the way of it.

The Beatles reflect this process of maturation. Their work gradually developed spiritually from year to year, album to album. They had an initial focus on personality desires, before reaching beyond the self. Spiritual awakening has been compared to a seed that blossoms into a flower. The point is not to leave the personality (seed), but to have it mature and radiate the soulful beauty (flowering) which envelops and sustains us. We might realize that we are intimately part of a broader organizing principle, that nature itself is as intelligent and alive as we are.

An astrology chart conveys the leftover work from our spiritual childhood, as well as intentions for growth in the present incarnation. Though that trajectory informs individual chart analyses, Part 2 also addresses many types of charts including events and album releases. The discussions intentionally focus on *what appears to be most relevant*.

261

Some sections will be more in-depth than others, tailored to their unique circumstances and importance in the story.

Regarding my astrological approach: The standard 10 planets and Chiron are included, as well as the major asteroids (Ceres, Juno, Athena, Vesta). The *Astrology of Awakening* approach examines the Moon and Sun from a *spiritual* perspective (compared to the more frequent associations with personality, gender or parental significations).

The Moon is understood as a window into the spiritual childhood, the early developmental organization of identity and needs. It points to our attachments and motivations, how we find a sense of self. Since we all begin as youngsters, there is something immature, unconscious or regressive with the Moon. If we don't mature, we perpetually stay in our spiritual childhood, playing out these attachments and tendencies. Maturation involves the loosening of attachments, letting go of the past and arriving more fully in the present. The central issue of the Moon is love. With a foundation of love inside, we become more poised to deal with the world. If not, we unconsciously scurry about trying to find it as it's so primal and central in our humanness (Moon).

The Nodes of the Moon encompass habitual patterns (or karma) stemming from our early emotional foundation (Moon), as well as their resolution. The Moon's South Node points to familiar areas and interests, unfinished patterns still in a process of development. Since we all begin in unconsciousness, there is generally something to clean up and release with the South Node (and associated factors). Some advocate that we should "move away" from the South Node; it's seen as a trap of the past. My view is to complete the work begun, to bring greater awareness and maturity to it.

The North Node is opposite the South and points to attributes, experiences and areas for new learning and integration. Opposite signs balance each other, so the North Node provides the important polarity to lift us from any entrenched patterns. Ultimately, we are developing the entire Nodal Axis, to do *both* the North and South Node consciously. Also, the planets in aspect or dispositing (often called "ruling") either Node are central players in the spiritual dynamics.

Many see the astrological Sun as personal identity. Here, the Sun is understood as a developmental *process*, the gradual becoming of the flower. Over time, we awaken into the soul self, and one's energy (Sun) connects beyond the confines of separation (Moon) and into all of life. Through our solar radiance, we project our energy out and experience unresolved patterns (Moon, Nodal lessons) in the present moment (Sun). As we mature and become more conscious, we navigate with increasing awareness and skill. In this analogy: the Moon is the seed (the core emotional self), the Nodes are the "gardening" (the spiritual lessons), while the Sun is the flowering into our spiritual potential. As we mature, we shine our beauty into the world and offer the fruits we've developed selflessly. Before such growth, we tend to reduce the Sun to personality, ego and a personal agenda (the more common conceptualization of the Sun in popular astrology).

The other planetary energies stem from this central organization, or exist around it in some way. Pluto points to material buried in the unconscious (deep in the "soil" of the Underworld), often called the shadow. Mercury (cognition, communication), Venus (sensuality, relational), and Mars (exertion of will) are personal energies that branch into the immediate environment. Jupiter and Saturn concern broader social and cultural participation, issues of purpose (Jupiter) and the structure of our contributions (Saturn). Saturn is an earth energy, relevant to what's occurring on the ground. It's the last visible planet and forms the structure of the mundane realm, what we typically experience as consensus reality.

Uranus pertains to the matrix, the metaphysical organization of spiritual issues, processes, lessons and soul intentions (including astrology). It's often called "The Great Awakener," as it might stimulate awareness of this other dimension. On a personal level, Uranus also relates to material that has been split off or disconnected in some way (sometimes due to trauma). Neptune involves consciousness itself: imagination, vision, inspiration, the stuff of dreams. It also involves issues of disenchantment, grief or existential malaise. Chiron involves areas of health and well-being, healing the bumps and grind of separation in order to venture beyond (it orbits between Saturn and Uranus, a bridge from the personal to the transpersonal).

Ceres, the "grain goddess," relates to nurturing and caretaking issues. Sharing the same root as cereal, it represents how we are emotionally and physically fed or nourished. The asteroids play supporting roles to the major archetypes. There is some overlap with the sign of Cancer and the Moon, which connects with home and domestic issues. Ceres specifically has associations with maternal issues as she is the "Great Mother," while Cancer/Moon involves broader issues of family, lineage, ethnicity, roots and tribe/clan membership. Athena relates to social issues, a public and cultural focus. She is the "warrior priestess," who makes a mark in the world by advocating a cause, fighting for justice.

Juno involves romance, a central focus of the band, especially in the early years. Libra/Venus concerns relating, the "I-Thou" dynamic between self and other (which may or may not involve romance). The romantic focus of Juno involves themes of jealousy, fidelity, idealism of a partner or trust issues—how we define the terms of our romantic relating. Vesta involves the honing of a craft, the devotion to a job well done. It's the sacred flame within, requiring inner focus and attunement to develop mastery.

In some analyses is a unique inclusion: the astrological attunement to the muse. John and Paul have a special relationship with this mysterious phenomenon and has major relevance in this story. The muse (signified by asteroid Euterpe) appears as a bird in some particular charts.

John Lennon

1: The 10th House is the area of ambition and professional stature. With his Aquarius Moon in this realm, John sought to occupy positions as a revolutionary, innovator or other progressive roles.

2: John's Moon-Pluto opposition relates to his painful family wounding dynamics (Pluto in the 4th). It's also the death signature, appearing throughout Beatles astrology. The Moon's square to Ceres steers the issue in the direction of maternal loss. Abandonment is a core issue with Aquarius, as well as general instability or restlessness. These lunar aspects illustrate John's grasping for emotional nurturance from outside sources.

3: Pluto in the 4th is a potential transformation into finding love within, which progressively blossomed in John and is seen in his message. It also matches the intention of the band itself.

4: The 7th House is the area of "others," often how we project the psyche into interpersonal realms. With Ceres in the 7th, it was natural for him to play out mother issues (Ceres) in relationships (7th).

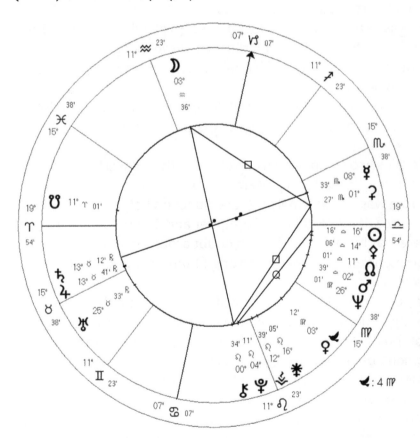

5: The "wounded child" signature is a T-Square: Ceres square his Moon-Pluto/Chiron opposition. The signature involves an initial blaming of others for his emotions and ultimately the transformation into more peaceable and loving relations.

6: Mercury is also a part of his "wounded child" T-square. It was conjunct Ceres—a desire to communicate (Mercury) with his dead mother (Ceres in Scorpio), connected to the healing of trauma (Aquarius Moon).

7: Aries South Node in the 12th House. War scenarios (Aries) are part of the archetypal scope of this conflictual signature. When John starred as a soldier in the film *How I Won the War*, this signature was being set off, supporting the notion of karma of this variety.

8: 6th House Libra North Node, the point of karmic reconciliation or balancing.

9: John had an overwhelming focus on the arts and relationship (Libra): his leadership (Mars), activism (Athena), the point of karmic reconciliation (North Node) and his process of spiritual awakening (Sun).

10: John's natural attunement to style, creativity and likability is found with the preponderance of Leo and Libra planets. The blend can be highly engaging and entertaining.

11: Venus in Virgo in the 5th House is the dispositor ("ruler") of the North Node. The planet is like the "ambassador" of the North Node, how its intentions become worked on. He specifically carried a soul intention to become an entertainer or performer (5th House), one who becomes professional, diligent, grounded, focused and technically savvy (Virgo).

12: Right next to his Venus is the muse (Euterpe), illustrating a creative (5th House Venus) work (Virgo) partnership. John's Venus-Euterpe conjunction displays how his creative expression (Venus, 5th) is inexorably tied to working (Virgo) with the muse.

13. His Libra North Node in the 6th House involved working with others, for John to learn to collaborate and establish productive partnerships.

14: John's Libra Sun was exactly quintile Pluto in Leo (highlighted in the above chart, its orb is only 5' or 1/12th of a degree). The quintile is the aspect of potential genius and John's was in entertainment (Leo) and cultural (Libra) signs. His Sun was also conjunct Athena in Libra, correlating with peace advocacy.

15: The gift of Libra is aesthetics, style, being pleasing. Combined with John's progressive instincts (Aquarius Moon), his attunement was perfect for shifting artistic trends.

Also of note is John's Aries Ascendant which correlates with his assertive approach to life and brings forward his artistic-leadership Mars in Libra (dispositor of ASC) into expression. Also in his 1st House was an extremely tight conjunction between Jupiter and Saturn in Taurus. The 1st is an area of leadership, while Jupiter and Saturn involve societal and professional issues. There was initial insecurity and doubt around cultural leadership, so the spiritual work was to mature into someone strong (Taurus) enough to handle it (rather than his karmic pattern of retreat).

Jupiter-Saturn was opposite Mercury, providing a vocational focus to communications (singing, songwriting). The combination was also square Vesta-Juno in Leo: John was learning to polish his creative (Leo) romantic (Juno) craft (Vesta), connected to the development of his writing (Mercury) maturation (Jupiter-Saturn). Uranus in Taurus in the 2nd House echoes his Aquarius Moon (initial insecurity, instability). Upon developing greater poise and confidence (Taurus), his breakthrough (Uranus) occurs in artistic ways (Uranus square 5th House Venus). Uranus-Venus contacts are found with the revolutionaries and visionaries of new cultural and artistic trends.

Paul McCartney

1: Leo Moon in the 11th House, a desire for recognition from the collective. He is driven by a need to perform for the masses (Leo, 11th), to satisfy an unfulfilled desire in his soul. The Moon is a window into our karmic inheritance, and Paul is a natural entertainer.

2: Mars-Pluto in Leo: aggression or anger (Mars) in the shadow (Pluto) related to the unfulfilled creative and performance desires (Leo).

3: South Node in Pisces in the 6th House, a karmic pattern of service and sacrifice (Pisces) in the realm of work (6th House). Disposited by Neptune in Virgo on the Ascendant suggests further sacrifice in his actions (1st House). Neptune on the Ascendant is also his "dreamy" presentation or demeanor, a persona of compassion and caring.

4: The Mars-Pluto in Leo conjunction is the "I'm in charge" signature.

5: The Pisces South Node also involves sadness or grief. Neptune (the dispositor) is opposite maternal Ceres, pointing directly to karma with maternal loss.

6: Paul has Venus in Taurus in the 8th House, positioning a financial planet in a financial sign in a financial house. Paul's Leo Moon is square Venus, illustrating deep emotional friction with others concerning money. The defense mechanism of a Leo Moon can look at the bright side of life, which can also lead to the evasion of the shadow and emotional pain.

7: The "expression of grief" signature involves his Gemini Sun, making his Neptune-Ceres opposition a T-square. As the energy of awakening in the present, the work of the Sun is to give voice (Gemini) to his maternal grief. He can find catharsis and completion, while also emotionally connecting with his audience. The "expression of grief" signature makes aspects to his muse at 26° Capricorn (Sun quincunx muse, Neptune trine muse, Ceres sextile muse), which resides in his 5th House of creative expression.

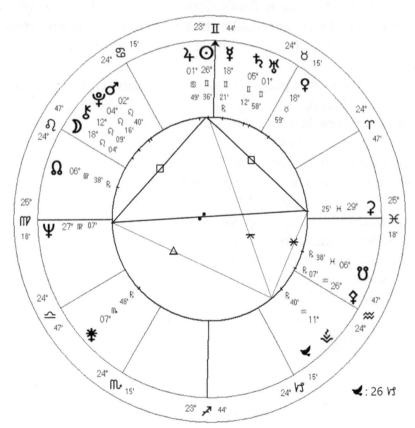

8: Virgo North Node in the 12th is developing the proficiency (Virgo) to experience imaginative or intuitive realms (12th), potentially to craft (Virgo) inspired works. Mercury (the dispositor) learns to communicate from such experiences, to teach (Gemini) broader truths (9th House).

9: "Karmic credit" is related to his 6th House Pisces South Node, his selfless devotion, responsible disposition and helpfulness.

10: Almost everything in Paul's chart is above the horizon. The upper hemisphere of the chart involves public, professional and cultural areas. His potential for realizing success is found with his Sun-Jupiter conjunction at the pinnacle of his chart. The message of his Gemini Sun is developing a philosophy (Jupiter) of love (Cancer).

11: Paul's ethic is found in his workmanlike Virgo Ascendant as well as his karmic pattern of dedication and service (6th House South Node).

12: Paul's Mercury is retrograde, correlating with his initial challenges with schooling, his decision to be primarily self-taught musically, and with appreciating trends from the past. Not only was he the Beatle most steeped in music history, his songs pay homage to older genres and his signature song is "Yesterday." He developed the knack to write intuitively, the gift of working through the initial challenges with education.

13: With Neptune square his Sun, the potential is to awaken into broader spiritual or archetypal themes. As a Gemini, his gift might capture such dynamics through storytelling. His incredible knack for melody and subtlety is found with this aspect and he has famously said that songs have arrived in his dreams.

14: Gemini has a focus on songwriting, interest in sound, and the ability to express himself melodically and through multiple instruments.

Also of note is Paul's Gemini Sun quintile his Virgo North Node—an especially expansive (and potentially brilliant) link between ideas (Gemini) and inspired craftsmanship (Virgo). Paul has become one the most successful songwriters in world history.

The karmic pattern of sacrifice (Pisces) with long hours and drudgery (6th House) has been limiting. Squaring the Nodal Axis are both Uranus and Saturn in Gemini in the 9th House. There is restriction (Saturn) with learning and adventure, so breakthrough (Uranus) occurs in these very areas. The intention is to be free (Uranus) to become his own authority (Saturn) and travel the world (9th House). The current lifetime is about expansion and a breadth of new experiences.

Paul has Vesta in Aquarius in the performance related 5th House signifying creative (5th House) craftsmanship (Vesta) of new inventive trends (Aquarius). Vesta is square Juno in Scorpio, adding romantic dimensions to such creativity. Juno in Scorpio square Pluto suggests deep frustration about being met intimately, with lots of passion and urgency. His Sun is also trine Athena in Aquarius, which involves progressive activism and social/civic outreach.

George Harrison

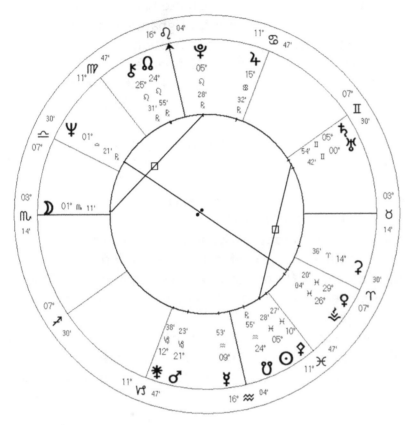

1: Scorpio Moon in the 12th House is consistent with both his need for spiritual connection and a defense mechanism of retreat from the world.

2: His Moon square Pluto in the 9th House was George's emotional angst towards dark teachings. He was likely wounded (Pluto) by ideas that didn't sit well in his heart (Moon), from the area of religion or beliefs (9th).

3: George's Moon was quincunx both Venus in Pisces in the 5th House and Uranus-Saturn in Gemini in the 7th. Both of these aspects involve yielding to others, a relational style (Venus) that might surrender (Pisces). The quincunxes suggest he would like to shift this, to hold his power (Scorpio Moon).

4: Uranus is square George's Sun. As he individuates and discovers his spiritual truth, he becomes more non-attached towards the demands or influences from others.

5: Aquarius South Node in the 4th House conveys an underlying restlessness or instability at his core. The breakthrough (Aquarius) into deeper self-love and stable familial experiences (4th House) heals the pattern.

6: The path of awakening (Sun) was also in the 4th. As he develops spiritually (Pisces Sun), finding his inner (4th) light (Sun), he discovers and resides in the spiritual sanctuary he has been longing for.

7: Leo North Node in the 10th is about as powerful as it gets. The cutting edge of his growth involved leadership (10th House) through celebrity (Leo), to be maximally visible. Disposited by his Pisces Sun, the intention brings spirituality and mysticism to such outreach, to shine his inner light (4th House Sun) publicly (brought to the 10th).

8: George's 5th House Venus in Pisces (creative spiritual expression, entertainment) connects to Neptune in Libra in the 11th, seeking global togetherness through spirituality and artistry.

9: 9th House Jupiter in Cancer develops a philosophy of greater heart. Interestingly, it was in aspect to Ceres in the 6th, which correlates with the maternal issues (Ceres) of his workmates (6th House). Jupiter in the 9th has a broad reach, a signature of the teacher.

10: Uranus in the 7th House is interested in progressive relationships, to find a new paradigm connected to individual truth rather than external influences.

11: The outer planets connect with collective, cultural and spiritual issues. George had all of them notable in his chart (Neptune-ruled Sun, Pluto-ruled Moon, Uranus square Sun).

12: Mercury in Aquarius in the 3rd House, a highly unique (at times quirky) intelligence and use of words or sounds. His mind focused on metaphysics and humanitarian concerns.

13: Pisces is equated with soulfulness, compassion, healing and universal spiritual and humanitarian principles to bring people together.

Also of note is his Scorpio Ascendant, an approach and style that can be introverted and mysterious. George also had Vesta in Pisces conjunct his Venus in the 5th. He was learning proficiency with bringing the sacred (Pisces) into creative expression. His Mars in Capricorn in the 3rd House was interested in becoming a thought leader by building a body of work based on his ideas or message.

Chiron conjunct his Leo North Node echoes the karmic pattern of reluctance with visibility. The turnaround and growth involved the willingness to share his creativity publicly. Athena conjunct his Pisces Sun relates to spiritual activism and cultural empowerment.

Ringo Starr

1: Leo Moon conjunct Mercury in the 5th, an unfulfilled desire for play and sharing.

2: Moon conjunct a Mars-Pluto conjunction, a pent-up need to perform.

3: Aries South Node in the 1st conveys a pattern of loneliness or autonomy. Mars (the dispositor), connects loneliness to his frustrations about performing. The more developed version of his South Node is to become strong and potent, even a leader (Aries).

4: Cancer Sun, a path of awakening through love. The prior loneliness resulted from externalizing a need for attention or validation (Leo Moon); further development involves finding it within (Cancer).

5: Sun-Chiron conjunction squaring the Nodal Axis, suggesting health matters at the karmic crossroads, a central issue of his soul work.

6: The challenge of his 4th House planets is staying hidden or inside.

7: Ringo and Paul share the same emotional strategy, to present as agreeable and likable (Leo Moon) as a cover for deeper frustrations (Mars-Pluto).

8: The resolution of his Moon is to perform (5th House) in highly assertive or physical ways (Mars in Leo) for both catharsis and sharing.

9: North Node in Libra in the 7th House. As he heals his frustrations and upset, further growth involves finding partnership and collaboration to heal his loneliness. Like John, Ringo has also been an advocate for peace and togetherness (Libra).

10: Venus in Gemini in the 4th House is the dispositor of his North Node, circling back to home and family.

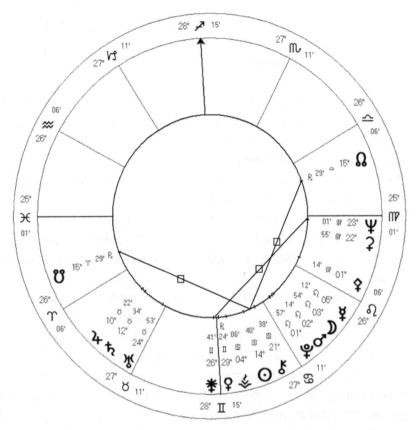

Karmic resolution involves communication (Gemini)—the lack of which may have contributed to his prior isolation (Aries South Node) and not feeling seen (Leo Moon). Now, the work is to communicate (sing, write, etc.) from his heart (4th House). Venus-Juno square Neptune brings a romantic orientation, fitting perfectly with The Beatles.

11: Jupiter, Saturn and Uranus are in Taurus in his 2nd House—substantial work in claiming his personal value, overcoming self-doubt or insecurity.

12: Jupiter (dispositor of his Sagittarius Midheaven) finds broader causes to advocate. Ringo has travelled the world (Sagittarius) to advocate peace and bring joy through his likability (Libra North Node), entertainment and celebrity (Leo planets).

13: Heart is associated with Cancer. Ringo is the only Beatle to share his Sun sign with the band. His inclusion set the emotional foundation for them to rise.

Chapter 2 – The Band

Soul Group Dynamics

1: John's loneliness was indicated by his Aquarius Moon (brilliance, disconnection) and 12th House South Node (removal). Paul's grief is his Pisces South Node (with Neptune opposite Ceres, regarding his mother). George's disconnection involves his Aquarius South Node and 12th House Moon. Ringo's loneliness and independence is his 1st House Aries South Node. All of their respective North Nodes (karmic resolution) involve some kind of motion toward connection.

2: They all had the emotional body (Moon) in connection with deep-seated fears and wounds (Pluto), which involves death. John had his Moon opposite Pluto. Paul and Ringo have their Moons conjunct Pluto (as part of Leo stelliums), and George had Moon square Pluto.

3. Each of their Moons was in a fixed sign and were square and opposed to each other. There can be great intensity or friction, depending on how it's managed.

4: The lunar contacts among them bring this tight (potentially frictional) familial bonding. Also, the band itself has the Sun in the sign of family (Cancer).

5: Leo relates to performance. Paul, Ringo and John all had a major emphasis in this entertaining sign. George was the least innately Leonine by *planetary* placements, but he carried an intention to become maximally commanding and visible with this archetype (Leo North Node in the 10th). Leo is the sign that follows Cancer—their emotional issues (Cancer) can naturally flow into creative expression (Leo) for release.

6: The Beatles typify the evolutionary spirit of Pluto in Leo. They were initially eager and urgent for applause, then radically shifted to using celebrity (Leo) for cultural and spiritual transformation (Pluto).

7: Three Beatles had major aspects between Mercury and Pluto: John (square), George (opposition) and Ringo (conjunction). Paul's Mercury (in Gemini) is precisely sextile his (Leo) Moon, which in turn is connected to Pluto (via his Leo stellium).

8: John had Mars conjunct his North Node in Libra—he was learning a more judicious use of power, an intention for leadership in the arts and for peace. Paul and Ringo have Mars conjunct Pluto—they were resolving inner intensity and frustration around performance. George had Mars square Ceres, a combination that can be bound up in weakness. His Mars in Capricorn in the 3rd House claims power by developing his professional voice.

Additionally, Venus involves creative expression. John (Virgo) and Paul (Taurus) had Venus in earth signs. They were chiefly responsible for making the music tangible and organized through their song craftsmanship. George's Venus in Pisces added inspired flourishes to the music, and brought it to the transcendent. Ringo's Venus in Gemini has dexterity and improvisational skill.

The Ascendant is a behavioral approach and style, how the chart expresses. Since the Ascendant is so up close, it's most noticeable through interactions with others. Here's how their personality styles (Paul-Virgo, John-Aries, George-Scorpio, Ringo-Pisces) are described in the available literature. "Paul was meticulous and organized: he always carried a notebook around with him, in which he methodically wrote down lyrics and chord changes in his neat handwriting. In contrast, John seemed to live in chaos: he was constantly searching for scraps of paper he'd hurriedly scribbled ideas on...John was impatient, always ready to move on to the next thing."[360] George is described as "introverted," "dour," "furtive," with "a sarcastic wit"; "He always seemed suspicious of everyone outside the Beatles inner circle." Adjectives used to describe Ringo include "easygoing," "good humor," and "laid back."[361]

As for the Sun, the group is organized by the elements. John (Libra) and Paul (Gemini) have their Suns in air signs (writing, ideas, aesthetics). Libra is cardinal (leadership) and it was John who formed the band and set the artistic tone. Paul the Gemini contributed a broad range of ideas and skills as a multi-instrumentalist and writer. George (Pisces, spirituality) and Ringo (Cancer, emotionality) have the Sun in water signs, providing an anchor to the loftier air. The air (John, Paul) and water (George, Ringo) Sun placements organizes the band in a 2-tiered fashion, often how it's discussed.

Most any planet in a chart is in aspect to a few other planets, and that is the case with all of their Suns. However, a pattern is noted with this group when a single planet is isolated, one that seems to have great importance in their biographies (Sun). The tightest aspect in John's chart was Pluto quintile his Sun. Paul has Neptune on his Ascendant and square his Sun. George had Uranus square his Sun, while Ringo has Saturn sextile his Sun. John represented power (Pluto) as the leader, with an eye towards the transformation of culture. Paul shines inspiration (Neptune), bringing us together. George was an innovator (Uranus), involved with new trends. Ringo provided structure (Saturn), assisting group cohesion and mainstream inclusion. The John-Paul-George-Ringo hierarchy reflects the planetary organization of Pluto-Neptune-Uranus-Saturn with their attunement to these key planets.

Sibling Hierarchy

1: John's "oldest brother" orientation: 10th House Moon and Aries South Node, a combination of dominance and leadership. Paul's "middle brother" dynamic: Leo Moon square Venus in the 8th House, conveying friction (square) around power dynamics with others (8th House). George's "youngest brother" orientation: Uranus in the 7th House (dispositor of South Node), a karmic pattern of deferring to others. Ringo's only child status is found with his independent 1st House Aries South Node. He grew to become the anchor (Cancer Sun in his 4th House) to the Beatles family.

1: Libra Moon in the 10th House: a need for love and public appreciation at the pinnacle of the chart ("toppermost"). The Moon is trine Venus-Jupiter in the 7th House, reinforcing the need for a jubilant reception from others. The Moon/MC conjunction in Libra is an accessible and charming public image. The shadow of Libra is selling out to popular sentiments or superficiality.

2: The Venus-Jupiter conjunction (the "Beatles signature") is the most dominant energy in the chart. They have an abundance (Jupiter) of artistic and creative energy (Venus), which brought much acclaim and expansion (Jupiter) into culture (Venus). Venus in Gemini places a premium on songwriting and variety, while the airy connection to the Libra Moon creates the classic Beatles breezy and sweet melodies. Their incredible popularity is found here, as well as their indulgent and hedonistic tendencies.

The Jupiter-Venus conjunction is the most outstanding signature in the chart for a few reasons. First, Jupiter is the most angular planet (only 1° from the Descendant), and therefore the one that "pops" into action most. Next, the chart has a Sagittarius Ascendant, so Jupiter is the dispositor of the 1st House (often called the "chart ruler"). Venus is the dispositor of the Midheaven (the angle of public life), as well as the planets in Libra and Taurus (both of these artistic signs are strongly represented).

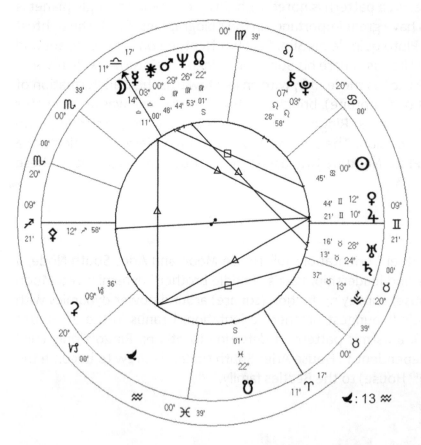

3: Mercury conjunct Juno in Libra pairs writing and singing (Mercury) with romantic energy (Juno) in a romantic sign (Libra). The combination is harmonious, perhaps even seductive. The Cancer Sun squares the pairing, adding friction to emotionally deepen. The more the awakening process unfolds (a more developed Sun), the more the writing and singing would reflect such depth.

4: Sagittarius Ascendant with Athena (the "warrior priestess"), opposite the "Beatles signature." Athena seeks to make an impact in the world, to advocate a cause. Her opposition to Jupiter-Venus suggests the cause is to entertain the masses in an inviting and jovial way. The opposition can also pull matters apart. Athena opposite Venus can be rivalrous, an interpersonal dynamic (Venus) based on competing (opposite) agendas (Athena).

5: The Sun is in Cancer, the archetype of family, heart and bonding. An example of bringing the world together through love was the One World broadcast featuring "All You Need is Love." Their Sun is at 0º Cancer, which is notable. The first degree of the cardinal signs heralds the entrance into a new season, a powerful new beginning. The Sun reaches the peak at the summer solstice (Cancer), having the most visibility and intensity at this time. This elevated Cancer Sun typifies summer energy, the pure feeling (Cancer) of being alive. Cardinal signs are leadership oriented, and the band is seen as not only leading the "British Invasion," but also the lead rock band in the world.

The Sun's opposition to Ceres in Capricorn further emphasizes family. It also suggests that the path of awakening (Sun) connects with maternal energy from the past (Ceres in Capricorn).

6: The dispositor of the Pisces South Node was Neptune in the 9th in Virgo, a seeking towards broader experiences and more diligence on the path. They might expand their horizons through travel and philosophy (9th House), learning the skills (Virgo) to be contemplative and receptive (Neptune).

7: The South Node in the 3rd House (mind) and Pisces (shared consciousness) represents their "group mind." Detailed in Beatles literature, they had an uncanny ability to sense and know what was occurring with each other and the band itself.

8: The Pisces South Node also correlates with the divine worship projected on them. The spiritual lesson was to deliver important teachings; a shadow dynamic is the devouring quality of Beatlemania.

9: 9th House Virgo North Node: They traveled (9th House) to Hamburg and worked grueling hours (Virgo) to hone their musical skill. Since they lacked formal training, their growth required discipline. The more focused they were, the more their spiritual work became realized (as seen with the long hours and focus for *Sgt. Pepper*). They also traveled to India as part of their questing.

10: Their Virgo North Node was supported by Epstein (Virgo Sun) and Martin (Virgo Moon) who provided necessary management, organization and production.

11: Mars-Neptune conjunct the North Node in Virgo—a lesson of selflessness and humility, modeling what a spiritually-conscious (Neptune) male (Mars) could be.

12: Saturn-Uranus conjunction in Taurus in the 6th House: the potential for manifesting (Saturn) brilliance (Uranus) in artistic (Taurus) projects (6th House). It signifies the novel business model of Apple, as well as the collective impact (Uranus-Saturn) of their work.

13: Pluto in the 8th House is an edgy and intense signature. Not only did the death of their mothers bond John and Paul, original bassist and friend Stu Sutcliffe suddenly died of a brain aneurysm in 1962, while manager Brian Epstein died in 1967. In 1969 the world was agog with the "Paul is dead" hoax. John Lennon was murdered at the age of 40, and George Harrison also died young at 58, after a brutal stabbing a couple years prior. Charles Manson was allegedly inspired by "The White Album" to lead his followers to murder.

14: Pluto conjunct Chiron correlates with health issues.

15: John's Libra Sun was on the group Moon. He founded the band and drove them up the mountain towards the "toppermost." Paul has the most attunement to Gemini (Sun, Mercury, Saturn & Uranus), a personal embodiment of the "Beatles signature." George's Pisces planets fall in the band's 3rd House, the area of message. Ringo's Cancer Sun matches the band's Cancer Sun and was the emotional anchor.

Also of note is Uranus trine the Virgo (North Node, Neptune, Mars) and Libra (Juno, Mercury) energies, sparking advances with writing (Mercury), spirituality (Neptune), leadership (Mars) and also potentially shifting what romance (Juno) means.

Their Vesta was in artistic Taurus, located in the performance arena of the 5th House—a devotion (Vesta) to crafting creative entertainment. Vesta was trine Ceres, suggesting that bonding and family (Ceres) are strengthened when they create music (5th House) as a unit. It also suggests their creative craft (Vesta) was in connection with mothers (Ceres).

Another variable is when a planet is "out-of-bounds," by declination. Occasionally, a planet ventures beyond the range that the Sun travels (23°27'), north or south of the celestial equator. Out-of-bounds planets are thought to operate in non-typical ways, to go beyond the planet's usual functioning. There is often a unique condition, issue or gift that is noteworthy. Initially, there might be something "off," which can be transformed into some kind of novel skill or awareness. In the south (depths), an out-of-bounds planet is buried deeply in the psyche, tending to operate privately for personal resolution. They tend to be heavier, even depressed at times. In the north (heights), out-of-bounds planets hover beyond our normal grasp, learning to touch into divine inspiration. They might initially be quixotic, ungrounded or manic. Out-of-bounds planets are often in aspect to in-bounds planets, helping them enter consensus reality.

Their Ceres at 23°55' southern declination and Pluto at 23°34' north, which is technically contra-parallel, was a type of connection. Deep shadow work (south) regarding maternal/nurturing issues (Ceres) was in need of attendance. The out-of-bounds Pluto in the north can explode into the heights of fame (Leo), connecting with the deep maternal (Ceres) work. Their composite Sun at 23°26' north declination (the Sun remains in bounds but very close to the threshold, only minutes from Pluto), was tightly in connection with this distinctive Ceres-Pluto combination, bringing it to life while also staying in bounds. The Sun was not only in conventional aspect to Ceres (opposition), it was also contra-parallel. This situation is yet another example of how profoundly Ceres is woven into the astrology. The inclusion of Pluto adds the element of death (and its transformation) as part of the path of awakening (Sun), connected to the maternal.

The Beatles composite chart features the muse (Euterpe) at 13° Aquarius. This point is trine their Moon at 14° Libra, and the "Beatles signature" (Jupiter at 10° Gemini, Venus at 12°), making a flowing air Grand Trine. The muse directly connects to their performance desires (Libra Moon) and their abundant musical creativity (Jupiter-Venus) in a most harmonious way. Air signs correlate with birds, while the diversity of Jupiter-Venus would include flutes and other wind instruments.

John & Paul – The Leaders (John: inner, Paul: outer)

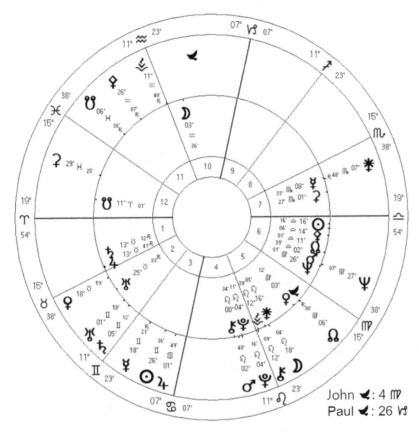

John ☽: 4 ♍
Paul ☽: 26 ♑

1: John's Aries South Node in the 12th House was his need to heal (12th) from war (Aries).

2: Paul's Pisces South Node (in his natal 6th House) is his sacrificial nature (Pisces) to a work ethic (6th).

3: John's Aquarius Moon was in tension (opposing signs) with Paul's Leo Moon.

4: One point of synthesis of Leo-Aquarius is rock & roll, revolutionary amped up (Aquarius) fun and entertainment (Leo).

5: Paul's Vesta in Aquarius was opposite John's in Leo. They could bridge the tension of their Moons (also in Leo-Aquarius) through collaboration in their craft (Vesta).

6: John's Mars in Libra was precisely sextile Paul's Mars in Leo. Both had Venus in earth signs (Virgo, Taurus), which grounds their Martial passion.

7: John's Venus was on Paul's Virgo North Node, a signature of a destined (North Node) partnership (Venus).

8: John's Jupiter in Taurus was conjunct Paul's Venus, and Paul's Jupiter in Cancer was sextile John's Venus in Virgo (reinforcing the "Beatles signature"). Paul's Mercury in Gemini was trine John's Libra Sun, landing in his 3rd House (writing).

9: In the composite chart (see below), their Moon was exactly quintile (72°) Mercury: innate (Moon) creativity (5th House) connects in an inspired way (quintile) with entertainment (Leo) writing (Mercury). Uranus square Mercury is a combination for breakthrough writing. Jupiter in Gemini is quintile their Leo Sun—inspired or intuitive writing (Jupiter in Gemini in the 12th House), brilliantly expressed through entertainment (Leo Sun).

10: John's Mercury in Scorpio was conjunct Paul's Juno, while Paul's Mercury in Gemini was sextile John's Juno in Leo. These Mercury-Juno contacts echo the Beatles composite chart, featuring Mercury conjunct Juno ("love songs").

11: Both have Ceres in the 7th House, the projection of mother issues onto relations.

The composite chart has a Scorpio Moon in the creative 5th House, a desire for creative expression to work out underlying issues. Its conjunction with Vesta and Euterpe adds focus and discipline, geared to transform hurt and pain (Scorpio Moon) into a performance (5th House) craft (Vesta) with the muse. The transformation of emotional intensity and death issues is further emphasized by the Pluto-Chiron conjunction in Leo square their Moon.

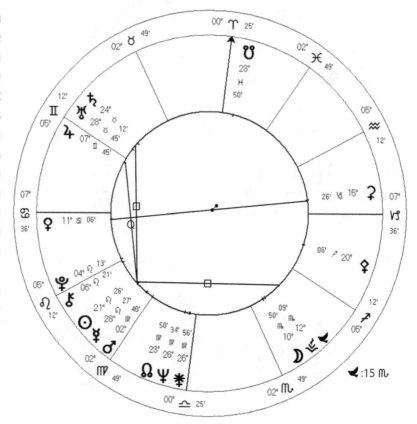

The 7th House Ceres in Capricorn points to their shared maternal issue, which becomes projected onto relations. Ceres was opposite Venus in Cancer in the 1st House, bringing maternal issues to artistic (Venus) expression (1st House), as well as a creative partnership (Venus) with the mothers (opposite Ceres). Venus on the Ascendant was the pair's attractiveness (stylistically, musically), in ways that evoked feeling (Cancer). Venus in Cancer is the sign of the Beatles Sun, and their musical (Venus) bond (Cancer) played the major role in the life of the band.

The North Node in Virgo in the 3rd House conjunct Neptune and Juno—an intention to develop a spiritual (Neptune) and romantic (Juno) message (3rd House). Their work (Virgo) involved transcendent notions of love, a maturation from the initial obsession (Scorpio Moon) with performing for applause (5th House). Mercury in Leo disposits the North Node, suggesting that entertainment (Leo) is fitting for such communications.

The composite Sun was in Leo, sign of visibility, entertainment and (potential) celebrity. The Sun's square to Uranus adds uniqueness and innovation, while its square to Saturn correlates with their vocational focus and historical longevity. Saturn-Uranus in the 11th House has reach into the world in a sign of artistry (Taurus). Uranus was precisely square Mercury in Leo—the development into brilliant (Uranus) creative (Leo) writers (Mercury).

Jupiter in Gemini in the 12th House was near Uranus, a voluminous (Jupiter) library (Gemini) of inspired (12th) songs. The 12th is an area of spiritual receptivity, available for them to "download" their ideas (Gemini) from the ethereal realms (12th). This Jupiter plays a significant role in the astrology with their mothers (reviewed in later chapters). Also note Jupiter's conjunction with the "Beatles signature" in the band's composite chart. Their ability to harness inspired ideas was a key ingredient in the band's success.

John & George – The Mystic Guitarists (John: inner, George: outer)

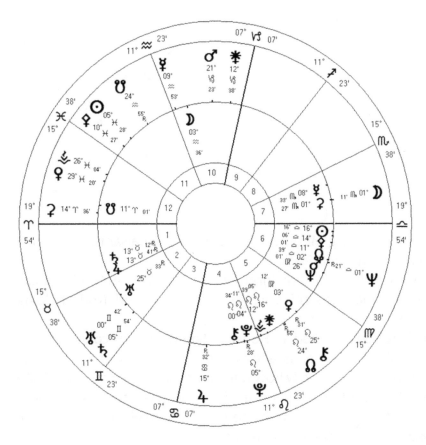

1: Their composite chart (see below) features both the Sun and Moon in Sagittarius. They are situated in the balsamic phase, which is like a hallway between worlds at the darkest point of the cycle. Their spiritual quest (Sagittarius) involved exploring consciousness.

2: John's Aquarius Moon was square George's Scorpio Moon.

3: John's Mercury in Scorpio was on George's Moon, while George's Mercury in Aquarius was on John's Moon. Each of their minds (Mercury) was innately connected to the other's emotional body (Moon). The spiritual work was to communicate (Mercury) emotion (Moon). The combination played out in a musical context as an intuitive feel (Moon) for each other's sound (Mercury).

4: John's Venus in Virgo was opposite George's Pisces Sun, bringing inspiration (Pisces) into form (Virgo) through collaboration. They blended to develop techniques (Virgo) to create soundscapes (Pisces). Their composite chart features a Jupiter-Venus conjunction in Gemini in the 5th House, strongly resembling the "Beatles signature" in the area of performance. Competitiveness is found with George's Mars in Capricorn square John's Libra Sun and John's Mars in early Libra opposite George's Venus in late Pisces.

278

5: Neptune was particularly strong in their composite chart, in the spiritual seeking 9th House and square their Sagittarius stellium (Sun, Moon, Mercury, Athena). The trine to their Uranus-Saturn conjunction in Taurus in the 5th brings it to artistic performance.

6: John's had an Aquarius Moon, while George's had an Aquarius South Node. The composite chart features Uranus opposite Mars, which can behave in rebellious or highly individuated ways.

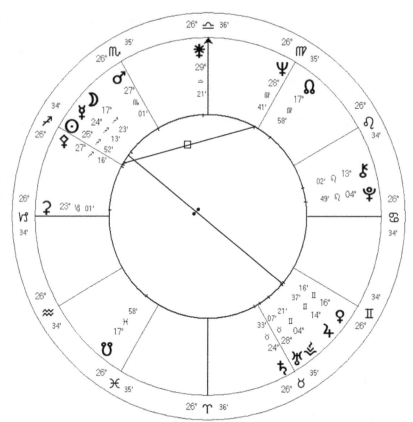

7: In the composite chart, Mercury was between the waning Moon and the Sun (in the balsamic "zone"), a position of releasing attachment and identification.

8: John's Leo planets (and Venus in early Virgo), were all in George's 10th House, supporting his career as an entertainer. George's Ceres was on John's South Node, helping him heal his conflictual past with loving energy.

The composite chart featured a packed 5th House. A Saturn-Uranus conjunction in Taurus straddled the cusp, while Vesta, Venus and Jupiter in Gemini were in it. The "Beatles signature" was evident, almost exactly how it appeared in the band's composite chart. Vesta in Gemini involved the crafting of sound and it's 6° from Uranus, the planet of experimentation. Uranus trine Neptune in Virgo in the 9th House might bring ethereal, perhaps even psychedelic dimensions to their techniques.

The Sagittarius Moon in the 11th House promoted purpose into culture. The Moon and the Venus-Jupiter conjunction in Gemini were all square the Nodal Axis, challenging them to bring their vision (Pisces South Node) into form (Virgo North Node). The North Node in the 8th required working through emotional or power dynamics to see to that realization. Pluto in the 7th House echoes the issue.

Sun-Athena conjunction on the 12th House cusp involved their spiritual questing, reflecting the "gunslinger" quality found in the Beatles composite chart. They carried a bravado, a spiritual passion (Sagittarius) that was untamed. Mercury's inclusion involved ideas and dialogue concerning metaphysics. The Libra Midheaven was their likability and brought forth their creative Venus publicly. Juno in Libra in the 10th House signified the

279

romantic orientation of their art and their appeal. Mars in Scorpio in the 11th House was their masculine sexuality, a drive for power in the world. The Capricorn Ascendant, disposited by Saturn in Taurus, illustrates their serious commitment to art.

Paul & George – The Improvisators (Paul: inner, George: outer)

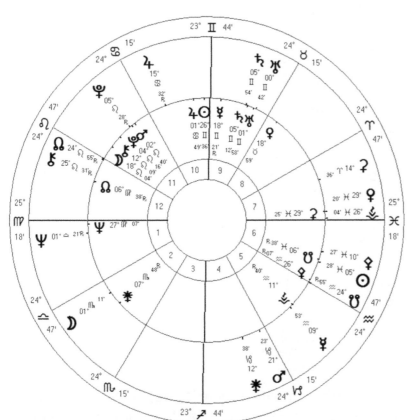

1: Paul has 4 planets in Gemini, the Nodal Axis in Pisces/Virgo, as well as the ASC and MC in mutable signs. George had 4 planets in Pisces (with asteroids) and 2 in Gemini.

2: Support is found with George's Venus in late Pisces trine Paul's Mars in early Leo; George's Mars in Capricorn trine Paul's Venus in Taurus. George's Mercury in Aquarius trine Paul's Gemini planets. The friction is found with the natural square between Gemini and Pisces.

3: Paul is amiable and seeks collaboration (Leo Moon), while George's style was giving and willing to sacrifice (Venus in Pisces).

4. In becoming leaders, both were relaxing the pattern of always having to be amiable or sacrificial.

5: George was developing leadership with his 10th House Leo North Node. The resolution of Paul's Mars-Pluto enables him to rise into creative empowerment.

6: Paul's Leo Moon (bright) and George's Scorpio Moon (dark).

7: George's Mars in Capricorn was quincunx Paul's Leo Moon. The composite chart displays Mars in Libra opposite Venus in Aries, a competitive tension.

8: Paul's Leo planets (particularly the Moon) were on George's North Node. George's Pisces planets (particularly the Sun) were on Paul's South Node.

The composite chart featured a Taurus Sun in the 7th House, conjunct Venus in fiery Aries. They joined together (7th House) to sculpt and manifest (Taurus) enthusiastic art (Venus in Aries). These planets were in opposition to Mars in Libra in the 1st, signifying a competitive edge. The Libra ASC led with a smooth and accessible vibe, though how they managed the feisty Venus in Aries (ASC dispositor) influenced how it played out.

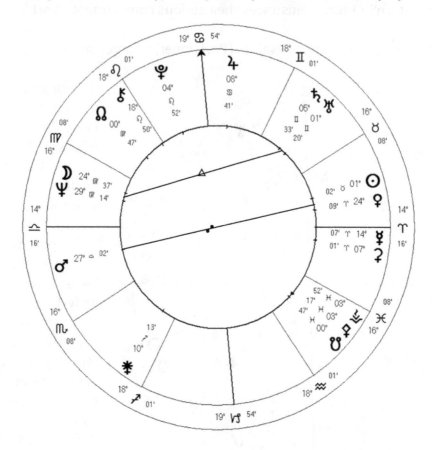

The South Node involved further growth (South Node) towards a creative, performance (5th) vision (Pisces). Its conjunction with Vesta and Athena adds seriousness and a cultural scope. Neptune (the dispositor of the South Node) was conjunct the Moon in Virgo in the 12th, a lesson to work with creative inspiration and iron out the details. Their North Node in Virgo in the 11th brought their work (Virgo) to the world stage (11th). Mercury in Aries on the 7th House cusp (dispositor of the North Node) was conjunct Ceres. They bonded (Ceres) through communications (Mercury), and this combination also might verbally hurt feelings if poorly managed. Mercury's square to Jupiter in Cancer in the 9th House sought to develop a broad message of love.

Pluto in Leo in the 10th conveys their worldly power as entertainers. Its sextile to Saturn in Gemini connects such power into the mainstream (Saturn) through sound and message (Gemini). Also of note is Ceres opposite Neptune, another example of familial healing through the band.

1: Irreverence is found with Uranus, which is strong in the composite chart (see below): Uranus square Sun-Mars and trine Mercury. With the Sun in the 5th House, their Uranian vibe played out in playful and comedic ways.

2: Uranus-Mercury often involves novel or unusual use of language.

3: Craftiness is found with their composite Virgo Sun, which seeks to ground ingenuity into form. Located in the 5th, the outlet is through performance.

4: John's Aquarius Moon was exactly opposite Ringo's Leo Moon. The Aquarius-Leo exchange connects irreverence with play. In contrast to the competitive dynamic between John and Paul along this axis, John and Ringo managed it much differently due to their roles in the band. They also had Sun square Sun (Cancer, Libra) but they were not competitive about leadership.

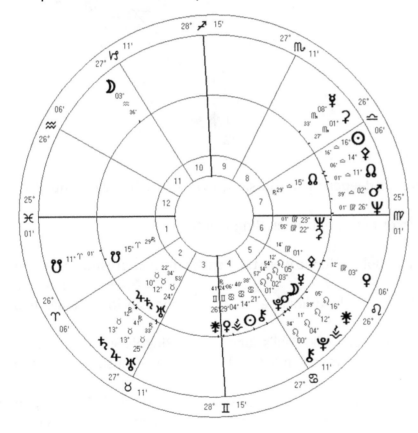

5: Their composite chart had Ceres conjunct the North Node in Libra, signifying development of a new, more peaceable and supportive, form of emotional nourishment.

6: John's Libra planets hit Ringo's North Node.

7: Ringo's Cancer Sun was sextile John's Jupiter-Saturn in Taurus. Ringo's Ceres in Virgo was trine John's Uranus in Taurus.

8: The Nodal Axis, as well as Jupiter, Saturn, Uranus, Neptune and Pluto are all conjunct each other's.

9: Their mutual support was further augmented by Venus sextile Venus (John's in early Virgo, Ringo's in late Gemini). Venus, being the ruler of both of their Libra North Nodes, is most supportive of growth and inclusion.

The composite chart had an Aries Ascendant, so Mars was the dispositor, located in the area of performance (5th House). The Libra North Node was disposited by Venus in Leo (conjunct Pluto), echoing a similar sentiment of deep and collaborative artistic partnership.

Similar to both of their natal charts, Jupiter-Saturn-Uranus in Taurus was in the 2nd House, which structures (Taurus) art professionally. They both were healing prior issues of insecurity, a development towards confidence and calm. Also of note is the packed 4th House, a deepening of roots, the joining in a "family" context.

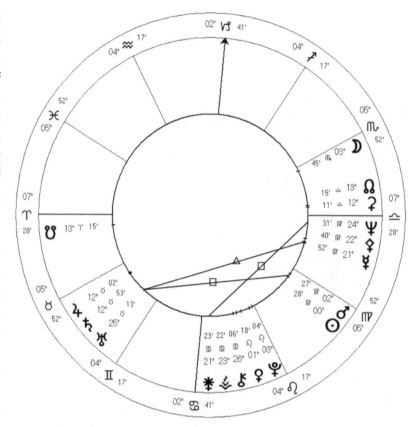

Paul & Ringo – The Performers (Paul: inner, Ringo: outer)

1: With their Leo Moons, Paul and Ringo were the Beatles most interested in touring and performing.

2: Paul's karmic situation involved limiting financial responsibilities. Ringo had health restrictions.

3: Ringo's Juno is on Paul's Sun while Paul's Juno is trine Ringo's Sun. This double Sun/Juno interchange reinforces the sweet, romantic vibe both in the music as well as in their presentation.

4: Ringo's Ceres in Virgo connects with Paul's "expression of grief" T-square, an activation of familial and nurturance issues. The composite Sun is in Cancer conjunct Ceres (loose but in orb).

5: Ringo's Venus is conjunct Paul's Jupiter, while Paul's Venus is conjunct Ringo's Jupiter. Their composite chart features a Jupiter-Venus conjunction in Gemini reflecting the "Beatles signature."

6: Both men have a Mars/Pluto conjunction.

7: The affection can be seen in the Jupiter-Venus contacts and also Ringo's Venus on Paul's Sun.

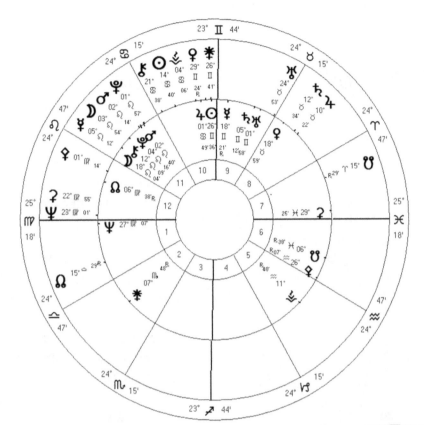

8: The composite Sun for the band is at 0° Cancer. The composite Sun for Paul-Ringo is at 5° Cancer, the closest of any dyad.

Over the years, Ringo and Paul have stated that the Beatles were about love. Their composite Sun in Cancer resides in the 1st House (advocating love), with a communicative Gemini Ascendant. Ceres in Gemini reinforces the dissemination of this message.

Their South Node on the Pisces Midheaven can easily become swept up (Pisces) in public roles and activities (10th House). The Virgo North Node in their 4th is an intention to inform their public roles as representatives of this soul (Neptune conjunct North Node) family (4th House). Paul and Ringo are the spokesmen of the Beatles family.

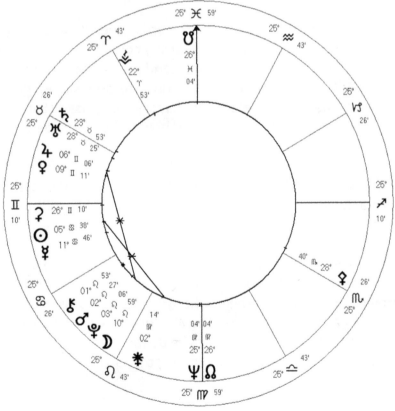

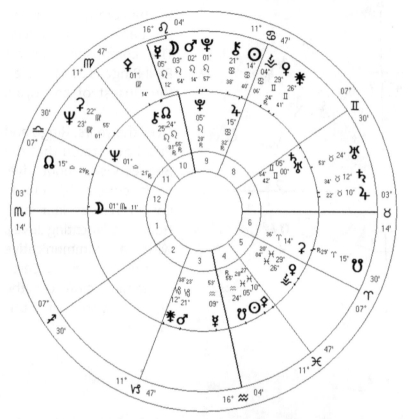

1: Ringo's Cancer and George's Pisces planets add depth and soulfulness to complement John and Paul's airiness.

2: Cancer trine Pisces, a naturally flowing and supportive watery aspect (bonding).

3: George's Scorpio Moon was square Ringo's Leo Moon.

4: George's Venus in Pisces was square Ringo's Venus in Gemini.

5: George's complicated existential and spiritual orientation stretched the band towards other dimensions (Mercury in Aquarius), while Ringo's more simple and playful quality connects it to youthful themes (Mercury in Leo). Together, they contributed to the band's incredibly broad appeal.

6: George's Mercury in Aquarius was opposite Ringo's Mercury in Leo.

7: The composite chart had a major emphasis (Saturn, Uranus, Athena, Jupiter) in the 5th House—they were learning how to be adept performers to make an impact into culture.

8: Both men were resolving karma with being marginalized or removed.

9: George's Ceres was on Ringo's South Node, assisting with healing his familial karma. Ringo's Ceres was opposite George's Venus, ideal for relating as members of this "family."

The composite chart's Virgo Moon emphasized skill development. Virgo can also identify as secondary or following. It featured a 7th House Pluto, a placement that can project power onto others. The 4th House Taurus planets provided a foundation of strength and dependability. The 4th House involves family and roots; George and Ringo were anchors. In the context of The Beatles, George and Ringo were expected to be solid (Taurus), with powerful (Pluto in the 7th) partners (John & Paul) in charge.

The North Node in the 9th House conjunct the Moon and Neptune was their worldly travel, an investment in broader causes or projects. Mars in Libra in the 10th House directed assertive energy towards public cultural pursuits. The Capricorn Ascendant had a reserved yet professional orientation, with Saturn serving as the dispositor in the entertainment 5th House.

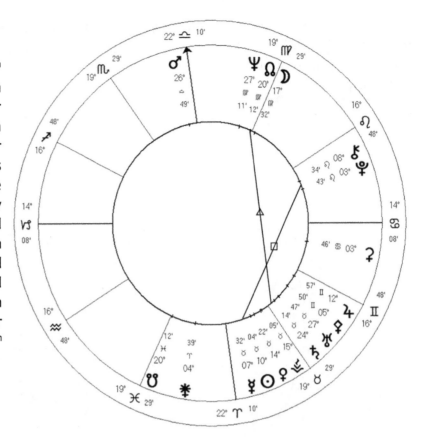

Major Influences

Lonnie Donegan's chart around The Beatles.

1: The Beatles Moon (roots) was at 14⁰ Libra, exactly on Donegan's South Node, a connection with his cultural and artistic (Libra) legacy (South Node). Donegan's Moon at 24⁰ Virgo hit The Beatles North Node, supporting their growth through technique and craft (Virgo).

These Moon-Nodal contacts in both directions, rare in astrology, involve maturation (Moon) towards soul intention (Nodes). Donegan's Taurus planets in the Beatles 5th House, and his Mars in Leo on their Pluto, light the fire of entertainment possibility.

Elvis Presley

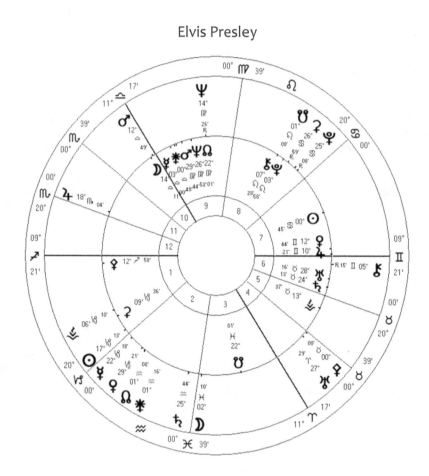

2: Elvis's ASC at 12° Sagittarius (not shown) was conjunct the Beatles ASC at 9° Sagittarius. Dispositing his Ascendant was Jupiter in Scorpio, which expressed his sexuality. The Beatles had Jupiter in Gemini, a more upbeat, carefree and bouncy presentation.

3: Elvis had Pluto conjunct Ceres in Cancer, revealing a similar theme of familial and maternal wounding issues that is seen in Beatles astrology.

4: Elvis's Pluto-Ceres conjunction in Cancer reflects John's 4th House Pluto square Ceres in Scorpio, a very similar assemblage of astrological factors.

5: Twins have astrological relevance with the astrology sign Gemini, interestingly linking Elvis to the band. Elvis had Chiron in Gemini, correlating with his twin wound. His Chiron was on the "Beatles signature," an interesting link between healing and communication.

6: In his natal chart, Elvis had Uranus in Aries in the 5th House, as the dispositor of his Aquarius North Node. The resolution of his painful karma (Pluto-Ceres conjunct South

287

Node) is through becoming courageous (Aries) with self-expression (5th House) as a breakthrough (Uranus) artist. His ability to model emotional catharsis through performance was influential to the Beatles.

7: Elvis's emotional coping through substances is found with his Pisces Moon. The Beatles had a Pisces South Node, which conveys their overall pattern with the archetype.

Buddy Holly

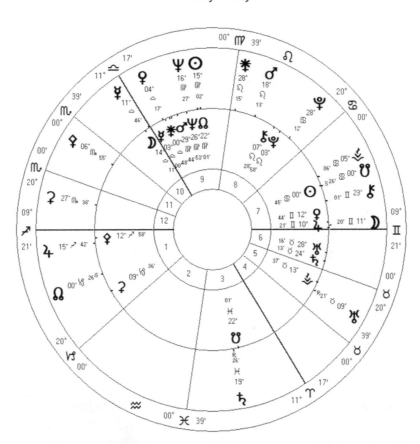

8: Holly had his Gemini Moon on the "Beatles signature," Sun on the Beatles Virgo North Node (craftsmanship), Jupiter on their Sagittarius ASC (life direction), Saturn on their Pisces South Node (structuring inspiration), Mercury on their Libra MC and Moon (influencing writing). Holly also had his Venus on the Beatles Mercury-Juno in Libra ("love songs"), Uranus on their Vesta in Taurus (influencing artistic craft), Ceres in Scorpio opposite their Uranus-Saturn in Taurus (connecting with tragedy), and his Nodal Axis on their Cancer Sun!

9: Holly's Nodal Axis on the Beatles Sun conveys the passing of the torch. Most interestingly, this even took form with the band names (Crickets, Beatles).

10: Holly had Ceres in Scorpio just like John. The tragedy of Holly's death in 1959 was another event during John's dark passage that added to his pain.

11. Paul's Mercury in Gemini is conjunct Holly's Gemini Moon, connecting Holly's legacy to Paul's writing and the rights to his song catalog.

Chuck Berry

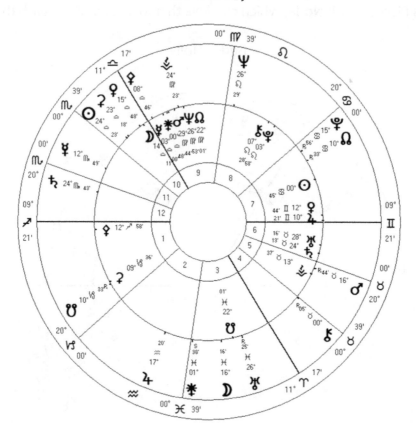

12: Berry had a Libra stellium (Sun, Ceres, Venus, Athena) in the Beatles 10th House, influencing their cultural contribution and ambition. The reflective Venus-Libra archetype might imitate, model or influence style. The Beatles adapted much of Berry into their act, especially John who was similarly a Libra Sun and Berry's Venus in Libra was right on it.

13: Berry had a Beatlesque Jupiter-Venus aspect (the trine), and he also expanded the reach of music into the collective.

14: Berry had Vesta in Virgo on the Beatles North Node, influencing the construction of their craft. His Mars was in the Beatles 5th House, modeling a testosterone-infused quality to their showmanship. Berry's Moon and Uranus in Pisces conjunct the Beatles South Node stimulated their imagination. Berry's North Node-Pluto conjunct the Beatles Sun also involved the passing of the torch.

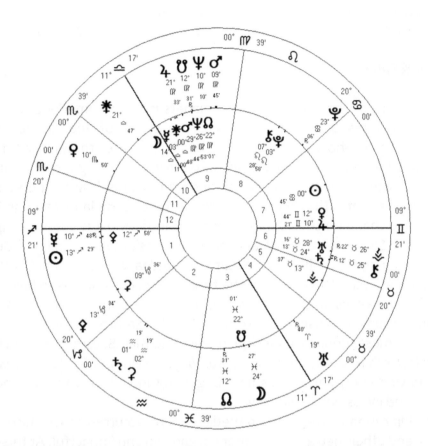

15: With his Mercury on The Beatles Ascendant, Little Richard directly influenced their singing (Mercury) style (ASC). His buoyant Sagittarian Sun was right there too (and opposite the "Beatles signature"), an uplifting, cheerleader-like influence. Richard's Moon was conjunct the Beatles Pisces South Node (inspiration), while his Jupiter in Virgo (with other planets nearby) was on their North Node supporting life purpose. Richard's Venus in Scorpio (his magnetism), was quincunx the "Beatles signature," influencing a deeper and more sexual undertone. His Juno in Libra in the band's 10th invited them to adorn their public image (10th House) with seductive appeal.

16: Richard's Jupiter is on Paul's Virgo Ascendant, reflecting the uplift (Jupiter) to his work (Virgo). His Venus in Scorpio was on George's Moon-ASC, supporting his artistic expression.

17: The 4 major influences all have significant placements in Pisces: Elvis (Moon), Holly (Saturn), Berry (Moon, Uranus), Richard (Moon, North Node). The Beatles absorbed (Pisces) these influences, helping them mature and develop (South Node). These figures also significantly supported the Beatles growth in the Virgo (North Node) direction: Elvis (Neptune), Holly (Sun/Neptune), Berry (Vesta), Richard (Mars, Neptune, South Node, Jupiter).

Chapter 4 – Setting the Stage

Additional astrological information on the social (Jupiter, Saturn) and personal planets (Mercury, Venus, Mars), as well as the Nodal Axis and eclipses, is found here.

Jupiter & Saturn

The influence of these social/cultural planets is more immediate (than the outer planets) and structures the everyday milieu. The scope of Jupiter includes politics, education and religion—how we make sense of life. It relates to our quest for meaning and clarification of purpose, how we expand into the world and "go for it." Saturn is more organizational, the infrastructure to systems and frameworks, how we personally mature and contribute to society. They partner to create the cultural landscape with particular trends, norms and characteristics. Jupiter has an orbit of almost 12 years, occupying a sign for roughly a year. Saturn has a 29.5 year orbit, so it transits every sign for about 2.5 years.

In February 1961, Jupiter and Saturn formed a conjunction at 25° Capricorn, beginning a 20 year cycle. This event set the tone for the 60s and 70s to have a Capricorn quality, which emphasizes status, big money, business expansion and the promotion of individuals and groups who rise to the top. The Jupiter-Saturn conjunction activated the Beatles chart in a most supportive fashion. It was trine their Saturn-Uranus in late Taurus, as well as their North Node-Neptune-Mars late Virgo stellium. A Grand Trine was formed, a circuit of flowing energy from this new beginning in culture to their innovative art, broader vision and inclusion into society.

The solidification of the modern media culture occurred at this time. Television, movies, music and other media became more organized and impactful. At the start of this cycle, there were fewer choices for radio or television. Everybody knew who The Beatles were; the Capricorn orientation enabled them to attain great prominence within this concentrated exposure. In contrast, there are many talented artists and entertainers today who remain anonymous.

Saturn moved forward from Capricorn to enter Aquarius in 1962, Pisces in 1964, Aries in 1967 and it first entered Taurus in 1969. Its residence in each of these signs brought different chapters to the story. Moving more quickly, Jupiter transited several signs in the 60s (about 1 year in each sign) and acted like a trigger planet on the collective level. It tends to amplify the sign it's in, ideally providing direction and meaning. The Beatles were particularly attuned to Jupiter energy, so we'll be tracking the changes relative to Jupiter's sign placement and aspects.

When Saturn transited Pisces from 1964—1967, it was opposite the Uranus-Pluto conjunction to various degrees, climaxing in 1966. The tension of the opposition was between conservative and progressive, the past with the future, the old ways against the upsurge of revolution. The integration was to bring modernization into form and thereby tangibly change culture and society. The challenge was polarization, which leads to conflict, instability and potentially mayhem.

Jupiter applied to the Uranus-Pluto conjunction shortly after the tension with Saturn began separating. Jupiter was amplifying entertainment areas with its transit through Leo in 1966—67. Upon its entrance into Virgo in late 1967, it was in the same sign as the Uranus-Pluto conjunction and applying, strengthening the energetic interface. Jupiter was exactly conjunct Pluto in 1968, signifying a cycle of "psychological intensification," corresponding with upheaval and violence (assassinations, riots, social unease). 1968 has been dubbed the "year of unraveling," which is quintessentially Plutonian and depicts the downward motion of the "arc of awakening." Jupiter moved forward to conjoin Uranus in Libra in later 1968 and 1969, correlating with a surge of "cultural expansion."

Venus & Mars Retrogrades

Venus and Mars are quicker moving "trigger" planets that set off the broader themes of the slower social (Saturn, Jupiter) and collective/transpersonal (Uranus, Neptune, Pluto) planets. Venus takes about a year to circle the chart, while the orbit of Mars is roughly 2 years. When these planets turn retrograde, a period of reassessment or reinvention of the planetary function occurs. The retrograde periods of Venus and Mars had an impact on the Beatles artistic/relational (Venus) and leadership (Mars) development. Mercury is also an inner planet and turns retrograde much more frequently. It'll also be addressed when relevant.

Below are the retrograde periods of Venus and Mars in the 1960s. Venus retrograde periods occur every year and a half and last 40 days. Mars retrograde periods come roughly every 2 years and last between 2 and 3 months. These times figure significantly in the development of the band.

Venus Retrograde Periods

There were 6 Venus retrograde periods in the 1960s. As the analysis reveals, each of them correlated with significant artistic and/or personal processes. Below is a listing of them as well as a brief description of their meaning.

March 20, 1961 – May 2, 1961 (Aries) Beginnings: Back from Hamburg, they were sorting out questions of how to move forward (Aries). Stu's involvement was under review and he left the band at this time.

October 23, 1962 – December 3, 1962 (Scorpio) Negotiations: There were contractual issues with EMI. Ringo was newly installed as the drummer and they were cutting the first singles. "Please Please Me" was re-recorded under this retrograde and became their first #1 hit.

May 29, 1964 – July 11, 1964 (Cancer-Gemini) Realization, Celebration: During this passage, Venus would crisscross their Sun 3 times at the height of Beatlemania, correlating with enormous popularity.

January 5, 1966 – February 15, 1966 (Aquarius-Capricorn) Implementation of Vision: Venus went retrograde in Aquarius back to Capricorn, inviting greater experimentation (Aquarius) into the mainstream (Capricorn). This passage opens the Transcendence phase and they would soon begin sessions for the revolutionary *Revolver*.

August 8, 1967 – September 20, 1967 (Virgo, Leo) Craftsmanship: Issues of focus and management (Virgo) of creative (Leo) direction were highlighted as they were filming *Magical Mystery Tour*.

March 18, 1969 – April 29, 1969 (Aries) Independence: This final Venus retrograde correlates with the "divorce" of the John-Paul partnership and major moves towards individuation.

Mars Retrograde Periods

The '60s had 5 Mars retrograde periods, and each of them involved processes with leadership and the assertion of will.

November 20, 1960 – February 6, 1961 (Cancer) Emotional Development: Resolving adolescence and family expectations to emerge independently.

December 26, 1962 – March 16, 1963 (Leo) Fame: Preparing for Beatlemania.

January 28, 1965 – April 19, 1965 (Virgo) Focus, diligence: Mars retrograde hit the band's Neptune. There was a marked increase in substance use. They were using marijuana liberally during the shooting of *Help!* and first took LSD at this time.

March 8, 1967 – May 26, 1967 (Scorpio-Libra) Negotiations, Conflict: Leadership changed during the creation of *Sgt. Pepper*.

April 27, 1969 – July 8, 1969 (Sagittarius) Expansion, Life Direction: Mars crossed their Ascendant 3 times as the band was breaking up. Each member was challenged to find his own purpose and direction.

Eclipses & The Nodal Axis

A solar eclipse is a New Moon on either the North or South Lunar Node, while a lunar eclipse is a Full Moon along the Nodal Axis. Both events are striking. The Sun is obscured by the Moon creating darkness for a solar eclipse. The Moon disappears, reappears as orangey-red, then goes back to its normal expression during a lunar eclipse. Something eerie or ominous is occurring. The link between eclipses and the Nodes signifies major karmic amplification and potential resolution. Eclipses herald breakdown or breakthrough (or a bit of both) of our spiritual lessons.

A pair of eclipses (sometimes 3) occur approximately every 6 months. Therefore, for the time frame of this analysis (1956—1970) there's a great many of them. Instead of commenting on all of them, they will be brought in when most relevant to the discussions.

The transiting Nodal Axis in itself conveys how spiritual lessons unfold through the various signs. The motion of this important cycle will be included in the discussion. It spends about 18 months in each polarity and moves "backwards" through the zodiac.

Below are the dates for the residence of the Nodes in the signs, with the South Node mentioned first followed by the North Node.

December 16, 1959 – June 11, 1961 (Pisces–Virgo): Nodal return, beginnings.
June 11, 1961 – December 23, 1962 (Aquarius–Leo): Penetrating into the collective.
December 23, 1962 – August 25, 1964 (Capricorn–Cancer): Realization of stature.
August 25, 1964 – February 20, 1966 (Sagittarius–Gemini): Diversity, direction.
February 20, 1966 – August 19, 1967 (Scorpio–Taurus): Negotiations of artistry.
August 19, 1967 – April 19, 1969 (Libra–Aries): Self-interests vs. collaboration.
April 19, 1969 – November 2, 1970 (Virgo–Pisces): Reverse Nodal return, endings.

The other major astrological technique is progressions (abbreviated with a "p"). To understand progressions, the seed/flower analogy is appropriate in this context too. The natal chart is like a seed, while progressions reveal how the seed becomes a flower. Transits are the outside (cosmic) weather in which the seed develops. Progressions are highly individual as they directly stem from the composition of a person's natal chart, moving through time using a day for a year formula. By applying this formula, the celestial activity occurring 10 days after one's birth plays out in the 10th year of life.

As this book is a coming-of-age story, progressions are an excellent way to understand spiritual development. A major variable is a person's status within their p-lunar cycle. We all have a p-New Moon roughly every 29 years. These times signify major new beginnings, while a p-Full Moon is a time of maximal illumination and climax.

One technical note: The astrology for the release of the albums is discussed. The charts are cast for 12am on the release days, set for London, England (home of EMI/Parlophone), and configured around the band's composite chart. Beatles music was packaged and distributed differently in the UK compared with the U.S and North American releases. Since the albums were made in England by Parlophone and first released there, those release dates will be used. The one exception is *Magical Mystery Tour*, which was not an official release in the UK. The Capitol (U.S.) release of it is included.

The Lennon Family Comes Apart

Below is John's chart with his transits that day.

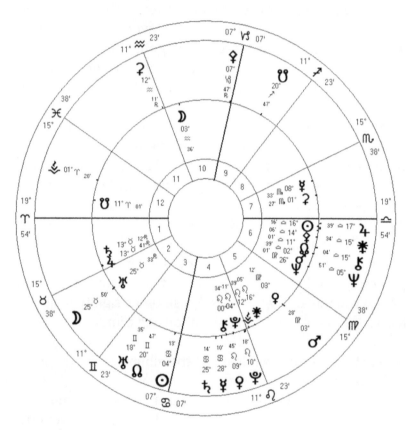

1: The t-Sun in Cancer was square John's Nodal axis—family (Cancer) at the point of his karmic crossroads (Nodes) —and he was literally in the middle of a family coming apart. Saturn in Cancer reflects the gravity (Saturn) of the emotional (Cancer) circumstance, transiting John's area of home (4th House).

A grouping of Libra planets was opposite his South Node, suggesting a painful (Chiron) loss (Neptune) of love (Juno) and meaning (Jupiter). Further strife is echoed by t-Venus on his Pluto (relational crisis) in his 4th (home) and t-Mars was precisely on his Venus, pointing to a volatility (Mars) in relations (Venus).

2: T-Ceres in Aquarius was in the middle of 3 exact hits to John's Moon. It was retrograde, signaling a return of issues. Ceres was triggering familial (Moon) estrangement (Aquarius), connected to basic childhood need (Ceres). His "wounded child" (Moon-Ceres-Pluto/Chiron) T-square, John's deep-seated anxieties and emotional vulnerabilities, was activated by this transit.

3: The Uranus-North Node conjunction in John's 3rd House suggests the event could eventually fuel writing as a way to heal. This combination was not only on the "Beatles signature," but also Paul McCartney's Mercury and Sun.

Below is a biwheel of John's progressions that day around his natal chart.

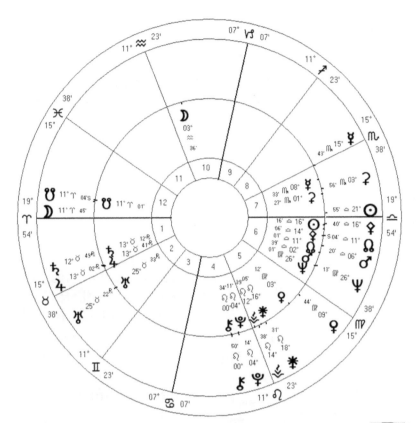

4: John's p-Moon was exactly on his South Node at 11° Aries, illuminating his "axis of conflict." He was re-experiencing his karmic pattern (South Node) of painful dissolution (12th House), which angered him (p-Aries Moon), potentially contributing to his belligerent tendencies in his youth. His p-Ceres had moved from 1° Scorpio to 3°, tightening to precisely square both his Moon and Pluto (family wounds).

John and his parents share a similarity of astrological factors consistent with family instability and abandonment issues. Here are the charts for Alf (inner wheel) and Julia's (outer wheel).

(Birth times unknown, both charts cast for midday.)

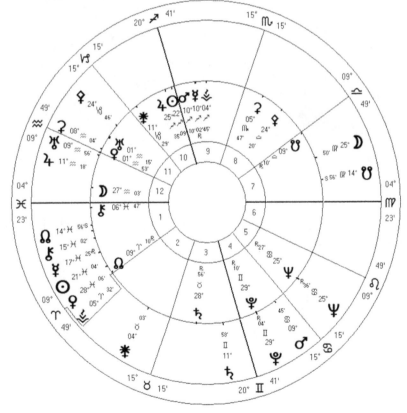

296

John had his Aquarius Moon square Ceres in Scorpio, while Alf (almost certainly) had an Aquarius Moon too. He also had Ceres in Scorpio square Uranus (the planetary ruler of Aquarius). Julia had Uranus conjunct Ceres, also linking familial nurturance with instability. Julia's Moon was square her Pluto, while John had the opposition. Alf's Moon was connected to Pluto via trine. It was also conjunct Chiron, reflecting the Moon-Chiron opposition in John's chart.

Ringo's Battle

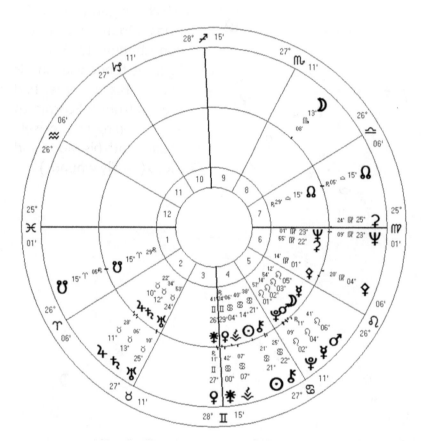

1: Ringo's natal Cancer Sun is square his Aries South Node (battle), and conjunct Chiron (health). This chart depicts his progressions on his 7th birthday. Ringo's p-Sun moved forward to activate his Chiron (at 21° Cancer), triggering the karmic health battle.

2: The p-Sun (and other planets) would be in the 4th House (inside) for several more years.

3: Ringo's p–Moon was in Scorpio in the 8th House, pointing strongly to the emotional fears of death.

4: The chart to the right features Ringo's p-Sun moving to Leo at the age of 16. Not only did it progress to Leo, it would visit his Pluto-Mars-Moon-Mercury Leo stellium for the next 5 years. He would transform (Pluto) himself into a performer (Leo) in his late teens.

5: Even after passing his Leo stellium, Ringo's p-Sun would be in Leo in his 5th House for the next couple decades, including his tenure with the Beatles. He was poised to be an entertainer for years.

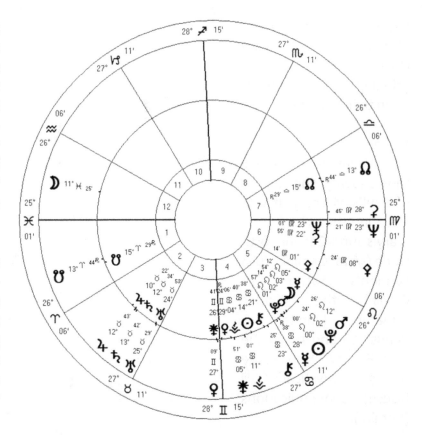

Also in 1956 Ringo's p-Venus was at 27 Gemini, 2° away and approaching a Venus return. Born with Venus retrograde, Ringo had initial challenges socializing and getting his art out. With the childhood issues resolving, he was primed to renew (return) his creative (Venus) passion and connect socially. In 1956 his p-Mars was at 12° Leo square his Saturn (and Jupiter), pressuring him to make his creative passion (Mars in Leo) a vocation he can get paid for (Saturn in Taurus). Born into poverty, Ringo desperately wanted to make music a viable life for himself.

Mary McCartney's Death

Below is Mary's chart. With an unknown birth time, 12pm is used. The house layout is not accurate, though the planetary aspects are.

Mary's chart features the muse (Euterpe) conjunct her Sagittarius South Node. She had a karmic familiarity with the role, a soul purpose to further develop it in the Gemini direction. Her North Node involves communication and writing (Gemini) of a romantic nature (conjunct Juno). Mary specifically carried the intention to serve in the role of muse as a romantic songwriter!

She had a T-Square composed of Mars in Pisces, Pluto in Gemini and Jupiter in Virgo. This configuration involved meaningful work collaboration (Jupiter in Virgo), inward intuitive focus (Mars retrograde in Pisces) and communications involving death (Pluto in

Gemini). Mary had a Full Moon, which was quite close to the T-square, bringing this configuration to illumination.

1: The solar eclipse on 6/8/56 was at 18⁰ Gemini (not shown), the degree of Paul's Mercury. It was also in the vicinity of Mary's Juno-Gemini North Node (9⁰,10⁰ Gemini), Julia Lennon's Saturn (11⁰ Gemini), the "Beatles signature" (Jupiter 10⁰, Venus 12⁰) and fell in the John-Paul 12th House (see p. 277); mystical (12th House) communications (Gemini).

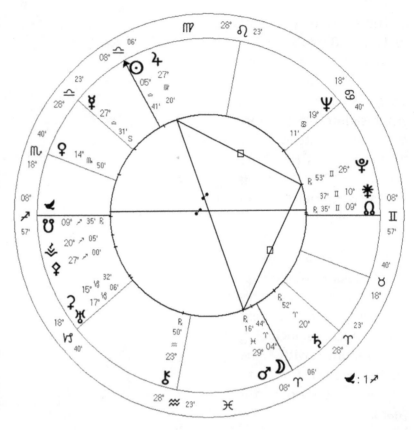

Paul's transits when Mary died.

2: Paul was at a Ceres return.

3: T-Libra Moon was challenging him to care (Moon) for himself and use solitary time (1st) for artistic (Libra) development (it was also conjunct the Beatles Libra MC, Moon, and John's Sun). T-Venus-Jupiter (echoing the "Beatles signature") was on his ASC and Neptune, opposed to Ceres, linking creativity to mother issues. T-Pluto

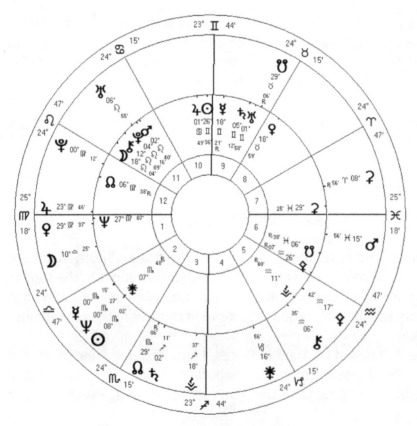

(death) was in his 12th House (spirituality, loss). The t-Scorpio Sun (death) was conjunct t-Neptune-Mercury (spiritualism).

Below is Mary's chart around Paul's.

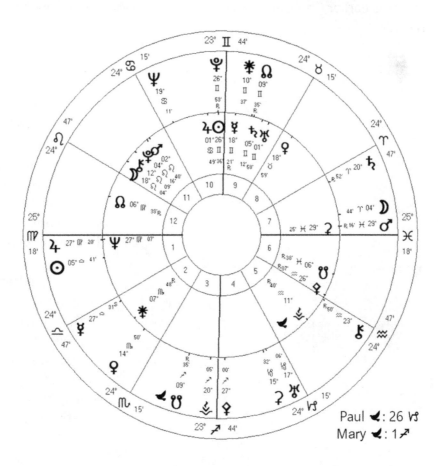

Paul ☾: 26 ♑
Mary ☾: 1 ♐

4: Paul's "expression of grief" T-square consists of Neptune in Virgo, Sun in Gemini and Ceres in Pisces. Mary's T-square falls *exactly* on his, precisely triggering the issue! Mary's Pluto on Paul's Sun at 26⁰ Gemini is central. His life (Sun) was transformed by her death (Pluto), with a communication linkage (Gemini) from her death (Pluto) to his life (Sun). Mary's Mars at 29⁰ Pisces on Paul's Ceres was like a lance (Mars), triggering his maternal issues for healing and resolution. Her Jupiter at 27⁰ Virgo on his Neptune stimulated him to find spiritual (Neptune) meaning (Jupiter), and ultimately grace.

5: Mary's Juno-North Node conjunction in Gemini was close to both Paul's career signature (Saturn in Gemini) and his writing (Mercury). Mary's Juno-North Node also falls *exactly* on the Ascendant/Descendant axis of The Beatles composite chart (not shown), conjunct the "Beatles signature."

300

Below are Paul's progressions on Oct 31, 1956 when Mary died.

At this time, Paul's p-Moon was in Pisces (grief, loss), about 3.5° away from his South Node (karmic lessons) and separating. She was diagnosed with advanced stages of cancer a few months earlier (in August 1956), when his p-Moon was exactly on his grief-stricken South Node.

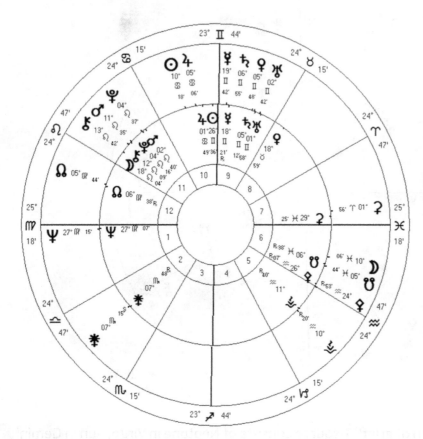

Paul was born with Mercury retrograde. It stationed direct by progression when he was a small child. Here at the age of 14, he was having a p-Mercury return, a new beginning in his writing.

Paul's p-Venus was conjunct Saturn, the maturation (Saturn) of his art (Venus). P-Mars was on his Chiron, triggering pain and anger which can ideally become expressed creatively (Leo).

John & Paul Meet

The Quarrymen performed an afternoon and an evening set. The two boys met in between sets, "in the early evening," according to Beatles historian Mark Lewisohn. The time being used is 6pm. Here's John and Paul's composite chart, surrounded by the transits for this seminal event.

1: At 6pm in Liverpool that day, the Moon was at 12° Scorpio. When Paul arrived to see the start of the show (presumably around the 3pm start time of the first set), the Moon was at 10° Scorpio, the exact degree of his composite Moon with John!

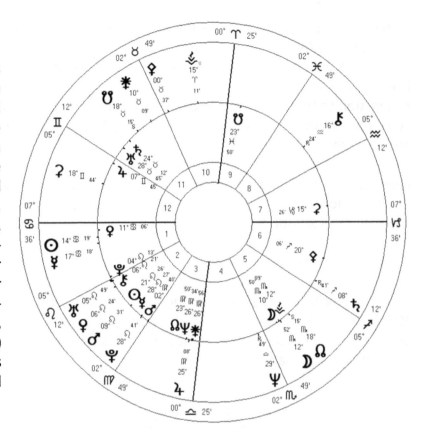

2: The t-Moon was conjunct t-North Node (karmic destiny), and together were lighting up their composite Vesta (craftsmanship) in the area of performance and creative expression (5th). T-Vesta was in Aries, located in their public-career 10th House. Their work (Vesta) together was starting (Aries). T-Saturn (maturation, vocational development) was at 8° Sagittarius (conjunct the eventual Beatles ASC).

3: The John-Paul chart (p. 277) had the brilliant quintile aspect between their performance-driven 5th House Moon and Mercury in Leo (creative writing). This aspect was being precisely triggered by the t-Moon quintile t-Pluto at 28° Leo. Pluto transiting their composite Mercury was enough to catalyze their writing partnership, and here it's *brilliantly and uniquely linked to emotional wounds* (Scorpio Moon). Additionally, t-Pluto was approaching their Mars (at 2° Virgo), catalyzing their competitive writing rivalry (Mercury-Mars). In the years to come, they would feed off of the competitive energy (Mars) and write (Mercury) the early catalog of Beatles music and transform (Pluto) culture.

T-Mercury was also out-of-bounds at 23°54' northern declination, connecting directly to the Ceres-Pluto out-of-bounds situation in the Beatles composite chart. John and Paul would grow to attain the heights (northern) of acclaim for their writing partnership. The lyrics of their songs would reflect the Ceres-Pluto dynamic, the transformation of maternal death issues.

4: T-Juno was at 10° Taurus conjunct the South Node (18° Taurus), something unfinished from the past (South Node) regarding romance (Juno) was coming to the world stage (11th). The Sun was in Cancer on that fateful day, transiting their 1st House (new familial beginnings) and conjunct their Venus (partnership). The Cancer Sun was also conjunct Mercury, emphasizing communications. T-Ceres (mothers) was in Gemini (communication) in their 12th House (divine inspiration). Ceres was at 18° Gemini, Paul's

302

Mercury degree as well as the solar eclipse degree from the prior year! It was also conjunct the "Beatles signature."

In addition to Pluto in Leo, Venus, Mars and Uranus were transiting the sign of the Lion. Uranus in Leo pertains to breakthrough creativity, new innovations, and it was in connection to both creative partnerships (Venus in Leo) and a drive to perform (Mars in Leo). The Leo planets were setting off Paul's planets in early Leo (Moon, Mars, Pluto) as well as John's Pluto-Moon opposition.

5: T-Jupiter was exactly on Paul's Ascendant, suggesting a new beginning with his purpose. T- Pluto was about to enter Virgo, and would soon hit his North Node (destiny) as well as John's Venus (partnerships). The Moon-North Node in Scorpio was on John's Mercury in his 7th House (writing partnerships).

Enter George Harrison

Below is George's chart around the time of the auditions (March 1958). It is cast for March 20, the New Moon that month. As we are looking at his transits during this general time frame, the exact moment of the auditions are not needed. George was going through a life-changing passage.

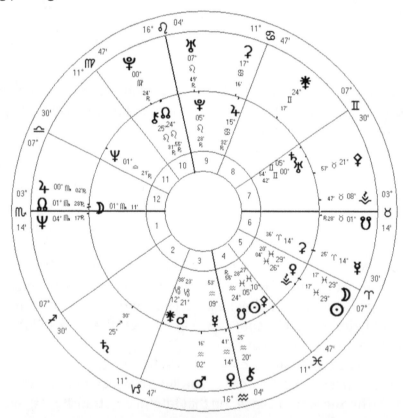

1: T-Saturn in Sagittarius was in George's 2nd House, a challenge for him to prove his worth and live his path. Saturn would soon move to Capricorn, and begin transiting his

Mars. In his later teens, he would come into his manhood (Mars) by maturing in his profession (Capricorn).

2: The New Moon on 3/20/58 was on George's Venus, triggering his musical dreams to be a performer as well as his relational (Venus) pattern of sacrificing (Pisces) to others. T-Saturn was square his Venus, reflecting the hierarchical relating structure he would enter, and his limitations within it.

3: T-Uranus was conjunct his Pluto and quincunx his Sun, dramatically challenging him to rise to his creative power. T-Pluto was recently on his North Node-Chiron in Leo, quenching his desires for entertainment as a youngster. It would soon be opposing George's Sun, challenging him to appear publicly (10th House) with his skills.

4: The Ascendant involves new beginnings. At this time, George had t-Jupiter, Neptune and the North Node on his Ascendant, stirring his dreams (Neptune) as he embraced his chosen life path (Jupiter). His natal Moon was also being transited by these planets, stimulating him to break out of hiding (12th) and claim his power (Scorpio).

Around the time of the auditions, on March 22, 1958, George's p-Moon entered Gemini, Sun sign of his buddy Paul McCartney (who advocated his inclusion), and also the sign of the "Beatles signature." The shift from Taurus (fixed earth) to Gemini (mutable air) can be a launch into a frenzy of new activity. George's p-Moon entered this sign of sound and variety (Gemini), illuminating his Uranus-Saturn (career individuation).

Below is his progressed chart (around his natal) at this pivotal time.

His p-Moon was both waxing and becoming more elevated in the chart—George was on the ascent and building momentum. His p-Sun was in the creative 5th House and sextile his natal Mars in Capricorn (claiming power). His p-Mercury recently entered Pisces (here at 1°) heading towards his Sun, bringing the issue of communications to his life force. His voice and message would become more developed as this progression perfected during his tenure with the Beatles.

304

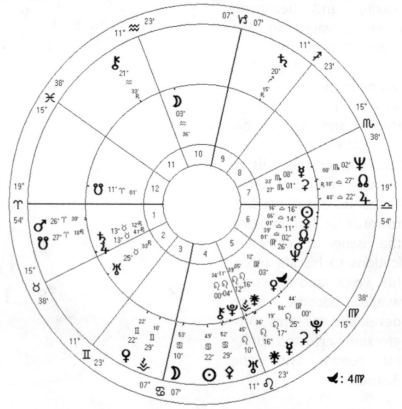

Julia had the muse in Pisces, like her North Node, Chiron, Mercury, Sun and Venus. She was learning to be intuitive and inspirational. Saturn in Gemini was square her Pisces planets, adding a writing focus. Pluto in Gemini connects ideas and communications with death. Her Ceres in Aquarius conjunct Jupiter-Uranus was a unique mix of nurturance with the metaphysical. Julia had a Full Moon, having been born just after a lunar eclipse, highlighting the drama she lived. In late Virgo-Pisces, it fell on the Nodal axis of the Beatles chart.

Here's the transits to John's chart when Julia was killed.

1: John's "wounded child" T-square was being transited by Neptune in Scorpio (painful loss, sadness). It was just a half degree from his Ceres. The t-balsamic Moon at 10⁰ Cancer (endings) was square John's Nodal "axis of conflict." John's violent karma (Aries South Node), involving loss (12th House), was being hit by the familial Cancer Moon in the area of home. At the time of the accident,

Mars in Aries was conjunct the South Node, consistent with violent themes. T-Mars-South Node in late Aries was only a few degrees from his "wounded child" T-square, filling it out into a frictional Grand Cross. In particular, Mars in (late) Aries opposite his Ceres in (early) Scorpio could feel like a dagger (Mars) stabbing (Scorpio) his most vulnerable, youngest self (Ceres).

Pluto pertains to death and transformation. It was transiting John's 5th House, approaching his Venus-Euterpe: the expression (5th House) of psychological processes (Pluto) into creative pursuits and partnerships (Venus), including with his muse (Euterpe). T-Pluto was traveling with Ceres, connecting the maternal with death. There was a Jupiter-Venus trine reflecting the "Beatles signature." Jupiter was conjunct John's Libra Sun, challenging him to find artistic purpose. Venus in Gemini was in John's 3rd House (writing) and conjunct Paul's Mercury (not shown), pointing to his writing partner.

Below is Julia's chart around John's (their composite chart will be discussed later).

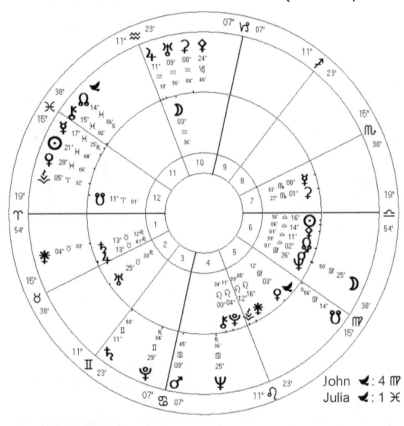

2: Julia's Ceres was on John's Moon, pointing to the emotional depth of their connection. Her Ceres was with Jupiter and Uranus, a unique form of love, consistent with nurturing from a distance (Aquarius, meta-physical). This archetype (Uranus-Aquarius) also involves trauma, insta-bility and abandonment issues.

Julia's Pisces energy resided in John's 12th House (loss, endings, soul connection). Her Virgo South Node was not too far from John's Venus and Euterpe, suggesting a karmic link to his artistic creativity involving his muse.

Julia's Virgo Moon was on John's 6th House Neptune, inspiring him to bring his vision (Neptune) into form (6th House). Neptune-Moon could also be a connection through consciousness or dreams, perhaps inspiration from beyond the veil. Her Mars in Cancer resided in his 4th House and was square his Nodes, violently setting off his karma from the sensitive area of the home. (As noted above, the Moon was here at the time of the accident.) Her Neptune was in late Cancer, also falling in his 4th House (family grief), and opposite his Moon. This not only reflects deep loss; it also may involve spiritual redemption and another link to the otherworldly. Her Neptune was square his wounded 7th House Ceres in Scorpio, another link between the mother (Ceres) and "loss" (Neptune).

Julia's Saturn at 11° Gemini (maturation with writing) was in John's writing-oriented 3rd House, while also conjunct the "Beatles signature." It was trine his 6th House Libra planets, a potential work relationship involving communications.

Below are John's progressions when his mother died, providing further illumination about this time in his life.

John's p-Sun (evolving biography) was right in the middle of his "wounded child" T-square. It was coming off an exact conjunction with his natal Ceres, a time when their bond became deeper (Scorpio). Julia supported John's musical interest and they spent more time together in his teens. At the time of her death, John's p-Sun moved forward to exactly square his Moon-Pluto opposition, triggering his unresolved emotional wounds.

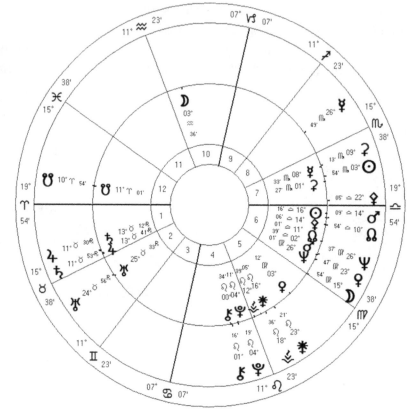

At this early age, John was completing the lunar cycle in which he was born. The waning p-Moon was in Virgo in his 6th House, applying to his p-Venus—he was learning (Virgo) to be a musical (Venus) performer and he met his main collaborator (Venus in Virgo).

His p-Vesta was conjunct natal Juno, exact a few years earlier when he was getting into music as a child and early teen. This combination pairs craftsmanship (Vesta) with romantic themes (Juno) in creative/expressive Leo. Much of the music in the 1950s was about youthful romance, and his development as a performer (5th House) relied heavily on this. John's p-Mercury (in Scorpio) was sextile his natal Neptune. The 8th House and Scorpio relate to deep soul work and commitments, a sense of shared destiny with another. Not only does this correlate with inspired, mystical writing potentials, it also captures the significance of the burgeoning Lennon-McCartney partnership.

Hamburg

The chart below is The Beatles arrival in Hamburg.

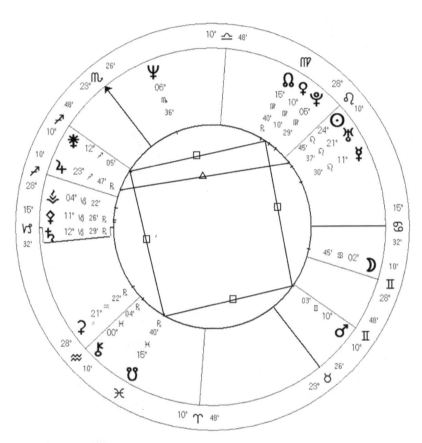

1: The North Node was in Virgo conjunct Venus and Pluto: a focus on work, long hours (Virgo) and intensity (Pluto) with connections (Venus). Saturn in Capricorn was rising, another emphasis on work and maturation. It was opposite a young-hearted Cancer Moon, challenging them to grow up. Saturn was trine the industrious Virgo North Node (skill development). Mars in Gemini (on the "Beatles signature") was square the Nodal Axis, suggesting issues with masculine empowerment. Juno in Sagittarius was also square the Nodes, pointing to the exotic foreign allure and the romance of Stu and Astrid. Jupiter in Sagittarius relates to the travel and adventure, while Neptune in Scorpio trine the Cancer Moon is a pull of seduction.

The Cavern Club

Below is the chart for their first performance as "The Beatles" at the fabled club.

1: Sagittarius Moon involves life direction and purpose. Its square to the Nodal Axis and Pluto suggests the working through of such issues. Mars at 0° Cancer foreshadows the eventual Beatles composite Sun. Mars square Venus in impetuous Aries is a competitive edge. Uranus in Leo adds a burst of celebratory energy, the hallmark of Beatlemania.

Venus sextile Juno was their romantic focus, an appeal to female fans. Uranus was opposite the revolutionary Aquarius Sun---something new and unique was emerging. It was also quincunx Jupiter and Saturn in Capricorn, seeking to penetrate the mainstream culture. The Sun was conjunct Athena in Aquarius, depicting an unrelentingly progressive force urging them to not hold back.

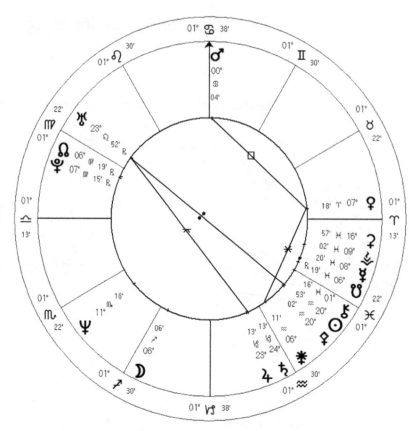

Stuart Sutcliffe

1: Stu had Jupiter, Saturn and Uranus in Taurus, the North Node in Libra, and a Vesta-Sun-Venus stellium in the 5th House—all pointing to artistry. Venus retrograde suggests an issue in figuring it out. The process leading to his departure also occurred under Venus retrograde.

2: Like the rest of The Beatles, Stu had a fixed sign Moon. Similar to John's, his Aquarius Moon involved themes of disconnection, emotional

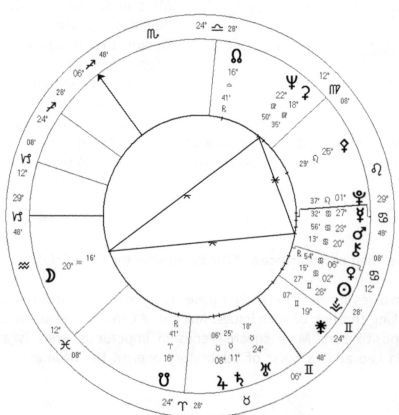

trauma and turbulence. His Moon was quincunx Neptune-Ceres and Mars-Chiron (a Yod), a complex signature involving unmet emotional needs and healing from conflict.

3: Also similar to John, Stu had an Aries South Node. Its residence in the 2nd House points to issues of physical safety and security.

4: The dispositor of his South Node was Mars in the 6th House conjunct Chiron, suggesting that compromised health conditions connect to the conflictual karmic pattern. Sustaining debilitating injuries through fighting precisely fits with this configuration.

Below are Stu's transits the day he was attacked.

5: Mars retrograde (violence, connected to the past) was transiting Stu's Sun. The T-Cancer Moon triggered his Mars-Chiron conjunction (wounds-Chiron, through battle-Mars). Saturn was transiting his 12th House (loss, confusion), exactly opposed to his sensitive Mars-Chiron, like a dead weight of karmic reality.

Also at this time was a Chiron-Pluto opposition, which fell along the Nodal axis, bringing forth health issues (Chiron) buried in the shadow (Pluto). Stu's karmic drama with John was in full manifestation.

6: In their individual charts, John and Stu both had an Aries South Node disposited by Mars in the 6th House—a signature of conflict (Aries) relating to workmates (6th House). A karmic past as soldiers together would fit.

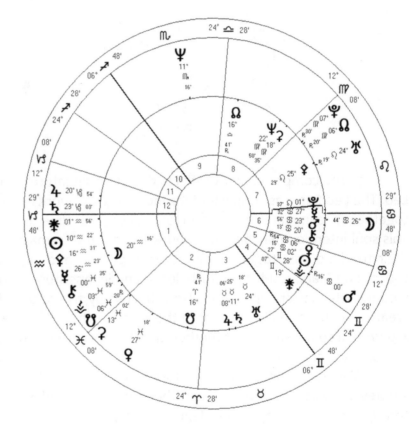

310

Below is the John-Stu composite chart.

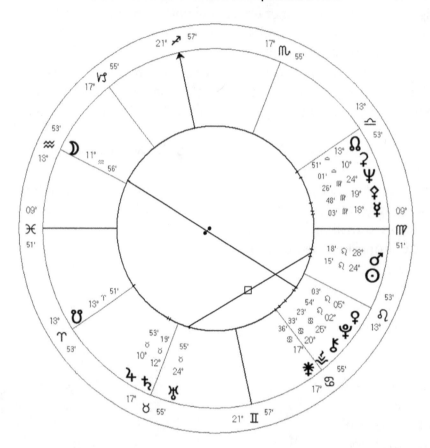

7: The composite chart reflects the same signature (Mars in the 6th), appearing in Leo. The Leo Sun was conjunct Mars, indicating the work in the present (Sun) was to join together as teammates once again (6th House), this time to develop as performers (Leo). This soul intention may be why John wanted Stu to remain a Beatle, so they could heal their troubled past together. However, they also had unpredictable Uranus in Taurus square Sun-Mars, resulting in turbulence and inconsistency. Their intention to transform wounds into performance was also reflected by the packed 5th House, which included creative Venus in Leo (dispositor of the Libra North Node). In addition to music, John and Stu were also art students together, another example of how this stylistic and creative combination could manifest.

Venus conjunct Pluto ventures into the psychological depths to transform whatever lurks there from the past. There was some kind of interpersonal dynamic to sort through, one involving some degree of intensity. The karmic pattern of being in the trenches together (Mars in the 6th House), resulted in a connection (Venus) that endured wounds (Pluto).

When Stu died on April 10, 1962, the t-Sun was at 20° Aries, on his South Node and square his Chiron-Mars conjunction. The Sun was also on John's South Node, stimulating a major loss (12th House) triggered by violence (Aries). The t-South Node (spiritual lessons) was in Aquarius (trauma, shock), the Moon sign for both Stu and John.

311

First Recording Session

1: The Cancer Sun and Libra Moon were in the same location as their counterparts on the Beatles composite chart (a solar and lunar return), a new beginning in their history.

2: Mercury retrograde can suggest unreadiness to move forward.

3: Juno (romance) is not particularly noteworthy.

4: Mars conjunct Uranus on the Leo North Node points to their eventual role as breakthrough (Uranus) leaders (Mars) in entertainment (Leo).

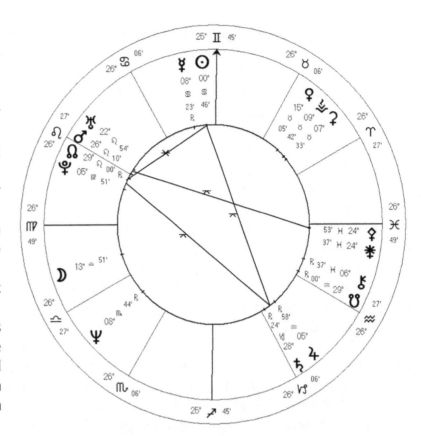

Discovery & Brian Epstein

1: Brian's Virgo Sun was conjunct the Beatles North Node, portraying a soul intention to have him organize and ground their talent (not shown).

2: Brian had a 1st House Virgo Sun, with a Virgo Ascendant and a Venus-Neptune conjunction in Virgo also present. He could manage (1st House) the details (Virgo) of artistic efforts (Venus) entering the collective consciousness (Neptune). Brian's Sun was square Juno in the 5th House, matching the Beatles motif

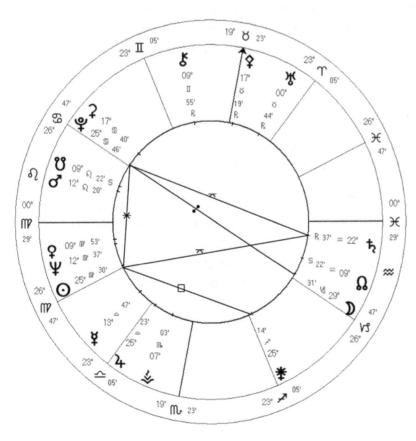

of romantically-oriented (Juno) entertainment (5th). He also had Saturn in Aquarius in the 6th House, which added structural form (Saturn) to innovation (Aquarius), with an eye on progressive trends.

3: His Saturn was trine Jupiter in Libra, a flowing energetic circuit for expansion (Jupiter) into culture (Libra). Brian also had Mercury in Libra, giving him an ear for what could be popular and pleasing. It was conjunct The Beatles Libra Moon, and he went to The Cavern to listen in and discover them.

4: There is no astrological signature for homosexuality; the lessons and themes astrology reveals are less specific. In this case, Brian's Mars in Leo in his 12th House suggests keeping passions (Mars) hidden in the proverbial closet (12th). It's well documented that Brian was infatuated with John. John's romantic Juno in Leo was conjunct Brian's Mars, a potentially erotic energetic circuit. However, it's completely up to them how it's managed, contingent on desires, intentions and circumstances.

5: Brian had a Capricorn Moon in the 6th House, the ideal placement for management (Capricorn) of projects (6th House). Capricorn can be professional and refined, sometimes shutting down emotion to appear in control. Similar to all of the Beatles, he had a Moon-Pluto aspect (the opposition). Like the band members, he was learning to find deeper self-love and acceptance, to be with prior emotional pain.

6: Brian's Venus-Neptune conjunction in Virgo was precisely square the "Beatles signature." The square is an aspect of friction. He had a vision (Neptune) and urged them (square) to realize the bounty of their potential. However, it can also manifest in problematical ways. Brian made some questionable business decisions which would cost the band. His unstable (some might say neurotic) behaviors were less than helpful at times. Nevertheless, he did light up the "Beatles signature" and they became famous soon after the partnership was established.

John's New Beginning

1: John's p-New Moon was at 7° Scorpio, presenting an opportunity to forge a new relationship with death, the core issue of his wounds. The sign also involves the rising into power, intimacy and partnerships.

2: The p-New Moon was on his Mercury in the 7th House, creating a focus on writing and communications with partners. His p-Sun would move forward to exactly conjoin his Mercury in March 1963, right when The Beatles first album came out, solidifying his identity (Sun) as a writer (Mercury). In February 1963, John's p-Mercury stationed retrograde in Scorpio. His writing increasingly became confessional, personal, psychological and revealing of his inner world.

3: Also of note is p-Mars on his Sun. John was the undisputed leader (Mars) of the band at this time.

Additionally, transiting Jupiter and Saturn in Capricorn were moving through his commanding 10th House (not shown), the "toppermost", urging him to claim his stature in his career. These social and cultural planets would soon make their way to his 11th House, the "world stage."

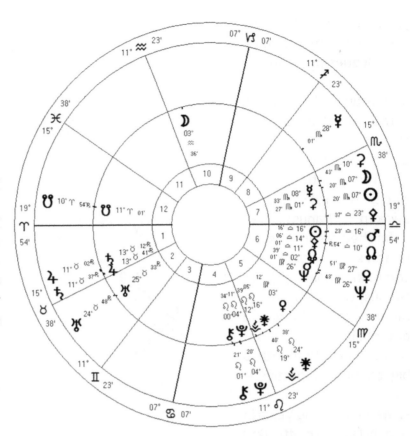

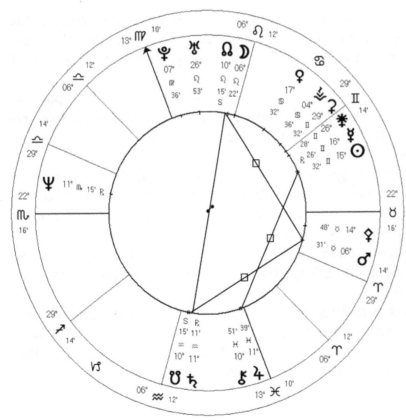

The Audition & George Martin

1: The audition chart features a Moon-North Node conjunction, fore-telling the birth (Moon) of a new entertainment (Leo) direction (North Node). The Sun (North Node dispositor), appears at 15° Gemini, on the "Beatles signature," pointing to the band.

2: Juno (romance) at 26° Gemini was conjunct Ceres (maternal) at 29° Gemini, on the 8th House cusp (death).

3: Mercury retrograde was at 16° Gemini, also on the "Beatles signature."

4: Martin's chart (right, with the Beatles) had Uranus at 22° Pisces, exactly (to the minute!) on The Beatles South Node. His role was to awaken (Uranus) their unfinished dream (Pisces) in areas of message and communications (3rd). His Uranus was also square Mercury in Sagittarius, a potential for brilliant sound innovation with a big-picture perspective.

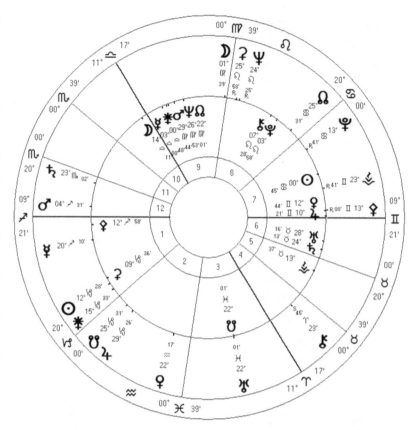

5: Martin also had Vesta in Gemini (sound craftsman) making his Uranus-Mercury a T-square, as well as connecting this signature directly to the Beatles Sun (from late Gemini to early Cancer). He had Athena in Gemini directly on the "Beatles signature" (and opposite their Athena), accentuating clever strategies to work with sound/voice.

 6: His Capricorn Sun was conjunct the band's Ceres. As a man, this added paternal support to the familial signature. Martin's Sun was conjunct Juno in Capricorn. Not only was he attuned to the romantic nature of their music, in Capricorn, his role was to structure and professionalize it.

 7: As a Capricorn Sun with a Virgo Moon, Martin provided the earth to ground their potential into reality. Also, his Jupiter in Capricorn (conjunct his South Node) finds success through business and the dominant cultural milieu. The Jupiter-Saturn conjunction in Capricorn in 1961 was exactly on his South Node, triggering his unfinished vocational work into action. Martin's Jupiter fell in the Beatles 2nd House (money, empowerment), and was trine their Uranus-Saturn in Taurus ("artistic genius"), as well as their Neptune-Mars-North Node in Virgo (spiritual destiny).

 8: Neptune in Leo has a flair for the theatrical. This creatively (Leo) inspired (Neptune) signature connects with others to fashion innovative artistic trends (opposite Venus in Aquarius). Martin's Neptune-Venus opposition was precisely square the Beatles "artistic genius" signature (their Saturn-Uranus conjunction in the work-oriented 6th House).

Here's Ringo's chart with transits when he joined the band.

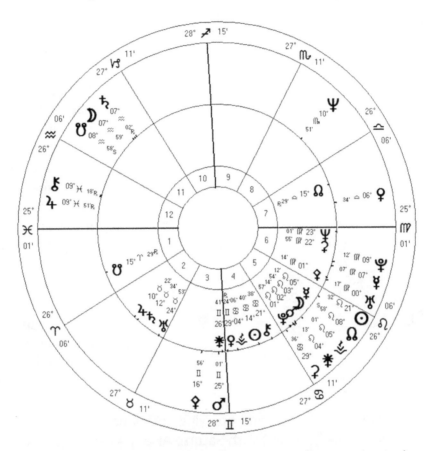

1: When Ringo entered the band, the North Node (karmic destiny) was transiting his 5th House (talent, performance). The t-Sun, Vesta and Juno were also there, adding creative energy (Sun) in crafting (Vesta) romantic (Juno) music. T-Mars in Gemini was hitting Ringo's natal Juno-Venus (romance, partnerships). T-Venus in Libra was in his 7th House, emphasizing artistic connections.

2: T-Saturn in Aquarius in his 11th House brought breakthrough (Aquarius) onto the world stage (11th House). Uranus and Pluto in his 6th House was trine his 2nd House Taurus planets; he was developing (6th House) stronger confidence (2nd House) in his trade. T-Neptune in Scorpio was opposite his artistic Taurus planets, and he was about to be swept up (Neptune) in a vortex of hysteria (Scorpio). T-Jupiter in Pisces was trine his Sun (opportunity, expansion) and soon to cross his Ascendant, signaling travel, and the adventurous ride to come.

Below are Ringo's progressions at this time.

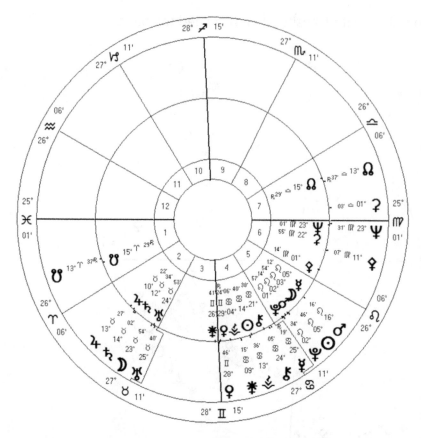

Ringo's 5th House Leo stellium is his desire for creative expression. With his p-Sun now at 5° Leo, for the last 5 years (p-Sun moves 1° a year) he had been working at its resolution. His p-Sun would travel through his 5th House for many years to come—Ringo would enjoy his life as a famous musician. The karmic struggle was over.

His p-Moon was at 23° Taurus conjunct his natal Uranus in Taurus, the moment of breakthrough (Uranus) for his art (Taurus). He was having a p-Venus return (it was now direct and less than a degree and applying to his natal Venus), and p-Mars was separating from the square (conflict) with Saturn. Also, p-Vesta was a degree away and applying to his Sun, placing a focus on skill development. Ringo's p-Moon arrived in Gemini in March 1963, the month *Please Please Me* was released.

The Marginalization of Pete Best

Below is Pete's chart (time unknown, cast for midday).

1: Pete also has the Moon in a fixed sign. It's in Aquarius like John and Stu and he shares the same issue of initial emotional disconnection from self. Due to the unknown birth time, his Moon degree is uncertain. However, it must be opposed Chiron in Leo (wounds with performance), as well as Pluto to some degree. Pete's situation fits with the pervading emotional wounds that typify Beatles astrology.

2: Feeling abandoned, an Aquarius Moon might act recklessly stemming from pain. John did this repeatedly, Stu took out his insecurity by charging at Paul, and Pete had a suicide attempt. The conscious resolution of the airy Aquarius Moon is to breakthrough into the emotional body and reconnect with self.

3: Should the seed (Moon) become cultivated with love, Pete's potential is to flower into spiritual direction (Sagittarius Sun) and develop a more engaging, fiery persona.

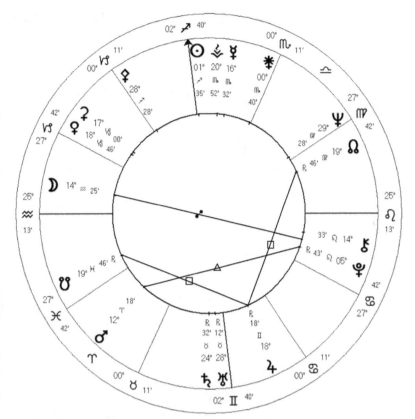

4: At the time of his dismissal, the t-South Node was in Aquarius (as well as an eclipse on his Moon), triggering his karma with abandonment or disconnection.

5: Venus in Capricorn can be reserved, measured or mechanical. The conscious version is utmost professionalism. Capricorn is ruled by Saturn (Kronos the Time Keeper), and his musicianship (Venus) on the drums keeps time. Pete's Venus is also out-of-bounds, way down at 25°12' southern declination. It is easy for him to feel like the outsider.

6: Pete has Jupiter in Gemini on the "Beatles signature." However, it's square his Nodal Axis, signifying major lessons. The potential is to become more improvisational, witty and engaging, which would've connected better with the band, both musically and interpersonally. His Venus in Capricorn is quincunx Jupiter suggesting that his reserved demeanor must be negotiated as part of the development. Ringo has Venus in Gemini, making him naturally more bouncy, dexterous and agile.

7: Pete has Pluto in Leo trine Mars in Aries, an underlying sexual magnetism. Like Paul, he also has a sexy Juno in Scorpio.

318

Below is the composite chart composed of John, Paul, George and Pete.

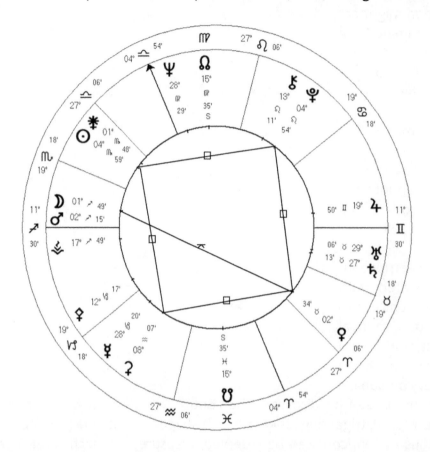

8: As Pete's birth time is unknown, this chart is likely to be a little off but we get a sense of the dynamic. It has a Scorpio Sun conjunct Juno (sexual magnetism, that was conjunct Pete's natal Juno). There is merit to the idea that Pete was seen as the sexiest in the group as his romantic magnetism (Juno in Scorpio) activates this group chart more than the others.

There is competitiveness: a Grand Cross composed of Pluto in Leo, Venus in Taurus and Ceres in Aquarius in frictional aspect (square, opposition) with the Sun. The configuration is relationally intense (Pluto square Venus), and connects with early-developmental abandonment issues (Ceres in Aquarius), so central in Beatles astrology.

This group chart also had a Moon-Mars conjunction in Sagittarius (emotionally charged competitiveness), which falls on Pete's Sun. Once again, the group chart strongly points to Pete, creating a challenge (perhaps a threat) to the front men. At one gig, the club owner wanted to have Pete's drum kit at the front of the stage so the girls could see him better. This did not go over well with the others and is illustrative of this sexually-competitive astrology.

Below is Cynthia's chart around John's.

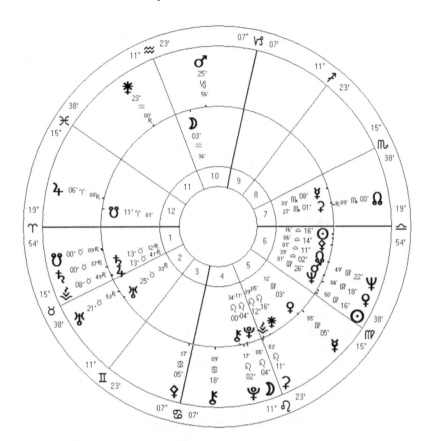

1: Cynthia's Moon was conjunct Pluto, a familiar emotional pattern in Beatles astrology. Her Moon was opposite John's, which brought it to a relational dynamic.

2: Cynthia's Moon-Pluto conjunction also included Ceres, reflecting John's "wounded child" signature. John's Juno in Leo was on Cynthia's Ceres, an example of the maternal-romantic transference in this story. John's Ceres was on Cynthia's Nodal Axis, suggesting a karmic nurturance connection of some sort.

3: Cynthia had a Leo Moon, another example of a fixed Moon in the story.

4: Cynthia had Pluto opposite Mars, which might play out issues of aggression relationally.

Below is John's chart with the transits on his wedding day.

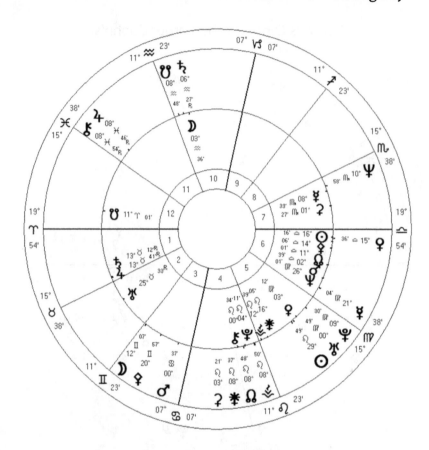

5: The Nodal Axis was on John's "wounded child" T-square, stimulating his love and home issues. The Leo North Node was conjunct Juno and Ceres, reflecting yet again this pairing: a romantic union (Juno) involving maternal issues (Ceres), geared for karmic resolution (North Node). However, John's Pluto in the 4th House was a deep wound with family, and his historical Aquarian patterns of family disengagement were activated. The issue was abandonment (Aquarius), as the t-South Node was activating his Aquarius Moon. (John would replay abandonment themes both with Cynthia and their son Julian.) T-Saturn was also conjunct the South Node (and his Moon) bringing reality to the pattern. John decided to do the "responsible" (Saturn) thing of getting married, which positioned him to address the underlying issues being triggered.

6: At the time of the marriage, Uranus was transiting John's Venus, consistent with a major shift in his relational life. T-Venus was on his Libra Sun, correlating with marriage. Interestingly, Venus was trine the Moon at 12° Gemini, conjunct the "Beatles signature." Gemini is a dualistic sign, and his emotional (Moon) allegiance was split. Mars was at 0° Cancer, on The Beatles Sun (not shown), illustrative of the family (Cancer) of men (Mars) that was his focus. Mars was out-of-bounds at 23°35' north, tightly parallel Ceres at 23°36', linking aggression (Mars) with nurturing issues (Ceres). Out-of-bounds can often manifest as out-of-sight, and later it became known that domestic violence was a part of their marriage.

321

Love Me, Please Me

Below is the release of the single "Please Please Me" with the band's chart.

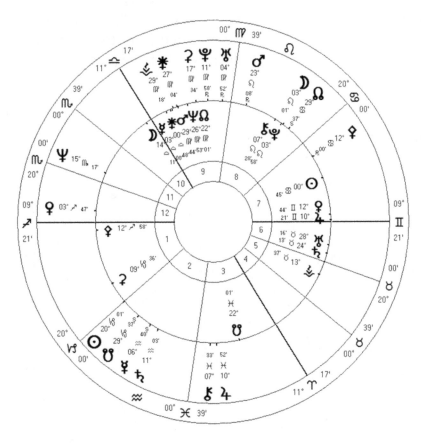

1: Ringo's 5th House Pluto in Leo suggests wounding with performance issues.

2: Ringo has Uranus in Taurus, a lesson of resolving unsteadiness and developing poise and calmness.

3: "Please Please Me" had a Jupiter-Venus square, directly in aspect (square, opposition) with the band's Jupiter-Venus, highlighting the potential of their creativity. Pluto at 11º Virgo was square the "Beatles signature" from one side, while Jupiter (expansion, opportunity) at 10º Pisces was squaring it from the other.

4: T-Mercury was direct for the release, but would station retrograde later that day. A planet has increased potency when it is standing still (stationing), concentrating its energy on a single point. Mercury was at 6º Aquarius, conjunct Saturn at 11º, suggesting the creation of a new (Aquarius) sound (Mercury) in the mainstream (Saturn). The Mercury-Saturn conjunction was trine the Beatles "love me" Libra Moon, as well as the "Beatles signature," smoothly connecting new cultural trends (Saturn in Aquarius) to the robust potential of their musicality.

A Juno-Vesta conjunction (romance with craft) was in late Virgo for the release. It was transiting the band's late Virgo/early Libra stellium (Neptune, Mars, Juno, Mercury). The asteroid Juno has about a 4 year orbit, so this was a Juno return. For the next 4 years their musical focus was on romantic themes, which shifted by the next Juno return.

T-Neptune was in their 11th House opposite their 5th House Vesta, connecting their musical craft (Vesta) up to the collective (11th House) in the glamorous and fantastical

(Neptune) way that became Beatlemania. The North Node (destiny) was at 29° Cancer. It would move towards their Sun (Nodes move "backwards") over the next year and half as the hysteria built and climaxed.

Shortly after the release of "Please Please Me" was a solar eclipse at 4° Aquarius on January 25th. The early degrees of fixed signs were a hot zone for all of them and this eclipse lit them up. It was conjunct John's Moon (who was recently married with a baby on the way), opposite Ringo's Moon, square George's Moon and on Paul's Leo planets. All of them had significant Leo energy, which this eclipse opposed from the collectively-oriented sign Aquarius. They were being awakened (Aquarius) into fame (Leo).

Twisting & Shouting

Below is the recording of "Twist and Shout."

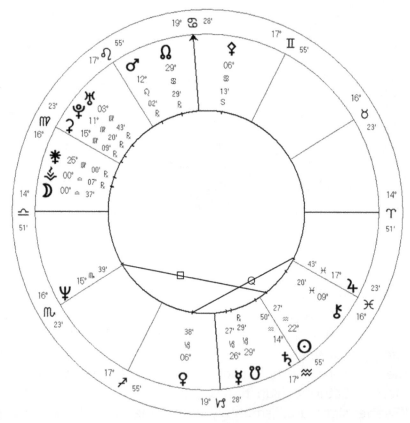

1: Venus was quintile Jupiter reflecting the familiar combination of the "Beatles signature," though with unusual novelty and brilliance (quintile). The innovative Aquarius Sun was in the realm of talent (5th House), while its conjunction to Saturn (and square to Neptune) involved entrance into the mass consciousness.

2: Throughout the day the Moon was transiting the later degrees of Virgo, illuminating the Beatles composite North Node, Mars and Neptune (realization of destiny, dream). For the recording of "Twist and Shout," the Moon entered Libra. The band's Mercury was in early Libra, so the Moon was directly on it. When recording for "Twist and Shout" began, the Ascendant was at 14° Libra, the degree of the band's Moon. The song was representative of their emotional passion (Moon) to connect (Libra) with their audience, their early desire to get to the "toppermost."

3: 14° Libra was also conjunct John's Sun and "Twist and Shout" contributed to the development of his artistic persona. Venus, the dispositor of the "Twist and Shout"

Ascendant, was in the 3ʳᵈ House in Capricorn—communication (3ʳᵈ). The song would go on to become classic (Capricorn).

Album #1 – *Please Please Me*

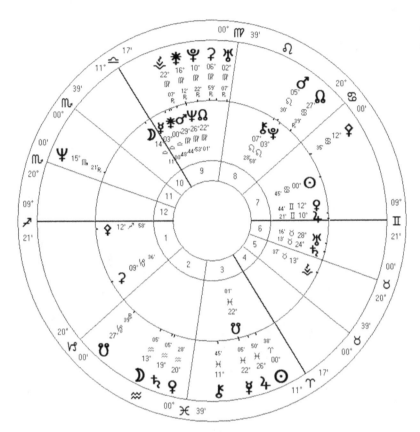

1: The Sun was at 0° Aries, the first degree of the zodiac, perfect for the release of their first album. The Sun was conjunct Jupiter in late Pisces, adding imaginative and inspiring elements. Mercury in Pisces was exactly on the band's South Node. The work they came to develop (South Node) was given sound (Mercury), and entered the collective consciousness (Pisces) through their lively (Sun-Jupiter) spirit.

2: Vesta was exactly on their Virgo North Node suggesting the realization of their craft. It connects via stellium to Juno (romance) and Pluto-Ceres-Uranus (reviewed below).

3: The album's Capricorn South Node involved mainstream culture and business, and it was trine the Beatles planets in Taurus (Uranus, Saturn) and Virgo (North Node, Neptune, Mars), creating a flowing Grand Trine. Saturn (dispositor of the South Node) in Aquarius brings organization (Saturn) to something new and innovative (Aquarius). Saturn was conjunct both the Moon and Venus in Aquarius, suggesting an underlying need (Moon) to capitalize (Saturn) on a new (Aquarius) artistic trend (Venus). These Aquarius planets were trine the "Beatles signature," creating a smooth connection for success. The Aries Sun was also trine Mars in Leo adding more fire, youthful expression and charisma. Mars in Leo was conjunct the North Node (in late Cancer) reflecting a similar signature in the Beatles chart.

4: In addition to appearing with Uranus and Pluto, there's another notable condition with Ceres. It is hovering above {out of bounds at 24°19' north declination}, just out-of-reach. It's close to the same declination position as their Pluto-Ceres situation seen in their composite chart, literally paralleling it. Therefore, Pluto and Ceres are connected by aspect for the album's release (conjunction), while the same energies connect by parallel to the Beatles chart itself. Out-of-bounds can be out of sight—the maternal (Ceres) death (Pluto) theme dominates this story, but as depicted astrologically, it is just removed from a consensus understanding.

The Birth of Julian Lennon

Below is Julian's chart around John's.

1: Julian has Ceres in Virgo conjunct Uranus and Pluto, indicating nurturance wounds similar to those of his father. John's Moon was conjunct Julian's South Node, creating a karmic link with family dynamics.

2: Julian has an (almost) Full Moon spanning Aries (Sun) — Libra (Moon), along John's Nodal axis, bringing illumination to his karmic issues. With his Libra Moon on John's North Node, Julian stimulated his father to invest (6th

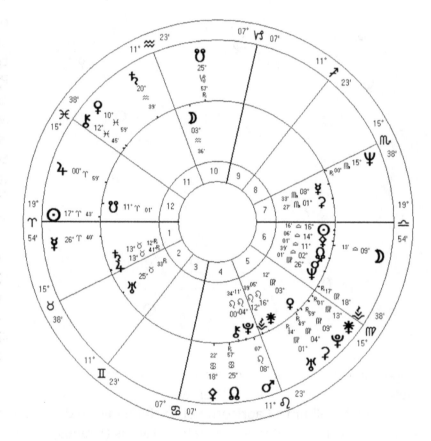

House) in sweet (Libra), loving connection (Moon). Julian's Aries Sun on John's South Node activates his tendency to check out (12th House) and be independent (Aries). As the Sun is always a process of becoming, there is a more conscious alternative. Aries in the 12th learns to choose (Aries) how to live with spiritual insight and grace (12th House), which can illuminate and partner with the relational Moon.

3: Julian's Mars in Leo was conjunct John's Leo planets, activating his core family wound (Pluto-Chiron in the 4th). The intention was to put such energy into creative performance (Leo), and both are musicians.

4: Julian's Sun is quite close to John's Ascendant, correlating with their strong resemblance.

5: Both John and Julian have Athena conjunct the North Node.

6: Whereas John's Athena-North Node was in Libra (peace activism through the arts), Julian's is in Cancer, pertaining to home, including our home planet.

Below is Jane's chart around Paul's.

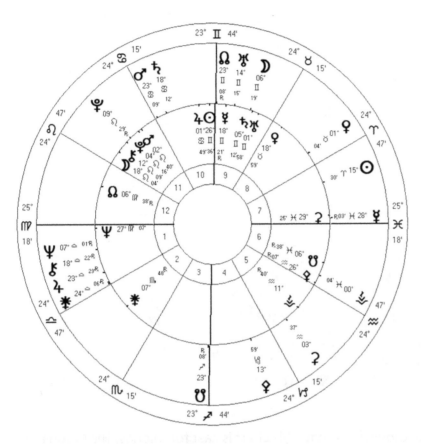

1: Jane's Venus in Taurus, fell in Paul's 8th House (intimacy) and opposite his passionate Juno in Scorpio. Her Jupiter-Juno in Libra was trine his Gemini Sun, further linking them together romantically. Jane's Aries Sun was trine Paul's Leo Moon. They also had libidinous Mars conjunct Mars (within 10° albeit different signs).

2: The air element (cool, conceptual, distant) is pronounced. Jane has a Gemini Moon, the same sign as Paul's Sun. However, they are 20° apart and Jane's Moon is conjunct Uranus, which can be emotionally cool or distant. Jane has Venus in Taurus just like Paul, but these planets are almost 18° apart. Jane's Jupiter-Juno trine Paul's Sun is very sweet and flowing, but the residence in air signs might indicate being enamored with the idea (air) of romance. Their relationship involved cultural sophistication, being socialites who mixed with the influential and glamorous. Jane's Juno is near Paul's, but once again, a distance to bridge (13° away and different signs).

3: Jane's Saturn in Cancer is learning to emotionally deepen (Cancer) and mature (Saturn). Paul's Jupiter in Cancer is an intention to expand the heart, as part of his path of awakening (conjunct Sun). These Cancer planets were once again many degrees apart. The legacy of their connection had some degree of missing each other. The dynamic replayed Paul's karmic issue of seeing love dissipate, as well as Jane's emotional pattern of airy removal. The potential for deepening was available, but it required focus and investment, which was a great challenge in the busyness of celebrity.

Below is Bob Wooler's chart around John's.

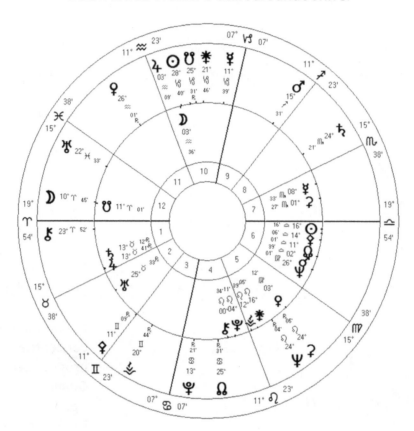

1: Due to Wooler's unknown birth time, his chart is cast for midday. His Moon must be between 3° and 16° Aries. Regardless of the unknown birth time, it was on John's Aries South Node, an emotional trigger to his violent karmic past. Wooler's Moon was square Pluto in Cancer (adding to the Moon-Pluto motif in the story). John's "wounded child" configuration was near Wooler's Nodal Axis, so the volatile dynamic went in both directions.

2: Wooler's Jupiter (amplification, enlargement) was on John's Aquarius Moon. In Aquarius, it could inflate reckless or anti-social behaviors; an emotional explosion is one possibility. Wooler also catalyzed a breakthrough (Aquarius) in expanding (Jupiter) John's professional desires (John's Moon in the 10th House) by introducing Brian Epstein. Regarding the beating, John was triggered (Moon) by his perception of Wooler's judgements and attitudes (Jupiter).

Jupiter involves opinions and belief systems, how we justify our behaviors. At the time of the attack, transiting Jupiter was in Aries on John's South Node, triggering his conflictual karma. Additionally, t-Mars was sandwiched between Uranus and Pluto. Buried aggression or violence (Mars) was being awakened to work through, or to play out. This grouping of energy was hitting John's Venus in his 5th house, a combination that socializes such energy (and the 5th House correlates with parties and recreational behavior).

Chapter 8 – The Meteoric Rise

The Beatlemania Astrology of the Musicians

This section is a brief summary of their individual astrology when Beatlemania exploded into the collective imagination and sets the stage for the next few chapters. The transits being discussed are for the next couple of years, so there is not a chart to encapsulate the activity.

Transiting Uranus was conjunct John's Venus during the march towards Beatlemania and its full-blown realization. Both his musical and personal lives were under radical (and breakthrough) change. T-Jupiter was in Aries in 1963-64, making its way across his Ascendant when he came to America for the first time. Along with travel and adventure, this transit also correlates with John's presentation of himself (1st House) in an empowered (Aries) manner. He was now the leader of the band spearheading the British Invasion. T-Saturn was in John's 11th House (collective, "world stage") opposite his 5th House Leo planets (Juno, Vesta), bringing realization to his romantic (Juno) craft (Vesta). T-Neptune in Scorpio was opposing his Jupiter-Saturn in Taurus, adding mystique and inspiration to his art (Taurus). In 1963-65, transiting Pluto was exactly trine his Jupiter-Saturn conjunction, echoing the explosion (Pluto) of his career (Jupiter-Saturn). In 1964, the transiting Nodal Axis hit his MC/IC axis (10th/4th Houses), sparking the realization of his karmic intentions. One of the biggest progressions of John's life occurred on his 23rd birthday, 10/9/1963, when p-Venus entered Libra. Considering that John was a Libra Sun (Venus-ruled), this is a titanic event, one that would be felt most potently. Indeed, John became famous and was adored by millions. His p-Moon entered Capricorn in 1965 and reached his Midheaven soon after, depicting his position at the "toppermost."

During the onset and blossoming of Beatlemania, Paul had t-Uranus conjunct his Virgo North Node, suggesting the realization of his destiny, the breakthrough into inspired (12th House) work (Virgo). The t-North Node was high in his chart, moving from the 11th House to the commanding 10th, and igniting the expansive potentials of his Sun-Jupiter conjunction. T-Jupiter (expansion) was steadily rising towards the top of his chart too. In 1964, Jupiter transited his Venus in Taurus 3 times, before entering his Sun sign, Gemini, as The Beatles were on top of the world. His p-Moon also moved to Gemini in March of 1963, correlating with the release of the first album. His p-Mercury was in late Gemini, applying to his Sun and Jupiter for the next few years as he became a famous and successful songwriter. Saturn was transiting his 5th House—he was hard at work developing his creativity and structuring his talent. T-Neptune was opposite his Venus, bringing the surreal quality of Beatlemania to his artistry. Paul was also the Beatle with the most romanticized (Venus) projections (Neptune) from the collective. During the years of The Beatles rise, transiting Pluto was relatively inactive for Paul. However, during the descent of the "arc," Pluto would have enormous importance and his life would irrevocably change.

George had t-Uranus in his 10th House (public life), directly opposite his Sun. He also had t-Pluto entering his 11th House (world stage), coming off of an opposition to his Pisces Sun during the formative years of the band. Jupiter rose above his horizon to the public hemisphere of his chart in 1964, and gradually elevated for the next few years. T-Saturn in Aquarius came to his Nodal Axis, presenting the issue of anonymity (Aquarius South Node) vs. boldly claiming his fire (Leo North Node). Saturn's movement into Pisces in 1964 brought spiritual (Pisces) maturation (Saturn) to his life force (Sun), and George forged his place as a visionary. After many years (and possibly lifetimes) of desiring to be recognized for his talent, George attained prominence. T-Neptune in Scorpio was trine his spiritual seeking 9th House Jupiter. He was in an energetic zone of possibility, freedom, adventure, spirituality, consciousness and a deeper connection with the world. His p-Moon was waxing towards fullness during Beatlemania and was completely full when he led the excursion to India.

During the height of Beatlemania, the North Node (karmic destiny) was in Cancer and Gemini where Ringo has his Sun (life force) and Venus (creativity). T-Jupiter went into Taurus in 1964 kicking off a Jupiter return, as well as expanding Ringo's Saturn (career) and Uranus (breakthrough). Saturn in Aquarius was moving through his 11th House (collective), and was trine his Venus-Juno in Gemini, structuring his art. Saturn's visit to Pisces connected by trine (flow) to Ringo's Cancer Sun. Uranus and Pluto were transiting his 6th House, challenging him to develop his skills and work with others. Neptune was exactly trine his Sun, as well as opposite his Jupiter-Saturn (cultural participation). Like Paul, Ringo's p-Moon entered Gemini (sign of the "Beatles signature") in March 1963 when *Please Please Me* debuted. It's been said that Ringo "was in the right place at the right time," when he joined the Beatles just before the explosion of Beatlemania. The collection of extremely supportive transits he had does not conflict with that idea!

Below is the recording of "She Loves You."

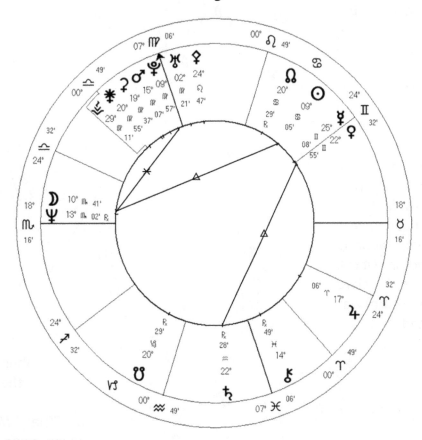

1: Moon-Neptune in Scorpio is a need for redemptive intimacy and spiritual healing through love. It was situated above the Ascendant when they recorded the song. About an hour earlier, it was exactly on the Ascendant (or closely approaching) during the eruption of Beatlemania at the studio. The 10° Scorpio Moon reflects the John-Paul composite Moon, as well as when they met on 7/6/57. "She Loves You" is a prime example of their need for redemption or reunion in their songwriting.

2: At the Midheaven were Pluto, Mars, Ceres and Juno, signifying the emergence of passion (Mars) from the shadow (Pluto), throwing off shame or limitation (Virgo). The combination of romance (Juno) with maternal (Ceres) was at the pinnacle in the sky.

3: Pluto-Mars is intensely passionate and urgent, while Jupiter in Aries in the 5th has abundant hormonal expression. Venus in Gemini, falling right in between the "Beatles signature" (mid Gemini) and Sun (0° Cancer) in their composite chart (not shown), portrays the light, breezy quality to the song,

Below is the astrology for the release of "She Loves You" with the Beatles chart.

330

The song was released 7 weeks later, so there are some similarities. The recording suggests the process that informs the song, while the release points to the outcome, an astrological "stamp." For the release, the Moon was conjunct both Juno and Ceres in Libra, highlighting the maternal, romantic transference. It's a need to find love (Moon) and nourishment (Ceres) from adoring women (Juno in Libra). Their "love me" Libra Moon (a lunar return) was highly activated.

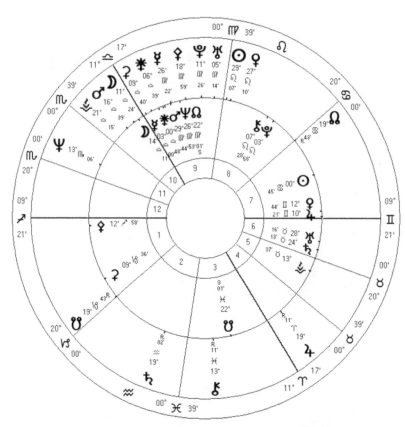

Album #2:
With the Beatles

1: The Moon was approaching the first quarter point, though not quite there. The faces on the album cover are similarly almost half illuminated. The faces are emerging from the dark, just like the Moon was emerging from the dark to become halfway full.

2: The album's Aquarius Moon (seed) involved healing estrangement. The maturation process (flowering) involved the processing of emotion and creative catharsis, Scorpio Sun.

3: Juno was conjunct Ceres, pairing romance with mother again. The combination was now in Scorpio (along with Neptune, which involves healing, dreams, transcendence). *With the Beatles* features 2 *dream* songs, both connected to the "call" theme. In contrast to the need for adoration in "She Loves You," this album desires deeper soul contact.

4: Spirituality is also found with the Sun-Vesta-Mercury stellium in the 12th House, a desire to learn (Vesta) how to call (Mercury) to beyond (12th House). The preponderance of "call" songs on the album correlates with Jupiter (abundance) opposite the group's Mercury (communications).

Opening Salvo of the British Invasion

The chart below is The Beatles appearance on The Ed Sullivan Show.

1: The Ascendant was at 22° Virgo, the degree of the Beatles North Node. At the conclusion of the hour long show, it moved to 4° Libra. During the broadcast, the Ascendant (activation, beginnings) triggered the band's North Node, Neptune, Mars, Juno and Mercury—their intention to bring a musical message to the world. During the show, the Midheaven degree (highest point in the sky) went from late Gemini to early Cancer, making a conjunction with their composite Sun.

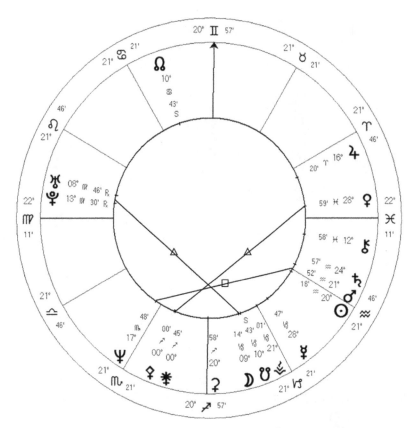

The Ascendant's dispositor was Mercury in Capricorn in the 5th House, suggesting a professional (Capricorn) performance, one that was enlivening (5th) the mainstream (Capricorn). Later in the 5th House was the Aquarius Sun, consistent with the illumination of a novel trend.

2: Venus in Pisces can be quixotic with romantic idealization. It was trine Juno in Sagittarius, suggesting romantic energy of a foreign or cross-cultural nature.

3: Athena (empowered feminine) was conjunct Juno, pointing to women taking charge of their desires. Jupiter in Aries (expansion of desire) was challenging prior domesticated conditioning to remain hidden (square Capricorn Moon in the 4th House).

4: The Aquarius Sun (collective) square to Neptune (consciousness) correlates with the untamed hysteria of Beatlemania.

The Sun Begins to Rise

Below is the recording of "And I Love Her."

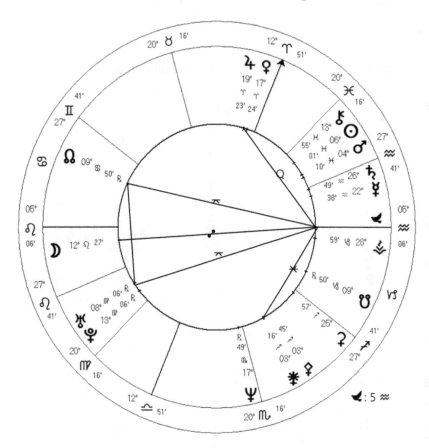

1: Sun-Mars-Chiron in Pisces concerns spiritual healing, and it's exactly on Paul's natal South Node at 6° Pisces (not shown).

2: The compassionate Pisces Sun illuminates a Leo Moon (conjunct Paul's), which was rising. The Moon was trine Venus-Jupiter at the Midheaven. It's seeking connection to above and reflecting the "Beatles signature."

3: The Leo Ascendant was disposited by the Pisces Sun, linking the emergence of solar songs with a transcendent (Pisces) archetype. The Pisces Sun was also trine a Cancer North Node in the 12th House, creating a focus on familial matters (Cancer) of a spiritual nature (12th).

4: Ceres was at 25° Sagittarius. This late mutable position powerfully connects to Paul's "expression of grief" T-square, appearing in the place to fill it out to a Grand Cross. Ceres was tightly quintile the Pisces Sun, suggesting that mother was uniquely connected to the solar energy.

5: The chart above highlights the aspects involving the muse, who was in contact with romantic expression (sextile Juno in the 5th), the need for solar connection (opposite the Leo Moon), and to creativity from above (quintile Jupiter-Venus). She also forms a Yod with the "arc of awakening" and the Cancer North Node in the 12th, factors relating to other dimensions. At 5° Aquarius, she was also applying to the muse in the Beatles chart (13° Aquarius), a Euterpe return. Note Uranus and Pluto exactly 5 degrees apart and applying, crossing the "inspiration line."

Below is the recording of "Anytime at All."

6: The 11° Gemini Sun was exactly on the "Beatles signature" and square the "arc of awakening." Its square to Pluto at 11° Virgo links the "call" (Gemini Sun) with death (Pluto).

7: The Aquarius Moon reflects John's, which was resolving disconnection. The Cancer North Node invites emotional opening and deepening. Venus in Cancer on the North Node is movement towards familial (Cancer) relations (Venus).

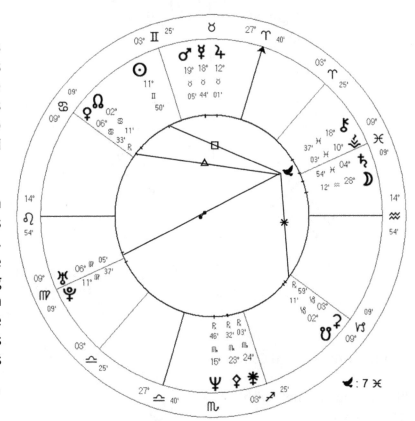

8: Ceres conjunct the Capricorn South Node involves maternal (Ceres) karma (South Node) being resolved from the past (Capricorn).

9: Neptune in the 4th requires a deepening into oneself.

10: As seen with "And I Love Her," the muse was in connection to the "arc" (by opposition) and the Cancer North Node (by trine). She was also linked to the mother (sextile Ceres) and the "call" (square Gemini Sun).

Things We Said Today

The chart below features the song with Paul's chart. The activity to his Nodal Axis is striking, the biggest stimulation yet. In addition to the muse (Euterpe) on his karmic portal to the past (South Node), the Moon, Saturn and Vesta were also present. Feelings (Moon) connected to his prior grief (Pisces) were activated, an intention to craft (Saturn-Vesta) them into inspired work. Uranus in Virgo was precisely on Paul's North Node, suggesting a breakthrough (Uranus) into his spiritual (12th House) work (Virgo), while Pluto (death, transformation) was close by. The t-Nodal Axis was accompanied by Ceres

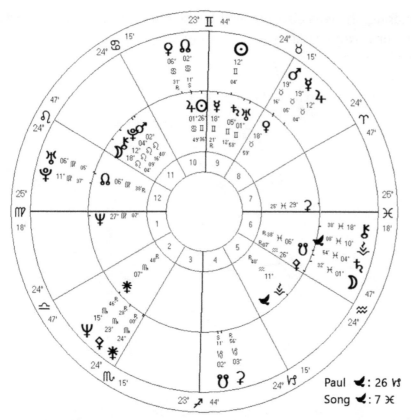

in Capricorn (conjunct South Node) and Venus in Cancer (conjunct North Node) illustrating the maternal work from the past and a motion towards reunion. The Nodal Axis was conjunct, and applying closer, to Paul's Sun (and his "expression of grief signature"). The Neptune-Mercury opposition (mystical communication) was on Paul's 8th House Venus, revealing a connection (Venus) in the area of death (8th). Also note the t-Sun at 12⁰ Gemini on the "Beatles signature."

Paul ☽: 26 ♑
Song ☽: 7 ♓

Another Unanswered Call

"I Call Your Name" with John's chart.

1: "I Call Your Name" had the North Node in Cancer (family) in John's 3rd, with Venus, Sun and Mercury in Gemini. Mars in Gemini was exactly quincunx John's Ceres. All of this involved communication with family and mother.
2: Ceres was out-of-bounds at 26⁰00' south, buried in the shadow.
3: Venus retrograde can manifest as an inability to connect.

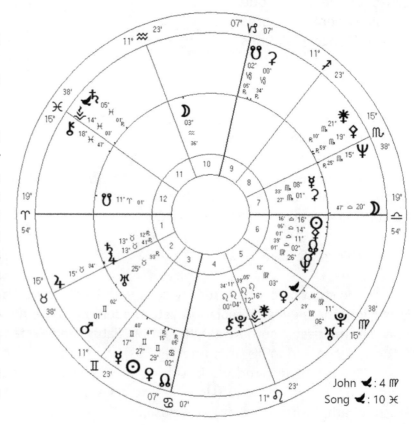

John ☽: 4 ♍
Song ☽: 10 ♓

335

A Hard Day's Night with the Beatles chart.

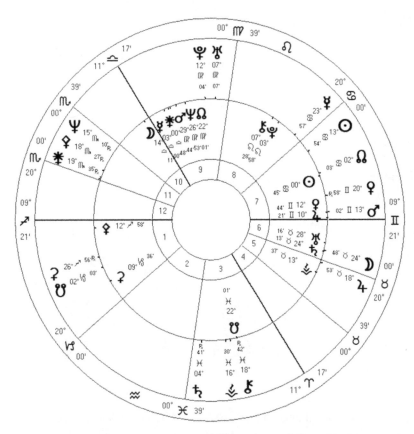

1: Mars at 13º Gemini (on their DSC) was located on the "Beatles signature").

2: Venus in Gemini was creating an extended Venus return. During the summer of 1964, their popularity (Venus) was enormous.

3: T-Jupiter was in their creative 5th House. The Moon was also in Taurus conjunct Jupiter, showcasing an underlying desire (Moon) for artistic (Taurus) expansion (Jupiter).

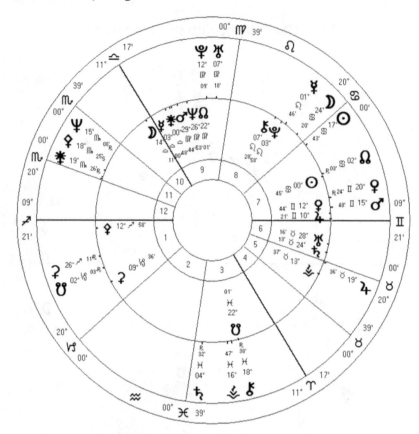

1: Paul's chart has natal Moon square Venus in Taurus in his 8th House (see p. 266), reflecting a complex dynamic between intimacy and finances.

2: Venus retrograde (along with Mars) was conjunct the "Beatles signature." Venus-Mars conjunction reflects the relational intensity on the album, including the first hints of aggression.

3: The album had a Mars-Pluto square, an aspect that often involves the shadow dynamics of aggression and sexuality.

4: Ceres conjunct the South Node and lurking way down in the depths (out-of-bounds at 27°02' south), connects with shadow areas of the psyche.

A Starr Has Fallen

Below is Ringo's chart the day he was hospitalized.

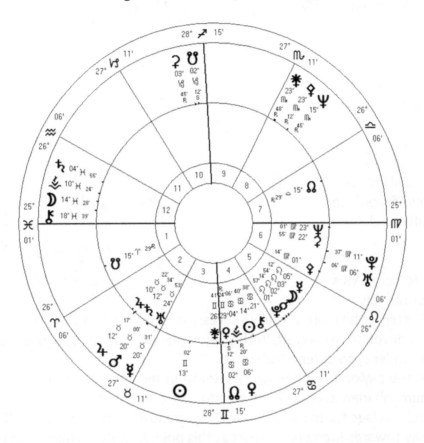

1: Ringo was having an extended Venus return during the Venus retrograde, involving 3 exact passes. His natal Venus (retrograde in the 4th House) was triggered for potential healing. T-Venus was also out-of-bounds (25°03' northern declination). Ringo was at the heights of Beatlemania (northern declination), but unable to connect (out-of-bounds).

2: Chiron (health, well-being) was transiting Ringo's 12th House (marginalization, karmic completion). Through grace and acceptance, the lesson was to arrive at newfound calm. T-Neptune in Scorpio was trine Ringo's Chiron in Cancer, also suggesting potential healing. The Ceres-South Node conjunction was in his 10th House, a public expression of the nurturance and family karmic dynamics.

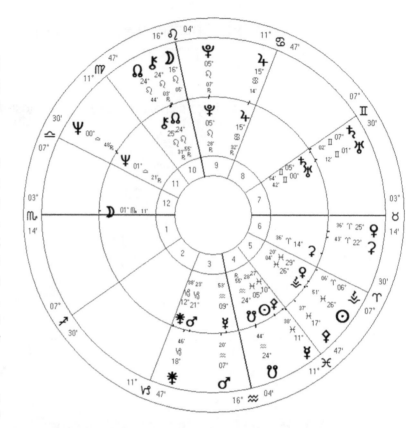

George Accepts His Path

George's p-chart (around his natal) in July 1964 when his p-Moon in Leo reached his Midheaven.

1: George's p-Moon entered Leo in March 1963, coinciding with the release of the first album. At this time in 1964, it moved forward to light up his Leo Midheaven, the place of maximal visibility. He was now forced to grapple with celebrity (Leo).

2: His p-Mercury was about to enter his 5th House, inviting him to be more verbally expressive, to become a songwriter. His p-Sun was on his Vesta, a devotion to his craft. With t-Saturn in Pisces on his Sun (not shown), he was maturing his tendency to defer to others.

When the p-Moon reached his 11th House in 1966, he became more interested in global and humanitarian issues. At that point the Moon progressed to Virgo, and he took on studies and tutelage for the sitar, expanding his musical craftsmanship. His P-Mars was making its way towards Mercury (2° apart at this point), another illustration that his voice would be developing greater empowerment over the years to come. His p-Sun was headed towards a conjunction with Venus (potential realization of his artistic contribution), an opposition with Neptune (integration with spirituality), and a sextile to his Uranus (innovation, metaphysics), then Saturn (attainment of greater stature), in communicative Gemini. All of this will be part of the spiritual developments in the latter part of the story. In 1964, the p-Sun's integration with Vesta would assist him in developing his musical proficiency to meet it.

Grieving Losers

Below is the recording "Baby's in Black" around the John-Paul composite chart.

1: T-Mercury was conjunct Pluto (voice with death) and trine their Ceres (mothers).
2: This song is a prime example of karmic maternal issues (Ceres-South Node) being worked through.

339

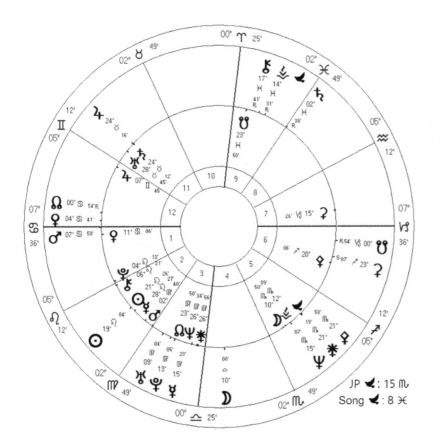

3: The t-Moon was in their 4th House (roots), making a t-square with their Venus-Ceres opposition: art (Venus) connected with the maternal (Ceres). The song's Venus-Mars conjunction in Cancer emphasizes family. The combination was on the John-Paul ASC and Venus, so central for them. The John-Paul chart was having a Venus and solar return, a defining song of their partnership. Mars in Cancer was at 23° 42' north declination: it's just out-of-bounds, triggering the Ceres-Pluto situation of the Beatles group chart.

"I'm A Loser"

1: Leo Sun (playful outer expression) was square a Scorpio Moon (internal wounding). Scorpio Moon was conjunct Neptune, illustrating grief and a desire for healing. The issue was still unresolved maternal issues (Ceres conjunct South Node). The Leo Sun's trine to Ceres was illuminating it creatively.

2: Mercury with Uranus-Pluto desires to speak psychological truth in realistic and accountable Virgo.

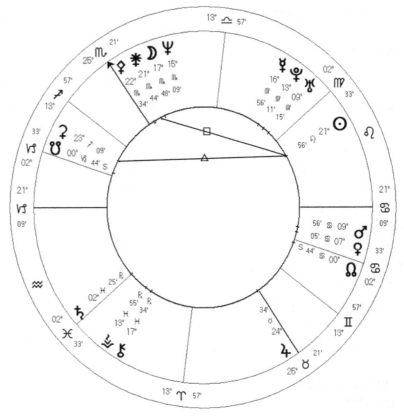

340

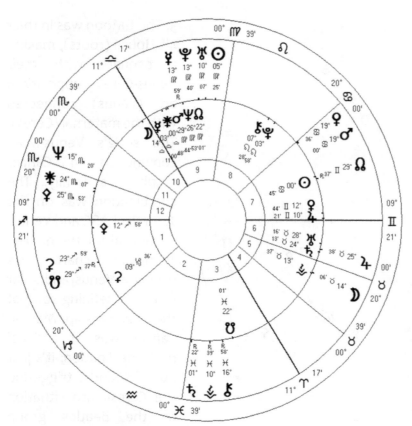

Beatles & The Bard

The Dylan meeting with the group chart.

1: Mercury retrograde was conjunct Uranus-Pluto and the Sun, while sextile Neptune.

2: Jupiter in Taurus was conjunct their "artistic genius" signature, the 6th House Saturn-Uranus conjunction.

Still No Answer

"No Reply" with John.

1: The Gemini North Node seeks to complete the call. Mercury in Virgo (dispositor) was square the Nodes—figuring out the lines of connection was the lesson. The North Node was transiting John's 3rd, consistent with the "call." The Ceres-South Node conjunction continued resolution of maternal karma. The Leo Moon with Mars was on John's "wounded child" signature, activating the intensity of his pain.

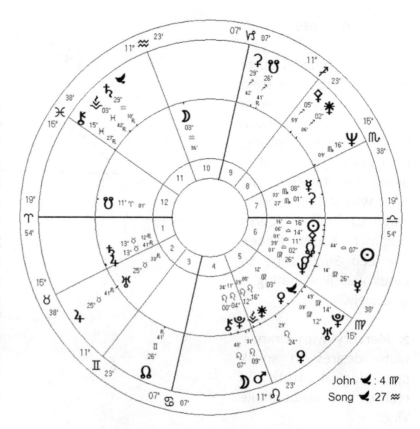

John ☽: 4 ♍
Song ☽ 27 ♒

341

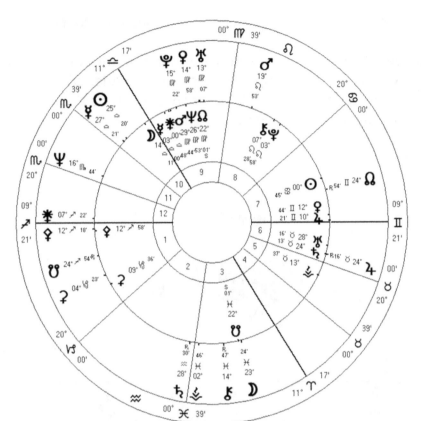

Rain and Sun

"I'll Follow the Sun" with The Beatles.

1: The song's Pisces Moon (with tender Chiron) was conjunct the Beatles South Node, giving voice to the internal rain storm of grief. The motion is to heal and emerge into light. The Libra Sun invites engagement. Mars in Leo desires to move forward (Mars) in pursuit of joy (Leo). This Mars was conjunct Paul's natal Moon, triggering his emotional yearning to have such connection.

Ill Feelings

Ringo (inner wheel) and Pete (outer wheel).

1: Pete has Chiron-Pluto opposite his Moon, suggesting ill (Chiron) feelings (Moon) that have dark psychological (Pluto) underpinnings. Ringo's Chiron is opposite Pete's Venus, connecting health issues interpersonally. Pete's Chiron-Pluto connects to Ringo's Leo planets, bringing health issues to entertainment (Leo) areas. Both men have

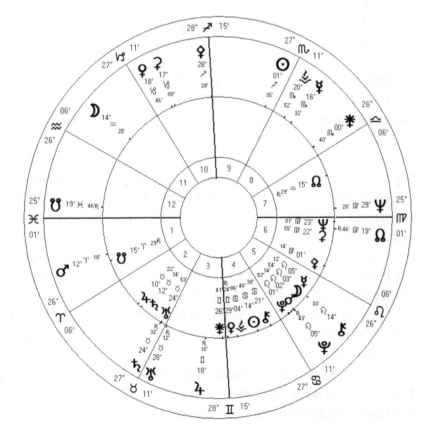

grave concerns about being sidelined and lonely due to the inability to perform adequately.

The antagonism between the men is found with Pete's Mars in Aries on Ringo's South Node, a karmic drama with conflict or competitiveness. Mars in Aries can be the loner, a condition both men wanted to avoid. Pete's Venus is square Ringo's Nodal Axis: the work involves the polarity of conflict (Aries) and peace (Libra).

Album #4 – *Beatles for Sale*

1: The balsamic Moon was opposite the "Beatles signature." Its tiresome nature impacted the usually buoyant and witty vibe in a more downbeat direction.

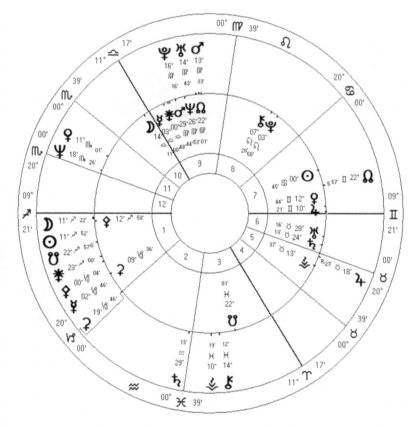

2: The album's Nodal axis was at 22° Sagittarius-Gemini, exactly square the band's at 22° Pisces-Virgo, indicating a crisis point of finding spiritual direction.

3: Saturn returned to Aquarius and was square (pressure) their "artistic genius" signature. Venus (finances) was conjunct Neptune in Scorpio, depicting an allure that can be marketed.

4: Venus in Scorpio was opposed to Jupiter in Taurus reflecting the "Beatles signature," though with tension (opposition) regarding money (Taurus-Scorpio are financial signs).

5: Juno was conjunct the Sagittarius South Node, romance (Juno) plays a central role in their successful formula (South Node). The Gemini North Node seeks to branch out and try new ideas, the habitual pull just perpetuates the pattern.

6: The balsamic Moon was squared by Mars/Uranus-Pluto in Virgo on one side and Chiron-Vesta in Pisces from the other—a need to break free from pressures to govern one's own destiny.

7: Ceres was out-of-bounds at 27°34' south, continuing the theme of transforming deep maternal issues for healing. It was no longer conjunct the South Node, but the band was having a Ceres return in Capricorn, strongly highlighting the issue.

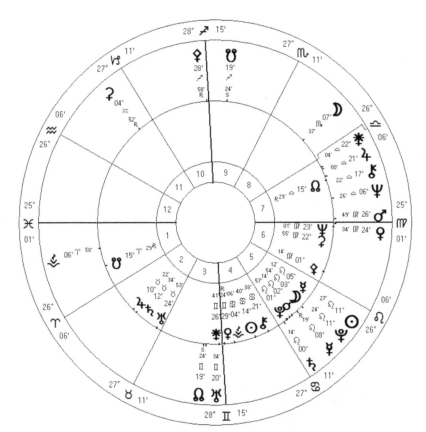

Ringo Gets Married

Maureen's chart around Ringo's.

1: Mo's Saturn in Leo was working through limits that inhibited her joy. She had Pluto conjunct Sun, as well as a Scorpio Moon, lots of seductive appeal.

2: Mo's Venus and Mars in Virgo were square Ringo's Juno-Venus in Gemini: openness (Gemini) vs. exclusivity (Virgo).

Maureen and George both had Scorpio Moons (secretive).

Ticket to Pride

"Ticket to Ride" and "Yes It Is" around John's chart.

1: Juno in Aquarius on John's Moon added a romantic dimension to his "wounded child" T-square, which was likely being fictionalized in song. Julia's natal Ceres (not shown) was also in early Aquarius, pointing to her involvement.

2: Ceres in Pisces (grief) was opposite John's 5th

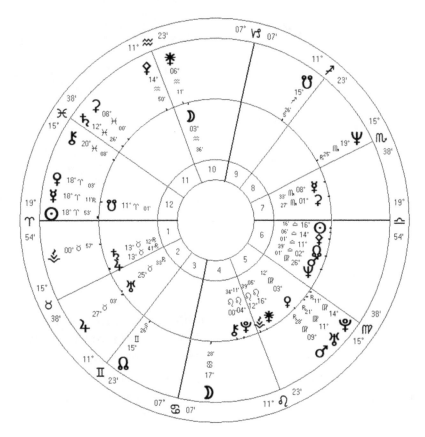

House Venus, bringing maternal energy into creative expression through entertainment. Ceres was opposite the Uranus-Pluto conjunction, signaling an awakening of such material for dispersal and potential healing.

The Cancer Moon was in John's 4th house, the area of home and roots. It was square his Nodal axis, and near where it was when Julia died. The Sun, Mercury and Venus were all in Aries, not far from John's South Node. Mercury was in the middle of 3 exact passes over his South Node and he was giving voice (Mercury) to his unresolved (South Node) relational dynamics (Venus). With these planets close to his Ascendant, John expressed his karmic themes outwardly.

The Reflection of Clowns

"You've Got to Hide Your Love Away" with John's chart.

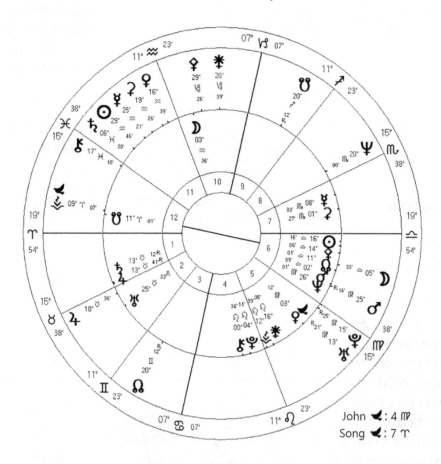

John ☽ : 4 ♍
Song ☽ : 7 ♈

The song's muse was on John's South Node, while a Libra Moon was on his North Node. Euterpe opposite Moon portrays a familial connection with the muse, here stimulating John's core lessons. Saturn at 6° Pisces was opposite John's natal Euterpe at 4° Virgo, structuring the inspired creative partnership and bringing it to the world (John's 11th). The combination also correlates with the *dream* theme (Pisces) of the song.

"Tell Me What You See" with Paul's chart.

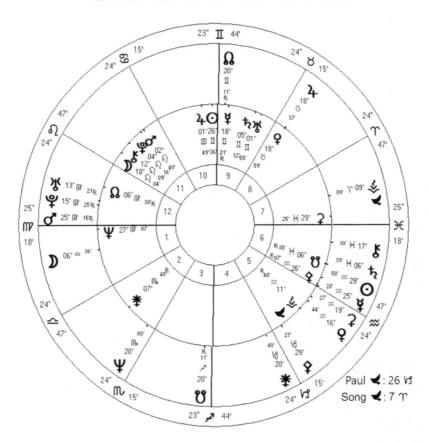

1: The "Tell Me What You See" North Node at 20° Gemini has a message, and it was finding voice through Paul's Mercury and Sun. Dispositing the North Node was Mercury in Aquarius, pointing to metaphysical communication. Mercury was conjunct Ceres in Aquarius (pointing to mom in another dimension). Mercury-Ceres was trine Paul's Sun and opposite his Leo Moon, further linking to his expression.

2: Paul's Moon was under major transits. Intuitive Neptune was squaring his Moon for a couple of years. For the song, other planets were also in aspect to his receptivity (Moon): Venus at 16° and Ceres at 19° Aquarius (opposite Moon) and Jupiter at 18° Taurus (square), were all connecting to his heart.

The "Tell Me What You See" Mars was at 25° Virgo, catalyzing his "expression of grief" T-square. The Moon was at 6° Libra, which is on Mary's Sun (her chart on p. 299), while the muse at 7° Aries was conjunct Paul's Ceres. Saturn in Pisces was exactly on Paul's South Node, activating his karmic history, while supporting manifestation to his inspirational (Pisces) work (6th House).

346

Below is the chart for the recording of "Help!"

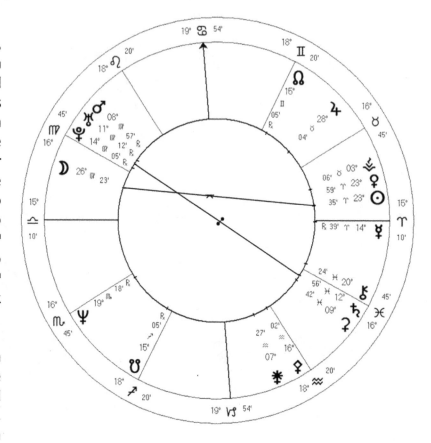

1: Virgo Moon is humble, and the 12th House is an area of grace and surrender. The Moon's opposition to Chiron in Pisces in the 6th House suggests a desire for self-development. There is an earnest feeling to this Moon, a need to uplift consciousness (12th House). Its quincunx to the Aries Sun in the 7th House learns to risk sharing from the heart.

2: Sagittarius South Node in the 2nd House works toward more solid self-worth with purpose. Gemini North Node in the 8th House supports open and honest communications. By working the Nodal lessons, awakening (Sun) into greater leadership (Aries) and connection to others (conjunct Venus, 7th House) becomes more possible. The Uranus-Pluto conjunction with Mars in the 11th House: breakthrough (Uranus) into power (Pluto-Mars) through publicly revealing (11th House) humility (Virgo). The opposition to Saturn in the 5th House connects the energy to a more mature self-expression.

3: Juno in Aquarius shifts the romantic focus of the early formula towards a universal form of love.

Chapter 10 – Inspiration

Yesterday: The Melody of Dreams

Below is the recording of "Yesterday" with Paul's chart.

1: Euterpe moved from 3° Gemini (at the Big Gemini eclipse) to 12° Gemini (for "Yesterday"), on the "Beatles signature" (not shown, below is Paul's chart with the song).

2: The "Yesterday" Sun was at 23° Gemini, same as Paul's MC. Mercury at 27° Gemini was on Paul's Sun (26° Gemini), a link to above with writing. His "expression of grief" signature was highly activated (with planets at all 3 points of the T-square). Recall that it precisely overlaps with the T-square in Mary's chart.

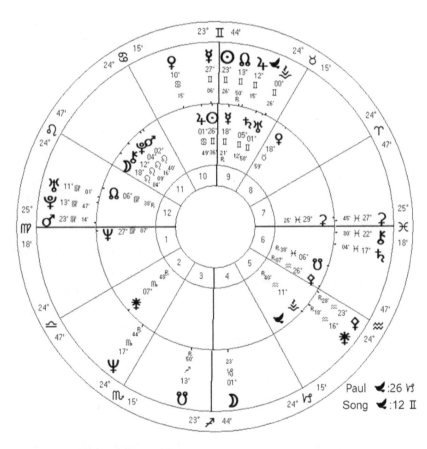

3: Mercury was out-of-bounds (24°42' north), another indication of connecting with above. It was parallel the Ceres-Pluto situation discussed in the Beatles group chart (maternal death transformation, p. 275).

4: Paul's natal Euterpe is at 26° Capricorn in his 5th House, inspiration is channeled through his creative expression (5th). The "Yesterday" Sun-Mercury in late Gemini was quincunx his Euterpe in Capricorn, bringing words (Gemini) to his professional (Capricorn) creativity (5th House). Additionally, the "Yesterday" Mars in Virgo and Ceres in Pisces were respectively trine and sextile his Euterpe, so his muse attunement was strongly activated.

5: The "Yesterday" chart itself (not shown) has 22° Virgo at the MC for the start of recording. The Beatles point of destiny (North Node) was pointing to the heavens.

6: The Jupiter return for the group chart (12° Gemini) was exact (not shown). "Yesterday" would become one of their most popular and successful songs.

7: The Big Gemini Eclipse (outer wheel) at 9° Gemini) was exactly on Mary's North Node and Juno (inner). She was also at a Nodal return, a time when spiritual lessons are particularly highlighted. Jupiter at 8° Gemini was also transiting her North Node, further amplifying her soul intentions and adding to the "big" spirit of this event. T-Euterpe at 3° Gemini was opposite her natal muse at 1° Sagittarius, both situated along the Nodal Axis (soul lessons, destiny).

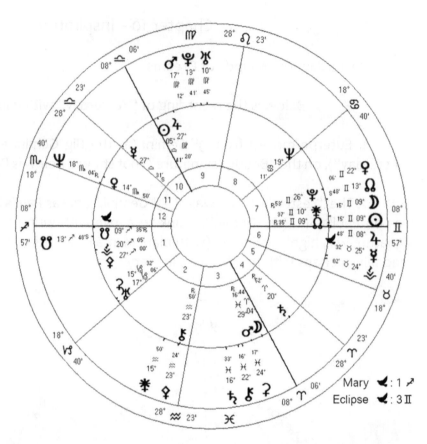

The Paul-Mary composite chart.

8: Due to Mary's unknown birth time, the precise Moon degree may be a few degrees off (a midday chart for Mary places it at 11° Gemini, right on the "Beatles signature"). It was activated by the Big Gemini Eclipse.

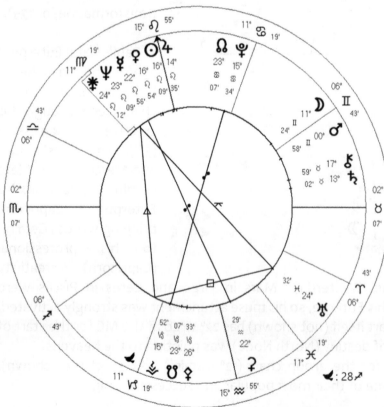

Paul-Mary had Pluto in Cancer on their North Node: the evolutionary motion (North Node) to love (Cancer) through death (Pluto). The Gemini Moon serves as the dispositor of the North Node, bringing that intention to their "writing" collaboration and the "Beatles signature." Ceres in Aquarius suggests a unique maternal-child bond, one with a metaphysical (Aquarius) orientation. Ceres is opposite the Leo stellium, connecting mom straight to abundant creativity.

The Paul-Mary Leo Sun was conjunct both Jupiter and Venus, a reflection of the "Beatles signature." They join to give light and creativity (Leo) to the same abundant musical joy (Jupiter-Venus) as seen with the band. They have Mercury, Neptune and Juno in Leo, adding transcendent (Neptune) romantic (Juno) communication (Mercury) to the creative (Leo) mix—also strongly reflecting the Beatles composite chart (which has the "love song" signature of Juno-Mercury).

Below is the release of the single "Yesterday" with Paul's chart.

9: The t-Sun was in Virgo (approaching Paul's ASC-Neptune) and opposite t-Ceres, so Paul was at a Ceres return in late Pisces. T-Jupiter at 29⁰ Gemini completes the T-square and falls on Paul's natal Sun-Jupiter conjunction (a Jupiter return) signifying how major this song is in his life.

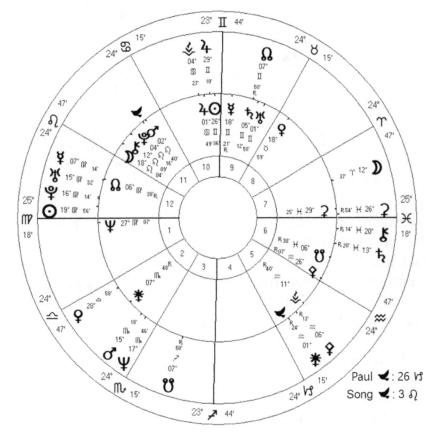

"Yesterday" had a Jupiter-Venus trine (echoing the "Beatles signature"). Its Jupiter was quintile Uranus (with Mercury nearby). These "Yesterday" planets were on Paul's natal configuration of Sun quintile North Node, so "Yesterday" reinforced and expressed the brilliance of the natal potential.

10: The Uranus-Pluto conjunction was almost exact and square to Paul's Mercury, supercharging his songwriting. As the outer planets move so slowly, he would have the square from Uranus-Pluto to his Mercury for the next few years to deepen further.

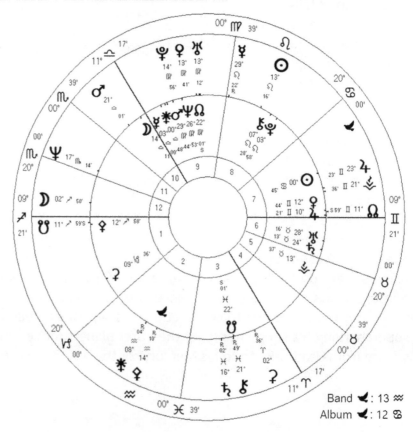

Things Said ☙: 7 ♓
Yesterday ☙: 12 ♊

Album #5: *Help!*

"Yesterday" around "Things We Said Today"

In "Things We Said Today," Paul sang about a prior agreement. The Moon for "Yesterday" in past-oriented Capricorn was on the "TWST" South Node, illustrating the link. The Gemini Sun for "TWST" was conjunct the "Yesterday" muse, so work with her fulfills the outstanding contract. The Sun-Euterpe link between the 2 songs occurs at 12° Gemini, precisely on the "Beatles signature" and the Big Gemini Eclipse.

1: As seen with *Beatles for Sale* (p. 343), *Help!* also had the Moon with the South Node: emotional (Moon) reconciliation (South Node).

2: The *Help!* Moon was in the group's 12th House (release, inspiration) and trine Ceres (mother) in their 3rd (writing).

3: The South Node was on the band's Ascendant (front and center).

4: The Leo Sun awakens into joy, free of the past.

Band ☙: 13 ♒
Album ☙: 12 ♋

351

5: Leo Sun square Neptune in Scorpio necessitates the balance of dark with bright. Deeper psychological insight and processes (Scorpio) are the fuel for the expansion of awareness (Sun).

6: The *Help!* Gemini North Node was on the "Beatles signature." Upon reconciliation of the past (South Node), new ideas become increasingly available. The dispositor of the North Node was Mercury retrograde in Leo, signaling a review (retrograde) of how the mind (Mercury) can be wrapped in personality desires (Leo). The suggested direction was to work with the mind (Gemini North Node), which is addressed on the next album (*Rubber Soul*).

7: The *Help!* Saturn-Chiron in Pisces was opposite Uranus-Venus-Pluto in Virgo—a tension between business pressures and the progressive potentials of the "arc."

8: Euterpe was at 12° Cancer for the album's release, just coming off of the band's Sun. It was conjunct their Sun over the summer of 1965 when the muse became central in the story. For the *Help!* album, she is opposite the band's natal Ceres at 9° Capricorn, linking directly with the mother.

Twinkle Twinkle Little Starr

Below is Zak's chart around Ringo's.

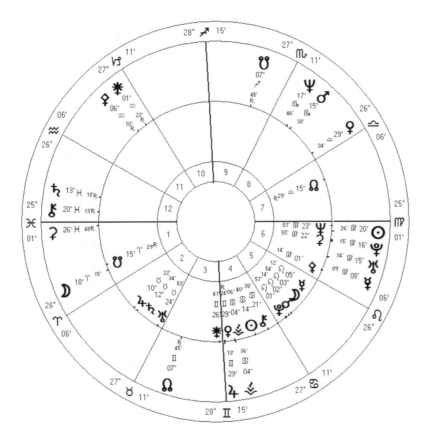

1: Zak's Aries Moon on Ringo's South Node shows a familiarity with independent themes, a karmic connection with aloneness.

2: Zak's has a Jupiter-Venus trine, reflecting the "Beatles signature." It directly touches Ringo's 4th House Venus, creating a Beatlesque home.

3: Both father and son have Vesta at 4° Cancer, their shared interest in developing skill (Vesta) in the home (Cancer); drumming.

Dead Little Girl and Lighting Fires

The recording of "Run for Your Life"

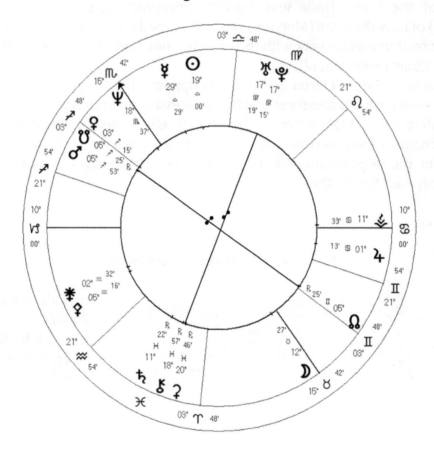

1: Mars on the South Node in Sagittarius points to entitled and fiery tendencies, wanting one's own way, while Venus brings it to relations. Synchronously, when Julia died, Mars was also on the South Node (see p. 305). This combination correlates with the violent karma, as well as leftover (South Node) anger (Mars). The Taurus Moon suggests it's been stuck inside—trine to Uranus-Pluto in the 8th House involves catharsis and release. The Ceres opposition to Pluto is the maternal death signature, while the Moon opposite Neptune conveys sadness.

2: North Node in Gemini in the 5th House invites communication (Gemini) through performance (5th House) for karmic resolution (North Node). Synthesis with the South Node-Venus-Mars in the 11th House connects to the world stage.

353

Next is the chart for "Norwegian Wood" later that evening.

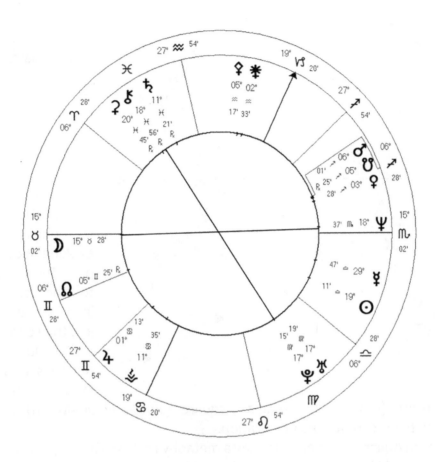

3: Paul's Pluto-Mars conjunction relates to anger in his shadow.

4: Mars can pertain to issues of selfishness. With Venus involved, it plays out with others. Also, the song's Mars-Venus-South Node stellium was in the 7th House (near 8th)—so another interpersonal dimension to the pattern.

5: The Libra Sun awakens into equality and peace.

6: Gemini North Node (karmic resolution) involves lightness and perspective, to "air" out the karmic heaviness through comedic dispersal.

Additionally, the Uranus-Pluto conjunction was in the 8th House for "Run for Your Life" (fidelity, conflict and drama, power dynamics). For "Norwegian Wood," the "arc" shifted to the 5th House (love affairs, playfulness, whimsy).

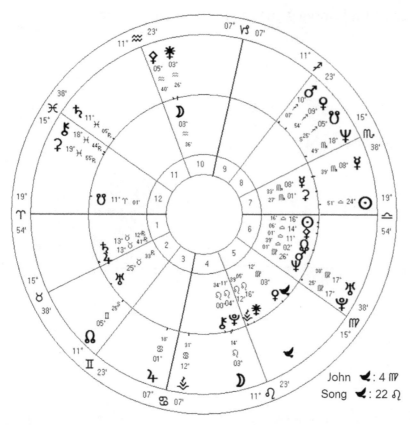

John ♋: 4 ♍
Song ♋: 22 ♌

"In My Life" around John's chart.

1: The "In My Life" Mercury was on John's Mercury-Ceres and gave voice to his "wounded child" signature. The song's Leo Moon was in his 4th House (home), right on his Pluto-Chiron, evoking wounds of the past. The transformation to the conscious Leo involves gratitude and joy, the sentiment of the song. Juno in early Aquarius was on John's Moon, romanticizing (Juno) his roots (Moon). The song's T-square (Juno-Mercury-Moon) was directly overlapping with his core natal configuration.

2: Juno in Aquarius was encouraging a metaphysical (and less egoic) understanding of love, which would increasingly develop from this point forward.

3: Prior activation to his "wounded child" configuration resulted in highly charged reactivity and cries for connection. John was "mellowing," a term used to describe his personality shift at this time.

4: The song's Leo Moon on John's natal 4th House Pluto emotionalizes (Moon) a familial (4th House) death issue (Pluto). "In My Life" also had a Ceres-Pluto opposition, the maternal death signature.

5: Neptune at 18° Scorpio was square John's Juno at 16° Leo. He was learning to bring broader consciousness to romance. Recorded at his Mercury return, this particular song launched a new start in his songwriting. The early formula was giving way to a new phase.

Additionally, John was almost at a Euterpe return in his 5th House. As it got closer, he would work with her in the songs to come. The resolution seen in "In My Life" potentially allowed him greater openness to the muse partnership.

355

"We Can Work It Out" with the John-Paul chart.

1: The song's South Node-Mars-Venus stellium was moving through the John-Paul 6th House, the area of work and craftsmanship. Venus at 11° and Mars at 12° Sagittarius were on the Beatles Ascendant (not shown) and opposite the "Beatles signature."

One of the defining astrological contacts in John-Paul synastry (not shown here) is John's Venus (3° Virgo) on Paul's North Node (6° Virgo), which encapsulates their karmic

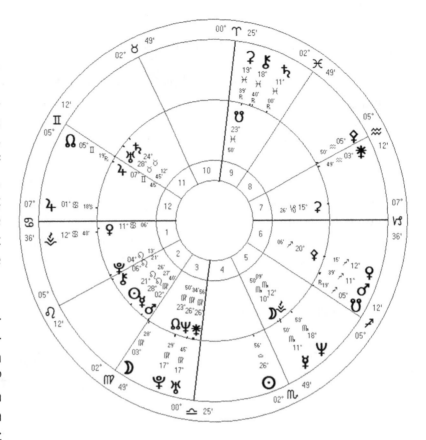

or destined (North Node) partnership (Venus). The "We Can Work It Out" Moon at 3° Virgo was lighting it up, further illustrating how the song involves the working out (Virgo) of emotion (Moon). The Virgo Moon was on the John-Paul Mars at 2° Virgo, emotionally highlighting their intention to put efforts (Mars) into craft (Virgo). Their Mars was conjunct Mercury at 28° Leo, adding a creative/entertainment (Leo) dimension. The challenge of Mercury-Mars can be adversarial communications, the devolution into fussing (Mercury) and fighting (Mars). The song's Mercury at 11° Scorpio was on the John-Paul Moon (10° Scorpio) Vesta (12° Scorpio) conjunction, which might bond deeply or splinter into conflict.

2: The John-Paul Nodal Axis was close to the Beatles Nodal Axis. Both charts were having Pluto coming to the Virgo North Node, while Ceres in Pisces was transiting the South Node at this time. The maternal death issue (Ceres opposite Pluto) was the underlying work to sort out.

3: The song's North Node (5° Gemini) was on their composite 12th House Jupiter (7° Gemini)—the resolution of the emotion being worked out leads to receptivity spiritually (12th House) with communications (Gemini).

Below is the recording of "Nowhere Man" around John's chart.

1: Mars was now tighter to the South Node than Venus—and the song is more about aloneness.

2: The song's Mercury-Neptune (intuitive receptivity) was on John's 8th House cusp (death), and his natal Mercury in Scorpio. Saturn in Pisces was trine his Mercury, structuring (Saturn) a transpersonal (Pisces) understanding (Mercury).

3: Ceres in Pisces was transiting John's 12th House, showing a mystical connection with the mother. Ceres was tightly trine Mercury/Neptune, further linking intuitive receptivity to the mother.

4: Euterpe was closing in for a return in John's chart. It was at 23° Leo in his creative 5th House for "Nowhere Man," now about 10° away.

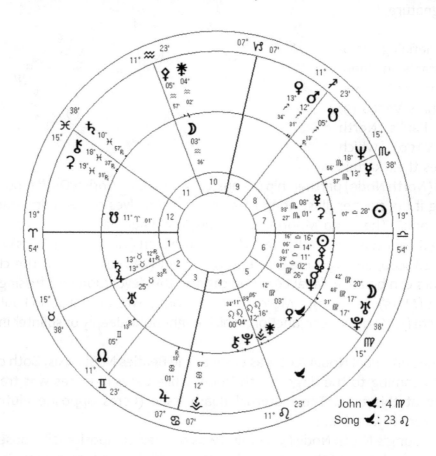

John ☽: 4 ♍
Song ☽: 23 ♌

Below is the composite chart for John and Julia. (Note that house placements are likely off due to Julia's unknown birth time.)

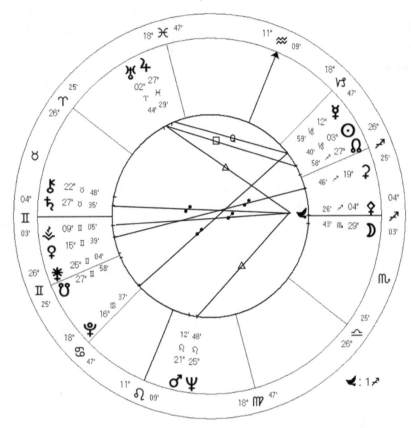

The John-Julia composite chart featured a Jupiter-Uranus conjunction, a metaphysical (Uranus) philosophical (Jupiter) scope. The combination was quintile Mercury in Capricorn, connecting it brilliantly to structured writing. Mercury was the dispositor of the Gemini South Node conjunct Juno, their unfinished work (South Node) with romantic (Juno) writing (Gemini). It reflects the Nodal work of Mary, who had Juno conjunct her Gemini North Node. They had a Venus-Vesta conjunction in Gemini, another suggestion of a writing partnership. The Big Gemini Eclipse was exactly on their Vesta (also on the "Beatles signature.") The lunar eclipse on 6/14/65 spanning 23° Gemini-Sagittarius was along the John-Julia Nodal axis with Juno, a major activation of the spiritual partnership, pertaining to romantic (Juno) writing (Gemini). Their Mercury was opposite Pluto, communications connected with death.

The John-Julia composite Euterpe was at 1° Sagittarius, conjunct their Moon (in very late Scorpio or early Sagittarius). (Interestingly, Mary McCartney's Euterpe was at 1° Sagittarius.) Their Moon-Euterpe was square Neptune encapsulating their unresolved grief, as well as an intuitive receptivity. Euterpe trine Uranus-Jupiter brings the muse directly to the metaphysical and philosophical scope mentioned above.

The Muse in Beatles Astrology

Here are a few more pieces of information on how the muse (Euterpe) ties into Beatles astrology. The composite Euterpe for Mary and Julia was 15° Capricorn. In the John-Paul composite chart (see p. 277) *their Ceres was this very degree*. John and Paul had Venus at 11° Cancer on their Ascendant, the embodiment of artistic creativity (Venus) with familial roots (Cancer), connected with their mothers (opposite Ceres). The Julia-Mary Euterpe at 15° Capricorn illustrates how they were the mothers playing the role of the muse. Euterpe was at 3° for the Big Gemini Eclipse and fell in the John-Paul 12th House (connection to other realms), conjunct their composite Jupiter, they learned to channel divine inspiration (12th House) into writing (Gemini).

The composite Euterpe for John and Paul was 15° Scorpio, which was on their Moon-Vesta conjunction in their 5th House. The intention was to focus (Vesta) their emotional (Moon) woundedness (Scorpio) into creative expression (5th House) with the muse (Euterpe).

The Mercurial Songs

Below is the recording of "Michelle."

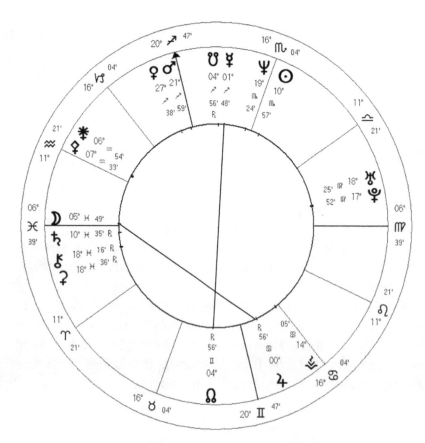

1: Mercury in the 9th House in Sagittarius points to cross-cultural communications. Its conjunction with the South Node signifies an unresolved issue. The Pisces Moon square Mercury-South Node portrays a deep longing, a desire to bridge distances and work through obstacles.

2: The "Michelle" Pisces Moon is conjunct Saturn (professional structure). It's also trine Jupiter in the 4th, echoing a longing to deepen. The "Michelle" ASC is the same degree as Paul's South Node (6° Pisces), linking to his unresolved grief.

3: Gemini North Node invites open, flowing dialogue. Mercury (the dispositor) circles back to the 9th House in Sagittarius, broadening its reach (Sagittarius) to include collective, universal and spiritual themes. Ultimately, the song is about bringing the world together. Paul's natal Gemini Sun (message) is conjunct Jupiter in Cancer (of love), precisely echoing this worldly sentiment.

Below is the recording of "Think for Yourself" with George's chart.

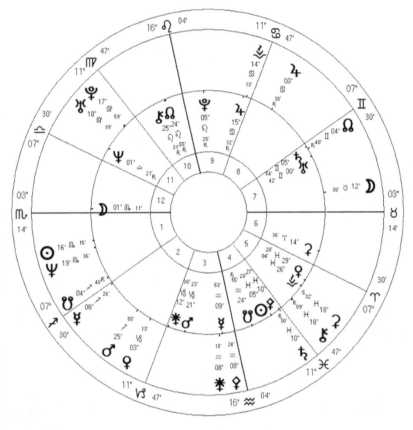

4: George's Uranus in Gemini in the 7th House was the dispositor of his South Node. Other people (7th) have influenced his mind (Gemini). Break-through (Uranus) was to think (Gemini) for himself.

5: George's 9th House Pluto suggests wounding from rigid teachings. Its square to his Scorpio Moon was his upset, why he's got "a word a two" to say about it.

6: A Pisces Sun awakens into direct spirituality through experiences. His Mercury-Pluto opposition was developing broader metaphysical understandings (Aquarius) to transform the Plutonian wounding.

The North Node was transiting George's Saturn-Uranus conjunction in Gemini, indicating a time to reclaim his mind. Also, empowered Athena was transiting his Mercury. Jupiter's residence in Cancer signaled the start of a Jupiter return, which would become much more pronounced in 1966. It would enter his 9th House and trigger his emotional immersion (Cancer) in Indian philosophy (Jupiter in the 9th).

Below is the recording of "The Word."

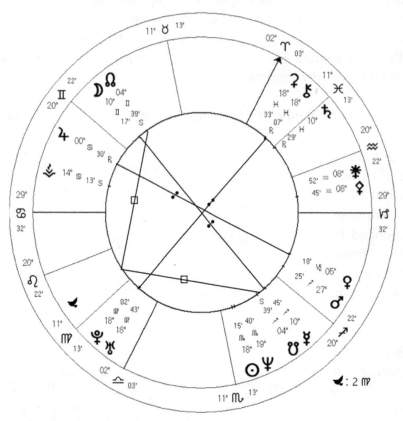

7: Mercury on the South Node was opposite a Gemini Moon on the North Node. The Mercury-South Node conjunction falls on the group's Ascendant (9⁰ Sagittarius, not shown here)—they were delivering their message.

8: "The Word" has the Gemini Moon-North Node conjunction in the 11th House, area of the world stage. The Gemini Moon-North Node conjunction was also on the "Beatles signature," (not shown) reinforcing the intention to bring message (Gemini) into cultural entertainment (Venus-Jupiter). The "arc" was in the 3rd House (message) for "The Word." The song's Gemini Moon also hits Julia's Saturn and Mary's North Node, the same signatures that were catalyzed for the Big Gemini Eclipse.

Additionally, the muse was now at 2⁰ Virgo, so John had reached his Euterpe return (his at 4⁰ Virgo). It was also opposite Julia's Euterpe (1⁰ Pisces) and square Mary's (1⁰ Sagittarius). The song also features a Beatlesque Jupiter-Venus opposition, and Jupiter was being informed from the mystical 12th House. Venus in the 6th House in Capricorn grounds inspiration into form.

361

1: Both *Beatles for Sale* (see p. 343) and *Rubber Soul* have the Sun on The Beatles Ascendant, a point of style and presentation. The fatigue at the time of *Beatles for Sale* (late balsamic Moon) contrasts with the waxing Pisces Moon for *Rubber Soul*, growing (waxing) in a transcendent direction (Pisces). The *Rubber Soul* Sun at 10° Sagittarius is exactly opposite the "Beatles signature" and the Big Gemini Eclipse point.

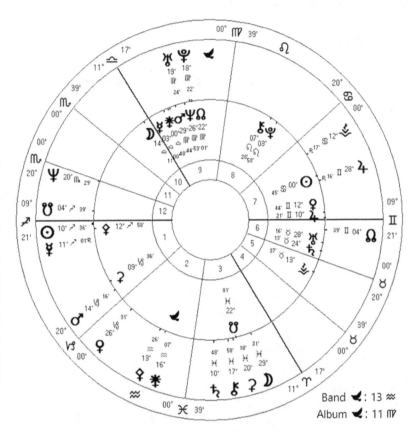

Band ☽: 13 ♒
Album ☽: 11 ♍

2: *Rubber Soul* had the Sun conjunct the South Node, consistent with the phase of resolution (Personality Reconciliation). The Moon conjunct Ceres in Pisces falls on the band's South Node (karmic patterns), signifying the dissolution (Pisces) of maternal (Ceres) attachments (Moon). *Rubber Soul* signaled a step in the process of letting mom go by working with the mind (3rd House).

3: The Pisces Moon transforms grief into spiritual vision. In the band's 3rd House, it involved the development of a spiritual viewpoint to relay a message.

4: Jupiter in Gemini was quincunx Venus in Capricorn, a complex integration involving spiritual discovery with business/financial interests. Mercury in Sagittarius was the dispositor of both Jupiter and the North Node in Gemini, further pointing to the delivery of a philosophical message. The *Rubber Soul* Jupiter (in late Gemini) was conjunct their Sun (in early Cancer)—the album is rife with Gemini themes and ideas.

5: The muse (Euterpe) was at 11° Virgo, exactly square the "Beatles signature" and conjunct the "arc of awakening." As the first record after the Big Gemini Eclipse, the muse was now highly activated, taking a central position in the astrology. The "arc" is closing in on the band's Virgo North Node, and will be exact for the Transcendence period.

Also of note is Juno in Aquarius, the shifting orientation of romance towards a conceptual and more non-attached (Aquarius) understanding. At this point, t-Neptune was opposite the band's Saturn, and had just entered their composite 12th House. Inspired creativity was being grounded by Saturn in earthy Taurus.

George Gets Married

Below is Pattie's chart around George's.

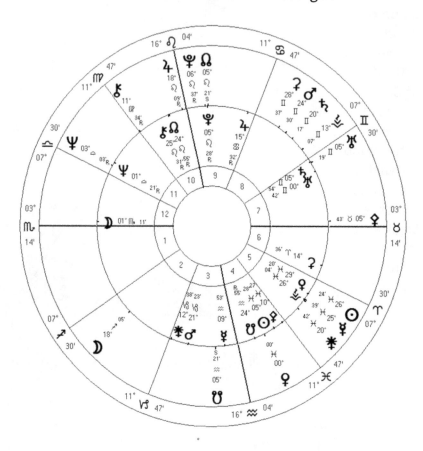

     1: Both were Pisces Suns, and both had Venus in Pisces on each other's Suns. Pattie's Juno in Pisces was also on George's Venus.

     2: Pattie's Mars in Gemini was square George's Venus in Pisces. Mutable signs seek a variety of experience, so the lesson was to negotiate boundaries.

Chapter 12
The Second Peak: The Mountaintop

1: The Venus retrograde passage involved the muse for the Beatles. Venus stationed at 13° Aquarius, the degree of their composite Euterpe. Transiting Venus (creativity) was stimulating her to innovate (Aquarius), and the most experimental collaborations soon followed. Paul's natal Euterpe is in late Capricorn, so he had a prolonged activation of t-Venus to his muse. Venus transited John's early Aquarius Moon 3 times in the passage, triggering his need (Moon) for revolutionary expression (Aquarius).

Below is John's progressed chart around his natal on 1/1/66 as the year opened.

2: Venus retrograde made a prolonged visit to John's professional area (10th House, not shown below). His p-Moon was in Capricorn, approaching his Midheaven, highlighting his public role of elevated visibility. His p-Sun was approaching an opposition to his natal Jupiter-Saturn in Taurus, involving artistic prominence, as well as business and financial issues. The Beatles created Apple Records when the progression perfected.

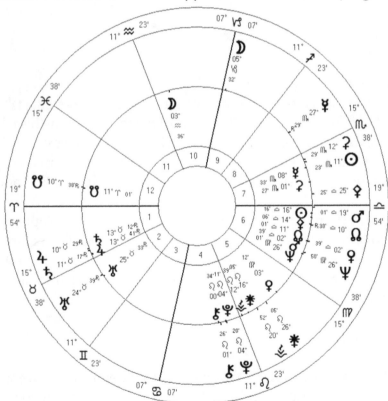

John's p-Venus was exactly conjunct his natal Mars, bringing up questions concerning collaboration (Venus) vs. independence (Mars) in his artistic work (Libra, 6th House). P-Mars was no longer on his Sun, the urgency for leadership wasn't as strong.

3: John's p-Sun was applying to conjoin p-Ceres, which was developing when he met, fell in love with and married Yoko Ono.

Controversy

Here's the interview with John's chart.

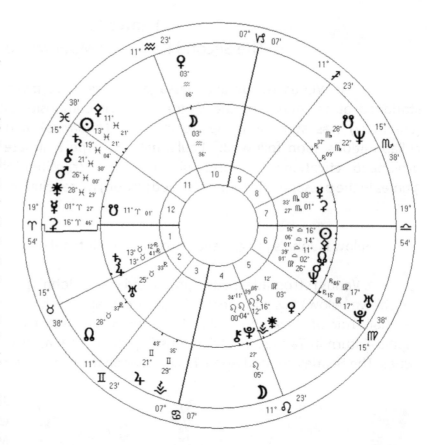

1: John had a strong desire to be seen as a breakthrough figure (Aquarius), though with underlying fears (Pluto-Chiron) of rejection (in Leo). At the time of the "Jesus" remark, the Moon was in early Leo emphasizing that fear, connected to Venus in Aquarius (on his 10th House Moon), playing out publicly in a reactionary (Aquarius) way. He was facing his worst demon, public humiliation (dark Leo) and marginalization (dark Aquarius).

With a 12th House South Node in his chart, the karmic pattern suggests retreat (12th) in anger (Aries), losing the fight and running away. With a slew of planets transiting his 12th at the time (including Ceres on his South Node evoking his historical maternal loss wound), he was feeling the familiar pattern. John's LSD use increased substantially. Pisces/12th House can involve substance use, as well as the development of spirituality and inspiration.

T-Neptune was opposite his Uranus, while t-Uranus was approaching his Neptune. This "double whammy" of wild, inspired and revolutionary energy was equally unstable and invigorating. During the next few years, John would grapple with taming his wild nature. He was at a time of increased intuitive sensitivity, further resolving his karmic issues. The synthesis was to make imaginative creations of his process.

The Sermon from the Mountaintop

1: Geoff Emerick (12/5/45, chart not shown) had Uranus at 15° Gemini opposite his Sun at 13° Sagittarius (hitting the "Beatles signature" and the band's Ascendant). Below is "Tomorrow Never Knows" with John's chart.

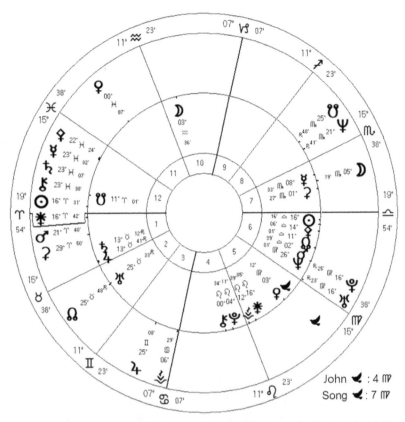

John ☾ : 4 ♍
Song ☾ : 7 ♍

2: The "Tomorrow Never Knows" Euterpe was 7° Virgo, conjunct John's natal position of 4° Virgo. He was at his Euterpe return, a time when the energy is potentially renewed at another level. Whereas John described the process in "Nowhere Man" as being receptive, more collaboration with the muse is speculated for this song (Euterpe conjunction in his 5th House).

3: Athena, Mercury, Saturn and Chiron were all in Pisces in John's 12th House. Additionally, Sun-Juno in Aries were also there and on his South Node, highlighting his unfinished visionary work. The "Tomorrow Never Knows" Sun was at 16° Aries, directly opposite John's Sun at 16° Libra. In the song, John sings about a shining (Sun) void (12th House), which connects with (opposition) his life force (natal Sun), located in the area of crafts and projects (6th House).

4: The Scorpio South Node involves the resolution of wounding, while the Taurus North Node seeks grounding and realism. The Taurus-Scorpio axis bridges the physical with the psychological.

5: The "Tomorrow Never Knows" North Node was in Taurus, suggesting an ongoing process of grounding the vision. It was at 25° Taurus, exactly on John's natal Uranus. He was making innovative (Uranus) art (Taurus), bringing his vision into tangible expression.

6: The song's Scorpio South Node was conjunct Neptune (spiritualism) in John's area of death (8th House). The Moon at 5° Scorpio highlights his natal Ceres and "wounded child" T-square. John was still processing through the death of his mother (perhaps with her assistance!).

7: Ceres was at 29° Aries, making his "wounded child" T-square into a frictional Grand Cross. It was opposed to his natal Ceres (4° and applying). This tension can lead to a tremendous catharsis, which is one way to comprehend the music. The exact Uranus-Pluto conjunction can be explosive and cathartic.

8: The Uranus-Pluto conjunction at 16° Virgo just entered John's 6th House. For the last several years, the planets were energizing his area of performance and development

(Virgo) of his talent (5th House). Now, the emphasis would shift to learning technical proficiency.

Sex & Drugs

"Love You To" with George's chart.

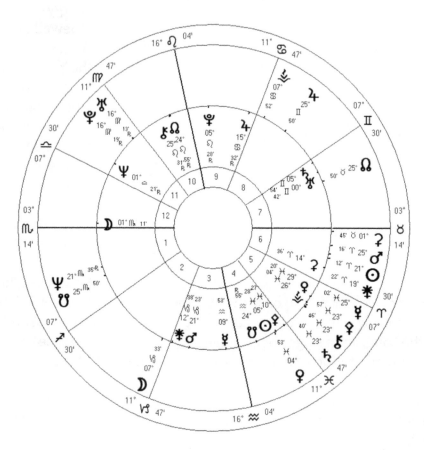

1: George had a Juno-Mars conjunction in opposition to his 9th House Jupiter, a desire (Mars) for romance (Juno) connected to a spiritual ideal (Jupiter, 9th). "Love You To" contains an echo: Sun (realization, presence) conjunct Juno-Mars and sextile Jupiter.

Additionally, "Love You To" had Venus in mystical Pisces on George's Sun. A stellium of planets (Saturn, Chiron, Athena, Mercury) was on his natal Vesta-Venus conjunction later in Pisces, signaling major stimulation (structure, new ideas) to his musical craft. The Uranus-Pluto conjunction was transiting George's 11th House (the world stage), and he was bringing such innovation into culture and society.

Below is Ravi Shankar's chart (cast for midday) around George's.

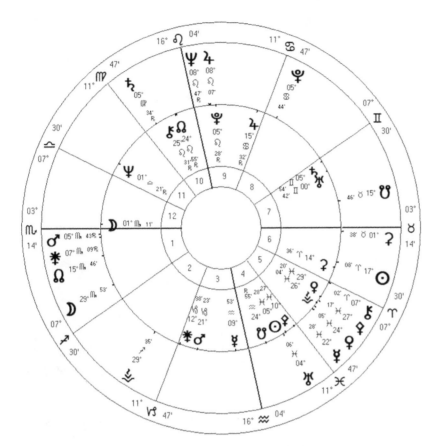

2: Ravi had Uranus in Pisces opposite Saturn in Virgo, bringing an integration of spirituality into workable forms. Virgo excels at tutelage and skill development. Ravi was a mentor and instructor, and George's Pisces Sun falls right on this aspect. They were connected through spiritual music (Venus conjunct Venus in Pisces). At this time, George's p-Sun was at 29° Pisces on his 5th House Venus (not shown); he was immersed in creating spiritual music.

3: Ravi had a Jupiter-Neptune conjunction (spiritual philosophy), which fell on George's 9th House Pluto, strongly supporting his questing (Jupiter-Neptune) and healing of prior karmic wounding from indoctrination.

4: Ravi's Mars in Scorpio was on George's Ascendant and Moon, challenging him to live with courage and passion.

Living the Dream

Below is the real Eleanor Rigby's chart around Paul's. With an unknown birth time, 12pm is used. At noon, the Moon appears at 3° Capricorn (and during the day it traveled between 25° Sagittarius and 8° Capricorn).

1: Eleanor's Ceres was at 27° Sagittarius, filling out Paul's "expression of grief" T-square into a Grand Cross. His core issue of sadness/loss is dramatically catalyzed by Eleanor's maternal energy (Ceres), so it's easy to transfer his mother issues to her.

2: Eleanor had a connection between mother and muse—her Euterpe at 20° Sagittarius conjunct her Ceres at 27°. The Paul-Mary Euterpe is 28° Sagittarius (p. 349), so Eleanor easily becomes part of their mother/muse dynamic.

3: The underlying issue is Mary's death. When she died in 1956, Euterpe was at 28° Sagittarius, the degree of the Paul-Mary Euterpe and on Eleanor's Ceres/Euterpe. Therefore, Eleanor is an easy representation of Mary's death—again, she links to both mothering (Ceres)

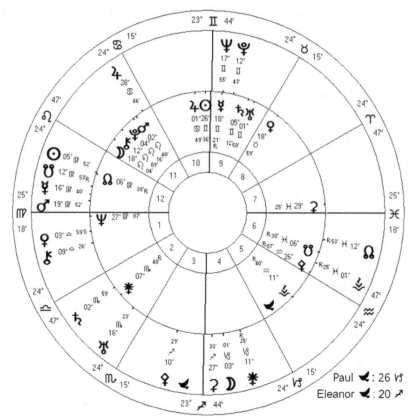

and the muse (Euterpe). The Big Gemini eclipse (9° Gemini) hit Eleanor's Pluto at 12° Gemini, catalyzing a message from beyond.

4: Eleanor's Pluto (12° Gemini) was exactly on the "Beatles signature." Her role was to bring a message (Gemini) through death (Pluto).

Additionally, Eleanor's Virgo Sun was exactly on Paul's North Node (less than 1°), encouraging his intention to compose spiritually-inspired (12th House) works (Virgo). Eleanor's Neptune (spiritual) in Gemini (message) was conjunct Paul's Mercury, reinforcing the same idea. Her Euterpe at 20° Sagittarius was opposite Paul's Mercury at 18° Gemini, linking the muse phenomenon to his writing. Eleanor's Saturn in Scorpio suggests her great work (Saturn) involved Scorpionic processes (death, transformation). It's square Paul's Pluto, another link between them involving death.

Venus is the planet of reflection and connection. Eleanor's Venus in Libra was on Mary McCartney's Sun in early Libra (see Mary's chart on p. 299), so it was easy for Paul to project his maternal issues onto Eleanor.

Below is the recording of "Eleanor Rigby" with Paul's chart.

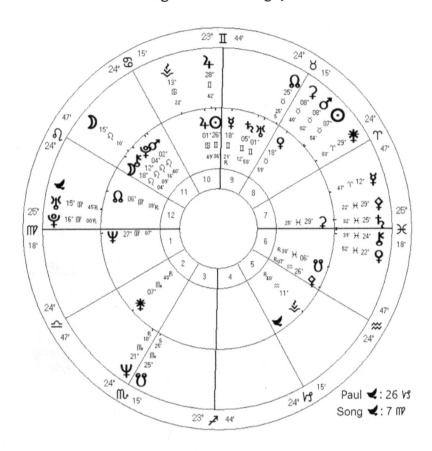

Paul ☽: 26 ♑
Song ☽: 7 ♍

The Neptune-South Node conjunction in Scorpio relates to spiritualism. For the recording of "Eleanor Rigby," it was on Paul's 3rd House cusp, the area of writing, and square his intuitive and familial Moon. He was having a Lunar return at the time, further accentuating his roots and desire to resolve his past (Moon) to feel happier (Leo). The muse was at 7° Virgo, precisely on Paul's North Node at 6° Virgo, residing in his 12th House. The astrology strongly supports her assistance for his critical soul work.

"Eleanor Rigby" has a large grouping of planets (Venus, Chiron, Saturn, Athena) on Paul's grief-oriented Ceres in Pisces, bringing artistry (Venus) healing (Chiron) and structure (Saturn) to his maternal grief process. His "expression of grief" T-square was being triggered by Jupiter at 28° Gemini on his storytelling Sun. The Uranus-Pluto conjunction was exact, located in his 12th House (spirituality, release), and square his Mercury in Gemini, bringing such processes to writing. Additionally, the "Eleanor Rigby" Sun was conjunct Ceres, shining the spotlight on maternal issues.

370

Below is the recording of "Yellow Submarine."

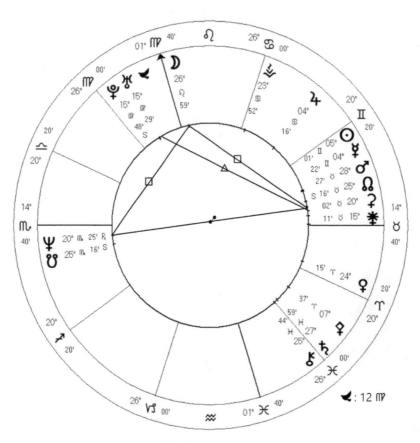

1: The North Node in the 7th (same as Ringo's natal placement) points to togetherness. It was joined by a slew of planets (Juno, Ceres, Mars, Mercury, Sun), adding lots of spirited energy to such social relating.

2: Neptune rising involves oceans and the dream world, and suggests a healing voyage. Joy relates to the Leo Moon, which was square to the Nodal Axis (and planets involved). It's caught in the middle of maternal grief issues (Ceres opposite Neptune, just like in Paul's natal chart), seeking to heal through togetherness (7th House North Node).

3: The Gemini Sun (communication) was on the "Beatles signature." "Yellow Submarine" has become a signature song, one of the few featuring dialogue. It is through communication (Gemini) and social connection (7th House) that underlying grief and loneliness (Neptune-South Node in the 1st) becomes resolved.

371

Chapter 13
The Third Peak: Gunfire

Dead Woman Talking

Below is the recording session for "She Said She Said."

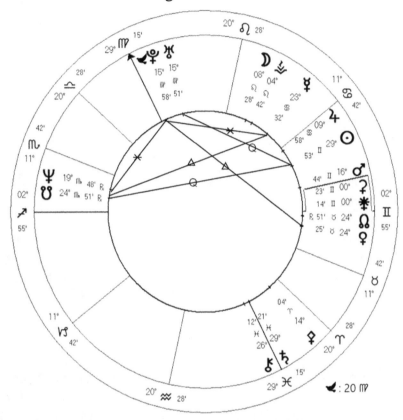

1: The "She Said" Gemini Sun was quintile Uranus-Pluto, intimating communications (Gemini) linked with the transpersonal nature of the "arc." The Sun was at 29⁰ Gemini (the final degree), suggesting a completion to communications. Furthermore, it's exactly (less than 1⁰ degree) biquintile the Scorpio South Node, creating another unique mystical link between communication (Gemini) and death (Scorpio).

2: Neptune conjunct the South Node in Scorpio (spiritualism) had just risen, and makes a trine to Mercury in the realm of death (8th). Neptune in Scorpio was with the South Node for the entire recording of *Revolver* (the <u>death</u> album).

3: Ceres was also in Gemini (communications involving mother) and conjunct the North Node (karmic resolution).

4: Euterpe (muse) was at 20⁰ Virgo, conjunct Pluto (death) at 18⁰ Virgo.

5: Euterpe (20⁰ Virgo) was conjunct the Beatles composite North Node (at 22⁰ Virgo, not shown). This particular song is a major example of spiritual work (North Node) involving a project (Virgo) with the muse (Euterpe).

1: The "upside down" Kite mentioned in Part 1: Moon (with Chiron and Saturn nearby) in Pisces is at the base (which was on the Beatles South Node). The Uranus-Pluto (at the tip) was on their North Node. At one wing was Venus-Jupiter-Mars in Cancer, while Neptune in Scorpio was at the other.

2: The "arc" will be even closer to the Beatles North Node for the next album, *Sgt. Pepper*, perhaps their defining work. However, it is in close proximity through-out the Transcendence period.

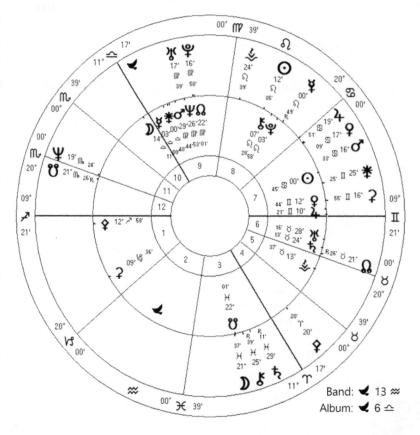

3: Mercury retrograde in Leo—sound (Mercury) entertainment (Leo) designed to make one rethink (retrograde). It correlates with the backwards effects, theme of dissolving the mind and the intentional confusion. Saturn (organization) in late Pisces (imagination, transcendence) was tightly trine Mercury, bringing professional organization to sound experimentation and message. Not only was the *Revolver* Mercury on the Beatles Pluto (death), so was the Sun (albeit looser). Both of these planets also fall in the group's 8th House, the area related to death.

4: The Leo Sun square Neptune in Scorpio reflects the synthesis of the solar (Sun) and dream (Neptune) threads. It also correlates with LSD use and spiritual questing, both of which were a part of this album's legacy.

5: The *Revolver* Euterpe at 6° Libra was conjunct the Beatles' Mercury. They were giving voice (Mercury) to the muse (Euterpe), and possibly partnering (Libra) with her.

Additionally, the album featured a Venus-Neptune trine (part of the Kite), correlating with great imaginative artistic works. This aspect is found in many masterpieces (visual, musical or otherwise). With Uranus-Pluto present, Neptune-Venus was given more power, thunder and explosiveness. Also, the album features a Pisces Moon square Juno in Gemini, suggesting a need to shift the lighter romantic focus towards greater spiritual depth.

Below is The Beatles chart with the transits for their final performance.

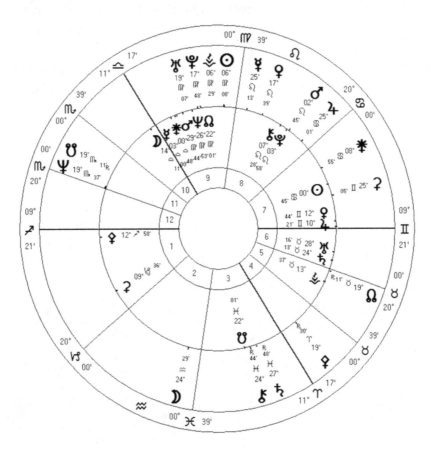

1: Not only did Mars return to Leo, Venus and Mercury were also in the sign of performance, highlighting matters in this area. Unlike 1963, Mars was direct at this time. They were moving forward, unimpeded by the demands of touring. The Aquarius Moon portrays a cooler and non-attached mood, in contrast to their prior enthusiasm.

2: The Scorpio South Node conjunct Neptune involves endings and dissolution. Neptune was on the verge of shifting from their 11th House (world stage) to the 12th House (behind the scenes), while the South Node was catalyzing a death/rebirth (Scorpio) to their public life (11th House).

3: The North Node in Taurus was entering their 5th House, bringing a focus to their art, particularly through craftsmanship (applying to their Vesta). Saturn in Pisces was transiting their South Node, signaling maturation of their vision. The Sun was exactly conjunct Vesta in Virgo, signaling a time to get to work.

Below is the release of *How I Won the War* with John's chart.

1: In addition to Saturn on his South Node, the Moon was also in the vicinity too. The karma being addressed circles back to his roots (spiritual childhood).

2: The Moon was nearing an eclipse, crossing John's Ascendant to get there. His prior belligerent style was being transformed. Biographers point to 1966 as the year John's personality considerably mellowed, which may be connected to some healing of his core wounds.

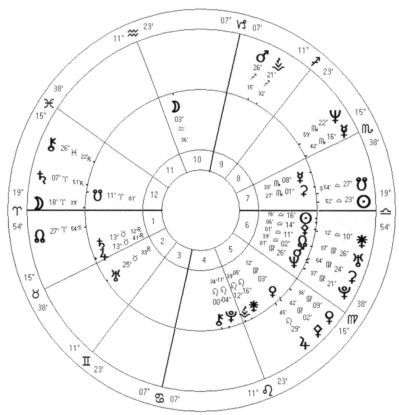

3: Ceres was sandwiched between Uranus and Pluto, suggestive of maternal dynamics in the wounding pattern. The movie's Nodal Axis was conjunct John's natal Ceres, echoing again how maternal issues were front and center in this drama.

4: For the movie release, Juno was in Libra, conjunct John's North Node. His point of karmic resolution was stimulated in a romantic way. The biwheel can also be looked at as the transits at the time. Juno was on John's North Node, coming to his Sun and 7th House soon. A new partnership was about to blossom.

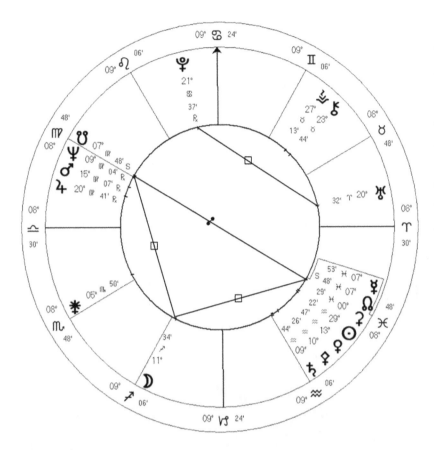

1: John's Moon (early) and Yoko's Sun (late) are both in Aquarius, sign of reform and revolution. The distance might allow freedom. The couple had a prolonged break in the early 1970s when they lived apart and John had another lover (May Pang).

2: Yoko's Aquarian energy, applied to the creative realm of the 5th House, correlates with highly unique (even eccentric) forms of art. True to the voluminous energy in this area (7 significant celestial signatures), Yoko has been a prolific artist and performer. Her Libra ASC is oriented to art and aesthetics, as well as to personal relations (and matches with John's strong Libra attunement).

3: Yoko's Ceres is at 0° Pisces, only 1° from her Sun. Recall that Julia had significant Pisces energy, so the transference of John's mother issues from Julia to Yoko was natural. Connected with the Nodal Axis, Yoko's karma involves grief and loss issues (Pisces) with nurturance (Ceres).

4: Yoko's South Node in Virgo in the 11th House portrays deep concern about collective evolution (11th House), a desire to do something helpful (Virgo) for the world. Her 12th House planets in Virgo (Neptune, Mars, Jupiter) are attuned to spiritual themes.

5: Yoko's Sagittarius Moon is square her Nodal Axis, suggesting clear direction for her humanitarian concerns has been a karmic challenge. Her Moon is extremely out-of-bounds at 27°31' south, corresponding with feeling (Moon) like a foreigner (Sagittarius) and an outsider (out-of-bounds).

6: A 10th House Pluto can correlate with challenges/wounding with public reputation. The racism and sexism she experienced was part of the darkness (Pluto) in her biography. Pluto involves transformation, and Yoko now enjoys the respect (10th House) she deserves.

7: When John and Yoko met, Vesta was at 11° Libra (on John's North Node). His peace activism intention was becoming grounded and realized at this time (Vesta).

The John-Yoko composite chart.

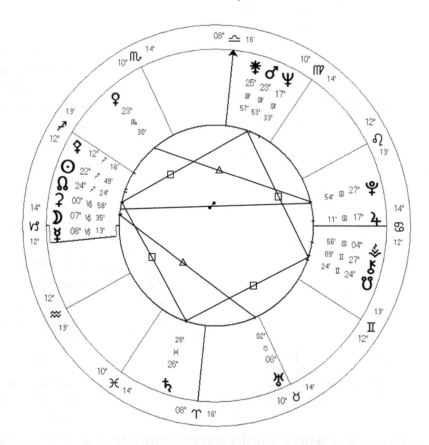

8: The Gemini South Node conjunct Chiron forges a message of healing. Disposited by Mercury in the 12th in Capricorn, it involved idealism and universal love (12th) for the mainstream (Capricorn): an anti-war message fits. Saturn in Pisces in the 3rd House squared the Nodes and echoed precisely the same sentiment, the organization (Saturn) of a message (3rd House) of love and compassion (Pisces). Neptune-Mars-Juno squared the Nodes from Virgo, which involved the dissolution (Neptune) of violence (Mars), connected with the energy of romance ("make love, not war").

The North Node in Sagittarius in the 12th House seeks to develop a focused spiritual mission. Disposited by Jupiter in Cancer in the 7th House, the mission was to learn to bridge differences (7th House) through love (Cancer). The Sun conjunct Athena in Sagittarius in the 12th House suggests purpose (Sagittarius) in advocating (Athena) a vision or ideal (12th).

9: The earth planet Saturn squared their Nodal Axis from one side, while the 3 Virgo planets squared it from the other. The spiritual lesson was to take measures to ground and materialize their message with inspired creativity.

10: Ceres was conjunct both their Moon and North Node, while Uranus resided in their 4th House. Both signatures involve processes to discover a deeper realization of calm, security and familial stability.

Below are Paul's, then John's, transits at the start of the *Pepper* sessions.

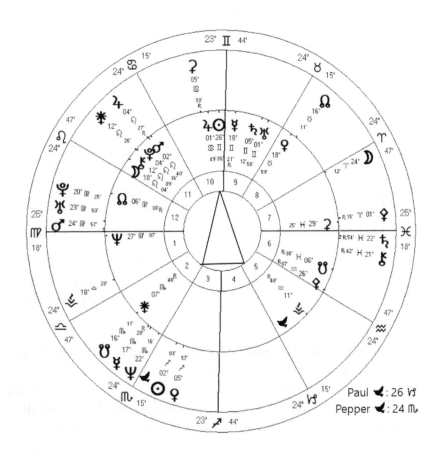

Paul ☾: 26 ♑
Pepper ☾: 24 ♏

When sessions began, Mars was crossing Paul's ASC, describing a new start with leadership. Mars would station in his 2nd house (in early 1967), bolstering his confidence. Jupiter in Leo was activating Paul's "I'm in charge" creative (Leo) drive (Mars). T-Uranus (breakthrough) was soon to cross Paul's ASC and square his Sun, heralding a major new beginning. The Yod (see chart) connects his Sun and his Euterpe with the *Pepper* Euterpe, signaling a profound connection with the muse for this album.

In contrast to Mars crossing Paul's ASC, John had the Moon on his when sessions began. John's lesson was to lead (ASC) with emotional support (Moon), though the shadow is competitiveness (Aries) and resentment. The yod pointed to this lesson. One leg of the yod landed in John's 8th House, the area which most relates to other people's power and agenda. The other one involved working with others (6th House). T-Jupiter was moving through John's 4th House, stimulating the area of roots and family. T-Saturn was transiting his 12th House, catalyzing historical themes of surrender or defeat. The lesson was to let go willingly.

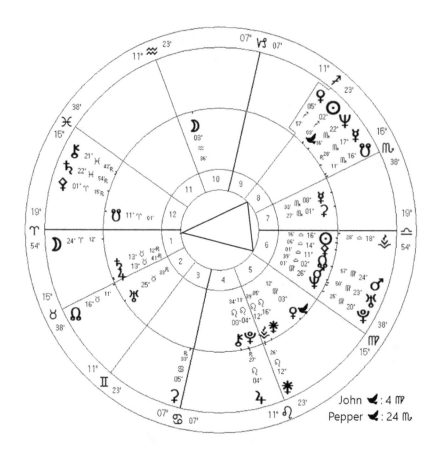

John ☽: 4 ♍
Pepper ☽: 24 ♏

Later in the sessions, Mars would enter his 7th House, signaling leadership (Mars) of a partner (7th House). It would turn retrograde right on his "wounded child" T-square, activating underlying emotionally-reactive dynamics. He was also in the midst of tremendous transpersonal stimulation: t-Neptune opposed his Uranus, while t-Uranus was conjunct his Neptune, bringing his psyche to the outer limits of intuition.

Below are George Martin's transits at the start of the sessions.

George Martin had a preponderance of planets in the early to middle 20 degree range of several signs. The transits were particularly emphasized at these degrees, making an assortment of major aspects to his chart. In his natal work area (6th House) were Saturn (career), Mars (will) and Mercury (sound). T-Neptune (imagination), Mercury and the South Node were traveling through this realm, along with the Sun and Venus in Sagittarius nearby. All of this energy suggests focused work on imaginative (Neptune) sound (Mercury) projects (6th House).

Martin had an Aquarius Midheaven (progressive trends) with Uranus in Pisces (visionary innovation) dispositing it from the executive 10th House. T-Saturn (manifestation) was on his Uranus, while the epic Uranus-Pluto conjunction, along with leadership Mars, opposed it. He had natal Pluto in Cancer opposite his Capricorn Sun: a desire to do something of major historical value.

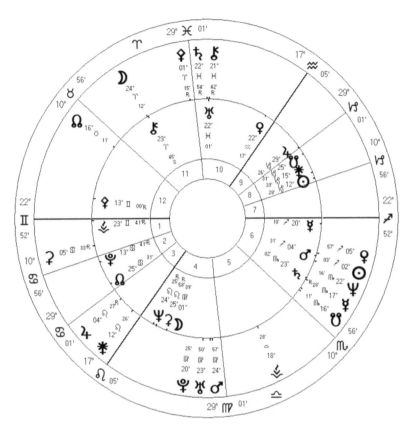

Fields of Dreams

Session for "Strawberry Fields Forever."

1: South Node-Mercury-Neptune-Euterpe stellium in Scorpio in the creative realm of the 5th House: creative work with the muse and her message.

2: John had Mercury in Scorpio himself, not far from the stellium. He was renewing his writing at a deeper level.

3: Jupiter at 4⁰ Leo was on John's natal 4th House Pluto, activating his "wounded child" signature.

4: With Jupiter residing in Leo, the spiritual purpose of this transit was to transmute the prior wounding into something creative and engaging.

5: Ceres was out-of-bounds at 24°11' (north) in early Cancer. It was also on the Beatles composite Cancer Sun (roots). The "Strawberry Fields" chart also featured a Cancer Ascendant, further accentuating an orientation to family.

A Journey through Time

Below is the first session for "When I'm Sixty-Four."

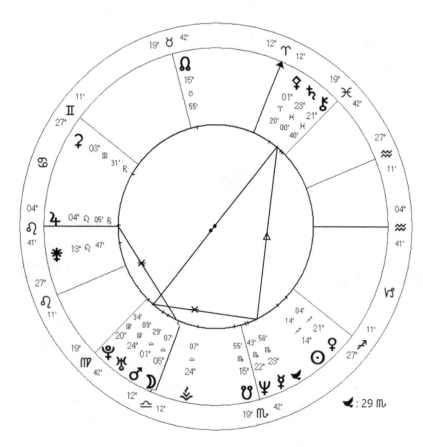

1: Jupiter on the ASC correlates with journeys, while Leo is theatrical. Jupiter sextile a 3rd House Moon is a message (3rd House) of loving (Moon) togetherness (Libra).

2: The performance area (5th House) has more about the journey. The Sun was in travel-oriented Sagittarius conjunct an out-of-bounds Venus (at 23°29' south); artistic (Venus) travels (Sag) of an unusual variety.

3: South Node-Neptune in the 4th House can idealize (Neptune) the past and roots.

4: Saturn in Pisces in the 9th House correlates with traditional values, which was in opposition to the changing tenor of the times (Uranus-Pluto).

Cleansing the Window of Perception

The "Penny Lane" Venus at 19° Capricorn was conjunct Paul's natal Euterpe at 26° Capricorn, linking the artistry of this song (Venus) and his muse attunement (Euterpe) in the sign of the past (Capricorn).

At this time, the Nodal Axis of the Beatles chart (22° Pisces-Virgo) was getting maximally set off. Uranus and Pluto were at 24° and 20° Virgo, while Saturn and Chiron were respectively at 23° and 21° Pisces. The stimulation points to the awakening of insight, spiritual maturation (Saturn) and healing (Chiron).

Interestingly, the Midheaven for "Penny Lane" is at 24° Aries, the same degree as the Moon for "Strawberry Fields Forever," linking these songs.

Below is the release of the 2 singles around the John-Paul composite chart.

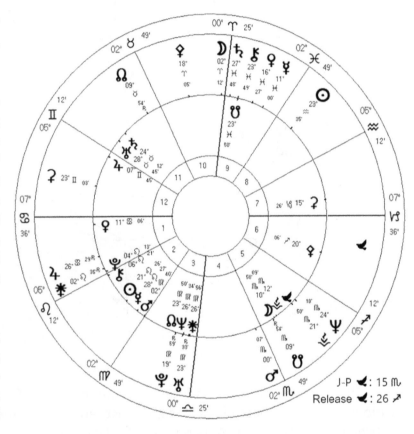

Euterpe was at 26° Sagittarius opposite Ceres at 23° Gemini, both squaring the central spiritual work of the John-Paul chart (Nodal Axis at 23° Virgo-Pisces). Ceres in Gemini was in their 12th House, correlating with a maternal (Ceres) message (Gemini) inspired from beyond (12th House). Euterpe in their 6th House brings the focus of the muse to work projects.

The South Node was at 9°54' Scorpio, right on their composite Moon-Euterpe conjunction. Recall when John and Paul met (9.5 years ago, half a Nodal cycle), the Nodal axis was at this same place only reversed, so these songs directly pick up on the purpose signified by their meeting (largely to heal maternal death issues). With the North Node now in Taurus, the lesson was to ground the emotional transformation (Scorpio Moon) they were experiencing into artistic form.

Transiting Juno was conjunct their composite Pluto, while transiting Uranus-Pluto was close and applying to conjoin their composite Juno. The romantic (Juno) orientation of their songwriting partnership (the early formula) was ending (Pluto). Emerging was further growth of their North Node-Neptune in the 3rd House, storytelling with a more mature level of spiritual insight. The Pluto-Juno activity also correlates with a shift in their "bromance" as John was beginning to detach from Paul and would soon deepen with Yoko.

Below is the "A Day in the Life" chart, emphasizing the aspects to the Sun.

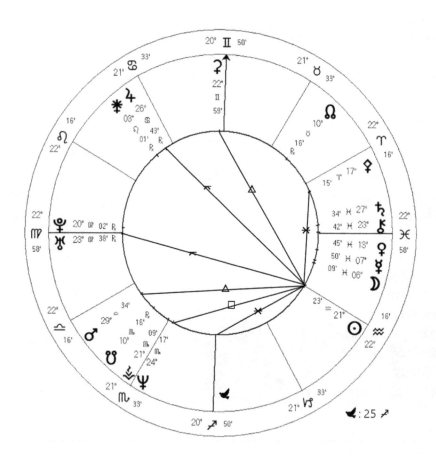

The theme of the song is interconnectedness. The Sun is the unifying energy in astrology, while the astrological sign most about our metaphysical Oneness and synchronistic relatedness is Aquarius. The "A Day in the Life" Sun in Aquarius makes an assortment of aspects to other planets, reflecting this theme. It is sextile Athena and connected to both the Kite (quincunx Uranus-Pluto, quincunx Jupiter, square Neptune-Vesta) and Grand Cross (sextile Euterpe, trine Ceres, quincunx Uranus-Pluto) from the 5th House (performance).

Additionally, Saturn-Chiron (at the base of the Kite) connects with more Pisces planets in the work-oriented 6th House. Venus and Mercury relate to artistic, mystical communication, while the Moon in Pisces is a need for transcendent experiences and healing.

Vesta (an earthy energy) in Scorpio joins Neptune at the lower wing of the Kite, supporting the grounding of its metaphysical scope in the manifest realm.

Chapter 15
The Dream of Lonely Hearts Part 2:
The Aeronautics of Consciousness

Mystical Kite Flying

Below is the chart for "Mr. Kite!," emphasizing the Sun's aspects.

Similar to "A Day in the Life," "Mr. Kite!" involves interconnectedness (Aquarius), here related to an event 124 years prior. The song's Sun is at 28⁰ Aquarius, conjunct the circus Sun at 25⁰ Aquarius (not shown)—illustrating synchronistic connectedness.

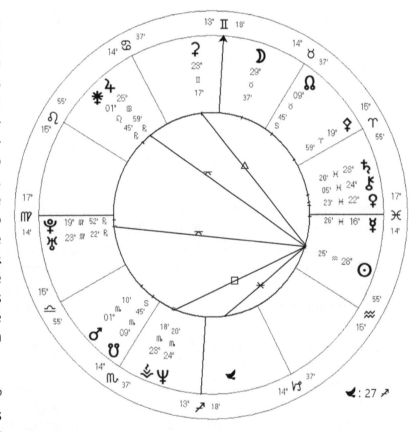

And like the prior song, the "Mr. Kite!" Aquarius Sun makes many aspects to other planets. The Sun's square to Neptune accentuates the transpersonal, revealing a multidimensional reach. It also relates to the swirling, psychedelic quality of the music. The Sun connects to planets that form the Kite (quincunx Jupiter & Uranus-Pluto, and square Neptune-Vesta), as well as the mother (Sun trine Ceres) and muse (Sun sextile Euterpe).

The song's Euterpe at 27⁰ Sagittarius opposite Ceres at 23⁰ Gemini profoundly connects to the John-Julia composite chart (see p. 358). They had their Nodal axis at 27⁰ Gemini-Sagittarius, so this song dynamically captures the potential of their spiritual work. "Mr. Kite!" is a shining example of the metaphysical reach of the John-Julia partnership and their other collaborations at this unique time also feature similar astrology.

The circus organizer, Pablo Fanque (3/30/1810) had the Nodes at 14⁰ Aries-Libra, conjunct John's (11⁰ Aries-Libra), illustrating their spiritual link.

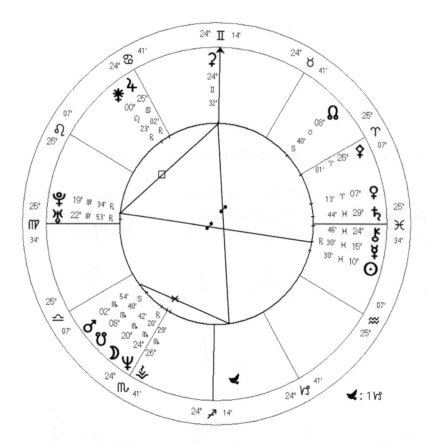

As Above, So Below:
The Girl Who Bridges
Worlds

The chart for "Lucy in the Sky with Diamonds" with additional aspects.

Mercury retrograde in Pisces loosely joins Saturn-Chiron at the Kite's base (its opposition to Pluto-Uranus is tighter). Mercury involves the dreamy and unusual psychedelic sounds in the song, as well as the metaphysical ideas and storyline.

Mars at 2° Scorpio plays a critical role. Early degrees of Scorpio hit John's natal "wounded child" aspects. His historical issues of pain, anger and loss were being worked through. The Mars-South Node conjunction in the "Lucy" chart involves violent (Mars) karma (South Node), echoes the same astrology as when Julia was fatally wounded in her accident (see p. 305) and underlies "Run for Your Life." Euterpe was sextile Mars, the muse was circling back to the violent karma for resolution. The Moon conjunct Neptune later in Scorpio further emphasizes the healing component of the reunion.

Additionally, the "Lucy" chart also had Pluto square Ceres, repeating the maternal death issue. Karmic resolution is found with the peaceable Taurus North Node, located in the 8th House. The reclamation of peace (Taurus) is found through sacred union (8th House), perhaps an artistic (Taurus) collaboration through death (8th House).

Ceres in Gemini was at the Midheaven—it is mom (Ceres) up in the sky (Midheaven) and calling (Gemini), connected with the muse (opposite Euterpe). "Lucy in the Sky with Diamonds" may not just be a John-Julia collaboration, it could also be a depiction of their reunion in John's psyche.

"Within You Without You" with the Beatles chart.

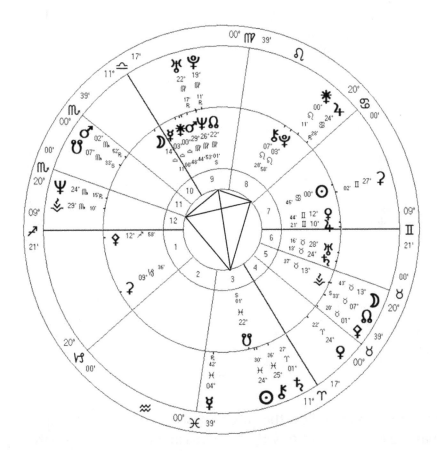

"Within You Without You" has Mercury retrograde in Pisces. The mind turns within (retrograde) in discovery (meditation, contemplation) of a shift in perception and understanding. The Moon conjunct the Taurus North Node signals a new relationship with the material realm and attachments. Like the Moon reflects the light of the Sun, we can exist in material form (Taurus Moon) as reflections of Spirit (illuminated by a Pisces Sun). The transcendent dimension can illuminate the earth realm, we can bring "heaven" to "earth," a grounded spirituality consistent with the "arc's" descent. In order to claim this promise, inflated self-interests (Mars conjunct Scorpio South Node) need to be addressed.

The Sun-Uranus opposition on the band's Nodal axis conveys the radical shift in their sound and message. George had a Sun-Uranus square, indicative of an attunement to making radical shifts, and this song is a prime example of his innovative streak.

The muse (Euterpe) was at 5° Capricorn, separating from its opposition to Ceres (at 27° Gemini). Compared to the dramatic connection between mother and muse in the earlier *Pepper* songs, this connection is peripheral and releasing. George's spiritual work involved study, particularly philosophy to heal his 9th House Pluto. By so doing, he could complement John and Paul's intuitive offerings. His 9th House Pluto was transforming from prior dogmatic wounding into love and togetherness, the message of the song.

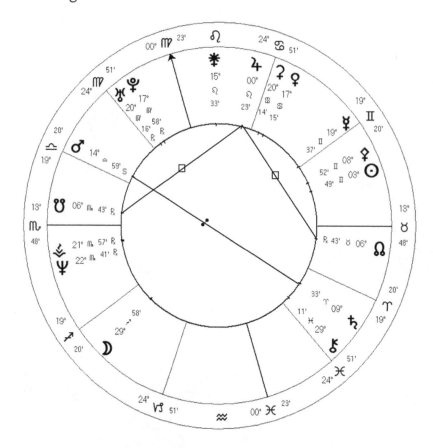

George continued to follow the "arc's" descent to a grounded spirituality. "It's All Too Much" has the North Node (growth) in Taurus in the 6th House (earth)—assisting the lofty South Node (12th, "show me that I'm everywhere") to settle down. The North Node dispositor (Venus in Cancer conjunct nourishing Ceres) seeks nurturing togetherness ("get me home for tea"), to make it real. Jupiter in Leo (too much) squares the Nodal axis. Its challenge is overindulgence, while the promise is to bask in the bounty of spiritual expansion ("All the world's a birthday cake"). Saturn opposite Mars signifies restraint and measured behavior choices.

The Sagittarius Moon is rooted in foreign philosophy and spiritual seeking. The philosophical Moon was way out-of-bounds at 28° 08' south, the mainstream didn't get the message. Mercury was out-of-bounds at 25° 02' north, right next to Venus at 24° 52'. The song was seen as "out there," a challenge for the listener to connect with the music (Venus) and message (Mercury). Nevertheless, George continued to be a main messenger of philosophical and spiritual ideas in Beatles music, fulfilling the high promise of his chart.

Below is the release of the album with additional astrological points and notes.

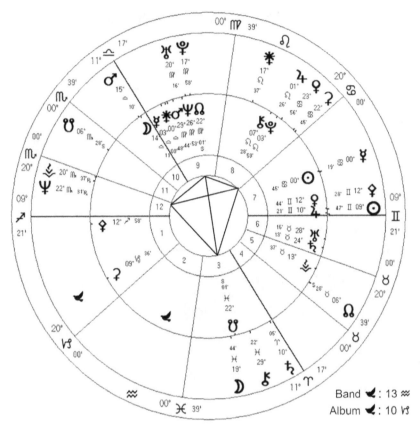

Band ◖: 13 ≈
Album ◖: 10 ♑

The album's Jupiter in Leo (conjunct Venus, echoing the "Beatles signature") correlates with its expansiveness and flashiness: colorful outfits and cover design, glissandos, circus, theatrics, etc. *Sgt. Pepper* is the only album with the Sun on the "Beatles signature," pointing to a signature work. There is a variety of sounds and genres on the album (Gemini), and the premise of being another band (alter egos, duality (Gemini)—seen with the 2 versions of them on the cover), and also points to Paul (a Gemini Sun, like the album), the creative visionary. The Sun was conjunct Athena ("warrior priestess"). They assumed the role of a military band, and are "armed" with instruments, a reflection of being musical gunslingers.

The *Sgt. Pepper* sound and message (Mercury) was right on the Beatles life force (at 0° Cancer, exactly on the Beatles composite Sun)—another reflection of their signature work, what is identified as their sound. Ideas were also streaming in from way up above (Mercury out of bounds north at 25°38'). The *Sgt. Pepper* Mars in Libra was on the band's Midheaven, signifying their position at the "toppermost" as cultural (Libra) leaders (Mars).

Chapter 16 – Descension

Paul's New Beginning

Below is Paul's p–New Moon (6/14/67) around his natal chart.

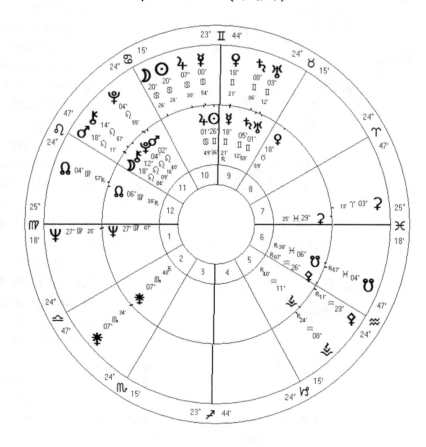

1: Paul's p–New Moon was in Cancer (heart) in the authoritative 10th House. It was the success of *Sgt. Pepper* that emboldened him to renew his career with confidence.

2: P-Mercury was within 1° of his natal Jupiter, correlating with the international expansion (Jupiter) he was now experiencing as a writer and singer (Mercury). Paul's p-Mercury was at the same degree as The Beatles Sun (0° Cancer). He was becoming the most prolific writer in the band and penned the most #1 hits from this point on. His p-Venus was exactly on his natal Mercury at 18° Gemini, reflecting the enormous popularity (Venus) of his songwriting (Mercury), as well as the youthful and breezy nature (Gemini) of much of his offerings.

3: P-Mars was exactly on his Leo Moon, another trigger (Mars) of his emotional need to shine (Leo). He would also experience emotional (Moon) strife (Mars) with John (and to a lesser extent, George & Ringo), and in his relationship with Jane.

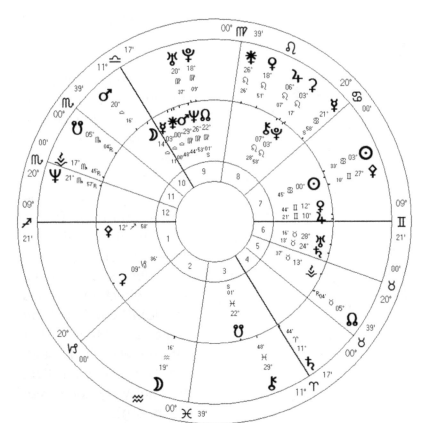

Relaying the Message

The Beatles chart with the Our World broadcast.

Athena in Gemini was conjunct the Cancer Sun, an activist (Athena) message (Gemini) of radiant love (Cancer Sun). Venus in Leo is celebratory: streamers, celebrities, etc. Jupiter was tightly conjunct Ceres in Leo, an enlargement (Jupiter) of loving bonds (Ceres). Mars in Libra is not far from their peace-loving Libra Moon, asserts the personal will (Mars) towards together-ness (Libra).

Baby, Mother and Guru

Ringo's chart (inner) and Jason's (outer).

1: Jason brings a pileup of energy (Uranus, Pluto, Juno, Venus) to Ringo's Ceres and Neptune. He connects with Ringo's longing for familial deepening. Like his dad, Jason also has 4 planets in Leo, mainly residing in Ringo's 5th House, the area of childhood joy and play. Jason entered the music business and played the drums, reflecting a similarity with creative pursuits.

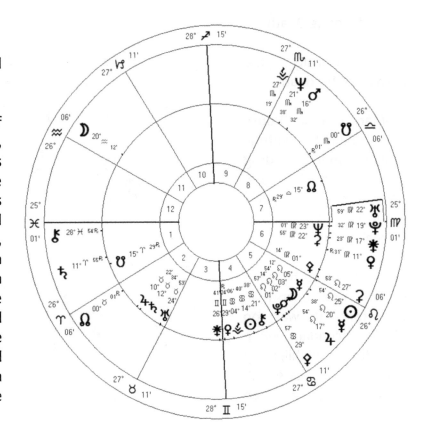

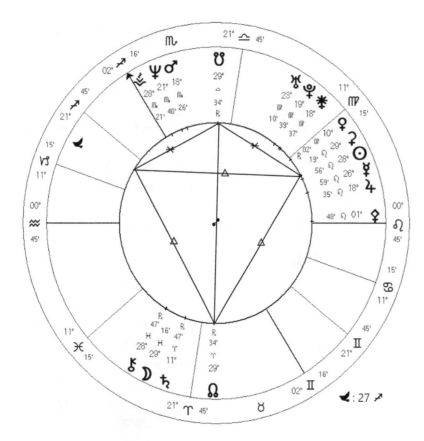

"Your Mother Should Know."

The Mercury-Sun-Ceres stellium was trine the muse, and forms a Kite with the Nodal Axis involving knowledge (3rd) and discovery (9th). The Kite's wings point to the mother and muse (Ceres trine Euterpe), while the Nodes involve partnership (Libra SNode) with a new direction (Aries NNode). The MC at 2° Sag suggests Mary (her Euterpe was at 1° Sag). The Leo planets reflect the Paul-Mary composite (see p. 349).

Confronting Death

Brian's transits the morning of his death.

1: T-Mars in his 4th House was conjunct Neptune (disillusionment, drug use), right at his core. Saturn (the "Reaper") was in Brian's 8th House, the realm of death.

2: Ceres is the perhaps the most central energy in this story. It was on Brian's Ascendant when he died, highlighting issues of self-care (1st House, Virgo). Virgo can

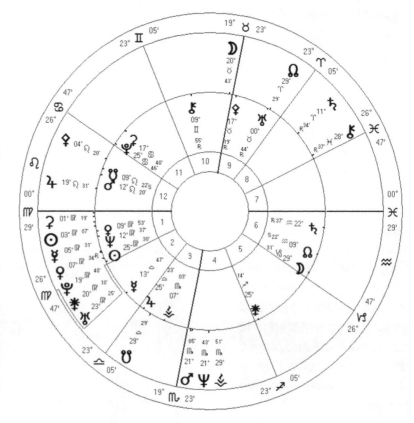

391

be harsh and self-critical. His feelings of unworthiness were connected to core nurturance themes (Ceres).

3: In the middle of the Uranus-Pluto conjunction was Juno, suggesting romantic struggles. These planets were square his natal Juno in Sagittarius, further echoing the issue. The Nodal Axis just shifted to Libra-Aries, also highlighting issues of relationship.

The Nodal Axis was about 1° from Brian's natal Uranus, indicating the sudden turn of events. It was also making a Grand Cross with his Pluto-Moon opposition, bringing his painful emotional wounds to the karmic crossroads.

Hello Walrus

Below is the release of "Hello Goodbye"/"I Am the Walrus" with the John-Paul composite chart.

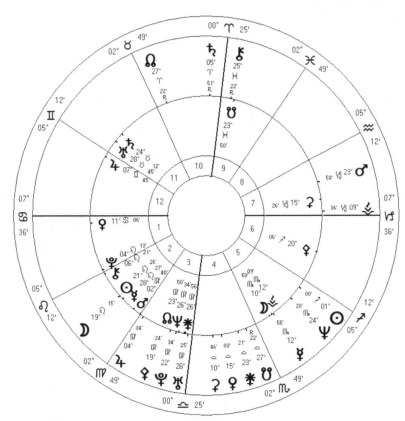

1: Bright vs. Dark: For the release of the singles, a Leo Moon (sunny) was square Mercury in Scorpio (dark). The Leo Moon was conjunct Paul's natal Moon, while the Mercury in Scorpio was conjunct John's natal Mercury!

2: Moon-Mercury can be an emotionally-charged dynamic (Moon) with ideas/writing (Mercury).

3: The Leo Moon was conjunct the John-Paul composite Mercury, spotlighting their rivalrous writing signature (Mars conjunct Mercury). Also, the singles' Mercury in Scorpio was conjunct their intense (and also rivalrous) Scorpio Moon. Jupiter in Virgo falls on their composite Mars, while Mars was in their 7th House—both pointing to amplified competitiveness.

The Muse in Flight

1: The South Node in Libra in the 8th House was at the Kite's tip, suggesting the familiar (South Node) enduring bond (Libra), connecting through death (8th House), was leading. The muse (Euterpe) at one wing was in travel-oriented Sagittarius up in the sky, not too far from the Midheaven. The Jupiter-Venus conjunction at the other wing straddles the point of partnership (Descendant).

2: The base of the Kite in Aries portrays the motion towards grounding (North Node in the 2nd House), and foreshadows (North Node) the Individuation (Aries) period to come. The evolutionary motion is towards empowerment, becoming whole in oneself.

3: As "Flying" was a John-led song, it is fitting that his muse (Julia) would be at the helm of the chart (her Euterpe at 1° Pisces, on the Ascendant). Julia's Euterpe at 1° Pisces will be strongly featured in another aerial song to come ("Across the Universe").

4: Venus (partnership) in the "Flying" chart was at 0° Virgo, conjunct John's natal Venus-Euterpe (3° and 4° Virgo) signifying his creative partnership with the muse. Additionally, the muse herself for "Flying" is in the same sign as Mary McCartney's muse, at the same degree when she died (28° Sagittarius) and (theoretically) assumed the role. Paul's Euterpe at 26° Capricorn is square the Nodal Axis of the "Flying" chart, connecting his muse attunement in as well.

The Sun Going Down

Below is the recording of "The Fool on the Hill."

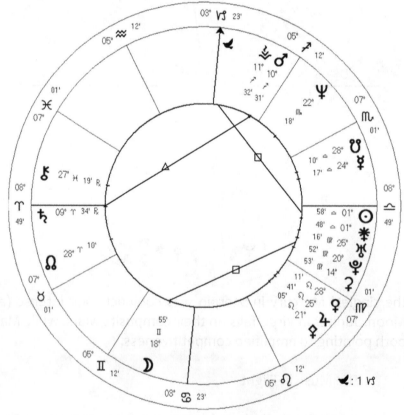

1: Euterpe was at 1° Capricorn for the song's recording, conjunct the Midheaven (the zenith in the heavens).

2: Euterpe was also square the Sun in collaborative Libra in the 6th House, bringing her inspiration into a work (6th House) partnership (Libra). Paul's natal Euterpe is in Capricorn, so he was beginning a Euterpe return. Recall that John was also beginning a Euterpe return for "Tomorrow Never Knows," another song involving a message inspired from above.

3: A Gemini Moon in the 3rd House desires learning. Mercury conjunct the South Node reflects the need to complete soul lessons regarding teaching/message. Mars (dispositor of the North Node) in the 9th House is evolutionary motion towards higher learning. The Moon at 18° Gemini was conjunct Paul's natal Mercury, which was highly activated at the time he (allegedly) made contact with the muse at the Big Gemini Eclipse (see p. 106-07).

4: The song had a Jupiter-Venus conjunction in Leo (entertainment). The square from Neptune in Scorpio deepens it in a contemplative or spiritual direction. The song's Mars at 10° Sagittarius was conjunct the band's ASC (not shown) and opposite the "Beatles signature," suggesting the higher truths discussed in the song can help mature their youthful and carefree signature.

5: Saturn's residence on the Ascendant suggests independence and maturity. The band was learning to be like the solitary wise figure in the song.

6: Mars is the dispositor of the North Node. The "Fool's" pursuits extend to philosophical and spiritual discovery (Mars in Sagittarius, 9th House), towards the heights of wisdom. Saturn was not only disposited by this Mars, it was tightly trine it—a connection between their advancing maturity (Saturn) and spiritual questing (Mars in Sagittarius in the 9th).

Album #9 – *Magical Mystery Tour*

(The album release with the Beatles chart)

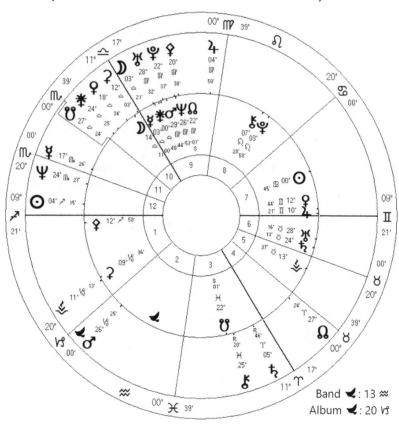

Band ☾: 13 ♒
Album ☾: 20 ♑

1: Saturn is the planet of vocational issues. For the album's release, it was square their Sun and opposite their Moon, applying major pressure. Neptune in Scorpio in their 12th House was opposite their Saturn. How does spirituality (Neptune) get packaged (Saturn)?

2: Mercury conjunct Neptune can manifest as intuition and inspiration, as well as communication issues and incoherence.

3: Saturn in Aries learns to develop professional (Saturn) self-alignment (Aries) and the willingness to be the lone wolf if necessary.

4: Jupiter in Virgo square the Sun in Sagittarius suggests a friction between spiritual direction (Sagittarius) and earthy pragmatics (Virgo).

5: The Sagittarius Sun was trine Saturn in Aries, a flowing aspect that bodes well for mainstream inclusion and endurance in the cultural milieu.

Additionally, the Libra South Node was conjunct Juno-Venus, representing their past (South Node), being musically appealing (Venus in Libra) and attractive (Juno). It also signifies the "beautiful people" mentioned on "Baby You're a Rich Man," the trappings of appearances (Libra).

The Aries North Node invites greater risk, leadership and fierceness. Mars in Capricorn disposits the North Node and is square the Nodal Axis. The work was to forge a newfound direction (Aries) and become their own authorities (Capricorn). Mars in Capricorn square Juno suggests frustration with their idealized romantic persona and a desire to assert their power (Mars).

Magical Mystery Tour Movie

Below is the movie release with the Beatles group chart.

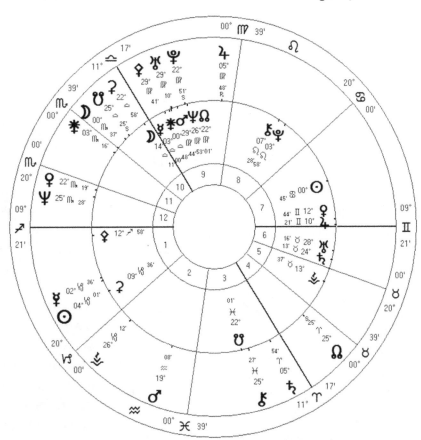

The astrology features a Grand Cross: the movie's Capricorn Sun square Saturn in Aries and Uranus-Athena in late Virgo, with the Beatles Cancer Sun.

Uranus at 29° Virgo was now moving swiftly away from Pluto (6°19') and about to change signs. When a planet reaches the end of a sign, it often goes out with a bang, bringing up related issues pertinent to the sign it's departing. Uranus can be erratic, while Virgo wants to be organized—and the movie was criticized for its erratic organization. Uranus was transiting their Mars, consistent with the jockeying for leadership and conflict. Uranus square the Beatles Sun can be unsettled.

Saturn in Aries square the Beatles Sun hammers reality home. There was pressure to mature (Saturn) and a desire for independence (Aries). The Capricorn Sun opposite their Sun adds additional tension with business and management issues.

396

Below is the recording of "Lady Madonna."

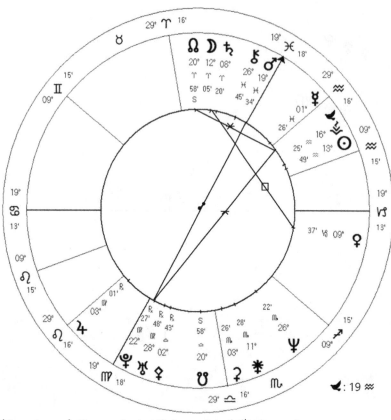

The Moon relates to underlying desires, what is seeking to mature and find greater fulfillment. Here, it resides in the 10th House and Aries, which together desire self-governance. However, such freedom is compromised (conjunct Saturn in Aries) due to tireless responsibilities to others (Moon square Venus in Capricorn in the 6th House). The South Node (karmic pattern) in Libra in the 4th House, is oriented to others (Libra) in the home (4th House). Its dispositor Venus is mired in responsibility (Capricorn) through dutiful service (6th House).

In the area of home (4th House) are the crises and challenges (Pluto) of domestic management (Virgo). Also in the 4th House is Uranus (conjunct Athena), which seeks to revolutionize (Uranus) the domestic dynamic (4th House), to birth a more empowered feminine (Athena) presence. Further development is found by independent (Aries North Node) assertion towards spiritual pursuits (the North Node dispositor Mars in Pisces).

The Aquarius Sun awakens towards the metaphysical. The Sun conjunct Vesta in Aquarius in the 8th House points to a new type of craft (Vesta), one that connects deeply with others (8th House). Euterpe is located at 19⁰ Aquarius (conjunct Sun-Vesta), suggesting the role of muse can be this innovative (Aquarius) new craft (Vesta). The "Lady Madonna" Sun at 13⁰ Aquarius is the very degree of the Beatles composite Euterpe! Therefore, the process of awakening (Sun) specifically relates to playing the role of the muse for the Beatles.

"Lady Madonna" was released as a single on March 15, 1968, coinciding with a late Virgo Full Moon, falling on Paul's "expression of grief" T-square. For the song's release, Euterpe moved from Aquarius to 7⁰ Pisces, which was right on Paul's South Node (6⁰ Pisces). The final astrological "stamp" for the song specifically featured the muse circling back to Paul crafting (6th House) a vision (Pisces) as a testament for karmic resolution (South Node).

Inner Visions #2: Julia's Poetry

A day can make a huge difference. The "Lady Madonna" Moon was in early Aries, in emotional resistance to the tiresome toll of continual service and responsibility (square 6th House Venus in Capricorn). For "Across the Universe," the spiritual work involved emotional reconnection: Moon conjunct the North Node. The Moon was at 24° Aries, the same degree as the (theoretically) muse inspired "Strawberry Fields Forever" (p. 380). Similarly, the Moon was in a Yod with Uranus-Pluto in Virgo and Neptune in Scorpio.

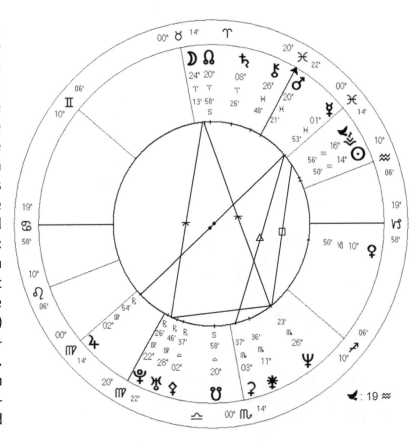

The reconnection (Moon on North Node) involved spirited new (Aries) journeys of exploration and soul healing (Yod with the outer planets). With a Cancer Ascendant, the Moon has direct expression and centrality.

Mercury in Pisces in the 9th House opposite Jupiter in Virgo in the 3rd is the journey (Jupiter) of words (Mercury) depicted in the song. The pileup of planets in the 4th House was the underlying familial karma being worked through. The Pluto-Mars opposition points to the disruptiveness of John and Julia's violent separation. Mars in Pisces is the dispositor of the North Node, pointing to spiritual travels as the way forward. The Sun conjunct Vesta and Euterpe in Aquarius portrays work (Vesta) with the muse (Euterpe).

Ceres in Scorpio involves the maternal death issue and it was right on John's corresponding placement in his chart. Not only was he having a Ceres return, (as noted before) he was experiencing a "double whammy" of t-Neptune opposite his Uranus, while t-Uranus was conjunct his Neptune. These interactions with the transpersonal planets would have no limitation to the vastness of consciousness and exploration.

398

Below is Julia's chart around "Across the Universe."

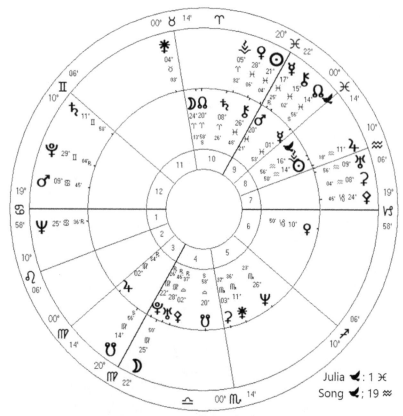

Julia ☾: 1 ♓
Song ☾: 19 ♒

In addition to Julia's Euterpe being exactly on the "Across the Universe" Mercury at 1° Pisces, her Pluto (death) in Gemini (communication) was trine to it too. Julia also had Mercury (poetry) in Pisces (metaphysical). Her Aquarian Jupiter-Uranus was conjunct the Sun-Vesta-Euterpe of the song, another connection between metaphysical understandings and work as the muse.

Julia's natal Virgo-Pisces Full Moon was on the "arc of awakening," with Chiron in Pisces involved.

There was deep spiritual healing occurring through these travels of consciousness. Her Neptune in Cancer (emotional reunion) was square the song's Nodal Axis and Aries Moon, another link to spiritual healing.

Inner Visions #3: The Light Within

Below is the release of "The Inner Light" with George's chart.

"The Inner Light" was released on a Virgo Full Moon. The song provides instruction to embody (Virgo Moon) the spiritual light (Pisces Sun). The Full Moon was conjunct George's global and spiritually-focused 11th House Neptune. The Pisces Sun was in George's 5th House, near his Venus, highlighting his spiritual creativity. Jupiter slid back to Leo in his 10th House, visiting his North Node and igniting the realization of his creative vision. The song's North Node was conjunct both Mars and Saturn in George's 6th House, reflecting the leadership (Aries) development (6th House) he was achieving.

There were Vesta-Sun contacts going in both directions. The song captured George's devotion (Vesta) to his inspired creativity (Pisces Sun). Venus and Mercury in Aquarius were on his South Node, activating unfinished metaphysical work, bringing creativity (Venus) and message (Mercury) forth in innovative (Aquarius) ways. Neptune in Scorpio was in his 1st House, signifying his spiritual leadership. It was trine his Venus, connected to his inspired music.

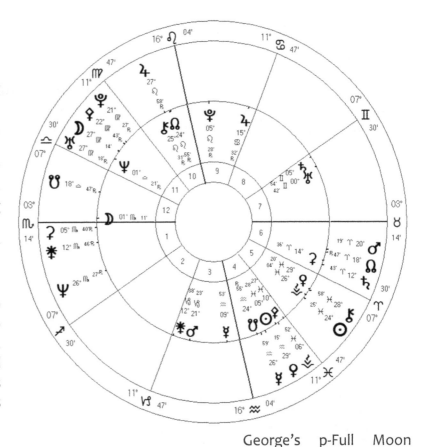

George's p-Full Moon (1/17/1968) around his natal chart.

In 1966-67, the "spiritual George" area of his chart was being accentuated (p-Sun on his Venus opposite Neptune) and George made huge strides with spiritually-oriented music. Towards the end of 1967, his path of development (p-Sun) shifted to greater leadership (Aries). Soon after, George led the band to India, put out his first solo album and continued to develop his proficiency as a writer. From this point forward, there

400

would be a new George in the Beatles, one who no longer identifies or behaves as secondary (p-Sun in Aries).

Early 1968 marked a time of realization, corresponding with his progressed Full Moon. The "youngest brother" was coming into his empowerment, and bringing it to the world (Moon in the 11th House). He personally initiated (Aries) the bridging of cultural divides to find greater unity and harmony (p-Moon in Libra, reaching his Neptune).

Chapter 18 – White Heat Part 1: Musings & Meltdown

Below is a group composite chart, cast with Yoko and the 4 Beatles.

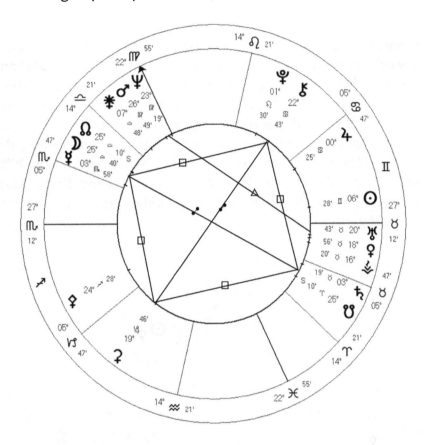

1: The Aries South Node conjunct Saturn in Taurus in the 5th House involves potential conflict (Aries) with creative direction (5th).

2: Saturn square Pluto in the 8th House adds drama and issues of power. The Scorpio Ascendant brings it forward.

3: Saturn-Pluto-Mercury T-square brought power issues to communications. The Libra North Node-Moon finds resolution through diplomacy. Ceres in Capricorn square the Nodes asks how the arrangement fits with family dynamics.

The recording of "Revolution"

The Ascendant at 0° Libra was a new beginning regarding peace, with the planet of revolution (Uranus) rising. The Nodal Axis spans peace (Libra South Node) and war (Aries North Node), hitting off John's natal chart along this axis. Saturn on the Aries North Node matures what is being fought for. Mars, the dispositor (of the Aries North Node), falls on the "Beatles signature" (with the Sun) placing an importance on message. The Cancer Moon square the Nodes positions love at the evolutionary crossroads, the necessary ingredient for peace. The Beatles message ("All You Need is Love") was shifting towards activism. Athena joined the Uranus-Pluto conjunction, adding fierce advocacy to its revolutionary scope. In the Beatles chart (not shown), she was coming to their Virgo North Node (destiny, soul intention).

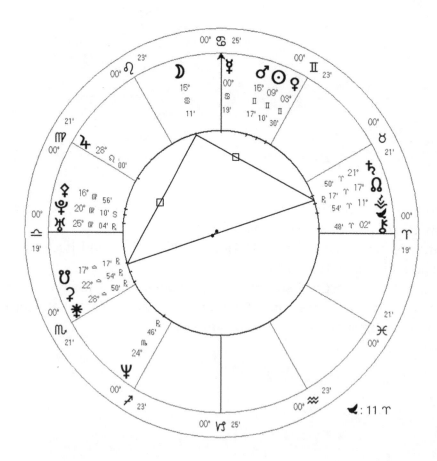

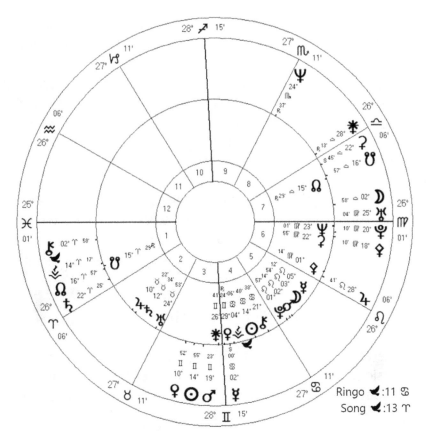

"Don't Pass Me By"
around Ringo's chart.

The Libra South Node-Ceres in Ringo's 7th points to the mother (Ceres) of a Libran ally (John). Moon-Uranus (also in the 7th) involves shock or trauma. The "Don't Pass Me By" Sun-Venus-Mars Gemini stellium was on the "Beatles signature;" the song relates strongly to the band. It falls in Ringo's 3rd House (writing), pointing to the man who authored the song.

Ringo ☽:11 ♋
Song ☽:13 ♈

Mercury retrograde relates to a song with roots in the past (Cancer).

Ringo's New Beginning

Ringo's p-Moon (on May 29, 1968, here around his chart) was in Leo, a new beginning with creative expression. He put out his first solo composition ("Don't Pass Me By") right when the cycle began. It would be the first of many songs he would write in a lengthy solo career that would ultimately land him in The Rock & Roll Hall of Fame. Up until this p-New Moon,

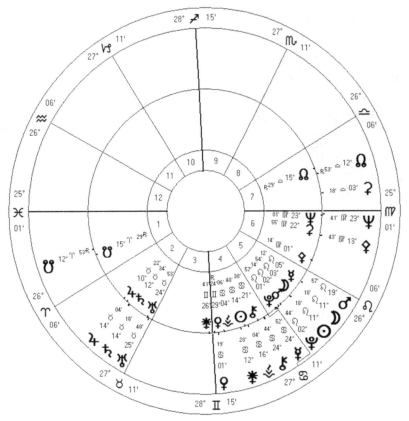

404

Ringo's progressed chart was playing out the lunar phase in which he was born. Similar to Paul, that time was for the resolution of his karmic issue of creative frustration. Now Ringo was poised to kickstart his career in a new way.

At the time of his p-New Moon, his p-Venus was at 1° Cancer. During the previous few years it was at 0° Cancer, exactly conjunct The Beatles composite Sun. His musical creativity (Venus) was identified with the band, and now it was separating (and Ringo would increasingly individuate). The p-New Moon at 11° Leo was square his Jupiter-Saturn conjunction (at 10° & 12° Taurus). Ringo was developing the confidence (Taurus planets in the 2nd House) to make it on his own. P-Mercury was at 24° Cancer, sextile his Uranus at 24° Taurus, as well as his Neptune at 23° Virgo. The developmental lesson was to infuse his writing with greater perspectives, intuition and inspiration. For his first song, he seemed to be able to channel spiritual processes in a way similar to his bandmates.

Blackbird #9

Below is the chart for the recording of "Blackbird."

"Blackbird" began with Ceres (and Juno) rising with the South Node in Libra. The Ascendant is a point of expression, but also the boundary between sky and earth. Maternal (Ceres) karmic issues (South Node) concerning the reclamation of peace (Libra) were literally rising into the light.

The ASC dispositor, Venus, was at 18° Gemini in the 8th House, the area of death. 18° Gemini is a significant degree in the "Yesterday" saga (see below). It's the degree of Paul's Mercury. Recall that he intuited the lyrics to "Yesterday" on his Mercury line in Portugal at that degree. Venus is quintile Jupiter at 29° Leo, creating the familiar combination of the "Beatles signature" in a uniquely brilliant way. The Sun at 20° Gemini was precisely square Pluto, signaling the

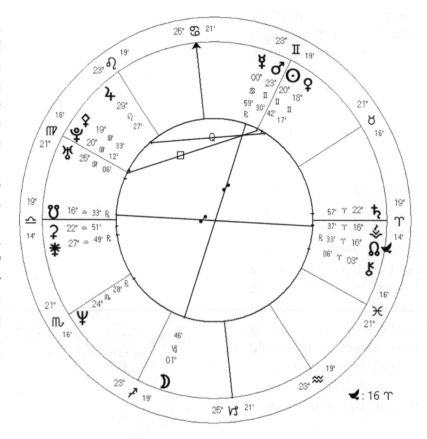

integration of light (Sun) into darkness (Pluto).

The Aries North Node-Ceres-Euterpe stellium was in the industrious 6th House—the muse (Euterpe) stepping forward (Aries) to craft (Vesta) a project (6th House). As the dispositor, Mars is found at 23° Gemini square the Uranus-Pluto conjunction. To move forward (North Node), the work was to find the courage (Mars) to awaken (Uranus) the anger in the shadow (Mars-Pluto). The Moon at 1° Capricorn connects emotionally with the past; at 28°44' southern declination, it's way down in the depths of the shadow. The Moon was opposite Mercury at 1° Cancer, connecting buried emotions to communication. Residing on the Beatles Sun (0° Cancer), the "Blackbird" Mercury gives voice to their process of emotional (Cancer) awakening (Sun).

Below is "Yesterday" situated around "Blackbird"

Miraculously, the Moon is at the same degree (1° Capricorn) for both songs, as well as being out-of-bounds in the shadowlands (south declination). The Suns are also close (less than 3° away) in Gemini, suggesting the awakening (Sun) of levity (Gemini) from the underlying shadow work. The dispositor of the "Blackbird" North Node is Mars at 23° Gemini, in the same degree as the "Yesterday" Sun. The resolution of "Blackbird" circles back to the awakening process (Sun) of the earlier song ("Yesterday").

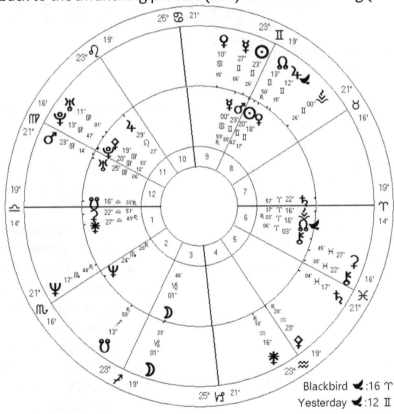

Blackbird ☾:16 ♈
Yesterday ☾:12 ♊

The Mercury-Mercury conjunction ties together these songs' message and scope. The "Blackbird" Venus at 18° Gemini falls on the North Node-Jupiter-Euterpe of "Yesterday." The communication and writing (Gemini) partnership (Venus) in "Blackbird" connects to the karmic resolution (North Node) of "Yesterday," which reflects purposeful (Jupiter) writing (Gemini) with the muse (Euterpe). All of these planets are on the "Beatles signature." Both are signature songs, emblematic of the Paul-Mary partnership.

406

"Revolution 9" with John's chart.

Ceres and the South Node opposite Euterpe-Vesta-North Node was on John's Nodal Axis—he was heavily involved with karmic resolution. Vesta-Euterpe on his South Node points to projects with the muse. Also, the "Revolution 9" Jupiter at 28⁰ Leo was conjunct John's 5th House Euterpe-Venus, an expansion and purpose to John's muse partnership. The Cancer Moon in John's 4th House evokes Julia (and this Moon was close to where it was when she died).

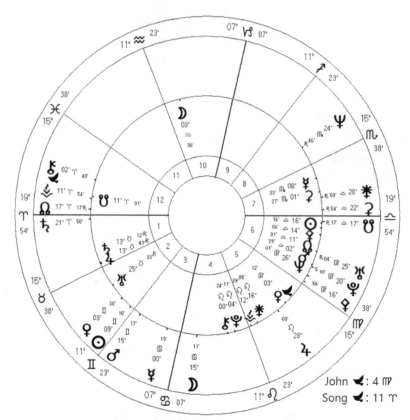

John 🕊: 4 ♍
Song 🕊: 11 ♈

Sleep Tight

The recording of "Good Night."

Euterpe at 23⁰ Aries opposite Ceres at 24⁰ Libra connects muse and mother. The opposition was in major aspect to Mercury at 23⁰ Gemini (by trine, sextile), which connects to message. The North Node in the 4th brings the focus to the home. The Moon at 8⁰ Leo was conjunct Ringo's, another indication of his deeper emotional role in the story.

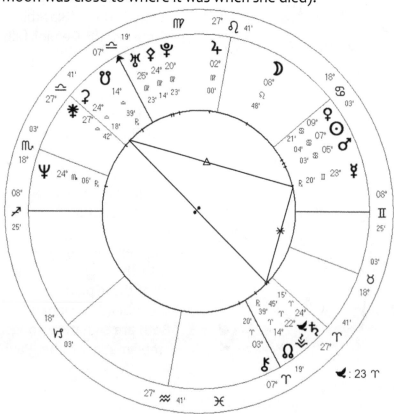

🕊: 23 ♈

Ob-La-Disaster

"Ob-la-di, Ob-la-da" with the Beatles chart.

The Sun-Mars conjunction in Cancer can be emotion-ally volatile. The inclusion of Venus directs it socially. They were opposed to the Beatles Ceres, triggering a heated process in the "family." Mercury square Uranus-Pluto correlates with the volatility of communications, while Saturn in Aries quincunx these planets adds more frustration.

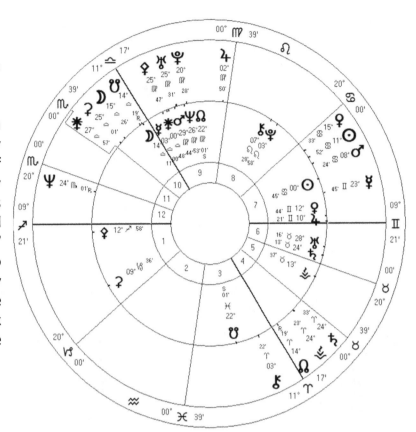

Screaming Babies

"Cry Baby Cry" with The Beatles chart.

The Moon at 15° Aries was square Mars 16° Cancer, a most emotionally volatile combination. The square was on the Nodal axis, bringing such emotion-ality to a karmic climax. The soul lesson was to consciously emote (cry, vent anger, communicate feelings, etc.), and if not, they would be prone to acting out like children (Moon) having temper tantrums (dark Aries).

Paul's transits at the start of sessions for "Helter Skelter."

Uranus, planet of new trends and innovation, is famous for unexpected and sudden shifts. At this time, it had just crossed Paul's ASC, so he was putting forth something completely new. It was exactly square his Sun, adding urgency (square) for breakthrough and liberation. Over the next time frame, Paul's Uranian passage would coincide with the break-up with Jane, his marriage to Linda, and also the break-up of The Beatles. "Helter Skelter" gives voice to the wild nature of Uranian energy—the emotionality in the song is a reflection of it transiting Paul's "expression of grief" T-square.

Chiron had moved to Aries, initiating healing (Chiron) of anger (Aries). It was conjunct Paul's Ceres in late Pisces, bringing the issue to his maternal wound. Mercury in emotional Cancer was square Chiron, giving it voice. Mars in Cancer involves the emotional expression of anger and it was square the Nodal axis (the crossroads of evolutionary growth). The Sun-Mars conjunction was still operable at 8⁰, but separating. Like the separating Uranus-Pluto conjunction, it involves release as it loosens.

Paul's Pluto-Mars conjunction is the anger in his shadow, what the muse in "Blackbird" was suggesting he attend to. For "Helter Skelter," Venus at 4⁰ Leo was on his Pluto-Mars, bringing it to creative expression.

"Hey Jude" with Paul's chart.

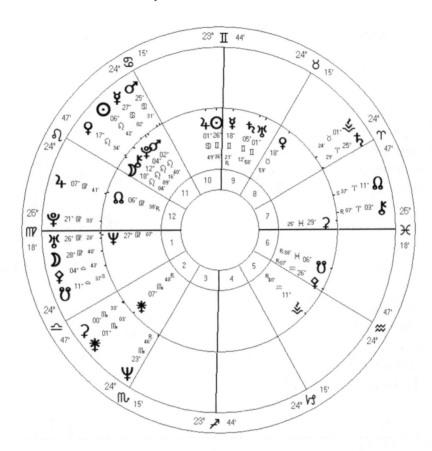

1: The "Hey Jude" Sun at 6° Leo was on Paul's "I'm in charge" (Pluto-Mars) signature. His p-Moon was also there at 3° Leo (not shown), adding increased emotionality. Venus at 17° Leo was on his Moon (18° Leo), correlating with the celebratory flavor of the song, his need for approval, and the song's great success.

2: The "Hey Jude" Moon at 28° Virgo conjunct Uranus captures the emotional changes in the song's subject matter. It also falls right on Paul's "expression of grief" T-square. His ability to be with his own emotional process (letting go of others) forms the underpinnings of the song.

Showdown at the Hoedown

Below is "Rocky Raccoon" around the Beatles chart.

1: Libra South Node involves issues of fairness and equality and was exactly on the Beatles Midheaven, their professional orientation. Athena was conjunct the Libra South Node, pointing to issues of justice. The Athena-South Node conjunction was exactly on John's Nodal Axis (not shown), which also has Athena in Libra, creating a strong reflection of his issues of selfishness vs. fairness.

2: The dispositor of the South Node was Venus in Virgo, addressing issues of production, the development of a body of work. In social contexts, Virgo can organize in ranks or hierarchies as seen in the military or with siblings, a jockeying for position. Venus was conjunct Mercury in Virgo, steering the issue towards writing and communications.

3: Venus was also conjunct Jupiter, raising issues of popularity while reflecting the "Beatles signature." The "Rocky" Venus-Jupiter was in a showdown (square, at the crossroads), with the "Beatles signature" in the composite chart. The Moon in the "Rocky" chart was in Taurus, on the band's 5th House Vesta, pointing again to underlying feelings (Moon) about crafting (Vesta) their art (Taurus).

4: The Aries North Node involves conflict management. Chiron in Aries on the Nodal Axis suggests some type of wound (Chiron) through battle (Aries), a theme of John's karma. Mars (dispositor of the North Node) was in Leo, embroiled in a romantic squabble—square Juno in Scorpio, sign of passion and betrayals. This Mars falls in the 8th House in the Beatles chart, conjunct their Pluto-Chiron conjunction, suggestive of wounds through fighting. The remedy is to bring such hurt and vulnerability to light (Leo), to come together in joy instead of pain. The healing of the Libra South Node is to renew the partnership, by working through conflict (Aries North Node). Then, the Leo Sun can awaken with a renewed vigor for performance and entertainment.

The Sun was at 22° Leo, directing us to a familiar duo. Below is "Rocky Raccoon" around the John-Paul composite chart.

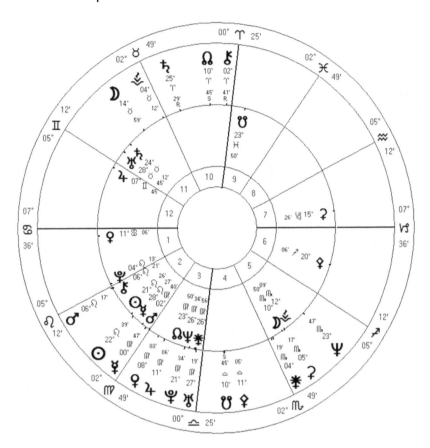

5: The "Rocky Raccoon" Sun was conjunct the John-Paul Sun, pointing to their partnership. Their Mercury-Mars conjunction (writing rivalry) had the "Rocky" Mercury *exactly* on it. The "Rocky" Jupiter-Venus falls in their 3rd House (writing again). Pluto and Uranus were also present, adding urgency to work through issues in this area. Pluto (and to a lesser extent, Uranus) was square the John-Paul Athena in Sag (fighting for justice) in the 6th House (work area). Chiron in Aries (the duel) was on the John-Paul Midheaven (broadcast to the world). The "Rocky" Mars in Leo was on the John-Paul Pluto-Chiron conjunction, suggesting additional activation of wounds from the preeminent trigger planet, Mars, which involves gunfights and other forms of competition and rivalry.

Turbulence

Ringo's transits when he temporarily quit.

The Moon was conjunct Mars in Leo, echoing Ringo's natal chart—a return of his frustrated need to perform. Not feeling validated (Leo Moon), he retreated, the fallback tendency of his Aries South Node. The Moon was balsamic, often seen with endings. Many planets were transiting his 6th House, raising questions about technical skill.

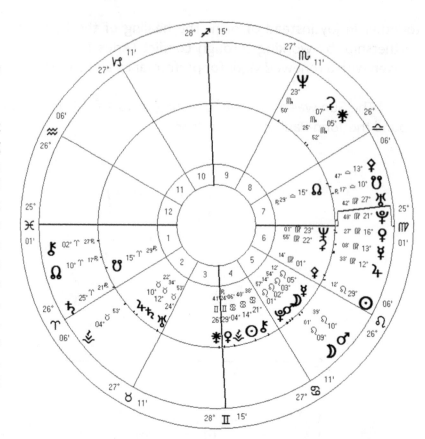

Playing in the Sun

The recording of "Dear Prudence" with the Beatles.

1: The band was at a Vesta return in the 5th House, a return to crafting songs with playfulness and spontaneity. Euterpe at 11° Taurus was conjunct Vesta, pointing to the muse ("bird" song) and the natural world (Taurus).

2: The 9th House (cross-cultural and spiritual

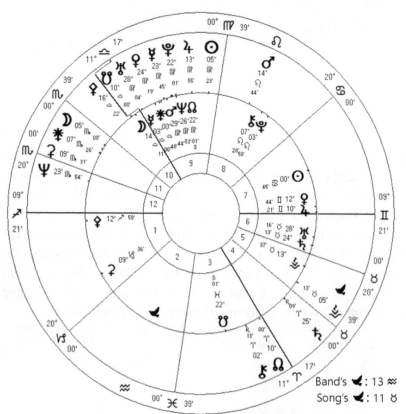

Band's 🕊: 13 ♒

Song's 🕊: 11 ♉

413

pursuits) was being heavily transited.

3: "Dear Prudence" strongly activates their Virgo North Node (grounded spirituality). The Sun, Jupiter, Pluto, Mercury, Venus and Uranus were all on it.

Jude's Revolution

The release of the singles with The Beatles chart.

The "Beatles signature" has the potential to bring people together through art and culture with optimism and inclusiveness. The release of these singles reflected that signature. Jupiter-Venus was on their composite North Node, stimulating their karmic destiny in this way. "Hey Jude" bonded millions together with its sing-a-long quality, and "Revolution" became an iconic song in the collective consciousness.

Mars in Leo could involve competitiveness with performance. It triggers Paul's Leo needs to be a celebrated performer and John's Aquarian revolutionary spirit (by opposition). The aggressive guitar riffs of "Revolution" give sound to John's activation, while the length of "Hey Jude" symbolizes Paul's need for self-expression.

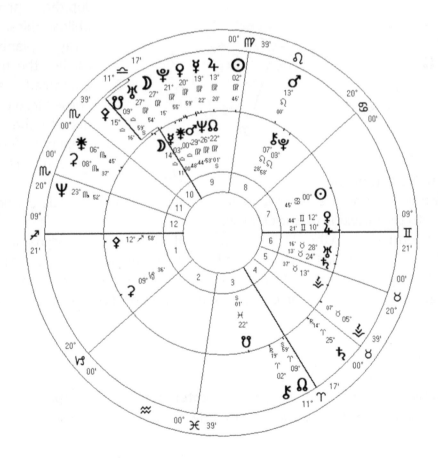

Below is the "While My Guitar Gently Weeps" session on 9/6/68.

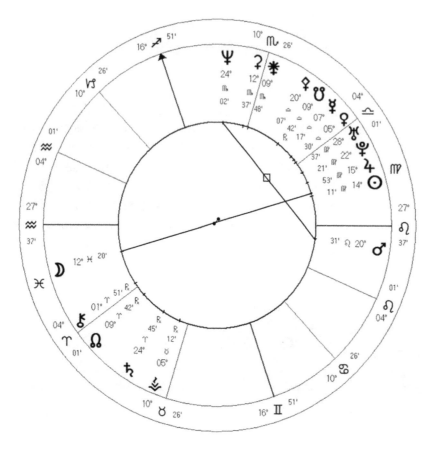

1: At a Full Moon, energy comes to a climax. For this historic session, the Moon was full in Pisces, the archetype most aligned with George and this signature song. The Moon would rise about a half hour into the session, right when they were really into it.

2: The Sun was conjunct Jupiter, providing a philosophical scope. The array of planets in Virgo further the message of embodied spirituality. These Virgo planets connect to the Full Moon, amplifying feeling. They were still traversing the Beatles North Node (not shown).

3: Uranus conjunct Venus represents a shakeup (Uranus) of personnel (Venus), correlating with the inclusion of Eric Clapton.

4: The South Node in the 8th House conveys the intense psychodynamics that were occurring. The North Node in the 2nd House ideally becomes calmer and more peaceful by managing intensity (Aries). Mars (North Node dispositor) in the 6th House in Leo suggests working together (6th House) for creative self-expression (Leo)—music as a form of therapy.

Birthday Piggies

Below is the recording of "Piggies" on September 19th. On the previous day for the "Birthday" sessions, the chart was almost exactly the same, with the Moon at 10° Leo.

Both songs show friction between Leo and Scorpio. They have Moon and Mars in Leo square a grouping of planets in Scorpio (Juno, Ceres, Neptune). Located in Leo in the 5th House, the Moon-Mars conjunction embodies creative and playful dimensions, while the 8th House Scorpio planets are the intensity.

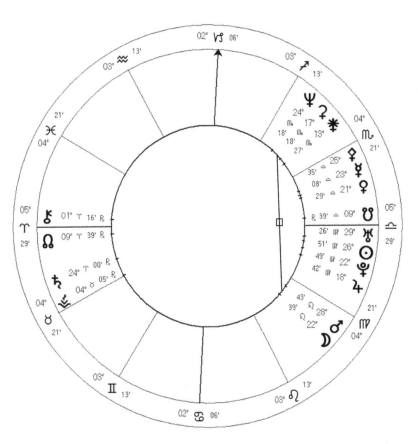

Finger on your Trigger

"Happiness is a Warm Gun" with John's chart.

The evolutionary edge in John's chart (North Node) was to learn how to cooperate (Libra) with others in work settings (6th House). For the recording session, there was a slew of planets in that area stimulating this lesson. Mars in Virgo was on John's Venus, inviting greater humility (Virgo) in creative areas (Venus in the 5th). The song's Venus was in his 7th

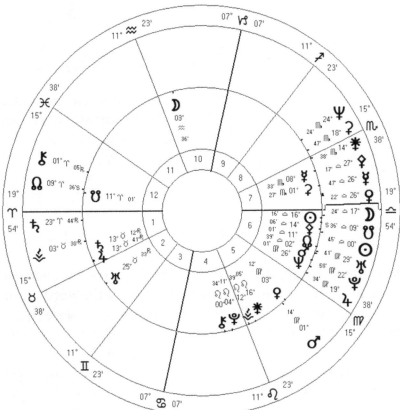

416

House, and John was relating to others in a more collaborative way. Perhaps the catharsis of "Helter Skelter" had been effective as there was now greater harmony. Jupiter had reached 19° Virgo (conjunct the band's composite North Node, (not shown), signifying a time of expansion (even celebration) of their purposeful (9th House) work.

A Song of Love

The recording of "Julia" with John's chart.

When Julia was killed on July 15, 1958, the Moon was at 10° Cancer, the same degree as when John began composing this signature song. At the age of 27, we have a reverse Nodal return—a time to examine our Nodal issues and potentially "turn them inside out," and work towards a resolution. The Moon was square the Nodes (the transiting Nodes, as well as John's natal ones).

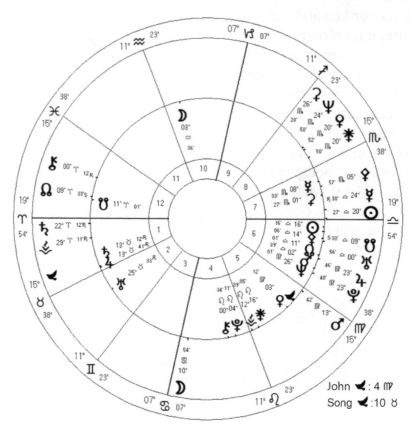

John ☽ : 4 ♍
Song ☽ : 10 ♉

It was the perfect time to put his emotion into creative expression, the central work of his chart. Furthermore, at the time of recording "Julia," the Cancer Moon was out-of-bounds at 27°22', way up in the sky. John was reaching up towards the heavens to emotionally connect with her.

George's Wonderwall

Below is George's chart with the transits for the release of *Wonderwall Music*.

When *Wonderwall Music* was released, the leadership archetype (Mars-Aries) was particularly emphasized in George's chart. In his 6th House (projects) were the North Node, Saturn and Vesta in Aries, challenging him to take initiative. Saturn and Vesta were square his natal Mars in Capricorn, providing a lesson to develop greater executive management. They were also square his 9th House Jupiter, reaching towards the foreign, exotic and philosophical. The album's Scorpio Sun was conjunct his natal 12th House Moon, picking up on his unfinished spiritual longing and bringing it forward (the Sun transiting his 1st House). Mars was in his globally-focused 11th House, along with the collective/transpersonal

417

planets Pluto, Uranus and Jupiter. The album had the Moon in visionary Pisces located in George's creative 5th House. Venus in Sagittarius bridges art between cultures, and it was out-of-bounds at 23°46' south. The album did not get much visibility or become popular. His natal Venus-Neptune opposition (spiritual artistry) was being set off by Uranus (innovation) and Chiron (development). Mercury in his 12th House (inspiration) was square his natal Mars: individuating towards claiming his voice.

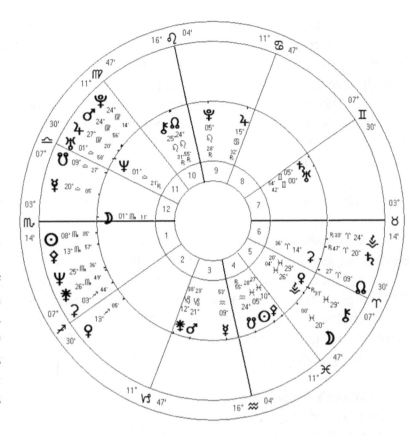

They Became Naked

Two Virgins with the John-Yoko composite chart.

1: The Midheaven (MC) is what we broadcast to the world. John and Yoko's had theirs in Libra (artistic partnership). For *Two Virgins*, Uranus (avant-garde) in Libra (art) was straddling their MC with the South Node, the point of unfinished spiritual work.

2: Venus (art, music) in Sagittarius was out-of-bounds at 25°10' south, down in the depths. It fell

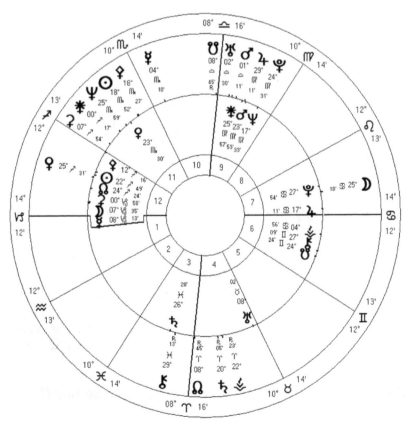

on the John-Yoko North Node-Sun conjunction, suggesting movement towards their purpose (Sagittarius Sun). The Cancer Moon was in their 7th House, highlighting their love. The *Two Virgins* Sun was in Scorpio on their 11th House Venus. Their art (Venus) would publicly reveal (11th House) their union (Scorpio).

3: The Scorpio Sun was conjunct both Neptune (consciousness) and Athena (activism), illustrating their empowered (Scorpio) visionary crusade (Neptune-Athena) into culture (11th House). Nearby in early Sagittarius was Ceres conjunct Juno, repeating the familiar Beatles motif of maternal energy connected to romantic union.

Album #10 – *The Beatles* ("The White Album")

1: The album's Sagittarius Moon in the 1st House was square the Nodal Axis of the Beatles, suggesting a crossroads in their spiritual quest.

2: The most pronounced archetype is Scorpio (Sun, Neptune, Athena, Mercury). The Scorpio planets were in the band's 12th (catharsis, release), and the album is noted for its psychological expression. "The White Album" Moon was square Pluto; shadow material emerged to clear from the emotional body. The Moon-Pluto square hits the Nodal Axis of the group chart, illustrating a major karmic process involving the death issue.

3: The album's Nodal Axis in Libra-Aries depicts the tension between collaboration and individuality. As the ruler of the North Node (karmic resolution), Mars appears in Libra (back on the South Node), synthesizing individuality with togetherness. The album is often described as having solo works under the broader Beatles banner. The Individuation period is also represented by the cluster of planets around the group's Ascendant, the point of individual expression.

4: "The White Album" Mars at 7° Libra was conjunct John's natal Mars at 2° Libra. His artistic (Libra) leadership sets the tone, and he was asserting (Mars) his partnership (Libra) with Yoko.

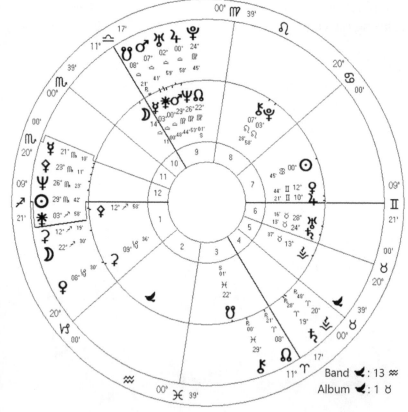

419

5: The album's Jupiter in Libra was square Venus in Capricorn, incorporating the planets that compose the "Beatles signature." Venus in Capricorn has a "classic" quality, and many songs pay homage to historical music genres. Uranus square Venus puts a unique progressive spin on it. Venus was also out-of-bounds in southern declination at 25°16', signifying a low point in their relations.

6: Mercury was in provocative and challenging Scorpio (the same as John's natal placement). It was also sextile Pluto in Virgo, amplifying the theme.

7: The album's Euterpe was at 1° Taurus, residing in the band's 5th House and sextile their Sun—representing nature themes and self-expression.

Manson & The Collective Shadow

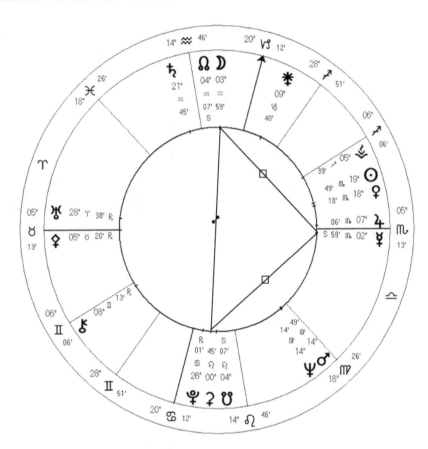

1: The Beatles Pluto (shadow) at 3° Leo (not shown) was conjunct Manson's South Node (4° Leo) and Ceres (0° Leo). Manson was sensitive to their psychology, reinforcing his core wounding. The shadow (Pluto) of Leo is narcissism, evidenced by the thought that Manson believed the band was speaking to him.

2: Manson's Ceres was conjunct Pluto and opposed to his Moon, echoing a striking similarity to John. At 3° Aquarius, Manson shared the same Moon degree as John, so he likely identified with him. Manson too had abandonment, childhood trauma and maternal issues. Manson's Sun was at 19° Scorpio conjunct his Venus at 18° Scorpio, typifying his intense and brooding demeanor. The promise would be awakening to greater

420

empowerment, the shadow is the abuse of power. He wanted to develop his musicianship (Venus), but was unsuccessful.

3: Paul's Moon is at 18⁰ Leo and Venus at 18⁰ Taurus, connecting tightly to Manson's Sun-Venus, displaying how profoundly affected Manson was by Paul's artistry (perhaps envious).

4: Manson's Mercury was at 2⁰ Scorpio, conjunct George's Moon at 1⁰ Scorpio, so the cult-leader could easily misinterpret (Mercury) George's motivations (Moon).

Recall that the Moon for "The White Album" was way out-of-bounds south, while also square Pluto. The intensity seen on the album is an expression of the overall Moon-Pluto motif in Beatles astrology, which Manson also shares. At 22⁰ Sagittarius, "The White Album" Moon was in Manson's 8ᵗʰ House, the area of psychological disturbance (at the shadow side).

Album # 11: Yellow Submarine

Below is the *Yellow Submarine* release around the Beatles group chart.

    1: The ASC for the "Yellow Submarine" song was 14° Scorpio (see p. 371), the same degree as the Moon (past) for the *Yellow Submarine* album. The Moon's residence in the Beatles 11th House shows the current dispersal of the prior work (Moon) into the collective (11th). The *Yellow Submarine* Venus in Pisces brings art (Venus) into oceanic (Pisces) themes. Venus for the song's recording in 1966 was at 24° Aries, the same degree as Vesta for this album. The creativity (Venus) of that song is now brought to this project (Vesta), while Saturn next to Vesta adds the corporate structure.

    2: The album had Mercury in Aquarius, relating to the airy and sophisticated (Aquarius) sounds (Mercury) in the orchestral arrangements. George Martin had his natal Venus in Aquarius, so he naturally had that style.

    3: *Yellow Submarine* had a Capricorn Sun square Saturn-Vesta in Aries, a focus on business. The Sun in the band's 2nd House is profit driven. Saturn-Capricorn can also rehash material from the past.

Jamming in January

Preston with the band.

1: Preston was friendly and agreeable, to which his surfeit of Libra planets (Neptune, Mars, Chiron, Jupiter, Venus, Juno) would attest.

2: Preston's Beatlesque Jupiter-Venus was in the band's 10th House (career, public life).

3: His Virgo Sun was square the "Beatles signature," while his North Node was conjunct it, making for important connections to work together.

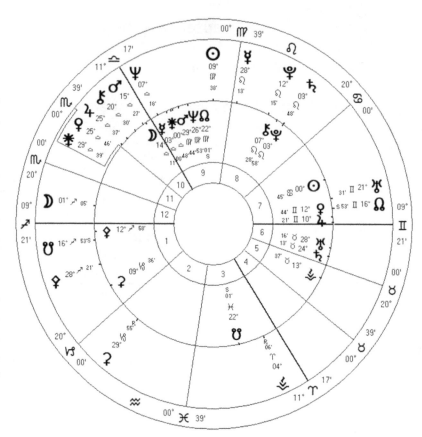

Singing on the Rooftop

1: The Moon at 6° Cancer was also conjunct the Beatles Sun (at 0° Cancer, not shown), highlighting emotionality.

2: The packed 12th House correlates with endings, particularly with Saturn. Venus, the dispositor of the ASC, was also in the 12th. It was opposite Pluto (death, transformation), further accentuating change.

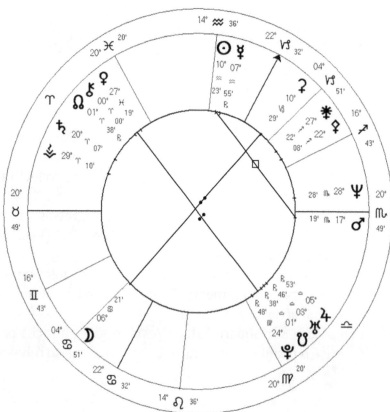

Marriages and Divorce

Paul & Linda

Paul and Linda both lost their mothers while young. Linda's mother Louise died in a plane crash on March 1, 1962 when Linda was 20 years old. Like Paul, she had significant Ceres issues with similar astrology. To the right is her chart. Like Paul, she had a Pisces South Node, indicative of karma with loss. As the dispositor, Neptune was square Ceres, pointing to maternal loss. The Ceres-Neptune square was on the Nodal Axis, signifying the centrality of this issue in her soul. Her Ceres was

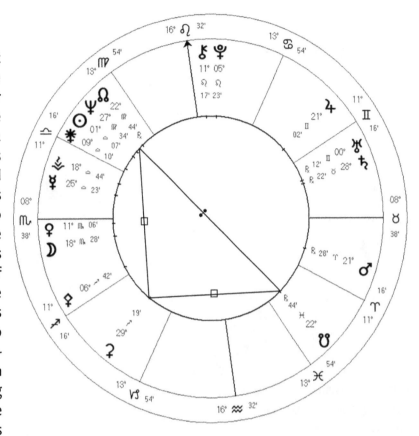

out-of-bounds (28°51' south), portraying deep internal work with this energy. She also had a Scorpio Moon which repeats the theme, indicating a necessity of working through prior emotional wounding with nurturing or familial themes.

Below is Linda's chart around Paul's. The Ceres connections between them are uncanny. Linda's Ceres at 29° Sagittarius falls in Paul's 4th House (home, familial roots). Her Ceres was exactly square Paul's at 29° Pisces. Both of them had Ceres in major aspect to Neptune (Linda had the square, and Paul the opposition), and all of these planets are in connection. Emotional resolution is found with the Moon contacts. Linda's Scorpio Moon was exactly square Paul's Leo Moon (and opposite his Venus in Taurus). As seen with the Ceres square, the opportunity was to work through underlying issues by creating a stable and loving home life.

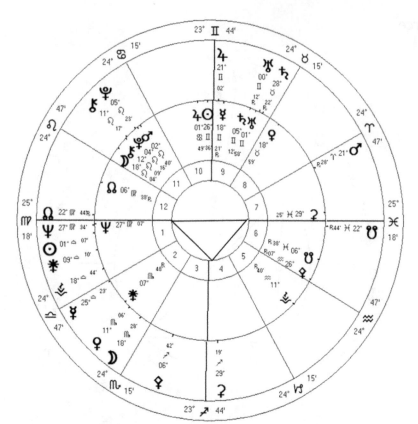

With Linda, Paul found a partner and lover with the same degree of intensity. Her Scorpio Ascendant (see above) was conjunct Paul's Juno, while her Venus (and Moon) were also in Scorpio close by. Her Juno in Libra was trine his Saturn in Gemini, boding well for a romantic (Juno) connection to last over time (Saturn). Linda had Jupiter in Gemini conjunct Paul's Sun (and Mercury), and they partnered together as a team on a mission through music and various causes.

John's transits at the start of the Amsterdam bed-in.

The Jupiter-Uranus conjunction in Libra correlates with peace activism. Jupiter in Libra is a philosophy of non-violence, while Uranus seeks revolution. The combination was transiting John's Mars and he was taking charge, becoming a leader (Mars) of the peace (Libra) movement.

Sun-Chiron conjunction was on John's Aries South Node, which was

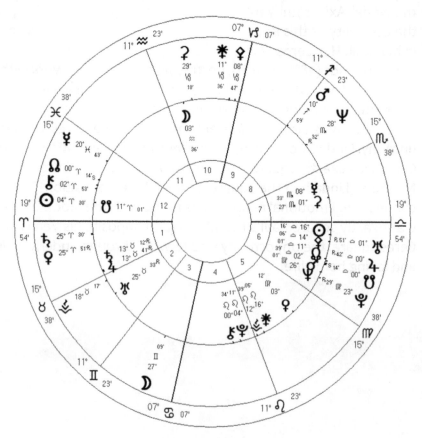

energizing (Sun) and healing (Chiron) his own prior violent (Aries) tendencies. Instead of the gruff, leather jacket persona of his youth (Aries), he had completely transformed. He wore white clothes, long hair and beard with glasses, and was inseparable from his partner. He was the embodiment of Libra, a leader (Mars) of the hippie movement (Uranus). Transiting the top of his chart (Midheaven) were Athena (advocacy) and Juno (romance) in Capricorn, broadcasting his message to the world through his activist romance.

Below is the astrology for 3/18/69 around the John-Paul composite chart. It is cast for the Solar Eclipse (when Venus was also turning retrograde). The "divorce" is abundantly clear.

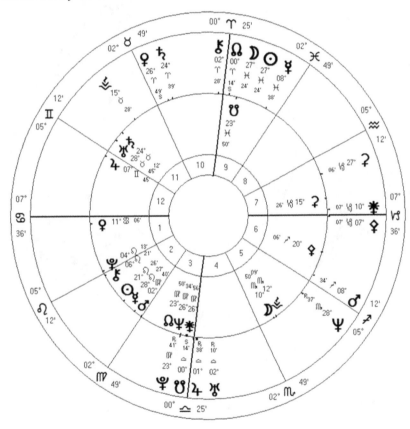

The eclipse was at 27° Pisces, less than 1° from opposing their Juno at 26° Virgo, a breakdown of their "bromance." The John-Paul Nodal Axis (23° Virgo-Pisces) was being activated by the eclipse, providing a turning point. The eclipse was opposite their Neptune at 26° Virgo too, adding the element of dissolution and grief.

Venus retrograde played a significant role. As the dispositor of the Libra South Node, it relates to prior (South Node) terms of relating (Libra), their shared past together. Turning retrograde and residing in Aries suggests a shift in the bond (Venus), to claim autonomy (Aries). Venus at 26° Aries was quincunx (stress, adjustment) their Juno at 26° Virgo, also applying pressure to their "bromance." Venus turned retrograde conjunct Saturn at 24° Aries—relations (Venus) were facing reality (Saturn).

Chapter 21 – Coming Apart and Together

The Ballad of John, Yoko & Paul

Below is the chart for the beginning of recording "The Ballad of John & Yoko." The John-Paul composite Mercury degree, 28⁰ Leo, was rising (see p. 277).

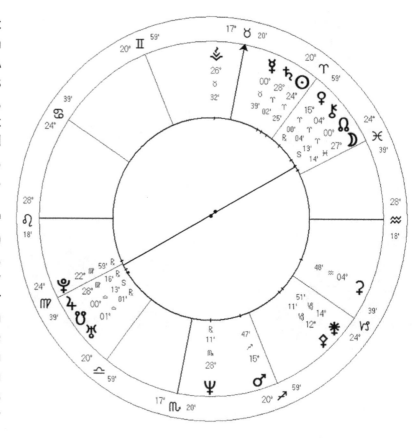

Dispositing the Ascendant was the Sun in Aries, which points to self-interests. A slew of planets in Aries (Sun, Saturn, Venus, Chiron), was conjunct John's natal ASC and South Node (see p. 264), pointing also to his desires.

The Moon was in the 8th House (deep relations) and opposite Pluto, illustrating the intensity and polarization of their passions. Moon-Pluto on the Nodal Axis brings the issue of healing pain (Moon) regarding death (Pluto) to a climax. It was one of the last times they truly collaborated.

Ringo's Summation: The Safe and Happy Garden

Below is "Octopus's Garden" with Ringo's chart.

1: Just prior to the recording of "Octopus's Garden," the North Node shifted from Aries to Pisces, archetype of the oceans. It was rising towards Ringo's Pisces Ascendant when the song was composed.

2: Ringo's Neptune conjunct Ceres yearns for more nourishing experiences. Pluto (transformation) was transiting this conjunction, and his familial life was changing.

427

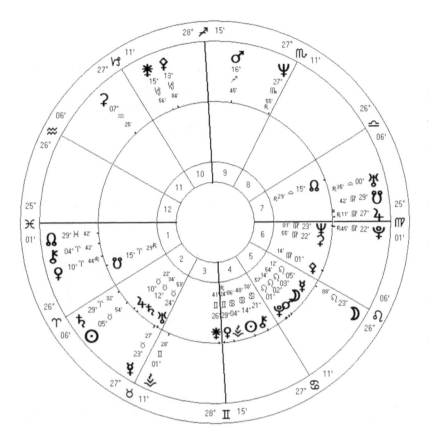

3: "Octopus's Garden" has a Leo Moon (similar to "Yellow Submarine") square Neptune in Scorpio, connecting a need for happiness (Leo Moon) with the oceanic bliss of Neptune. The song's Sun was in Taurus, conjunct Ringo's Jupiter in Taurus—his desire for increased (Jupiter) comfort and safety (Taurus).

John's Summation:
Giving Peace

The chart for the "Give Peace a Chance" event.

1: The romantic (Juno) activist (Athena) combo was on the Ascendant, along with the Moon, suggesting a desire to shape public consensus (Capricorn).

2: The peaceful Libra Midheaven was disposited by Venus in Aries, alluding to a fight for peace (matching the spirit of John's chart,

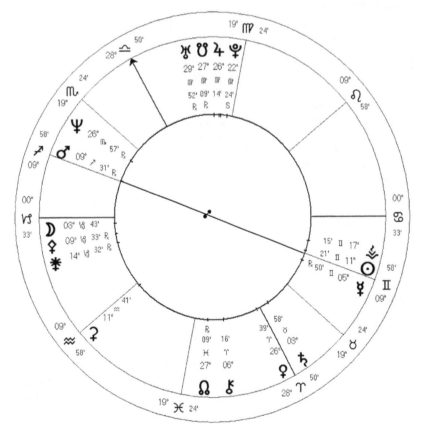

and this Venus was on his ASC).

3: The Sun at 11⁰ Gemini was on the "Beatles signature," (not shown) opposite Mars at 9⁰ Sagittarius (on their ASC). The relationship with Beatles astrology may explain why John initially felt the need to credit Paul. The song is sometimes (incorrectly) thought of as a Beatles song, possibly because it was composed before the band broke-up.

4: The "Give Peace a Chance" Mars was at 9⁰ Sagittarius, an individual assertion (Mars) of purpose (Sagittarius).

5: The North Node in Pisces involves global spiritual togetherness.

6: Chiron at 6⁰ Aries was conjunct the song's North Node, pointing to the healing of battle scars. Chiron was beginning to transit John's natal South Node. He was taking measures to heal his belligerent karma and transform it into a gift of peaceable world togetherness.

George's Summation: The Radiance of Being

Below is the recording of "Here Comes the Sun."

1: The "Here Comes the Sun" Pisces North Node involves the blossoming of spirituality. It was in the Sun-related 5ᵗʰ House. At the MC is Leo, sign of the Sun, which broadcasts to the world.

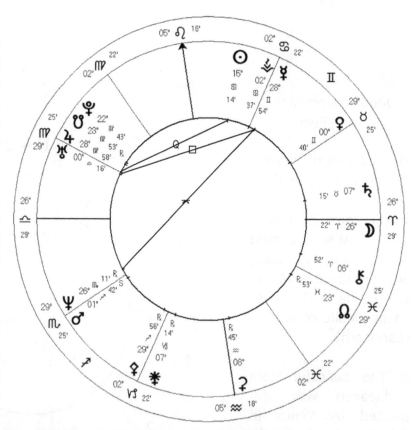

2: Pluto (darkness) was conjunct the Virgo South Node (past). A challenge of Pluto in Virgo is a negative outlook. Mercury, the dispositor, was square Uranus, coaxing it to shift or awaken. Mercury was also quincunx Neptune—the mind learning to see spiritual beauty.

3: The Cancer Sun reflected the Beatles Sun, the awakening through love. It was right on George's Jupiter in Cancer (not shown), representing his philosophical growth and message. The Sun was quintile Jupiter (as well as Uranus), suggesting a brilliant transformation of the prior contraction (Jupiter in Virgo conjunct South Node, Pluto), into a revolution (Uranus) of connection (Libra).

The Beatles Summation: The Awakening of Love

Below is the first session of "The End."

1: "The End" features flowing triangular astrology (different than the Kite configuration from 1967). The song had a triangle featuring 2 sextiles and a trine. The Leo Sun was trine Mars in Sagittarius, while both were sextile a Uranus-Jupiter conjunction in Libra. The individual's path (Mars in Sagittarius) is celebrated and expressed (Sun in Leo), linked by brilliant (Uranus) musical togetherness (Libra), uniting in joint purpose (Jupiter). The triangle harmoniously synthesizes individuality. The Sun is also opposed to Ceres in Aquarius, the sign of individuation.

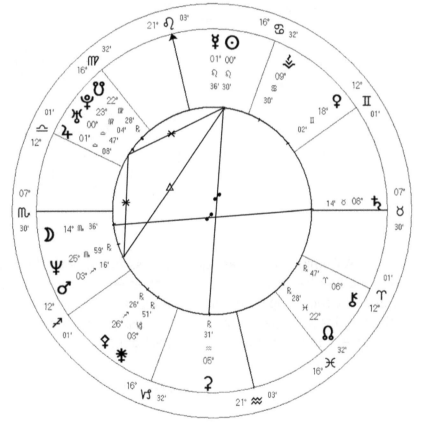

2: The North Node at 22° Pisces was on the Beatles South Node (and vice versa); the reverse Nodal return was exact. The return can be a revisitation of the underlying work, a final summation. The song's Pisces North Node resides in the Beatles 3rd House of message (not shown), suggesting a spiritual teaching (Pisces in the Beatles 3rd House). In the song's chart, 22° Pisces falls in the expressive 5th House— the message is given outlet through musical performance itself.

3: The Moon rising at 14° Scorpio reflects the John-Paul composite Moon, as well as George's natal Moon sign. Venus at 18° Gemini is on Paul's natal Mercury degree (he wrote the line and sang it). Middle Gemini is also the area of the "Beatles signature."

The Zebra walk with the band's chart.

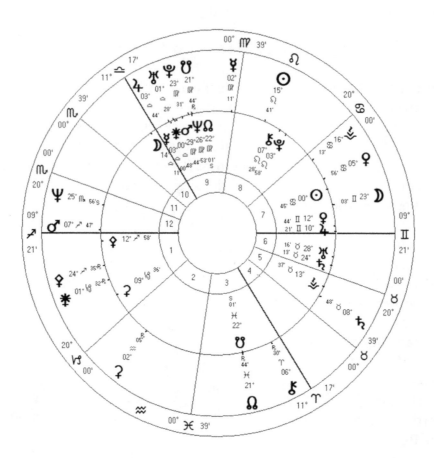

1: A Gemini Moon was square (crossroads) both the t-Nodal Axis, and the Nodal axis in the Beatles chart. The Moon involves emotional desire, while Gemini's intellectual and dualistic focus implies decision making, the fork in the road. Venus in early Cancer was on the Beatles Sun; the picture would be representative of their style and image (Venus) at this time. Venus was square Jupiter, echoing the "Beatles signature," their popularity.

Mary's (the daughter) chart around Paul's.

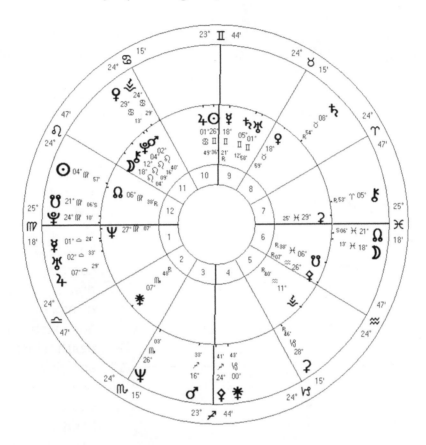

1: Paul's daughter Mary has Ceres in Capricorn, similar to his mother Mary (as well as where it's found in the Beatles composite chart). The signature weaves family with The Beatles for Paul. Mary's Ceres (28° Capricorn) is trine Paul's Neptune (27° Virgo) and sextile his Ceres (29° Pisces), while her Neptune (26° Scorpio) is trine his Ceres (29° Pisces)—a double signature of healing (Neptune) his maternal (Ceres) issues. Mary's Virgo Sun is on Paul's North Node, supporting the potential resolution of his karmic issues.

2: Mary's Athena is tightly opposed to Paul's Sun (and residing in his 4th House) and she would join his humanitarian activism.

432

Chapter 22 – The End

John's Departure

1: The solar eclipse at 18° Virgo on 9/11/1969 was on the Nodal Axis of the group chart, as well as squaring the "Beatles signature." Activation to the Nodes highlights their shared destiny and direction, while the stress (square) to the "Beatles signature" conveys the friction and crisis point they were at. The lunar eclipse (after John's announcement) at 1° Aries was square the Beatles Sun (0° Cancer), signifying the transformation towards independence.

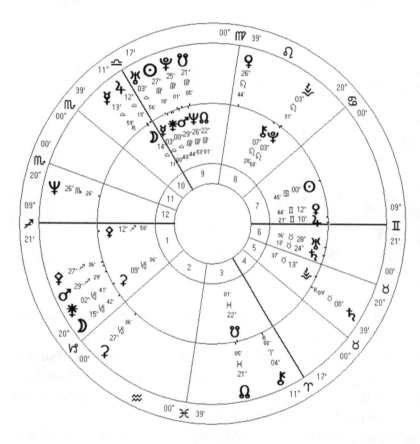

This chart is cast for the time of John's departure (with the Beatles chart).

T-Pluto was conjunct their composite Neptune, the dream (Neptune) was dying (Pluto). T-Pluto and Sun in late Virgo (conflict, death-rebirth) were applying to square the Beatles Sun. T-Pluto-Sun was also conjunct the band's Mars; the underlying conflict (Mars) had come to light (Sun). They were moving forward independently (Mars). T-Mars was at 29° Sagittarius, the end of its 7 month passage through the sign of spiritual direction. Mars was square Sun-Pluto (and opposite The Beatles Sun) adding a fierce intensity, urgently asserting the need for autonomy.

T-Uranus conjunct the band's Mercury saw the shift in songwriting collaboration (Libra). T-Jupiter on their Moon amplified feelings. John's Libra Sun was also here, so Jupiter was challenging him to claim a newfound mission or purpose. Recall when John's nuclear family came apart Jupiter was also transiting his Sun, another time of new beginnings. With his natal Saturn in Taurus, John was also in his Saturn return.

At this time, there were some key out-of-bounds planets in southern declination, the depths of the psyche: Ceres, Moon and Mars. Ceres was the most deeply buried at

433

31⁰21', while the Moon was at 27⁰52'. The mood was bleak, quite a difference compared to the heights of Beatlemania they shared just a few years previously. Mars was at 26⁰13' southern, challenging them to sink into their own individual power. Southern declination involves a descent, but what goes down eventually rises up. Their work from this point forward was to come up from the depths as men (Mars) who follow their hearts (Moon), ideally more healed from their historical nurturance and maternal (Ceres) issues.

Album #12: *Abbey Road*

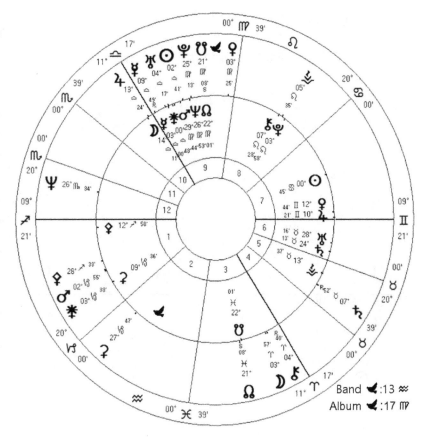

1: The Full Moon was near exact at the start of the day, still in the zone of a Lunar Appulse eclipse. Consistent with dramatic change, *Abbey Road* featured the last music they made together as a foursome. They were at the exact reverse Nodal return, correlating with a turning point in their spiritual work together.

2: The Lunar eclipse squared the Beatles Sun, highly suggestive of frictional change. The inclusion of the *Abbey Road* Mars in early Capricorn makes it a Grand Cross.

3: Not only was Mercury retrograde for this album, it was conjunct the band's Mercury. They were returning to familiar ways and sounds, including Martin's elegant production.

4: The criticism of "artificiality" is the shadow of Libra (where Mercury resides). Mercury was also conjunct Uranus, adding a hi-tech quality.

5: Venus in Virgo was trine Saturn in Taurus, a sober and industrious combination. The album lacks a Jupiter-Venus aspect. Instead, the Venus-Saturn combination concerns management of realities, including the financial strain that is referenced on the album.

6: Jupiter in Libra has a "teamwork" flavor, the coming together (Libra) in joint purpose (Jupiter). Libra also involves harmony and the album is noted for its harmonies.

434

7: The Moon in Aries desires independence. The dispositor of the Moon was Mars in Capricorn, representing a need for solo (Mars) ambition (Capricorn). Each would create a solo album shortly after *Abbey Road*. Mars was also conjunct Athena (in late Sagittarius) and Juno (in Capricorn), signifying the importance of women (Yoko, Linda) moving forward.

8: The muse was at 17° Virgo, appearing on their North Node, the point of realization. This degree is very close to the solar eclipse in earlier September. Perhaps she is ready to vanish (eclipse) and return fully back to her ethereal home.

Paul is "dead" and John's in "hell"

Below is Paul's chart with his transits when the hoax proliferated.

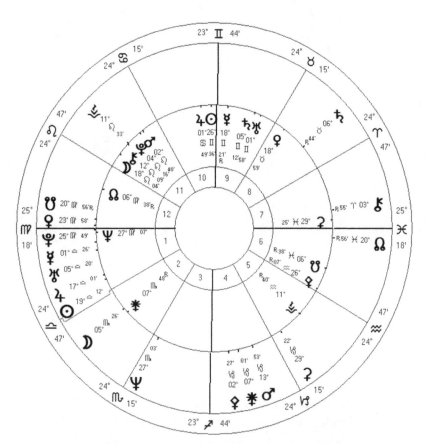

Pluto (planet of death!) was at 25° Virgo, the same degree as Paul's Ascendant and within 1° of squaring his Sun. The Moon was in Scorpio and square Paul's Pluto, highlighting death again. Recall that Neptune in Scorpio (p. 51), can correlate with conspiracy, confusion or misleading information, particularly with death.

Neptune was finishing its 14-year passage through the sign of death. Astrologers have noted that when a transiting planet is at the end of a sign, issues especially relevant to that sign tend to come to a head. The death thread is central to this story, particularly with respect to a spiritual (Neptune) understanding. The "Paul is Dead" hoax helped bring spiritualism forward into the mainstream. The fascination with finding clues in the music, album covers, playing songs backwards, etc., is consistent with many believing something supernatural was occurring, and the research of this book supports this idea. However, It is hypothesized that it was the dead mothers (not Paul) who were connecting from the other side of the veil.

Below is the release of "Let it Be" with Paul's chart.

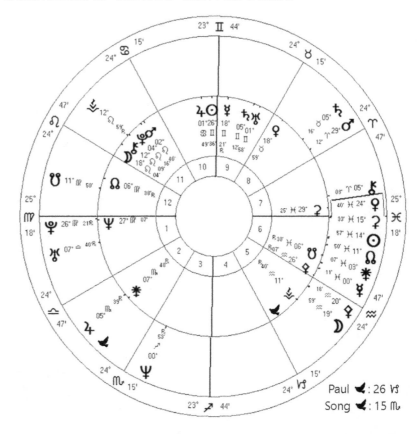

1: The "Let It Be" Pluto (transformation) was at 26° Virgo, precisely hitting Paul's expression of grief T-Square, activating his core issue. Venus was at 24° Pisces opposite Pluto, suggesting a partnership (Venus) through death (Pluto), and Venus was on Paul's Ceres, linking to his mother. Venus was leading a massive group of planets in the sign of Pisces, which included Ceres, Sun, North Node, Juno and Mercury. The Sun was conjunct Ceres in Pisces, shining light (Sun) on maternal (Ceres) healing and spirituality (Pisces). Additionally, Sun-Ceres was on the North Node, indicating movement in the direction of letting go (Pisces). This combination hits Paul's Pisces South Node, his central lesson concerning grief, and the crafting (6th House) of a vision based on its resolution.

2: Juno-Mercury on the Pisces North Node strongly reflects Mary's chart (she had North Node conjunct Juno in Gemini). The Neptune-Mercury square brings the transcendent (Neptune) into sound and words (Mercury). Neptune was square Paul's Nodal axis, triggering the healing of his central soul work. Neptune was now moving through his 3rd House, and he was writing about it.

3: The Moon was in Aquarius, John's Moon sign. He too was healing prior estrangement (Aquarius) from love (Moon). All of the Pisces energy for "Let It Be" strongly reflects Julia (see p. 305), highlighting her pileup of Pisces energy. In particular, the Sun for "Let It Be" is right on her Pisces North Node.

4: The "Let It Be" Euterpe was at 15° Scorpio, the same Euterpe degree in the John-Paul composite chart (see p. 277). The John-Paul chart had the Moon-Euterpe conjunction in the 5th House, indicating an emotional (Moon) connection with the muse (Euterpe) through death (Scorpio), which expresses creatively (5th House). "Let It Be" shows a completion (a planetary return) of that spiritual work.

The biwheel below displays the Beatles chart with Paul's press release.

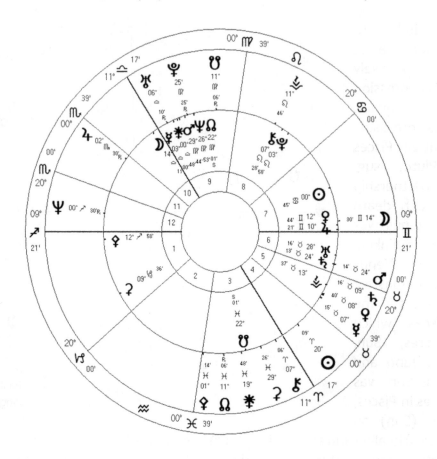

1: Similar to the zebra walk, a Gemini Moon was square the Nodal Axis, symbolic of major decision-making.

2: The Moon was on the "Beatles signature," pointing directly to their creativity and popularity. Also, Jupiter (in Scorpio) was opposite Venus (in Taurus), reflecting it. This opposition, as well as Venus conjunct Saturn, suggests the interpersonal and financial hardship that led to the break-up.

3: Additional hardship is noted with Mars transiting their Saturn, denoting a time of dealing with intractability in business realms (Saturn in Taurus).

4: Uranus was transiting their Mercury in Libra, consistent with a major change in their songwriting partnership. The Aries Sun involves independence, the movement towards solo careers.

1: Venus is a central energy in this story. They used Venusian motifs to attain popularity in the early days and were exceptional in producing music with broad appeal. At this time, Venus was returning to its position in the group chart, suggesting a completion to a cycle. Their art (Venus) had come full circle.

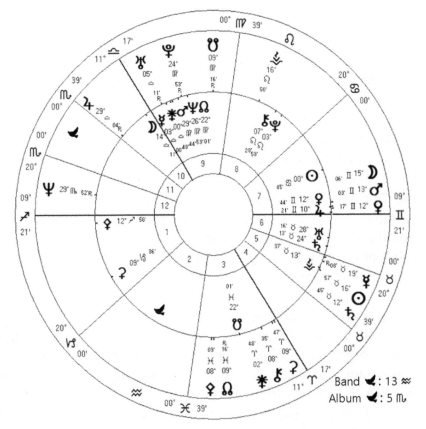

2: Mars and the Moon join Venus on the "Beatles signature," portraying the underlying emotional issues (Moon) with leadership and conflict (Mars), which were not communicated (Gemini) effectively in the album's making. The competitive rivalry (Venus conjunct Mars) was central to both their success and downfall.

3: The Moon was out-of-bounds (at 26°48' north), further echoing the challenges of communicating (Gemini) emotion. Mercury retrograde can also involve communication challenges, as well as the return ("retro") to roots. Mercury conjunct Saturn links with business interests (Saturn in Taurus).

4: Ceres in Aries opposite Uranus in Libra signifies the turbulence (Uranus) in the family (Ceres). Consistent with endings, both Neptune (in Scorpio) and Jupiter (in Libra) were at the final degrees of the signs they were transiting. Neptune in Scorpio was completing its lessons about death, including the death of the band. Jupiter retrograde in Libra was finishing the collaboration.

5: Euterpe at 5° Scorpio isn't making striking connections to either the group chart or the album. It is square the band's Pluto at 3° Leo, consistent with returning to the realm of death.

Extras

Summaries of the Threads

The 5 major and 5 minor threads are summarized in the following sections. Each summary describes how the thread took form throughout the story. The "arc of awakening" serves as the structure and backdrop for examination. A complete list of the songs in each thread is provided. First is a master graph depicting how each album registers in the 10 threads overall. Also included is a legend for the abbreviations used in the sections. There are a few issues to keep in mind before venturing in.

Yellow Submarine was not a studio album. The Beatle songs on it are leftovers from the Transcendence phase, material not previously released. With just 4 original songs (compared to 13 or 14 on most other albums), it doesn't register strongly in any thread. Additionally, "Across the Universe" was created in the Transcendence period. A most spiritually significant song, it registers in 5 threads. After being shelved for more than 2 years, it finally appeared on the *Let It Be* album. In the master graph below, the bar for *Let It Be* includes a shaded portion, signifying it's partially including this song from earlier. A similar shaded portion is also used in the *Let It Be* bars to account for "Across the Universe" in the 5 threads it's a part of. In the master graph below, imagine the 4 songs represented by the *Yellow Submarine* bar, and "Across the Universe" from *Let It Be*, in the Transcendence phase. It becomes clearer how precisely the elevation of the "arc" parallels the amplification of the threads.

The *Yellow Submarine* songs and "Across the Universe" are being noted in this way because they had official recording sessions and production in the Transcendence period. Other songs created earlier than their release, but not officially recorded, do not qualify for this notation. For example, "I'll Follow the Sun" was written about 4 years before its official release on *Beatles for Sale*, "When I'm Sixty-Four" about 6 years before *Sgt. Pepper*, and "One After 909" about 10 years before appearing on *Let It Be*. Since these songs were not recorded or produced when they were created, they enter the chronology when they were.

"The White Album" has 32 songs (including 2 singles), twice as many as the other albums. Fittingly, this double album is represented by 2 adjacent bars. Unlike *Yellow Submarine* (4 original songs), the elevation of the double bars for "The White Album" are an accurate visual depiction of its thread activation relative to the other albums.

The lyrical threads are best understood through listening to the music. In the listings below, certain songs have an asterisk* to highlight importance in the development of the theme. Some of them are focalizers of the threads, while others are particularly representative of the theme. It is suggested to listen to them in sequence to hear how the thread played out in the arc of the story.

439

Album Abbreviations

PPM = Please Please Me

WTB = With the Beatles

HDN = Hard Day's Night

BFS = Beatles for Sale

HLP = Help!

RBS = Rubber Soul

RVL = Revolver

SGT = Sgt. Pepper's Lonely Hearts Club Band

MMT = Magical Mystery Tour

WHT = The White Album

YSB = Yellow Submarine

ABR = Abbey Road

LIB = Let It Be

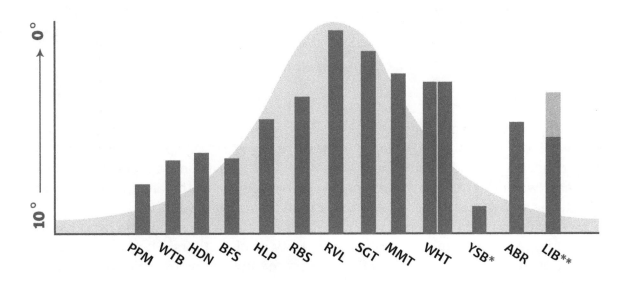

Song Threads

* YSB only has 4 original songs.

** LIB has "Across the Universe," from Transcendence period, registers in 5 threads.

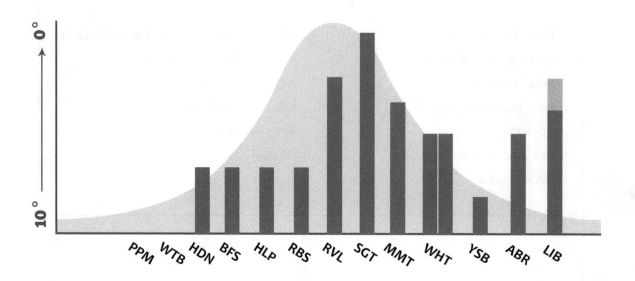

Solar Songs

There are 38 **solar** songs, with 5 containing a **solar** word in the song title. 8 (or 21%) were written in the first half (Personality phases) and 30 (or 79%) appeared in the second (Transcendence, Individuation). There were none at the beginning, a modest amount as the "arc" was rising, then a flourishing for the remainder of the albums. The pattern reflects the analogy of spiritual awakening, a seed gradually flowering.

Each **solar** song delivers a teaching about spiritual awakening. The hypothesis is that during a unique time of spiritual receptivity (with authors who were especially intuitive and with soul intentions to bring a message forward), word choices connect to a larger spiritual framework. However, some songs are more inspired than others. As a general rule, the higher the position of the "arc," the more connection to other levels of consciousness or dimensions. The first **solar** songs were developed when the "arc's" motion crossed the "line of inspiration" on the ascent. The line was crossed on the descent during the recording of "The White Album." The use of **solar** imagery in the songs created afterwards (*Abbey Road*, *Let It Be*) are hypothesized to be less inspired or not at all—perhaps how the wisdom of the journey became integrated in their personalities. Nevertheless, they provide additional ways to see and learn about the **Sun** (soulfulness, awakening, Oneness) in other contexts.

The first two **solar** songs ("And I Love Her," "Any Time at All") appear on the third album, *A Hard Day's Night*. With the juxtaposition of bright and dark terminology, both involve the initial emergence from darkness. Next came "No Reply," which concerns bringing light (awareness) to the emotions for self-awareness and potential healing. Another step is found with the first **solar** titled song, "I'll Follow the **Sun**," offering a pivotal lesson—an individual must choose to follow the light of the soul.

The "arc" elevated further for the *Help!* album, when the muse is hypothesized to be more active. Consequently, the teaching in "Tell Me What You See" is more advanced, building from "I'll Follow the **Sun**." After choosing to follow the soul, we can learn to trust life, for we are held within a broader context of spiritual experience. The final **solar** song in the personality phases is "The Word," which further informs us of this broader context—sunshine itself is the energetic nurturance of love.

The Transcendence phase featured a marked blossoming of **solar** songs, including many significant teachings. "Tomorrow Never Knows" picks up on "The Word" with instructions to directly embody and experience the sunshine of love. We might relax the mind and thereby *"float downstream"* in the **"shining"** (soul) presence. "Yellow Submarine" mimics the message, providing storybook animation to the process. We're all riding the waves together on the promise of transcendence (sailing to the **Sun**). These two songs integrate the **solar** and *dream* threads at the "arc's" peak.

"Rain" suggests the individual creates a unique experience of reality, influenced by one's quality of consciousness. "Here, There and Everywhere" teaches that love is eternal ("never dies") and could help heal heartache. "Good Day **Sunshine**" is an expression of the pure joy available when we bask in solar radiance. "When I'm Sixty-Four" involves the sustenance and usefulness of solar energy. "Good Morning, Good Morning" is a call to presence in the now, to show up fully and participate.

The Sun provides perceptual clarity. "Penny Lane" brings awareness of the past to understand prior experience. With the Sun (awareness) in her eyes, "Lucy in the Sky with Diamonds" points to the illumination of meaningful patterns in the sky. "With a Little Help from My Friends" informs us that within darkness is a creative spark of imagination. "A Day in the Life" involves synchrony, pointing to the interconnectedness (Oneness) that pervades all of life, a central solar theme. "Across the Universe" is a meditation on the interplay of Oneness with duality, how we meet the self and Spirit in a glorious game of projection and reflection. As the "arc" continued to descend, "The Fool on the Hill" brought the image of the Sun going down into the darker and denser earth realm. George's "The Inner **Light**" points to an inward connection with soul, the encouragement for an embodied spirituality.

The Individuation phase followed the process of spiritual awakening back down. "Mother Nature's Son" and "Dear Prudence" give voice to the beauty of the Sun's illumination of the mundane world. "Blackbird" brings solar presence/awareness into the depths of the psyche. "Good Night" depicts how the embodied personal consciousness (Moon) reflects soul/Spirit (Sun). "Let It Be" further grounds "heaven" to "earth." Instead of being stuck in the past and upset, there is now a forward-looking faith and optimism (**"shine** until tomorrow"). The final 2 **solar** songs, "Here Comes the **Sun**" and "**Sun** King," are both **solar**-titled songs celebrating our spiritual blossoming and the magnificence of the Sun.

Solar teachings derive from the context of solar words in the lyrics and from astrological analysis of each song's meaning. Below is a complete list of the **solar** songs and possibilities for their teachings.

1*: "And I Love Her" (*A Hard Day's Night*): "Bright are the stars that **shine**": Illumination comes from the celestial.

2: "Any Time at All" (*A Hard Day's Night*): "If the **sun** has faded away/I'll try to make it **shine**": We are able to partner (or co-create) with the Sun.

3: "No Reply" (*Beatles for Sale*): "I saw the **light**": Emotional awareness leads to healing.

4*: "I'll Follow the **Sun**" (*Beatles for Sale*): "Tomorrow may rain, so I'll follow the **sun**": Challenges are inevitable; it is the individual who must choose life.

5*: "Tell Me What You See" (*Help!*): "If you put your trust in me, I'll make **bright** your day": We awaken through trusting life.

6: "It's Only Love" (*Help!*): "Just the sight of you makes nighttime **bright**": People are a reflection of soul/Spirit.

7: "Norwegian Wood (This Bird Has Flown)" (*Rubber Soul*): "So, I lit a **fire**": Energy (fire) can be used constructively or destructively.

8*: "The Word" (*Rubber Soul*): "It's so fine, it's **sunshine**/It's the word, love": The Sun's nurturance is spiritual love.

9*: "Tomorrow Never Knows" (*Revolver*): "…surrender to the void/It is **shining**, it is **shining**": Beyond the mind is presence and being; there is freedom through transcendence.

10*: "Rain" (single): "Rain, I don't mind/**Shine**, the weather's fine": Each person creates their own experience of reality.

11*: "Yellow Submarine" (*Revolver*): "So we sailed up to the **sun**": Successful navigation of the *dream* leads to Oneness.

12*: "Good Day **Sunshine**" (*Revolver*): "When the **sun** is out/I've got something I can laugh about": Solar nourishment brings joy.

13: "Here, There and Everywhere" (*Revolver*): (**Solar** theme implied): Love is eternal.

14: "When I'm Sixty-Four" (*Sgt. Pepper*): "When your **lights** have gone/You can knit a sweater by the **fireside**": Solar energy provides sustenance for our survival.

15: "Penny Lane" (single—*Magical Mystery Tour*): "There beneath the blue suburban skies" (Implied): The Sun provides clarity of perception.

16: "Good Morning Good Morning" (*Sgt. Pepper*): (Implied): Spiritual awakening involves being present.

17: "A Day in the Life" (*Sgt. Pepper*): "…the **lights** had changed": Everything is interconnected. (This teaching relates to the broader context of the song.)

18: "Being for the Benefit of Mr. Kite!" (*Sgt. Pepper*): "Lastly through a hogshead of real **fire**!": The Sun (fire) provides animation to the grand theater of life.

19*: "Lucy in the Sky with Diamonds" (*Sgt. Pepper*): "the girl with the **sun** in her eyes": The Sun illuminates a scintillating panorama of patterned meaning.

20: "With a Little Help from My Friends" (*Sgt. Pepper*): "What do you see when you turn out the **light**?": In darkness lies a spark of creative imagination.

21*: "It's All Too Much" (*Yellow Submarine*): "The love that's **shining** all around here": Practice moderation, humility, appreciation.

22: "I Am the Walrus" (single—*Magical Mystery Tour*): "If the **sun** don't come/You get a tan from standing in the English rain": The entire world is ensouled.

23*: "Fool on the Hill" (*Magical Mystery Tour*): "The fool on the hill, sees the **sun** going down": There are levels of spiritual realization.

24*: "Across the Universe" (*Let It Be*): "Images of broken **light**, which/Dance before me like a million eyes": Spirit (Oneness) meets itself through the sacred reflection of separation.

"Limitless undying love, which/**Shines** around me like a million **suns**": Love is reflected throughout the realm of separation.

25*: "The Inner **Light**" (single): Soul is what we are.

26: "Blackbird" ("The White Album"): "Blackbird fly/Into the **light** of the dark black night": Spiritual awakening is furthered by illuminating darkness.

27*: "Good Night" ("The White Album"): "Now the **sun** turns out his light," "Now the moon begins to **shine**": The personal consciousness (Moon) reflects our soul connection to Spirit (Sun).

28: "Sexy Sadie" ("The White Album"): "Just a smile would **lighten** everything": It's our task to use our light responsibly.

29: "Mother Nature's Son" ("The White Album"): "Swaying daisies sing a lazy song beneath the **sun**": Nature reveals Spirit.

30*: "Dear Prudence" ("The White Album"): "The **sun** is up, the sky is blue/It's beautiful and so are you": We reflect the beauty of Spirit.

31*: "Julia" ("The White Album"): "Her hair of floating sky is shimmering, glimmering/In the **sun**": One's essence (soul) remains vital and present, connected to Source (Sun).

32: "Two of Us" (*Let It Be*): "Two of us wearing raincoats/Standing solo in the **sun**": Duality and Oneness coexist.

33: "I've Got a Feeling" (*Let It Be*): "Everybody had a wet *dream*/Everybody saw the **sunshine**": Our dreams form the seeds from which we blossom and awaken.

34: "Dig A Pony" (*Let It Be*): "You can **radiate** everything you are": We radiate the dream to meet self.

35*: "Let It Be" (*Let It Be*): "There is still a **light** that **shines** on me/**Shine** until tomorrow": Spiritual light is eternal.

36: "Octopus's Garden" (*Abbey Road*): "We would be **warm** below the storm": The Sun provides warmth for security, nurturance.

37*: "Here Comes the **Sun**" (*Abbey Road*): We blossom into an expression of the soul.

38*: "**Sun** King" (*Abbey Road*): The Sun's nourishing power is magnificent.

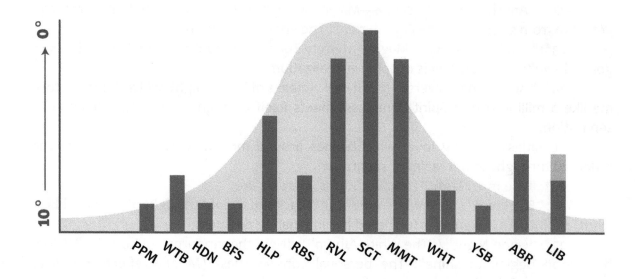

Dream Songs

The song catalog has a total of 43 *dream* songs, the most of any thread. 23 (or 53%) were written in the Transcendence period. Whereas **solar** songs gradually developed and flourished, *dream* songs follow the "arc's" trajectory. There are fewer *dream* songs at the start and finish, when the context tended to be conventional. *Dreams* were something anticipatory or what we did in sleep—a perspective from the lower position of the "arc" (down to earth). In the middle years, the context included life itself being a dream. The world is seen from another perspective (from on high).

In the Personality Expression phase, the first two *dream* songs ("There's a Place," "I'll Get You") foreshadowed the introspective direction of the thread. "All My Loving" exemplifies the anticipatory spirit of the conventional dream usage. As the motion of the "arc" crossed the "line of inspiration," "Things We Said Today" pointed to dreaming as the context for remembering a meaningful connection.

The Personality Reconciliation phase featured "I'm A Loser" and "You've Got to Hide Your Love Away," providing the first examples of people described as characters playing roles. As the "arc" neared its first peak, the hypothesized contact with the muse was made ("Tell Me What You See"). Paul wrote "Yesterday," which he famously intuited in his dreams, then "I've Just Seen a Face," which possibly remarks on the reunion ("I'll *dream* of her tonight"). John's "Nowhere Man" portrays the dream perspective, a striking illustration of our existential condition. Paul's "I'm Looking Through You" brings the perspective to a social context ("you're nowhere"), reconfiguring how we might understand others.

In the Transcendence phase, songs involving a dreaming process entered the songwriting. In "I'm Only Sleeping," John discusses his dreamtime and intuitive side, his way of witnessing the world from a removed position. Paul's "Fixing a Hole" and "Got to Get You into My Life" give voice to his wandering mind in his alone time. "Lady Madonna" mentions "lying on the bed" and listening inward to music, another suggestion of meditative time for creative processes.

It is hypothesized the John-Julia and Paul-Mary partnerships were most operable during the Transcendence phase. It featured many compelling *dream* songs, **perhaps the most visionary and multi-dimensional in this study.** The *dream* thread became increasingly philosophical and complex ("Tomorrow Never Knows," "Across the Universe"), as well as allegorical and literary ("Eleanor Rigby," "Penny Lane"). The synthesis with the **solar** thread ("Yellow Submarine," "Tomorrow Never Knows," "A Day in the Life") reveals broad perspectives of our spiritual condition, while integration with the <u>death</u> thread ("She Said She Said," "Eleanor Rigby") involves deep personal healing. "It's All Too Much" remarks on the projection of the dream onto the entire canvas of life ("show me that I'm everywhere").

Sgt. Pepper is the *dream* album. "When I'm Sixty-Four" is a journey of the imagination through time. "Within You Without You" describes life as an illusion. "Lucy in the Sky with Diamonds," perhaps the ultimate *dream* song, concerns the bridging of the dream realm with the everyday world. "Being for the Benefit of Mr. Kite!" is a dream within the dream of Sgt. Pepper, revealing how our imagination creates an experience in consciousness. "Lovely Rita" applies imagination to a real-life situation right outside Abbey Road studios.

At this point, the "arc" was descending, the dream perspective was becoming integrated back down. "Strawberry Fields Forever" and "Penny Lane" describe the past as being a "dream" or a "play." "All You Need is Love" and "Baby You're a Rich Man" also frame life as something we "play," asking listeners how we wish to navigate. "I Am the Walrus" is an exaggeration of the dream perspective, a depiction of the unlimited creativity of the mind. "Blue Jay Way" encourages greater mental clarity, a descent from the clouds to be more present on the ground.

During sessions for "The White Album," the "arc" descended below the "line of inspiration." The Individuation period further integrated the dream perspective to the everyday, returning to the more mundane context of sleep ("Good Night," "Golden Slumbers"), as well as conventional usage ("Rocky Raccoon," "You Never Give Me Your Money"). In "Revolution 9," John provides a window into the depths of his consciousness. "Let It Be" reveals Paul's reunion with the mother/muse in his dreams.

The song "Like Dreamers Do" did not appear on an album, so is not part of the official count. However, this early song is prescient as it begins with, "I saw a girl in my *dreams*." The final *dream* song, "The End," has the line, "Are you going to be in my *dreams* tonight?" These songs are like bookends to the theme. In between, connections were made with women in dreams, fittingly inspiring the dream perspective.

Whereas the **solar** thread is instructive, the *dream* thread is illustrative of our existential condition. Below is a list of the *dream* songs with a brief description of the context.

    1: "There's A Place" (*Please Please Me*): An introspective journey where *"there's no time."*

    2: "I'll Get You" (single): The imagination creates the experience of love.

    3*: "All My Loving" (*With the Beatles*): "And hope that my *dreams* will come true" is an early, conventional dream usage.

    4*: "Things We Said Today" (*A Hard Day's Night*): "Someday when we're *dreaming*" alludes to the reunion in consciousness to come.

    5*: "I'm A Loser" (*Beatles for Sale*): *"I'm not what I appear to be"* and *"Beneath this mask I am wearing a frown"* involve the playing of characters in a theater of make-believe.

    6: "You've Got to Hide Your Love Away" (*Help!*): "Gather round all you *clowns*" continues to frame others as characters in a theater.

    7: "Tell Me What You See" (*Help!*): Hypothesized message from the muse and her attempt to breakthrough into conscious awareness.

    8*: "Yesterday" (*Help!*): Paul famously discovered the song while dreaming.

    9*: "I've Just Seen a Face" (*Help!*): Mentions dreaming throughout; hypothesized to depict both audio and visual contact with the muse in dreamtime.

    10*: "Nowhere Man" (*Rubber Soul*): An illustration of existential aloneness in the dream space.

    11*: "I'm Looking Through You" (*Rubber Soul*): A perceptual shift towards the dream perspective, it references life as a "game" and applies the vision in "Nowhere Man" to a social context.

    12*: "Tomorrow Never Knows" (*Revolver*): Regards the dream journey in separation consciousness towards Oneness. It contains the lines, "listen to the *color of your dreams*" and *"float downstream"* (stream of consciousness), and another reference to life as a "game."

    13: "Got to Get You into My Life" (*Revolver*): Altered state of consciousness found in *"another kind of mind."* Paul shares his interest in exploring consciousness.

    14*: "I'm Only Sleeping," (*Revolver*): About sleep and meditative time, includes the lyric, *"float upstream."* John shares his interest in exploring consciousness.

    15*: "Eleanor Rigby" (*Revolver*): Eleanor *"lives in a dream,"* while she is *"wearing the face that she keeps in a jar by the door,"* a reference to being a character.

    16*: "Yellow Submarine" (*Revolver*): Regards the *dream* journey (water references) in separation towards Oneness (sailing to the **Sun**).

    17: "I Want to Tell You" (*Revolver*): *"The games begin to drag me down"* is another reference to life as a game as well as depicting the self in a lofty position.

    18*: "She Said She Said" (*Revolver*): Points to another dimension of consciousness, *"feel like I've never been born."* The song is hypothesized to reveal dialogue with the muse in the bardo realm.

    19*: "Strawberry Fields Forever" (single—*Magical Mystery Tour*): Mentions *"nothing is real"* and *"it's a dream."* It applies the dream perspective to childhood.

20: "When I'm Sixty-Four" (*Sgt. Pepper*): Depicts the imagination journeying through time.

21*: "Penny Lane" (single—*Magical Mystery Tour*): "…she's *in a play,*" references life as theater. The dream perspective is brought to the past to see it more clearly.

22: "Good Morning, Good Morning" (*Sgt. Pepper*): "Everyone you see is half *asleep*" is a reference to dreaming. The song echoes the existential situation in "Nowhere Man."

23*: "A Day in the Life" (*Sgt. Pepper*): Contains the lyric, "*I went into a dream.*" Additionally, "Read the book," suggests life as story.

24: "Fixing a Hole" (*Sgt. Pepper*): "And when my *mind is wandering*" further expresses Paul's journeys of consciousness.

25: "Being for the Benefit of Mr. Kite!" (*Sgt. Pepper*): Another adventure through time—theater within the theater of *Sgt. Pepper*, a dream within a dream.

26: "Lovely Rita" (*Sgt. Pepper*): The song begins with an aural depiction of imagination ("aaahhh-ah-ah-ahhhh"), which might "fly" down to create life's dramas.

27*: "Lucy in the Sky with Diamonds" (*Sgt. Pepper*): The prototypical *dream* song. The "*boat on a river*" journeys through consciousness in a dream world. "*Head in the clouds*" suggests the lofty experience of dreams. The song may be illustrating John's experience of his muse in an altered state.

28*: "Within You Without You" (*Sgt. Pepper*): Mentions a "*wall of illusion*" and "*life flows on,*" another water reference to consciousness.

29*: "It's All Too Much" (*Yellow Submarine*): "Show me that I'm everywhere" is the projection of consciousness onto all of life. A water/dream reference is found in "*floating down the stream of time.*"

30: "All You Need Is Love" (single—*Magical Mystery Tour*): "Learn how to *play the game*" references life as theater.

31: "Baby You're a Rich Man" (*Magical Mystery Tour*): "What are you going to *play?*" is another reference to people playing roles.

32*: "I Am the Walrus" (single—*Magical Mystery Tour*): Exaggeration of a dreamlike (psychedelic) landscape where pigs can fly, penguins can sing, and you can get a tan in the rain. John plays a character with intentionally ambiguous meaning.

33: "Blue Jay Way" (*Magical Mystery Tour*): Symbolic of coming out of the dream (fogginess) to be more attentive to life, it discusses those who "*lost themselves*" and George mentions "I may be *asleep.*"

34: "Lady Madonna" (single): Alludes to dreaming or meditation in, "lying on the bed/Listen to the music playing in your head."

35*: "Across the Universe" (*Let It Be*): John claims the song is a dream transmission. It discusses consciousness as having an unlimited capacity for projection.

36*: "Revolution 9" ("The White Album"): A portrayal of John's mindscape, revealing the subjective nature of consciousness.

37*: "Good Night" ("The White Album"): "*Dream sweet dreams* for me" returns to a conventional dream use.

38: "Rocky Raccoon" ("The White Album"): "His rival it seems had broken his *dreams*" also returns to a conventional dream use.

39: "I've Got a Feeling" (*Let It Be*): Mentions "wet *dream*," followed by "**sun shine**"—a metaphor for spiritual awakening.

40*: "Let It Be" (single—*Let It Be*): "I *wake up* to the sound of music"—the song describes the (hypothesized) reunion in a dream, revealing Paul's muse.

41: "You Never Give Me Your Money" (*Abbey Road*): "*One sweet dream*" is another conventional dream use.

42*: "Golden Slumbers" (*Abbey Road*): The song's topic is sleep and another conventional use.

43*: "The End" (*Abbey Road*): "Are you going to be *in my dreams* tonight?" completes the thread with a conventional use, while also harkening back to the early song "Like *Dreamers* Do."

Death Songs

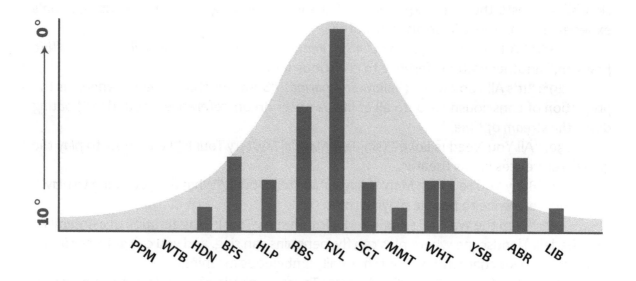

Death Songs

There are 30 death songs, generally following the pattern of the "arc." The death theme was initially absent, then minimally present in the early days. As the "arc" ascended, emotional and psychological material {Pluto} became awakened {Uranus}. The topic was addressed obliquely in "Baby's in Black," a song about managing grief. Further emotionality is heard on "No Reply," while "Run for Your Life" is filled with bitterness and resentment. "In My Life" is the first death song that discusses the issue more overtly, and perhaps, maturely. *Rubber Soul* had 5 death songs as the "arc" climbed to the peak.

Revolver (the <u>death</u> album), was released at the peak and contains 8 <u>death</u> songs. "Tomorrow Never Knows" provides an overarching philosophical context to potentially bring perspective and healing to the issue. "Eleanor Rigby" discusses a woman who dies and her funeral, the most graphic depiction of death in any Beatles song. The astrology points strongly to Mary, who had uncanny similarities to the real-life Eleanor. "She Said She Said" mentions death and sadness, another song directly confronting the issue. A possible spiritual dimension is a confrontation between John and Julia about her death. "For No One" expresses mourning, while "Here, There and Everywhere" claims that "love never <u>dies</u>," pointing to a resolution.

After the peak, <u>death</u> songs greatly diminished with the deescalating of intensity. A possible reason is the answering of the "call," which would affirm that love in fact never dies. The **solar** and *dream* threads were flourishing, with many thrilling examples from the hypothesized reunions. The death issue shifted to storytelling. "A Day in the Life" involves a vague incident with a car crash (reflecting Julia's demise), while "Good Morning, Good Morning" is also surreal, mentioning a life that could not be saved.

Death became further accepted and integrated in the Individuation phase. John worked through psychological turmoil in "Revolution 9," while Paul went into his "<u>dead</u>" of night in "Blackbird." Both wrote loving songs directly about their dead mothers ("Julia," "Let It Be"). <u>Death</u> songs make a minor comeback on *Abbey Road*, which has 3. However, they're intentionally humorous ("Maxwell's Silver Hammer") and light ("The Ballad of John & Yoko," "Oh! Darling"), possibly conveying some degree of resolution. Additionally, both "The Ballad of John & Yoko" and "Let It Be" intimate an afterlife, thus resolving the issue.

1*: "And I Love Her" (*A Hard Day's Night*): "A love like ours could never <u>die</u>."

2*: "Baby's in Black" (*Beatles for Sale*): Lacks a death word, but it's implied by a grieving woman wearing black for a man who'll "never come back."

3: "No Reply" (*Beatles for Sale*): "I nearly <u>died.</u>"

4: "Every Little Thing" (*Beatles for Sale*): "For I know love will never <u>die</u>."

5: "You've Got to Hide Your Love Away" (*Help!*): "If she's <u>gone</u> I can't go on."

6. "You're Going to Lose That Girl" (*Help!*): "You're going to find her <u>gone</u>."

7*: "Run for Your Life" (*Rubber Soul*): "I'd rather see you <u>dead</u>, little girl."

8*: "In My Life" (*Rubber Soul*): "Some are <u>dead</u> and some are living."

9: "What Goes On" (*Rubber Soul*): "... watch me <u>die.</u>"

10: "You Won't See Me" (*Rubber Soul*): "Since you've been <u>gone</u>."

11: "Girl" (*Rubber Soul*): "Will she still believe it when he's <u>dead</u>?"

12*: "Tomorrow Never Knows" (*Revolver*): "It is not <u>dying</u>," "mourn the <u>dead.</u>"

13: "Love You To" (*Revolver*): "Before I'm a <u>dead</u> old man."

14: "Rain" (single): "They might as well be <u>dead</u>."

15: "Taxman" (*Revolver*): "Now my advice for those who <u>die.</u>"

16*: "Eleanor Rigby" (*Revolver*): "Eleanor Rigby <u>died</u> in a church..."

17: "For No One" (*Revolver*): "... her love is <u>dead</u>."

18*: "Here, There and Everywhere" (*Revolver*): "love never <u>dies.</u>"

19*: "She Said She Said" (*Revolver*): "She said, 'I know what it's like to be <u>dead</u>.'"
20: "A Day in the Life" (*Sgt. Pepper*): "He blew his mind out in a car."
21: "Good Morning, Good Morning" (*Sgt. Pepper*): "Nothing to do to save his life…"
22: "Magical Mystery Tour" (*Magical Mystery Tour*): "…<u>dying</u> to take you away."
23*: "Blackbird" ("The White Album"): "Blackbird singing in the <u>dead</u> of night."
24*: "Revolution 9" ("The White Album"): "Afraid she'll <u>die</u>."
25*: "Yer Blues" ("The White Album"): "…wanna <u>die</u>/If I ain't <u>dead</u> already…"
26*: "Julia" ("The White Album"): About a dead person.
27*: "Let It Be" (*Let It Be*): About a dead person.
28: "The Ballad of John & Yoko" (single): "'Oh boy, when you're <u>dead</u>."
29: "Oh! Darling" (*Abbey Road*): "I nearly broke down and <u>died</u>."
30*: "Maxwell's Silver Hammer" (*Abbey Road*): "Made sure that she was <u>dead</u>."

"Call" (reunion) Songs

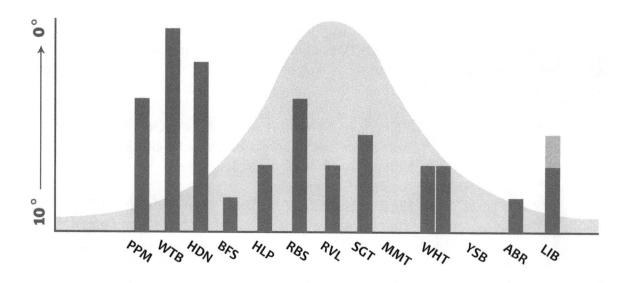

Call Songs

"Call" songs were most prevalent in the early years, when they were lonely, upset and grieving. Of the 35 "call" songs, 14 were released during the Personality Expression phase, enough for an entire album. All these songs concern reunion in some way, the bridging of distance with a beloved. The songwriters call out for the beloved by letter, verbal pleas (including requests to be called), in the imagination as well as in fictional scenes. Most express strong emotion about the issue—sadness or angst if the reunion isn't occurring ("Misery," "I Call Your Name," "No Reply"), or elation should it be possible ("From Me to You," "She Loves You," "It Won't Be Long").

As the "arc" neared the peak, the call was (hypothesized to be) answered ("Tell Me What You See"), then calls began to come in ("I've Just Seen a Face"). At the peak was "She Said She Said," which may reveal a dimension of communication between John and his muse. Calls continued to come in during the descent ("A Day in the Life," "Lucy in the Sky with Diamonds," "Across the Universe," "Don't Pass Me By"), including specific mentions of being called (or spoken to) by the dead mothers ("Julia," "Let It Be").

As seen with the <u>death</u> thread, the "call" theme also shifted towards humor. The outrageous comedy song "You Know My Name (Look Up the Number)" concerns phoning, while comedic elements are also found in "Hey Bulldog" and "Maxwell's Silver Hammer." They suggest some degree of emotional resolution was likely achieved.

1*: "P.S. I Love You" (*Please Please Me*): Letter requesting reunion.
2: "Misery" (*Please Please Me*): Request for reunion.
3: "There's A Place" (*Please Please Me*): Reunion imagined in consciousness.
4*: "From Me to You" (single): Letter to bridge distance with a beloved.
5: "She Loves You" (single): Facilitation of reunion.
6: "I'll Get You" (single): Anticipates reunion.
7: "This Boy" (single): Request for reunion.
8*: "It Won't Be Long" (*With the Beatles*): Anticipation of reunion.
9*: "All I've Got to Do" (*With the Beatles*): Calls for reunion.
10*: "All My Loving" (*With the Beatles*): Letter writing to bridge distance.
11*: "Any Time at All" (*A Hard Day's Night*): Calls for reunion.
12: "I'll Be Back" (*A Hard Day's Night*): Anticipates reunion.
13: "Things We Said Today" (*A Hard Day's Night*): About a future reunion.
14*: "I Call Your Name" (single): Calling out for the beloved.
15*: "No Reply" (*Beatles for Sale*): Calling for the beloved.
16*: "Tell Me What You See" (*Help!*): Hypothesized completion of the call.
17*: "I've Just Seen a Face" (*Help!*): "Calling" begins to come in.
18: "Michelle" (*Rubber Soul*): Bridging of distance.
19: "You Won't See Me" (*Rubber Soul*): Discusses phone communications.
20: "Wait" (*Rubber Soul*): Anticipates reunion.
21: "If I Needed Someone" (*Rubber Soul*): Mentions "call."
22: "Dr. Robert" (*Revolver*): "Ring my friend, I said you'd call..."
23*: "She Said She Said" (*Revolver*): Hypothesized communication with the muse.
24*: "A Day in the Life" (*Sgt. Pepper*): Receiving a call, leading to dream sequence.
25*: "Lucy in the Sky with Diamonds" (*Sgt. Pepper*): Lucy "calls" the singer (John).
26*: "You Know My Name (Look Up the Number)" (single): About telephoning.
27*: "Across the Universe" (*Let it Be*): John is "called" from across the universe.
28: "Hey Bulldog" (*Yellow Submarine*): Communications to allay loneliness.
29: "Don't Pass Me By" ("The White Album"): Singer receives news.
30: "Honey Pie" ("The White Album"): Bridging of distance.

31: "I'm So Tired" ("The White Album"): Mentions "call."
32*: "Julia" ("The White Album"): Julia "calls" John.
33: "One After 909" (written in the late 50s, on *Let It Be*): Anxiety about reunion.
34*: "Let It Be" (*Let It Be*): Paul/Mary reunion, he receives "words of wisdom."
35: "Maxwell's Silver Hammer" (*Abbey Road*): Mentions a phone call.

"Dark" Songs

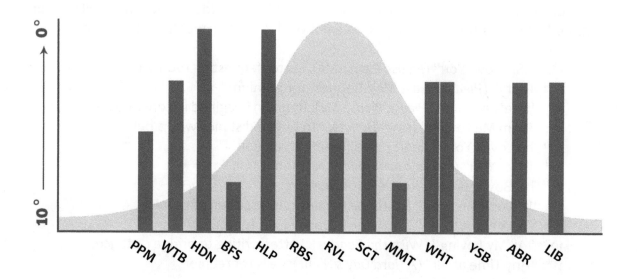

Dark Songs

There are 35 "dark" songs present throughout the 4 phases, albeit with an interesting pattern. The motion of the "arc" rises from darkness toward awakening and back down again. Consequently, there are fewer "dark" songs at the heights. The Personality Expression and Individuation phases, beginning and ending the journey, have the most "dark" songs (combining for 60%).

Darkness relates to unconsciousness, though the context and meaning of "dark" songs change. The Personality Expression songs suggest a fear of darkness, a need for reassurance ("I Saw Her Standing There," "I'll Get You," "It Won't Be Long"). George's "Don't Bother Me" is his version of darkness, an egoic defense mechanism of retreat. As the phase concluded, "And I Love Her," both a **solar** and "dark" song, shows the first inklings of awakening.

The working through of unconsciousness continued in the Personality Reconciliation phase. "Baby's in Black" connects darkness to the <u>death</u> thread, their core issue. "Tell Me What You See" and "It's Only Love" are **solar** and "dark" songs, signifying

453

further steps towards awakening. Paul brings the shadow out for examination in "Yesterday," a pouring out of longing and grief. "We Can Work It Out" states the desire for growth in the title. "Day Tripper" is an example of a "dark" song with taboo subject matter (prostitution).

Unconsciousness becomes even more transformed during the Transcendence phase. "Eleanor Rigby" and "Good Morning, Good Morning" provide perspective on existing of the darkness in the everyday world. "Lovely Rita" is a playful "dark" song, an invitation to bring soaring imagination down to life. "Lady Madonna" involves the mining of the unconscious for creativity and music. Not only is darkness nothing to fear, it can potentially be a great resource.

The Individuation Phase provided the test of living on the darker ground. Songs about healing the dark ("Blackbird," "Revolution 9," "Good Night") were followed by mature reflections on being with darkness ("The Long and Winding Road," "Let It Be"). As seen with the <u>death</u> and "call" threads, the "dark" theme also shifted. "The Ballad of John & Yoko," "Maxwell's Silver Hammer" and "Mean Mr. Mustard" are bouncy tunes with comedic elements. The thread concludes with George providing spiritual perspective. "I Me Mine" addresses the ego's attachments and emotionality, informed by the wisdom of the journey.

1*: "Please Please Me" (*Please Please Me*): "night"
2*: "I Saw Her Standing There" (*Please Please Me*): "night"
3: "I'll Get You" (single): "night"
4: "It Won't Be Long" (*With the Beatles*): "night"
5*: "Don't Bother Me" (*With the Beatles*): "night"
6*: "And I Love Her" (*A Hard Day's Night*): "dark"
7*: "I Call Your Name" (single): "night"
8*. "A Hard Day's Night" (*A Hard Day's Night*): "night"
9: "I'm Happy Just to Dance With You" (*A Hard Day's Night*): "night"
10*: "Baby's in Black" (*Beatles for Sale*): "black"
11*: "Tell Me What You See" (*Help!*): "black"
12*: "Yesterday" (*Help!*): "shadow"
13*: "The Night Before" (*Help!*): "night"
14: "It's Only Love" (*Help!*): "nighttime"
15: "We Can Work It Out" (single): "night"
16: "Day Tripper" (single): "night"
17: "Dr. Robert" (Revolver): "night"
18*: "Eleanor Rigby" (Revolver): "night"
19*: "Good Morning, Good Morning (*Sgt. Pepper*): "dark"
20: "Lovely Rita" (*Sgt. Pepper*): "dark"
21*: "Only A Northern Song" (*Yellow Submarine*): "night," "dark"
22*: "Lady Madonna" (single): "night"
23: "Hey Bulldog" (*Yellow Submarine*): "dark"
24*: "Blackbird" ("The White Album"): "night," "dark," "black"

454

25*: "Revolution 9" ("The White Album"): "night"
26*: "Good Night" ("The White Album"): "night"
27: "Cry Baby Cry" ("The White Album"): "dark"
28: "Yer Blues" ("The White Album"): "black"
29: "Back in the U.S.S.R." ("The White Album"): "night"
30*: "The Long and Winding Road" (single—*Let It Be*): "night"
31*: "Let It Be" (single—*Let It Be*): "darkness," "night"
32: "The Ballad of John & Yoko" (single): "night"
33*: "Maxwell's Silver Hammer" (*Abbey Road*): "night"
34: "Mean Mr. Mustard" (*Abbey Road*): "dark"
35*: "I Me Mine" (*Let It Be*): "night"

"Rain" Songs

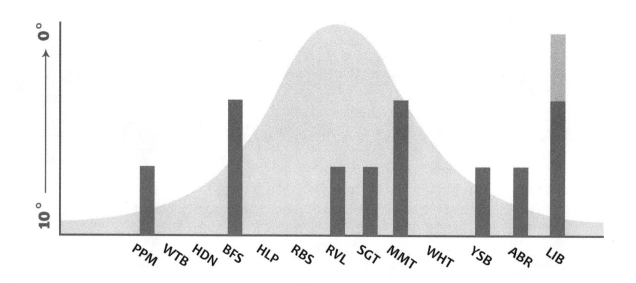

Rain Songs

There are 12 "rain" songs, that portray a fascinating development of the theme. The first 8, which run through the Personality and Transcendence phases, depict a step-by-step process of resolving sadness (rain). The Individuation phase features the final 4 "rain" songs, bringing an application of what was learned into the context of life.

In "Please Please Me" and "I'm A Loser," rain is a metaphor for expressing sadness, devoid of any resolution. "Please Please Me" petitions others for support and "I'm A Loser" wallows in self-pity. A step forward is found in "I'll Follow the **Sun**," also a **solar**

455

song. There's a hint of optimism amidst the melancholy, an intention to follow the light. Next comes "Rain," reconfiguring rain from being negative. Instead of being helpless to external circumstances, an individual determines the quality of his or her experience.

The next step is to take further responsibility for what we co-create through the projection of consciousness (or dreams). "Penny Lane" brings a refreshed perspective to the past by seeing how sadness (rain) colored the lens of perception. Another crucial step is found in "Fixing a Hole," which involves healing. An individual must get to the root of the underlying sadness and patch matters up. The next 2 rain songs provide spiritual perspective. The teaching in the multi-dimensional "I Am the Walrus" is rain (like everything else) is part of Oneness, our wholeness. In "Across the Universe," rain is further embraced as mystical nourishment, like manna from heaven for us on the ground. In just 4 years, rain is completely reconceptualized with striking insight, demonstrating a gargantuan leap of consciousness.

The remaining "rain" songs integrate the lesson. "Hey Bulldog" offers communication as a solution for upset and loneliness, "If you're lonely you can talk to me." The lack of open dialogue initially led feelings to become stuck, as seen with "always rain in my heart" in "Please Please Me." "Two of Us" is both a "rain" and **solar** song ("Two of us wearing raincoats/standing solo in the **sun**")—we can learn to be with rain (upset) while standing in our soul self. "The Long and Winding Road" returns to sadness, which is now managed with perspective, wisdom and grace. As seen with other threads, "The Ballad of John & Yoko" brings lightness to the theme, suggesting some degree of resolution.

1: "Please, Please Me" (*Please Please Me*): "rain"

2*: "I'm A Loser" (*Beatles for Sale*): "rain"

3*: "I'll Follow the Sun" (*Beatles for Sale*): "rain"

4*: "Rain" (single): "rain"

5*: "Penny Lane" (single— *Magical Mystery Tour*): "rain"

6*: "Fixing A Hole" (*Sgt. Pepper*): "rain"

7: "I Am the Walrus" (single—*Magical Mystery Tour*): "rain"

8*: "Across the Universe" (written in Transcendence, appears on *Let It Be*): "rain"

9: "Hey Bulldog" (*Yellow Submarine*): "rain"

10: "Two of Us" (*Let It Be*): "raincoats"

11*: "The Long and Winding Road" (single—*Let It Be*): "rain"

12: "The Ballad of John & Yoko" (single): "rainy"

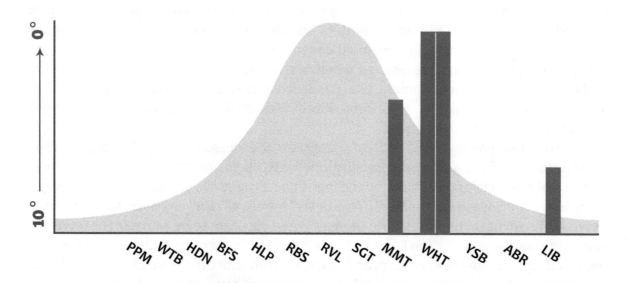

Mother Songs

There are 9 "mother" songs, all of them released in the second half. Given the emotional sensitivity of losing one's mother, it's understandable the topic wasn't addressed early on. Instead, the longing for reunion was projected onto romance. The first 2 "mother" songs were in the Transcendence period. The astrology for "Your Mother Should Know" portrays a link between knowledge, mother and muse, while "Lady Madonna" suggests Mary's transformation from mother to muse.

The remaining "mother" songs were authored in the Individuation period, with "The White Album" containing 6. True to the spirit of the phase, there's a variety of contexts. Of note are "Mother Nature's Son" and "Julia," which show healing and acceptance of the core issue of loss. Nurturing qualities are brought to a spiritual context, one that can be felt and experienced in nature. The final "mother" song, "Let It Be," dramatically concludes the thread by revealing the reunion ("mother Mary comes to me").

1*: "Your Mother Should Know" (*Magical Mystery Tour*): "mother"
2*: "Lady Madonna" (single): about motherhood
3: "Cry Baby Cry" ("The White Album"): "mother"
4*: "Mother Nature's Son" ("The White Album"): "mother"
5: "Yer Blues" ("The White Album"): "mother"

6: "Happiness is a Warm Gun" ("The White Album"): "mother"

7: "The Continuing Story of Bungalow Bill" ("The White Album"): "mom," "mommy"

8*: "Julia" ("The White Album"): John writes about his mother

9*: "Let it Be" (*Let It Be*): "mother"

"Bird" Songs

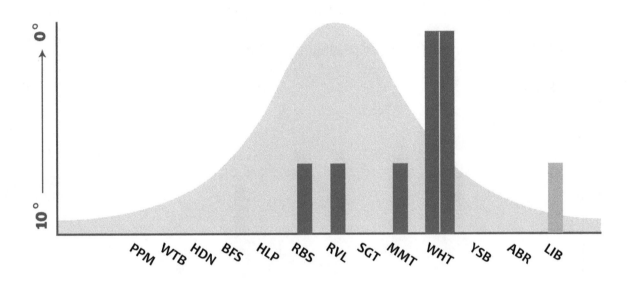

Bird Songs

Birds soar unbounded through the air like the muse traveling through consciousness. They bridge the realm above to below and are noted for their songs. There are 9 "bird" songs, emphasized in the second half of the story.

Bird symbolism enters the songwriting in 1965, at the time of the hypothesized reunions. The first two "bird" songs, "Norwegian Wood (This Bird Has Flown)" and "And Your Bird Can Sing," were penned at the "arc's" peak. "Across the Universe" was written in the Transcendence period and connects the "bird" theme to a vast reach of interstellar communication. This song is hypothesized to be the clearest example of actual words coming from the muse (Julia). One version is notable for opening with 20 seconds of bird sounds.

"The White Album" has 5 "bird" songs including "Blackbird," the preeminent song in this thread. Bird symbolism takes a darker turn (black), indicating the motion into the shadow. "Blackbird" and "Revolution 9" have elements of deep psychic transformation of underlying wounds. Both "Mother Nature's Son" and "Dear Prudence" are "bird" songs that celebrate nature and a return to simplicity.

1: "Norwegian Wood (This Bird Has Flown)" (*Rubber Soul*): "Bird" in title
2*: "And Your Bird Can Sing" (*Revolver*): "bird"
3: "Blue Jay Way" (*Magical Mystery Tour*): Blue jay is a type of bird
4*: "Across the Universe" (appears later on *Let It Be*): a version (heard on Past Masters) opens with bird sounds
5*: "Blackbird" ("The White Album"): "blackbird"
6*: "Revolution 9" ("The White Album"): "wings"
7: "Cry Baby Cry" ("The White Album"): "bird"
8: "Mother Nature's Son" ("The White Album"): "Listen to the pretty sound of music as she flies" alludes to birds
9*: "Dear Prudence" ("The White Album"): "birds"

"Flute" songs

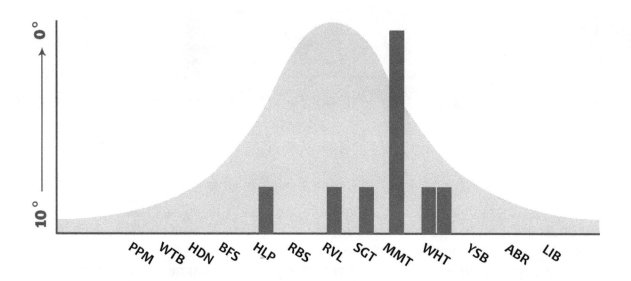

Flute Songs

The flute is the instrument of Euterpe, the muse. There are 10 "flute" songs, also dominant in the second half. The first one, "You've Got to Hide Your Love Away," was composed when the "arc" was climbing to the first peak. It was recorded the same day as "Tell Me What You See," the song hypothesized to suggest connection with the muse.

7 of the 10 "flute" songs appear in the Transcendence phase. "Tomorrow Never Knows," "Strawberry Fields Forever," "Penny Lane," "A Day in the Life" and "Fool on the Hill" are hypothesized to be major collaborations of the John-Julia and Paul-Mary partnerships. "Flying" is like a celebration of the muse with its flutelike atmospherics, aerial subject matter and overwhelming astrology pointing to her presence.

The Individuation phase included "Good Night," which describes a return to peaceful rest and a conclusion to the muse relationships. The final "flute" song is "Hey Jude." As the "arc" was returning to the ground, Paul was embodying the inspiration of the muse himself, within the context of a real-life situation.

1*: "You've Got to Hide Your Love Away" (*Help!*): flute

2: "Tomorrow Never Knows" (*Revolver*): Tape loop created from the sound of a mellotron on the flute setting

3*: "Strawberry Fields Forever" (single—*Magical Mystery Tour*): Mellotron creating flute sound

4*: "Penny Lane" (single— *Magical Mystery Tour*): flutes, piccolo

5: "A Day in the Life" (*Sgt. Pepper*): flute (in orchestra)

6*: "Flying" (*Magical Mystery Tour*): Mellotron creating flute sound

7*: "Fool on the Hill" (*Magical Mystery Tour*): flutes, recorder, penny whistle

8: "The Inner Light" (single): bansuri (bamboo flute)

9*: "Good Night" ("The White Album"): flute (in orchestra)

10: "Hey Jude" (single): flute (in orchestra)

"Violence" songs

"Violence" songs also proliferate in the second half of the story. The first 2 (of 13) appear on *Rubber Soul* at the "arc's" first peak. Consistent with awakening {Uranus} the shadow {Pluto}, "Run for Your Life" gives voice to John's violent tendencies. "Norwegian Wood" also expresses entitlement and underlying aggression. The Transcendence period also has 2 "violence" songs. "A Day in the Life" features a car crash and the astrology has echoes of Julia and her accident. "Getting Better" addresses the violence heard in "Run for Your Life," now with responsibility and sincerity to heal the issue.

7 "violence" songs appear on "The White Album," perhaps the record with the most psychological realism. The songs transmute aggression into creative catharses, the high promise of this soul group. "Don't Pass Me By" returns to the car crash theme, giving voice to the emotions involved. "Revolution 9" is a deep dive into John's psyche to work the roots of his violent tendencies. His personal revolution with the issue empowers collective revolution. "Helter Skelter" is Paul's loudest and most powerful emotional catharsis, perhaps leading "therapy" for the group. The astrology for "Rocky Raccoon" points to the rivalrous dynamic of the John-Paul partnership. Once again, song is a creative outlet to express underlying feelings.

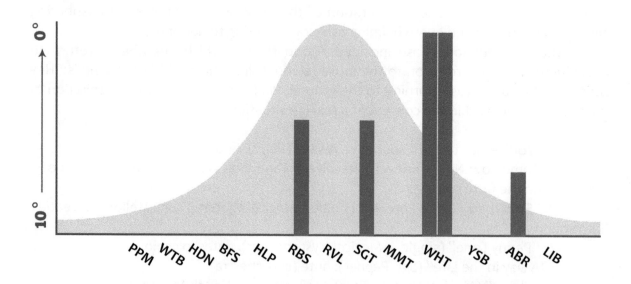

Violence Songs

John continued to write songs expressing different facets of his violent tendencies. "Yer Blues" mentions suicide, aggression towards the self. "Happiness is a Warm Gun" concerns the transmutation of aggression into sexual expression, part of his personal work with Yoko. "The Continuing Story of Bungalow Bill" concerns hunting, domination through force. John was denunciating such behavior, right when he was beginning his peace activism. George's "Piggies" expresses his aggression towards those who abuse power, a major issue of his soul work. The thread concludes with "Maxwell's Silver Hammer," another example of healing and transformation of the underlying issue through a humorous context.

1*: "Run for Your Life" (*Rubber Soul*): threat of violence
2: "Norwegian Wood" (*Rubber Soul*): insinuating arson
3: "A Day in the Life" (*Sgt. Pepper*): car crash, war reference
4*: "Getting Better" (*Sgt. Pepper*): domestic violence
5*: "Don't Pass Me By" ("The White Album"): car crash
6*: "Revolution 9" ("The White Album"): violent noise
7*: "Helter Skelter" ("The White Album"): "break you"
8*: "Rocky Raccoon" ("The White Album"): a shoot out
9: "Yer Blues" ("The White Album"): suicide
10: "Piggies" ("The White Album"): "damn good whacking"
11*: "Happiness is a Warm Gun" ("The White Album"): shooting guns

461

12*: "The Continuing Story of Bungalow Bill" ("The White Album"): hunting, killing
13*: "Maxwell's Silver Hammer" (*Abbey Road*): murder spree

Major Integrative Songs

Below is a chronological list of songs that integrate 2 or more of the lyrical threads. Some songs that register in 1 thread focalize the theme (for instance "The Word" (**solar**) and "Nowhere Man" (*dream*)). In contrast, each of these songs bridge themes in a unique way. All of them could be considered spiritually-significant songs in this study.

2: "Please Please Me" (dark, rain): Unresolved sadness (rain) resides within the unconsciousness (dark), with request for external support.

3: "I'll Get You" (*dream*, call, dark): The imagination (*dream*) is used to bridge estrangement (call) and alleviate loneliness (dark).

2: "There's a Place" (*dream*, call): The imagination (*dream*) is used to experience reunion with the beloved (call).

2: "It Won't Be Long" (call, dark): The anticipation of reunion to alleviate loneliness (dark).

2: "All My Loving" (*dream*, call): Paul *dreams* of a reunion with his beloved.

--------------------------------Line of inspiration--------------------------------

2: "And I Love Her" (**solar**, dark): The "**bright**" stars in the sky illuminate darkness. Paul becomes engaged in a broader mystery.

2: "Anytime at All" (**solar**, call): John requests to be called and pledges to make the Sun "**shine.**" He is becoming more engaged in his spiritual blossoming.

2: "Things We Said Today" (*dream*, call): *Dreaming* is the setting to follow up a prior pledge for reunion.

2: "I Call Your Name" (call, dark): John repeatedly calls out for his beloved from the well of his emotional pain (dark).

3: "No Reply" (**solar**, death, call): John becomes more aware (**solar**) of his feelings by his call remaining unanswered. The intensity of his reaction ("I nearly died") likely has roots in his unresolved death issue.

2: "I'll Follow the **Sun**" (**solar**, rain): The willingness to follow the soul (**solar**) as a means to ultimately heal sadness (rain).

2: "Baby's in Black" (death, dark): John and Paul address their death issue, which was emerging from their unconscious (dark).

3: "You've Got to Hide Your Love Away" (*dream*, death, flute): In working with his death issue ("If she's gone I can't go on"), John begins to see the world as theater (*dream*) in the first flute song (associated with the muse).

4: "Tell Me What You See" (**solar**, *dream*, call, dark) Through the completion of the "call" in a *dream* state, a **solar** perspective (trusting life) arrives to illuminate darkness.

2: "Yesterday" (*dream*, dark): In his dreamtime, Paul discovers a song in his unconsciousness (dark) that assists in reconciling his past.

2: "I've Just Seen a Face" (*dream*, call): Paul is repeatedly called and mentions his *dreams* as the setting for connecting with his beloved.

2: "Run for Your Life" (<u>death</u>, violence): John reveals his belligerent tendencies, which likely has roots in his <u>death</u> issue.

3: "Norwegian Wood (This Bird Has Flown)" (**solar**, violence, bird): This violence song is lighthearted, illustrating greater awareness (**solar**) about the issue. As the first bird song, perhaps the muse assists with an inspired perspective.

4: "Tomorrow Never Knows" (**solar**, *dream*, <u>death</u>, flute): The 3 most significant threads are synthesized at the "arc's" peak. John instructs relaxation into a **"shining"** presence, lighting the direction of *dreaming*. Upon loosening attachment to the mind, "it is not <u>dying</u>," we can trust the eternal flow of consciousness from life to life. As the second flute song, this vision is hypothesized to be inspired by the muse.

3: "Rain" (**solar**, <u>death</u>, rain): One determines the quality of life's experience regardless if it's rain or "shine." We can transcend negativity and fear ("might as well be <u>dead</u>") by attuning within.

3: "Eleanor Rigby" (*dream*, <u>death</u>, dark): A journey into the darkness of Paul's <u>death</u> issue (a woman's funeral, with parallels to Mary). Eleanor depicts the existential crisis of being lost and alone in the *dream*.

2: "Yellow Submarine" (**solar**, *dream*): Depicts the *dream* journey towards the **Sun** (soul realization).

2: "Here, There and Everywhere" (**solar**, <u>death</u>): The transcendence of <u>death</u> ("love never <u>dies</u>") through the eternality (**solar**) of love.

3: "She Said She Said" (*dream*, <u>death</u>, call): Hypothesized communication (call) between John and Julia (in an *altered state*, possibly the bardo) about her <u>death</u>.

2: "Strawberry Fields Forever" (*dream*, flute): Muse inspired vision (flute) applied to John's childhood. He's healing the suffering created by previously misunderstanding the *dream*.

4: "Penny Lane" (**solar**, *dream*, rain, flute): Through the healing and inspiring presence of the muse (flute), she assists in reconciling the sadness (rain) from the past by bringing radiant clarity (**solar**) to the *dream*.

4: "Good Morning, Good Morning" (**solar**, *dream*, <u>death</u>, dark): A man is <u>dying</u> in a world of darkness where people are "half *asleep*." The song is a rousing invitation to bring presence (**solar**) to life.

6: "A Day in the Life" (**solar**, *dream*, <u>death</u>, call, violence, flute): The only song connected to both muse/musician partnerships (flute). It portrays a violent car crash scenario involving <u>death</u> (recalling Julia), a reference to war and the receptivity to the call to enter a *dream* state. The **solar** teaching involves synchronistic interconnectedness.

2: "Being for the Benefit of Mr. Kite!" (**solar**, *dream*): The vivid animation (**solar**) of the *theatrical nature of life*.

2: "Lovely Rita" (*dream*, dark): The imagination (*dream*) can stimulate playfulness and story to animate our world of darkness.

3: "Lucy in the Sky with Diamonds" (**solar**, *dream*, call): John is called into a fantastic *dream* journey that reveals the patterned meaning of the sky from the girl with the **Sun** in her eyes.

2: "It's All Too Much" (**solar**, *dream*): Mentions the projection of the *dream* ("show me that I'm everywhere") onto all of life. We might connect with the love that's "**shining** all around," thereby synthesizing these two major threads.

3: "I Am the Walrus" (**solar**, *dream*, rain): Integration of the **solar** and rain threads in a psychedelic/symbolic (*dream*) way. The world is ensouled (**solar**)—everything (including rain) is part of energetic Oneness.

2: "Fool on the Hill" (**solar**, flute): Depiction of a wise figure above who sees the diminishment of spiritual awareness (**Sun**) on the ground in everyday life. The Fool may be allegorical of the muse (flute) herself.

3: "Lady Madonna" (*dream*, dark, mother): Portrayal of Mary's transformation into the muse, from domestic toil to discovering music in her consciousness (*dream*, dark).

5: "Across the Universe" (**solar**, *dream*, call, rain, bird): By connecting through consciousness (*dream*) from far away, John is contacted by his muse (call, bird) who delivers poetic teachings on our spiritual interconnectedness (**solar**) and mystical nourishment (rain) to refresh his heart.

2: "Don't Pass Me By" (call, violence): Hypothesized portrayal of Julia's car crash (violence). The singer receiving news (call) that the beloved is all right may symbolize a similar message from Julia for John.

4: "Blackbird" (**solar**, <u>death</u>, dark, bird): The muse (bird) brings an awakened perspective (**solar**) straight into the darkness of Paul's <u>death</u> issue for transformation and release.

5: "Revolution 9" (*dream*, <u>death</u>, dark, bird, violence): A surreal journey (*dream*) of the muse (bird) through John's shadow (dark) to heal the roots of his violent tendencies, including his unresolved emotions about <u>death</u>.

4: "Good Night" (**solar**, *dream*, dark, flute): A blessing from the muse (flute) to experience joy (**solar**) in the darkness of consciousness, to flow downstream safely in sleep.

----------------------------------Line of inspiration----------------------------------

3: "Cry Baby Cry" (dark, mother, bird): The resolution of emotions from childhood (dark), connected to maternal issues (mother, bird). Prior angst is transformed into storytelling.

3: "Mother Nature's Son" (**solar**, bird, mother): Muse inspired message of nature's vitality (daisies singing beneath the **Sun**) as Paul spiritualizes his connection with the maternal.

4: "Yer Blues" (<u>death</u>, dark, violence, mother): John's emotional catharsis about his mother's <u>death</u>, stemming from his unconscious (dark) reactivity (violence).

2: "Rocky Raccoon" (*dream*, violence): An allegorical portrayal (*dream*) of the John/Paul dynamic occurring in the band at this time. Their competitiveness was helpful in working through underlying aggression (violence).

2: "Dear Prudence" (**solar**, bird): Contains a message ("you are part of everything") from a bird (muse) about our interconnectedness (**solar**).

4: "Julia" (**solar**, <u>death</u>, call, mother): Julia "calls" John to relay the teaching that our energy (**solar**) does not extinguish with <u>death</u>, rather it merges "in the **Sun**."

6: "Let It Be" (**solar**, *dream*, <u>death</u>, dark, call, mother): The grand finale and only song that integrates the 5 major themes. Paul sings of his <u>dead</u> mother Mary, who communicates messages in his *dreams*. He is able to work through times of darkness due to the **"light"** he finds inside.

2: "I've Got A Feeling" (**solar**, *dream*): Emblematic of the personality's integration of the lyrical themes ("arc's" descent, back on the ground). John's idiosyncratic word usage ("wet *dream*" followed by **"sun shine"**) illustrates how these words and concepts resided in his psyche.

2: "The Long and Winding Road" (dark, rain): Paul's processing of grief (rain) in his unconscious (dark) as he advances on his spiritual path (road) home.

3: "The Ballad of John & Yoko" (<u>death</u>, dark, rain): John's lighthearted tune illustrates some degree of resolution of his underlying (dark) sadness (rain). It intimates an afterlife, resolving his <u>death</u> issue.

4: "Maxwell's Silver Hammer" (<u>death</u>, dark, call, violence): Paul's comedic and bouncy tune also wraps up the heavier threads from a place of humor. Maxwell is a dark, violent murderer who phones a victim, a complete transformation of these Beatles themes.

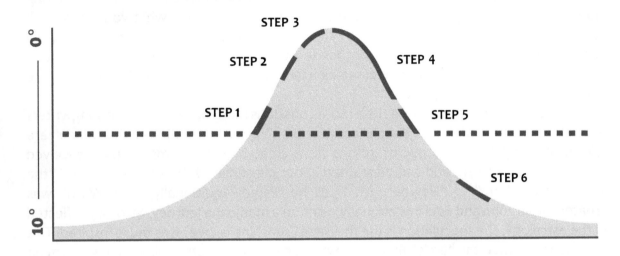

Muse Process

John and Paul have timeless soul bonds with their mothers, who are speculated to play the role of the muse in this story. The astrology for both mother/son dyads illustrates the soul intentions to partner in such a way. As these relationships are so foundational, much of the songwriting is likely influenced. Nevertheless, there are particular songs that are more central and revealing of these bonds and their work together.

The overarching structure of the "arc" also organizes the muse process in the same rhythm. The process involved 6 steps (1: description, 2: expression, 3: connection, 4: collaboration, 5: healing, 6: conclusion) and 29 songs. The ascent correlates with making contact, collaboration was at the peak, and the release of her influence for the descent. Step 1 occurred when the "arc" crossed the "line of inspiration" ascending, while Step 5 concluded when the "arc" crossed it again at the descent. Step 6 can be thought of like a curtain call, when the songwriters explicitly acknowledge her in the song lyrics. (Julia and Mary are the only examples of actual biographical people in their lives directly mentioned in song.)

Step 1 (description, 2 songs) is found in "I'll Be Back" and "Things We Said Today," songs that describe the nature of the soul contracts with the mother/muse. There is a spiritual necessity to depart and an underlying pledge to reunite. Of note are the lyrics, "I've got a big surprise" in "I'll Be Back" and "someday when we're *dreaming*" in "Things We Said Today." They foreshadow the reunion in dreamtime to come.

Step 2 (expression, 3 songs) involves the first examples of the muse's influence in both the music and lyrics. The flute (her instrument) first appeared in Beatles music on John's "You've Got to Hide Your Love Away" (recorded on 2/18/65), potentially signaling her presence. Later the same day "Tell Me What You See" was recorded, a song speculated to be a "channeled" message to Paul. From this perspective, the muse is asking "how can I get through?" The enchanting, "It is no surprise now, what you see is me," could be her giveaway. "I've Just Seen a Face" comes shortly afterwards. Paul writes, "I'll *dream* of her tonight." Here, it's hypothesized the muse is expressing herself through audio ("calling") and visual channels (seeing a face) in Paul's *dreamtime*. At this point, the "arc" was nearing its first peak.

Step 3 (connection, 3 songs) is a more conscious merging between the songwriters and their muse, pointing to a deeper connection. "Yesterday" and "Nowhere Man" are specifically said to be *discovered* rather than created. Paul claims to have received "Yesterday" in a dream and was concerned about plagiarism. John said he received "the whole damn thing" of "Nowhere Man" as he rested. Additionally, "The Word" was created when John and Paul intentionally went on a marijuana journey. Strongly reflected in the astrology, the speculation is the message (sunshine is love) was muse inspired. This step occurs right at the "arc's" first peak, when an opening to other dimensions was most available. It was the critical turning point that led to a fuller realization of the muse partnerships.

Step 4 (collaboration, 15 songs) finds the majority of muse inspired songs, all in the Transcendence period. It differs from the prior step (connection), in which the contact seemed to be baffling or surprising. Here, John and Paul have (some degree of) greater awareness that dreaming, meditation or enhanced journeys of consciousness are openings of the imagination to other realms. *The collaborations are at the soul level*, the fruits of the contracts to bridge worlds. The astrology overwhelmingly points to such partnerships, but the extent of involvement with their personalities is on a range of awareness. For instance, Paul denies any deeper meaning in "Yellow Submarine;" the song seems to be written instinctually. In contrast, John was aware that the soaring vision in "Across the Universe" was being delivered from an outside source ("I don't own it you know").

The songs in this step feature sophisticated teachings, otherworldly synchronicities and the aeronautics of consciousness. Each is "mind-blowing" in its own way, (to apply a term which literally means the transcendence of logic or reason). Other songs in the Transcendence period may also qualify for inclusion in this step, but the list is narrowed to the 15 clearest and most compelling examples. John-Julia collaborations tend to feature metaphysical visions, philosophical musings and a breathtaking scope. Paul-Mary collaborations are more literary, allegorical and personal.

The mature collaborations began right at the second (and absolute) peak of the "arc" with "Tomorrow Never Knows." The "sermon on the mountaintop" unites the major lyrical threads, illustrating the *dream* journey in separation back to Oneness. "Yellow Submarine" is Paul's more accessible counterpart, inviting the whole world to join on the voyage. "Rain" teaches how an individual creates a uniquely subjective version of reality.

"Eleanor Rigby" provides potential resolution of the <u>death</u> thread and features startling synchronicity involving Mary. At the third and final peak of the "arc," "She Said She Said" could be John's communication in the bardo realm with his muse (Julia), the climax of the "call" thread.

"Strawberry Fields Forever" informs us that life is indeed a *dream*. When we accept and integrate this notion, we can heal our pasts. "Penny Lane" involves the cleansing of perception to see life from this newfound awareness. Similar to "Eleanor Rigby," the teaching is provided through story, alluding to Mary herself. "A Day in the Life" is the only song resulting from both mother/son partnerships. Its vast scope reveals the synchronistic landscape (John), while also intimating personal receptivity to the *dream* realm to see it (Paul).

"Being for the Benefit of Mr. Kite!" illustrates the synchronistic relatedness of seemingly unrelated events. It points to a brilliant metaphysical organization, a great mind that envelops us. "Lucy in the Sky with Diamonds" portrays the concordance between the realms above (*dreams*, metaphysics) to below (manifest life). "Your Mother Should Know" specifically connects mother and knowledge with the muse, reflecting the idea of inspired teachings. "Flying" is a musical depiction of the aeronautics of consciousness, a celebration of the muse. "Fool on the Hill" has perspective from Paul-Mary, an allegorical portrayal of a spiritual being existing in the material world. "Lady Madonna" is Mary's story, illustrating her transformation from mother to muse. "Across the Universe" is Julia's poetry, a meditation on the interconnectedness of consciousness and love in a meaningful universe.

Step 5 (healing, 4 songs) unfolds on "The White Album" as the "arc" continues to descend, a motion towards the depths. The astrology suggests the muse was directly involved with karmic resolution {Euterpe conjunct North Node} and the synchronicities at this time were uncanny, if not spooky. Ringo put forth "Don't Pass Me By," pointing to Julia's accident. Shortly afterwards, John and Paul were in parallel processes, working on their personal healing simultaneously. "Revolution 9" has mysterious echoes of Julia's story, possibly including her transformation into the role of muse after her accident. "Blackbird" involves the muse's descent into **the dark night of Paul's shadow to regenerate his power. These 3 songs are linked lyrically ("and you lost your hair," "my wings are broken and so is my hair" and "take these broken wings and learn to fly"). After such intensity, "Good Night"** brings the issue to rest, providing a safe return to sleeping soundly in the manifest world.

Step 6 (conclusion, 2 songs) occurs as the "arc" gradually returns to the ground. The mother/muse is acknowledged by name in the songwriting and her presence in the songwriters' psyche is depicted. John reveals in "Julia" that his mother "calls me," she's a "shimmering" presence in the sky. In "Let It Be," Paul states that Mary visits him in his *dreams*. He awakes with music in his head and she stands "right in front of me." At the conclusion, "heaven" is brought to "earth." The partnerships with the muse have successfully bridged worlds.

John as Muse?

Paul is quoted in the Beatles Anthology, "Among ourselves we'd had a pact that if one of us were to die, he'd come back and let the others know if there was another side."[362] Similar to "Things We Said Today," it sounds like there was a prior agreement to be followed up on. As a fitting coda to this musical story, perhaps that is exactly what transpired.

John created a demo for a song titled "Free as a Bird" in 1977. It remained unfinished and unreleased. In 1995, the other Beatles got access to it and worked on it as part of the Anthology project. The song is a collaboration through the boundary of death on a "bird" song! We can only wonder how the song was completed. Were Paul, George and Ringo inspired by John? For his curtain call in this story, was John playing the role of muse? It'd be quite fitting for his trickster character!

According to Paul, the Beatles theme of channeling the dead seems to have taken this twist. He stated in a 2019 interview that John visits him in his dreams.[363] In fact, he says that both John and George have a strong presence in his life. In 2020, Paul claimed he also communicates with George, apparently through a tree the guitarist gifted him.[364]

It turns out that "Free as a Bird" has substantial significance in this study. It's not just a "bird" song, but a "mother" song too. At the end of the song John is heard saying, "Turn out nice again, mother." Perhaps he was speaking, or referring, to Yoko. Though maybe it involves Julia. John might have been relating to her as he composed this song about birds and the attainment of freedom. Being "free" might involve the liberation from prior suffering, an exit from the soul cage.

The lyrics include "wings" (which were previously "broken," as seen in "Blackbird" and "Revolution 9"). Here, John sings about flying without limitation, being "free." The lyrics also mention "home" several times, which is within the province of the archetype Cancer, the Beatles Sun sign. As reviewed, the Sun is in Cancer when it's highest in the sky (northern declination), and the Egyptians believed beetles could fly into the celestial planes and return with messages. "Free as a Bird" (written 3 years before John's death) may be eerily foreshadowing John at home in the sky with a bird's eye perspective. It might be a depiction of Julia's journey. Maybe both.

The video for the song (easily found on You Tube) follows the flight of a bird. Similar to "Across the Universe," it begins with bird noises. From on high, it flies down and ventures on a journey through dozens of references and depictions of Beatles songs and themes, including a car crash. The video captures the nostalgic flavor of Liverpool roots, a weaving back to the past for synthesis and completion of this epic story.

Consistent with that flight, the astrology also depicts the role of the muse for the Beatles. Whether or not John was somehow inserting himself into the role for this song, the chart below illustrates the message of the muse to wrap up the story.

Below is "Free as a Bird" with the Beatles chart.

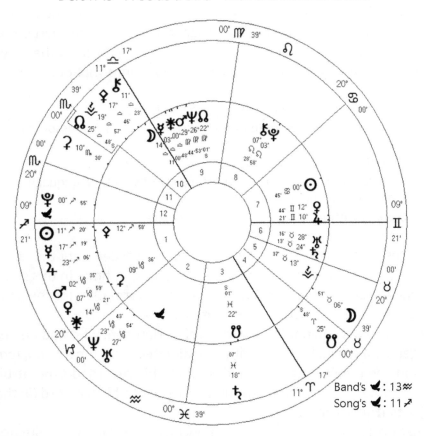

Band's ◗: 13 ≈
Song's ◗: 11 ♐

For "Free as a Bird," the muse was at 11° Sagittarius, conjunct the band's Ascendant and directly opposite the Beatles signature. Sagittarius involves travel with connotations of great distances, while the Ascendant is upfront and animated. The muse's residence here is most consistent with expressing the flight (Sagittarius) of a bird (muse), which is heard in the song and depicted in the video. Furthermore, the muse is exactly conjunct the Sun, a thematic joining to the **solar** thread. She has been integral in the awakening process in this story.

Part of such awakening is the transformation of death. In addition to the muse conjunct the Sun for "Free as a Bird," she is also conjunct Pluto, planet of death (just shy of 1° Sagittarius). So, the chart features the combination of awakening (Sun), the muse (Euterpe) and death (Pluto), a most fitting conclusion. Also, at this position in early Sagittarius, the "Free as a Bird" Pluto is tightly connected to both Mary (conjunct her Euterpe at 1° Sagittarius) and Julia (square hers at 1° Pisces). It is also brilliantly connected to the muse attunement of the Beatles (exactly quintile their Euterpe at 13° Aquarius). The muse transforms our understanding (Sagittarius) of death (Pluto). As written in "Julia," we merge with the eternality of an ever present and aware life force (Sun). And as heard from both Julia and Mary, the muse delivers words of wisdom and calls to those below.

470

Chart Data

There are different types of astrology charts featured in this book: birth (or natal) charts, transits, progressions and events. This section provides the chart data.

For birth charts, the day, place and time is given, as well as the universally used "Rodden Rating," a system used to rank the reliability of information.

AA: Accurate data as recorded by the family or state
A: Accurate data as quoted by the person, kin, friend, or associate
B: Biography or autobiography
C: Caution: no source of origin
DD: Dirty Data: two or more conflicting quotes that are unqualified
X: Data with no time of birth
XX: Data without a known or confirmed date

Birth times were not consistently and reliably recorded until the later decades of the 20th Century. Therefore, some birth charts lack an exact time. In this situation, charts are cast for midday (12pm). Thankfully, there is sound information for the band members, so their natal charts, and the group's composite chart, are precise.

However, there is a minor issue with George Harrison, who had his chart rectified by an astrologer. As a result, his chart with an estimated birth time of 11:42pm on 2/24/43 can be found in the public domain. For this study, his recorded time at birth is used. According to the notes in Astrodatabank, his sister states a birth record (in their mother's handwriting) lists 12:10am on 2/25/1943.

Information for transit charts is not included below. Most discussions about transits are for an extended time frame. For instance, the transits the musicians were experiencing for Beatlemania occurred over a few years. Transits are often configured around another chart (natal, composite) in a biwheel. They represent the astrological activity at a given time, which is addressed in the main text. Progressions stem from natal charts, so chart data is not necessary. The times for the progressed charts are also noted in the text.

Chart data for event charts is found below. In some cases, precise times are lacking. For instance, the band met Bob Dylan sometime in the late afternoon or evening on 8/28/1964, and Brian Epstein died sometime in the morning of 8/27/1967. Like transits, event charts are generally displayed around other charts. The meeting with Dylan is depicted around the Beatles composite chart and Epstein's death is viewed as the transits that morning to his natal chart. These estimations should not be a concern to the reader. Over the course of any given day, the positions of the planets do not change very much at all. The one exception is the Moon, which travels about 12^0 a day. Therefore, if a midday chart is used for an event with an unknown time, the Moon is guaranteed to be within 6^0 of its actual place (and all other planets within 1^0). All of the charts featured in this study are completely useful for our purposes.

There are many charts for the beginning of song recordings. The information is from *The Complete Beatles Chronicle*, by Mark Lewisohn. All of the songs were recorded in London, so just the day and time is listed below. There is no exact time for the release of the music (both albums and singles), just a day. To generate charts, 12am (the start of the release day), is used.

John Lennon: 10/9/1940, 6:30pm, Liverpool, England: A
Paul McCartney: 6/18/1942, 2:00pm, Liverpool, England: A
George Harrison: 2/25/1943, 12:10am, Liverpool, England: A
Ringo Starr: 7/7/1940, 12:05am, Liverpool, England: A
Lonnie Donegan: 4/29/1931, 3:00am, Glasgow, Scotland: AA
Elvis Presley: 1/8/1935, 4:35am, Tupelo, MS: AA
Buddy Holly: 9/7/1936, 3:30pm, Lubbock, TX: A
Chuck Berry: 10/18/1926, 6:59am, St. Louis, MO: B
Little Richard: 12/5/1932, 2:50pm, Macon, GA: C
Alfred Lennon: 12/14/1912, unknown, Liverpool, England: XX
Julia Lennon: 3/12/1914, unknown, Liverpool, England: XX
Mary McCartney: 9/29/1909, unknown, Liverpool, England: XX
Mary McCartney's death: 10/31/1956, unknown time, Liverpool, England
John Meets Paul: 7/6/1957, afternoon/evening (6pm estimate), Liverpool, England
George's Auditions: 2 auditions in March 1958, days unknown. The New Moon on 3/19/1958 is used to capture his astrological activity around this time
Julia's Death: 7/15/1958, evening in Liverpool
Arrival in Hamburg: 8/17/1960, "early evening" (6pm estimate), Hamburg, Germany
The Cavern Club: 2/9/1961, evening, Liverpool
Stu Sutcliffe: 6/23/1940, 11:25pm, Edinburgh, Scotland: AA
Attack on Stu: 1/30/1961, unknown, Liverpool, England
First Recording Session: 6/22/1961, unknown, Hamburg, Germany
Brian Epstein: 9/19/1934, 4:30am, Liverpool, England: C
Audition at EMI: June 6, 1962, 7pm, London, England
George Martin: 1/3/1926, 2:29pm, London, England: A
Ringo Joins: 8/14/1962, unknown, London, England
Pete Best: 11/24/1941, unknown, Madras, India: XX
Cynthia Powell: 9/10/1939, unknown, Blackpool, England: XX
John/Cynthia Wedding: 8/23/1962, unknown time, London, England
Release of "Please Please Me": 1/11/1963, UK
Recording of Twist & Shout: 2/11/1963, 10pm
Release of *Please Please Me*: 3/22/1963, UK
Julian Lennon: 4/8/1963, 7:45am, Liverpool, England: B
Jane Asher: 4/5/1946, 10pm, London, England: A
Bob Wooler: 1/19/1926, unknown: XX
Recording of "She Loves You": 7/1/1963, 5pm
Release of "She Loves You": 8/23/1963, UK

Release of *With the Beatles*: 11/22/1963, UK
Appearance on Ed Sullivan: 2/9/1964, 8pm, New York, NY
Recording of "And I Love Her": 2/25/1964, 2:30pm
Recording of "Anytime At All": 6/2/1964, 10am
Recording of "Things We Said Today": 6/2/1964, 2:30pm
Release of "I Call Your Name": 6/19/1964, UK
Release of the film *A Hard Day's Night*: 7/6/1964, UK
Release of the album *A Hard Day's Night*: 7/10/1964, UK
Ringo's Hospitalization: 6/3/1964
Recording of "Baby's in Black": 8/11/1964, 7pm
Recording of "I'm a Loser": 8/14/1964, 7pm
Meeting with Bob Dylan: 8/28/1964, late afternoon/evening, New York, NY
Recording of "No Reply": 9/30/1964, 10:30pm
Recording of "I'll Follow the Sun": 10/18/1964, 2:30pm
Release of *Beatles for Sale*: 12/4/1964, UK
Maureen Cox: 8/4/1946, unknown, Liverpool, England: XX
Release of "Ticket to Ride" and "Yes It Is": 4/9/1965, UK
Recording of "You've Got to Hide Your Love Away": 2/18/1965, 3:30pm
Recording of "Tell Me What You See": 2/18/1965, 6:30pm
Recording of "Help!": 4/13/1965, 7pm
Recording of "Yesterday": 6/14/1965, 7pm
Release of "Yesterday": 9/13/1965, UK
Release of *Help!*: 8/6/1965, UK
Zak Starkey: 9/13/1965, 8am, London, England: B
Recording of "Run for Your Life": 10/12/1965, 2:30pm
Recording of "Norwegian Wood": 10/12/1965, 7pm
Recording of "In My Life": 10/18/1965, 2:30pm
Recording of "We Can Work it Out": 10/20/1965, 2:30pm
Recording of "Nowhere Man": 10/21/1965, 7pm
Recording of "Michelle": 11/3/1965, 2:30pm
Recording of "Think for Yourself": 11/8/1965, 9pm
Recording of "The Word": 11/10/1965, 9pm
Release of *Rubber Soul*: 12/3/1965, UK
Pattie Boyd: 3/17/1944, 4am, Taunton, England: B
Maureen Cleave Interview ("more popular than Jesus"): Published 3/4/1966
Recording of "Tomorrow Never Knows": 4/6/1966, 8pm
Geoff Emerick: 12/5/1945, unknown, England: XX
Recording of "Love You To": 4/11/1966, 2:30pm
Ravi Shankar: 4/7/1920, unknown, Benares, British Raj: XX
Eleanor Rigby: 8/29/1895, unknown, England: XX
Recording of "Eleanor Rigby": 4/28/1966, 5pm
Recording of "Yellow Submarine": 5/26/1966, 7pm
Recording of "She Said She Said": 6/21/1966, 7pm

Release of *Revolver*: 8/5/1966, UK
Beatles final concert: 8/29/1966, 8pm, San Francisco, CA
Release of *How I Won the War*: 10/18/1967, UK
Yoko Ono: 2/18/1933, 8:30pm, Tokyo, Japan: A
John and Yoko Meet: 11/9/1966, unknown, London, England
Recording of *Sgt. Pepper* (beginning with "Strawberry Fields Forever"): 11/24/1966, 7pm
Recording of "When I'm Sixty-Four": 12/6/1966, 7:45pm
Recording of "Penny Lane": 12/29/1966, 7pm
Release of "Strawberry Fields Forever"/"Penny Lane": 2/13/1967, UK
Recording of "Sgt. Pepper's Lonely Hearts Club Band": 2/1/1967, 7pm
Recording of the orchestral event for "A Day in the Life": 2/10/1967, 8pm
Recording of "Being for the Benefit of Mr. Kite!": 2/17/1967, 7pm
Recording of "Lucy in the Sky with Diamonds": 3/1/1967, 7pm
Recording of "Getting Better": 3/9/1967, 7pm
Recording of "Within You Without You": 3/15/1967, 7pm
Recording of "It's All Too Much": 5/25/1967, 7pm
Release of *Sgt. Pepper's Lonely Hearts Club Band*: 6/1/1967, UK
Our World Broadcast of "All You Need is Love": 6/25/1967, 8:54pm, London, England
Jason Starkey: 8/19/1967, 3:25pm, London, England: A
Recording of "Your Mother Should Know": 8/22/1967, 7pm
Brian Epstein's Death: 8/27/1967, unknown, London
Recording of "Flying": 9/8/1967, 7pm
Recording of "Fool on the Hill": 9/25/1967, 7pm
Release of "Hello Goodbye"/"I Am the Walrus": 11/24/1967, UK
Release of *Magical Mystery Tour* album: 11/27/1967, US
Release of Magical Mystery Tour movie: 12/26/1967, UK
Recording of "Lady Madonna": 2/3/1968, 2:30pm
Recording of "Across the Universe": 2/4/1968, 2:30pm
Recording of "The Inner Light": 2/6/1968, 2:30pm
Release of "Lady Madonna/"The Inner Light": 3/15/1968, UK
Recording of "Revolution": 5/30/1968, 2:30pm
Recording of "Don't Pass Me By": 6/5/1968, 2:30pm
Recording of "Blackbird": 6/11/1968, 3:30pm
Recording of "Good Night": 6/28/1968, 7pm
Recording of "Ob-La-Di, Ob-La-Da": 7/3/1968, 8pm
Recording of "Cry Baby Cry": 7/15/1968, 9pm
Recording of "Helter Skelter": 7/18/1968, 10:30pm
Recording of "Hey Jude": 7/29/1968, 8:30pm
Recording of "Rocky Raccoon": 8/15/1968, 7pm
Ringo quits the band: 8/22/1968
Recording of "Dear Prudence": 8/28/1968, 5pm
Release of "Hey Jude"/"Revolution": 8/26/1968, UK
Recording of "While My Guitar Gently Weeps": 9/6/1968, 7pm

Recording of "Birthday": 9/18/1968, 8:30pm
Recording of "Piggies": 9/19/1968, 7:15pm
Recording of "Happiness is a Warm Gun": 9/23/1968, 7pm
Recording of "Julia": 10/13/1968, 7pm
Release of *Wonderwall Music*: 11/1/1968, UK
Release of *Two Virgins*: 11/11/1968, US
Release of "The White Album": 11/22/1968, UK
Charles Manson: 11/12/1934, 4:40pm, Cincinnati, OH: AA
Release of *Yellow Submarine*: 1/13/1969, UK
Billy Preston: 9/2/1946, unknown, Houston, TX: XX
Rooftop Concert: 1/30/1969, "lunchtime," London, England
Linda Eastman (McCartney): 9/24/1941, 10am, New York, NY: A
Amsterdam Bed-in: 3/25/1969, Amsterdam
Recording of **"The Ballad of John & Yoko"**: 4/14/1969, 2:30pm
Recording of "Octopus's Garden": 4/26/1969, 4:30pm
Recording of "Give Peace a Chance": 6/1/1969, 10pm, Montreal, Canada
Recording of "Here Comes the Sun": 7/7/1969, 2:30pm
Recording of "The End": 7/23/1969, 2:30pm
Zebra Walk: 8/8/1969, 11:35am, London, England
Mary McCartney (daughter): 8/29/1969, 1:30am, London, England: B
John's Departure: 9/21/1969, unknown time
Release of *Abbey Road*: 9/26/1969, UK
"Paul is Dead" Hoax (radio broadcast): 10/12/1969, unknown, Detroit, MI
Release of "Let It Be" single: 3/6/1970, UK
Paul's Press Release: 4/10/1970, unknown, London, England
Release of *Let It Be*: 5/8/1970, UK
Release of "Free as a Bird": 12/4/1995, UK

Notes

For the opening quotes of the book: McCartney's words were spoken in a Q & A session, "Paul McCartney Answers the Web's Most Searched Questions" and can be found on YouTube: https://www.youtube.com/watch?v=5Pf19jV1NYw&t=255s

John's first quote is in *All We Are Saying: The Last Major Interview with John Lennon and Yoko Ono*, by David Sheff (St. Martin's Press, 2000), p. 267

The second quote was also delivered shortly before his death. It is in *Revolution in the Head: The Beatles' Records and the Sixties, 3rd Edition*, by Ian MacDonald (Chicago Review Press, 2007) p. 173. The quote is in the first footnote which reads, "Lennon described his favourite experiences in songwriting in terms of being passively 'in tune' with the 'music of the spheres': 'My joy is when you're like possessed, like a medium you know' (Interview with Andy Peebles for the BBC, 6th December 1980)."

1: *The Beatles: The Biography*, by Bob Spitz (Back Bay Books, 2005), p. 536

2: https://www. astrologynewsservice.com/news/how-the-beatles-rocked-with-astrology/, 3/10/2014

3: *Lennon: The Man, the Myth, the Music—The Definitive Life*, by Tim Riley (Hyperion, 2011), p. 595

4: *All the Songs: The Story Behind Every Beatles Release*, by Jean-Michel Guesdon & Philippe Margotin (Black Dog & Leventhal, 2013), p. 440

5: See Riley, p. 160; *Tune In, The Beatles: All These Years, Vol. 1*, by Mark Lewisohn (Three Rivers Press, 2013), p. 54-55, 208; or Spitz, p. 149, 310.

6: *Here, There and Everywhere: My Life Recording the Music of The Beatles*, by Geoff Emerick and Howard Massey (Avery, 2007), p. 10; *All You Need Is Ears* by George Martin (St. Martin, 1979), p.200

7: Lewisohn, p. 101

8: *Paul McCartney: The Life* by Philip Norman (Little, Brown and Company, 2016), p. 61

9: Lewisohn, p. 207-208

10: Spitz, p. 116

11: Lewisohn, p. 45, 47, 79-80; Spitz, p. 336-337

12: *Revolution in the Head: The Beatles' Records and the Sixties, 3rd Edition*, by Ian MacDonald (Chicago Review Press, 2007) p. 216

13: Guesdon & Margotin, p. 502

14: Lewisohn, p. 159-160; Spitz, p. 125; 136, Emerick, p.11

15: Paul refers to George as his "little baby brother" in an Uncut interview, 7/1/2008

16: In Rolling Stone magazine 9/15/2016 Ringo is quoted, "I'm an only child, and I felt like I suddenly had three brothers."

17: Emerick, p. 104; MacDonald, p. 247

18: Spitz, p. 200, 319

19: Lewisohn, p. 291-2, 301-4

20: https://historyplex.com/egyptian-scarab-beetle, "The Significance of the Egyptian Scarab Beetle Through the Ages"

21: "The scarab is a classical rebirth symbol. According to the description in the ancient Egyptian book Am-Tuat, the dead sun God transforms himself at the tenth station into Khepri, the scarab, and as such mounts the barge at the twelfth station, which raises the rejuvenated sun into the morning sky", Jung's Red Book, Footnote 62.

22: *Ringo Starr: A Life* (2nd Edition) by Alan Clayson (Sanctuary, 2005), p. 182-184

23: *You Never Give Me Your Money: The Beatles After the Breakup* by Peter Doggett (HarperCollins, 2009), p. 120-122

24: *The Beatles Anthology* (Chronicle, 2000), p.312

25: *The Beatles Diary Volume 2: After the Break-up 1970-2001* by Keith Badman (Omnibus Press, 2001), p.135

26: https://outsider.com/news/entertainment/elvis-presley-the-tragic-story-of-his-twin-brother-jesse-garon-presley/, 2/24/2021

27: Spitz, p. 132

28: https://www.the-paulmccartney-project.com/artist/buddy-holly/

29: https://www.beatlesbible.com/songs/johnny-b-goode/, 4/8/2020

30: https://www.beatlesbible.com/features/drugs/

31: https://en.wikipedia.org/wiki/Etymology_of_hippie

32: Ian MacDonald's *Revolution in the Head* is the source for the song numbers.

33: The "choice" is portrayed in *John Lennon: The Life* by Phillip Norman (Harper Collins, 2008), p. 20-21 and Spitz, p. 29-30, but Lewisohn, *Tune In*, p. 41–42 doesn't agree. He writes, "There was no choice at all," and provides an account from a witness (Billy Hall).

34: Lewisohn, p. 117; Riley, p.35

35: Lewisohn, p.45, 79-80; Spitz p. 332-39

36: Ibid

37: Spitz, p.86

38: Norman (McCartney bio), p. 61

39: Lewisohn, p. 157-58

40: Lewisohn, p. 181-84

41: Riley, p. 88-89

42: Ibid

43: Lewisohn, p. 187

44: https://www.beatlesbible.com/songs/hello-little-girl/

45: Lewisohn, p. 152

46: Spitz, p. 243-44

47: Lewisohn, p. 356-57

48: Lewisohn, p. 358

49: Spitz, p. 247; Lewisohn, p. 280

50: Spitz, p. 247

51: Norman (McCartney), p. 125

52: Lewisohn, p. 451-52

53: Lewisohn, p. 411

54: Ibid

55: *The Beatles Shadow: Stuart Sutcliffe & his Lonely Hearts Club* by Pauline Sutcliffe (Pan, 2002), p. 82; Norman (Lennon) p. 133-136

56: Sutcliffe, p. 132-33

57: Spitz, p. 270-74

58: Martin, p. 123

59: Martin, p. 133, 139, 167

60: Martin, p. 123

61: Lewisohn, p. 651; Spitz p. 299

62: https://www.beatlesbible.com/people/pete-best/3/

63: Spitz, p. 299, 322

64: Riley, p. 88-89; https://en.wikipedia.org/wiki/Cynthia_Lennon

65: MacDonald, p. 64; *The Beatles Lyrics* by Hunter Davies (Little, Brown and Company, 2014), p. 32

66: Martin, p. 130

67: *The Beatles Recording Sessions* by Mark Lewisohn (Harmony, 1988), p. 24-26

68: MacDonald, p. 70, 75

69: MacDonald, p. 69-70

70: Spitz, p. 394--99

71: Norman (McCartney), p. 197-98

72: Spitz, p. 415

73: The Beatles Anthology, p. 98

74: Emerick, p. 65-68

75: Spitz, p. 425

76: Spitz, p. 462

77: Martin, p. 164

78: https://en.wikipedia.org/wiki/With_the_Beatles

79: https://en.wikipedia.org/wiki/The_Ed_Sullivan_Show

80: MacDonald, p. 327

81: https://www.mentalfloss.com/article/66739/10-writing-tips-stephen-king

82: https://en.wikipedia.org/wiki/Euterpe

83: In *The Beatles Off the Record* by Keith Badman (Omnibus , 2000), p.91

84: Lewisohn, P. 184

85: https://en.wikipedia.org/wiki/A_Hard_Day%27s_Night_(film)

86: https://www.beatlesbible.com/1964/04/04/beatles-billboard-hot-100-top-five/

87: The Beatles Anthology, p.131

88: Badman, p. 101

89: Guesdon & Margotin, p. 171

90: Spitz, 535-36

91: Ibid

92: Guesdon & Margotin, p. 176

93: https://www.beatlesbible.com/1964/10/28/interview-playboy/

94: https://www.ultimateclassicrock.com/beatles-pete-best-lawsuit/

95: Ibid

96: Guesdon & Margotin, p. 200-01

97: In *John, Paul, George, Ringo and Me*, by Tony Barrow (Thunder's Mouth Press, 2006), p. 143

98: Guesdon & Margotin, p. 236

99. MacDonald, p. 143

100: Guesdon & Margotin, p. 228-29

101: In *Lennon and McCartney: Songwriters—A Portrait from 1966*, by Michael Lydon, 2014.

102: Guesdon & Margotin, p. 220

103: https://www.beatlesstory.com/blog/2017/05/29/george-harrison-the-beatles-and-indian-music/

104: Spitz, p. 551

105: Riley, p. 272-74

106: The Beatles Anthology, p. 191

107: https://en.wikipedia.org/wiki/The_Beatles_(TV_series)

108: The Beatles Anthology, p. 175

109: Ibid

110: Ibid

111: MacDonald, p. 157

112: Spitz, p. 160-63

113: Guesdon & Margotin, p. 216-18

114: Ibid, p. 242

115: MacDonald, p. 162

116: https://en.wikipedia.org/wiki/Norwegian_Wood_(This_Bird_Has_Flown)

117: MacDonald, p. 164

118: In *All We Are Saying: The Last Major Interview with John Lennon and Yoko Ono* (St. Martin's Press, 2010), p. 178

119: MacDonald, p. 169-70

120: Ibid

121: *Playboy*, September 1980

122: MacDonald, p. 173

122: Ibid

123: Ibid

124: Guesdon & Margotin, p. 270-72

125: Norman (Lennon), p. 415

126: MacDonald, p. 167

127: https://en.wikipedia.org/wiki/Rubber_Soul

128: Davies, p. 129

129: Clayson (Harrison), p. 223-24

130: Doggett, p. 209

131: Spitz, p. 627-29

132: Ibid, p. 608

133: Ibid, p. 619-22

134: MacDonald, p. 191

135: Ibid, p. 185

136: Ibid, p. 192-93

137: Ibid, p. 191

138: Ibid

139: Emerick, p. 116

140: Ibid, p. 112

141: MacDonald, p.190

142: Spitz, p. 665-666; Norman (Lennon), 464-465

143: Davies, p. 176

144: https://en.wikipedia.org/wiki/Love_You_To

145: Ibid

146: Guesdon & Margotin, p. 344

147: Ibid, p. 360

148: In *Paul McCartney: Many Years from Now*, by Barry Miles (Holt and Company, 1997), p. 280

149: Guesdon & Margotin, p. 362-63

150: MacDonald, p. 203

151: https://en.wikipedia.org/wiki/Eleanor_Rigby

152: Ibid

153: MacDonald, p. 203

154: Guesdon & Margotin, p. 334-35

155: https://www.the-paulmccartney-project.com/song/yellow-submarine/

156: Norman (McCartney), p. 245

157: Spitz, p. 580-81

158: Ibid

159: MacDonald, p.185; Davies, p. 176-77

160: Spitz, p. 580

161: Guesdon & Margotin, p. 337

162: https://en.wikipedia.org/wiki/Revolver_(Beatles_album)

163: Ibid

164: In *George Harrison: Living in the Material World* by Olivia Harrison (Abrams, 2011), p. 204

165: Spoken by Paul on 8/24/66 in Los Angeles at a press interview, seen on YouTube: https://www.youtube.com/watch?v=O8MgItRRaTo&t=810s

166: https://en.wikipedia.org/wiki/How_I_Won_the_War

167: Spitz, p. 652-53

168: https://en.wikipedia.org/wiki/Yoko_Ono

169: Norman (McCartney), p. 256

170: Ibid, p. 257

171: Spitz, p. 643-44

172: https://en.wikipedia.org/wiki/Sgt._Pepper's_Lonely_Hearts_Club_Band

173: MacDonald, p. 212

174: Martin, p. 200-01

175: https://www.rollingstone.com/music/music-lists/500-greatest-songs-of-all-time-151127/the-beatles-strawberry-fields-forever-48149/

176: MacDonald, p. 220

177: Ibid, p. 221

178: Spitz, p. 86

179: MacDonald, p. 235

180: Ibid

181: In *Paul McCartney's Guide to the Beatles Songbook* by Alan Aldridge, published in the Los Angeles Times on 1/14/1968

182: Guesdon & Margotin, p. 388

183: In *The Complete Beatles Chronicle* by Mark Lewisohn (Harmony, 1992), p. 244

184: Ibid

185: Guesdon & Margotin, p. 404

186: Miles, p. 380, Spitz, p. 672

187: Spitz, p. 660

188: MacDonald, p. 230

189: Spitz, p. 669

190: Martin, p. 206

191: Spitz, p. 669-70

192: MacDonald, p. 239

193: Ibid

194: MacDonald, p. 240

195: Ibid

196: Norman (Lennon), 497-99

197: https://en.wikipedia.org/wiki/Lucy

198: https://en.wikipedia.org/wiki/Through_the_Looking-Glass

199: *Playboy*, January 1981

200: Spitz, 670-71

201: Guesdon & Margotin, p. 394-95

202: MacDonald, p. 243

203: Martin, p. 203

204: MacDonald, p. 245

205: Lewisohn (*Complete Beatles Chronicle*), p. 249

206: https://www.huffpost.com/entry/paul-mccartney-said-he-and-john-lennon-masturbated-together-with-friends_n_5b97e059e4b0cf7b0043fa94

207: MacDonald, p. 246

208: https://www.thebeatles.com/album/sgt-peppers-lonely-hearts-club-band

209: https://www.beatlesbible.com/features/drugs/

210: Spitz, p. 683; Emerick, p. 164

211: Emerick, p. 179

212: *The Beatles Anthology*, p. 242

213: MacDonald, p. 261

214: https://www.beatlesbible.com/1967/06/25/the-beatles-on-our-world-all-you-need-is-love/

215: https://en.wikipedia.org/wiki/All_You_Need_Is_Love

216: Spitz, p. 568-569

217: Ibid

218: Ibid, p. 518

219: https://en.wikipedia.org/wiki/Brian_Epstein

220: *Rolling Stone*, 1/21/1971

221: Spitz, p. 698-99

222: Ibid, p. 720

223: https://www.beatlesbible.com/songs/i-am-the-walrus/

224: In *Meet the Beatles: A Cultural History of the Band that Shook Youth, Gender, and the World* (Harper Collins, 2005), p. 220

225: In *The Beatles Diary Volume 1: The Beatles Years*, by Barry Miles (Omnibus, 2001), p. 275-76

226: https://en.wikipedia.org/wiki/Blue_Jay_Way

227: Guesdon & Margotin, p. 434

228: Ibid, p. 432

229: https://en.wikipedia.org/wiki/The_Fool_on_the_Hill

230: https://en.wikipedia.org/wiki/Magical_Mystery_Tour

231: *Rolling Stone*, 1/21/1971

232: Guesdon & Margotin, p. 444

233: Spitz, p. 88-89

234: In *All We Are Saying: The Last Major Interview with John Lennon and Yoko Ono*, by David Sheff (St. Martin's Press, 2000), p. 267

235: Ibid, p. 265

236: https://en.wikipedia.org/wiki/Across_the_Universe

237: Ibid

238: Guesdon & Margotin, p. 446

239: https://en.wikipedia.org/wiki/The_Inner_Light_(song)

240: Emerick, p. 223

241: https://en.wikipedia.org/wiki/The_Beatles_in_India

242: Ibid

243: Spitz, p. 756-57

244: Ibid, p. 757

245: Ibid, p. 757-58

246: Ibid, p. 760

247: Ibid, p. 771-72

248: Ibid, p. 775

249: Emerick, p. 234

250: Ibid, p. 230

251: https://en.wikipedia.org/wiki/Revolution_(Beatles_song)#Revolution_1

252: Emerick, p. 243

253: https://en.wikipedia.org/wiki/Don%27t_Pass_Me_By

254: Guesdon & Margotin, p. 476

255: In *Lennon on Lennon: Conversation* by Maurice Hindle (Chicago Review Press, 2017), p. 53

256: https://www.beatlesbible.com/songs/everybodys-got-something-to-hide-except-me-and-my-monkey/

257: Emerick, p. 246

258: https://en.wikipedia.org/wiki/Ob-La-Di,_Ob-La-Da

259: Emerick, p. 257-58

260: Lewisohn (*Complete Beatles Chronicle*), p. 289-90

261: Guesdon & Margotin, p. 501

262: Norman (McCartney), p. 334

263: https://en.wikipedia.org/wiki/Jane_Asher

264: Spitz, p. 782

265: https://www.beatlesbible.com/songs/hey-jude/2/

266: https://en.wikipedia.org/wiki/Yer_Blues

267: Guesdon & Margotin, p. 480

268: Clayson (Starr), p. 183-84

269: Spitz, p. 804

270: Ibid, p. 806

271: Guesdon & Margotin, p. 458

272: https://www.beatlesbible.com/songs/revolution-1/

273: The Beatles Anthology, p. 312

274: Spitz, p. 785

275: Ibid

276: Lewisohn (*Complete Beatles Chronicle*), p. 298

277: https://www.beatlesbible.com/songs/glass-onion/

278: https://www.beatlesbible.com/songs/piggies/

279: Ibid

280: MacDonald, p. 318

281: *The Beatles Anthology*, p. 306

282: Guesdon & Margotin, p. 508

283: Ibid, p. 472

284: https://www.beatlesbible.com/songs/the-continuing-story-of-bungalow-bill/

285: Ibid

286: Guesdon & Margotin, p. 484

287: Ibid, p. 488

288: Ibid

289: https://www.beatlesbible.com/1968/10/18/john-lennon-and-yoko-ono-are-arrested-for-drugs-possession/

290: https://www.beatlesbible.com/people/george-harrison/albums/wonderwall-music/

291: https://en.wikipedia.org/wiki/Unfinished_Music_No._1:_Two_Virgins

292: Ibid

293: Ibid

294: Riley, p. 422

295: https://www.beatlesbible.com/albums/the-beatles-white-album/

296: Ibid

297: Ibid

298: Ibid

299: https://www.beatlesbible.com/features/charles-manson/

300: https://en.wikipedia.org/wiki/Helter_Skelter_(scenario)

301: https://en.wikipedia.org/wiki/Let_It_Be_(Beatles_album)

302: Ibid

303: Spitz, p. 808

304: Ibid p. 806

305: Ibid

306: https://en.wikipedia.org/wiki/Let_It_Be_(Beatles_album)

307: https://www.beatlesbible.com/albums/yellow-submarine/

308: https://en.wikipedia.org/wiki/Only_a_Northern_Song

309: https://en.wikipedia.org/wiki/All_Together_Now

310: Spitz, p. 809, 814

311: MacDonald, p. 335

312: https://en.wikipedia.org/wiki/Don%27t_Let_Me_Down_(Beatles_song)

313: https://www.beatlesbible.com/1969/01/30/the-beatles-rooftop-concert-apple-building/

314: MacDonald, p. 337

315: https://en.wikipedia.org/wiki/Let_It_Be_(Beatles_song)

316: Ibid

317: Norman (McCartney) p. 410

318: https://en.wikipedia.org/wiki/Abbey_Road

319: Ibid

320: https://en.wikipedia.org/wiki/I_Want_You_(She%27s_So_Heavy)

321: https://en.wikipedia.org/wiki/Old_Brown_Shoe

322: https://en.wikipedia.org/wiki/Something_(Beatles_song)

323: https://en.wikipedia.org/wiki/May_Pang

324: https://www.beatlesbible.com/1969/03/25/john-and-yokos-first-bed-in-for-peace/

325: Ibid

326: Ray Connolly, April 1970, *The Evening Standard*, Spitz, p. 848-49

327: Spitz, p. 805

328: Guesdon & Margotin, p. 550

329: Emerick, p. 269-270

330: https://en.wikipedia.org/wiki/The_Ballad_of_John_and_Yoko

331: Spitz, p. 817-20

332: Norman (Lennon), p. 605-07

333: Spitz, p. 838

334: Ibid, p. 839

335: Interview with *Rolling Stone*, January 2008

336: https://en.wikipedia.org/wiki/Maxwell%27s_Silver_Hammer

337: Miles (*Paul McCartney: Many Years from Now*), p. 554

338: Guesdon & Margotin, p. 594

339: Ibid, p.598

340: Spitz, 844-45

341: Spitz, p. 847

342: https://en.wikipedia.org/wiki/Abbey_Road

343: Ibid

344: https://en.wikipedia.org/wiki/Paul_is_dead

345: https://en.wikipedia.org/wiki/Cold_Turkey

346: Riley, p. 462

347: Guesdon & Margotin, p. 620

348: https://en.wikipedia.org/wiki/I_Me_Mine

349: https://en.wikipedia.org/wiki/Instant_Karma!

350: https://en.wikipedia.org/wiki/Sentimental_Journey_(Ringo_Starr_album)

351: Spitz, p. 848

352: https://en.wikipedia.org/wiki/McCartney_(album)

353: Norman (McCartney), p. 413

354: Norman (Lennon), p. 647-52

355: https://en.wikipedia.org/wiki/All_Things_Must_Pass

356: Ibid

357: en.wikipedia.org/wiki/Let_It_Be_(Beatles_album)

358: Ibid

359: Ibid

360: Emerick, p. 100

361: Ibid p. 101-02, https://www.biography.com/musician/ringo-starr

362: *The Beatles Anthology*, p. 69

363: https://www.dailymail.co.uk/tvshowbiz/article-7503571/Sir-Paul-McCartney-reveals-visited-late-bandmate-John-Lennon-dreams.html

364:https://people.com/music/paul-mccartney-talks-george-harrison-spirit-through-tree/

Bibliography

Aldridge, Alan. *Paul McCartney's Guide to the Beatles Songbook*. Los Angeles Times, January 14, 1968.

Badman, Keith. *The Beatles Diary Volume 2: After the Break-up 1970-2001*. Omnibus Press, 2001.

Badman, Keith. *The Beatles Off the Record*. Omnibus Press, 2000.

Barrow, Tony. *John, Paul, George, Ringo and Me*. Thunder's Mouth Press, 2006.

Beatles, The. *The Beatles Anthology*. Chronicle, 2000.

Burger, Jeff (Ed.) and Maurice Hindle. *Lennon on Lennon: Conversation*. Chicago Review Press, 2017.

Clayson, Alan. *Ringo Starr: A Life*. Sanctuary, 2005.

Clayson, Alan: George Harrison. Sanctuary, 2003.

Davies, Hunter. *The Beatles Lyrics*. Little, Brown and Company, 2014.

Davies, Hunter. *The Beatles* (2nd Edition). Norton, 1996.

Doggett, Peter. *You Never Give Me Your Money: The Beatles After the Breakup*. HarperCollins, 2009.

Emerick, Geoff and Howard Massey. *Here, There and Everywhere: My Life Recording the Music of The Beatles*. Avery, 2007.

Goldsmith, Martin. *The Beatles Come to America*. Wiley & Sons, 2003.

Gould, Jonathan. *Can't Buy Me Love: The Beatles, Britain and America*. Three Rivers Press, 2007.

Guesdon, Jean-Michel, and Philippe Margotin. *All the Songs: The Story Behind Every Beatles Release*. Black Dog & Leventhal, 2013.

Harrison, Olivia. *George Harrison: Living In the Material World*. Abrams, 2011.

Jung, Carl. *The Red Book*. W.W. Norton & Company, 2009.

Kane, Larry. *Ticket to Ride*. Running Press, 2003.

Leary, Timothy, and Richard Alpert. *The Psychedelic Experience*. University, 1964.

Lennon, John. *A Spaniard in the Works*. Jonathan Cape, 1965.

Lennon, John. *In His Own Write*. Jonathan Cape, 1964.

Lewisohn, Mark. *Tune In, The Beatles: All These Years, Vol. 1*. Three Rivers Press, 2013.

Lewisohn, Mark. *The Complete Beatles Chronicle*. Harmony, 1992.

Lewisohn, Mark. *The Beatles Recording Sessions*. Harmony, 1988.

Lydon, Michael. *Lennon and McCartney: Songwriters—A Portrait from 1966*. Rock's Backpages (online archive), 2014.

MacDonald, Ian. *Revolution in the Head: The Beatles' Records and the Sixties*, 3rd Edition, Chicago Review Press, 2007.

Martin, George and Jeremy Hornsby. *All You Need Is Ears*. St. Martin, 1979.

Miles, Barry: *The Beatles Diary Volume 1: The Beatles Years*. Omnibus, 2001

Miles, Barry. *Paul McCartney: Many Years from Now*. Holt and Company, 1997.

Norman, Philip. *Paul McCartney: The Life*. Little, Brown and Company, 2016

Norman, Philip. *John Lennon: The Life*. HarperCollins, 2008.

Norman, Philip. *Shout! The Beatles in Their Generation*. Elm Tree, 1982.

Riley, Tim. *Lennon: The Man, the Myth, the Music—The Definitive Life*. Hyperion, 2011.

Saltzman, Paul. *The Beatles in India*. Insight, 2018.

Sheff, David. *All We Are Saying: The Last Major Interview with John Lennon and Yoko Ono*. St. Martin's Press, 2000.

Sheffield, Rob. *Dreaming The Beatles: The Love Story of One Band and the Whole World*. HarperCollins, 2017.

Spitz, Bob. *The Beatles: The Biography*. Back Bay Books, 2005.

Stark, Steven: *Meet the Beatles: A Cultural History of the Band that Shook Youth, Gender, and the World*. HarperCollins, 2005.

Sutcliffe, Pauline and Douglas Thompson. *The Beatles Shadow: Stuart Sutcliffe & his Lonely Hearts Club*. Pan, 2002.

Taylor, Alistair. *Yesterday: The Beatles Remembered*. Sidgwick & Jackson, 1988.

Turner, Steve. *Beatles '66: The Revolutionary Year*. HarperCollins, 2016.

Acknowledgements

I am grateful to the colleagues, clients, family and friends who supported me during the 4+ years it took to complete this work—thank you from the depths of my heart. I want to further acknowledge those who played significant roles in the book's production and my process.

Thanks to my Virgo editors, Sue Hillyard and Shelley Madsen, who both exercised incredible patience and irreplaceable precision in helping to craft this work. Bill Streett handled the graphic design and interior figures with impeccable artistry and professionalism; you've been a terrific friend and support for many years. The cover art was created by David Holtz—thank you for an exceptional job in capturing the book's essence. Thanks to Armand Diaz, Arielle Guttman, Sol Jonassen, Mark Jones and Rick Levine, who all gave such kind and generous endorsements. Special gratitude to Corrina Porterfield for taking the back cover photograph and for being my muse. The love, longing and reunion I experienced inspired every step of this journey. You profoundly catalyzed the *feeling* of this story in all of its transformative beauty.

My parents, Alan and Lois Meyers, provided me a home and an understanding of life to get me started on my journey. It is my hope that I've returned the favor, that this work nurtures and provides you some insight as you move forward on yours. Thank you for your unconditional love, acceptance and having *Sgt. Pepper* waiting for me when I was born. I know I played it endlessly (still do, and likely always will...) and now we know why.

Gratitude to Viktoria Blüm for our reunion and soulful connection, Josh Levin for being a fellow journeyer/explorer and Cristie Kephart-Downs for being a window into the ethers. Thank you Heather McCloskey Beck, Reuvain Bacal, Rick Snyder, Merryl Rothaus, Cathy Lindsey, Richard Fragomeni, Medora Woods, Glenn Ostlund, Julene Louis, Lloyd Raleigh, Valerie D'Ambrosio, Tami Palmer, Andrew Smith, Lucian Schloss, Kevin DeCapite, Dena DeCastro, Rebecca Crane, Christa Holtz, Emily Duhaime, Jen Berlingo, Andy Mione, Steve Sperber, Spenta Cama, Vince Buscemi, Sajit Greene, Drew Meyers and Blaze for friendship, guidance and personal support.

To John, Paul, George and Ringo—it has been the greatest honor in my life to partner with you this way. You have changed me forever, as you have this world. I want to acknowledge the extraordinary contribution of Mary and Julia to this music and story, truly bringing it to another dimension. It is miraculous and meaningful that love never dies and neither did you. I am forever inspired to trust the sublime benevolence of this world. And finally, thank you to the universe itself for weaving this profound, multi-leveled, heartfelt intelligence and awareness throughout every corner, quark and crevice of this existence.